ADMINISTRATIVE JUSTICE IN THE UNITED KINGDOM

This book critically examines the development and operation of administrative justice in the UK.

Every day, people have millions of interactions with government and public services. Administrative justice is concerned with the fairness of these interactions and the redress mechanisms people can use when things go wrong. Administrative justice is a large and expanding part of the legal system and of governmental activity in the United Kingdom. It includes initial administrative decision-making, the delivery of public services as well as redress and scrutiny mechanisms, principally tribunals, complaint-handling and ombudsmen. Administrative justice encompasses a far greater number of decisions than the caseloads of the courts.

This book explores what administrative justice is, why it is important, how it has evolved, how it works in practice and how it could be improved. Combining theoretical and empirical analysis, the book examines various contexts in which administrative justice operates, including benefits and special educational needs and disability. It also examines the social and political forces that drive the development of administrative justice and critically analyses the creation, operation and effectiveness of redress institutions.

Administrative Justice in the United Kingdom

Robert Thomas

•HART•
OXFORD • LONDON • NEW YORK • NEW DELHI • SYDNEY

HART PUBLISHING
Bloomsbury Publishing Plc
Kemp House, Chawley Park, Cumnor Hill, Oxford, OX2 9PH, UK
1385 Broadway, New York, NY 10018, USA
Bloomsbury Publishing Ireland Limited, 29 Earlsfort Terrace, Dublin 2, D02 AY28, Ireland

HART PUBLISHING, the Hart/Stag logo, BLOOMSBURY and the Diana logo are trademarks of Bloomsbury Publishing Plc
First published in Great Britain 2026

1

A catalogue record for this book is available from the British Library.

Library of Congress Cataloging-in-Publication Data

Names: Thomas, Robert (Writer on Administrative justice) author

Title: Administrative justice in the united kingdom / Robert Thomas.

Description: First edition. | Oxford ; New York : Hart Publishing, 2026. | Includes bibliographical references and index. | Summary: "This book critically examines the development and operation of administrative justice in the UK. Everyday, people have millions of interactions with government and public services. Administrative justice is concerned with the fairness of these interactions and the redress mechanisms people can use when things go wrong. Administrative justice is a large and expanding part of the legal system and of governmental activity in the United Kingdom. It includes initial administrative decision-making, the delivery of public services as well as redress and scrutiny mechanisms, principally tribunals, complaint-handling and ombudsmen. Administrative justice encompasses a far greater number of decisions than the caseloads of the courts. This book explores what administrative justice is, why it is important, how it has evolved, how it works in practice and how it could be improved. Combining theoretical and empirical analysis, the book examines various contexts in which administrative justice operates, including benefits and special educational needs and disability. It also examines the social and political forces that drive the development of administrative justice and critically analyses the creation, operation and effectiveness of redress institutions"–Provided by publisher.

Identifiers: LCCN 2026030552 (print) | LCCN 2026030553 (ebook) | ISBN 9781509983810 hardback | ISBN 9781509983773 paperback | ISBN 9781509983803 epub | ISBN 9781509983797 pdf

Subjects: LCSH: Administrative law–Great Britain | Administrative procedure–Great Britain | Administrative courts–Great Britain | Judicial review of administrative acts–Great Britain | Ombudspersons–Great Britain

Classification: LCC KD4879 .T46 2026 (print) | LCC KD4879 (ebook)

LC record available at https://lccn.loc.gov/2026030552

LC ebook record available at https://lccn.loc.gov/2026030553

ISBN: HB: 978-1-50998-381-0
ePDF: 978-1-50998-379-7
ePub: 978-1-50998-380-3

Typeset by Lumina Datamatics Ltd

For product safety related questions contact productsafety@bloomsbury.com

To find out more about our authors and books visit www.hartpublishing.co.uk. Here you will find extracts, author information, details of forthcoming events and the option to sign up for our newsletters.

ACKNOWLEDGEMENTS

This book has had a long gestation period. I have worked in the broad area of administrative justice for over a quarter of a century. This work has included empirical research projects and academic publications, but also being part of the broader administrative justice community in the UK, going to conferences organised by the old Council on Tribunals, being a member of the Administrative Justice Council, being involved in the peer review of the Parliamentary and Health Service Ombudsman and so on.[1] I have also had practical experience of administrative justice through, for a number of years, chairing school admission appeal panels and school exclusion review panels in my local area. There have also been significant changes to administrative justice throughout this period. In light of all of this, I felt that there was a need for an overall analysis of what administrative justice is, how it works and how it could be improved. Such a book seems timely. The last overall analysis of administrative justice was Patrick Birkinshaw's *Grievances, Remedies and the State*, published in 1994, an excellent account, although inevitably much has happened since.[2] This book therefore looks at administrative justice afresh. While this is a long book, it feels that there are many large issues of administrative justice that have been left out here, but which I hope others will pursue. I must acknowledge my debts to many people, too many to name individually. I have also benefitted from discussions with people who work within the various world – or rather worlds – of administrative justice and would therefore prefer to remain anonymous, including tribunal judges, complaint-handling staff, ombudsmen and government officials. I am greatly indebted to many colleagues and would like to thank Guy Baldwin, Cosmo Graham, Luke Graham, Matthew Groves, Javier Garcia Oliva, Richard Kirkham, Alistair Mills, Joe Tomlinson and Shiling Xiao for discussions and for commenting on drafts. Finally, I need to thank my wife, Nicola, and our children, Penelope, Rosamund, Constanza, Edward and Gwendolyn.

Robert Thomas
Hartford

[1] A Pottakis, M Englman, A Keenoy and R Thomas, *Ombudsman Peer Review of The Parliamentary and Health Service Ombudsman, UK* (Manchester, PHSO, 2022).
[2] P Birkinshaw, *Grievances, Remedies and the State*, 2nd edn (London, Sweet & Maxwell, 1994).

CONTENTS

ABBREVIATIONS

AJC	Administrative Justice Council
AJTC	Administrative Justice and Tribunals Council
CHC	Continuing Health Care
ECHR	European Convention on Human Rights
EHCP	Education, Health and Care Plan
DWP	Department for Work and Pensions
FTTIAC	First-tier Tribunal (Immigration and Asylum Chamber)
FTTSEC	First-tier Tribunal (Social Entitlement Chamber)
HMCTS	HM Courts and Tribunals Service
HMRC	HM Revenue and Customs
ICIBI	Independent Chief Inspector of Borders and Immigration
LEAP	Legal Entitlements and Administrative Practices
LGSCO	Local Government and Social Care Ombudsman
MoJ	Ministry of Justice
NAO	National Audit Office
NHS	National Health Service
NIPSO	Northern Ireland Public Services Ombudsman
PAC	House of Commons Public Accounts Committee
PACAC	House of Commons Public Administration and Constitutional Affairs Committee
PASC	House of Commons Public Administration Select Committee
PHSO	Parliamentary and Health Service Ombudsman
PSOW	Public Services Ombudsman for Wales
SEND	Special Educational Needs and Disability
SPSO	Scottish Public Services Ombudsman
UTAAC	Upper Tribunal (Administrative Appeals Chamber)
UTIAC	Upper Tribunal (Immigration and Asylum Chamber)

INTRODUCTION

This book is about administrative justice in the UK. The phrase 'administrative justice' is approached expansively and from a range of perspectives. It is used to cover the interactions people have with government, administration and public services, and the justice or otherwise which ensues from them. Overall, the purpose of the book is to explain, understand, analyse and critically evaluate administrative justice as it has developed and how it operates in the UK.

The book presents a 'big picture' and long-term analysis by charting, examining and assessing the development and evolution of administrative justice in the UK over approximately the last century or so. It is a study of administrative institutions and administrative justice redress and scrutiny institutions, in particular tribunals, ombudsmen, complaint-handling and other oversight bodies. The book examines how these institutions work in practice. It also analyses a wide range of problems that administrative justice has to grapple with and that cut across various sectoral and governmental contexts: substantive decision-making on people's entitlements; the handling of people's complaints; the design and operation of administrative systems; how government takes decisions that have a rationing element; administrative delay; government communications; using lessons to improve government and public services; and so on. In doing so, the discussion is informed by the empirical literature, data gleaned from freedom of information requests, the academic and other literature, and the author's own practical knowledge and experience of administrative justice. The book adopts a law in context and in action approach. The formal structures of administrative justice matter enormously, but they only make sense when understood and analysed in terms of how things actually work in practice and in the context of the wider social, economic, political and governmental forces in play. The intention is that the book will contribute to and consolidate the UK's tradition of administrative justice and the accompanying literature.

The notion of administrative justice does not lend itself to easy definition. It spans multiple areas of administration, law and policy. There are many ways in which administrative justice manifests and how it operates. It includes administrative and tribunal decision-making, but also a variety of other functions; administrative actions and inactions; the delivery of public services; policy implementation; complaint-handling; ombudsman investigations; audit and scrutiny; and so on. Administrative justice is concerned with the interactions people have with government, administration and public services, and the 'justice' or otherwise which characterise these interactions. The phrase 'administrative justice' is used in both a descriptive sense and a normative sense.

Descriptively, administrative justice often refers to the collection of mechanisms people can use to seek redress against government, principally tribunals and ombudsmen, complaints and administrative review. However, administrative justice cannot and should not be confined solely to individualised external redress after the event. It also includes governmental operations and the many types of interactions people have with government and public services. Core redress institutions, such as tribunals and ombudsmen, are important and receive detailed treatment here. Non-redress institutions, such as audit and inspection bodies, are similarly important and are a key aspect of administrative justice.

Administrative justice is also used in a normative sense to prescribe how people ought to be treated by government. There are various principles and standards of fair and good administration. Government should, for instance, get it right, make good decisions, treat people fairly, be responsive to their needs, be open and accountable, put things right, learn for the future and so on. These and other principles are underpinned by social and political attitudes and expectations concerning how people should be treated by administration. At the same time, administrative justice cannot be approached and understood solely from the position of the individual; it also has to be seen and understood from the governmental perspective.

The thesis of this book is that administrative justice is an inherent aspect of the relationship between the individual and the state. It is deeply embedded in people's expectations of fair treatment by government. However, securing administrative justice is a highly problematic and comprised endeavour. Fairness and justice for the individual are important, but they are not absolute values. They must be considered alongside and reconciled with a host of other competing forces, including: the policies adopted by government; administrative efficiency; the organisational challenges of delivering public services; and the political, financial and other pressures forces that bear down upon government and redress institutions. Administrative justice makes demands on the institutional competence and capacity of government to design and operate administrative systems that can both implement policy effectively and provide fairness for individuals. The need for administrative justice arises from people's experiences of unfair treatment from government. Yet, improving matters also depends on government, which is responsible for the unfairness. Not all demands for administrative justice can be satisfied within the limits of political and organisational realities. At the same time, it is necessary to consider how administrative justice can be reformed, enhanced and improved. In one sense, 'administrative justice' is what results from the tensions between the competing demands of the individual's expectations and the political forces and institutional competence which motivate and constrain government. The realistic goal for administrative justice can never be the attainment of some perfect, idealised vision of justice, but at most, trying to achieve the best within the limits of the possible – and even this has become increasingly challenging.

Key Questions

The book asks a number of interrelated questions. First, what is administrative justice? What does it actually mean and involve? What are the basic features and aspects of administrative justice? And how do they shape how administrative justice works in practice? What are the different conceptions of administrative justice that have evolved in the UK?

Second, why does administrative justice exist? Why, despite obvious interests to the contrary and at some financial cost and administrative inconvenience, has government not only grudgingly recognised the need for administrative justice, but also positively supported, promoted and expanded its role and scope? After all, government is concerned with exercising authority and making and implementing policy. Additional procedures and redress and scrutiny institutions to ensure administrative justice inevitably increase costs and delays, and thereby potentially compromise the ability of government to perform its principal activities. Why then does government establish and operate administrative justice institutions? It is necessary to explore the underlying dynamics that generate the need for administrative justice and drive its growth and development. Administrative justice did not just appear from nowhere. Calls for just treatment emanate from individuals who have been treated unfairly by administration. These demands occur at the micro-level, but also at the wider macro-level as to how society – both as a whole and in terms of its specific constituencies – expects to be treated by government. This inquiry therefore involves consideration of the basic social and political forces in play that drive the need for just treatment by administration and how the tension between governmental authority and efficiency on the one hand is reconciled with the need for fair and just administration on the other.

A third set of questions concerns the particular ways in which administrative justice has evolved and developed in the UK. The growth and operation of administrative justice is deeply intertwined with the evolving functions and structures of government, and changing social and political attitudes towards government. But this does not explain why administrative justice redress institutions have developed in the way they have. Why has there been a preference for non-court mechanisms? Why is the basic structure of administrative justice in the UK characterised by a division between, on the one hand, individualised administrative decision-making and tribunal appeals and, on the other hand, other types of administrative actions, complaint-handling and ombudsmen? To what extent is this division helpful? And to the extent that it is unhelpful, what, if anything, can be done about it? Having operated as non-judicial bodies for many decades, why were tribunals then brought into the formal judiciary? And what have been the consequences of this? By comparison, why have some ombudsmen been reformed? Any why have other ombudsmen, principally the Parliamentary and Health Service Ombudsman (PHSO), been relatively overlooked and remain unreformed?

A fourth set of questions concerns how administrative justice operates in practice. How do governmental systems, tribunals, ombudsmen and complaint-handling actually work and function? How effective are they? What is the impact and influence of redress institutions upon government? This involves examining the principal problems that administrative justice has to deal with, its effectiveness and its impact upon government. What are the benefits of individualised redress and scrutiny as opposed to more systemic scrutiny? There is a need here to include but also go beyond procedure. From one perspective, administrative justice can be viewed as a set of procedures through which people interact with government bodies and then, potentially, redress institutions. But while procedures are important, it is important to avoid an excessively formalistic or proceduralistic approach to administrative justice. No one interacts with government or appeals to a tribunal or complains to a public body (and then potentially escalates their complaint to an ombudsman) solely in order to go through those procedures for their own sake; they only do so in an effort to secure a positive benefit or decision on their substantive entitlements and to obtain redress against a perceived wrong. In addition to considering procedures, it is equally important to examine the substantive aspects of administrative justice and how these features are embedded within governmental operations. The analysis presented here is framed in terms of different variants of administrative justice – the systemic and the pathological – and the differences between autonomous law and responsive law, and the impact of redress mechanisms upon government.

Fifth, how could administrative justice be reformed, enhanced and improved? In recent years, there has been a general sense that while individuals retain rights of redress, the effectiveness of those rights have in practice been weakened and that the system as a whole does not function as it should. Moreover, there is a perception that the salience of administrative justice within government has been diminished as a result of cost pressures and policy choices. There have been significant efforts at reforming and improving administrative justice, but concerns remain. How then could administrative justice be reformed? What proposals for reform could be realistically implemented? At the same time, there are areas in which the scope for reform and improvement is highly constrained and limited. Given the pressures on government and the strains within its operations, achieving a genuine and authentic form of administrative justice is either difficult to achieve or largely unobtainable.

Parameters

The scope of the inquiry and its limitations need to be clarified. The focus is on the core aspects of administrative justice in the UK and its most visible aspects. No book could ever conceivably cover the entirety of this large, diverse, unwieldy and shifting landscape. Administrative justice is simply too large and diverse. Moreover, much of the action of administrative justice in practice – especially when it occurs within government – is not easily accessible except through extensive empirical research into specific focused contexts. There have also been significant shifts in the understanding of the topic. For instance, topics such as complaints against the police and utilities regulation were previously considered as aspects of administrative justice, but have now been hived off into their specialist domains.[1] Such topics are not considered here, although they are undoubtedly important. Another important omission is public inquiries. There have been several large and important public inquiries over recent years: Grenfell Tower, Post Office Horizon, infected blood and the grooming gangs scandal amongst others. Public inquiries are undoubtedly a topic of great importance, although they are not examined here for reasons of space and the consequent inability to do the topic justice.[2]

[1] P Birkinshaw, *Grievances, Remedies and the State*, 2nd edn (London, Sweet & Maxwell, 1994) 228–41; N Lewis and P Birkinshaw, *When Citizens Complain: Reforming Justice and Administration* (Buckingham, Open University Press, 1993) ch 9; N Creutzfeldt, C Gill, M Cornelis and R McPherson, *Access to Justice for Vulnerable and Energy-Poor Consumers Just Energy?* (Oxford, Hart Publishing, 2021).

[2] See M Elliott and R Thomas, *Public Law*, 5th edn (Oxford, Oxford University Press, 2024) ch 17; F Donson and D O'Donovan, 'Public Inquiries and Administrative Justice' in M Hertogh, R Kirkham, R Thomas and J Tomlinson (eds), *The Oxford Handbook of Administrative Justice* (Oxford, Oxford University Press, 2022).

Another limitation is that the traditional focus of administrative law – judicial review in the higher courts – is here pushed largely to the periphery. The book examines administrative justice redress and scrutiny mechanisms not as an alternative to the courts, but as the core means through which people experience just (or otherwise) administration and how they seek redress. The courts are important, but they are not at the centre stage of administrative justice as it has developed in the UK. This point highlights something of a disjuncture. The traditional focus of the administrative law literature is on the courts and judicial review. However, for most people most of the time, administrative justice is the mainstream. It is the core concern people have in their interactions with and normative expectations of government, their use of redress mechanisms and also the scrutiny and improvement of government. Many more people use administrative justice redress mechanisms than the courts. Despite its low profile, administrative justice deals with many more decisions, actions and challenges than the courts will ever have the capacity to handle. Further, administrative justice goes beyond redress by including how administration and government work in practice and how they could be improved. Administrative justice is where most of the action is in practice and is therefore an area in need of increased study and analysis.

Despite its largely overlooked role and scale, administrative justice has something of an image problem. The courts possess a prestige and history that administrative justice lacks. The forums of administrative justice – government offices in which caseworkers take decisions and handle complaints, public services, tribunal hearing rooms, ombudsmen offices and increasingly online – are often unglamorous locations, far less illustrious than the Royal Courts of Justice. The principles and practices of administrative justice – good customer service, the principles of good administration, tribunal hearings, fact-finding and making decisions – may seem banal, mundane and to lack conceptual sophistication. They do not carry the sense of urgency implied by the courts enforcing the rule of law to ensure that the government complies with the principles of legality as handed down in a Supreme Court ruling. But, the vast majority of people who have a problem with a public body do not want to go to the courts, even if they could. Instead, they want their problems resolved through more informal, less costly and quicker procedures. Moreover, while administrative justice is less high profile than the courts, it can also exert a more pervasive influence. It is through routine administrative procedures and systems that people experience administrative justice (and injustice). It is also through those same procedures and systems that government can be enhanced and improved.

A related point is that administrative justice goes wider than judicial review not just in terms of caseloads, but also in terms of its principles. The principles of good administration overlap with and also go beyond the grounds of judicial review. They assume considerable importance when, for instance, a public body is found to have made systematically incorrect decisions on people's entitlements, failed to communicate important changes that affect millions of people or simply failed to deliver public services to people who depend upon them. Administrative justice is concerned with matters of substance, namely decisions concerning people's entitlements and other types of administrative actions and the delivery of public services. It is also concerned with improving administration and public services. Administrative justice raises wider issues concerning, for instance, how public bodies are organised, the knowledge and skills they possess, and the institutional cultures that both infuse and are generated from within their operations.

Administrative justice also needs to be delineated from human rights law. There are some overlaps in this respect. In terms of substantive law, Article 3 of the European Convention on Human Rights (ECHR) (the prohibition of torture, inhuman or degrading treatment or punishment) and Article 8 (the right to respect for their private and family life) play a prominent role in the immigration context. Article 6 (the right to fair trial) applies to various tribunal systems, although the notion of procedural fairness goes wider and is deeply embedded in legal procedures. Human rights law has some limited role in social security appeals, but also in how groups of vulnerable people are treated (eg, people in care). Ombudsmen also increasingly refer to human rights law as a matter to be taken into account by a public body, although their investigations rarely engage with human rights law directly because their jurisdiction is one of maladministration or service fault, not unlawfulness. Despite these overlaps, for the most part, administrative justice and human rights law exist in relative isolation from each other. A person's outrage at the injustice done to them can sometimes prompt complaints that their human rights have been breached. But more often than not, 'human rights' is being used in such instances to dress up someone's complaint in the language of rights, but without adding much substantive bite to it. Alternatively, it is being used as a synonym for providing a person with individual attention to their case and circumstances.

Administrative justice is more concerned with how policy is administered and how public services are delivered. A fair amount of administrative justice concerns social welfare programmes. The welfare state involved the creation of social rights (in a broad sense) to a range of public services, including social security, healthcare, housing and education. These social rights are secured through administrative schemes and public services, which have changed and evolved over time. The nature and content of these social rights are determined by government policy. Accordingly, someone qualifies for an entitlement or service only if they fulfil the relevant eligibility requirements, which typically are provided for in the detailed statutory rules, regulations and guidance made by government and which embody government policy. There are no overriding higher-level judicially enforceable social rights which confer entitlements over and above what the detailed statutory rules and regulations prescribe.

In practice, most administrative justice decisions and actions concerning people's entitlements depend not upon the invocation of human rights or social rights. Instead, they turn upon matters that, although commonplace, are nonetheless of decisive importance. These include: the interactions people have with government and public services; the methods of collecting evidence; the exercise of judgement when finding facts and making decisions; the detail and application of the relevant rules and guidance; the quality of individual decisions and their accompanying reasons; the competence and capacity of caseworkers and the volumes of decisions they process; how effectively government is organised and managed; how government communicates with people; the requirements of good administration and how they are applied by government; and so on. These tasks take place within wider administrative systems and their accompanying institutional cultures, which inform how any particular policy is actually implemented in practice. Most of the time, the principal determinant that conditions administrative justice and its quality is government – that is, government policy and how it is administered and implemented. It is government that makes and funds the policies which determine people's eligibility for public services. It is government that establishes the administrative structures and processes through which people interact with it. It is also government that makes policy about redress institutions and manages and funds them. The degree to which redress institutions have a wider impact upon government – that is whether improvement recommendations become embedded within administrative practices – is similarly dependent on government. Accordingly, any study of administrative justice is also an examination of government itself and its attitudes and approaches to administrative justice.

Another matter to be highlighted is the increasing differentiation of administrative justice within the UK given the devolution of many public services to Scotland, Wales and Northern Ireland, such as health, education and social care. Over time, differences in administrative justice and redress mechanisms have become more apparent. Ombudsmen and some tribunals are now devolved. There are also some significant procedural and policy differences. Scotland's developing social security system – based explicitly on respecting the dignity of individuals – has been framed in contradistinction to the perceived stringency of the Department for Work and Pensions.

Structure

The structure of the book is as follows. Chapter 1 explores the various meanings of administrative justice and why it exists. From a higher altitude, administrative justice is something which concerns and emerges from the relationship between the state and society. From a ground-level perspective, it concerns a wide range of activities, including social security caseworkers deciding claims, tribunals hearing appeals and a mass of complaint-handling. There is administrative justice as external redress, but also justice within administration, systemic administrative justice and so on. Even within the first category – administrative justice as external redress – there are significant differences. Both tribunals and ombudsman are external redress mechanisms, but they are altogether quite different institutions and reflect different understandings of administrative justice.

Chapter 2 examines the formative period in the development of administrative justice in post-war Britain by considering the key landmarks, principally the growth of the welfare state, the Franks Report on tribunals (1957) and the 1961 JUSTICE report that recommended the creation of an ombudsman. It is argued that administrative justice needs to be understood in the context of the wider relationship between the state and society. When the power of the state expands, there is a corresponding reaction from society to protect liberty and to make the state accountable. This tension resulted in administrative justice institutions, such as tribunals and ombudsmen, being reconfigured and created to make the state more accountable and responsive to people, by providing redress and making government accountable. The development of both tribunals and ombudsmen needs to be understood against the background of public concerns about the growth of administrative power and the unfair treatment of the individual. Administrative justice is an important aspect of the tension between the state and society. It is also part of a wider process of state building, in particular making government accountable.

Chapter 3 surveys the contemporary administrative justice landscape, in particular the development of tribunals and ombudsmen. A key development here was the big reform of tribunals in the 2000s, which involved moving them into the formal judiciary and the creation of the current tribunal system, the First-tier and Upper Tribunals. The chapter also considers the development of ombudsmen. A period of reform in the 2000s has since been followed by a fundamental shift in the wider ethos and effectiveness of administrative justice as a result of austerity policies introduced after the global financial crisis. The chapter also examines the appeal-complaints dichotomy and the role of non-redress scrutiny mechanisms in administrative justice.

Having considered the development of administrative justice in general, the book then proceeds to undertake the detailed examination of how specific parts of the machinery of administrative justice operate in practice and their effectiveness. Chapter 4 examines administrative decision-making and tribunals, the nature of such decision-making, the quality of initial decision-making, the role of internal administrative review, the role, operation and procedures of tribunals and the Upper Tribunal, how to improve decision-making and also automated decision-making.

Chapter 5 examines the initial handling of complaints by public bodies, another large and diverse area of administrative justice. Initial complaint-handling is itself a public service and a redress process undertaken by and within government. This chapter examines how government bodies handle complaints, the quality of such complaint-handling and the increased use of complaint standards frameworks by ombudsmen in order to provide benchmarks for complaint-handling in order to improve their quality.

Chapter 6 explores the role and work of ombudsmen in detail. It investigates the following: how ombudsman handle routine complaints; the principles of good administration (and how those principles interact and overlap with administrative legality and human rights); the series of big investigations undertaken by the PHSO and its changing relationships with government and Parliament; the impact of ombudsmen upon government; and the issue of ombudsmen and own-initiative powers of investigation.

Subsequent chapters examine various cross-cutting themes of administrative justice by exploring administrative practices and the responses and interventions of redress and scrutiny bodies. Chapter 7 is concerned with systemic administrative justice. It examines various case studies of systemic administrative justice failures over recent years and their underlying causes. Chapter 8 examines government communications and the problems that arise with how government communicates with people and how effectively it provides information to people. Chapter 9 investigates a range of problems which fall under the rubric of 'pathological administrative justice'. These problems include: administrative decisions that have a rationing aspect; disciplinary administrative justice; and administrative delay. Finally, Chapter 10 concludes the book by providing an overall assessment of administrative justice in the UK and its strengths and weaknesses, and then considering how it could be reformed and enhanced, as well as its prospects.

1

Investigating Administrative Justice

Getting Started

To investigate and understand administrative justice, it is first necessary to consider what it is, but this is not straightforward. Administrative justice arises in manifold contexts and assumes different meanings from those contexts. An elusive and amorphous notion, it cannot be confined within a single and fixed definition. It is better to approach administrative justice as something to be problematised and to think not in terms of a single concept, but of different conceptions of administrative justice. It also evolves over time. Nonetheless, we need to begin somewhere and the following can serve as a preliminary starting point.

Administrative justice has the following key features. First, it is concerned with government and how people are governed. The basis of all government is to govern society by making decisions that affect people. With the expansion of administrative governance over the last two centuries, there has been a whole series of fundamental changes concerning the role, tasks and functions of government. Modern government is an instrumentality for meeting people's needs, their security, prosperity and well-being. To this end, government operates many administrative systems and delivers large-scale public services to millions of people. These systems perform a wide range of important social functions, including: administering social security to relieve poverty and to help people with disabilities; collecting taxes; administering immigration and asylum policies; and delivering public services such as health and social care; education; and so on. These systems and services are deeply embedded within the structure and patterns of daily life. People rely heavily upon them. The idea of *administrative* justice only became both conceptually possible and necessary with the expansion of administrative governance.

Second, administrative justice is concerned with the relationship between the individual and government, and the interactions that occur within that relationship. People rely on government. They often have little or no option but to interact with government to receive their entitlements or to access public services or because they are subject to governmental controls. In the UK, the paradigmatic administrative justice situation involves a person who applies for social security benefits and then experiences some problem or other in the handling of their claim or it is rejected; what then can they do? In this situation, the claimant is typically unaware of the system and perhaps experiencing a degree of vulnerability. They are also often entirely dependent upon government. There is a risk that the claimant may do nothing and therefore potentially not receive her entitlements or seek redress. This would compound the inequality of power between them and a large administrative bureaucracy. Administrative justice is therefore required.[1] It concerns both people's interactions with government and also redress mechanisms. The treatment and needs of individuals are therefore central; so are the behaviours and operations of government. From the perspective of the individual, what matters is their own personal interactions with government and their personal circumstances. Matters look different from the governmental perspective. Government engages with not just with one individual, but millions. There is an inherent tension between the consideration of one person's situation on the one hand and the administrative need for system, uniformity and efficiency on the other.

Third, administrative justice is often used to describe the collection of non-court redress mechanisms by which people can challenge administrative decisions and actions. These institutions comprise tribunals, ombudsmen and other types of complaint-handling. In the UK, tribunals decide appeals against various initial administrative decisions.[2] Ombudsmen investigate complaints of maladministration and service failure. 'Administrative justice' has been used in this descriptive sense to delineate such redress mechanisms from a traditional court-focused conception of administrative law in which judicial review is the centre of attention. Redress institutions, such as tribunals and ombudsmen, differ significantly from the higher courts and have sometimes (and wrongly) been viewed as inferior to them. Accordingly, they have been categorised under the heading of 'administrative justice' as a way of highlighting their distinctiveness from the courts and also their legitimacy. When viewed together, tribunals and ombudsmen comprise the principal administrative justice redress mechanisms, although they are themselves quite distinct and different from each other. They reflect a broad division of governmental tasks inherent within administrative justice. There is individualised decision-making about people's entitlements and there are other types of administrative actions and public service delivery. When government takes individualised administrative decisions, there is often (but not always) a right of appeal to a tribunal. When government performs a wider range of other administrative actions and public service delivery, then people can complain to the public body concerned and then, if they remain dissatisfied, to an ombudsman. This distinction between individualised decision-making and other types of administrative actions and service delivery permeates the structure of and thinking around administrative justice both within government and redress institutions.

Fourth, administrative justice embodies a range of normative principles, values, expectations and best practices as to how people ought to be treated by government and public services. These principles include getting things right, treating people fairly, being open and accountable, and putting things right. In this sense, administrative justice has significant normative content which both government and redress mechanisms

[1] Administrative justice manifests in other contexts, such as business regulation. For instance, utility companies can appeal against decisions of the Competition and Markets Authority to the Competition Appeal Tribunal, but this belongs more to the area of regulatory law and justice.

[2] On tribunals outside the UK, see S Thomson, M Groves and G Weeks (eds), *Administrative Tribunals in the Common Law World* (Oxford, Hart Publishing, 2024).

should live up to and against which they can be assessed. Various reports over the years have articulated a range of principles, such as the need for tribunals to be open, fair, expert, independent, impartial and focused on the needs of the people who use them. Ombudsmen have adopted their principles of good administration (considered below) to articulate a set of standards and expectations for the public and government. Other principles of administrative justice include accessibility, procedural fairness, the quality of decision-making, applying the law correctly and giving reasons for decisions. It is preferable to think of the principles of good administration not as fixed and static, but as part of an evolving process as new problems and issues arise.

Fifth, administrative justice is highly conditioned by government policy and behaviours on a number of levels. Overall government policy towards administrative justice has, at times, shifted considerably. During the 2000s, the then Labour government sought to improve public services and also undertook a significant reform of tribunals. Following the global financial crisis of 2008, austerity policies have led to an overall weakening of administrative justice, reduced resources and less commitment to its norms. Administrative justice is also influenced by the specific substantive policies relating to particular administrative systems and also the departmental structure of government. In UK central government, the government department is the principal unit of government.[3] The relevant government department – for instance, the Department for Work and Pensions – both makes substantive policy and administers it.[4] It also decides whether to have redress mechanisms and their scope. This has resulted in a fragmented system of administrative justice, which itself reflects the departmental and pluralistic character of British government. Administrative justice is also deeply contextual because each administrative system or public service performs a unique social function and operates within its social, economic and political context. What happens within one area (eg, social security) is never quite the same as happens in other contexts (eg, tax or immigration). The UK does not have a general administrative procedure law as exists elsewhere.[5] Administrative procedures are determined by the relevant government department through rules, regulations, guidance and administrative practices. This illustrates the typically ad hoc and pragmatic approach of government responding to particular problems, although it can lead to anomalies and inconsistencies. However, there are some regularities, such as the requirements of procedural fairness, the relatively uniform nature of tribunal procedure rules and the principles of good administration. There have also been occasional efforts by the centre of government, for example, to improve the quality of government complaint-handling through initiatives such as the Citizen's Charter (1991).

Despite its fragmented character, a sixth feature is that administrative justice has also increasingly come to be seen as a distinct 'justice system' in its own right alongside the criminal, civil and family justice systems. Traditionally, administrative justice was not seen as a system or even given much priority within either the Ministry of Justice

[3] T Daintith and A Page, *Executive Self-Government and the Constitution* (Oxford, Oxford University Press, 2025).

[4] In some contexts, policy is both made and administered by the government department (eg, social security, immigration and tax); in other contexts, delivery is for local authorities and other public bodies.

[5] For example, the US Administrative Procedure Act 1946, the German Administrative Procedure Act 1976 and the Dutch General Administrative Law 1994.

or across government as a whole. Administrative justice was less a 'system' and 'more a jungle of intersecting agencies and jurisdictional divisions'.[6] In response, there have been various efforts to work towards a more coherent administrative justice system, although this remains very a much work in progress. The Ministry of Justice is not responsible for the entirety of administrative justice or even all tribunals. Ombudsmen are not integrated with tribunals or each other.[7] This is to say nothing of administrative justice within government. In short, the movement towards achieving a more coherent administrative justice system takes place against the pervasive reality that such a system does not exist or, to the extent that it does, then it is quite unsystematic.

Definitions

These points assist, at a general level, in clarifying the British tradition of administrative justice, but they do not define it. While the book does not adopt a single definition of administrative justice, various definitions have been advanced and are considered here.

The phrase 'administrative justice' itself suggests that the concept it embodies is composed of two aspects: administration or government and justice or fairness. Administration presumes the existence of a system of administrative governance in which administrators and public servants make and implement policy and deliver public services. The second aspect is justice. This can be understood as a normative concept which requires that individuals who interact with government and public services should be treated fairly and justly. 'Justice' can also refer to a justice system, such as the criminal justice system. Either way, administrative justice refers to how people are treated by government and whether they receive fair and just treatment. In this sense, administrative justice implies a set of normative standards or principles that should inform the activities of administrative institutions and the quality of their interactions with people.

A traditional definition of administrative justice is that it is concerned with the resolution of disputes through external redress machinery, especially tribunals.[8] This way of viewing administrative justice emphasises the external control of administration and doing justice for people who have appealed initial administrative decisions to tribunals. Underpinning this definition is a division between administration and government on the other hand and tribunal adjudication on the other. Government is responsible for administration and processing high volumes of initial decisions. By contrast, tribunals adjudicate upon individual appeals by considering each case on its own merits through a judicial approach. This approach was strongly associated with the culture of tribunals

[6] R Rawlings, 'Into the Jungle' (1987) 50 *MLR* 110.

[7] For instance, the Parliamentary and Health Service Ombudsman handles complaints against the UK government and NHS England, whereas the Local Government and Social Care Ombudsman handles complaints against English local government and social care.

[8] HWR Wade, *Towards Administrative Justice* (Ann Arbor, University of Michigan Press, 1963); HJ Elcock, *Administrative Justice* (London, Longmans, 1969); M Partington, 'Restructuring Administrative Justice? The Redress of Citizens' Grievances' (1999) 52 *Current Legal Problems* 173, 175–76: 'much writing and research on administrative justice tends to be on the secondary and tertiary decision-making which occurs after an initial decision has been taken'.

and it served the purpose of emphasising their separation and independence from government and political influences and pressures. By tying administrative justice to external redress, it was possible to try to quash the notion that tribunals were somehow part of the governmental process; instead, tribunals could be understood as independent and impartial adjudicatory bodies, albeit not then part of the formal judiciary.

This approach to administrative justice has something to it. It reflects differences of institutional structures, cultures and perspectives. Governmental institutions are administrative bureaucracies. For instance, the Department for Work and Pensions – the UK's largest public service delivery department – makes millions of decisions each year on people's claims for benefits. Such an organisation focuses on processing the entire caseload of all claims it receives and therefore it naturally prioritises values such as efficiency and speed in the delivery of services. By contrast, redress mechanisms focus on providing justice in the individual case through fair procedures. Consequently, tribunal adjudication and complaint-handling are often seen as preferable to governmental administration because they provide a higher standard of justice, fair treatment and substantive decision-making.

At the same time, a criticism of this approach to administrative justice has been that it prioritises external redress and thereby overlooks the great mass of initial administrative decision-making. All decision-making starts – and most of it ends – within government. If so, then such decision-making is itself an important area for investigating administrative justice in order to, for instance, assess the quality of such decisions and to raise their quality. A related matter is that there is, in practice, no hard-edged distinction between administrative decision-making and tribunal adjudication: 'administration merges imperceptibly into adjudication'.[9] Both government officials and tribunals apply the same rules to make decisions. What is then required is a conceptual reversal. Rather than defining administrative justice solely in terms of external redress, it makes more sense to view it as encompassing all initial administrative decisions made by government in addition to onward levels of review and appeal. This approach is reinforced by the fact that while redress systems, such as tribunals, ombudsmen and other processes, certainly undertake a considerable volume of work, it is actually quite small compared with the huge volume of initial administrative decisions taken by government. From this perspective, to focus exclusively on external redress is to neglect the greater part of administrative justice in practice. It also overlooks both the need for and challenging of getting decisions right first time.

Accordingly, administrative justice has been redefined as the 'justice inherent in administrative decision-making'.[10] The focus here is on the handling of claims and the making of initial decisions. This approach is closely associated with an analytical framework that identifies competing models of administrative justice which exhibit different characteristics and are often in tension with each other. A bureaucratic model prioritises the quick and efficient processing of claims and decisions. A legal model emphasises procedural fairness and the impartial application of the rules. And a professional judgement model underlines the importance of specialist professional knowledge, such as

[9] ibid 176.

[10] M Adler, 'A Socio-legal Approach to Administrative Justice' (2003) 25(4) *Law & Policy* 323.

medical expertise. Each model has its own strengths and weaknesses. There are tensions between these models and trade-offs must be made between them.[11]

This way of understanding administrative justice from the level of initial administrative decision-making upwards has been influential upon both scholarship and practice. The only official definition of administrative justice ever adopted to date in the UK was contained in the Tribunals, Courts and Enforcement Act 2007, which brought together most of the previously disparate tribunals into a unified tribunal system: the First-tier and Upper Tribunals. This will be examined in depth later on. For present purposes, the key point is that the 2007 Act defined the 'administrative justice system' as comprising 'the overall system by which decisions of an administrative or executive nature are made in relation to particular persons, including: the procedures for making such decisions; the law under which such decisions are made; and the systems for resolving disputes and airing grievances in relation to such decisions'.[12]

This definition was introduced to clarify the ambit and role of the then Administrative Justice and Tribunals Council, which had been established to keep the system under review. It was an independent statutory body that replaced the Council on Tribunals, which had been created in 1958, to oversee tribunals.[13] As it happens, only six years after the 2007 Act, the Administrative Justice and Tribunals Council was abolished as part of the then government's 'bonfire of the quangos'.[14] The definition of the 'administrative justice system' was also repealed.[15] The short life of the Administrative Justice and Tribunals Council demonstrates the low value placed by government on external oversight of administrative justice.

These matters will be examined later on. In the meantime, working with the definition in the 2007 Act, it seems clear that administrative justice is a system that involves administrative bodies taking decisions that affect specific people. That system also concerns the procedures for taking such decisions and the large body of laws and rules that are applied by administrative officials when taking those decisions. On top of these administrative processes, there are further systems which handle and resolve disputes and grievances concerning these initial decisions. All of this put together comprises the overall system of administrative justice.

Administrative justice is then about systems. It is also concerned with the relationship between government and individuals, and the onward redress systems for handling and resolving the disputes and grievances that people have about government. Administrative justice is also concerned with the procedures and policies which are embodied in the relevant rules. The definition includes a core concern of administrative justice: taking decisions about people's legal entitlements and rights. This occurs in areas of mass administration such as social security, immigration, tax, school admissions and

[11] JL Mashaw, *Bureaucratic Justice: Managing Social Security Disability Claims* (New Haven, Yale University Press, 1983); J Mashaw, 'Models of Administrative Justice' in M Hertogh, R Kirkham, R Thomas and J Tomlinson (eds), *The Oxford Handbook of Administrative Justice* (Oxford, Oxford University Press, 2022). Other models have been identified and disputed: Adler (n 10); M Adler, 'Understanding and Analysing Administrative Justice' in M Adler (ed), *Administrative Justice in Context* (Oxford, Hart Publishing, 2010); S Halliday, *Judicial Review and Compliance with Administrative Law* (Oxford, Hart Publishing, 2004).

[12] Tribunals, Courts, and Enforcement Act 2007, sched 7, para 13(4).

[13] Tribunals and Inquiries Act 1958, s 1.

[14] Public Bodies Act 2011.

[15] Public Bodies (Abolition of Administrative Justice and Tribunals Council) Order, SI 2013/2042.

compensation decisions. Government and Parliament have created many administrative schemes which are then implemented by officials who take individual decisions about people's entitlements and legal rights. Such schemes span the range of policy contexts for which government is responsible. Another feature of the definition is that it includes both initial administrative decision-making within government bodies and the onward systems for resolving disputes and airing grievances in relation to those initial decisions. These onward systems include the judiciary, and hence judicial remedies provided by the courts and tribunals, and also non-judicial remedies.

This definition captures a significant area of administrative justice activity. However, it has its weaknesses. There are many other types of administrative actions and public service delivery that fall outside the relatively narrow category of individualised decision-making. These include the other types of executive actions of government, the interactions people have with government, how government communicates with people, how administrative systems operate, and the delivery of public services, such as health, social care, education and local public services. Some 80 per cent of the caseload of the Parliamentary and Health Service Ombudsman (PHSO) concerns complaints about healthcare. It is a distortion of language to describe the provision of healthcare including medical operations and treatments as 'administrative decision-making'. The same applies to other administrative justice concerns such as other types of administrative actions and inactions. These include the entire range of other types of governmental activity, such as policy-making, implementation and delivery, and the operation of large-scale systems and processes which in turn frame and condition individualised decisions and actions. If administrative justice is to be extended beyond external redress, then it makes little sense to limit that extension solely to initial decisions and thereby exclude the various other administrative actions through which people interact with government. Redress for such matters is typically provided by ombudsmen and the internal redress processes within public bodies, such as initial complaint-handling.

Another aspect missing from the definition in the 2007 Act concerns the range of norms and principles which inform the substance of administrative justice. The challenge here is that while such norms exist, they are often in tension with each other. For instance, people who apply for social security benefits are entitled to receive good-quality and correct decisions. The procedures used to make such decisions should also be fair. Decisions should also be made reasonably quickly, efficiently and within available resources. This suggests that administrative justice is not as simple as solely ensuring people receive just and fair treatment and correct decisions. The concept embodies tensions between competing values and norms and how trade-offs between them are reached.

These points are illustrated by a paper presented at a seminar on administrative justice in 2006 by the senior official responsible for administrative justice policy at the time of the Tribunals, Courts and Enforcement Act 2007.[16] The focus of the paper was on the core aspects of an effective administrative justice dispute resolution process. Such a mechanism would be informed and evaluated by three values and criteria: the ability to make good quality and correct decisions; the fairness of the process; and the resource

[16] P Stockton, 'Proportionate Dispute Resolution: What are the Options?' (Nuffield Foundation, Administrative Justice Seminar, 23 January 2006).

implications. There had been a tendency to view these criteria as essentially linear in nature. Fair procedures are the only or best way of ensuring correct decisions and so the resources required have to be provided so that people can receive correct decisions. However, in practice, the relationships between the three criteria are not linear at all; instead, they are more like three points of triangle that are often in tension with each other. It is impossible to know in any objective sense whether decisions are correct, especially when they are fundamentally about issues of fact, not law. Inevitably, the procedures used to consider the evidence and to make findings of fact are imperfect. Moreover, deciding what evidence to accept or reject involves the exercise of judgement and discretion – as does the application of the facts to the applicable standards. Nonetheless, decisions must be made. Furthermore, the resources required to fund the process are always limited and there is always competition with other areas that need to be funded.

The three values – fair process, correct decisions and resources – influence and impact upon one another in a multiplicity of different ways. A change to one value invariably influences the others. Additional procedural safeguards might well increase fairness and the accuracy of decisions, but they might also increase costs, thereby impacting upon other parts of the wider system. There are no simple or settled answers as the nature of the relationships between these values or to the problems posed. The practical operation of administrative justice requires trade-offs between competing principles and values, and there will often be disagreement about the nature of those trade-offs. At the same time, the system needs to be able to work in practice.

Another set of issues concerns the nature of the administrative justice system itself. This can be defined, in accordance with the definition within the 2007 Act, as the overall system of remedies by which people can secure redress. This 'horizontal' perspective makes sense because it views different tribunals (social security, tax, immigration etc) along with ombudsmen and other remedies as an overall coherent system of remedies. However, administrative justice also needs to be viewed from a 'vertical' and contextual perspective. In addition to there being a single overarching administrative justice system composed of redress mechanisms, the problems people experience always occur in the context of specific systems of administration and public services. Each redress body occupies just part of these larger functional systems. Social security, tax and immigration tribunals all hear appeals against initial decisions, but they also differ from each other as they operate within their own silos. Their work is influenced by both the wider social and administrative systems and governmental behaviours, and also the general legal principles and rules that apply to all tribunals. The same point applies to ombudsmen.

Despite these points, the definition in the 2007 Act was innovative in that it included initial administrative decision-making within the scope of administrative justice. Further, such definitional problems are unsurprising. Administrative justice is a jumble of different institutions, processes and principles. It can be approached from a range of different perspectives. Discussions of administrative justice often have a sense that all perspectives have a substantial degree of validity and they are adopted for convenience depending on the specific subject matter and the approach adopted.

Administrative justice it is not itself a discrete area of law. It covers many different areas of law and also the wider social and other contexts in which the law is administered. Administrative justice is also concerned with a wide range of institutions. In addition to government bodies and redress bodies, there are also parliamentary select committees, audit agencies, inspectorates, public sector regulators and other scrutiny bodies. There are also other entities: society; stakeholders; pressure groups; the media and non-governmental organisations. The particular issues and problems of administrative justice that arise depend heavily on the specific area of social policy concerned, what government is trying to do in that particular area, the challenges involved and the clash of different interests.

Descriptions

It may be preferable to abandon definitions in favour of describing what exists and how it has evolved. One feature of this approach is that administrative justice is a socially constructed notion which is (re-)created through human interactions, the wider overarching relationship between the state and society, and changes in policy, administration and public service delivery. Various conceptions of administrative justice have arisen and evolved as a result of changing social, economic and political forces and developments which influence and determine the work of government and the delivery of public services. These conceptions have emerged from and are rooted within specific periods of time and reflect the development of government and public services. At the risk of some repetition, these different conceptions can be identified.

To begin with, it must be recognised that in the British governing tradition, the redress of grievances has long been principally a function of the political process.[17] One of the oldest tasks of Parliament, dating back centuries, is to provide a forum for ventilating complaints and for the redress of grievances.[18] This now occurs through the constituency casework of Members of Parliament and correspondence with ministers, petitions to Parliament, and questions and debates in Parliament. This remains an important means of redress. However, with the growth of the responsibilities of government, the redress of grievances through Parliament has necessarily been supplemented by other institutional arrangements.

During the early twentieth century, government established a number of administrative schemes that involved individualised decision-making on people's entitlements in areas such as immigration and asylum, pensions, tax and unemployment insurance.[19] In each instance, two questions arose: what happens if people are aggrieved by decisions? What redress mechanism is appropriate? The answer was to establish tribunals to decide appeals. The tribunals were part of the administrative process. This was an ad hoc, gradual and, at times, controversial development. The new schemes of social administration were seen by some as a troubling assertion of governmental power at the expense of

[17] FF Ridley, 'The Citizen against Authority: British Approaches to the Redress of Grievances' (1984) 37 *Parliamentary Affairs* 1; T Cogswell, 'A Low Road to Extinction? Supply and Redress of Grievances in the Parliaments of the 1620s' (1990) 33 *Historical Journal* 283; M Knights, '"The Lowest Degree of Freedom": The Right to Petition Parliament, 1640–1800' (2018) 37 *Parliamentary History* 18.

[18] See, eg, art 13 of the Bill of Rights 1689: 'for redress of all grievances, and for the amending, strengthening and preserving of the laws, parliaments ought to be frequently held'.

[19] Aliens Act 1905; Old Age Pensions Act 1908; Finance Act 1910; National Insurance Act 1911.

individual liberty. Tribunals were seen not as supplementing, but as undermining the role of the ordinary common law courts. Traditionalist lawyers, such as Dicey and Hewart, viewed tribunals as inherently inferior to the courts because they were at risk of political interference. For Dicey, the conferral of 'judicial' decision-making powers on administrative officers and tribunals – as opposed to the common law courts – marked a significant decline in the ancient veneration and respect for the rule of law, which meant the rule of the higher courts.[20] The scepticism towards administration was widespread. A senior judge noted that 'administrative action generally meant something done by' a faceless official 'sitting at a desk in a government office, very apt to be a despot if free from the interference of the Courts of Justice'.[21] Tribunals were viewed as a threat to the established role of the ordinary courts. The notion of 'administrative justice' was an oxymoron.

Yet, tribunals evolved in large part because of the inadequacies of the courts. These included procedural defects, the inability of the courts to handle large numbers of cases arising from administrative decision-making and the lack of appropriate doctrinal tools. Moreover, there was a lack of sympathy on the part of the judiciary with the new positive functions of government. The discouraging experience of workmen's compensation, which had relied on the courts, resulted in many injured workmen not receiving compensation because they lacked legal advice and the means to pursue their claims in court. Following this, the government deliberately bypassed the courts by creating bespoke specialist tribunals that used more informal and inquisitorial methods, which could handle the volume of cases and which also possessed an appreciation of the administrative scheme and its underlying social purpose.[22] Tribunals came to be accepted as a pragmatic response to the need for swift, inexpensive and expert adjudication without all of the legalistic procedures and trappings of the higher courts. 'Administrative justice' now meant redress against government through tribunal adjudication. This conception, associated with the Franks Report on tribunals (1957), was focused on external redress by tribunals that provided justice through single-instance hearings and decisions.

This understanding was augmented by the establishment of the ombudsmen to investigate complaints of maladministration. There was also significant continuity with the established redress of grievances through Parliament. When the Parliamentary Ombudsman was established in 1967, its purpose was to provide Members of Parliament with a better means of securing the redress of individuals' grievances against government and thereby to enhance political scrutiny of administration. Over time, the need to separate tribunals from their parent government departments grew. This movement reached its high-water mark in the Leggatt Report on tribunals (2001) and the Tribunals, Courts and Enforcement Act 2007, which brought tribunals within the formal judiciary. Administrative justice was viewed as a system of tribunals for resolving disputes between individuals and the state.

[20] AV Dicey, 'Introduction to the Eighth Edition' in *Introduction to the Study of the Law of the Constitution*, 8th edn (London, Macmillan, 1915) xxxviii. See also G Hewart, *The New Despotism* (London, Benn, 1929).

[21] 'Encroachments of the Executive: The Master of the Rolls on a Modern Danger' *The Times* (4 May 1911). See also 'Exaltation of the Executive' *The Times* (2 September 1909).

[22] B Abel-Smith and R Stevens, *Lawyers and the Courts: A Sociological Study of the English Legal System 1750–1965* (London, Heinemann, 1967) 115–17.

From the 1980s onwards, a new perspective emerged. Rather than viewing administrative justice solely as external redress – that is, putting things right after the event – it made more sense to supplement this with a bottom-up perspective focused on getting things right from the outset. On this approach, administrative justice is also concerned with governmental operations: the initial handling of people's applications, administrative procedures and decisions, and public service delivery. Administrative justice includes tribunals and ombudsmen, but also includes people's interactions with government and initial decision-making on their entitlements. The real challenge is to raise the overall quality of initial decisions and actions through, amongst other things, feedback from redress mechanisms.

This conception of 'justice within administration' represented an advance, although it was still largely focused on individualised decision-making. It has now been supplemented by a wider conception of 'systemic administrative justice'.[23] Many of the problems people experience with administration and public services often stem from structural weaknesses embedded deep within the systems, processes, policies and behaviours of government. This systemic conception of administrative justice is predicated upon the organisational nature of administration. The challenge is then to understand the design and operations of the wider administrative system that people interact with and to diagnose and address any systemic failures that may arise. This conception of administrative justice emerged in the 2000s and can be seen reflected in various ombudsmen reports and the conferral of own-initiative powers on some ombudsmen to investigate systemic maladministration. It is also reflected in reports by parliamentary select committees and the National Audit Office. From this perspective, individual redress is a small part of the larger project of promoting good administration.

These approaches to administrative justice broadly reflect a linear progression. They embody different emphases and differences of degree which can merge into differences of kind. Further, these conceptions of administrative justice are by no means exhaustive. The purpose is not to create a rigid conceptual straightjacket, but a broad and open-ended framework of analysis. The functions of redress, appeals, complaints, systemic scrutiny, improving administration, and public accountability are part of a continuum, not separate subjects.[24] The character of administrative justice varies according to context. Administrative justice concerning the performance of administrative functions is different from, for instance, healthcare. The broad conceptions outlined here can provide a useful way of thinking about administrative justice, its development and how it works in practice. Administrative justice is a constantly evolving area that responds to a wide range of factors: social, economic and political developments and changes in the administrative systems and schemes which then prompt administrative justice to assume various and new forms and understandings. Needless to say, there are different ways of analysing administrative justice and overlaps between different analytical frameworks.

[23] R Thomas, 'Analysing Systemic Administrative Justice Failures: Explanatory Factors and Prospects for Future Research' (2021) 43 *Journal of Social Welfare and Family Law* 339; see also ch 7.

[24] P Birkinshaw, *Grievances, Remedies and the State*, 2nd edn (London, Sweet & Maxwell, 1994) 21.

Why Do We Need Administrative Justice?

Despite its fragmented and contextual nature, administrative justice also possesses some core common features cut across its various manifestations. These features also justify the need for administrative justice. At the core of administrative justice are the interactions people have with government and public services. These can be single-instance interactions or a continuing process of multiple interactions stretching out over much longer timescales, sometimes years and decades. A particularly important feature in this respect concerns the impact of such interactions on people and the justice – both procedural and substantive – or injustice which occurs. Moreover, one person interacts with many different systems. In the context of contemporary administrative governance, the whole pattern of people's everyday lives is so enmeshed within different systems of decision-making and public services that one error or problem can have consequences in other areas of a person's life. Administrative systems and public services do not exist in isolation from each other and the many other contexts of human life. Yet, government is functionally differentiated. Government bodies habitually think solely in terms of their own silos, whereas the people concerned interact with many different systems which may or may not align with each other.

There are two other inherent features of direct concern to administrative justice: the huge inequality and disparity of power between the individual and government, and the individual's lack of choice. Government possesses immeasurably more power than any individual. Its scale and influence create inequalities by subordinating people and placing them in a weak and often powerless position. Public services often require people to think and behave like bureaucrats.[25] Government institutions can prioritise their own interests above people's needs. Moreover, government is monolithic and monopolistic. People have no choice but to interact with government. Someone applying for benefits has no option but to interact with the Department for Work and Pensions, as there is no alternative provider. The only choice is between approaching government or forgoing the possibility of receiving such entitlements altogether. These features – the inequality of power and the individual's lack of choice – reinforce the need for distinct principles and procedures to ensure that individuals have, at the very least, a reasonable opportunity of securing the entitlements and services which they qualify for. Without administrative justice, a person will be almost entirely powerless and is unlikely to receive their entitlements. Even if people do not qualify, they still deserve to be treated fairly and with dignity, and to receive a reasoned decision.

Another rationale for administrative justice arises from people's practical experiences of governmental behaviours, how they impact upon people, and the political and social reactions to them. Government and public services can be competent and effective, but they can also make mistakes and errors which harm people who depend upon them. People can feel that they have been treated unfairly and insensitively by an uncaring and impersonal bureaucracy. These mistakes and errors inform people's lived experiences of government. Not all errors and failures by government result in harm and injustice to those concerned, although many do. The consequences range

[25] R Sennett, *The Culture of the New Capitalism* (New Haven, Yale University Press, 2005) 33.

from minor inconvenience and frustration to truly life-changing injustices and harms. This is far from a new phenomenon.[26] The growth of administrative governance has exponentially increased the scope for administrative injustice.

People's negative experiences of government and the sense of injustice can generate a range of emotions: outrage, frustration, disappointment, powerlessness, withdrawal and alienation. They can create wider public dissatisfaction with government and the consequent need to put things right. This also prompts the articulation of normative principles and standards as to how people should be treated by government. Government and public services should take good-quality decisions, deliver good-quality services, consider the position of individuals and be responsive to their needs, and follow the principles of good administration (see below). When government does not follow these principles, then people should be able to access and secure redress. It is the very sense of injustice and outrage arising from administrative failures that drives the need for administrative justice. This can generate political forces for enhanced redress mechanisms and greater scrutiny and improvement of government.

Administrative justice cannot be separated from politics. There are arguments for administrative justice from both the political right and left. It can be framed as both protecting the little person and their liberty and property rights against the state, and as a means of ensuring that people can secure their social rights and welfare entitlements. In both instances, administrative failures causing injustice to people can generate demands for enhanced administrative justice.

The reasons why administrative faults and mistakes arise are complex and various. Some arise from the structural relationship between the individual and government. Officials are in a position of power over people. This can result in indifference and sometimes the abuse of power. The scope for human error by officials is increased by the intricacy of individual situations and the complexity of rules and their rigidity or the flawed exercise of discretion. Other causes stem from the nature of organisational life. Officials work within large, complex institutions composed of many different levels. These organisations tend to look inwards rather than outwards. They often focus on process over outcomes, hierarchies rather than teams, rules rather than initiative, and detachment from rather than engagement with human interests.[27] They often overlook the needs of the people they are supposed to serve. There is also ineffective and inefficient organisation, and the sheer social and institutional complexity and difficulty of what government is trying to do. Such ordinary features are exacerbated by the financial pressures on government. Society's demands on government often exceed its resources and institutional capacity to deliver.

The issue of redress itself generates practical challenges for people in terms of seeking to challenge government or otherwise simply absorbing the harms that arise. The burden is placed on people who have suffered injustice to seek redress. Many people will not seek redress even though they might succeed if they did so. Conversely, many people whose grievances are without merit seek redress. A further point is that the only way of providing redress and controlling large administrative institutions is to establish separate redress institutions. These bodies are imbued with their own cultures and processes.

[26] 'The insolence of office, and the spurns that patient merit of th'unworthy takes' (*Hamlet*, Act 3, Scene I).
[27] J Bourn, *Public Sector Auditing: Is it Value for Money?* (Chichester, Wiley, 2007) 18–22.

Redress institutions can themselves operate as a different form of bureaucracy and there is no necessary reason to suppose that they necessarily always dispense justice. They often operate as microcosms of the sectors they operate within and are informed by the same social and institutional tensions. In this sense, while redress mechanisms are independent, they are not necessarily separate from government; they operate as part of the wider overall system.

Put together, the above features – people's interactions with government, the inequality of the individual–state relationship, people's lack of choice, governmental behaviours, people's lived experiences of government and the need for appropriate and effective redress mechanisms when things go wrong – justify the need for and drive the development of administrative justice. They also influence its design and operation.

Another rationale for administrative justice derives from people's happiness and how people view and cooperate with government. In 1809, Thomas Jefferson noted that 'the care of human life and happiness, and not their destruction, is the first and only legitimate objective of good government'.[28] How people are governed – and the quality of that governance – affects the quality of their lives and overall happiness. Indeed, the quality of government is a principal determinant of people's happiness – more so than their wealth and income.[29] People interact with government at a distance when they vote and when they observe government through the media. But people also experience government close up through their quotidian interactions with particular administrative systems and public services. These interactions shape and determine people's views of government. People who experience unfair administrative treatment have lower levels of satisfaction with government and public services.[30] Such interactions will play a significant role in determining their happiness. Administrative justice is one aspect of people's well-being and contentment. Exercising voice – for instance, through redress mechanisms – can mitigate the negative impacts of unfair administration, although it carries its own burdens. Pursuing redress can be stressful and the processes involved may themselves sometimes feel oppressive. Related to this is another rationale for administrative justice. People are more likely to accept and view government as legitimate and to cooperate with it if they feel that they have been treated fairly and justly. If government wants people to follow the rules and to comply with its requirements, then people are more likely to do so if they both are and feel that they are treated fairly by government itself. Such cooperation can enhance the capacity of government to manage and govern society.

The pursuit of administrative justice is therefore important and necessary. It is also a messy and problematic endeavour – both at the micro-level of individuals' interactions with government and the macro-level of governmental systems and behaviours. There

[28] Thomas Jefferson to the Republicans of Washington County, Maryland, 31 March 1809.

[29] JF Helliwell and H Huang, 'How's Your Government? International Evidence Linking Good Government and Well-Being' (2008) 38 *British Journal of Political Science* 595; JC Ott, 'Government and Happiness in 130 Nations: Good Governance Fosters Higher Level and More Equality of Happiness' (2011) 102 *Social Indications Research* 3; S Kim and D Kim, 'Does Government Make People Happy? Exploring New Research Directions for Government's Roles in Happiness' (2012) 13 *Journal of Happiness Studies* 875; S Holmberg and B Rothstein, *Good Government: The Relevance of Political Science* (Cheltenham, Edward Elgar, 2012).

[30] J Du and X Zhu, 'Bureaucratic Encounter, Voice Behaviour and Citizen Satisfaction' (2024) *Public Management Review* 1.

is an overarching and inherent tension within administrative justice between what should happen and what actually happens – and how that gap can then be closed or at least ameliorated. Government should follow the principles of good administration and embed them within its structure and operations. However, these normative standards and aspirations are often defeated by the behavioural realities of government. At the macro-level, government should operate effective and just administrative systems, and keep redress institutions up to date and, if necessary, enhance and expand their role and powers. Society's aspirations for administrative justice may exceed what government is capable of achieving. There is only so much time and money that can be devoted to administrative justice. Yet, demands for administrative justice can push government to do better. This normative-behavioural dynamic is inherent within administrative justice. It can never be fully resolved and the tensions fluctuate from one context to another and also over time.

Another way of clarifying administrative justice is to consider what it is not concerned with. Administrative justice is principally concerned with how policies are implemented, how public services are delivered and how people interact with government. Administrative justice is not concerned with the intrinsic merits or otherwise of government policy itself; these are political matters. Neither tribunals nor ombudsmen can scrutinise government policies. Tribunals decide appeals by applying the relevant rules, which embody government policy. Similarly, ombudsmen investigate complaints of maladministration; they cannot question the merits of decisions and actions taken without maladministration.[31]

Yet, the dividing line between policy and administration, and by extension administrative justice, is fuzzy. Issues of policy, its implementation and administrative justice overlap. Policy conditions administrative justice and vice versa. A policy may be so harsh in its consequences that it cannot be administered fairly. Further, redress mechanisms themselves raise policy issues. The question whether to create tribunal appeals or to reform ombudsmen is a policy decision for government. The operation of redress mechanisms can also have significant consequences for government policy and how it is administered. When tribunals allow many appeals or when ombudsman recommend that government pay high-value financial remedies, this can raise policy questions for government. Nonetheless, broadly speaking, there is often a discernible difference between policy and administrative justice; redress institutions are conscious of the need not to exceed their role.

Administrative Justice and Administrative Law

Administrative justice also needs to be distinguished from the dominant model of administrative law which is centred on the courts, judicial review, legal doctrine and the legality of administrative action. Administrative justice means something more and different. It is concerned with good administration and what happens within the legal limits of administration. This includes promoting and ensuring fairness, in a wider sense,

[31] Parliamentary Commissioner Act 1967, s 12(3); Local Government Act 1974, s 34(3).

in the interactions people have with administration. Such interactions involve individualised hearings, but also, for instance, how government communicates to people. Administrative justice is also concerned with good-quality substantive decision-making. This involves not just knowing the legal rules being applied but also the craft of holding fair hearings, making reasoned findings of fact and making decisions. Another aspect of administrative justice is the idea that government and redress mechanisms should understand and take account of people's circumstances and needs, how they are affected by governmental (in)action and what should then be done to ensure fairness and good administration. This occurs at both the level of individual interactions and large-scale mass interactions.

Administrative justice redress differs from judicial review in various ways. Tribunals decide appeals de novo on issues of fact and law. Their decisions are legally binding on government unless challenged through onward appeal. The utility of tribunals is illustrated by the fact that they have always been the principal redress mechanism against individualised decisions in areas such as benefits, tax and immigration. When benefit schemes were first established in the early twentieth century, the choice as to redress was never between the courts or tribunals; it was only ever between tribunals or no redress at all. It has always been recognised that in the context of individualised decision-making, tribunal appeals provide a more substantive, effective, efficient, quicker and accessible remedy than judicial review. Instead of sending wrong decisions back to be re-determined by a government body, tribunals make their own substantive decisions. They are aided in this respect because they specialise in particular areas of government, whereas courts are generalist bodies.

Similarly, ombudsmen were created, in large part, to provide a remedy when people had suffered injustice as a result of administrative failures which cannot be accommodated within a traditional construct of legal rights and legal principles. For instance, a person complains that a public body has delayed taking a decision. Alternatively, a public body has failed to deliver a certain service to a person as a result of a lack of joined-up working by different units within that body. In such circumstances, there is typically no remedy by way of judicial review or a tribunal because there is no legal error or decision to appeal against. These are precisely the types of informal administrative actions which ombudsmen can deal with. Their investigatory procedures differ significantly from the adversarial and legalistic procedures and culture of the courts. They investigate complaints themselves at no cost to the complainant and they apply the principles of good administration in a flexible and responsive manner. While tribunals and the courts are judicial, ombudsmen are not and this is reflected in how they operate.

Another difference between judicial review and administrative justice redress is caseload. A traditional rationale for examining administrative justice is based on a complaint of neglect. In contrast with the higher courts, administrative justice redress has been largely 'unseen, ignored and unloved'.[32] It is 'the cinderella branch of the justice system deals with more cases than any other – yet it operates largely in the shadows'.[33] Far more people use administrative justice redress than judicial review. Between 2000 and 2025, there were, on average, 5,692 judicial review claims lodged per year with the

[32] F Gibb, 'Administrative Justice and Tribunals Service Comes out of the Shadows' *The Times* (10 February 2010).
[33] ibid.

Administrative Court of England and Wales, leading to 408 substantive hearings, of which 161 were decided in favour of the claimant.[34] Of course, some judicial review claims granted permission are conceded by the public body concerned. By contrast with the courts, tribunals handle over half a million appeals per year and ombudsmen collectively handle several thousands of complaints. There is also a large amount of redress within government, including internal administrative reviews of initial decisions and a large volume of complaint-handling. Further, other forms of non-judicial scrutiny, such as the National Audit Office and public sector inspectorates and regulators, scrutinise the operation of administrative systems without having to be activated by a claimant.

None of this implies that judicial review is of minor importance or that administrative justice is without its own problems and difficulties. Judicial review performs unique functions: interpreting legislation and clarifying the law; issuing declarations of incompatibility under the Human Rights Act 1998; and ensuring that government acts lawfully. There is the precedent-setting function and radiating effects of court judgments.[35] Judicial review is also the default remedy when a public body makes initial decisions that do not attract a right of appeal. This type of litigation arises across a variety of areas (immigration, prisons, education, health etc). It comprises largely individualised challenges which rarely end up in a final court hearing or judgment. By contrast, in other large decision contexts, such as tax and benefits system, almost all routine individualised challenges are contained within administrative reviews and tribunals, except for a small number of policy challenges that go to the higher courts. Another development is some types of judicial reviews are now undertaken by the Upper Tribunal. Overall, the judicial review caseload is relatively small. The capacity of the higher courts is tightly constrained. Whenever the Administrative Court has received a high volume of repetitive challenges, caseload pressures have prompted it to restrict access or to shift those cases elsewhere.[36] There is also the limited availability of legal aid, the legalistic and adversarial nature of court litigation, and the inhibiting effects of the costs regime (by which the losing litigant pays both their own costs and those of the winning side).[37] Most people have no reasonable access to the courts. Judicial review is a costly, exclusive and largely inaccessible process, and its impact on government is variable.[38] The courts undoubtedly have an important role to play in terms of providing a practical remedy when they are used and also in terms of articulating general legal principles, but there are large areas in which their role is either non-existent or at best relatively limited.

[34] Ministry of Justice, 'Judicial Review Data Visualisation Tool', judicial-reviews-app.apps.live.cloud-platform.service.justice.gov.uk.

[35] See TT Arvind, S Halliday and L Stirton, 'Judicial Review and Administrative Justice' in M Hertogh, R Kirkham, R Thomas and J Tomlinson (eds), *The Oxford Handbook of Administrative Justice* (Oxford, Oxford University Press, 2022).

[36] This has been achieved by tightening up the permission threshold (eg, homelessness cases in the 1980s), shifting the caseload to the Upper Tribunal (eg, immigration judicial reviews in 2013) and by requesting that a particular route of challenge be reduced (eg, *Cart* judicial reviews in 2020–22). See M Sunkin, 'What is Happening to Applications for Judicial Review?' (1987) 50 *MLR* 432; R Thomas and J Tomlinson, *Immigration Judicial Reviews: An Empirical Study* (London, Palgrave Macmillan, 2021); *R (Cart) v Upper Tribunal* [2011] UKSC 28; *Independent Review of Administrative Law* (CP 407, 2021); Judicial Review and Courts Act 2022, s 2.

[37] T Hickman, 'Public Law's Disgrace' *UK Constitutional Law Blog* (9 February 2017), https://ukconstitutionallaw.org/2017/02/09/tom-hickman-public-laws-disgrace/.

[38] Halliday (n 11); M Hertogh and S Halliday (eds), *Judicial Review and Bureaucratic Impact: International and Interdisciplinary Perspectives* (Cambridge, Cambridge University Press, 2004).

As Fuller noted, there are 'serious disadvantages in any system that looks solely to the courts as a bulwark against the lawless administration of the law'.[39]

Administrative justice redress institutions have both a different role and a larger caseload than judicial review. Furthermore, administrative justice goes beyond redress to include the operations of administration itself as well as its scrutiny and improvement. The volumes of tribunal appeals and complaints far exceed that of judicial reviews, but are themselves small compared with initial governmental decision-making and the delivery of public services. The level of external redress is only the tip of the iceberg. Beneath this level, there is an intermediate level of redress within government (administrative reviews and initial complaint-handling). There is then the truly enormous scale of administrative activities and public service delivery: huge volumes of initial decisions and a wide range of other administrative actions and public services. The bottom of the pyramid is extremely large, variegated and spans multiple different contexts that people interact with. It is difficult even for those well acquainted with administrative justice to comprehend the size, scale and diversity of what happens within government and public services. It is this level that ombudsmen and the various other forms of non-judicial scrutiny – auditors, inspectorates and regulators – are concerned with evaluating and improving. They have none of the self-imposed limitations of legal doctrine. They can identify the underlying causes of systemic maladministration and injustice in a way that tribunals and the courts will never be able to. They also recommend service improvements, which go beyond the scope of judicial remedies.

Three further points deserve mention. The first is legal culture. The courts are centuries old. They form one of the basic building blocks of the legal system. By contrast, administrative justice is a much more recent development. The higher courts possess a degree of esteem and prestige which other redress bodies do not. For decades, tribunals had something of an inferiority complex. They were viewed – and often viewed themselves – as not 'proper courts'. By contrast, ombudsmen remain quite distinct and separate; they are not easily accommodated within a legal culture focused on judicial procedures. However, veneration for the courts should not obscure the fact that the scale of administrative justice exceeds that of the courts. It also performs a complementary role.

Second, many of the theoretical and doctrinal controversies concerning judicial review do not arise in the context of administrative justice. For instance, the debates over the constitutional foundations of judicial review and the standard of review do not arise in the administrative justice context.[40] Tribunals and ombudsmen both have a statutory basis. Tribunals can decide appeals only because they have the statutory jurisdiction to do so. The same applies to ombudsmen.

A third and related point concerns legal research methodology. Conventional legal analysis of administrative law is often based on the assumption that law is an autonomous discipline separate from administration and politics. From within this framework, case law and the principles of judicial review are subject to legal analysis in the search for conceptual coherence in legal doctrine. Not all of the judicial review literature adopts this approach, although a significant amount does. However,

[39] LL Fuller, *The Morality of Law* (New Haven, Yale University Press, 1969) 81.
[40] C Forsyth (ed), *Judicial Review and the Constitution* (Oxford, Hart Publishing, 2000).

this methodology is inapplicable to administrative justice. What is more important for administrative justice are the design and operation of administrative processes, the institutional behaviours of government, the role and impact of redress and scrutiny institutions, and the pursuit of good administration. Another essential aspect is the experiences and needs of people who rely upon government and use redress mechanisms – and those who do not. Administrative justice exists at the intersection of law, politics and administration. Accordingly, the appropriate methodology to investigate and analyse it is empirical, normative and evaluative. The focus of administrative justice is not the search for conceptual coherence. Instead, the animating concerns are the very real problems created by administration and people's interactions with government; the grinding, relentless practical challenges of seeking to secure just treatment for people and to enhance the workings of government.

The Principles of Good Administration

Given their centrality to administrative justice, the principles of good administration need to be highlighted. Some of the principles are taken from the nature of judicial decision-making. Other principles are embedded in good administrative practices and people's expectations of just administration.

In typical British fashion, various principles of good administration have evolved ad hoc over time as part of the development of administrative justice. Consider procedural fairness and reason-giving. Fair process is embedded within judicial practice and has been adopted by tribunals. It enables people to participate in decisions that affect them; it also improves the quality of decisions. Consider reasons for administrative decisions. The importance of giving adequate, proper and intelligible reasons has long been recognised. In 1932, the Donoughmore Committee on ministerial powers recommended that tribunals should observe the principles of natural justice and give reasons for their decisions.[41] The position of ombudsmen is that public bodies should be open and accountable by giving reasons for their decisions. Giving reasons enables people affected by decisions to understand the basis upon which they have been taken. It can also raise public confidence and enable people to challenge poor decisions.[42]

The Franks Report on tribunals (1957) emphasised that tribunals be informed by the principles of openness, fairness, and impartiality.[43] The 1961 JUSTICE report recommended the creation of ombudsmen to investigate administrative actions which had been flawed by maladministration. The report recognised that the circumstances giving rise to such complaints were of infinite variety and assumed different forms: the abuse of power; oppressive behaviour; unequal treatment; negligence or error; and so on.[44] The report considered that it was too early to develop general principles of administrative conduct. However, over time, the momentum for an agreed set of principles of

[41] Donoughmore Committee, *Committee on Ministers' Powers* (Cmd 4060, 1932) 99–100.

[42] Precisely the same arguments for reason-giving were forcefully made by a civil servant writing in 1836: H Taylor, *The Statesman* (New York, Mentor Books, 1958 [1836]) 102–03.

[43] Franks Committee, *Report of the Committee on Administrative Tribunals and Enquiries* (Cmnd 218, 1957).

[44] JUSTICE, *The Citizen and the Administration: The Redress of Grievances* (London, Stevens, 1961) 34–35.

good administration grew. Such principles were required to clarify the standards of behaviour that people could expect from government. The principles would also be used by ombudsmen to assess governmental actions and performance.[45] There were also wider European developments in this direction.[46] The counter-argument was that a formal code of principles of good administration could generate bureaucratic rigidity and reduce the flexibility required when unforeseen situations occur.

Eventually, ombudsmen published their principles of good administration.[47] This was a consequence of the broader formalisation of administrative justice, the need for agreed principles and the accumulated casework experience of ombudsmen. There was a perceived need to reverse the traditional retrospective focus on maladministration, which could generate defensive administration, by elaborating principles to promote good administration.[48] The then Parliamentary and Health Service Ombudsman argued that far from being a tame and unexciting aspiration, good administration is 'a critical component of much that we continue to value most in public life and in public service delivery'; good administration is 'the space where much of our theory collides with practice in situations of most acute concern' to people.[49]

The principles of good administration are: getting it right; being customer-focused; being open and accountable; acting fairly and proportionately; putting things right; and seeking continuous improvement. Each principle is broken down into more specific components.[50] In summary, the principles embody a broad concept that when people interact with administration, they should be treated fairly and humanely. They are used by ombudsmen to evaluate the quality of administrative actions to determine and whether public bodies have engaged in maladministration or service failure. The principles also provide guidance for and clarify what people can expect from government.

The principles of good administration generally concern administration actions. By contrast, individualised decision-making by government and tribunals has its own generally accepted set of principles. When a public body makes individualised decisions, it should ensure that applicants can access and understand the process and the criteria that decision-makers apply. Decision-makers should be competent, well trained, and understand the rules and guidance they apply. The process should be efficient. Decisions should be taken within a reasonable period of time and should consider relevant and material evidence. Decisions should be taken by applying the relevant rules

[45] JUSTICE later recommended a code of principles of good administration: JUSTICE, *Administration under Law* (London, Stevens, 1971); JUSTICE-All Souls Review, *Administrative Justice: Some Necessary Reforms* (Oxford, Oxford University Press, 1988) ch 2.

[46] Council of Europe, *Recommendation on the Protection of the Individual in Relation the Acts of Administrative Authorities* 28 September 1977 R(77)31; Council of Europe, *Recommendation of the Committee of Ministers Concerning the Exercise of Discretionary Powers by Administrative Authorities* 11 March 1980 R(80)2; European Ombudsman, *The European Code of Good Administrative Behaviour* (2001); S Nason, 'The Impact of Pan-European General Principles of Good Administration on United Kingdom Administrative Law: Shared Principles in a Strained Relationship' in U Stelkens and A Andrijauskaite (eds), *Good Administration and the Council of Europe: Law, Principles, and Effectiveness* (Oxford, Oxford University Press, 2020).

[47] Local Government Ombudsman, *Good Administrative Practice* (London, Commission for Local Administration in England, 1993) (Appendix E); Parliamentary and Health Service Ombudsman, *Principles of Good Administration* (2007) (Appendix A).

[48] A Abraham, 'Good Administration: Why We Need it More Than Ever' (2009) 80 *Political Quarterly* 25.

[49] ibid.

[50] See Appendix A.

and guidance. Decision-makers should consider the circumstances of individual claims, be impartial and approach each case with an open mind. They should give adequate, proper and intelligible reasons for their decisions and there should be some route of onward redress, whether by way of administrative review, tribunal appeal, internal complaint and/or complaint to an ombudsman or other body.

All of these principles are grounded in casework experience. They prescribe how people ought to be treated by government and the values which should inform those interactions. They are also used to evaluate and assess administration. Ideally, government bodies would internalise and embed the principles of good administration. To some extent, this happens, but not always. The central and perennial challenge of administrative justice concerns the degree to which government lives up to the principles of good administration in practice and how people are then affected. The principles are conditioned by and take colour from their context and application. These points are typical of the way that administrative justice has unfolded over time and how it is practised. There is always scope to adjust and mould the principles in response to particular instances. The nature of the principles also evolves over time. For instance, the principle of seeking continuous improvement requires public bodies to review their policies and procedures to ensure that they are effective. Public bodies should then take account and act upon feedback so that they learn appropriate lessons in order to improve their services and performance. This aligns with the notion of organisational learning.

Matters can become more complex. The principles of good administration are not always consistent with each other. They are also contingent in terms of their precise nature and how they are applied in practice. There is an obvious tension between a decision-making process being both fair and efficient and deciding where the optimum balance lies. How the principles are applied depends on both the context and the forces in play, who is applying them and the weight given to one principle over another. Just to state the need for administrative justice only begs the question as to what it actually requires in any particular area and situation and, of course, this will differ from one context to another.

The evolving notion of systemic administrative justice has also generated discrete principles of good administration, which reflect the complex nature of institutional problems that occur within administrative systems. These principles themselves assume an institutional and structural character. For instance, when a caseworker takes individualised decisions, the decision-maker needs to understand the applicant's case and treat them fairly. By contrast, a more systemic approach to good administration requires that the government body concerned possesses a sufficient institutional understanding and appreciation of the position and needs of the whole cohort of people who use a particular public service. This understanding needs to be present not just at the level of front-line operational delivery, but also at the higher policy-making level. Another principle concerns the need for internal controls. Whenever government operates a large decision-making process, it will know that a certain number of decisions may well be wrong. Accordingly, government should establish and operate appropriate internal and quality assurance systems to monitor and guard against the risk of error. Such internal systems must themselves be effective in identifying systemic errors. Finally, government should be aware that the institutional cultures embodied within administrative systems can generate – and indeed normalise – systemic maladministration, thereby disadvantaging a whole group of people. Front-line officials are typically focused on processing decisions and lack the perspective to identify such systemic maladministration precisely because they are too deeply embedded within that system and its institutional culture, and can thereby become desensitised to what can be significant injustices. These and other principles of systemic good administration will be examined later on.

Overall, administrative justice is an ongoing project of governing, treating people fairly, making administration accountable and seeking its improvement. It is always in the process of being created and re-created. It is generated by the problems people experience in their interactions with government, which then prompts the articulation of relevant principles as normative standards to assess the justice of such interactions. Administrative justice needs to be understood from the perspective of both the individual and government. It involves trade-offs as to which changes are possible to improve justice while also ensuring the efficient implementation and delivery of services. It is a very practical endeavour and can only be understood in context by examining specific issues and problems. Figure 1.1 provides a very simplified version of the overall structure of administrative justice in the UK. Having outlined administrative justice, we can examine how it has developed and evolved.

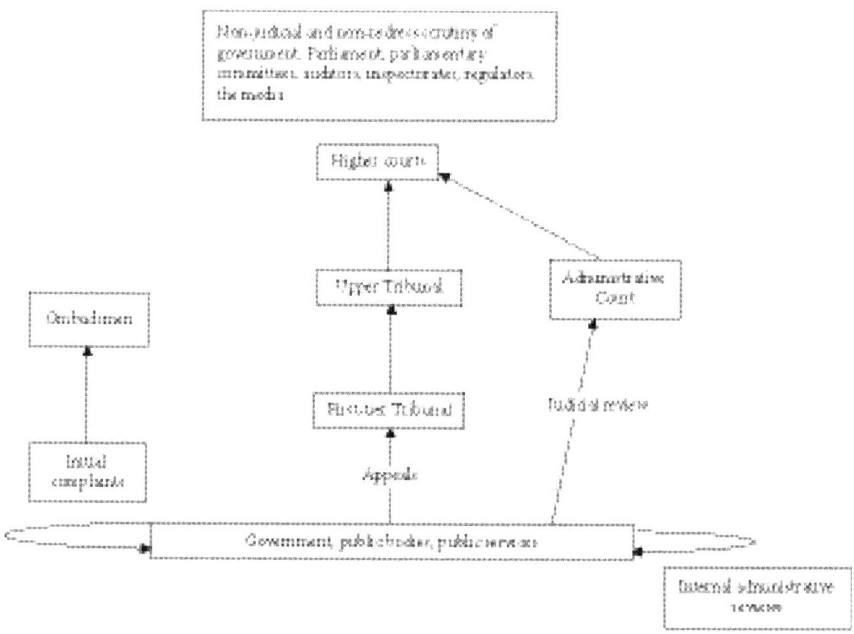

Figure 1.1 The overall structure of administrative justice in the UK

2

State, Society and Administrative Justice

To understand administrative justice, it is necessary to appreciate its historical development and how it has evolved. To this end, this chapter examines the growth of administrative justice in the twentieth century. More specifically, it considers the expansion of the post-war welfare state and the challenges this posed in terms of providing people with effective means of securing redress for their grievances. The chapter examines two major episodes in the evolution of administrative justice: the Franks Report on tribunals, which brought them into the formal constitutional landscape; and the establishment of ombudsmen, a relatively innovative development that created a new institution that was hitherto without parallel in the UK. However, before considering these matters, the chapter commences by exploring the dynamic that underpins and drives the progression of administrative justice, namely the tensions inherent in the relationship between the state and society. And to explore this, we will start not in post-war Britain, but in Renaissance Venice.

Bocche di leone and the Narrow Corridor of Liberty

In Venice, dotted around the city, are the famous Lions' Mouths (*bocche di leone*). These carved receptacles are built into the stone walls of public buildings. Each of them has a face, often that of a lion. The oldest Lion's Mouth dates from 1618. It is embedded within the Doge's Palace and is still intact today. A lion's face was used because the winged lion of St Mark is the symbol of Venice. There is an ancient bronze winged lion sculpture in the Piazza San Marco in Venice.[1]

During the Renaissance, the Lions' Mouths had a particular purpose. They were the means by which Venetian citizens could lodge complaints against other Venetians and also against the government. Each state department had its own Lion's Mouth. Venetian citizens submitted their complaints by inserting their hand-written letters into the Lion's Mouth. The legend beneath one of the Lion's Mouth faces reads: *denontie secrete in materie di stato* ('secret denunciations in matters of the state'). Another reads: *denontie secrete contro chi occultera gratie et officii o colludera per nasconder la vera rendita d essi* (secret denunciations against anyone who conceals favours and services or will collude to hide the true revenue from them).

[1] en.wikipedia.org/wiki/Lion_of_Saint_Mark. See generally A Zorzi, *Venice 697–1797: City, Republic, Empire* (London, Sidgwick & Jackson, 1983).

By law, anonymous complaints were accepted only if made against public officials. The complaints were read and considered by the relevant state department. Complaints signed and supported by witnesses were often considered by Venice's highest main governing body, the Council of Ten, which had authority over all government actions. Complaints could be used, amongst other things, to accuse officials of misusing their powers. The system of government in Venice was an oligarchic republic led by its ruler, the Doge. Venetian citizens generally supported the system of government, and Venice was known locally as *La Serenissima* (the most serene Republic of Venice). It has been argued that, by enabling citizens to make complaints, the Lions' Mouths played a part in creating a strong republic in Venice. They enabled citizens' grievances against officials to be aired and taken seriously.[2] Consequently, Venetian citizens felt that their government listened to and was responsive to their concerns. Both the Venetian state and its society prospered. When Napoleon occupied Venice in 1797, its reputation of being a calm and orderly republic came to an end. Many of the Lions' Mouths were destroyed.

One theme that arises from this is the degree to which the provision of a specific mechanism for considering people's grievances enabled the Venetian government to become more acceptable to its people and more responsive to their needs. People could lodge anonymous complaints against officials who were misusing their powers. These complaints were considered and taken seriously by those in authority. This helped to create a strong republic because the views of ordinary citizens were given weight. Accordingly, Venice came to enjoy a remarkable degree of liberty and prosperity.

There are grounds for questioning this account. In addition to enabling people to complain against officials, the Lion's Mouths also allowed people to make secret denunciations against adulterers and those expressing anti-republic sentiments. Complaints provided the authorities with a source of information and served as a form of surveillance and social control.[3] Moreover, the image of Venice as a bastion of calm serenity and orderliness compared with other Italian republics ridden and toppled by internal conflicts is now seen by some as something of a myth.[4] Nonetheless, the history of the Venetian Lion's Mouths suggests a wider point about the development of administrative justice, how it operates and the basic social and political forces underpinning it.

At the centre of administrative justice is a tension between the state and society. The state exercises power over people's lives in order to protect society, to provide public services and to manage the economy. When exercised with care, such power is beneficial to people and society. The state provides public security and thereby ensures people can live safe lives. It provides public services that support people and meets their needs. And it manages the economy to secure economic security and growth. However, the state can also exercise its powers in ways that are unfair, harm people and create injustice. When this happens, then there will likely be a corresponding reaction by society. People will

[2] K Dietz, 'Need to Complain? Here's How Renaissance-Era Venetians Did it' *National Geographic* (31 December 2020).

[3] RA Sparling, 'Corruption and Whistleblowing: Beccaria and Montesquieu on Secret Crimes and Secret Accusations' (2020) 61 *The Eighteenth Century* 413, 414–18.

[4] J Johnson, *Venice Incognito: Masks in the Serene Republic Unmasked* (Berkeley, University of California Press, 2011); M van Gelder and F de Vivo, 'Papering over Protest: Contentious Politics and Archival Suppression in Early Modern Venice' (2023) 258 *Past & Present* 44.

become concerned about the extent and exercise of the state's powers. Society will want the state's powers to be controlled and held accountable. Individual people will have grievances and these will often reflect wider social concerns about the behaviours of the state. Accordingly, mechanisms must be devised so that people can seek redress against the state – to ensure fairness and to make it accountable and responsive to people's needs. Such mechanisms include many basic constitutional arrangements, including elections, representative government, parliamentary scrutiny and so on. Another set of mechanisms include administrative justice redress processes – complaints, tribunals, ombudsmen and so on. It is these mechanisms that resolve grievances on an individual basis and thereby make the exercise of state power accountable and responsive to people's needs.

If this analysis is credible, then the area known as administrative justice is deeply embedded within the wider relationship between the state and society and the tensions inherent within it. Further, many of the developments in administrative justice and also its problems reflect and embody these frictions between the state and society. These tensions relate to different perspectives about how state power should be exercised and how people should be treated by the state, how they can seek redress against it and how to make it accountable.

This theory has been elaborated by Acemoglu and Robinson in their book *The Narrow Corridor*.[5] Their purpose is to explain why some societies have achieved liberty and why others have fallen into either authoritarianism or anarchy. In essence, their theory is that for liberty to emerge and flourish, both the state and society must be strong. A strong state is required to protect civil order, to resolve disputes, to provide public services and to create the right conditions for economic growth. This gives people the ability to make and pursue their own choices. Without the state, there would be a Hobbesian state of nature in which life would be short, nasty and brutish. However, the state can also become too powerful, abuse its power and infringe upon people's liberty. A strong, mobilised society is therefore needed to control and influence the state – to ensure it protects people's liberty. Without a strong society, the state may become a 'despotic Leviathan'. When this happens, liberty is weak or non-existent and an authoritarian state dominates. The influence of society is eroded and people are unable to resist and challenge the state.[6]

The cause of liberty therefore depends on an ongoing competition between the state and society. If liberty is to flourish and be preserved, then the growth of state power must be met by social demands that such power be subject to control and thereby made accountable. In this way, the state becomes more responsive to people's needs. Society can do this through collective social action. People can come together to challenge the state, to influence or oppose it, and bring it under control and make it accountable. This involves both non-institutionalised action – for instance, public protests and demonstrations – and institutionalised controls such as elections, legislatures and parliamentary scrutiny.

[5] D Acemoglu and JA Robinson, *The Narrow Corridor: States, Societies, and the Fate of Liberty* (New York, Penguin, 2019).

[6] The other extreme is an 'absent Leviathan'. In this model, society is too strong and the state is weak. The problem is not the state having excessive power, but it being either non-existent or too weak and ineffectual, potentially leading to anarchy.

If society is unable to challenge and influence the state, then government is likely to act in a high-handed way and become a law unto itself.

This tension between the state and society can never be resolved once and for all. Achieving liberty is an ongoing and evolving process. It is an essential aspect of developing an effective government that is responsive to people's needs and subject to control and scrutiny – a 'shackled leviathan'. In this situation, the state has power and authority, but it is exercised for the benefit of its people. It is subject to checks and controls through representative institutions and other mechanisms, including legal controls and administrative justice mechanisms. This type of state emerges when there is a balance between the power of the state and the ability of society to control and influence it. Countries that have developed this type of balance are within 'the narrow corridor of liberty'.

The process of managing the tensions between the state and society is called the 'Red Queen' effect.[7] This refers to the situation in which both the state and society have to keep running in order to maintain an equilibrium with each other. When the state accumulates more power, then society must respond. It needs to compete with the state to check and control it. The more powerful the state becomes, the more powerful and vigilant society must become to make the state accountable. The state will also keep developing. It needs to do so to develop its capacity in the face of new and formidable challenges posed by social, economic and technological changes. This is essential if the state is to enforce the law, provide public services and protect liberty. The space created by the competition between the state and society in which both work together with each other constructively is the narrow corridor of in which liberty is created, negotiated and preserved.

How the 'Red Queen' effect plays out in practice is often messy, contingent and unpredictable. It cannot be easily planned or designed in advance. In extreme situations, it involves protest, violence and internal conflict. In other contexts, more civil means are used to discipline and influence the state. On some occasions, the demands of society for the state to be made more accountable and responsive will be met with a counter-reaction by the state to weaken and dilute those demands. On other occasions, both sides will recognise the need for compromise. The 'Red Queen' effect is necessary for human progress and liberty. It makes both the state and society more capable. It reconfigures the nature of state institutions by making them more accountable and more responsive to people's needs. It also involves the design and creation of new institutions through which people can hold the state to account.

This theory provides a big picture framework of why liberty exists and how it develops. It is also clear that there is a direct link with administrative justice. For a start, there is a deep connection between the redress of people's grievances against government and the concept of liberty. In 1644, the English poet John Milton noted:

> For this is not the liberty which we can hope, that no grievance ever should arise in the Commonwealth – that let no man in this world expect; but when complaints are freely heard, deeply considered and speedily reformed, then is the utmost bound of civil liberty attained, that wise men look for.[8]

[7] In Lewis Carroll's *Through the Looking Glass*, the Red Queen advises Alice that 'it takes all the running you can do, to keep in the same place'.

[8] J Milton, *Areopagitica* (1644). See W Chernaik, 'Civil Liberty in Milton, the Levellers, and Winstanley' (1999) 22 *Prose Studies* 102.

No one expects government to be perfect and for complaints not to arise. However, people do expect government to listen to their grievances, consider them and act upon them. When this happens, the cause of liberty is advanced. For Milton, liberty and freedom needed to be strenuously defended as they could easily be lost. Milton defined civil liberty as comprising, in part, people's freedom to complain and the willingness of those in power to listen to and consider such grievances and to provide redress. Similarly, William Walwyn, a Leveller and contemporary of Milton, argued that: 'The greatest glory of authority is to protect the distressed; and for those that are Judges in other mens causes to beare themselves as if the afflicted mens cases were their owne.'[9] The redress of grievances is therefore one site – and an important one at that – in which the state and society compete with each other and through which the pursuit of liberty can be either advanced or diminished. Only countries already within the narrow corridor of liberty use administrative justice as a means of protecting liberty.

A second point is that we now live in an administrative state which assumes positive responsibility for providing public services for the collective public good. The tension between the state and society endures, but it has assumed a different character, given the nature of administrative governance. The notion of administrative justice only becomes conceptually possible in the context of a state apparatus in which public services are delivered and policies are implemented first and foremost by public servants and administrative institutions. With this growth of governmental responsibilities and activities, the risks to liberty become more acute. The state can infringe people's liberty by limiting their freedoms. It can also do so by not providing people with their legal entitlements and the public services – health, benefits, housing and education – which they depend upon. In the process, the concept of liberty has itself been transformed. It now assumes both a negative and a positive meaning. Liberty no longer means solely the absence of state intervention or dominance; it also requires effective and competent action by government to provide public services. The state can infringe upon people's liberty by invading their personal freedom and by not providing public services upon which they rely.

Overall, administrative justice concerns the relationship between the state and society. More specifically, administrative justice is about how people are affected by the exercise of administrative powers and how society reacts to the exercise of administrative powers by the state. This is important because administration is how the state implements its policies and what people interact with. Administrative justice is then directly connected to the relationship between the individual and the state, how that relationship has developed over time, and society's expectations of fair treatment and how government should behave towards people. The growth of administrative justice should therefore be situated and understood within the context of the wider relationship between the state and society.

How then does this theory apply to the development of administrative justice in Britain? To examine this question, we need to consider the controversies concerning administrative justice that occurred in the 1950s and 1960s. But before considering the debates of those decades, we need to start in the 1940s.

[9] W Walwyn, 'The Compassionate Samaritane' (1644) in JR McMichael and B Taft (eds), *The Writings of William Walwyn* (Athens, GA, University of Georgia Press, 1989) 123.

The Post-war British State and the Redress of Grievances

At the height of the Second World War, William Beveridge, then director of the London School of Economics, published his report entitled *Social Insurance and Allied Services.*[10] This revolutionary report set out detailed proposals for addressing social inequality by introducing the welfare state. Beveridge's guiding principles included the provision of social welfare support to citizens as part of a comprehensive policy of social progress. There were 'five giants' that prevented people from living better lives and which had to be addressed: want; ignorance; squalor; idleness; and disease. Beveridge was clear that positive action by the state was needed to address these evils; philanthropy alone was insufficient.

The Labour Party promised to implement Beveridge's proposals if elected to government. The proposals were very popular. Having won a landslide victory in the 1945 general election, the Labour government proceeded to put the Beveridge plan into action. This involved enacting numerous statutes, including the National Health Service Act 1946, the National Insurance Act 1946 and the National Assistance Act 1948.[11] This created a comprehensive from 'the cradle to grave' system of social insurance. The National Health Service was established to provide free healthcare to people based on need rather than their ability to pay. To address the shortage of housing, the Town and Country Planning Act of 1947 introduced planning controls and played an important role in the expansion of council housing. The Labour government also nationalised various industries to support employment and to enable the government to manage the economy. The British state now assumed responsibility for people's well-being in ways that would have been unimaginable only a decade earlier. The crucial experience of the war was that the central state could and would direct and command the economy and society during the war effort; it could now do the same in peacetime for the purposes of post-war reconstruction and to create the welfare state.[12]

All of this involved a significant expansion and deepening of state capacity. The growth of administration was grafted onto and reinforced the pre-existing top-down structures of British central government. The key institutional features were the centralisation of the state and its organisation into government departments responsible for policy and its administration.[13] The pervasive governing assumption was that central government had the almost universal right to decide on matters of policy and administration because government ministers were elected and responsible to Parliament. The public interest was what ministers said it was, subject to parliamentary scrutiny. It was for civil servants to advise ministers and to give effect to their wishes. The views of affected people counted for relatively little. Moreover, there was the legacy of the

[10] W Beveridge, *Social Insurance and Allied Services: Report by Sir William Beveridge* (Cmnd 6404, 1942) (hereinafter 'Beveridge Report').

[11] An earlier statute, the Education Act 1944, was written by Rab Butler MP, then Secretary of State for Education.

[12] P Hennessy, *Never Again: Britain 1945–51* (London, Penguin, 2006); D Kynaston, *Austerity Britain 1945–51* (London, Bloomsbury, 2007).

[13] WJM MacKenzie and JW Grove, *Central Administration in Britain* (London, Longmans, 1957); DN Chester and FMG Wilson, *The Organization of British Central Government 1914–1956* (London, Allen & Unwin, 1957).

wartime experience which naturally induced government to prioritise the public interest and to give short shrift to anyone who complained.

Given its commitment to central economic planning, nationalisation and the welfare state, the Labour Party viewed a powerful executive as an essential precondition for implementing its policies. This extension of governmental power and the provision of new public services were controversial, but received widespread public support. The Labour government was concerned that unelected conservative elements in the constitution, in particular the House of Lords and the judiciary, might obstruct its programme for government. There was resistance to the courts having any role in the social welfare system. Given his experience as a barrister, Beveridge doubted both the efficacy and impartiality of 'needlessly expensive' court ligation; it was 'obviously desirable as a matter of social policy' to remove disputes from this 'arena of litigation and conflict' and for them to be handled instead by tribunals.[14] In 1946, Aneurin Bevan, then Health Secretary, spoke of his fear of 'judicial sabotage of socialist legislation'.[15] This distrust of lawyers and the judiciary was complemented by faith in political institutions. There had been warnings from some, such as Friedrich Hayek, that socialist state planning and the management of the economy would undermine individual liberty and the rule of law, although at the time such concerns attracted little support.[16] The Conservative government elected in 1951 did not seek to reverse or abolish the welfare state. To a large extent, it continued the same the economic policies as Labour – a mixed economy and Keynesianism as part of the post-war consensus.

Public attitudes towards governmental administration had been hugely influenced by the war effort and the need for social and economic change following it. The public were largely deferential to those in power, although there was a degree of scepticism towards low-level bureaucrats ordering people about and telling them what they could and could not do. The phrase that 'the gentleman in Whitehall really does know better what is good for people than the people know themselves' became notorious.[17] The growth of administrative power was, of course, also highly political. Despite the broad consensus between Labour and the Conservatives, there was a deep-seated ideological difference in certain policy areas, especially the Town and Country Planning Act 1947.[18]

The expansion of administrative power in the post-war years and increased state control of people's lives inevitably raised the problem of arbitrary government and the position of the individual aggrieved by high-handed officialdom. Such concerns arose from various administrative schemes, some of which directly affected property rights: town and country planning; housing; and agriculture. In Britain, the redress of

[14] Beveridge Report (n 10) 37, 46, 130 and 148; J Fulbrook, *Administrative Justice and the Unemployed* (London, Mansell, 1978) 140.

[15] HC Deb (series 5) 23 July 1946, vol 425, col 1983 (Aneurin Bevan MP). See also HWR Wade, 'Administrative Tribunals and Administrative Justice' (1981) 55 *Australian Law Journal* 374.

[16] FA Hayek, *The Road to Serfdom* (London, Routledge, 1944).

[17] D Jay, *The Socialist Case* (London, Faber & Faber, 1937) 317. For a revisionist appraisal, see P Toye, '"The Gentleman in Whitehall" Reconsidered: The Evolution of Douglas Jay's Views on Economic Planning and Consumer Choice, 1937–47' (2002) 67 *Labour History Review* 187.

[18] P Weiler, 'Labour and the Land: From Municipalization to the Land Commission, 1951–71' (2008) 19 *Twentieth Century British History* 314, 321–22.

grievances had always been principally a function of the political process.[19] For centuries, Parliament had been the forum for airing grievances through petitions and MPs. In the 1770s, Burke had suggested that 'an openness, approaching towards facility, to public complaint' was one of the 'true characteristics of a House of Commons'.[20] Even by 1946, a leading constitutional lawyer, ECS Wade, still maintained that the 'primary function of Parliament … [was] the remedying of grievances and not the passing of legislation'.[21] However, given the advent of mass administration, parliamentary mechanisms of redress had become increasingly unsuited to securing individual redress. As the former Labour Minister, Lord Silkin, explained:

> Parliamentary democracy would become impossible if every single administrative act of a Minister were to become a subject of debate, of delay and of controversy. One recognises that Parliament has every right to deal with policy, and no one wishes to stifle discussions on policy. But on the detailed day-to-day implementation of policy it can really become very burdensome, and the machine could be entirely clogged if every single decision were subject to the possibility of public debate in this House or another place.[22]

A senior judge, Lord Cooper, similarly noted that the doctrine of ministerial responsibility, by which all administrative decisions were taken by ministers who were then answerable to Parliament, had become a myth. 'In 99 cases out of 100 the decision is a decision of departmental officials' about which the minister knew nothing, except when he was provided with a departmental brief to answer questions on the matter in Parliament.[23] The minister was 'normally the mere mouthpiece of his officials'.[24] Accordingly, 'as an effective safeguard to an aggrieved individual, a Parliamentary challenge' by an MP was 'worth next to nothing'.[25] Parliament enabled MPs to scrutinise and discuss of policy and ask questions of ministers, but such methods were an entirely inappropriate means of checking the millions of individual decisions taken by civil servants. Relying on Parliament as a way of securing redress was not only inadequate, but also constrained Parliament in undertaking its other principal functions.

If parliamentary controls were an inappropriate means of reconsidering individual administrative decisions and actions, then more suitable mechanisms were required. What remedies did exist were controversial. Various types of administrative decisions could be appealed to tribunals, adjudicative bodies which were not then part of the formal judicial system. Tribunals had developed in a haphazard and ad hoc manner.[26] Their use and growth had been closely associated with the social legislation of the early

[19] FF Ridley, 'The Citizen against Authority: British Approaches to the Redress of Grievances' (1984) 37 *Parliamentary Affairs* 1.

[20] E Burke, 'Thoughts on the Present Discontents' (1770) in I Kramnick (ed) *The Portable Burke* (London, Penguin, 1999) 132.

[21] House of Commons Select Committee on Procedure, Third Report (HC 1945–46, 189) Q 5150 (ECS Wade, Downing Professor of Laws, University of Cambridge).

[22] HL Deb 17 February 1954, vol 185, cols 982–83 (Lord Silkin). Silkin had been Minister of Town and Country Planning (1945–50).

[23] Lord Cooper, 'Administrative Justice' (1954) 32 *Public Administration* 165, 167.

[24] ibid.

[25] ibid.

[26] WJL Ambrose, 'The New Judiciary' (1910) 26 *LQR* 203; CT Carr, *Concerning English Administrative Law* (New York, Columbia University Press, 1941) ch 4; RSW Pollard (ed), *Administrative Tribunals at Work: A Symposium* (London, Stevens, 1950); CK Allen, *Administrative Jurisdiction* (London, Stevens, 1956).

twentieth century. In 1906, the Liberal government had won a landslide parliamentary majority to improve living conditions for working-class and under-privileged people.[27] Its programme of social reform included: old age pensions; unemployment insurance; public health; tax; education; local government; and housing and town planning. Various administrative schemes were introduced, which involved individualised decision-making in areas such as old age pensions and unemployment insurance. There was a need for the quick and effective adjudication of disputes arising from the implementation of these new social policies. Tribunals had been established to judicialise a specific segment of the wider administrative process.[28] They would combine justice with efficiency.[29] Tribunals were used instead of the higher courts for various reasons. The slow, expensive, adversarial and legalistic procedures of the courts were ill-suited to handling a large number of appeals from people who could not afford legal representation. Judicial review as it operates today did not exist. Moreover, the attitudes and culture of the judiciary were often hostile to the underlying social purposes of the new administrative schemes. In some contexts, these tribunal systems included both first-tier and also second-tier tribunals, such as the unemployment insurance Umpire (a barrister) who decided onward appeals against decisions of the first-tier appeal bodies, the Courts of Referees.[30]

There was a real ambiguity about the constitutional status of tribunals. They were administrative and not part of the formal judiciary, although they made individualised 'judicial' decisions concerning people's legal rights and entitlements. As a pragmatic matter, administrative adjudication through tribunals was vastly preferable to the heavily judicialised procedures, delays and costs of the higher courts and their hostility to the new positive social policies.[31] The tribunals were free and legal representation was not required. Moreover, the tribunals were applying a new type of law quite unknown to the courts; neither common law precedents nor rules of private law, but evolving regulatory standards concerning matters such as medical treatment, sanitation, housing and education, which took their substance from changing social environments and needs. The rationale for tribunals was functional: administrative-judicial decisions had to be taken so that government could get its work done.[32] However, tribunals had evolved piecemeal on an ad hoc basis without any sense of them comprising an overall

[27] C Cross, *The Liberals in Power (1905–1914)* (London, Pall Mall Press, 1963); JR Hay, *Origins of the Liberal Welfare Reforms, 1906–14* (London, Macmillan, 1975); I Packer, *Liberal Government and Politics, 1905–15* (London, Palgrave Macmillan, 2006) ch 7.

[28] The generic label 'tribunals' risks implying a far more consciously designed system from what actually existed. 'Tribunals' were known by various titles – a Commissioner, a Board, a Court of Referees, an Umpire, an appellate body and so on. They developed and operated on an ad hoc basis in isolation from each other. As RE Wraith and PG Hutchesson, *Administrative Tribunals* (London, Allen & Unwin, 1974) 43 noted, the phrase 'administrative tribunals' was 'unfortunate and misleading … the nomenclature of the subject is chaotic'.

[29] E Barker, 'The "Rule of Law" in *Church, State and Society* (London, Methuen, 1930) 178–90. Central government departments also decided appeals against various local government decisions: FHC Wiltshire, 'The Appellate Jurisdiction of Central Government Departments' (1924) 2 *Public Administration* 370.

[30] Selected decisions of the Umpire were published. See, eg, Ministry of Labour, *Unemployment Insurance Acts 1920–1929: Selected Decisions Given by the Umpire From 19th April 1920, to 12th March 1930 Respecting Claims to Benefit* (HMSO, 1930).

[31] B Abel-Smith and R Stevens, *Lawyers and the Courts: A Sociological Study of the English Legal System 1750–1965* (London, Heinemann, 1967) 111–21.

[32] S Leathes, 'The Alleged "New Despotism": Reply to the Lord Chief Justice: The Civil Service View' *Daily Telegraph* (10 October 1929).

system. The logical response would have been to amalgamate them together into a comprehensive system of administrative law, as recommended by Robson.[33] However, this was at odds with the Diceyan tradition and its emphasis upon the higher courts; constructing a distinct system of administrative law composed of tribunals was viewed as inherently antithetical to the received understanding of the rule of law.

With the advent of the post-war welfare state, tribunals grew exponentially. As CK Allen noted in 1956, 'nothing is more remarkable in our present social and administrative arrangements than the proliferation of tribunals of many different kinds. There is scarcely a new statute of social or economic complexion which does not add to their number'.[34] Tribunals were established in many areas, including social security, agricultural land, rent assessments, health and local valuation. While tribunals had previously been an 'unobtrusive and rarely used piece of machinery', they had, within a relatively short period of time, become a ubiquitous and immensely influential means of settling conflicts between government and people.[35] Tribunals could handle a far larger caseload than the courts and were also more efficient. The tribunals were administrative and departmental. They were the means through which judicial procedures were widely used and integrated within the functions and structures of specific government departments. Some of the 'administrative judges' in the tribunals were officials and lay people appointed by the relevant department. Some were lawyers appointed from outside the civil service. They were de facto independent and had security of tenure.[36] Traditions of legal procedure were pervasive.[37] However, there was no overarching tribunal system, only a plethora of different tribunals, each with its own practices. The system lacked intelligibility rather than fairness.[38]

The legal establishment was deeply sceptical. Tribunals were not seen as 'proper courts', but inferior bodies likely to act unfairly and not be independent of government. They had developed rapidly and were unsystematic and 'sadly lacking in consistency of principle'.[39] Tribunals were appendages of their parent government departments which also controlled tribunal procedures and their administration.[40] By contrast, others, such as Robson, viewed tribunals as inherently connected with changed social conditions and the expansion of governmental functions. Tribunals were here to stay and they needed to be improved and rationalised.[41] However, tribunal procedures were criticised. People could not be represented and legal aid was unavailable. Some tribunals did not give reasons for their decisions. There was a perception that tribunals approached appeals from a policy perspective. This led to complaints that tribunals were not disinterested,

[33] WA Robson, 'The Report of the Committee on Ministers' Powers' (1932) 3 *Political Quarterly* 346, 351; WA Robson, *Justice and Administrative Law: A Study of the British Constitution*, 3rd edn (London, Stevens, 1951).

[34] Allen (n 26) 1.

[35] Editorial in the *Law Society Gazette* discussing the Franks Report, quoted in Fulbrook (n 14) 198. See also E Summerskill, 'The Functions of Tribunals within the Modern State' (1954) 1 *British Journal of Administrative Law* 93.

[36] For a notable exception, see N Wikeley, 'Tribunals and Judicial Independence in the Post-war Welfare State: GL Haggen and the "Practical Man's" Approach to "Good Cause"' (2024) 31 *Journal of Social Security Law* 19.

[37] MacKenzie and Grove (n 13) 397.

[38] ibid 400.

[39] Allen (n 26) 97.

[40] *Local Government Board v Arlidge* [1915] AC 120 (HL); KB Smellie, 'Some Aspects of English Administrative Law' (1927) 5 *Public Administration* 276.

[41] Robson, *Justice and Administrative Law* (n 33).

but were influenced by policy considerations and that the parties were not allowed to know the whole of the case against them. There was also a degree of amateurism in some tribunals, as evidenced by the variable quality of procedures and substantive decisions and the handling of evidence and fact-finding.[42] Further, tribunals were not subject to correction on points of law or procedure by the higher courts.[43] Until *Shaw*, tribunals were only reviewable on the ground of jurisdictional error.[44] Having extended the scope of judicial review to errors of law on the face of the record, another anomaly arose: tribunals did not have to give reasons. If they gave no reasons, then there was no record for that a court could review. Accordingly, tribunals needed to give reasoned decisions.[45] Overall, tribunals attracted little attention, but social concerns about the growth of officialdom and bureaucracy had been accumulating.

While the prospects for reform seemed slim, a series of high-profile cases of injustice caught the public mood. The classic case was the Crichel Down affair in 1954. This uncovered governmental ineptitude and became a beacon for many other similar grievances.[46] Before the Second World War, the Air Ministry had compulsorily purchased farm land in Dorset for use as a bombing range. Some years later, the land was transferred to the Ministry of Agriculture. The former owner's son-in-law, Lieutenant Commander Marten, had sought to buy the land back or become the tenant farmer, but officials had decided to let the land to another tenant. Angry at his unfair treatment, Marten pursued the matter vigorously through political channels. An ad hoc public inquiry severely criticised civil servants.[47] *The Times* described the episode as 'almost unbelievable in its catalogue of errors of judgement and misleading advice and in the arrogant temper which it discloses among those who are meant to be public servants'.[48] The case became a major controversy and attracted considerable public attention and questions in Parliament. The Secretary of State for Agriculture, Sir Thomas Dugdale, resigned.

If the British public had long assumed that the civil service provided a Rolls-Royce service, then Crichel Down provided the classic example of bad government and thereby illustrated the helplessness of the ordinary citizen subject to arbitrary officialdom. The affair came to wider attention partly because Commander Marten had been a determined and capable man. However, the case was only the tip of the iceberg in terms of the injustices caused to ordinary people by an uncaring, faceless and unaccountable officialdom. CJ Hamson, a Cambridge law professor, explained that the real lesson of Crichel Down was the desperate and defenceless position of ordinary citizens when confronted with ministerial powers exercised by civil servants who possessed 'a

[42] Cooper (n 23) 171, noting 'the obscurantism which disfigures many of the efforts of the Executive to discharge as amateurs judicial functions'.

[43] A Denning, *Freedom and the Law* (London, Stevens, 1949) 80–83.

[44] *R v Northumberland Compensation Appeal Tribunal ex p Shaw* [1952] 1 KB 338; [1952] 1 All ER 122 (CA).

[45] A Denning, 'Law in a Developing Community' (1955) 33 *Public Administration* 1, 7–8. Denning later contributed to House of Lords debates on the Tribunals and Inquiries Bill 1958, which required tribunals to give reasons for their decisions.

[46] DN Chester, 'The Crichel Down Case' (1954) 32 *Public Administration* 389; IF Nicolson, *The Mystery of Crichel Down* (Oxford, Oxford University Press, 1986).

[47] *Report of the Public Inquiry Ordered by the Minister of Agriculture into the Disposal of Land at Crichel Down* (Cmd 9176, 1954).

[48] 'The Question of Responsibility' *The Times* (20 July 1954) 9.

collective anonymity which has as little soul as it has human face'.[49] Ministerial responsibility was simply no longer an effective means of redress given the delegation of powers to civil servants. On the contrary, it operated as 'a powerful shield to a department responsible only to the Minister'.[50] Consequently, there was 'no process, no machinery of any kind, by which a normal citizen can as of right bring before any court or any other impartial person an act done by a Ministry within its enormous departmental powers, not even if the act is as grossly misdone as was the Crichel Down affair'.[51] There was an urgent need for redress when a government department had acted within the ambit of its powers, but had nonetheless proceeded to cause injustice to a person as a result of its administrative failings. As FH Newark noted, compared with French administrative law, English law was 'living in a state of decayed gentility … we have come to tolerate an arbitrariness in governmental administration which not infrequently produces the rankest of injustices'.[52]

Crichel Down was the iconic case, although there were others. Another controversial case, now forgotten about but which attracted widespread attention at the time, concerned Mr Ted Pilgrim of Romford, Essex. Mr Pilgrim had purchased a small plot of land adjoining his property. As part of the post-war housing drive, Romford Borough Council later decided to compulsorily purchase this plot of land to build new homes on it. Under the Town and Country Planning Act 1947, the Council could only pay Mr Pilgrim the existing use value of the land. As the small plot had been used for agricultural purposes and not for building houses, Mr Pilgrim was entitled to far less compensation than what he had actually paid.[53] Having his land expropriated by the state for considerably less than its real value caused Mr Pilgrim acute financial distress and he committed suicide. The local newspaper described the case as 'surely the greatest possible indictment against an age gone mad with a rigmarole of rubber stamps, restrictions, and baffling red tape'.[54] The case was discussed at the highest levels within government and a national newspaper led a campaign to vilify the officials in both Romford Council and the Ministry of Housing.[55] Beneath these headline cases, there were numerous smaller concerns about the position of the individual vis-a-vis bureaucratic administration.

Both the Crichel Down and Pilgrim cases reinforced and consolidated the hardening public mood towards governmental arbitrariness.[56] The overall effect was to light

[49] CJ Hamson, 'The Real Lesson of Crichel Down' (1954) 32 *Public Administration* 383.

[50] ibid 385. Ministerial responsibility was later described as 'a cloak for a lot of murkiness, muddle and slipshoddery within the Departments': HC Deb 12 November 1970, vol 806, col 648 (Frederick Willey MP).

[51] Hamson (n 49) 385.

[52] FH Newark, Book review (1955) 71 *LQR* 571.

[53] Pilgrim had purchased the land for £400. The repayments on his mortgage totalled around £550. As the plot of land was used for agricultural purchases, its existing use value was only £65, resulting in a significant loss. See J Davis, 'Macmillan's Martyr: The Pilgrim Case, the "Land Grab", and the Tory Housing Drive, 1951–9' (2008) 23 *Planning Perspectives* 125.

[54] *Romford Times* (6 October 1954), quoted in D Kynaston, *Family Britain, 1951–57* (London, Bloomsbury, 2009) 418.

[55] ibid. Prime Minister Winston Churchill questioned the Minister of Housing, Harold Macmillan MP, as he finished his breakfast in bed: 'Why have you done this man to death – you and your minions?' Davis (n 53) 127. A 'Pilgrim' clause was subsequently inserted into the Town and Country Planning Act 1954 to allow discretionary payments to Mrs Pilgrim. See D Heap, 'New Developments in British Land Planning Law – 1954 and after' (1955) 20 *Law and Contemporary Problems* 493, 509–10.

[56] B Keith-Lucas, 'Mr Pilgrim and Crichel Down' (1962) 69 *Queen's Quarterly* 135.

'a long-smouldering mass of public grievance and indignation that otherwise would perhaps have continued for much longer to smoulder without bursting into fire'.[57] As HWR Wade noted, the storm over Crichel Down 'touched off a large accumulation of discontents connected with the more formal proceedings of tribunals and public inquiries'.[58] In short, society was expressing concerns about the behaviours of the expanding bureaucratic state. After the end of the war, the public – society – had instructed the political elites to create the welfare state. A decade later, there was deep public concern about the high-handedness of officials. The public recognised the need for government, but it was now also demanding fair and effective remedies for people who suffered as a result of government errors and mistakes. The key question was how the governing elites would respond to these concerns.

Until the mid-1950s, neither of the two main political parties had given any thought to the problem of administrative justice and the adequacy of remedies against government. With Crichel Down, the public and political mood changed entirely. Both political parties became acutely aware of the problems of administrative justice and the need both to do something and to be seen to be doing something. The parties approached the issue from different starting points. For the Conservative Party, the key issue was protecting the little man and his property rights against the new socialist bureaucracies. There were concerns that the 'Crichel Down disease' had infected other ministries. The Inns of Court Conservative and Unionist Society published an influential report that made wide-ranging recommendations, including the establishment of an Administrative Division of the High Court.[59] An indication of the depth of public concern, the Conservative Party's election manifesto for 1955 promised that a 'strong advisory Committee' would examine 'the problems of administrative law and recommend action':

> [I]n exercising the normal powers of Government in a modern State, a just balance should be struck, and seen to be struck, between the interests of the individual and those of the community. There is no ground for belief that, as a general rule, justice is not substantially done; but we consider that there is room for further improvement in the machinery of tribunals, of public inquiries and of departmental decisions affecting individual interests and property. The public has a right to be assured on these matters.[60]

Opinion within the Labour Party also changed. Richard Crossman MP, a leading left-wing thinker, was concerned that the Conservatives would use Crichel Down to monopolise the debate and to argue against the use of executive power for socialist ends and for a return to pre-war limited government. Crossman therefore sought to reframe the debate. Instead of understanding the growth of administration solely as a benevolent means for implementing socialist policies, he argued that 'the growth of a vast centralised state bureaucracy' also constituted 'a grave potential threat to social democracy. The idea that we are being disloyal to our socialist principles if we attack its excesses or defend the individual against its incipient despotism is a fallacy'.[61] For Crossman,

[57] HL Deb (series 5) 1 April 1958, vol 208, col 611 (Lord Salter).
[58] HWR Wade, 'Tribunal and Inquiries Act 1958' (1958) 16 *CLJ* 129, 130.
[59] Inns of Court Conservative and Unionist Society, *Rule of Law* (London, Conservative Political Centre, 1955).
[60] Conservative Party, *Election Manifesto* (1955).
[61] RHS Crossman, *Socialism and the New Despotism* (London, Fabian tract No 298, 1956) 6.

the redress of grievances was another means by which the over-concentration of power could be challenged and social equality secured.[62]

While both political parties approached the issue from different positions, they arrived at essentially the same conclusion: there was a real need to reform, improve and modernise the mechanisms by which individuals could seek redress for grievances generated by government. As Robson noted, 'the climate of opinion had changed to the extent that both the political parties had become increasingly conscious of the problem of executive justice and injustice, and anxious that something be done about it'.[63]

The Franks Report on Tribunals

Having won the 1955 election, the Conservative government established the Franks Committee to consider in response to public concerns of arbitrary administration. However, from the outset, the terms of reference of the Franks Committee had been severely limited by senior civil servants, a classic defensive bureaucratic move.[64] Instead of a wide-ranging inquiry into the broad problem, the inquiry would be focused narrowly on tribunals. There was an intermingling of political and administrative problems. There was a political need for government to quell public disquiet following Crichel Down and to restore public confidence. There was also a perceived need within government to maintain the status quo, to retain the essential administrative powers of government and to avoid repeating the problematic episode of the Donoughmore Committee of a generation earlier. The wide-ranging nature of that earlier committee had generated much heat but little light about the constitutional place of ministerial powers, delegated legislation and tribunals. As the permanent government, the civil service also had its self-interests in mind. Senior officials were concerned that introducing a general administrative tribunal with the ability to reverse all types of government decisions – as had been proposed by Robson – would weaken ministerial responsibility, the authority of government departments and the powers of officials.[65]

The solution was then to establish a committee to consider matters, but to focus its attention on existing tribunals and inquiries. This would enable the government to respond to public disquiet and to restore the public reputation of the civil service, but without undertaking extensive reforms that could radically unsettle established practices and constitutional conventions.[66] The Franks Committee's terms of reference had therefore been deliberately restricted to considering situations where an appeal or review had already been provided. Whitehall officials could not obstruct or dampen the general spirit of social discontent and the need for government and Parliament to respond to it, but they could redirect its focus and thereby narrow and minimise its potential disruptive

[62] Labour Party, *Personal Freedom: Labour's Policy for the Individual and Society* (London, Labour Party, 1956). See also G Borrie, *Justice and the Administration* (London, Fabian Research Series, No 185, 1957).

[63] WA Robson, 'Administrative Justice and Injustice: A Commentary on the Franks Report' [1958] *PL* 12, 13.

[64] HC Deb (series 5) 3 July 1958, vol 590, col 1655 (Charles Fletcher-Cooke MP).

[65] See the memorandum 'The Civil Service and the Public' (26 July 1954) by Sir Edward Bridges, then Head of the Home Civil Service, quoted in WH Greenleaf, *The British Political Tradition: Volume Three. A Much Governed Nation Part 2* (London, Methuen, 1987) 625–26.

[66] TT Arvind and L Stirton, 'The Curious Origins of Judicial Review' (2017) 133 *LQR* 91, 104.

effects. Paradoxically, the Franks Committee, which was established following Crichel Down, ended up examining tribunals, whereas Crichel Down itself had not concerned the operation of tribunals at all, but the exercise of administrative discretion resulting in maladministration and injustice. The focus of the promised committee had thereby been directed away from the general problem which had prompted it. This move was all the more self-serving because the fundamental defect exposed by Crichel Down had been the culture and mentality of officials, an attitude of mind simultaneously 'shaped by the consciousness of power' and the 'lack of a sense of public responsibility'.[67]

Despite its inauspicious beginnings, the Franks Committee proved to be an important episode. The Committee considered extensive evidence and reported in 1957.[68] What is notable about the report is that, right at the outset, it situated administrative justice and the effective redress of grievances within the wider relationship between authority and the individual, between the state and society. As the report noted, this relationship was not static, but a dynamic and developing one which varies over time. At different times in British history, it had been necessary to adjust this relationship and to seek a new balance between private right and public advantage, between fair play for the individual and administrative efficiency. The report then highlighted its specific focus:

> Since the war the British electorate has chosen Governments which accepted the general responsibilities for the provision of extended social services and for the broad management of the economy. It has consequently become desirable to consider afresh the procedures by which the rights of individual citizens can be harmonised with wider public interests.[69]

The Franks Committee explicitly recognised that its task of considering and making recommendations concerning the constitution and workings of tribunals directly implicated the relationship between the state and society. The expansion of the power of the state in the post-war period had prompted concerns on the behalf of society that people were being subject to and at future risk of arbitrary and unfair treatment by civil servants. The Committee's task was then to examine tribunals, their procedures and constitution and to make recommendations to their improvement so as to satisfy public concerns about their operation. This was required in order to strike a new balance between the state and society. This notion of achieving a balance between individual rights and the public interest is now commonplace, although at the time, it had 'a slightly radical air'.[70] The assumption that pervaded the top-down structures of British government was that the 'administrative view' dominated and rarely, if ever, needed to be balanced against the interests of affected individuals before a neutral forum.[71]

The overall thrust of the Franks Report was that tribunals had become a 'permanent feature of our society' and of the system of law and government.[72] The social, economic and political changes of the preceding decades meant that tribunals had 'come to stay'.[73] The increasing tendency for disputes arising from legislative schemes of social regulation

[67] JAG Griffith, 'The Crichel Down Affair' (1955) 18 *MLR* 557, 569–70.
[68] Franks Committee, *Report of the Committee on Administrative Tribunals and Enquiries* (Cmnd 218, 1957).
[69] ibid [5].
[70] G Marshall and GC Moodie, *Some Problems of the Constitution* (London, Hutchinson, 1971) 103.
[71] ibid.
[72] Franks Committee (n 68) [44].
[73] ibid [37].

meant that the need for tribunals was more likely to grow than diminish. Both tribunals and administrative procedures 'were essential to our society'.[74] Tribunals possessed advantages over the courts: their cheapness, accessibility, freedom from technicality, expedition and expert knowledge of their particular subject. Indeed, it was because of these advantages that Parliament had given people the right to take their cases to a tribunal. If all such decisions were to be automatically vested in the ordinary courts, then they would become entirely overburdened. Given this situation and the pragmatic need for tribunals, the important matter was to consider what improvements and safeguards could be introduced into the present structure of tribunals.

Tribunals were not ordinary courts, but nor were they part of the machinery of administration. They were adjudicative bodies. When Parliament had introduced tribunals, it had deliberately moved the final decision outside of the government department concerned. Principles were therefore needed to inform the procedures of tribunals. These were openness, fairness and impartiality. Tribunal procedures had to be open. If decisions were taken in secret, then they would lack confidence and acceptability. Tribunals also had to proceed fairly by ensuring the people appearing before them could state their case. Tribunals also had to be impartial. Anyone appearing before a tribunal had to feel that the tribunal had approached their case with an open mind. Tribunals applied the rules and policies of the department concerned, but they had to do so impartially.

The Committee then made a number of recommendations. Tribunal members had to be qualified and appointed independently. Tribunal procedures had to be more orderly. Tribunals had to give reasons for their decisions. The Committee was 'firmly of the opinion, that all decisions of tribunals should be subject to review by the courts on points of law'.[75] Any error of law in a tribunal's reasons needed to be scrutinised by a higher judicial body and this could only be achieved by introducing an onward right of challenge to identify and correct such errors. There could be no exclusion of the courts. Furthermore, a new Council on Tribunals would oversee and monitor tribunals. The government accepted almost all of the recommendations. The Tribunals and Inquiries Act 1958, one of the major pieces of statutory administrative law in the post-war period, was swiftly enacted. A short statute, the Act created the Council on Tribunals to oversee tribunals, required tribunals to give reasons for their decisions and introduced both an onward right of appeal from tribunals to the courts and a no-ouster clause. The Act was 'a bundle of heterogeneous provisions aimed at practical problems'.[76]

The significance of the Franks Report and the 1958 Act was not just their technical detail. Both embodied a wider and decisive policy choice by both the government and Parliament to reform and improve administrative justice remedies in response to the public concerns about unfair and arbitrary administration. Speaking for the Bill at second reading, the Home Secretary, Rab Butler, told the House of Commons:

> It is a long time since Parliament deliberately legislated to regulate the balance between the individual and the State. The growth, during the past quarter of a century, of great welfare services and the larger measure of equality which they have brought about have increased,

[74] ibid [406].
[75] ibid [107].
[76] Wade (n 58) 131.

> rather than diminished, the need for strengthening the processes whereby the citizen can be satisfied that he is being fairly and considerately treated. To make these processes more judicial in kind and to ensure their subjection to the courts on matters of law is a powerful way of giving the citizen this satisfaction. De Tocqueville put it like this: 'The strength of the courts of law has ever been the greatest security which can be offered to personal independence; but this is more especially the case in democratic ages: private rights and interests are in constant danger if the judicial power does not grow more extensive and more strong to keep pace with the growing equality of conditions.' It is in that spirit that we commend the Bill to the House.[77]

Underpinning Butler's analysis was the tension between the state and society. Increased administrative power created a risk for individual freedom. Irrespective of the political rights or wrongs of that, 'what is wrong is that the judicial system – the courts of law, tribunals and inquiries – has not been adapted and extended so as to guarantee full protection to the interests of the individual'.[78] The purpose of the 1958 Act was then 'to protect the individual against the arbitrary exercise of the growing powers of the State'.[79] What Butler described as the 'idea or spirit of Franks' – essentially, the underlying social forces and currents sparked off by Crichel Down – would also inform other legislation and administrative action. The general tenor of the parliamentary debates was that a highly organised society involved the growth of administrative power – and the more this trend continued, the greater the need to create and strengthen safeguards to prevent those powers from being exceeded and abused. The Franks project would be a long-term work in progress. The 1958 Act was only a modest first step in the right direction.

A sense of the wider shift in the tectonic plates is illustrated by the speech of Lord Salter, a former Conservative minister: 'The real problem before us is much bigger than anything that has been touched upon in this Bill or has been dealt with by the Franks Committee.'[80] The balance between the individual and the state had been 'profoundly disturbed' by 'the immense extension of the sphere of government'.[81] The growth of government had, to a large extent, been inevitable. What was also apparent was a more fundamental set of changes in terms of how law was being used and where power now resided. The bulk of laws were no longer made by Parliament, but by government. The vast majority of 'judicial' decisions – those affecting individuals – were no longer made by the courts, but by government officials and tribunals.[82] Furthermore, within government itself, the balance between ministers and officials had moved in the direction of officials possessing greater influence. It was not possible to restore the old notion of the balanced constitution between the legislature, the executive and the judiciary, which had protected personal freedom and rights in the nineteenth century. Instead, the problem of replacing what had been lost through the growth of government would be a

[77] HC Deb 3 July 1958, (series 5) vol 590, col 1606 (Rab Butler MP, Secretary of State for the Home Department).
[78] ibid cols 1614–15.
[79] ibid col 1615.
[80] HL Deb 1 April 1958, (series 5) vol 208, col 612 (Lord Salter).
[81] ibid.
[82] The earlier report of the Donoughmore Committee had contained much conceptual wrangling and confusion about how the 'judicial' was to be distinguished from the 'administrative': *Report of the Committee on Ministers' Powers* (Cmd 4060, 1932).

difficult and a long one. It would remain a 'great problem of our Constitution and of our system of government, now and for long to come'.[83]

The forces unleashed by both Crichel Down also exerted a deep influence upon the civil service and its culture. Crichel Down became a powerful symbol of governmental ineptitude and of a bureaucratic attitude within the civil service towards the public which could not be tolerated. Many years later, a senior official, John Delafons, noted that the effect was to instil within the civil service the need to ensure that administrative processes, particularly those affecting private interests, were both fair and seen to be fair by the public. Crichel Down influenced the collective consciousness of the civil service for some years about how not to treat the public and the attendant risks of doing so.[84]

The wider lesson from the whole episode illustrates the importance of the underlying competition between the state and society. The Franks Report itself drew a direct link between the role of tribunals, the need for their decisions to be acceptable, and the wider principle that government depended upon public consent. Parliament had decided that many types of administrative decisions were not to be remitted to the ordinary courts. But nor had it decided that such decisions should be left solely to the administration. Government and Parliament had then sought to balance two competing pressures. The first was the need for administration to be efficient in the sense that policy objectives could be secured without delay. The second was the need for government to satisfy the general body of citizens that it was proceeding with reasonable regard to the balance between the public interest which it was promoting through its actions and the private interests affected by it.

This is reflected in the detail of the Franks Report. Tribunal decisions had to be acceptable to the public. They had to be properly made and be seen to have been properly made. For the Committee, it was natural that Parliament should have taken this view of what constituted good administration: 'In this country government rests fundamentally upon the consent of the governed. The general acceptability of [tribunal] adjudications is one of the vital elements in sustaining that consent.'[85] In other words, social demands for the extension of the state to be acceptable and accountable required not only that tribunals existed, but also for their decisions were considered to be acceptable. The Franks Committee had clearly been channelling demands from society that the extension of state power through the creation of the welfare state should be subject to improved levels of scrutiny and control. Individuals affected by administrative decisions had to have a means of challenging them. Further, while the mechanisms for challenging decisions had to be efficient, they also had to be acceptable to the public and society.

Together, the Franks Report and the 1958 Act were an important step forward. Yet, the Committee had been significantly constrained from the outset. Its terms of reference had prevented it from considering what remedies were required in other situations, as exemplified by Crichel Down, in which the problem had not been the lack of fairness or independence on behalf of a tribunal, but one of maladministration causing

[83] HL Deb 1 April 1958, (series 5) vol 208, col 612 (Lord Salter).

[84] J Delafons, 'Working in Whitehall: Changes in Public Administration, 1952–1982' (1982) 60 *Public Administration* 253, 257.

[85] Franks Committee (n 68) [22].

injustice that had arisen from informal procedures used by officials that did not infringe a person's legal rights and which could not be appealed to tribunals. The Committee recognised this significant omission. Over most of public administration, there was no formal procedure by which affected people could raise objections as to what was being proposed by government or for deciding on such objections. There was no other body to which an individual could approach if the responsible administrative authority had decided upon a course of action that could result in a detriment to him. The aggrieved individual could, of course, complain to the appropriate administrative authority, to his Member of Parliament, to a representative organisation or to the press. But there was no formal procedure which the person could use.[86] It was precisely this open-ended realm of injustice arising from faulty administration which the Committee had been prevented from considering: 'It may be thought that in these cases the individual is less protected against unfair or wrong decision. But we are not asked to go into questions of maladministration which may arise in such cases.'[87] As JAG Griffith noted, the Franks Committee had been told to look at procedures which were predominantly open, fair and impartial, and had been asked to see if they could be made any more so: 'And the Committee answered that they could in a few small ways. But into the closed, dark and windowless procedures the Committee was not asked to let air and light.'[88] A perennial theme of administrative justice is what happens within government, how administrative decisions are taken, their quality and the procedures used. However, these matters are usually difficult to investigate owing to the reluctance of government to open itself up to scrutiny.

There were at least two other weaknesses of the Franks Report. One was the Committee's insistence that tribunals were part of the machinery for adjudication rather than part of the machinery of government. This was prompted by the need to assimilate tribunals into a more judicial framework and thereby enhance their separateness from government. However, as Griffith argued, the dichotomy between adjudication and administration was false.[89] When tribunals adjudicated upon appeals, they were also functioning as part of the wider overall process by which policy is administered. Tribunals are both adjudicative and administrative.

Another weakness was Franks' complete antipathy to re-establishing tribunals as a distinct and coherent system of administrative courts which would replace the role of the common law courts. It was widely recognised at the time that the ordinary courts were largely incapable of exercising an effective form of judicial review over government. Robson had argued for the creation of a new administrative appeal tribunal to hear appeals from first-instance tribunals and against harsh or unfair administrative decisions in that large area of administration in which no tribunal appeal or inquiry procedure existed. This could have provided the institutional basis for a more robust and coherent system of administrative law, informed by a new philosophy. An appellate tribunal outside the structure of the ordinary courts would enable a proper and coherent tribunal system to develop. However, this was a step too far for the Franks

[86] ibid [10].
[87] ibid [14].
[88] JAG Griffith, 'Tribunals and Inquiries' (1959) 22 *MLR* 125, 127.
[89] ibid 129. See also K Bell, *Tribunals in the Social Services* (London, Routledge & Kegan Paul, 1969) 31.

Committee. Establishing a new administrative appeal tribunal beyond the supervision of the ordinary courts would undermine the 'unifying control' of the ordinary courts.[90] There was also the potential for having different systems of law in operation 'with all the evils attendant on this dichotomy'.[91] In short, while tribunals operated as useful, pragmatic adjudicatory bodies, the Diceyan tradition of access to and oversight by the common law higher courts and their pre-eminent status was confirmed and reinforced.

Overall, the episode reflected the tension between the state and society. The extension of the state in the post-war period had revealed the weak position of the individual at the hands of government. Social concerns prompted the government to establish the Franks Committee, although senior civil servants had limited the Committee's role. However, there remained a significant gap in the protection of the individual for which tribunals provided no remedy. This concerned the position of an individual who had suffered injustice as a result of faulty administration which was not itself unlawful or had infringed their legal rights. There was a need to create a new remedy for such cases, but how?

Assimilating the Ombudsman into British Government

The gap in the protection of the individual arising from faulty administration had not escaped attention. Robson considered it 'deplorable' that the Franks Committee had been prevented from considering this.[92] Yet, in retrospect, the emasculation of Franks had its benefits. It is highly unlikely that either the Franks Committee or Whitehall officials would have possessed either the imagination or ability to find innovative and constructive solutions to the problem of maladministration causing injustice. The established conventional modes of legal and governmental thought were binary; something was either administrative or judicial. The notion of an investigatory body had some resemblance in public inquiries, although Whitehall officials would likely have lacked the curiosity to look elsewhere for inspiration.

Within this milieu, the initiative for change came not from government, but from academia and civil society. The broad solution that began to surface was the notion of a non-judicial institution that would examine people's grievances, investigate government and secure redress. The idea of introducing an ombudsman emerged and was widely discussed.[93] An institution similar to the Swedish ombudsman or Commissioner for Justice was needed.[94] This would be an independent officer to investigate people's complaints about unfair government action caused by official mistakes, bias, favouritism or incompetence. The Swedish ombudsman had free access to government information

[90] Franks Committee (n 68) [122].

[91] ibid [123].

[92] Robson (n 63) at 14 and 31. See also HL Debs 1 April 1958, vol 208, cols 605–06 (Lord Denning) (arguing for a new remedy in cases of maladministration).

[93] In 1958, the Danish Ombudsman gave a lecture tour in Britain: S Hurwitz, 'The Folketingets Ombudsmand' (1958) 12 *Parliamentary Affairs* 199; S Hurwitz, 'The Danish Parliamentary Commissioner for Civil and Military Government Administration' [1958] *PL* 236; IM Pedersen, 'The Danish Parliamentary Commissioner in Action' [1960] *PL* 115; IM Pedersen, 'The Parliamentary Commissioner: A Danish View' [1962] *PL* 15.

[94] D Mitrany, 'Protecting the Citizen. I – The Swedish System' *Manchester Guardian* (6 August 1957); D Mitrany, 'Protecting the Citizen. II – A Warden of Rights' *Manchester Guardian* (7 August 1957).

and could secure redress for people. In doing so, the office also helped to improve the working of government. The idea took hold.[95] Ombudsmen had been established in Denmark in 1953 and in New Zealand in 1962.[96] Why not also in Britain? By investigating people's complaints against government, the ombudsman would assist Parliament in holding government to account and also try to get government to improve.

In 1961, an expert working group created by the then new non-governmental organisation, JUSTICE, published the Whyatt Report.[97] This report consciously picked up from where Franks had finished. The report's central point was that there was a gap in the protection of individuals against unfair administrative action which could not be challenged to the courts or tribunals. This gap needed to be filled by a new institution, an ombudsman, which would investigate complaints of maladministration.

The Whyatt Report framed itself as part of the wider process in which society had to respond to the expansion of administrative power. In the foreword, Lord Franks noted that 'the struggle between liberty and authority which characterises all human societies is unending and has attracted a good deal of concern and discussion in Britain over the last fifteen years'.[98] A major part of this broad subject concerned the redress of grievances for people who had found themselves badly treated by those in authority. Lord Shawcross elaborated on the theme. The report would provide a 'Charter for the little man'.[99] Given the ever-growing complexity of the modern state, central and local government intervened more than before in the lives and affairs of ordinary citizens. For the most part, such interventions were for benevolent purposes and had good results. The standards of administration were generally high. Nonetheless, the existence and interventions of a great bureaucracy inevitably meant that many injustices would arise through official error, carelessness and indifference.

New machinery was therefore required to provide the citizen with a remedy against maladministration. This would be achieved by establishing a permanent and dedicated officer to investigate complaints of maladministration and then to report the findings and recommended remedies to Parliament. In this way, the new ombudsman – or Parliamentary Commissioner – would secure justice for individuals adversely affected by governmental errors. The office would assist Parliament in holding government to act. It would also highlight lessons for government. The fundamental role of the ombudsman would be to deal with complaints where government bodies had failed to observe proper standards of conduct and behaviour when undertaking official duties and exercising their administrative powers. There was a great variety of different kinds of such behaviour, including the abuse of power, oppressive behaviour, inefficiency, negligence, error and partiality. It was impossible precisely to define in a legalistic way the entire range of such behaviour. Instead, the ombudsman required flexibility when handling complaints that arose when officials had not adhered to standards of good

[95] FH Lawson, 'An Inspector-General of Administration' [1957] *PL* 92; L Blom-Cooper, 'An Ombudsman in Britain?' [1960] *PL* 145; TE Utley, *Occasion for Ombudsman* (London, Johnson, 1961).

[96] Parliamentary Commissioner (Ombudsman) Act 1975 (New Zealand); LB Hill, *The Model Ombudsman: Institutionalizing New Zealand's Democratic Experiment* (Princeton, Princeton University Press, 1976).

[97] JUSTICE, *The Citizen and the Administration: The Redress of Grievances* (London, Stevens, 1961) (hereinafter 'Whyatt Report'). The Committee was chaired by Sir John Whyatt.

[98] Lord Franks, 'Foreword' in ibid xi.

[99] Lord Shawcross, 'Preface' in ibid xiii.

administrative conduct. The expansion of governmental activity, particularly in social and economic fields, had greatly increased both the risk of maladministration and the consequent need for better protection for the citizen.

A crucial feature was that the Whyatt Committee could not, like the Franks Committee, be deliberately hamstrung by the debilitating dead hand of Whitehall which feared plunging 'into reckless courses which might lead … Heaven knows whither'.[100] Had the proposal for an ombudsman solely been a matter for government, then it would likely never have progressed at all. The Whyatt Committee was then a direct means by which progressive experts could set the agenda for improving administrative justice by tapping into and responding to the evident public and social concerns without being emasculated by senior officials.

Nonetheless, some of the report's recommendations seem distinctly conservative and deferential from a contemporary perspective. Some restrictions, such as the ombudsman's limited access to internal minutes and allowing ministers to veto an investigation, were never implemented. However, other limits were adopted and still remain in place. For instance, complaints against central government departments could only be considered for investigation by the ombudsman if they had been forwarded by the complainant's Member of Parliament: the MP filter. The Whyatt Committee had deliberately constrained itself so as not to offend either government or MPs and thereby jeopardise its success. However, in other respects, the Committee went too far. Part of the report proposed extending tribunals to the discretionary decisions taken by ministers. This did not find favour. Tribunals had previously only been used in areas in which the issues were defined and could be decided in accordance with settled rules; tribunals were considered inappropriate when decisions were largely discretionary and involved policy considerations.[101]

Commentators welcomed the proposed ombudsman, but criticised the report's diffidence. JAG Griffith thought that an ombudsman was a 'comparatively uncontroversial' and 'fundamentally sound' idea.[102] It was necessary to strengthen complaints for the simple reason that current procedures – parliamentary, judicial and administrative – did not provide an adequate and independent means by which ordinary citizens could have their grievances investigated. However, the Whyatt Report had erred too much on the side of caution 'which, in the reform of public administration is generally the wrong side to err on'.[103] Allowing ministers to veto investigations was misconceived and the MP filter was spoilt by the suggestion that it was necessary for MPs to insulate the ombudsman from complaints. For Robson, the widespread interest in ombudsmen reflected 'a belated recognition of the inadequacy of parliamentary control of ministerial power on the one hand and the insufficiency of judicial review of administrative action on the other to safeguard the rights and interests of the citizen'.[104] The only tenable position was to accept the expansion of the modern state and its welfare policies and to insist that the larger the powers conferred on government, then the greater the need

[100] FM Cornford, *Microcosmographia Academica: Being a Guide for the Young Academic Politician* (London, Bowes & Bowes, 1908) 15.
[101] HL Deb 7 December 1961, vol 236, col 218 (Viscount Dilhorne, Lord Chancellor).
[102] JAG Griffith, 'Comment' [1962] PL 1, 3.
[103] ibid.
[104] WA Robson, *The Governors and the Governed* (Baton Rouge, Louisiana State University Press, 1964) 29.

to provide people with adequate safeguards and remedies. Political control alone was insufficient. The ombudsman idea was therefore welcome. However, the Whyatt Report's recommendations had been so 'hedged about with qualifications, so elaborately careful to avoid the slightest encroachment on parliamentary rights and ministerial power, that they might accomplish little in practice beyond serving as a symbol to mark the widespread dissatisfaction with the present position'.[105] An ombudsman would not solve all of the problems, but it would be a step in the right direction.[106] Similarly, KC Wheare considered the proposal to be 'practicable, sensible and worth trying', but the report's recommendations did not go far enough; consequently, the results of these recommendations would be both 'meagre and disappointing'.[107] The modest nature of the proposal could lead to a loss of confidence in the ombudsman which could render the office ineffective, but until the experiment was tried, it would be impossible to know one way or the other. By contrast, JDB Mitchell thought that the proposed ombudsman would be a very poor substitute – a distraction – from what was really required, namely, an entirely new and robust system of administrative courts along the lines of continental models that could subject government to extensive and deep legal control.[108]

In an insightful analysis, Chapman emphasised the wider political and constitutional differences between Sweden and Britain.[109] The Swedish system was based on an altogether different set of assumptions about the relationship between government and governed from those in Britain. In Sweden, the policy and administrative functions of government were separated from each other as far as possible through the use of administrative boards. Official documents were available for public inspection. The policy function of the Cabinet was constantly supervised by parliamentary committees. There was a distrust of secret administration and an emphasis on public control of government. The Swedish ombudsman fitted naturally within this wider culture of openness, scrutiny and close parliamentary supervision of government. By contrast, in Britain, power was concentrated within central government and its control was above all a political matter to be resolved through political means via the doctrine of ministerial responsibility. Yet, Parliament had failed to provide effective scrutiny of administration. It was an indication of the decline of Parliament and the resultant muddled thinking that it was now being proposed to create an ombudsman to protect the citizen, as opposed to strengthening parliamentary institutions to meet this new and urgent need. If controlling administration was inherently political in Britain, then an ombudsman would not resolve the problem. There was a risk of two equally unsatisfactory outcomes. If the ombudsman intervened thoroughly in the workings of government and criticised administration, then it risked being drawn into political matters. On the other hand, if the ombudsman confined itself to only considering individual complaints that raised no issues of wider public interest, then it would occupy a narrow and limited role and

[105] ibid 23.

[106] ibid 26. See, similarly, SA de Smith, 'Anglo-Saxon Ombudsman?' (1962) 33 *Political Quarterly* 9; AW Bradley, 'The Redress of Grievances' (1962) 20 *CLJ* 82, 95–98.

[107] KC Wheare, 'The Redress of Grievances' (1962) 40 *Public Administration* 125, 127.

[108] JDB Mitchell, 'The Ombudsman Fallacy' [1962] *PL* 24; JDB Mitchell, 'Administrative Law and Parliamentary Control' (1967) 38 *Political Quarterly* 360; JDB Mitchell, 'The Irrelevance of the Ombudsman Proposals' in DC Rowat (ed), *The Ombudsman: Citizen's Defender*, 2nd edn (London, Allen & Unwin, 1968).

[109] B Chapman, 'The Ombudsman' (1960) 38 *Public Administration* 303.

thereby struggle to gain a prominent position. The ombudsman could end up being a relatively unimportant institution that only operated on the periphery of the administrative process and could be largely ignored by government.

The Whyatt Report led the debate and had a considerable impact, although it was initially resoundingly rejected by the Conservative government in 1962.[110] Senior ministers and officials were distinctly unenthusiastic about the proposed ombudsman, which they viewed as an esoteric matter only of interest to academic lawyers and of little, if any, relevance to the general public. The proposed ombudsman could not be reconciled with the principle of ministerial responsibility. It would 'seriously interfere with the prompt and efficient dispatch of public business'.[111] There was already adequate provision under long-established constitutional and parliamentary arrangements and practices for the redress of any genuine complaint of maladministration, in particular by means of the citizen's right of access to their MP. Accordingly, the proposed ombudsman was misguided, contrary to long-established constitutional arrangements and unnecessary.

The government's rejection was strongly criticised. Griffith considered the government's response to be 'disreputable' and beyond complacent. It was 'almost unbelievable' that the government could produce a statement which revealed 'a state of mind which is exactly what all the fuss is about'.[112] Each of the points made was centrally at issue in the debate. Enhanced redress of grievances was necessary because of the ineffectiveness of ministerial responsibility. Yet, the government had invoked 'ministerial responsibility' as an unassailable conclusion to reject the need for considering the evidence and the facts concerning the nature of the problem and the need for reform. Ministerial responsibility was being used, not for the first or last time, by the government as a defensive shield to limit scrutiny. In fact, it had come to mean ministerial irresponsibility. Ministers who were constitutionally responsible could, when called upon to account for themselves, simply absolve themselves by saying that they were not actually responsible on this or indeed most other occasions. The government's disavowal that any problem existed, the lack of considered engagement with the Whyatt Report's arguments and the whole complacency of its response illustrated an attitude of the official mind which was at once 'so self-sufficient that it thinks a reasoned statement superfluous, so limited that it cannot free itself from the constraints of its private mythology and so obtuse that it will not see the effect of its own arrogance'.[113] This attitude of mind had prompted the whole inquiry into whether or not an ombudsman was required and it reflected how the government had failed to even acknowledge that the problem even existed.

As with Franks but much more so, the government was pushing back against arguments for enhanced redress and scrutiny mechanisms. Nevertheless, despite the rejection of the ombudsman, there were deep social concerns about the inadequacy of existing remedies. At the 1964 general election, the Conservatives showed some sign of coming round to the idea, but without explicitly committing themselves. They promised the immediate establishment of a select committee to consider reforms in

[110] HC Deb 8 November 1962, vol 666, cols 1124–25 (Sir John Hobson, Attorney-General).
[111] ibid.
[112] JAG Griffith, 'Comment' [1962] *PL* 391.
[113] ibid 392.

parliamentary procedure, including whether adequate means were available to MPs to secure the redress of genuine complaints of maladministration by their constituents.[114] But given the rejection of the ombudsman proposal only two years earlier, this pledge was castigated as a 'ludicrously insincere' instance of 'death-bed repentance'.[115]

By contrast, the Labour Party saw the opportunity to take the lead. Labour had been out of office since 1951 and used its 1964 election manifesto set out an ambitious programme of government.[116] There would be a focus on making government itself more efficient. The tasks of government had grown more numerous and more complex. The machinery of government required modernisation and new techniques and skills.[117] Then, in a statement straight out of the 'Red Queen' playbook, the Labour manifesto stated:

> [N]ew ways must be found to ensure that the growth of government activity does not infringe the liberties of the subject. This is why we attach so much importance to humanising the whole administration of the state and that is why we shall set up the new office of Parliamentary Commissioner with the right to investigate the grievances of the citizen and report to a select committee of the House.[118]

The Labour leader Harold Wilson developed the theme. The more government intervened in society, the more essential it became to maintain and extend mechanisms to safeguard the rights and liberties of the individual: 'Never must the individual feel that he is helpless against the juggernaut of the modern state.'[119] Further, 'the complexity of legislation and administrative processes over the past half century is such that it is urgent to provide safeguards'.[120]

Labour was clearly sensitive to criticisms from the Conservatives that a socialist government and the idea of a planned economy would enable a large centralised bureaucracy to trample upon and undermine people's rights.[121] However, the Conservatives' outright rejection of the ombudsman proposal in 1962 enabled Labour to seize the idea in order to counter such criticisms. Labour therefore promoted the ombudsman as a symbolic way of broadening the party's electoral appeal by reassuring voters that a more interventionist governmental system would be compatible with British traditions of individual liberty. Electoral concerns were clearly important, but they also reflected deeper sentiments concerns about the balance between the individual and the state.

Having been elected into office in the 1964 election, the Labour government published its White Paper on the ombudsman.[122] The paper noted that the various remedies for the individual – inquiries, tribunals and the courts – did not cover every instance in which

[114] Conservative Party, *1964 General Election Manifesto: 'Prosperity with a Purpose'* (1964).
[115] B Crick, *The Reform of Parliament* (London, Weidenfeld & Nicolson, 1964) 194.
[116] Labour Party, *Labour Party Election Manifesto 1964: 'The New Britain'* (1964).
[117] The Fulton Report on the civil service was published in 1968. See K Jenkins, *Politicians and Public Services: Implementing Change in a Clash of Cultures* (Cheltenham, Edward Elgar, 2008) 24–29.
[118] Labour Party (n 116).
[119] H Wilson, speech to the Society of Labour Lawyers (20 April 1964); 'Wilson Hint of Annual Law Reform Bill' *The Times* (21 April 1964); H Wilson, *Liberty and the Law* (London, Labour Party, 1964).
[120] H Wilson, speech at Stowmarket, Suffolk (3 July 1964); 'An Ombudsman for Britain' *The Times* (4 July 1964) 8.
[121] WB Gwyn, 'The Labour Party and the Threat of Bureaucracy' (1971) 19 *Political Studies* 383, 402.
[122] Prime Minister, *The Parliamentary Commissioner for Administration* (Cmnd 2767, 1965).

a person had suffered injustice as a result of faulty administration. Having examined arrangements elsewhere, the government would supplement the ability of MPs to take up their constituents' grievances by creating an ombudsman. Parliament was the place for ventilating grievances. The government did not want to erode this function, but to strengthen it by giving MPs a better instrument they could use to protect the citizen: the proposed 'Parliamentary Commissioner for Administration'.

Some insight into the challenges involved in creating an ombudsman can be gained by comparing it with the relatively unproblematic reform of tribunals in the 1950s. The Franks Committee had clear and limited parameters – to bring tribunals within the constitutional fold and improve them. Moreover, as tribunals were essentially court-substitutes, there was a clear paradigm of judicial procedures which informed them and against which they could be measured. Tribunals were also an autochthonous set of institutions that had evolved in the UK. By contrast, the ombudsman was an entirely new type of institution inspired by the Scandinavian experience. Precisely how the ombudsman would be assimilated into long-standing constitutional arrangements was a much more controversial and fraught matter compared with the consolidation of tribunals undertaken by the Franks Committee. There was considerable discussion within government as to the precise details and how the ombudsman would be transplanted into established British constitutional principles and institutions. The specific issues concerned citizens' access to the ombudsman; the filtering of complaints; the ombudsman's precise role and also its jurisdiction – just central government, or also local government and the nationalised industries?[123]

After much discussion within government about the details of the scheme, a Bill to create the new Parliamentary Commissioner for Administration was published. As the Minister, Richard Crossman MP, told the House of Commons, the current system for redress by Parliament lacked 'the cutting edge of a really impartial and really searching investigation into the workings of Whitehall – an investigation designed primarily to deal not with great scandals but with those secondary acts of injustice against the individual which, if permitted to fester, arouse what is often a grossly unfair prejudice against the Civil Service'.[124] The ombudsman would investigate complaints of alleged maladministration by central government. It would not replace established parliamentary procedures by which MPs could scrutinise government, but instead would provide them with 'a new and powerful weapon': the possibility of impartial investigation into alleged maladministration by government.[125] As a servant of Parliament, the ombudsman would provide MPs with an 'extremely sharp and piercing instrument of investigation' into alleged maladministration.[126] Complaints would be accepted for investigation only if forwarded to the Parliamentary Commissioner for Administration

[123] For detailed accounts, see F Stacey, *The British Ombudsman* (Oxford, Oxford University Press, 1971); R Gregory and P Hutchesson, *The Parliamentary Ombudsman: A Study in the Control of Administrative Action* (London, Allen & Unwin, 1975); R Gregory and P Giddings, *The Ombudsman, The Citizen, and Parliament: A History of the Office of the Parliamentary Commissioner for Administration and Health Service Commissioners* (London, Politico's, 2002) chs 4 and 5 (on internal governmental and parliamentary debates on the precise details of the ombudsman scheme).

[124] HC Deb 18 October 1966, vol 734, col 42 (Richard Crossman MP, Leader of the House of Commons).

[125] ibid col 43 (Richard Crossman MP, Leader of the House of Commons).

[126] ibid col 60 (Richard Crossman MP, Leader of the House of Commons).

by a MP. The ombudsman's authority would be supported by a parliamentary committee. The minister also provided an indicative list of maladministration – the 'Crossman catalogue' – 'bias, neglect, inattention, delay, incompetence, inaptitude, perversity, turpitude, arbitrariness, and so on'.[127] The Parliamentary Ombudsman would not be directly concerned with the merits of the administrative action or decision complained of, but rather the way in which a government department had acted. Moreover, the ombudsman would have virtually unrestricted ability to interview officials and access to private government papers that would otherwise never come to light.

The Bill was controversial both within Parliament and government, but was ultimately enacted.[128] In retrospect, the scheme introduced seems conservative, but at the time, it was – and to some extent still remains – a fairly radical reform given deep Whitehall resistance towards parliamentary and other forms of scrutiny and 'interference'. For Crossman, the advantage was that the ombudsman could examine the detailed workings of central government and thereby 'get well behind the façade of ministerial responsibility to Parliament to see how decisions are really taken in a Department'.[129] By contrast – and for precisely the same reason – Roy Jenkins, then Home Secretary, had objected to the ombudsman on the ground that it would alter 'the whole constitution by destroying the doctrine of ministerial responsibility'.[130] There is, of course, an inherent ambiguity in the notion of ministerial responsibility. It can mean either ministerial responsibility *to* Parliament or ministerial responsibility *for* policy and administration, according to the intentions of those using it.[131] This tension is especially evident in the ombudsman's big investigations into central government.

Standing back from the detail, the creation of the Parliamentary Ombudsman was clearly the product of the society's demands for more effective means of challenging faulty administration. It reflected other deep-seated social currents. Economic growth and consumerism had certainly benefitted some people, but left many behind. The welfare state had developed to respond to such problems, but part of its weakness was its complexity: bureaucratic form-filling and procedures for vulnerable people either unaware of their entitlements and/or experienced difficulties in such navigating systems. This produced a continuous flow of minor complaints of little public interest, but which were important to those concerned. The combined effect of social inequality and bureaucratic complexity was fertile soil for implanting an ombudsman.[132] At the same time, as with the Franks Report, there had been a corresponding counter-reaction from within government to contain and limit the role of the ombudsman.

Following the creation of the Parliamentary Commissioner for Administration, there remained sufficient momentum to extend the mechanism beyond central government. In the 1970s, ombudsmen were created for the National Health Service and local

[127] ibid col 51 (Richard Crossman MP, Leader of the House of Commons). See also G Marshall, 'Maladministration' [1973] *PL* 32.

[128] Parliamentary Commissioner Act 1967.

[129] R Crossman, *The Diaries of a Cabinet Minister: Volume Two* (London, Cape, 1976) 150.

[130] ibid.

[131] M Elliott and R Thomas, *Public Law*, 5th edn (Oxford, Oxford University Press, 2024) 455–58.

[132] G O'Hara, 'Parties, People, and Parliament: Britain's "Ombuds" and the Politics of the 1960s' (2011) 50 *Journal of British Studies* 690, 700–02.

government.[133] However, a persistent theme has been the relatively limited nature of the scheme. Unlike its Swedish equivalent, the Parliamentary Ombudsman was not seen as a protector of citizens' rights, but as an officer of Parliament who would assist MPs to hold government to account. The MP filter, the lack of own-initiative powers of investigation, the length of time taken for complaints to be investigated and the relatively low profile of the office have been perennial and continuing concerns. From one perspective, the creation of the Parliamentary Ombudsman was 'a symbol of declining deference' to authority and the civil service.[134] Yet, from a different perspective, the ombudsman's 'undoubtedly botched' statutory framework meant that it would have a limited scope and purpose; conservative forces within government and the civil service had won an 'infamous victory' by emasculating the institution from the outset.[135]

By 1977, JUSTICE concluded that the new institution had worked well, but only within a very restrictive statutory framework which constrained its scope and effectiveness. If the ombudsman was to become a more effective safeguard for protecting the citizen against government, then it needed to be reformed in several significant respects. Again, the key dynamic underpinning administrative justice resurfaces. The continued growth of administration in terms of its size, functions and power required 'a parallel development of effective checks and balances if the citizen [was] not to be submerged by bureaucracy'.[136] However, the government had no interest in enhancing or expanding the role of the ombudsman. The wider point is that the assertion of principled and logical arguments for improving administrative justice is necessary, but insufficient. These arguments also need to be supported by wider social and political concerns about administrative behaviours in order to get government to act.

Conclusion

The period from the mid-1940s to the 1960s was one of major political and social change in Britain. It was also the formative period of administrative justice reform and institution-building. Tribunals and ombudsmen remain the core administrative justice institutions and have grown and developed since. Indeed, given the path-dependent nature of institutions, it is unsurprising that many of the contemporary issues with these institutions can, in large part, be traced back to the debates of the 1950s and 1960s. This was also an exercise in state-building in two senses. First, there was the creation of the post-war welfare state. This was the product of demands from society that government

[133] National Health Service Reorganisation Act 1973; JUSTICE, *The Citizen and His Council: Ombudsmen for Local Government?* (London, JUSTICE, 1971); Local Government Act 1974; Local Government (Scotland) Act 1975. In practice, the same office-holder has always been both the Parliamentary Commissioner for Administration and the Health Service Commissioner. Ombudsmen were also established in Northern Ireland: Parliamentary Commissioner Act (Northern Ireland) 1969; Commissioner for Complaints Act (Northern Ireland) 1969.

[134] R Lowe, *The Official History of the British Civil Service: Reforming the Civil Service, Volume 1: The Fulton Years, 1966–81* (Abingdon, Routledge, 2011) 365.

[135] G Marshall, 'The British Parliamentary Commissioner for Administration' (1968) 377 *The Annals* 87, 91 and 97. See also H Street, *Justice in the Welfare State* (London, Stevens, 1968) 116 (the 1967 Act was 'unfortunately … a half-hearted affair, hinged about with restrictions and exceptions').

[136] JUSTICE, *Our Fettered Ombudsman* (London, JUSTICE, 1977) 18.

assume a more active role in providing social welfare services. Yet, the extension of state power also prompted concerns about the position of the individual. Government responded to pressures from society to construct the new institutional machinery of administrative justice to protect individuals. The second dimension of state-building was then the recognition of the need for and expansion of administrative justice to give people rights of redress, to make administration accountable and to make government more legitimate.

The effect of all of this was to create a new relationship between the state and society, administration and the individual. The expanded administrative state was accepted – provided it was accompanied by new machinery for the redress of grievances. Society had succeeded in emphasising the importance of administrative justice. The recognition in the Labour Party's 1964 manifesto of the need to find new ways to ensure that the growth of government activity did not infringe people's liberties illustrates how governing elites had internalised society's demands for fair and just administration. The new bureaucratic state had to act fairly towards people. Tribunals had to be open, fair and impartial. Ombudsmen would investigate complaints of maladministration by government. Consequently, government institutions would have to be on their guard as they would be subject to enhanced accountability for their decisions and actions. All of this would take some years to become fully effective, but the institutional machinery now existed.[137] A related point is the implicit recognition that redress institutions should share certain core characteristics. To be credible, tribunals and ombudsmen must be independent, inclusive and participatory institutions. People who use them should be able to engage directly and participate in the process. Their views should be listened to and they should be treated with dignity and respect. These institutions are also inclusive in the sense that they are not as legalistic as the courts.

While the episode demonstrates the growth and development of administrative justice, it also illustrates the challenges involved. The contest between the state and society is a perennial one and it can never be finally resolved. The world is constantly facing new social, economic, political and technological innovations and challenges. The state will also change in terms of what it does and how. This in turn will prompt concerns from society that new machinery of administrative justice is required. Administrative justice will then be in a perpetual condition of simultaneous decay and renewal. This explains why administrative justice can never stand still and why parts of its machinery will, over time, become overtaken by wider changes and become rusty and require reform, improvement and redesign. Further, the ways in which the tensions between the state and society play out in practice is unpredictable. While there is a reaction from society to the growth of state power, there is also a corresponding reaction from the state to dilute and weaken the social forces calling for more accountable government. Both the Franks Report and the establishment of the ombudsman exemplify this dynamic in action.

The general point here is that there will often be compromises involved and that government almost always has the final say on how administrative justice is structured.

[137] There were, of course, also significant developments in judicial review during this period: TT Arvind, R Kirkham, D Mac Síthigh and L Stirton (eds), *Executive Decision-Making and the Courts: Revisiting the Origins of Modern Judicial Review* (Oxford, Hart Publishing, 2021).

This applies not just to people's interactions with government, but also the redress mechanisms that aggrieved people use when they challenge government itself. The concept of administrative justice that emerges from this is then a complex and multi-faceted one. It is not fixed in stone for all time. It changes and develops in response to wider social and political changes and developments in both the scope of administrative power and the reality of administrative behaviours that people experience. Moreover, the contest between the state and society in the 1950s and 1960s that prompted significant reforms to administrative justice only marks the start of the inquiry. It raises questions about how administrative justice has developed since, how redress institutions operate in practice, and their adequacy and effectiveness. These issues will be explored in the following chapters.

3

The Contemporary Landscape

The principal building blocks of administrative justice were laid in the 1950s and 1960s, but much has happened since. The tasks of government have become more complex and administrative justice has continued to evolve. This chapter examines the development of administrative justice 'landscape' up to the present day. It starts by considering the growth and development of tribunals and ombudsmen since the 1960s and then proceeds to examine the reforms of tribunals introduced by the Tribunals, Courts and Enforcement Act 2007 and the impact of austerity policies in the 2010s. It then examines two cross-cutting issues: the pervasive appeals/complaints dichotomy and the role of alternative and non-redress mechanisms in administrative justice. Prominent themes concern the role of politics in influencing administrative justice and the degree to which administrative justice has become more coherent.

The Development of Tribunals

Following the Franks and Whyatt Reports, there continued to be concerns about the position of the individual subject to administrative power. Whereas the 1950s and 1960s was a period of institution-building, the next phase of administrative justice focused on consolidating and expanding upon what was already in place. Changing social attitudes reflected concerns about administrative injustice extending far beyond property owners, as in Crichel Down, and the mainstream population. The introduction of Mental Health Tribunals in 1959 reflected changing social attitudes towards people with mental health issues and recognition of their rights. The tribunals provided an independent check on detention in mental health facilities, an important safeguard for personal liberty. The previously closed world of prisons and criminal justice began to be opened up to judicial scrutiny and standards of fairness.[1]

Similarly, during the 1960s, immigration had emerged as a major area of government responsibility and political controversy. Successive governments had limited Commonwealth immigration in response to public opinion. This exercise of state power prompted concerns from within parts of society – and within the then Labour government – that immigrants were potentially being denied fair process and being

[1] D Feldman, 'Changing Boundaries: Crime, Punishment and Public Law' in JNE Varuhas and S Wilson Stark (eds), *The Frontiers of Public Law* (Oxford, Hart Publishing, 2020).

wrongly refused without any redress or appeal.[2] The courts had recognised the need for fair procedure.[3] To dispel criticism that immigration decisions were based on prejudice, a Home Office committee recommended the introduction of tribunal appeal rights.[4] An appeal system was required to restore public confidence that decisions were not being taken arbitrarily, but were not being properly considered. However well the immigration system was administered, it was fundamentally wrong and inconsistent with the rule of law that decisions affecting a person's whole future should be in the hands of executive officers without any independent redress.[5] An important tribunal system was therefore created and has grown significantly since.[6] The model adopted was a two-tier appeal structure comprising first-tier immigration adjudicators and a second-tier appellate tribunal, the Immigration Appeal Tribunal, to decide onward challenges. This was supported by a wider system of advisors and legal aid. Nonetheless, viewed from a contemporary perspective, this system was, like all tribunals of the time, inchoate. The immigration adjudicators deciding appeals were themselves appointed by the Home Office, whereas members of the second-tier Immigration Appeal Tribunal were appointed by the Lord Chancellor. The wider point is that the frontier dividing the 'administrative' from the 'judicial' had shifted with changing social and political circumstances and attitudes, and would continue to evolve.[7]

Tribunals had become 'one of the most important institutions of government' and 'an integral part of the machinery of justice'.[8] The point is illustrated and confirmed by comparing the courts and tribunals. The classic judicial revival of the rules of natural justice in *Ridge v Baldwin* has considerable symbolic importance in terms of the post-war reinvigoration of judicial review and procedural fairness, although the actual practical impact of the ruling was quite modest.[9] Then and since, the courts have rarely imposed requirements of procedural fairness across large swathes of administrative decision-making. Doing so involves administrative organisation, resources and personnel. On the contrary, the widest and deepest insertions of procedural fairness into the administrative process have been undertaken not by the courts, but by the government itself through the creation of tribunals to judicialise the administrative process. Government had taken this project forward because it had itself internalised the social need for administrative justice and the importance of inserting fair process into administration, and thereby enabling its own decisions to be challenged to tribunals. Given the scale of their initial decision-making, government departments did not want the trouble of resolving disputes. They were not interested in how individual cases were

[2] C Thornberry, 'Non-British Justice' *The Guardian* (11 August 1965); 'Criticism of Powers of Discretion in Migration Proposals' *The Guardian* (16 September 1965).

[3] *Re HK (An infant)* [1967] 2 QB 617 (QBD).

[4] Home Office, *Report of the Committee on Immigration Appeals* (Cmnd 3387, 1967).

[5] ibid 27–28.

[6] Immigration Appeals Act 1969; Immigration Act 1971.

[7] RE Wraith and PG Hutchesson, *Administrative Tribunals* (London, Allen & Unwin, 1974) 232–33.

[8] JA Farmer, *Tribunals and Government* (London, Weidenfeld & Nicolson, 1974) ix; B Schwartz and HWR Wade, *Legal Control of Government* (Oxford, Clarendon Press, 1972) 162.

[9] *Ridge v Baldwin* [1964] AC 40 (HL); R Thomas, '*Ridge v Baldwin*: Executive and Judicial Approaches to Administrative Law before and during the Quartet Years' in TT Arvind, R Kirkham, D Mac Síthigh and L Stirton (eds), *Executive Decision-Making and the Courts: Revisiting the Origins of Modern Judicial Review* (Oxford, Hart Publishing, 2021).

decided, provided that it was in accordance with their regulations. The answer then was for government to create tribunals, which then proliferated.[10] It was government that assumed responsibility for designing, funding and managing tribunals.

Yet, while tribunals were relatively accessible and offered fair process, they were sometimes seen as amateurish. In the 1970s, social security tribunals were widely criticised on various grounds: ad hoc procedures; the subjective discretion of panels; the variable quality of decisions and reasons; their unclear structural position; and the disorderly nature of the 'system'. Part of the welfare rights movement, the literature was empirical, realist, critical and reformist.[11] For '90 per cent of people 90 per cent of the time, tribunals are *the* courts and social security tribunals are the most important courts'.[12] However, these tribunals were the 'slums' of the legal system, 'the lowest form of tribunal life'.[13] Often seen as incapable of performing their minimal role satisfactorily, the real purpose of these tribunals was to defend government from criticism and to provide a symbolic fig leaf of legality.[14]

The tribunals 'system' was notably unsystematic and ad hoc. Tribunals were not independent of their parent government departments, which retained significant influence and control over 'their' tribunals through appointments, providing the administrative support for tribunals and also writing their procedure rules.[15] Another concern was the unprofessionalised culture of tribunal members, who were then overwhelmingly lay non-legal members. Training and appraisal systems were non-existent or very rudimentary.[16] What was needed were better personnel, procedures and the separation of tribunals from their parent departments.[17] Traditional adversarial judicial procedures simply prevented unrepresented people from understanding let alone participating effectively in their appeals. Instead, tribunals were inquisitorial and appellants received

[10] *cf* HWR Wade, *Towards Administrative Justice* (Ann Arbor, University of Michigan Press, 1963) 13–15, noting that 'Government departments … seize every chance of setting up new machinery for handling administrative matters judicially' and had 'become thoroughly tribunal-minded'; tribunals had 'multiplied at a phenomenal rate' and had 'become a standard technique of administration … no one would say that the hearings provided are not, on the whole, fair … the natural instinct of government departments is to entrust new problems to new tribunals'. See also JAG Griffith, 'Tribunals and Inquiries' (1959) 22 *MLR* 125, 129–30.

[11] M Herman, *Administrative Justice and Supplementary Benefits: A Study of Supplementary Benefits Appeal Tribunals* (London, Bell, 1971); N Lewis, 'Supplementary Benefits Appeal Tribunals' [1973] *PL* 257; K Bell, P Collison, S Turner and S Webber, 'National Insurance Local Tribunals: A Research Study' (1974) 3 *Journal of Social Policy* 289; M Adler and AW Bradley (eds), *Justice, Discretion and Poverty: Supplementary Benefit Appeal Tribunals in Britain* (Abingdon, Professional Books, 1975); J Fulbrook, *Administrative Justice and the Unemployed* (London, Mansell, 1978).

[12] H Calvert, 'Appeal Structures of the Future' in Adler and Bradley (n 11) 201.

[13] H Rose, 'Who Can De-label the Claimant?' in Adler and Bradley (n 11) 150; HL Deb 9 July 1974, vol 353, col 511 (Lord Gardiner) (Gardiner had been Lord Chancellor during the 1964–70 Labour government and was closely involved in the establishment of the Parliamentary Ombudsman). For a less strident, although somewhat critical assessment, see: H Street, *Justice in the Welfare State* (London, Stevens, 1968).

[14] *cf* T Prosser, 'Poverty, Ideology, and Legality: Supplementary Benefit Appeal Tribunals and their Predecessors' (1977) 4 *British Journal of Law and Society* 39.

[15] S McCorquodale, 'The Composition of Administrative Tribunals' [1962] *PL* 298; WE Cavenagh and D Newston, 'The Membership of Two Administrative Tribunals' (1970) 48 *Public Administration* 449; WE Cavenagh and D Newston, 'Administrative Tribunals: How People Become Members' (1971) 49 *Public Administration* 197.

[16] M Partington, 'The Status of Administrative Judges in the UK: Recruitment, Tenure, Training and Appraisal' (2001) 21 *Journal of the National Association of Administrative Law Judges* 315, 316–20.

[17] N Harris, 'The Reform of the Supplementary Benefit Appeals System' (1983) 5 *Journal of Social Welfare Law* 212.

little advice or representation. Further, both attendance rates at hearings and success rates were low.[18] Tribunals remained closely connected to their parental government department. Until 1984, social security tribunals were administered by the then Department of Health and Social Security, which also took the initial decisions and was responsible for appointing tribunal members, who were recruited and then assessed by the Department's own local office managers. However, in practice, there was a strong tradition of independence amongst initial decision-makers and adjudication officers. The tribunals operated in an independent manner, despite not being fully institutionally separate from the Department.

Over time, the situation improved. In response to criticisms, social security appeals were reformed and amalgamated in 1984 in order to improve their quality and make them more structurally independent. The tribunals were placed within a new separate administrative structure led by a president, who, along with the regional chairmen, was appointed by the Lord Chancellor. Responsibility for appointing and overseeing the second-tier Social Security Commissioners, which decided onward appeals against first-tier social security tribunals, was transferred from the then Department of Health and Social Security to the then Lord Chancellor's Department, as with judicial appointments.[19] The new tribunal structure still depended on the Department for its personnel and resources. Nonetheless, the close relationship between the Department of Health and Social Security, tribunals and regional chairmen had its benefits. Tribunal members contributed to the training of the Department's adjudication officers who took initial decisions. There was a culture of adjudication focused on careful deliberation to ensure that claimants received their entitlements.[20] This was reinforced by the Chief Adjudication Officer, an independent office-holder within the Department who reported on the standards of adjudication.[21] The chairs of social security tribunals now had to be experienced legal practitioners.[22] Social security tribunals were overhauled again in the late 1990s. By this time, the focus had shifted away from improving adjudication standards and towards enhancing speed and efficiency. The structure of independent adjudication officers and the Chief Adjudication Officer was dismantled. Decision-making was transferred to the Secretary of State. The culture of adjudication was replaced by a focus on processing benefit claims efficiently.[23]

A similar change affected immigration tribunals. There were concerns about immigration adjudicators being appointed by the Home Office, the perception of structural

[18] K Bell, *Research Study on Supplementary Benefit Appeal Tribunals. Review of Main Findings: Conclusions; Recommendations* (HMSO, 1975); A Frost and C Howard, *Representation and Administrative Tribunals* (Abingdon, Routledge, 1977).

[19] Transfer of Functions (Social Security Commissioners) Order, SI 1984/181.

[20] N Warren, 'The Adjudication Gap: A Discussion Document' (2006) 13 *Journal of Social Security Law* 110.

[21] R Sainsbury, 'The Social Security Chief Adjudication Officer: The First Four Years' [1989] *PL* 323.

[22] Health and Social Services and Social Security Adjudication Act 1983, sch 8, pt II; AW Bradley, 'Recent Reform of Social Security Adjudication in Great Britain' (1985) 26 *Les Cahiers de Droit* 403.

[23] Department of Social Security, *Improving Decision-Making and Appeals in Social Security* (Cm 3328, 1996); Social Security Act 1998; M Adler, 'Decision-Making and Appeals in Social Security: In Need of Reform?' (1997) 68 *Political Quarterly* 338; R Sainsbury, 'The Reform of Social Security Adjudication' in M Harris and M Partington (eds), *Administrative Justice in the 21st Century* (Oxford, Hart Publishing, 1999); N Wikeley, 'Burying Bell: Managing the Judicialisation of Social Security Tribunals' (2000) 63 *MLR* 475.

bias and the overall effectiveness of the appeals system.[24] Eventually, a select committee recommended that immigration adjudicators be appointed by the Lord Chancellor's Department to maintain public confidence.[25] When the number of asylum claimants increased in the late 1980s, the lack of a right of appeal became increasingly anomalous. While judicial review was available, it cannot resolve the key issue in dispute which typically involves fact-finding. Given the increased number of asylum judicial reviews (tiny in comparison with later volumes), the Home Office created a right of appeal in asylum cases.[26] In other contexts, the introduction of appeals reflected wider changes in government policy. For instance, greater choice in public services resulted in parental choice of schools and the introduction of school admission appeals.[27]

A key issue concerned the constitutional place of tribunals. By this stage, tribunals were now important, albeit overlooked and rather marginal entities 'floating around in a no man's land somewhere between the judicial and the administrative systems'.[28] Tribunals were not courts, but they were not wholly governmental either. They were separate from government, but were not formally independent either. Tribunals themselves understood their distinctive role and place. Their culture was based on providing accessible ground-level justice. In the public consciousness, 'courts' are closely associated with the criminal courts and defendants being subject to cross-examination. Designating tribunals as courts would likely dissuade many social security and other claimants from appealing at all. At the same time, tribunals lacked the confidence to articulate their place and role. They were looked down upon by lawyers and court judges, and often suffered from and internalised something of an inferiority complex.

Linked to this is the question of how judicialised tribunal procedures should be. The concept of 'judicialisation' carries a range of potential meanings. In one sense, to judicialise an area of decision-making denotes that the decisions concerned can properly be taken not just by administrators but also by tribunals. As noted above, changing social attitudes have played a more important role in this regard than a priori conceptual categories as to whether a particular matter is or should be judicial or administrative. But in another sense, judicialisation can refer to the degree to which tribunals are independent, use fair procedures and make impartial, reasoned and good quality decisions. Judicialisation can also refer to the degree to which tribunals function more like the courts by, for instance, adopting formal, adversarial and court-like judicial procedures. On the whole, tribunals have sought to become more judicial in the sense of becoming more independent and separate from their parent government departments, and using fair and accessible procedures, especially for unrepresented appellants. However, tribunals have largely sought to avoid adopting fully court-like formal and adversarial procedures precisely because this would make them less accessible to unrepresented appellants and thereby reinforce the inequality of the individual vis-à-vis government.

[24] R Moore and T Wallace, *Slamming the Door: The Administration of Immigration Control* (London, Martin Robertson, 1975).

[25] House of Commons Home Affairs Committee, *Immigration and Nationality Department of the Home Office* (HC 1984–85, 277) [58]; Transfer of Functions (Immigration Appeals) Order, SI 1987/465.

[26] Asylum and Immigration Appeals Act 1993, ss 8–9.

[27] Education Act 1980, s 7.

[28] G Drewry, 'The Judicialisation of "Administrative" Tribunals in the UK: From Hewart to Leggatt' (2009) 28 *Transylvanian Review of Administrative Sciences* 45, 47.

However, there is an inherent tension between tribunals being accessible for unrepresented appellants while also applying increasingly complex legal rules and case law and not being too informal. There is also the risk of an unintended drift towards formal court-like procedures.

Another marked feature was that tribunals were not collectively thought of as a justice system in their own right. Each tribunal operated within its own silo and was overseen by the same government department responsible for policy and initial decision-making. The old Lord Chancellor's Department had focused almost exclusively on the higher courts and the judiciary. It was not at that stage a Ministry of Justice with responsibility for managing the overall justice system. Administrative justice existed, but only in a fragmented and incoherent sense. To some degree, such unsystematic arrangements are inherent in the nature of administrative justice itself. What works depends heavily on the particular context and what government is trying to do in that context. The evolution of tribunals has often been driven by sectoral-specific forces emanating from government, select committees, lawyers lobbying government and MPs. This resultant accretion of such changes is scattered amongst various sources: Council on Tribunals reports, parliamentary debates, ministerial decisions and tribunal and case law, and so on. The minutiae of amendments to tribunal procedure rules and practice directions often seems obscure, but can have a significant practical impact in terms of both procedure and substantive decision-making.

Studies emphasised the tensions within tribunal practices.[29] The rules governing benefits, immigration and tax had become increasingly complex, making legal advice and representation all the more important and thereby weakening the Franks idea of tribunals being free from technicality. There was a tension between cheap, quick, simple and informal hearings and the need for correct, reasoned and consistent decision-making. There was no coherent policy answer as to how the various tensions were to be resolved in practice, resulting in an ad hoc approach that was largely dependent on tribunal panels. Similarly, in theory, tribunals were inquisitorial and informal, but in practice, they could be adversarial and formal.

One modest unifying feature was the Council on Tribunals, a small, low-key and part-time body. The Council's formal role was to keep under review the constitution and working of tribunals and report on relevant matters to the Lord Chancellor.[30] The Council had emerged from a suggestion by Robson to the Franks Committee, although what actually emerged was far narrower than the more wide-ranging entity Robson had envisaged. Instead of overseeing the entirety of administrative justice in the widest sense (including initial decision-making), the Council's remit was narrowly focused on tribunals. Even then and despite producing valuable work, it often struggled to influence government. An attempt by the Council to secure an enhanced remit to become a general advisory body in the wider field of administrative justice, including initial

[29] J Baldwin, N Wikeley and R Young, *Judging Social Security: The Adjudication of Claims for Benefit in Britain* (Oxford, Clarendon Press, 1992); H Genn, 'Informal Justice and Tribunals' (1993) 56 *MLR* 393; H Genn, 'Tribunal Review of Administrative Decision-Making' in G Richardson and H Genn (eds), *Administrative Law & Government Action: The Courts and Alternative Mechanisms of Review* (Oxford, Oxford University Press, 1994).

[30] Tribunals and Inquiries Act 1958, s 1.

decisions, unsurprisingly failed.[31] Government has always resisted opening up front-line administration to external scrutiny. Instead, it preferred to maintain the Council on Tribunals as a part-time, minor and low-key body. As Robson noted, the Council was 'a worthy body struggling hard against adverse conditions largely imposed upon it by the narrow-minded outlook and lack of imagination of successive Lord Chancellors and their Department'.[32] In the 1990s, the Council warned the government that the workings of tribunals were being compromised by financial pressures and greater use of internal administrative review.[33] The Council reaffirmed the Franks principle that nothing less than independent tribunals were required when administrative decisions affected a citizen's liberty, livelihood, status or other basic rights. It also wanted improved training for tribunal members and clearer guarantees of their independence. Overall, tribunals remained, like administrative justice as a whole, an overlooked and unglamorous backwater. The Council did much valuable behind-the-scenes work, but it always remained a relatively obscure body that was easily ignored by government.[34]

Ombudsmen

What then of ombudsmen? Establishing the Parliamentary Ombudsman had been a major innovation. The UK had been the first country with a large population to create an ombudsman. Yet, ever since the Parliamentary Ombudsman had been proposed, there were significant reservations about whether it would amount to anything more than a palliative or a halfway measure.[35] A familiar jibe was: 'ombudsman or ombudsmouse?'.[36] A persistent theme was – and remains – the relatively limited nature of the scheme. Moreover, established to reassure the public about how people were treated by government, office-holders were themselves often former senior civil servants and establishment figures. They had insider knowledge of government, but the office had a low public profile. Indeed, the Parliamentary Ombudsman did not personally interact with complainants; all correspondence went through the complainant's MP. The volumes of complaints received were small and the number of investigations was smaller.[37] Many MPs chose not to use the ombudsman and paid little attention to it. Nonetheless, some complaints were investigated and the office undertook some notable high-profile investigations, including the refusal of compensation to British servicemen detained at the Sachsenhausen concentration camp during the Second World War and the collapse

[31] Council on Tribunals, *The Functions of the Council on Tribunals: Special Report by the Council* (Cmnd 7805, 1980).

[32] WA Robson, '*Justice and Administrative Law* Reconsidered' (1979) 32 *Current Legal Problems* 107, 115.

[33] Council on Tribunals, *Annual Report 1989/90* (HC 1990–91, 64) 2-5.

[34] JF Garner, 'The Council on Tribunals' [1965] *PL* 321; DCM Yardley, 'The Functions of the Council on Tribunals' (1980) 2 *Journal of Social Welfare Law* 270; DGT Williams, 'The Council on Tribunals: The First 25 Years' [1984] *PL* 73; O Lomas, 'The 25th Annual Report of the Council on Tribunals: An Opportunity Sadly Missed' (1985) 48 *MLR* 694.

[35] JDB Mitchell, 'The Ombudsman Fallacy' [1962] *PL* 24; JDB Mitchell, 'The Irrelevance of the Ombudsman Proposals' in DC Rowat (ed), *The Ombudsman: Citizen's Defender* (London, Allen & Unwin, 1965).

[36] WB Gwyn, 'The British PCA: "Ombudsman or Ombudsmouse?"' (1973) 35 *Journal of Politics* 45.

[37] R Gregory and A Alexander, 'Our Parliamentary Ombudsman' (1972) 50 *Public Administration*; (1973) 51 *Public Administration* 51.

of the holiday firm Court Line in the 1970s.[38] An investigation into the revocation of TV licences sharply criticised the Home Office's high-handed actions. As the Court of Appeal noted, 'no criticism of a government department could be more devastating than that contained in the Parliamentary Commissioner's Report'.[39]

In the early 1980s, Street declared that the Parliamentary Ombudsman was 'an essential concomitant of any acceptable system of accessibility to the judicial system'.[40] A key aspect was the ombudsman's ability to investigate complaints and its access to otherwise private government documents. This contrasts sharply with the usual position in court litigation, in which the claimant has the burden of trying to uncover such information. Street considered that the history of the Parliamentary Ombudsman had conclusively demonstrated that the citizen was given help in his confrontation with the administration that was not available from any other source. Overall, the Parliamentary Ombudsman had made its mark by investigating complaints and exerting some influence on central government.[41]

The Parliamentary Ombudsman had been supported in its work by a dedicated House of Commons Select Committee. The Committee had three principal roles: scrutinising the government when it had rejected the ombudsman's reports, thereby resulting in unremedied injustice for aggrieved individuals; using the ombudsman's reports to undertake follow-up scrutiny of government to ensure improvements to administrative systems; and examining the adequacy of the ombudsman's powers.[42] The Committee had achieved some successes in terms of improved administration and challenging instances of unremedied injustice, although it largely failed to convince the government to enhance the ombudsman's role and powers.[43] Nonetheless, the relationship between the Committee and the ombudsman became embedded as an essential aspect of the scheme and its role in assisting parliamentary scrutiny of administration. The ombudsman had worked well, albeit within a restrictive statutory framework. Familiar concerns were and remain as follows. The need for complainants to have their complaints referred to the Parliamentary Ombudsman by their MP – the MP filter – and the consequent lack of direct public access. Some complaints were inevitably lost in the process.[44] The ombudsman's relatively low public profile meant that it was not widely known and was under-used. Investigations needed to be undertaken more quickly. Ombudsmen

[38] R Gregory and P Hutchesson, *The Parliamentary Ombudsman: A Study in the Control of Administrative Action* (London, Allen & Unwin, 1975) chs 11 and 12; GK Fry, 'The Sachsenhausen Concentration Camp Case and the Convention of Ministerial Responsibility' [1970] *PL* 336; G O'Hara, 'The Parliamentary Commissioner for Administration, the Foreign Office, and the Sachsenhausen Case, 1964–68' (2010) 53 *Historical Journal* 771; R Gregory, 'Court Line, Mr Benn and the Ombudsman' (1977) 30 *Parliamentary Affairs* 269.

[39] Parliamentary Commissioner for Administration, *Television Licences* (HC 1974–75, 680); *Congreve v Home Office* [1976] QB 629 (CA), 654 (Roskill LJ).

[40] H Street, 'Access to the Legal System and the Modern Welfare State: A European Report from the Standpoint of an Administrative Lawyer' in M Cappelletti (ed), *Access to Justice and the Modern Welfare State* (Florence, European University Institute, 1981) 295, 311–12.

[41] Gregory and Hutchesson (n 38).

[42] R Gregory, 'The Select Committee on the Parliamentary Commissioner for Administration, 1967–1980' [1982] *PL* 49.

[43] JUSTICE, *Our Fettered Ombudsman* (London, JUSTICE, 1977); House of Commons Select Committee on the Parliamentary Commissioner for Administration, *Parliamentary Commissioner for Administration (Review of Access and Jurisdiction)* (HC 1977–78, 615 and 444).

[44] The 'councillor filter' for complaints to the Local Government Ombudsman was removed in 1988.

elsewhere had 'own-initiative' powers. These and other reforms were required. The debate continued throughout the 1990s to the present day.[45]

In 1978, Harlow argued for a reassessment.[46] Little attempt had been made to define what ombudsmen should do. The operation of the MP filter had been criticised for its inaccessibility, but the Parliamentary Ombudsman's investigatory procedures would never be suited to mass complaint-handling. It struggled with an annual caseload of 1,500 complaints, whereas tribunals handled many times that volume. For Harlow, the primary role of the Parliamentary Ombudsman should be one of investigating general administrative problems and recommending improvements to administrative systems. Individual complaints should be used as a vehicle to this end. Two implications flowed from this. First, the ombudsman should focus on problems arising from the mainstream of the administrative process and not stray into areas outside its competence. Second, the real issue with accessing the ombudsman was not the MP filter, but the need for it to have own-initiative powers of investigation similar to those possessed by its counterparts in New Zealand and Denmark, which had been used profitably, albeit rarely.

There is an inherent tension within the ombudsman institution. Should it focus on 'fire-fighting'/'swatting flies' or 'fire-watching'/'hunting lions'?[47] The former refers to the ombudsman handling high volumes of routine, ordinary complaints that raise no wider public interest. The latter involves the ombudsman investigating significant administrative problems in order to benefit a wider population. Neither metaphor is perfect, although both capture something of the competing roles within the ombudsman enterprise. In a 'fire-fighting' or 'swatting flies' mode, ombudsmen reactively investigate individual complaints one at a time to resolve specific and typically low-level problems. By comparison, in a 'fire-watching' or 'hunting lions' mode, ombudsmen undertake more systemic and big investigations where a problem has affected a whole cohort of people. Alternatively, they use individual complaints to draw attention to wider administrative deficiencies or undertake own-initiative investigations into potential systemic maladministration. This latter role is typically accompanied by the ombudsman issuing wide-ranging service improvement recommendations to government. Both approaches have their advantages and disadvantages. The independent and expert investigation of individual complaints is important, but is taken too far, meaning that the ombudsman risks becoming overwhelmed with a high volume of relatively routine complaints. Alternatively, undertaking a smaller number of big high-profile investigations widens and deepens the ombudsman's role, but risks both distancing it from the mass of complainants and creating tensions with government and potential non-compliance. Government has a natural self-interest in confining ombudsmen to routine complaint-handling rather than diagnosing structural problems. More generally, there is a subtle and finely graded spectrum between the two extremes of fire-fighting and fire-watching which ombudsmen have to negotiate carefully. As with all dilemmas, there are strong arguments both ways and no single right answer.

[45] House of Commons Select Committee on the Parliamentary Commissioner for Administration, *Report of the Parliamentary Commissioner for Administration for 1989* (HC 1989–90, 129); House of Commons Public Administration Select Committee, *Time for a People's Ombudsman Service* (HC 2013–14, 655).

[46] C Harlow, 'Ombudsmen: In Search of a Role' (1978) 41 *MLR* 446.

[47] C Harlow, 'Ombudsmen: "Hunting Lions" or "Swatting Flies"' in M Hertogh and R Kirkham (eds), *Research Handbook on the Ombudsman* (Cheltenham, Edward Elgar, 2018).

A general view was that the Parliamentary Ombudsmen had not been a dismal failure, but nor had it really achieved its full potential.[48] By contrast, a wide-ranging review of administrative justice had concluded that in many situations, ombudsmen had become a more effective way of securing redress against administration than recourse to the courts.[49] They had extended redress beyond the lawfulness of administration action to include maladministration. However, the number of investigations undertaken by the Parliamentary Ombudsman had been quite low. There had also been delays and difficulties in getting the right issues investigated. The Parliamentary Ombudsman had 'a record of valuable but for the most part unspectacular achievements'.[50] The Local Government Ombudsman received more complaints than the Parliamentary Ombudsman, although it sometimes encountered resistance from local government.

In 1990, Harlow and Drewry found that the Parliamentary Ombudsman was held in low esteem both inside and outside Parliament.[51] The average amount of time taken to investigate a complaint was 12 months. As one MP noted, the ombudsman's investigations had been 'so deplorably slow' that the office could not provide 'the effective channel of redress that Parliament intended'.[52] Few MPs rated the ombudsman highly, while the office seemed unaware of how MPs worked. Successive ombudsmen were establishment figures and the office functioned more as a different part of the government machine.

The Parliamentary Ombudsman's jurisdiction was gradually extended, although it remained a low-profile body.[53] However, the Barlow Clowes investigation – the office's 'most complex, wide-ranging and onerous investigation' ever undertaken – then brought the ombudsman to prominence.[54] Inadequate regulation of a fraudulent investment scheme had caused injustice for investors. The ombudsman found a lack of rigorous regulation by government. A key strength was that the Parliamentary Ombudsman had the time, the resources and the right of unrestricted access to civil servants and government papers, and was therefore able to undertake a far more extensive and formidable fact-finding exercise than MPs, the media or litigants before the courts. 'Rarely, if ever, can any record of administration have been so closely scrutinised, and reconstructed in such detail.'[55]

In 1996, the remit of the Health Service Ombudsman was significantly widened. Previously, the ombudsman could not exercise clinical judgement when investigating

[48] WB Gwyn, 'The Ombudsman in Britain: A Qualified Success in Government Reform' (1982) 60 *Public Administration* 177; R Gregory and J Pearson, 'The Parliamentary Ombudsman after Twenty-Five Years' (1992) 70 *Public Administration* 469; P Giddings, 'Whither the Ombudsman?' (2001) 16 *Public Policy and Administration* 1; R Gregory and P Giddings, *The Ombudsman, The Citizen, and Parliament: A History of the Office of the Parliamentary Commissioner for Administration and Health Service Commissioners* (London, Politico's, 2002).

[49] JUSTICE-All Souls Review, *Administrative Justice: Some Necessary Reforms* (Oxford, Oxford University Press, 1988) 99.

[50] R Gregory and G Drewry, 'Barlow Clowes and the Ombudsman: Part 1' [1991] *PL* 192.

[51] G Drewry and C Harlow, 'A "Cutting Edge"? The Parliamentary Commissioner and MPs' (1990) 53 *MLR* 745.

[52] ibid 763.

[53] Parliamentary Commissioner (Consular Complaints) Act 1981; Parliamentary and Health Service Commissioners Act 1987; Parliamentary Commissioner Act 1994; and the many Parliamentary Commissioner Orders; AW Bradley, 'Sachsenhausen, Barlow Clowes – and Then?' [1992] *PL* 353.

[54] Parliamentary Commissioner for Administration, Second Report Session 1988–98: Annual Report for 1988 (HC 1988–89, 301) [62].

[55] R Gregory and G Drewry, 'Barlow Clowes and the Ombudsman: Part 2' [1991] *PL* 408, 439.

healthcare complaints concerning the diagnosis of an illness or the medical care or treatment of a patient.[56] This limitation was then removed.[57] The consequence was that the ombudsman came to perform a major role in investigating complaints about medical treatment; the clinical judgement of health professionals was no longer sacrosanct. The long-term effect was that the Parliamentary and Health Service Ombudsman (PHSO) came to operate first and foremost as a handler of health care complaints, which now account for 80 per cent of its caseload.

Overall, while ombudsmen matured and evolved, they remained something of an oddity in a legal culture focused upon the courts. Unsurprisingly, Ann Abraham (PHSO, 2002–11) noted her perception that, in the eyes of lawyers, the work of ombudsmen seemed unfamiliar and, indeed, 'sometimes suspect'.[58] Nonetheless, she emphasised that the ombudsman model was not merely 'a sub-standard form of adjudication' that lacked all of the procedure and culture of the full judicial process. Its work went far beyond the resolution of individual disputes by issuing service improvement recommendations. In this way, ombudsmen had the ability to transcend the individual case and to identify wider patterns of deficiency, and to make recommendations for systemic change that went beyond individual redress. At the same time, the breadth of this role meant that such recommendations are not legally binding and it was queried whether government actually took the Parliamentary Ombudsman's reports seriously in terms of their wider impact.[59]

A wider structural feature of administrative justice concerned the pervasive distinction between tribunal appeals and complaints on the one side and ombudsmen on the other. Tribunals adjudicate upon appeals against initial administrative decisions. Both front-line officials and tribunals take decisions by applying a body of fixed and detailed rules concerning particular administrative schemes (for example, benefits, tax and immigration). By contrast, complaint-handlers and ombudsmen investigate complaints when something has gone wrong within government or public services. They are designed to remedy instances of faulty administration that adversely affect people (for example, financial payments) and to identify wider lessons to improve for the future. The distinction is obviously important on a practical level, with people's problems being filtered into two entirely separate and different systems. It is also deeply embedded at the conceptual level. The distinction is then enduring, but it is necessary? This is a question to which we shall return.

New Labour, New Administrative Justice

By the end of the 1990s, various structural factors prompted a new phase of 'system building' of administrative justice, specifically of tribunals. The New Labour government led a wide-ranging effort to improve public services and to make them more

[56] Health Service Commissioners Act 1993, s 5.

[57] Health Service Commissioners (Amendment) Act 1996, s 6.

[58] A Abraham, 'The Ombudsman and Individual Rights' (2008) 61 *Parliamentary Affairs* 370, 375.

[59] G Drewry, 'Ombudsmen and Administrative Law: Bright Stars in a Parallel Universe?' (2009) 17 *Asia Pacific Law Review* 3, 15–16.

responsive to people's needs.[60] There had been significant constitutional reforms: devolution and the Human Rights Act 1998. The government also recognised that the time had come to reform tribunals by organising them into a coherent system, clarifying their constitutional status, raising the profile of administrative justice and ensuring that its significance for ordinary citizens was much better understood.[61] The major landmarks here were the Leggatt Report (2001), the *Transforming Public Services* White Paper (2004) and the Tribunals, Courts and Enforcement Act 2007.

The Leggatt Review of Tribunals had concluded that the tribunal 'system' was inefficient and incoherent.[62] Tribunals had evolved in an entirely haphazard way. The 'system' had never been properly designed and amounted to little more than a patchwork of various tribunals with no overall sense that, put together, they amounted to part of the justice system of similar importance to that of criminal and civil justice. The Human Rights Act 1998, in particular the right to a fair trial (Article 6 ECHR), required access to an independent and impartial decision-maker to determine a person's civil rights. The appointment of tribunal members by parent government departments was no longer acceptable. Tribunals now had to be and be perceived to be as independent as the courts. Tribunal chairs and adjudicators wanted an equivalent status as court judges. Leggatt recommended wide-ranging radical reforms aimed at making the tribunals system more coherent. Tribunals were to be entirely separated from their parent government departments. A new unified tribunals system was required.[63] Responsibility for tribunals would come under the remit of the justice department rather than delivery departments. The incoherent and confused systems of onward appeal rights from first-tier tribunals had long been in need of rationalisation.[64] Above all, tribunals existed for their users – not the other way round. The needs of tribunal users were paramount and tribunals had to ensure that they met these needs and were as accessible as possible.

The government accepted the Leggatt proposals and wanted to go beyond them. An important White Paper, *Transforming Public Services* (2004), signalled a significant change in governmental attitudes towards administrative justice.[65] The Ministry of Justice would 'turn on its head' its traditional top-down emphasis 'first on courts, judges and court procedure, and second on legal aid to pay mainly for litigation'.[66] Instead, its focus would be the real-world problems people face. The aim was to develop a range of policies and services that would, so far as possible, help people to avoid problems and legal disputes in the first place. Where this was not possible, the aim

[60] Prime Minister, *Modernising Government* (Cm 4310, 1999); M Barber, *Instruction to Deliver* (London, Politico's, 2007).

[61] M Partington, 'Restructuring Administrative Justice? The Redress of Citizens' Grievances' (1999) 52 *Current Legal Problems* 173.

[62] A Leggatt, *Tribunals for Users – One System, One Service: Report of the Review of Tribunals by Sir Andrew Leggatt* (London, Lord Chancellor's Department, 2001).

[63] See also M Alder and AW Bradley, 'The Case for Systematic Reform and the Establishment of a Unified Administrative Tribunal' in M Partington (ed), *The Leggatt Review of Tribunals: Academic Seminar Papers* (Bristol, Bristol Centre for the Study of Administrative Justice, 2001).

[64] H Woolf, 'A Hotchpotch of Appeals: The Need for a Blender' (1988) 7 *Civil Justice Quarterly* 44.

[65] Department for Constitutional Affairs, *Transforming Public Services: Complaints, Redress, and Tribunals* (Cm 6243, 2004).

[66] ibid [2.2]

would be to provide tailored solutions to resolve disputes quickly and cost-effectively. A key concept was proportionate dispute resolution. The methods and costs of resolving disputes had to be proportionate to the issues at stake for the parties concerned. Furthermore, the 'sphere of administrative justice' embraced 'not just courts and tribunals, but the millions of decisions taken by thousands of civil servants and other officials'.[67] It also included the needs of users who wanted to navigate the process in order to access justice. The focus needed to be on improving the whole end-to-end process. Good public service delivery organisations had to be designed with the needs of users in mind. Redress systems had to be accessible, efficient and responsive to the needs of users. However, tribunals were not as good as they could or should be. They needed to be modernised and thereby contribute to the government's wider reform of public services. For decades, tribunals had been viewed as doing important but unglamorous work and were compared unfavourably with the higher courts, but now it was their turn to be reformed.

The White Paper's ambition extended further. It was important not just to put things right after the event, but also to get things right in the first place. People did not want to go to tribunals; they wanted their problems to be resolved quickly and fairly. The first requirement of a fair and effective administrative justice system was to give person the opportunity to explain their circumstances clearly and comprehensively to the initial decision-making department. In many cases, tribunals allowed appeals on factual matters which, had they been known or considered initially, would have resulted in a different decision at the outset. Consequently, 'all the money and effort spent on overturning' initial decisions was 'a waste, putting unnecessary pressure on the individual and tying up resources which could have been spent on direct services to the public'.[68] The end-to-end process was fragmented, as illustrated by feedback from tribunals to government on the quality of initial decisions. The president of social security tribunals had published annual reports on the standards of initial decision-making to the Department for Work and Pensions. By contrast, other tribunals were simply the end stage of the overall decision-making process, with no formal means of feeding back their views on initial decisions. There was no expectation that tribunals would share their views of the quality of initial decisions or that if they did, that this would be acted upon. The new tribunals system would seek to stimulate improvements in the quality of initial administrative decisions. People would also be supported to make the best possible case at the stage of initial decisions, thereby enabling government departments to get things right first time.[69]

This shift of approach towards administrative justice was consolidated by cultural and organisational changes concerning the role, priorities and responsibilities of the justice department. The old Lord Chancellor's Department had neither operated nor viewed itself as a public service delivery department. It had been mostly focused on the higher courts, judicial appointments, and administering the courts and legal aid. Tribunals had been largely ignored and overlooked, even though people were many times more likely to use a tribunal than a court. The White Paper was based on a very

[67] ibid [1.6].
[68] ibid [10.5].
[69] ibid [6.32].

different set of presuppositions and this was later reflected in the creation of the Ministry of Justice in 2007.[70]

Many of the structural reforms proposed by Leggatt and the 2004 White Paper were then implemented by the Tribunals, Courts and Enforcement Act 2007. This Act established two general tribunals: the First-tier Tribunal and the Upper Tribunal. The First-tier Tribunal determines first-instance appeals on issues of fact and law, while the Upper Tribunal decides onward appeals on error of law grounds. The Upper Tribunal replaced other second-tier appellate tribunals, including the Social Security and Child Support Commissioners and the Immigration Appeal Tribunal.

Both the First-tier and Upper Tribunals are organised into specialist chambers that handle appeals from particular contexts, such as social security, immigration, tax, special educational needs and disability, and mental health. Administrative support is provided by HM Courts and Tribunals Service (HMCTS), an executive agency of the Ministry of Justice. Tribunal chairs became judges of equivalent standing to District Judges, the most junior level of civil judge. The statutory guarantee of judicial independence was extended to the tribunals judiciary.[71] The post of Senior President of Tribunals was created to provide senior judicial leadership. This post has always been held by a Court of Appeal judge.[72] Tribunal procedure rules are no longer made by government departments, but by the Tribunal Procedure Committee.

The First-tier Tribunal is, in essence, a specialist low-level administrative court that decides appeals against certain initial administrative decisions, principally those taken by central government departments, such as social security, immigration and tax. In practice, the First-tier largely operates as a fact-finding and rule-application body that is organised into various chambers. It focuses on holding fair hearings, collecting the relevant evidence, applying the relevant rules and then making decisions supported by adequate reasons. The Upper Tribunal is principally a specialist second-tier appellate tribunal.[73] Like the First-tier Tribunal, the Upper Tribunal is organised into specialist chambers. Its principal functions are to decide onward appeals on error-of-law grounds and to clarify important wide-ranging issues of law and practice.

Onward appeals from the Upper Tribunal go to the Court of Appeal and are subject to the second-tier appeals criteria – that is, a case must raise an important point of principle or practice or possess some other compelling reason why it should be heard.[74] A distinctive aspect of the Upper Tribunal is that it would be greater than the sum of its parts. It was envisaged that the Upper Tribunal would operate as a strong and dedicated appellate body at the head of the new system. The intention was that the Upper Tribunal would 'come to play a central, innovative and defining role in the new system, enjoying a position in the judicial hierarchy at least equivalent to that of the Administrative Court

[70] R Percival, 'The Challenge of Public Law Law Reform: Reflections on a Failed Law Commission Project' (2019) 41 *Journal of Social Welfare and Family Law* 372, 378–80. The Lord Chancellor's Department in 2003 became the Department for Constitutional Affairs, which in 2007 became the Ministry of Justice.

[71] Tribunals, Courts and Enforcement Act 2007, s 1.

[72] Respectively, Sir Robert Carnwath (2007–12); Sir Jeremy Sullivan (2012–15); Sir Ernest Ryder (2015–20); and Sir Keith Lindblom (2020–25); and Sir James Dingemans (2025–).

[73] The Upper Tribunal's non-appellate jurisdiction is principally its judicial review function.

[74] Tribunals, Courts and Enforcement Act 2007, s 13(6).

in England and Wales'.[75] The 2007 Act designated the Upper Tribunal as a superior court of record.[76] This means that it has an equivalent status as the High Court and that it can both set precedents and can enforce its decisions (and those of the First-tier Tribunal) without needing to ask the High Court to intervene. The 2007 Act also enabled certain types of judicial reviews to be transferred from the Administrative Court to the Upper Tribunal to reduce the burden on the former. Judicial review cases can be transferred, either individually or as a general class of case, from the Administrative Court to the Upper Tribunal.[77] The principal bulk transfer has been immigration judicial reviews.[78]

Another aspect of the reform package was that the old Council on Tribunals was remodelled as the new Administrative Justice and Tribunals Council (AJTC) and given an expanded remit to keep the wider administrative justice landscape under review. The AJTC would oversee not just tribunals but also administrative justice as a whole, starting with initial governmental decision-making and including internal and external complaint procedures, dispute resolution outside tribunals, and the role of tribunals and mechanisms to encourage feedback, learning and improvement. It would ensure that the administrative justice system was accessible, fair and efficient, and met users' needs. It would be consulted on procedure rules. It could also scrutinise and comment on legislation concerning tribunals and make proposals for research. It could now potentially undertake a more expansive and effective role to oversee not just tribunals, but also initial decision-making and the overall system.[79] As with the Council on Tribunals, members of the AJTC continued observing tribunal hearings, how appellants were treated and how tribunals approached their decision-making. Tribunal judges found the feedback helpful.[80]

The AJTC started its work by articulating a set of principles to inform the evolving administrative justice system.[81] The system needed to: make users and their needs central, treating them with fairness and respect at all times; enable people to challenge decisions and seek redress using procedures that are independent, open and appropriate for the matter involved; keep people fully informed and empower them to resolve their problems as quickly and comprehensively as possible; produce well-reasoned, lawful and timely outcomes; be coherent and consistent; work proportionately and efficiently; adopt the highest standards of behaviour; and seek to learn from experience and continuously improve. Allied to this was the 'right first time' agenda: the role of the

[75] Tribunal Service, *Transforming Tribunals: Implementing Part 1 of the Tribunals, Courts and Enforcement Act 2007* (CP 30/07, 2007) [178].

[76] Tribunals, Courts and Enforcement Act 2007, s 3(5). In Scotland, such appeals go to the Court of Session and in Northern Ireland to the Court of Appeal in Northern Ireland.

[77] Tribunals, Courts and Enforcement Act 2007, ss 15–21.

[78] R Thomas and J Tomlinson, *Immigration Judicial Reviews: An Empirical Study* (London, Palgrave Macmillan, 2021).

[79] As variously advocated by: JUSTICE-All Souls Review (n 49) ch 4; AW Bradley, 'The Council on Tribunals: Time for a Broader Role?' [1991] *PL* 6; N Lewis, 'Filling in the Gaps: A Standing Administrative Conference for the United Kingdom' in Harris and Partington (n 23); Partington (n 61) 193. Overseas models have included the Administrative Conference of the United States and the Australian Administrative Review Council.

[80] House of Commons Work and Pensions Committee, *Oral Evidence: Employment and Support Allowance and Work Capacity Benefits* (HC 2014–15, 1212) (7 May 2014) (HH Judge Robert Martin, President of the First-tier Tribunal (Social Entitlement Chamber)) Q 159.

[81] Administrative Justice and Tribunals Council, *Principles for Administrative Justice* (AJTC, 2010).

new tribunal system in stimulating improvements in initial decision-making.[82] This had obvious attractions. Improved and robust initial decisions would mean better outcomes for individuals, less work for tribunals and lower costs for government departments. The new reforms would focus more on learning from tribunals and getting primary decisions right first time.

Overall, this amounted to the most significant overall reform of tribunals. They had been fully brought inside the formal judiciary. There was a centralising impetus behind the reforms. Responsibility for tribunals would rest with a single government department, the Ministry of Justice, rather than individual delivery departments, such as the Department for Work and Pensions (DWP). The new unified tribunal system and the Senior President of Tribunals were also centralising measures. Administrative justice had long been overlooked and sidelined in favour of criminal and civil justice systems, but with the reform programme, administrative justice had finally emerged from the shadows. Unlike the experience of the 1950s and 1960s, the reforms of the 2000s were not prompted by social demands for better redress motivated by concerns of arbitrary administrative behaviour or poor decision-making. They were more of an elite, top-down and benevolent project initiated and led by government and taken forward by senior officials with ministerial support.[83] At the same time, the reform package reflected deeper social needs to modernise and update tribunals by bringing them fully within the judiciary. While this was a major institutional change, it was of little wider public interest, being more of 'a quiet revolution'.[84]

However, there were some weaknesses. The 2004 White Paper had been the first cross-government general policy towards administrative justice, but it was far from a comprehensive policy. The Ministry of Justice was concerned to reform and enhance the position of tribunals, but ombudsmen were left untouched. Moreover, the new tribunals system is not fully comprehensive; it does not include all appeal and adjudicatory bodies. The various chambers of the First-tier and Upper Tribunals predominantly handle appeals against decisions of central government departments, such as the DWP, HM Revenue & Customs and the Home Office. It excludes the many other adjudicatory-type bodies, including those that operate in the local government context, such as school admission and exclusion panels, the Traffic Penalty Tribunal and the Valuation Tribunal. There are also specialist court-like tribunals (for example, the Competition Appeal Tribunal) and those which handle national security matters: the Special Immigration Appeals Commission and the Investigatory Powers Tribunal.[85] It is highly unlikely that these bodies will be incorporated into the First-tier and Upper Tribunals because of their specialist and distinct functions.[86]

[82] Department for Constitutional Affairs (n 65) [6.32].

[83] The support of Lord Filkin (Parliamentary Under-Secretary of State for Constitutional Affairs, 2003–04) was crucial in terms of getting the 2004 White Paper published.

[84] R Carnwath, 'Tribunal Justice: A Quiet Revolution' (Presidential Address of the Holdsworth Club, Birmingham, University of Birmingham Law School, 2005).

[85] At the same time, some local authority tribunals are incorporated within the First-tier and Upper Tribunal system. For instance, the First-tier Tribunal (Special Educational Needs and Disability) hears appeals against English local authority decisions. The equivalent tribunals outside of England are: the Special Educational Needs Tribunal for Wales; the Scottish Additional Support Needs Tribunals for Scotland; and the Northern Ireland Special Educational Needs and Disability Tribunal.

[86] This is so for various reasons. For instance, school admission and exclusion panels are operated by local authorities and panel members are volunteers. It is extremely unlikely that the Ministry of Justice would want to assume responsibility for them – or the cost.

Another matter was the relative lack of practical efforts to improve initial front-line administration or to introduce effective feedback mechanisms from tribunals to public bodies. The White Paper emphasised the need to adopt a bottom-up perspective on administrative justice, but its only lasting legacy was the structural reform of tribunals. The explanation is that the writ of the Ministry of Justice was and remains limited to the formal legal system. It lacked the authority within central government to exert much, if any, significant influence upon large casework departments, such as the DWP and the Home Office. Overall, the 'right first time' agenda and the wider ambition of constructing a wider holistic administrative justice system was more grand aspiration than concrete action.

The Leggatt Report and the 2004 White Paper also embodied some inherent policy and practical tensions essentially between fairness and cost, a wider tension of administrative justice. An important point from the Leggatt Report was that tribunals existed for users and not the other way round. At the time, publicly funded advice, though not representation, was available in social security and other tribunals, but why not extend publicly funded representation for everyone who needed it? The obvious answer was cost. Leggatt had taken the view that tribunals could adopt an 'enabling' approach so that unrepresented appellants could participate effectively in their cases. Tribunal procedures would enable most users to prepare and present their own cases without representation. By contrast, stakeholder and advice and representation groups argued that representation would help users to participate and to overcome the inevitable imbalance of power and the challenges involved in understanding and overcoming procedural and legal complexities.[87] There were doubts about how effectively an enabling approach would work in practice.

Another concern was that the distinctiveness of tribunals – when compared with the more formal and adversarial culture of the courts – might be lost. Tribunals have long seen themselves as different from the courts in terms of their expertise, flexibility and user-friendliness. While bringing the tribunals together into one system more firmly secured their position, there was a general feeling that tribunals needed to remain distinct from the courts and that they should not be assimilated into a more formal and court-like culture.

There was also uncertainty as to what 'proportionate dispute resolution' actually meant and how it would work in practice.[88] Proportionate dispute resolution must be distinguished from *alternative* dispute resolution (ADR) mechanisms, such as mediation and conciliation. By contrast with ADR, proportionate dispute resolution concerns the relationship between the importance of the issues at stake for the parties concerned and the costs involved in resolving disputes through formal the redress machinery, in particular tribunals. This implies some assessment and balancing of the value of a case and the costs of handling it. However, it was unclear precisely how this assessment would be undertaken. The Ministry of Justice was interested in the greater use of 'early

[87] M Adler, 'Who is Afraid of Sir Andrew Leggatt?' (2002) 9 *Journal of Social Security Law* 177, 191–93; M Adler, 'Waiting in the Wings: The Leggatt Report and the Reform of Tribunals' (2006) 13 *Journal of Social Security Law* 73.

[88] M Adler, 'Tribunal Reform: Proportionate Dispute Resolution and the Pursuit of Administrative Justice' (2006) 69 *MLR* 958.

neutral evaluation' prior to a full tribunal hearing for social security appeals. This would involve a preliminary assessment by a tribunal judge of the facts, evidence and/or legal merits of an appeal. If the judge thought that the appellant was likely to lose on appeal, then they would be given an explanation of the decision and advised to submit more evidence. Alternatively, if the judge was unable to form a view of the likely tribunal outcome, then the appeal would proceed for a substantive hearing before a tribunal. The idea was to increase efficiency and enable disputes to be resolved without formal hearings. However, an evaluation of a trial of in social security tribunals was equivocal. Some of the evidence suggested that early neutral evaluation provided more proportionate resolution, but there was limited evidence in respect of timeliness.[89] Further, the cost savings were limited. The idea was dropped and has not since resurfaced, but has been overtaken by the greater use of internal administrative review in the immigration and social security contexts.

As regards ADR itself, this has traditionally been resisted in the administrative justice context. The principal concern is that the use of mediation or conciliation in disputes between an individual and a government body would likely reinforce the inequality of power inherent in that relationship to the detriment of claimants, especially those without advice and representation (which is now the majority of them). People may well feel pressurised to settle for less than their full legal entitlements, thereby surrendering to a compromise outcome.[90] In administrative justice, there is an underlying public interest in ensuring correct decisions and that people receive their entitlements irrespective of their status. Even in the unlikely event of there being a level playing field between the parties, it is rarely possible to split the difference or to reach a compromise solution. Administrative decisions are typically binary: someone either qualifies for social security benefits or asylum or they do not. Further, ADR would result in the de facto removal of the independent fact-finding function of first-tier tribunals, thereby significantly weakening the principal function of first-tier tribunals. The pervasive risk is that many claimants may unwittingly 'mediate away' their entitlements. None of this implies that ADR has no role at all. It is used, to varying degrees, in tax and special educational needs and disability and also by the PHSO. However, the use of ADR is a subsidiary one at best and its usefulness depends very much on the context, volume and the willingness of both sides to engage.

The principal effect of the 2007 Act was to enhance the status of tribunals. The attitude of the higher courts towards tribunals also shifted – as exemplified by various comments from Baroness Hale.[91] While tribunals had once been regarded with deep suspicion, they were now an essential part of the justice system.[92] The right of access to tribunals was just as important and fundamental as the right of access to the ordinary courts.[93] Further, second-tier appellate bodies, such as the Upper Tribunal and its predecessors, were to be recognised as expert and specialist legally qualified bodies. The higher courts had to exercise an appropriate degree of caution before interfering on

[89] C Hay, K McKenna and T Buck, *Evaluation of Early Neutral Evaluation: Alternative Dispute Resolution in the Social Security and Child Support Tribunal* (London, Ministry of Justice, Research Series 2/10, 2010).

[90] Street (n 40) 310-311; Adler (n 88) 977–78.

[91] Baroness Hale was a former member of the Council on Tribunals. See also B Hale, 'Courts and Tribunals' (London, Annual Upper Tribunal (UTAAC / UTIAC) Lecture, 14 October 2021).

[92] *Gillies v Secretary of State for Work and Pensions* [2006] UKHL 2; [2006] 1 All ER 731 (HL) [36] (Baroness Hale).

[93] *R v Secretary of State for the Home Department ex p Saleem* [2001] 1 WLR 443 (CA) 458 (Hale LJ).

matters within the tribunal's area of expertise.[94] Tribunals had also become more judicialised, as evidenced by an increasingly large body of detailed precedents from various chambers of the Upper Tribunal and the higher courts.[95] Tribunals had then come full circle. Initially viewed with suspicion, after the 2007 Act, they were now recognised as proper and legitimate judicial bodies at the core of a modernised and integrated concept of administrative justice. By 2021, a strategic objective of senior judges was to complete the move to 'one judiciary'; it was no longer helpful to think of the judiciary as being divided between court and tribunal judges.[96]

A cross-cutting development was devolution. Traditionally conceived as being a unitary state, the UK does not have a federal system, but is better described as asymmetrical quasi-federalism. The consequence for administrative justice is that the three smaller nations (Scotland, Wales and Northern Ireland) can, within their areas of devolved competence, develop and experiment with their own approaches to administrative justice. Devolved public services have meant devolved redress mechanisms. This has naturally affected the structure and nature of administrative justice depending on which governmental functions have been devolved.[97] For instance, services such as health and education have been devolved in all three smaller nations, which also have devolved competence of redress institutions. By contrast, areas such as immigration and tax (mostly) remain at the UK level. Social security is mostly administered at the UK level, although some social security functions have been devolved to Scotland (such as disability benefits) with appeals going to the Scottish First-tier Tribunal Social Security Chamber. Social security has not been devolved in Wales. In Northern Ireland, social security is devolved, but there is parity with the UK, meaning that social security law and administration are the same as in Britain. Appeals are heard by Appeal Tribunals for Northern Ireland. Mapping exercises of devolved and non-devolved administrative justice illustrate the level of complexity involved.[98]

As regards the building of devolved tribunal systems, the Scottish Parliament in 2014 legislated for a two-tier structure for Scottish tribunals – the First-tier and Upper Tribunals for Scotland – thereby introducing a coherent tribunal system.[99] Devolved Welsh tribunals are being brought together into a unified coherent tribunal common structure comprising the First-tier Tribunal for Wales and the Appeal Tribunal for Wales.

[94] *Cooke v Secretary of State for Social Security* [2001] EWCA Civ 734; [2002] 3 All ER 278 (CA) [15] (Hale LJ); *AH (Sudan) v Secretary of State for the Home Department* [2007] UKHL 49 (HL) [30] (Baroness Hale).

[95] T Buck, 'Precedent in Tribunals and the Development of Principles' (2006) 25 *Civil Justice Quarterly* 458. In the 2000s, the Immigration Appeal Tribunal (now the Upper Tribunal (Immigration and Asylum Chamber)) started issuing 'country guidance' precedents. See R Thomas, *Administrative Justice and Asylum Appeals: A Study of Tribunal Adjudication* (Oxford, Hart Publishing, 2011) ch 7.

[96] Senior President of Tribunals, *Annual Report 2021* (2021) 5–6.

[97] That is, whether the policy function is at the UK level (eg, immigration, defence, foreign affairs and most tax functions), Britain (eg, most social security functions) or England (eg, education and health) and England/Wales/Scotland/Northern Ireland.

[98] M Anderson, A McIlroy and M McAleer, *Mapping the Administrative Justice Landscape in Northern Ireland: Report on Research Undertaken on the Administrative Justice System in Northern Ireland* (Belfast, Northern Ireland Ombudsman's Office, 2014); Scottish Tribunals and Administrative Justice Advisory Committee, *Mapping Administrative Justice and Tribunals in Scotland* (2015); S Nason, *Understanding Administrative Justice in Wales* (Bangor, University of Bangor, 2015).

[99] Tribunals (Scotland) Act 2014. The First-tier Tribunal for Scotland is organised into the following chambers: General Regulatory Chamber (Charity Appeals and Parking and Bus Lane Appeals); Health and Education Chamber (Additional Support Needs); Housing and Property Chamber; Social Security Chamber and the Tax Chamber. There are other tribunals that sit outside of this structure. See www.scotcourts.gov.uk/courts-and-tribunals/scottish-tribunals.

The purpose is to keep tribunals up to date and ensure that they can respond flexibly to the future needs of tribunal justice.[100] By contrast, tribunals in Northern Ireland remain unreformed. Overall, administrative justice policy has become increasingly fragmented, a natural consequence of devolution and a trend that is likely to develop further. At the same time, the dynamics of devolution has created new opportunities for innovation and partnerships that would be more difficult to pursue on a wider UK basis, although this comes with additional complexity and fragmentation.[101]

Ombudsmen Again

Devolution also impacted heavily upon ombudsmen. Up to the late 1990s, the PHSO dealt with complaints against UK government departments, and ombudsmen in England, Scotland and Wales had dealt with local government complaints. In Northern Ireland, separate ombudsmen were created in the late 1960s: the Commissioner for Complaints (local government, housing and employment) and the Northern Ireland Ombudsman (complaints against Northern Ireland government departments and their agencies).[102] Following devolution, each of the smaller nations reformed their ombudsmen by adopting the model of the single public services ombudsman to handle all complaints against devolved services and public bodies. The ombudsmen are: the Scottish Public Services Ombudsman; the Public Services Ombudsman for Wales; and the Northern Ireland Public Services Ombudsman.[103] These ombudsmen were also given new and additional functions beyond traditional complaint-handling. One was the complaint standards authority function of ombudsmen. This involves the ombudsman in overseeing, monitoring and improving the complaint procedures of public bodies within their remit.[104] This complaint standards function has been pioneered by the Scottish Public Services Ombudsman and has since been adopted in Wales and Northern Ireland. Another important innovation, to date adopted only in Northern Ireland and Wales, was to give ombudsmen own-initiative powers to investigate systemic maladministration.[105]

[100] H Pritchard, 'Building a Welsh Jurisdiction through Administrative Justice' in S Nason (ed), *Administrative Justice in Wales and Comparative Perspectives* (Cardiff, University of Wales Press, 2017); Law Commission, *Devolved Tribunals in Wales Report* (Law Com No 403, 2021); Welsh Government, *A New Tribunal System for Wales: White Paper* (Cardiff, Welsh Government, 2023).

[101] B Thompson, 'Opportunities and Constraints: Reflections on Reforming Administrative Justice Within and Across the United Kingdom' in Nason (n 100); L Edwards and S Nason, 'Judicial Review and Administrative Justice within and across the UK Nations: A Tale of Divergence and Convergence' in M Aronson and G Weeks (eds), *Controlling the Administrative State: Essays in Honour of Matthew Groves* (Oxford, Hart Publishing, 2025).

[102] Parliamentary Commissioner Act (Northern Ireland) 1969; Commissioner for Complaints (Northern Ireland) Act 1969; Commissioner for Complaints (Northern Ireland) Order 1996; Ombudsman (Northern Ireland) Order 1996; HJ Elcock, 'Opportunity for Ombudsman: The Northern Ireland Commissioner for Complaints' (1972) 50 *Public Administration* 87.

[103] Scottish Public Services Ombudsman Act 2002; Public Services Ombudsman (Wales) Act 2005; Public Services Reform (Scotland) Act 2010.

[104] Scottish Public Services Ombudsman Act 2002, s 16A–G (as inserted by the Public Services Reform (Scotland) Act 2010, s 119); Public Services Ombudsman Act (Northern Ireland) 2016; Public Services Ombudsman (Wales) Act 2019; C Gill, 'The Ombud and "Complaint Standards Authority" Powers' in R Kirkham and C Gill (eds), *A Manifesto for Ombudsman Reform* (London, Palgrave Macmillan, 2020).

[105] Public Services Ombudsman Act (Northern Ireland) Act 2016, ss 8–9; Public Services Ombudsman (Wales) Act 2019, ss 4–5; C Gill, 'The Ombud and Own-initiative Investigation Powers' in Kirkham and Gill (n 104).

By contrast, in England/the UK, the traditional central government-local government divide between the PHSO and the Local Government and Social Care Ombudsman (LGSCO) remains in place. Whereas tribunals were subject to big reform following the Leggatt Report, ombudsman reform has languished and stagnated. In 1996, the select committee concluded that there was a pressing need for the reform of the 1967 Act to expand the Parliamentary Ombudsman's jurisdiction and to enhance its role.[106] A 2000 review commissioned by the New Labour government concluded that the statutory framework was restrictive and distorted the ombudsman service. A radical overhaul was required. This included the merger of the three English ombudsman schemes – the Parliamentary Ombudsman, the Health Service Commissioner and the Local Government Ombudsman – into a single ombudsman service.[107] The review – a cautious and modest one – was mostly welcomed.[108] The Labour government had intended to act, but nothing then happened.[109] However, while the government had proceeded with tribunal reform, albeit at a slow pace, ombudsman reform ground to a halt. A reasonable suspicion is that senior civil servants, wary of enhanced scrutiny of their departments, wanted to kick ombudsman reform into the long grass.

In 2003, the Public Administration Select Committee criticised the government for its inaction. Ombudsmen had a vital role to play in maintaining and improving the quality of public services. Reform of the office was necessary, but there had been a 'history of delay' in relation to the matter; 'a roll call of talk rather than action'.[110] The need for ombudsman reform had become more pressing in light of worrying trends: increased complaints to the Parliamentary Ombudsman; its jurisdictional restrictions and the cumbersome methods imposed on the office by the 1967 Act; and disturbing evidence of routine administrative failures, including departmental indifference and political intrusion into administrative matters.[111] These trends went to the heart not only of the operational capacity of the office, but also to the wider issue of the quality of public administration that citizens should expect. The Committee noted that the problems were compounded by lengthy delays by government departments when responding to the Ombudsman's investigations. Indeed, there was a double standard by central government departments. They imposed strict deadlines on complainants, but then themselves took too long to put things right when complaints had been upheld by the ombudsman. Very few people in central government knew how the Parliamentary Ombudsman worked. Furthermore, there was an increasing tendency for government departments to take a harder line and to be less co-operative with the ombudsman. Investigations had consequently become lengthy and uphill work. The Parliamentary Ombudsman noted that given the downwards pressures on departmental operating costs, it had become more likely that things would go wrong thereby resulting in more

[106] House of Commons Select Committee on the Parliamentary Commissioner for Administration, *Open Government* (HC 1995–96, 84) [114].

[107] Cabinet Office, *Review of the Public Sector Ombudsmen in England: A Report by the Cabinet Office*, (London, Cabinet Office, 2000).

[108] M Seneviratne, '"Joining up" the Ombudsmen: The Review of the Public Sector Ombudsmen in England' [2000] *PL* 582; B Thompson, 'Integrated Ombudsmanry: Joined-up to a Point' (2001) 64 *MLR* 459.

[109] HC Deb 20 July 2001, vol 372, cols 464–465W.

[110] House of Commons Public Administration Select Committee, *Ombudsman Issues* (HC 2002–03, 448) [4]–[11].

[111] ibid [12]–[18].

maladministration. The Committee strongly argued for reform of the Parliamentary Ombudsman and the government giving greater emphasis to the ombudsman's role in assisting the government to improve public services. The government therefore needed to produce a draft Bill to implement the review of the ombudsman. Again, nothing happened.

The 2004 *Transforming Public Services* White Paper subsequently emphasised the importance of ombudsmen in improving service delivery and promoting better administration.[112] The Local Government Ombudsmen were highlighted not just for their flexible and informal style of investigation, but also for their role in providing guidance on good administrative practice and their 'powerful influence on administrative practice within local government generally, to the benefit of many more citizens that actually complain'.[113] It would be difficult to find a similar effusive commendation about the fire-watching function of ombudsmen in many other formal government documents, let alone a White Paper. It was further noted that investigations by the Parliamentary Ombudsman had revealed faults in procedures or systems that would lead to the government department or public body concerned revising their procedures so that other people did not suffer the same difficulties. The ability of the Parliamentary Ombudsman to undertake a big investigation had, on occasion, led to the resolution of disputes for many thousands of people. The office ought naturally to be an integral component of attempts to plan and to improve public service delivery. Further, to mitigate the negative effects of lengthy investigations, the Parliamentary Ombudsman had increasingly sought to settle disputes by making informal enquiries with government departments and agreeing recommendations for settlement rather than launching formal statutory investigations. Nonetheless, the prospects of wider ombudsmen reform advanced little. While tribunals were now overseen by the Ministry of Justice, the PHSO and the LGSCO came under the jurisdiction, respectively, of the Cabinet Office and the Ministry of Housing, Communities and Local Government. Ombudsmen continue to be a low priority within government. A review led to a minor change of the PHSO and the LGSCO being able to collaborate with each other by undertaking joint investigations.[114]

Various cross-currents were in play beneath the surface. Since the late 1960s, successive Parliamentary Ombudsmen had been mostly former senior Whitehall officials. The appointment of Ann Abraham in 2002 marked a distinct change as she had come from a different career path – the advice sector. The old-style Parliamentary Commissioner for Administration and the Health Service Commissioner were rebranded as the PHSO in 2005. During Abraham's tenure, there were an unprecedented number of big investigations finding systemic maladministration that affected groups of people.[115] There was a distinct sense of a concerted effort by the PHSO to make a deep imprint and enlarge its role and authority in this broad scrutiny space. The second Labour term (2001–05) was heavily focused on improving public services through additional investment and reform. Abraham situated the PHSO's work as part of the government's

[112] Department for Constitutional Affairs (n 65) [4.20].
[113] ibid [4.12].
[114] Regulatory Reform (Collaboration etc between Ombudsmen) Order 2007, SI 2007/1889.
[115] R Kirkham, 'Auditing by Stealth? Special Reports and the Ombudsman' [2005] *PL* 740. See further ch 6.

reform agenda.[116] This was achieved by adopting a conciliatory and collaborative tone and approach towards government. At the same time, this role involved more thorough and robust challenge to government, which proved to be controversial and high-risk at times.

Other investigations sought to protect the rights of groups of citizens against oppressive administration.[117] They shed important light upon the systematic neglect of cohorts of vulnerable people and the service failures across both health and social care experienced by people with learning disabilities and older people.[118] Through such investigations, the ombudsman was realising its role in advancing the rights of vulnerable groups by revealing patterns of neglect and the need for more responsive and humane public services. The trend is also reflected by the Local Government Ombudsman having responsibility for investigating complaints concerning privately funded social care.[119] Abraham also reframed the PHSO's role. Instead of criticising government for maladministration, the office would take a more proactive role in promoting good administration. The principles of good administration were devised as a blueprint for humanising administration, 'a template for shaping administrative practice to fit the needs of citizens, not the other way around'.[120] However, there were distinct points of friction with government. In three big investigations – Debt of Honour (2004), the regulation of occupational pensions (2006) and Equitable Life (2008) – the government rejected the PHSO's reports and there was protracted scrutiny by both the select committee and the courts.[121] As the New Labour period of government wore on, the challenges of improving public services became more acute and the prospects of ombudsmen reform faded. Under the Conservative–Liberal Democrat coalition government (2010–15), calls for a Leggatt-style review of ombudsmen were ignored despite the pervasive sense of the PHSO being 'stuck in time' with an outdated statutory framework.[122] A subsequent review and 2016 draft Bill would have combined the PHSO and the LGSCO, although the government lost all interest in the issue in the light of Brexit.[123]

[116] A Abraham, 'Preface' in PHSO, *The Parliamentary Ombudsman: Withstanding the Test of Time* (HC 2006–07, 421) 2.

[117] AW Bradley, 'The Role of the Ombudsman in Relation to the Protection of Citizens' Rights' (1980) 39 *CLJ* 304, 312–14.

[118] PHSO, *Six Lives: The Provision of Public Services to People with Learning Disabilities* (HC 2008–09, 203); *Care and Compassion? Report of the Health Service Ombudsman on Ten Investigations into NHS Care of Older People* (HC 2010–12, 778); *Report by the Parliamentary and Health Service Ombudsman on Complaints about Disability Issues* (HC 2010–12, 1512).

[119] Local Government Act 1974, ss 34A–T (as inserted by sch 5 of the Health Act 2009).

[120] A Abraham, 'Good Administration: Why We Need it More Than Ever' (2009) 80 *Political Quarterly* 25, 26. See also R Kirkham, T Buck and B Thompson, 'Putting the Ombudsman into Constitutional Context' (2009) 62 *Parliamentary Affairs* 600.

[121] These episodes are examined in ch 6, 195–212.

[122] T Buck, R Kirkham and B Thompson, 'Time for a "Leggatt-Style" Review of the Ombudsman System?' [2011] *PL* 20; Law Commission, *Public Services Ombudsmen* (Law Com No 329, 2011); House of Commons Public Administration Select Committee, *Time for a People's Ombudsman Service* (n 45); House of Commons Communities and Local Government Committee, *The Work of the Local Government Ombudsman* (HC 2012–13, 431); R Kirkham, 'A 2020 Vision for the Ombudsman Sector' (2016) 38 *Journal of Social Welfare & Family Law* 103.

[123] R Gordon, *Better to Serve the Public: Proposals to Restructure, Reform, Renew and Reinvigorate Public Services Ombudsmen* (London, Cabinet Office, 2014); Cabinet Office, *Draft Public Service Ombudsman Bill* (Cm 9374, 2016).

What then of administrative justice under New Labour? Important advances had been made, principally the creation of the new tribunals structure. Yet, there were many concerns about the poor quality of initial decisions made by government, especially on benefit claims and immigration and asylum applications. In 2003–04, the Home Office sought to introduce a wide-ranging ouster clause to exclude judicial review of immigration and asylum decisions.[124] This was dropped following a backlash, but it had raised concerns about a lack of governmental commitment to the rule of law and administrative justice.

The sense of dislocation within administrative justice is illustrated by comparing the assessments of two prominent leaders of the day: the then Senior President of Tribunals, Sir Robert Carnwath, and the then PHSO, Ann Abraham.

According to Carnwath, tribunals reform had been a successful effort to make the system more coherent and independent.[125] There had been a profound change of culture both within tribunals and within government towards tribunals. Tribunals were now part of the formal judiciary. While there remained some unfinished business – principally the 'right first time' agenda – the new two-tier system introduced by the 2007 Act amounted to a 'radical restructuring of the existing tribunal jurisdictions into a coherent two-tier model'.[126] The Upper Tribunal would bring procedural advantages through the 'welcome rationalisation of the confused and illogical network of appeal routes' which tribunal appellants previously had to negotiate. A coherent system of tribunal justice had been successfully achieved.

By contrast, for Abraham, administrative justice was 'in a muddle, not just in any particular way but in general: a muddle for those who work in it and a muddle for those who have to use it'.[127] Nobody could definitely say what administrative justice was about, whether it concerned courts and tribunals or whether it also included first-instance decision-making, ombudsmen and other complaint-handlers too. Nobody was certain about the purpose of administrative justice and what it was for: was it merely about 'fire-fighting' or also 'fire-watching' or 'fire-prevention', that is, improving administrative systems and the culture of public services? Within all this, ombudsmen occupied 'a special, and especially muddled, niche' characterised by ambiguity about their design, coverage and scope.[128] Each of the various public sector ombudsmen had different structures, powers and remits. This muddled coverage existed because the different ombudsmen operated within arbitrary and increasingly fluid boundaries, both sectoral and jurisdictional. The sense of disarray was reinforced by the lack of public awareness concerning what ombudsmen actually did, the absence of coherent government policy, and by fragmentation of delivery. Consequently, the notion of an integrated and coordinated administrative justice 'system' remained more of 'a distant aspiration rather than

[124] Asylum and Immigration (Treatment of Claimants, etc) Act 2004; R Thomas, 'Evaluating Tribunal Adjudication: Administrative Justice and Asylum Appeals' (2005) 25 *Legal Studies* 462; R Rawlings, 'Review, Revenge and Retreat' (2005) 68 *MLR* 378; R Thomas, 'After the Ouster: Review and Reconsideration in a Single Tier Tribunal' [2006] *PL* 674.

[125] R Carnwath, 'Tribunals Reform: Five Years on' (AJTC, 12 November 2009).

[126] R Carnwath, 'Tribunals Justice: A New Start' [2009] *PL* 48, 69.

[127] A Abraham, 'Making Sense of the Muddle: The Ombudsman and Administrative Justice, 2002–2011' (2012) 34 *Journal of Social Welfare and Family Law* 91.

[128] ibid.

a present reality'.[129] This unsatisfactory state of affairs was 'especially frustrating since not so long ago the future of administrative justice' had been 'so much brighter'.[130] The cause of the darkening outlook was the introduction of austerity.

Austerity and Administrative Justice

The reforms of the 2000s were the high-water mark of administrative justice. The Leggatt Report (2001) and the 2004 White Paper had both been comparatively innovative and had produced a flurry of interest. The Tribunals, Courts and Enforcement Act 2007 had created the First-tier and Upper Tribunals. It was a successful transition. There were constructive interactions between policy-makers, judges, academics and stakeholders.[131] There was a sense that administrative justice had finally emerged from the shadows and had become recognised as an important part of the legal system in its own right. For many years, it had been argued that there was a need for a holistic vision of administrative justice as a coherent justice system in its own right.[132] This was something that could potentially be achieved through the new Administrative Justice and Tribunals Council with its expansive remit to keep the entirety of administrative justice under review.

Yet, just as it seemed that everything had improved for the better, the economic and political context altogether changed. The decisive turning point was, of course, the global financial crisis (2008–09) and its wider and ongoing consequences. Between 1997 and 2007, the Labour government faced a relatively benign economic context and had focused on improving public services. The global financial crisis changed all of this. The coalition government introduced austerity policies to reduce public spending. This significantly impacted upon many policy areas relevant to administrative justice. Public service reform took on a very different meaning: reduced budgets, services and entitlements. Many public services, including the justice system, came under intense funding pressures. Two of the principal contexts of administrative justice – benefits and immigration – were subject to restrictions, including the benefit cap, tougher benefit sanctions and the hostile immigration environment.[133] A related strand of government policy was to open up public services to external competition through contracting out to outsourcing suppliers, potentially prioritising profits over good administration.[134]

Three particular restrictions need to be highlighted. The first of these was the weakening of various appeal rights. In 2011, challenges against school exclusion decisions

[129] ibid 92.

[130] ibid.

[131] In 2005–06, the Nuffield Foundation held a series of seminars on administrative justice with practitioners and academics. In 2006–07, there was an ESRC seminar series on administrative justice: M Adler (ed), *Administrative Justice in Context* (Oxford, Hart Publishing, 2010).

[132] B Thompson, 'Administrative Justice: Towards the Millennium, Towards Integration?' in Harris and Partington (n 23); B Thompson, 'Current Developments in the UK: System Building: From Tribunals to Administrative Justice' in Adler (n 131).

[133] See generally R Thomas and J Tomlinson, 'Mapping Current Issues in Administrative Justice: Austerity and the "More Bureaucratic Rationality" Approach' (2017) 39 *Journal of Social Welfare and Family Law* 380.

[134] R Thomas, 'Does Outsourcing Improve or Weaken Administrative Justice? A Review of the Evidence' [2021] *PL* 542.

were downgraded from appeals to a review on judicial review principles.[135] There was also much greater use of internal administrative review as either a compulsory stage prior to appeals or to replace appeals altogether.[136] Various immigration appeal rights were abolished.[137] Fees were introduced for some tribunals.[138] These restrictions were pursued by separate government departments. Nonetheless, there was evidently a wider move to weaken access to tribunals.

The second restriction was the abolition of the AJTC in 2013. Despite a good start, the AJTC had soon found itself fighting for its existence.[139] The government's rationale was that the major structural changes to the tribunal system had been completed. Effective oversight of tribunals could be better undertaken by the Ministry of Justice than the AJTC. Reforms to make the system fairer, more efficient and effective would continue from within government and this did not require the oversight of a purely advisory publicly funded body. Therefore, there was no compelling reason to continue funding a statutory body such as the AJTC. However, the government's reasons seemed more like post hoc justifications. The real weakness in the government's argument was that it overlooked the AJTC's ability to provide independent and expert scrutiny of a kind that officials in the Ministry of Justice could not. For instance, administrative justice covers a range of adjudicatory bodies outside of the formal First-tier and Upper Tribunals about which Ministry of Justice officials were likely uninformed about and uninterested in. Further, the AJTC's independence enabled it to scrutinise and criticise future government proposals relating to administrative justice, something that the Council on Tribunals had previously undertaken, but which civil servants were unlikely to.

The Commons Public Administration Select Committee strongly criticised the government for wanting to abolish the AJTC. Administrative justice may seem 'obscure and technical', but 'it touches upon the lives, the standards of living, and rights of millions of citizens every year'.[140] Its importance was underscored by persistent criticism of the quality of initial decisions and the high numbers of successful appeals. The Committee regarded the high proportion of successful appeals and complaints against government departments as evidence of 'widespread administrative failure'.[141] There was a real need for improvements; the scale of the injustice and the cost to the taxpayer caused by poor decision-making was wholly unacceptable. Consequently, the role of the AJTC and its independent oversight of this enormous system was a matter of 'vital

[135] Education Act 2011, s 4.

[136] Welfare Reform Act 2012, s 102.

[137] Immigration Act 2014, s 15.

[138] Ministry of Justice, *Court and Tribunal Fees* (Cm 9181, 2015); House of Commons Justice Committee, *Courts and Tribunals Fees* (HC 2015–16, 167). Fees were introduced for immigration tribunals, but not social security tribunals. The momentum behind this effort was effectively stopped by *R (Unison) v Lord Chancellor* [2017] UKSC 51, in which the Supreme Court held that fees for employment tribunals were unlawful.

[139] AJTC, *Right First Time* (London, AJTC, 2011); AJTC, *Putting It Right – A Strategic Approach to Resolving Administrative Disputes* (London, AJTC, 2012); AJTC, *Securing Fairness and Redress: Administrative Justice at Risk?* (London, AJTC, 2011); AJTC, *Future Oversight of Administrative Justice: The AJTC's Response to the Justice Committee Report* (London, AJTC, 2013); C Skelcher, 'Reforming the Oversight of Administrative Justice 2010-2014: Does the UK Need a New Leggatt Report?' [2015] *PL* 215.

[140] House of Commons Public Administration Select Committee, *Future Oversight of Administrative Justice: The Proposed Abolition of the Administrative Justice and Tribunals Council* (HC 2010–12, 1621) 3.

[141] ibid [18].

national importance'.[142] While policy responsibility for administrative justice rested with the Ministry of Justice, there remained a need for independent oversight by the AJTC. The Ministry of Justice lacked the resources and expertise to undertake effective scrutiny, particularly given that substantial elements of the administrative justice system were outside of its remit.

The government remained unpersuaded. The AJTC was therefore abolished in 2013, despite its minimal costs and good work.[143] The episode highlights a wider continuity going back to the Council on Tribunals. Any administrative justice oversight body will always struggle to get its voice heard and to exert impact upon government owing to the multiple fields of its subject matter and governmental attitudes. The end of the AJTC symbolised and reinforced the overall downward trajectory. In its place, a diluted form of non-statutory oversight was provided initially by the Administrative Justice Forum (2014–16) and then the current Administrative Justice Council (AJC, 2016–).[144] These bodies undertook discussions amongst those within the administrative justice community, namely, the advice sector, academics, tribunal judges, ombudsmen, complaint-handlers and Ministry of Justice officials. They have largely been unable to exert much impact upon government or even to get government to engage with them. The AJC is certainly better than having nothing at all, although it would be preferable to have a funded and statutory body with formal powers, such as the AJTC.

The third – and most controversial and impactful – reform was significant cuts to publicly funded civil legal aid.[145] Such provision dated back decades.[146] It had never been particularly generous; it was subject to both a financial means test and a merits test. However, following the 2013 changes, legal aid has been largely decimated.[147] The reductions in legal aid had been vigorously opposed and seen as a means of restricting much-needed access to justice for people who would otherwise be without assistance. The restrictions had wider impacts. Publicly funded legal aid work is rarely economically viable and many providers have exited the market, leading to advice deserts. This added considerable pressures and challenges to the wider advice sector, the various voluntary and charitable bodies that provide advice, particularly on interrelated issues such as indebtedness, housing and benefits.[148] The scheme for exceptional case funding has been highly limited in practice. There were many legal challenges against the new funding regime with some successes.[149] There was also a programme of closing court centres, which prompted concerns about access to justice.[150] When combined with

[142] ibid. See also HL Deb 23 November 2011, vol 732, cols 1076–89; HL Deb 22 July 2013, vol 747, cols 1125–35.

[143] Public Bodies (Abolition of Administrative Justice and Tribunals Council) Order, SI 2042/2013.

[144] The Administrative Justice Council is chaired by the Senior President of Tribunals.

[145] Legal Aid, Sentencing and Punishment of Offenders Act 2012.

[146] Legal Aid and Advice Act 1949.

[147] S Hynes, *Austerity Justice* (London, Legal Action Group, 2012); House of Commons Justice Committee, *Impact of Changes to Civil Legal Aid under Part 1 of the Legal Aid, Sentencing and Punishment of Offenders Act 2012* (HC 2014–15, 311); E Palmer, T Cornford, A Guinchard and Y Marique (eds), *Access to Justice: Beyond the Policies and Politics of Austerity* (Oxford, Hart Publishing, 2016).

[148] S Kirwan (ed), *Advising in Austerity: Reflections on Challenging Times for Advice Agencies* (Bristol, Policy Press, 2017).

[149] See, eg, *R (Public Law Project) v Lord Chancellor* [2016] UKSC 39 (the residence test, a near-blanket exclusion from legal aid for anyone not lawfully resident in the UK, was unlawful).

[150] House of Commons Justice Committee, *Court and Tribunal Reforms* (HC 2019, 190) [92]–[130].

under-funded and crumbling courts and tribunals, there is deep and persistent concern that access to justice is in crisis.[151]

Overall, New Labour's administrative justice legacy has not been entirely dismantled. The structure of the First-tier and Upper Tribunals has endured. However, the whole policy emphasis behind the 2004 White Paper of improving administrative justice has altogether dissipated and has been reversed in some key respects.[152]

Having considered the development of administrative justice, we now consider two wider issues. The first concerns the structure of administrative justice, namely the deep and pervasive dichotomy between appeals and complaints, the degree to which this is problematic and, if so, what can be done to address it. The second issue concerns the growth of other forms of non-judicial redress and scrutiny bodies beyond tribunals and ombudsmen.

The Appeals/Complaints Dichotomy

In Manchester city centre, two quite large office buildings stand almost next to each other. In one building are the offices of the PHSO, in which a few hundred staff handle complaints against central government departments and the National Health Service. In the other building, First-tier Tribunal judges hear and decide appeals concerning matters such as immigration and asylum, criminal injuries compensation, and war pensions and armed forces compensation. Each building houses an administrative justice redress institution. Yet, despite their physical proximity and their broadly speaking homologous character, these institutions inhabit entirely separate and mutually exclusive worlds. Tribunals and ombudsmen very rarely, if ever, interact or engage with each other. They do not share their decisions with each other. Senior leaders do not meet to discuss matters of shared common interest, let alone liaise with each other to coordinate the exercise of their respective jurisdictions. Both institutions work within their own silos and seem to exist in parallel universes. Nonetheless, they have two commonalities: they handle people's grievances against government and they are the principal redress institutions of administrative justice. Given the bifurcated way in which administrative justice has developed, the appeal/complaint dichotomy is far more than a surface-level procedural difference. It embodies the two quite different models and cultures of administrative justice, which in turn structures and informs much of the thinking about it.

Tribunals decide appeals against initial administrative decisions. They are judicial. They are not concerned with the quality of initial administrative decisions, but only with making their own decisions on appeal by using fair procedures and applying the

[151] JUSTICE, *Delivering Justice in an Age of Austerity: A Report by JUSTICE* (London, JUSTICE, 2015); Bach Commission on Access to Justice, *The Crisis in the Justice System in England & Wales* (2016), https://fabians.org.uk/publication/the-crisis-in-the-justice-system-in-england-wales.

[152] M Adler, 'The Rise and Fall of Administrative Justice: A Cautionary Tale' (2012) 8 *Socio-Legal Review* 28; N O'Brien, 'Administrative Justice: A Libertarian Cinderella in Search of an Egalitarian Prince' (2012) 83 *Political Quarterly* 494; J Tomlinson and R Kirkham, 'Revisiting the Administrative Justice Legacy of New Labour' in M Gordon and A Tucker (eds), *The New Labour Constitution: Twenty Years on* (Oxford, Hart Publishing, 2022).

relevant rules, which embody government policy. An appeal hearing before a tribunal is, for all intents and purposes, the same as a hearing before a lower court. Tribunals also specialise in areas such as social security, tax and immigration. Their jurisdiction is often highly specific. They can only hear and decide appeals against specified initial administrative decisions. They can only allow an appeal if the appellant has demonstrated that their case fulfils the eligibility criteria laid down in the relevant rules. Tribunal appeals and hearings are routine and repetitive. Their decisions are legally binding. There are also onward rights of appeal on error of law grounds to the Upper Tribunal and then to the higher courts.

By contrast, ombudsmen are non-judicial – or, rather, the distinctive nature of ombudsmen means that they do not fit comfortably within a traditional separation of powers framework of analysis. Instead, ombudsmen sit across the conventional division of executive, legislative and judicial powers. As one Parliamentary Ombudsman once noted, the office 'stands curiously poised between the legislature and the executive, while discharging an almost judicial function in the citizen's dispute with his government; and yet it forms no part of the judiciary'.[153] Ombudsmen are best understood as being part of the administrative and political process. They do not use judicial procedures such as hearings; they use paper-based investigatory procedures. Unlike tribunals, ombudsmen are typically generalist, not specialist bodies.[154] They have a wide-ranging jurisdiction to investigate complaints against government and public services irrespective of policy context. They are not organised by governmental function, but by territory and the level of government – central, local and devolved. By contrast with tribunals, ombudsmen are concerned with assessing the quality of administrative actions and decisions against the principles of good administration, which are broad and flexible standards, not legal rules. Like tribunals, they make findings of fact, although their findings and decisions are not legally binding, but are overwhelmingly accepted in practice. They also recommend improvements to public services, which tribunals do not. This would be viewed as stepping far beyond the judicial function into the realm of administration. There is no appeal against ombudsmen decisions. Ombudsmen have their own internal quality review mechanisms. The only external route of onward challenge is through judicial review. Whereas tribunals reflect a court-based model that emphasises the need for separation from politics, ombudsmen rely on the political process and public bodies wanting to improve. They can lay reports before Parliament and elected committees. Further, they sometimes speak to the media, something that no tribunal judge would ever do.

The appeal/complaint dichotomy is deeply embedded within the roles, functions and cultures of tribunals and ombudsmen. It is also internalised by government. Appeals and complaints are handled within government by different teams and in quite different ways.

Despite these differences, both appeals and complaints are essentially concerned with the same underlying issues: the need for an individual to secure redress arising from poor quality service delivery. The point was highlighted by the report of

[153] Parliamentary Commissioner for Administration, *Annual Report for 1983* (HC 1983–84, 322) 1.

[154] There are some specialist public sector ombudsmen, such as the Prisons and Probation Ombudsman.

the National Audit Office (NAO) on *Citizen Redress*.[155] This found that public sector redress systems had developed piecemeal over time and in isolation from each other. The division between appeals and complaints results in unnecessary duplication and compels aggrieved individuals to make what can sometimes be ill-informed choices about which redress route is most appropriate to resolve their problems. The choice for the citizen is between two superficially similar but really quite different redress systems. Some people may use the wrong process and thereby waste their time with the result that their problem cannot be satisfactorily resolved. From this perspective, the appeal/complaint dichotomy is reflective of a wider dysfunctional administrative justice system which operates on the basis of silos and procedures that have little, if any, meaning for members of the public. The overall system is not properly designed around and focused on the needs of individual users.

In reality, the typical administrative justice situation concerns a person who has a problem with a public body and wants to have it resolved. However, instead of the overall system being responsive to people's needs and problems, they have to fit their case within the structures determined by the system. People can view the distinction between complaints and appeals as an official 'trap' that is almost 'designed to help partition a complex original cause for concern into small parts about which citizens [can] more easily be fobbed off'.[156] The division between appeals and complaints has therefore been described as 'one of the most pervasive, important and counter-productive concepts in British official and administrative law culture'.[157] The distinction has no meaning for most people because few understand it. Further, silo-based working and fragmentation within both government and redress institutions typically inhibits effective working across such contexts. A reformed approach would focus on making the system more responsive to people's lives as opposed to requiring them to fit in with the system. There has been a lack of holistic thinking about the ways in which people's grievances against public bodies are dealt with across the whole administrative justice landscape.[158] In a similar vein, it has been suggested that tribunals and ombudsmen should be fused together into a unified and holistic model of redress that would deliver decisions, provide redress in individual cases, address wider administrative problems and undertake systemic reviews to improve for the future.[159]

What then is to be made of this? The diagnosis and critique have some force. People do sometimes fruitlessly pursue a complaint or a tribunal appeal when the alternative process would have better suited to their circumstances.[160] Tribunals can only apply the law to determine a person's entitlements, but they cannot correct service failures. Complaint procedures can redress service failures, but they cannot apply the law to

[155] National Audit Office, *Citizen Redress: What Citizens Can Do if Things Go Wrong with Public Services* (HC 2004–05, 21); P Dunleavy, S Bastow, J Tinkler, S Goldchluk and E Towers, 'Joining up Citizen Redress in UK Central Government' in Adler (n 131).

[156] ibid 426.

[157] ibid 424.

[158] A Le Sueur, 'Designing Redress: Who Does it, How and Why' (2012) 20 *Asia Pacific Law Review 1; V Bondy and A Le Sueur, Designing Redress: A Study about Grievances against Public Bodies in England and Wales* (London, Public Law Project, 2012).

[159] C Hodges, *Delivering Dispute Resolution: A Holistic Review of Models in England and Wales* (Oxford, Hart Publishing, 2019) 436–38.

[160] Independent Case Examiner, *Annual Report 2024–25* (2025) 14–17.

determine a person's entitlements. Going down the wrong road – unwittingly using the wrong redress mechanism – inevitably leads to problems, delay or the loss of any opportunity to secure redress. It is not unusual, according to the Independent Case Examiner, the second-tier complaint-handling body for social security complaints, for someone to appeal to a social security tribunal only for the judge to signpost them to the DWP's complaints process to remedy an administrative fault, such as being given incorrect advice, a matter which a tribunal cannot resolve. Conversely, some people complain about problems that can only be resolved by tribunals.[161]

The appeal/complaints dichotomy can then lead to practical difficulties for people, although it is now known how frequently such problems arise in practice. Despite this, the suggested solution of fusing tribunals and ombudsmen into a single unified redress institution is less convincing. The structure of administrative justice is bifurcated. There are different redress institutions, procedures and remedies. Tribunals and ombudsmen embody quite different models of redress. However, it is far from obvious what alternative institutional designs could be adopted to transcend the appeal/complaint dichotomy and how a new unified redress model could be made to work in practice. The academic team behind the *Citizen Redress* report focused principally on critiquing existing administrative justice arrangements. They emphasised how citizens have to grapple with two very different concepts of redress, instead of a more integrated concept of 'putting things right'. However, they did not advance any alternative design to replace the appeal/complaint dichotomy. Moreover, there are wider governmental-institutional forces in play here. Responsibility for administrative justice is distributed across government departments. The fragmented nature of administrative justice as a whole reflects the departmental character of UK central government. Government does not think in terms of grand utopian designs; it responds to specific practical problems. Even if a credible alternative holistic model of administrative justice could be devised, there would be obvious practical challenges with implementing it, not least the lack of any political will across government for reform and the likely need for additional resources. Current arrangements are imperfect, but they are not altogether broken either.

Another point is that government is unlikely to undertake any reform that would open it up to more criticism. For instance, government typically feels less apprehensive of tribunals allowing appeals. It often argues that appeals are allowed not because of poor initial decisions, but because new evidence has been presented or elicited on appeal, which then shifts the basis for decisions. By contrast, government is more sensitive to criticism by ombudsmen of defective administrative procedures. Consequently, it seems unlikely that government would willingly remodel existing redress mechanisms into a unified institution that both redetermined decisions and identified defective processes – precisely because this would open up government to more criticism and blame.

One response to the problems generated by the dichotomy is then simply a 'we-are-where-we-are' acceptance of reality and the practical challenges of reform. Administrative justice is a sprawling landscape. It has developed piecemeal in response to specific matters of social concern and not according to any grand plan. It has many centrifugal forces and pressures: the social and political contexts in which people's

[161] ibid.

justice problems arise; devolution and the fragmented departmental nature of government; and practical pressures, especially caseloads. In contrast, the centripetal forces are weak. Administrative justice is also path-dependent and there is an in-built bias for retaining the status quo subject to incremental changes.[162] It is just too fragmented for anyone working within it to spend too much time trying to understand it as a whole or to interact with others. Each redress institution faces enough of its own operational challenges to be concerned about working together to develop a more coherent and joined-up vision of an administrative justice system. Instead, practical problems, such as the fragmented handling of grievances within government and limited learning, would be better addressed through smaller-scale improvements such as better information for people, better signposting for people and more focused collaborative working as opposed to wholesale reform.

There has though been some consideration as to how closer joint working could be achieved. In 1990, Lord Woolf highlighted the differences and emerging relationships between ombudsmen, tribunals and the courts: 'The way in which the Ombudsman seeks to redress the complaints of the citizen as to maladministration bears no resemblance to the adjudicative powers of a court or tribunal.'[163] Ombudsmen had ready access to government papers and documents, whereas the courts rarely order the discovery of private government files. The inquisitorial investigations of ombudsmen were more searching than the courts. Woolf knew from first-hand experience 'the dread' created within government by ombudsmen investigations.[164] The recommendations of ombudsmen were not legally binding, but they were almost always followed. Further, victims of maladministration receive financial payments in circumstances in which the courts have no power to award damages. Building on this, Woolf suggested that ombudsmen should have a power, where appropriate, to refer a matter to the higher courts to clarify a point of law of wider significance or in circumstances in which the courts were better placed to provide a remedy. This power could be exercised by the ombudsman before, during or after an investigation. Conversely, the courts could refer a matter for investigation by the ombudsman when an inquisitorial investigation would be more effective than adversarial court procedures, especially with regard to accessing government documents.[165] This could make the best of both systems available to the public. However, these suggestions were not acted upon.

Some decades later, another judicial reformer, the then Senior President of Tribunals, Sir Ernest Ryder, updated Woolf's recommendations.[166] Both the Administrative Court and the tribunals should have the ability to refer matters that were prima facie maladministration to an ombudsman, which could then investigate. Giving ombudsmen a corresponding power to refer to the Upper Tribunal any issues requiring guidance by judicial determination or individual redress would enable ombudsmen to receive

[162] See generally N Creutzfeldt and R Kirkham, 'Understanding How and When Change Occurs in the Administrative Justice System: The Ombudsman/Tribunal Partnership as a Catalyst for Reform?' (2020) 42 *Journal of Social Welfare and Family Law* 253.

[163] H Woolf, *Protection of the Public: A New Challenge* (London, Stevens, 1990) 88.

[164] ibid 89.

[165] ibid 90.

[166] E Ryder, 'Driving Improvements: Collaboration and Peer Learning' (Belfast, Ombudsman Association Conference, 2019).

authoritative legal rulings and also enhance redress for the individual. Ryder further suggested career interoperability – that is, enabling judges to work as ombudsmen and vice versa. This exchange of career paths would break down the respective cultures in tribunals and ombudsmen, thereby creating an integrated culture of administrative justice.

These were fairly radical ideas that could have positive effects, although, unsurprisingly, nothing happened. Achieving positive improvements in administrative justice is possible, but it is often an uphill and long-haul endeavour. One issue is that ombudsmen, as statutory public bodies, are themselves subject to judicial review challenges. It might seem odd if the courts coordinated their role with ombudsmen who are, on occasion, a respondent in judicial review litigation which the courts adjudicate upon. Another reason is simply that the senior judges work within a long-established court-based model of adjudication and do not necessarily see it as their role to coordinate their work with ombudsmen. Alternatively, the courts are more concerned with addressing their own challenges, not least caseloads and case management – as opposed to some abstract notion of constructing a joined-up and coherent administrative justice system. All of this maintains the status quo. For their part, ombudsmen may harbour concerns that the distinctiveness and advantages of their model of administrative justice may, over time, be weakened if they come under pressure to become judicialised. Whatever the reason, ombudsmen have often felt misunderstood and uncertain about their status in a legal culture focused heavily on judicial adjudication as the predominant model and which tends to view departures from that model as suspect.[167] In any event, redress and scrutiny bodies other than tribunals and ombudsman have come to play an increasing role.

Other Redress and Non-redress Scrutiny Mechanisms

There are other redress and scrutiny bodies beyond tribunals and ombudsmen. These include other non-judicial redress bodies and also non-redress bodies that scrutinise and inspect government and public services.

One model of non-judicial redress that is quite different from tribunals and ombudsmen was the Independent Review Service which reviewed Social Fund decisions. The Social Fund was introduced in 1988 as a discretionary welfare scheme.[168] Initial decisions were taken by the DWP. Refused claimants could seek a review by the Independent Review Service as opposed to appeal to tribunals, the normal redress process for social security decisions. This was controversial because the review of decisions by another official was seen as inherently inferior to a right of appeal to an independent tribunal.[169]

Despite this inauspicious start, the Independent Review Service developed into a relatively successful and distinctive form of administrative justice. The process involved

[167] It was only in 2019 that senior leaders from tribunals and ombudsmen met to discuss the potential for cross-working: Administrative Justice Council, Ombudsman and Tribunals Familiarisation Workshop (11 October 2019). Little came from this.

[168] The aim was to support families on low income with certain one-off or occasional expenses through Budgeting Loans, Sure Start Maternity Grants, Funeral Expenses Payments and Cold Weather Payments.

[169] Council on Tribunals, *Social Security: Abolition of Independent Appeals under the Proposed Social Fund* (Cmnd 9722, 1986).

a review by Social Fund Inspectors, who were experts in the Social Fund, although they were themselves officials, albeit quite separate from the DWP. This was a unique form of administrative justice redress because it combined both a review and an appeal function that dealt with issues of legality and whether the decision was right in all the circumstances of the case. Moreover, the decision was legally binding. What was notable was that over time, the Independent Review Service came to provide accessible, timely, proportionate and fair decisions with high user engagement in the process and high user satisfaction at a relatively low cost. The ethos of inspectors was to: prioritise and be responsive to the needs of claimants; deliver simplicity with the required level of clarity; provide clear reasons; and conduct reviews as quickly as possible.[170] The system was based on the following values: independence; inquisitorial procedures without hearings; delivering high-quality decisions promptly with understandable reasons; being responsive and tailored to the needs of individuals; easy to access; and proportionate and cost-effective. The service handled some 50,000 cases per year and inspectors completed 95 per cent of urgent cases within 24 hours and a similarly high proportion of all other cases within 21 working days. Such performance is entirely beyond the capacity of any tribunal or ombudsman.

The Independent Review Service was a bespoke and a relatively successful form of administrative justice within government. It was viewed by justice policy-makers as an impressive success.[171] However, no effort was made to adapt this model into other areas. Various government departments – principally the DWP and the Home Office – have since developed their own internal administrative review processes by which officials review decisions either before or instead of a tribunal appeal. These administrative review systems tend to suffer from the same pressures and dysfunctions that afflict large initial casework organisations. By contrast, the separateness of the Independent Review Service in part enabled it to develop into a successful form of external-internal expert administrative review. Another form of non-judicial redress is initial complaint-handling by public bodies (see Chapter 5).

A different institutional form of administrative justice is through non-redress mechanisms that undertake scrutiny and oversight of administrative justice matters. Tribunals and ombudsmen differ in various ways, but both are reactive redress institutions in the sense that they handle grievances from those individuals who appeal or complain. Individualised administrative justice is long-established, but it is not necessarily the most effective or efficient option. Many people do not seek redress. Moreover, individual administrative justice denotes a relatively confined and limited understanding of the concept based on mass transaction processing. By contrast, the notion of collective

[170] Social Fund Commissioner, *Annual Report 2012/2013* (2013). The Independent Review Service was abolished in 2013 when the Social Fund was itself abolished and replaced by various models. In England, there is a locally based provision delivered by local authorities with internal reviews and then complaints to the Local Government and Social Care Ombudsman. Scotland has locally based provision with *appeals* going to the Scottish Public Services Ombudsman. See C Himsworth, 'A Cuckoo in the Nest of the Scottish Ombudsman' [2020] *PL* 14. Both Northern Ireland and Wales retained devolved centralised administration, with the former keeping the previous redress model (see Office of the Discretionary Support Commissioner, *Annual Report 2023–24* (2024)). In Wales, there are tiered levels of reviews and complaints, ultimately to the Public Services Ombudsman for Wales.

[171] P Stockton, 'Proportionate Dispute Resolution: What are the Options?' (Administrative Justice Seminar, Nuffield Foundation, January 2006) [32].

administrative justice has increasingly come to be recognised.[172] It typically arises when a group of similarly situated people share common characteristics and experience a collective justice problem. This problem reflects, but also transcends, those individuals' specific circumstances. For instance, the group of people rely on a government body or public service, the delivery of which is systemically flawed in a structural, cultural and/or behavioural way. In such situations, the need for collective administrative justice is naturally associated with – and often by generated by – underlying systemic failures which adversely affect the wider group of people. Collective administrative justice requires more wide-ranging and encompassing modalities than individual redress. These include proactive monitoring, investigation, inspection and scrutiny of government to get it to improve. This is exemplified by the own-initiative powers of ombudsmen to investigate systemic maladministration.[173] However, the wider scrutiny space also includes a range of different bodies which, while not necessarily thought of as administrative justice institutions, have nonetheless come to play an important role: the NAO, inspectorates, public sector regulators, monitoring bodies, advisory committees, commissioners and public inquiries.

Established to examine whether government provides value for money, the NAO has, over time, served a dual mission of helping Parliament hold government to account and recommending improvements.[174] It has increasingly focused on scrutinising the performance of government departments and improving operational delivery by identifying good practices and lessons learned.[175] One distinctive contribution is that the NAO adopts a 'whole system' approach which is focused on how effectively administrative systems operate, including administrative decision-making.[176] Both the NAO and the House of Commons Public Accounts Committee have, at times, examined administrative justice issues by investigating and reporting on the underlying systemic causes of problems that would otherwise have been neglected by the otherwise predominant focus on individual redress.[177]

Other relevant oversight bodies include the Social Security Advisory Committee and the Independent Chief Inspector of Borders and Immigration – both of which have reported on the quality of initial administrative decisions and administrative

[172] R Thomas, 'The Northern Ireland Public Services Ombudsman's Report into Personal Independence Payment and Collective Administrative Justice (Part 1)' (2023) 30 *Journal of Social Security Law* 143, 145–46. See also C Hodges and S Voet, *Delivering Collective Redress: New Technologies* (Oxford, Hart Publishing, 2018); M Molavi, *Collective Access to Justice: Assessing the Potential of Class Actions in England and Wales* (Bristol, Bristol University Press, 2021).

[173] See ch 6 228–234.

[174] National Audit Act 1983; M Power, 'The Theory of the Audit Explosion' in E Ferlie, LE Lynn and C Pollitt (eds), *The Oxford Handbook of Public Management* (Oxford, Oxford University Press, 2005); D Morin and M Hazgui, 'We are Much More Than Watchdogs: The Dual Identity of Auditors at the UK National Audit Office' (2016) 12 *Journal of Accounting & Organizational Change* 568; HC Midgley, L Ferry and AD Murphie, *Holding Government to Account: Democracy and the National Audit Office* (Abingdon, Routledge, 2024).

[175] See, eg, National Audit Office, *Improving Operational Delivery in Government: A Good Practice Guide for Senior Leaders* (London, NAO, 2021).

[176] National Audit Office, *Getting it Right, Putting it Right: Improving Decision-Making and Appeals in Social Security Benefits* (HC 2002–03, 1142).

[177] In addition to the above, see National Audit Office, *Improving the Speed and Quality of Asylum Decisions* (HC 2003–04, 535); National Audit Office, *Helping Those in Financial Hardship: The Running of the Social Fund* (HC 2004–05, 179); idem, *Compensating Victims of Violent Crime* (HC 2007–08, 100) amongst other reports.

review systems.[178] When the government abolished various immigration appeal rights in 1993 owing to their cost and delay, an Independent Monitor was appointed to monitor overseas entry clearance visa decision-making and to make recommendations.[179] The Independent Monitor was later absorbed into the Independent Chief Inspector of Borders and Immigration that was established following deep-seated failures by the Home Office.[180] Other important bodies include: the Equality and Human Rights Commission; public inquiries; reviews into healthcare scandals; independent ad hoc reviews (such as the Windrush Lessons Learned Review); parliamentary select committees; and a number of different commissioners (the Children's Commissioner, the Victims Commissioner, the Armed Forces Commissioner and the Windrush Commissioner).[181] There are also inspectorates such as Ofsted, which inspects schools, and the Care Quality Commission, the independent regulator of health and adult social care in England. It has reported on people's struggles in accessing quality health and social care, waiting list delays and the pressures on mental health services, although the Care Quality Commission has itself been criticised for its poor operational performance.[182]

Overall, individual redress through tribunals and complaints have been complemented by more systemic oversight and scrutiny, which has become increasingly more prominent and important. The wider picture is one of incoherence. By the 2000s, the PHSO's health jurisdiction had eclipsed its traditional parliamentary jurisdiction; the institution had become now part of the wider realm of public sector regulation and inspection. The PHSO was also part of the complaint-handling structures, including second-tier complaint-handlers. These two domains – public sector regulation and inspection and complaint-handling – have developed ad hoc in response to specific problems and were fragmented and incoherent, thereby reinforcing the overall sense that administrative justice was increasingly disjointed and unsystematic.[183] Yet, this jumble can be seen as both an innate characteristic and a positive attribute. It embodies a degree of redundancy within oversight and scrutiny, and while imperfect, it reflects the importance attributed to administrative justice and its diversity.

[178] Social Security Advisory Committee, *Decision Making and Mandatory Reconsideration: A Study by the Social Security Advisory Committee* (London, Occasional Paper No 18, 2016); ICIBI, *An Inspection of Asylum Casework* (2024).

[179] Asylum and Immigration Appeals Act 1993, s 10.

[180] UK Borders Act 2007, ss 48–56.

[181] B Kirkup, *The Report of the Morecambe Bay Investigation* (London, Stationery Office, 2015); *Independent Review of Maternity Services at the Shrewsbury and Telford Hospital NHS Trust* (HC 2021–22, 1219); *Maternity and Neonatal Services in East Kent: 'Reading the Signals' Report* (HC 2021–22, 681); W Williams, *Windrush Lessons Learned Review* (HC 2019–20, 93). On public inquiries, see generally M Elliott and R Thomas, *Public Law*, 5th edn (Oxford, Oxford University Press, 2024) ch 17. On commissioners, see P Cox, R Lamont and M Sunkin, 'Constitutionalising Regulatory Governance: The Case of the Victims' Commissioner' [2025] *PL* 283.

[182] Department of Health and Social Care, *Review into the Operational Effectiveness of the Care Quality Commission: Full Report* (London, DHSC, 2024).

[183] A Abraham, 'The Parliamentary Ombudsman and Administrative Justice: Shaping the Next 50 Years' (London, JUSTICE, 2011) 28.

Conclusion

This chapter has examined the development of the contemporary administrative justice landscape. The discussion has highlighted the diversity and evolving nature of administrative justice. The criminal and civil justice systems have a relative unity and coherence in terms of both the law being applied and the judicial processes. Administrative justice is altogether different. It applies across many different and disparate areas of public administration. There are judicial processes, but also ombudsmen and other complaint-handling bodies. Another important area for investigating administrative justice is the operations and behaviours of public bodies themselves. Administrative justice is also heavily conditioned and influenced by government policy on a number of levels. Many recent developments have been underpinned by political choices about public spending and specific areas of substantive policy. At the same time, administrative justice embodies core values – individual redress and fairness for individuals and, increasingly, systemic scrutiny. The development of administrative justice has a sense of progression and then regression. Positive developments, such as the reforms to tribunals, have been followed by restrictions to legal aid. Nonetheless, the notion of administrative justice remains deeply embedded within people's expectations and governmental and judicial structures. Having considered the overall landscape and its development, we now need to consider in detail how administrative justice works in practice. We will start by examining individualised decision-making by government and tribunals.

4

Administrative Decision-Making and Tribunals

Every year, government takes tens of millions of decisions about people's entitlements and liabilities. In high-volume systems – social security, immigration and tax – government departments operate as huge machines that churn out enormous volumes of decisions. In other contexts – special educational needs, adult social care, homelessness, criminal injuries compensation, school exclusions and so on – the volumes are lower, but the decisions are just as important and life-changing. Following initial decisions, there are administrative reviews and tribunal appeals. Put together, all of this casework comprises a huge amount of work by government and tribunals.

In this context, the primary demand of administrative justice is to make accurate and good-quality decisions.[1] People are entitled to receive well-considered and reasoned decisions on their entitlements. The consequences of poor-quality decisions are significant: people living in poverty not receiving their benefits; asylum claimants potentially being returned to face persecution; children wrongly excluded from school; children and/or young people with special educational needs and disabilities not receiving the educational support they require; and so on. Good decisions are required to ensure people receive their legal entitlements and that policy is administered effectively. The quality of decision-making is also directly related to trust in government. Poor-quality decisions generate costly and lengthy disputes and appeals, and undermine trust in the system, whereas many people will not seek redress, but will simply absorb the harms that arise. On the other hand, the number of decisions required and the 'tyranny' of casework requires mass-volume processing and presents significant challenges for government.

This chapter examines how administrative decision-making, administrative reviews and tribunals work in practice and their effectiveness. It considers the quality of decision-making, the strengths and weaknesses of current decision-making systems, and what could realistically be done to improve them in practice. The issues are complex and evaluative, and there are inevitably trade-offs involved. An overall theme is that government could and should do more to improve the quality of decision-making. At the same time, decision-making is not solely a technocratic exercise; it is also influenced by institutional cultures.

[1] R Sainsbury, 'Administrative Justice: Discretion and Procedure in Social Security Decision-Making' in K Hawkins (ed), *The Uses of Discretion* (Oxford, Oxford University Press, 1992) 302.

Initial Decision-Making

Government decision-makers take decisions, but what is an administrative decision? There is sometimes a tendency to focus on the individual decision received by a claimant as a single isolated phenomenon. In reality, a decision is one of many (often very many) other decisions which flow through a public body. Decisions are the products of a wider process which starts before anyone makes an application. This background comprises many layers: the social interests in play; government policy; the detailed rules being applied; the design and operation of decision processes; forms to be completed; the presentation and collection of evidence; and the competence of caseworkers to exercise judgement and make robust decisions.[2] If the claim is granted, then the claimant receives their entitlements. If refused, then the question arises as to whether the claimant wants to challenge that decision and, if so, how.[3] There are various redress mechanisms: administrative reviews, appeals and complaints. Decision-making can be straightforward or complex. It often involves the careful assessment of human situations and circumstances upon which has been superimposed a detailed and intricate body of rules and case law. The quality of decision-making depends heavily on the competence of decision-makers, the procedures they use and the wider institutional arrangements in they which operate. To make findings of fact, caseworkers have to apply standards of proof, which involves careful judgement and the handling of the evidence.

Decision-makers need knowledge and understanding of the contexts they work within, the skills to elicit and discern relevant information, and the ability to exercise sound judgement to produce informed and reasoned decisions. Deciding whether a person's entitlement to disability benefits involves an assessment and requires an understanding of how different medical and disability conditions affect a person's functional capacity to undertake ordinary daily activities. Asylum decision-makers have to assess whether an asylum claimant would be at risk of persecution or torture on return to their home country and whether they are telling the truth. There is usually no corroborating evidence. Claimants will not normally speak English, but have their story translated. They will also come from an entirely different culture from that of the decision-maker and will possibly be a victim of torture. Asylum decision-makers must also make judgements about the conditions in the country from which asylum is being sought – for instance, the social attitudes towards gay men in Iran and the effectiveness of laws in Sierra Leone prohibiting female genital mutilation and how they are enforced in practice.[4] School admission appeal panels must weigh up a child's case to be admitted to a school with the needs of children already there. This requires local knowledge about routes to schools, travel distances, social and family contexts and school capacity. Much decision-making involves evaluating the evidence and exercising judgement when applying the relevant standards.

While much of the focus has typically been on tribunals, the largest volume of administrative justice activity occurs within government. From the perspective of claimants,

[2] On application forms, see: A Ryan, 'The Form of Forms: Everyday Enablers of Access to Justice' (2023) 32 *Social & Legal Studies* 690; J Meers, 'Forms of Fettering: Application Forms and the Exercise of Discretion in the Welfare State' (2020) 42 *Journal of Social Welfare & Family Law* 221.

[3] Some decisions are binary (eg, asylum decisions and school admission appeals), whereas other decisions operate on a sliding scale (eg, disability benefits have lower and higher rate entitlements).

[4] R Thomas, *Administrative Justice and Asylum Appeals: A Study of Tribunal Adjudication* (Oxford, Hart Publishing, 2011).

the consideration of their claims initially is far more important than going to a tribunal. Initial decision-making is a largely closed and hidden world, although its general features and the wider forces which impact upon it can be identified.

Initial decisions are usually taken by relatively junior front-line officials. Being a caseworker is typically a low-pay, low-status position. It is not recognised as a professional role within government. Caseworkers typically have relatively little professional autonomy. They are often under pressure to decide – or process – large volumes of cases quickly. Caseworkers may want to make good-quality decisions, but their endeavours are heavily constrained by the wider systems, processes, environments and cultures in which they work. The training and experience of caseworkers varies. Applying complex legal rules and sensitively exercising discretion can be challenging, especially in borderline cases. The application of standards of proof such as the balance of probabilities can be nuanced and challenging. Many caseworkers do not understand concepts like the standard of proof and how to weigh up evidence. Giving proper and adequate reasons for decisions is easier said than done.

There are procedural variations in how decisions are taken. In some contexts, caseworkers interview claimants in person. People applying for disability benefits undergo an assessment. Increasingly, many decisions are taken on the papers/online. This has coincided with institutional pressures to process applications quickly with the obvious risk that targets take priority over making good-quality decisions.[5] Inevitably, this leads to a culture in which the facts, nuances and circumstances of individual applications do not necessarily receive the type of detailed and careful assessment that they deserve. When caseworkers are disconnected from claimants and unable to ask them questions to resolve evidential gaps and difficulties, they are less likely to understand the difficulties facing claimants or to exercise empathy.[6] This can change the nature of decision-making to impersonal case processing which is focused on speed and efficiency. In some contexts, caseworkers make decisions on the evidence presented. In other contexts, they may have discretion as to whether to collect further evidence themselves, although they may not necessarily exercise it in practice. In some contexts, caseworkers may write a 'minded-to' pre-decision letter to claimants outlining concerns and then inviting the claimant to respond. In other contexts, this does not happen. Even when decision-makers do meet claimants, there are the non-rational and emotional responses of decision-makers to factor in. When decision-making involves assessing the truthfulness or credibility of a person's story (as in asylum cases), caseworkers may fear being duped by dishonest claimants.[7] All human decision-making is vulnerable to cognitive biases, including confirmation bias, the tendency to search for and interpret information in a way that confirms or supports their beliefs.[8] Such biases can

[5] See, eg, 'DWP Civil Servants Describe "Unbearable" Workloads amid "All-Time Low Staffing" Levels' *Civil Service World* (4 December 2023), www.civilserviceworld.com/professions/article/excl-dwp-civil-servants-describe-unbearable-workloads-amid-alltime-low-staffing-levels.

[6] KPR Bartels, 'Public Encounters: The History and Future of Face-to-Face Contact between Public Professionals and Citizens' (2013) 91 *Public Administration* 469; RA Kagan, 'Varieties of Bureaucratic Justice' in NR Parillo (ed), *Administrative Law from the Inside out* (Cambridge, Cambridge University Press, 2017) 247, 265; S Paul, 'Administrative Empathy: A New Value in Administrative Justice' [2025] *PL* 670.

[7] S Halliday, 'Administrative Justice and Street-Level Emotions: Cultures of Denial in Entitlement Decision-Making' [2021] *PL* 727.

[8] D Kahneman, *Thinking, Fast and Slow* (London, Penguin, 2012).

be reinforced by repeated exposure to grinding casework and rules of thumb that sort claimants into predetermined categories.

Decision-making also poses organisational challenges for government. An increased number of claims places additional demands on caseworkers and can exceed their capacity, thereby leading to backlogs and delays. This can then lead to efforts to manage the flow through streamlining processes and the prioritisation of specific categories. Quality can be sacrificed to productivity, with poor-quality refusal decisions being shifted onto review and appeal systems. Decision-making also occurs within institutional and political environments and is influenced by government policy to the potential detriment of some claimants. This has been particularly evident in certain contexts. In recent years, government has sought to reduce spending on disability benefits and to enforce a hostile immigration environment to reduce immigration. These wider political forces clearly impact upon the quality and culture of initial decision-making. A Home Office commitment in 2022 to clear the asylum backlog involved frequent and significant changes to processes with a focus on productivity and outputs. The overburdening of caseworkers resulted in high staff turnover and extremely low morale.[9] Asylum caseworkers have been subject to targets which may be unachievable without undermining quality.[10] Government bodies can seek to mitigate caseload pressures by having internal checks on decision-making, including quality assurance checks and having a 'second pair of eyes' – that is, reviews by other caseworkers before decisions are sent out. There are also significant differences in the quality of decisions across government. Some government departments have a reputation for poor-quality decisions (eg, the Home Office and the Department for Work and Pensions), whereas others have a better reputation (eg, HMRC). The quality of decisions within the same department can vary between one unit and another, and can also vary over time.

The widely shared assumption is that the quality of initial decision-making across government is variable and not as good as it could be. It is unrealistic to expect initial decisions to be of a uniformly high standard. But how are we to assess whether decisions are of good or inferior quality? The most frequently relied-upon metric is the proportion of allowed appeals. A very high rate of allowed appeals is often pointed to as evidence of poor-quality initial decisions. However, appeal outcomes provide one only indicator of the quality of initial decisions and are at best a limited proxy measure. Tribunals only consider a small proportion of all initial decisions. Appeals can be allowed for reasons unrelated to the quality of the initial decision. New evidence unavailable to the initial decision-maker may be presented to or collected by tribunals and thereby shift the basis for the decision. There are also procedural differences between initial decision-making and decision-making of tribunals. The notion of the quality of decision-making is itself problematic. It is impossible to know in any objective sense whether decisions are accurate and correct, especially when they are fundamentally concerned with issues of fact rather than issues of law. Fact-finding is a judgemental and evaluative task that involves assessing the evidence presented and deciding how much weight to place upon

[9] Independent Chief Inspector of Borders and Immigration (ICIBI), *An Inspection of Asylum Casework* (2024). See also 'Over half of DWP disability assessors quit in a year over feeling "despised"' *The Independent* (31 January 2025). One assessor noted: 'We all got in healthcare for altruistic reasons and that maybe isn't the case in this job … you're a cog in the machine doing bureaucratic work.'

[10] ICIBI (n 9). See also 'Home Office Says Only Half of UK Asylum Decisions Meet its Quality Standards' *The Guardian* (8 December 2024).

it and which evidence to accept or reject. A crucial aspect of the quality of decisions is therefore the quality of the reasons given. Decision-makers must give reasons for their decisions which state the criteria applied, and the evidence that was taken into account and how it was considered, and must explain why they have reached the decision in a way that the applicant can understand. A decision outcome might be correct, but if it is supported by inadequate reasons, then it is of poor quality. There has been extensive criticism of the quality of reasons of initial decisions. Poorly explained decisions weaken people's confidence in the quality of those decisions. Taking account of all these points and qualifications, the quality of initial decision-making often appears variable and sometimes inadequate, and therefore in need of improvement.

This in turn raises the issue of redress. The conventional means of redress involves tribunal appeals, although administrative review has increasingly been inserted either before or instead of tribunals. The overall decision structure has been progressively concatenated into: initial decision; administrative review; tribunals; and the courts. A related issue concerns the degree to which people actually seek redress.

Much of this chapter focuses on redress mechanisms and their effectiveness, but before proceeding further, it is appropriate to highlight some wider points concerning administrative justice. Indeed, some aspects of the prior discussion pose challenges for articulating the meaning of that term. For instance, is it preferable for government to process a large caseload quickly and therefore accept a low quality of decision, or to accept delays as the inevitable price of ensuring better decisions? What skills and competences in its decision-makers can government afford? What does 'consistency' mean when huge volumes of decisions are taken by thousands of caseworkers? There are no simple answers to these questions. They illustrate the inevitable and often difficult compromises involved. There are higher-level overarching principles of administrative justice and then there are the imperfect realities of what happens. It is inherent in the notion of administrative justice that our collective aspirations for justice must inevitably, to a greater or lesser degree, be moderated when they collide with the real-world realities of government.

A wider point is that administrative justice includes, but is not limited to, the quality of individual decisions. It also encompasses a broader sense of the fairness and acceptability of the overall decision process. A fundamental aspect of any administrative decision process is that it both seeks to be and is seen as fair and effective by the people who use it. A decision process should command general acceptance even though specific decisions may well be contestable and wrong. People should be able to understand decisions and believe that they have been fairly assessed. Poor decision-making can adversely affect people by denying them their entitlements, forcing them to proceed through lengthy and complex redress processes. Poor decision-making also contributes to a wider sense that the decision process as a whole is unreliable and inadequate, not working as it should and therefore not authentic or legitimate. It is therefore necessary to consider not just individual decisions, but also the decision-making process as a whole and its operations. Redress mechanisms are needed, although their existence can, paradoxically, weaken administrative justice. Government bodies can implicitly assume that there is less need for them to get initial decisions right, because claimants can always appeal. The onus is then placed on claimants to challenge decisions, sometimes through multiple stages, shifting the caseload to tribunals. This is not just inefficient; it also overlooks the fact that many people do not seek redress and the need for government to ensure legitimacy in its decision-making. Overall, decision processes labour under various pressures and tensions, and do not always necessarily operate in the way that they should.

Yet, there is another side of the coin. Debates over the quality of decision-making have a distinct negativity bias. Attention and criticism are almost entirely focused on claimants being wrongly refused and their access to and the fairness of onward rights of redress. However, if the quality of initial decisions is variable, then it is problematic to assume that errors always go against claimants. It is just as likely that some errors go in their favour. Some people will receive incorrect positive decisions – for instance, to benefits or asylum. However, there is little, if any, scrutiny of the quality of positive decisions.[11] This highlights a wider structural and attitudinal feature of administrative justice in general. The redress apparatus is entirely focused on correcting wrong initial refusal decisions through reviews and appeals. By contrast, potentially flawed initial positive decisions in favour of claimants remain hidden away and cannot be challenged. Tribunals only decide appeals against refusal decisions and can only be activated by refused claimants. Viewed objectively, the concept of administrative justice requires all decisions, both positive and negative, to be of good quality in order to ensure that people receive their entitlements – no more or less. There is a risk that some claimants receive more than they should. The anxiety is increased once it is appreciated that one way for government, when under pressure to clear huge volumes of claims, is to streamline by, for instance, replacing personal interviews with dealing with claims solely on the papers.[12] Caseworkers may sometimes be incentivised simply to waive claims through by allowing them. After all, this obviates any troublesome obligation to give reasons and the additional work this and appeals involve. If so, then the lack of scrutiny of initial positive decisions seems like a major gap in administrative justice. However, no one knows about the quality of initial positive decisions, few are interested and the issue is very difficult to investigate. Nonetheless, it is important to guard against any easy assumption that only initial refusal decisions are of poor quality. We can now consider redress mechanisms.

Administrative Review

Administrative review involves a paper-based review of an initial refusal decision by a different official within the same government body. It has become the principal stage of the redress either before or instead of a tribunal appeal. The rationale is that administrative review enables initial decisions to be reviewed quickly and efficiently without the delay and cost of tribunals. By contrast, the Council on Tribunals once stated that administrative review could not 'in any sense be regarded as a proper substitute for

[11] In some contexts, such as immigration, there is internal quality assurance of initial decisions, although such processes can be weak. One problem that exceeds the ability of administrative justice to address and belongs more to the criminal process concerns corrupt decision-makers: see '"Corrupt" Home Office Worker Took Thousands in Bribes to Grant Asylum Claim' *Manchester Evening News* (24 June 2025) (a corrupt Manchester-based Home Office caseworker took over £3,000 in bribes to grant an asylum claim and was jailed for four-and-a-half years); '"Mass-Scale Fraud" Feared in Council Lettings' *BBC News* (17 January 2026) (an investigation into council housing fraudulently allocated by 'corrupt housing officers for personal gain' with links to organised crime).

[12] 'Migrants Granted Asylum without Face-to-Face Interviews: Fast-Track Measure Aimed at Clearing Backlog, But Home Office Experts Warn of "Massive" Risks' *Daily Telegraph* (7 December 2025).

a right of appeal'.[13] Leggatt took a middle position: undertaken properly, administrative review could ensure that only the right cases would proceed to tribunals. Review processes could be used to identify problems in the system if public bodies looked at their own decisions critically and adopted the same 'kind of independent-mindedness and impartiality which can be expected from tribunals'.[14] This would involve some time, but reviews should not simply have the effect of protracting appeals.[15]

Administrative review processes are owned and designed by the relevant government department. Only certain types of initial decisions attract a review, whereas others do not, thereby potentially creating a redress gap. The Local Government and Social Care Ombudsman has taken the approach that where there is no right to a statutory review, it is good practice for councils to conduct a non-statutory review when a complainant raises concerns.[16] The PHSO has not adopted the same position as regards central government.

The role and prominence of administrative review has increased in recent years. There are now various different models: compulsory review before going to tribunals (social security); administrative review instead of appeals and then judicial review (most immigration decisions); an administrative review and then appeal on point of law to the County Court (homelessness); or a choice between a review and an appeal (tax). Administrative reviews offer speed and efficiency. A quick and informal review of an initial decision should enable errors to be corrected without incurring the delay of a tribunal, although practice sometimes suggests otherwise. However, there are significant institutional and procedural differences between administrative reviews and tribunals. Reviews are undertaken by different officials within the same department. They may be located in a different unit, but they are not structurally independent in the way that tribunals are. Reviews are decided on the papers on the basis of documentary evidence, although in some instances reviewers may phone claimants. By contrast, tribunals are institutionally separate from government and undertake a de novo consideration of a person's case. Beneath such practical differences, there is an underlying difference between administrative processing and the judicial approach of tribunals.

To illustrate the operations of reviews, Figure 4.1 shows Personal Independence Payment (PIP, a disability benefit) decisions over the years 2018–25 and those cases that proceed to 'Mandatory Reconsideration' (the administrative review stage in social security decision-making) and then to tribunal appeals. PIP is only one benefit amongst many and there are many other decision systems. Nonetheless, the figure is indicative of how administrative review works in practice. The volume of decisions reduces as cases proceed throughout the overall process. Most decisions start and finish at the initial and review stages. Tribunals handle significant volumes, but this is relatively small compared to initial and review decisions.

[13] Council on Tribunals, *Annual Report 1989/90* (HC 1990–91, 64) [1.9]. See also R Sainsbury, 'Internal Reviews and the Weakening of Social Security Claimants' Rights of Appeal' in G Richardson and H Genn (eds), *Administrative Law & Government Action* (Oxford, Oxford University Press, 1994).

[14] A Leggatt, *Tribunals for Users: One System, One Service: Report of the Review of Tribunals by Sir Andrew Leggatt* (London, Lord Chancellor's Department, 2001) [9.6] and [9.8].

[15] ibid.

[16] LGSCO, London Borough of Newham (23003461) [12] and [44]. See also London Borough of Lambeth (23010081) (the council took seven months to undertake a homeless review when it should have been carried out within eight weeks).

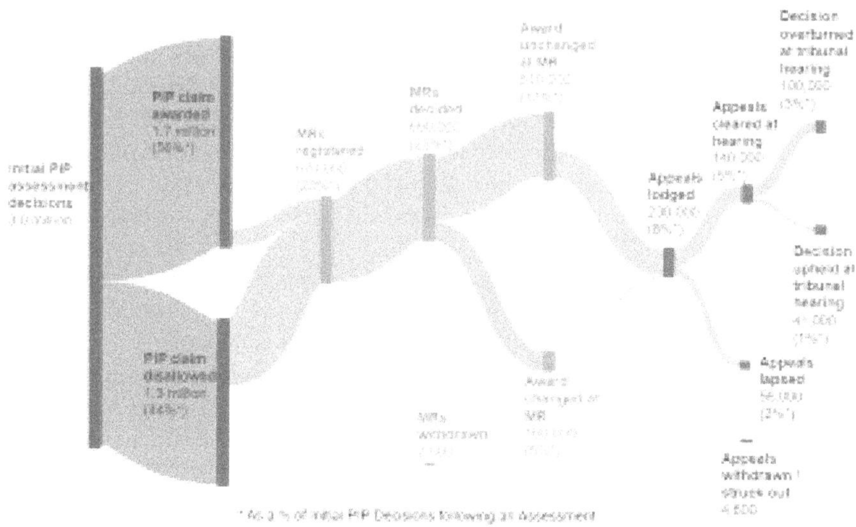

Figure 4.1 PIP decisions, 2018–25.[17] This figure shows the numbers of decisions concerning entitlement to PIP from initial claims, through mandatory reconsideration (MR) to tribunals

It is difficult to reach definitive conclusions about how administrative review works in practice. As with so much of administrative justice, practice varies both from one system to another and within each system. Both good and inferior practice can co-exist within the same system. Much depends upon the attitude and approach adopted within government, which is typically difficult to investigate. Nonetheless, drawing upon the available evidence, the quality of administrative reviews is variable and sometimes poor. The handling and consideration of reviews is often informed by the same processing mentality and institutional pressures as initial decision-making. Initial refusal decisions are more likely to be upheld through administrative review unless the claimant provides a strong argument or clear evidence that justifies overturning the initial decision. We can consider the experience of administrative reviews in the social security and immigration contexts.

Mandatory reconsideration was introduced in the social security context in 2012.[18] Prior to this, initial decisions were internally reviewed upon the lodging of appeals (so-called 'lapsed appeals'). Claimants must now seek a review before then lodging an appeal to access a tribunal. The president of social security tribunals expressed concern that mandatory reconsideration was of 'dubious advantage' and 'regressive'.[19]

[17] Department for Work and Pensions, *Personal Independence Payment: Official Statistics to January 2025* (2025), gov.uk/government/statistics/personal-independence-payment-statistics-to-january-2025/personal-independence-payment-official-statistics-to-january-2025.

[18] DWP, *Mandatory Consideration of Revision before Appeal* (TSO, 2012); Welfare Reform Act 2012, s 102; Social Security and Child Support (Decisions and Appeals) Regulations, SI 1999/991, reg 3ZA; Universal Credit, Personal Independence Payment, Jobseeker's Allowance and Employment and Support Allowance (Decisions and Appeals) Regulations, SI 2013/381.

[19] House of Commons Work and Pensions Committee, *Oral Evidence: Employment and Support Allowance and Work Capacity Benefits* (HC 2014–15, 1212, 7 May 2014) (HH Judge Robert Martin, President of the First-tier Tribunal (Social Entitlement Chamber)) Q96.

It built in an additional step, requiring claimants to make two successive applications – mandatory reconsideration and then appeal. This takes longer and operates as an informal filter process which further tests people's willingness to challenge. It will dissuade some claimants from going to a tribunal, especially those who lack advice and do not appreciate the differences between administrative reviews and an independent and judicial tribunal. [20] It can deter people who may have legitimate grievances – and for reasons unrelated to their prospects of success. Empirical research has found that many claimants do not appeal following a mandatory reconsideration because they think the process would be too stressful, they do not expect the award to be changed or they are too unwell.[21] Some find it difficult to navigate the appeals process or consider that the stress and anxiety involved would be detrimental to them. The cynical view is that mandatory reconsideration represents a procedural tightening designed to make it more difficult for people to challenge decisions. It would be politically unacceptable to abolish or weaken social security tribunals, so government has indirectly added a further hurdle for claimants.

Mandatory reconsideration could be of value if it involved a much more rigorous re-appraisal by the Department of its decisions than under previous processes. However, the quality of mandatory reconsideration decisions is generally considered to be variable.[22] Before 2012, DWP decision-makers were often unwilling to reconsider – or 'revise' – their decisions unless claimants supplied fresh medical or other third-party evidence.[23] There is little to suggest that things have changed greatly since then; the perception is that initial decisions are unlikely to be overturned unless the claimant presents additional evidence. In 2020, it was reported that DWP caseworkers undertaking reviews were putting claimants under pressure by giving them 'take it or leave it' offers over the telephone, thereby possibly accepting less than their full entitlements.[24] This was criticised as an underhand tactic.[25] A judicial review against the practice was settled out of court, with the DWP agreeing that decision-makers contacting claimants would inform them that they retained a right of appeal against revised decisions and that claimants should not feel pressured into accepting these offers.[26] Following this, it was reported in 2024 that for some benefits, the DWP was not issuing a formal mandatory reconsideration decision notice, but was instead giving the claimant an 'explanation

[20] ibid; see also social security tribunal judge quoted in Social Security Advisory Committee, *Decision Making and Mandatory Reconsideration* (London, Paper No 18, 2016) 24. An early empirical study found that local authority officers used administrative review to control claimants' access to tribunals: T Eardley and R Sainsbury, 'Managing Appeals: The Control of Housing Benefit Internal Reviews by Local Authority Officers' (1993) 22 *Journal of Social Policy* 461.

[21] DWP, *Personal Independence Payment Claimant Research: Final Report Summary* (DWP, 2018) 9.

[22] House of Commons Work and Pensions Committee, *Health Assessments for Benefits* (HC 2022–23, 128) 47–48, 77–79 and 91.

[23] President's Report Social Entitlement Chamber, *Report by the President of the Social Entitlement Chamber of the First-tier Tribunal on the Standards of Decision-Making by the Secretary of State and Child Maintenance and Enforcement Commissioner 2008–09* (London, Tribunals Service, 2010) [1.7].

[24] F Ryan, 'DWP Accused of Offering Disabled People "Take it or Leave it" Benefits: Lower Value "Deals" Allegedly Offered to Vulnerable People Appealing against Decisions' *The Guardian* (2 March 2020).

[25] In the 1970s, similar concerns were raised that administrative reviews were being used to 'buy off' claimants by offering them increased benefits, but less than their full entitlements, thereby 'stifling appeals'. In other instances, decisions were reconsidered by more knowledgeable officials. See J Fulbrook, *Administrative Justice and the Unemployed* (London, Mansell, 1978) 200–01 and 238.

[26] *R (K) v Secretary of State for Work and Pensions* (CO/4263/2020) (Consent Order) (13 July 2021).

call' which reiterated the reasons already given, but did not inform claimants of their appeal rights.[27] The DWP was also issuing formal decisions with standardised reasoning, thereby not giving a sufficient explanation for the new decision and generating the impression, if not the reality, that initial decisions were being 'rubber-stamped'. Such practices are of dubious legality and will likely prevent some claimants from appealing, even though they might have good chances of success. Overall, informal, low-visibility administrative procedures can in practice weaken access to justice, in the same way as high-profile restrictions, such as tribunal fees and legal aid cuts.

The Upper Tribunal has intervened to blunt some of the sharp edges of mandatory reconsiderations. Initially, the DWP adopted the approach that applications for mandatory reconsideration made out of time did not generate a right of appeal to the tribunal. Instead, the DWP's entirely unrealistic view was that claimants could seek a judicial review of its decision not to allow a mandatory reconsideration. However, the Upper Tribunal (Administrative Appeals Chamber) ruled against the DWP, holding that there was a high risk that vulnerable claimants with good claims could miss the time limits, a risk exacerbated by the reduction in legal aid and advice services.[28] The Upper Tribunal concluded that the DWP had improperly assumed the role of gatekeeper to the tribunal system. Consequently, the Upper Tribunal ruled that such claimants retained a right of appeal to the First-tier Tribunal (Social Entitlement Chamber) (FTTSEC). Overall, mandatory reconsideration is seen as both producing variable quality of decisions and serving a gatekeeping function. Benefit advisers would always prefer cases to proceed to tribunals to secure fuller consideration.

What of immigration administrative reviews? There are long-standing concerns about the variable quality of initial Home Office refusal decisions.[29] Criticisms have focused on the poor reasoning of refusal decisions and findings of fact and inferences.[30] It has been repeatedly argued that there is a culture of disbelief within the Home Office. The argument is that decision-makers start from the assumption that claimants are not to be believed or are abusive and that the Home Office often unreasonably rejects applicants and seeks to undermine the credibility of people seeking asylum.[31] Given the politics of immigration, there is little trust amongst claimants, representatives and stakeholder groups in the ability of the Home Office to make good-quality decisions.

In 2013–14, various immigration appeal rights were withdrawn altogether and replaced with administrative reviews.[32] The Home Office's view was that 'too many' people had been using the First-tier Tribunal (Immigration and Asylum Chamber) (FTTIAC). The appeals system had become 'a never-ending game of snakes and

[27] Child Poverty Action Group, *Mandatory Reconsideration in 2024: A Briefing* (London, CPAG, 2024).

[28] *R (CJ) v Secretary of State for Work and Pensions* [2017] UKUT 0324 (AAC).

[29] Independent Chief Inspector of Borders and Immigration, *An Inspection of Asylum Casework* (London, ICIBI, 2021).

[30] L Schuster, 'Fatal Flaws in the UK Asylum Decision-Making System: An Analysis of Home Office Refusal Letters' (2020) 46 *Journal of Ethnic and Migration Studies* 1371.

[31] See, eg, J Anderson, J Hollaus, A Lindsay and C Williamson, *The Culture of Disbelief* (London, Refugee Studies Centre, 2014); Freedom From Torture, *Lessons Not Learned: The Failures of Asylum Decision-Making in the UK* (London, Freedom from Torture, 2019).

[32] Crime and Courts Act 2013, s 52 (withdrawing family visitor appeals of which there used to be 40,000 such appeals per year); Immigration Act 2014, s 15 (withdrawing other immigration appeal rights).

ladders'.[33] The Home Office argued that the costs and delays of appeals were 'not fair to applicants'.[34] A minister explained that administrative review would be 'a central part of improving decision quality, dealing with case working errors and feeding back review outcomes much better to decision makers'.[35] In response, it was argued that administrative review was not being introduced to secure fairness and justice, but to reduce the number of immigrants who would have succeeded had they been able to put their case to a tribunal.[36] One MP noted that the Home Office's response to the fact that tribunals allowed around half of all appeals was 'not to seek to improve the quality of their decision making, but rather to reduce the opportunities for challenge'.[37] This made no difference. The Joint Committee on Human Rights invoked the dictum of Hale LJ: 'In this day and age a right of access to a tribunal or other adjudicative mechanism established by the state is just as important and fundamental as a right of access to the ordinary courts.'[38] Withdrawing appeal rights undermined access to justice.[39] But the Home Office was implacable: only fundamental rights cases justified the expense and delay of an appeal. Immigration decisions do not fall within the right to a fair trial (Article 6 ECHR).[40] The result is that only around 12 per cent of the 3.5 million immigration decisions per year now attract a right of appeal. Immigration decisions can only now be appealed on asylum and human rights grounds.[41] Some appeals can only be brought from outside the UK.[42] Immigration decisions that are not appealable can be challenged through administrative review and then judicial review.[43] Some appeals are non-suspensive – that is, heard and decided outside the UK.

What then is the quality of immigration reviews? Review decisions have often reiterated the same reasons for refusal contained in initial decisions, but without addressing the applicant's grounds of challenge. An initial inspection found that there was significant room for improvement in terms of administrative reviews identifying and correcting case working errors, and in communicating those decisions to applicants.[44] Some reviews were taken by staff with no experience of initial decision-making. There was an over-reliance in review decisions on initial refusal decisions. Review decisions often reiterated the same reasons for refusal

[33] Home Office, *Immigration Bill Factsheet: Appeals* (London, Home Office, 2013); R Thomas, 'Immigration and Access to Justice: A Critical Analysis of Recent Restrictions' in E Palmer, T Cornford, Y Marique and A Guinchard (eds), *Access to Justice: Beyond the Policies and Politics of Austerity* (Oxford, Hart Publishing, 2016).

[34] Home Office (n 33) 1.

[35] House of Commons Public Bill Committee: Immigration Bill (2013–14) 5 November 2013, col 199 (Mark Harper MP, Minister of State for Immigration).

[36] HL Deb, 5 March 2014, vol 752, col 1353 (Lord Avebury).

[37] HC Deb 22 October 2013, vol 569, col 199 (Barry Gardiner MP). See also HC Deb 22 October 2013, vol 569, col 189 (Fiona MacTaggart MP).

[38] *R v Secretary of State for the Home Department ex p Saleem* [2001] 1 WLR 443, 458 (Hale LJ).

[39] Joint Committee on Human Rights, *Legislative Scrutiny: Immigration Bill* (2013–14 HL 102 HC 935) [39].

[40] Home Office, *Government Response to the Joint Committee on Human Rights, Eighth Report of Session 2013–14* (2014) 2.

[41] Immigration Act 2014, s 15.

[42] These include asylum and human rights claims which are certified by the Home Office as clearly unfounded.

[43] Immigration Rules Appendix Administrative Review.

[44] Independent Chief Inspector of Borders and Immigration, *An Inspection of the Administrative Review Processes Introduced Following the 2014 Immigration Act* (London, ICIBI, 2016) 2.

without addressing the applicant's points. Subsequent inspections identified some improvements.[45] Review decisions were generally effective at identifying and correcting objective errors, generally well written, factually accurate and engaged with all thc points raised by applicants. Nonetheless, weaknesses were identified. Reviewers were limited to considering only the same evidence that initial decision-makers had previously considered. The review process was therefore geared more towards demonstrating that the Home Office had not made an error rather than reaching the most appropriate outcome for the applicant.[46] Some reviews demonstrated 'a readiness to side with the original decision-maker's opinions about the weight of the evidence provided that raised questions about institutional thinking'.[47] In seeking to improve administrative reviews, the Home Office needed to go beyond merely 'tweaking' its processes and assess whether the administrative review system had delivered the benefits claimed for it would during the passage of the Immigration Act 2014. The quality of immigration reviews is then mixed.

The ad hoc nature of administrative review – and by extension administrative justice as a whole – is illustrated by the episode of international students accused of cheating in their English language tests. Over the years 2014–18, the Home Office revoked the visas of some 35,000 students at some financial and human cost to them.[48] The Home Office considered that the majority of students had cheated. Some had, but the Home Office had overreacted by wrongly penalising thousands of students who had not cheated.[49] Following years of protracted, expensive and time-consuming appeals and litigation, the then Home Secretary, who was sympathetic towards the students, had agreed to introduce a swift administrative review process by which students who felt that they had been unfairly treated could have their cases reconsidered by the Home Office.[50] However, the next day, a new Prime Minister and Home Secretary took over with a different set of priorities and the proposed review process was dropped.[51] This episode illustrates how redress can be driven just as much, if not, more so by short-term political considerations than by a principled commitment to administrative justice. Such policy decisions are typically taken by central government departments, the same departments responsible for causing the failures that adversely affect people which in turn generate the demand for effective redress mechanisms.

[45] Independent Chief Inspector of Borders and Immigration, *A Re-inspection of the Administrative Review Process* (London, ICIBI, 2017); Independent Chief Inspector of Borders and Immigration, *An Inspection of Administrative Reviews* (London, ICIBI, 2020).

[46] Independent Chief Inspector of Borders and Immigration, *An Inspection of Administrative Reviews* (n 45) [3.24].

[47] ibid [3.25].

[48] '"It Destroyed My Life": The Students Accused of Cheating in English Tests' *The Guardian* (11 February 2024).

[49] R Thomas and J Tomlinson, *Immigration Judicial Reviews: An Empirical Study* (London, Palgrave Macmillan, 2021) 176–88; 'English Test Scandal: Home Office Accused of "Shocking Miscarriage of Justice"' *The Guardian* (9 February 2022); 'English Test Scandal: Students Renew Fight to Clear Names after 10 Years' *The Guardian* (11 February 2024).

[50] HC Deb 23 July 2019, vol 663, col 117WS (Sajid Javid MP, Secretary of State for the Home Department).

[51] 'English Test Scandal: Reprieve Plan was Derailed by Government Reshuffle' *The Guardian* (13 February 2024).

Administrative review operates in other contexts. Homelessness reviews are of variable quality.[52] By contrast, tax reviews undertaken by HMRC are generally considered to be of reasonably high quality, thereby reflecting that department's emphasis on customer service.[53] In general terms, administrative reviews will likely always be inferior compared with tribunal appeals. However, reviews should be assessed on their own terms as a paper-based process. A quick review can correct poor decisions and provide justice. The speed and lack of formal procedures can be a virtue. Even so, administrative reviews can be inadequate. Part of the problem is that government does not see administrative review principally as a mechanism of administrative justice, but as another efficiency-focused administrative process. Moreover, the shift towards greater use of administrative reviews in the 2010s can only be understood as one part of the then government's wider policy agenda to reduce benefit spending and tighten up on immigration. Government has then repeatedly reformed decision-making structures in a way that conditions or limits people's rights of challenge to tribunals, thereby reducing the number of appeals going to tribunals.

The growth of administrative reviews at the expense of tribunal appeals suggests two wider points. First, procedures influence substantive outcomes. People's substantive legal rights and entitlements are likely to become ineffective or less effective whenever procedural guarantees are reduced. Second, the weakening of procedural rights has gone hand in hand with government's policy objectives to reduce demand. The prospects for positive reform seem low. In 2017, the Law Commission proposed to undertake a cross-government examination to improve the operation of reviews, but unsurprisingly this stalled because of a distinct lack of enthusiasm from government, particularly the DWP and the Home Office.[54]

Tribunals

Tribunals are now low-level specialist administrative courts that decide appeals against specified administrative decisions. 'Appeal' is understood in contradistinction to judicial review. While some tribunals are limited to exercising a judicial review function, the vast majority of tribunals decide appeals de novo on issues of both fact and law. Tribunal appeals involve: fact-finding, the application of the relevant eligibility rules, and the substitution of substantive decisions for those of the initial government body. In this way, tribunals are the judicial component of the wider decision process. Tribunals must adopt fair procedures and hearings, make reasoned findings of fact and apply the relevant rules correctly. Their decisions are legally binding on the parties unless successfully challenged, although, unlike the courts, tribunals cannot

[52] Homelessness (Review Procedure etc) Regulations 2018 SI 2018/223. The quality of reviews may depend upon the nature of the local authority – rural or urban – and the pressures upon it.

[53] HMRC, *Statutory Review Process: Quantitative Research to Understand Customers' Experience and Perception of the Statutory Review Process* (London, HMRC, 2014).

[54] R Thomas and J Tomlinson, 'A Different Tale of Judicial Power: Administrative Review as a Problematic Response to the Judicialisation of Tribunals' [2019] *PL* 537; Law Commission, *Thirteenth Programme of Law Reform* (Law Com No 377, 2017) 13–14.

enforce their own decisions; instead, the successful claimant has to go to the courts to do so.[55] However, this is rarely a problem as government almost always follows tribunal decisions, albeit that the Home Office sometimes ignores tribunal and court rulings, whether intentionally or through administrative error and a lack of internal coordination.[56]

Tribunals are intended to provide a form of legitimacy as regards decisions that affect people. When government makes high volumes of decisions, it will necessarily engage in administrative processing and the quality of decisions will vary. Any decision is only one amongst many, but it is very important to the person concerned. Those refused may well feel that they have been wrongly refused and want a reconsideration. Tribunals enable someone who has been refused initially to re-present their case to an independent body. The arguments for the legitimacy of tribunals vary. Tribunals are independent and separate from government. Their procedures enable people to participate on a more equal footing. A person should be able to feel they have had a fair hearing of their case irrespective of the outcome. There is also the experience of tribunals in handling appeals, their ability to understand the individual case and to make a sound decision, the adequacy of the tribunal's reasons, and onward rights of challenge. If someone's appeal is allowed, then they have succeeded. If an appeal is dismissed, then the person has gone through the tribunal process, had their opportunity to re-present their case and been given reasons why their appeal has been dismissed. Tribunals must also be understood from the governmental perspective. Government has willingly handed over responsibility for final decisions to tribunals. This implies a recognition by government that its decisions may be wrong and that a more judicial and enhanced process is required to remake decisions. Further, tribunals are costly. They are funded by government and involve some delay in terms of administering policy. There are limits to what tribunals can provide. They cannot be used to challenge the policies underpinning the rules being applied; that is essentially a political matter for government. However, the Upper Tribunal plays an important role in interpreting such rules.

The basic structure of appeal routes is to have a first-instance appeal on issues of both fact and law to the First-tier Tribunal and then onward challenges (with permission) to the Upper Tribunal on error of law grounds. First-instance tribunals are principally fact-finding bodies. There is no general right of appeal against all administrative decisions; that would be enormously expensive and impose considerable burdens and delays on government. Instead, there are specific statutory rights of appeal against specific decisions on specific grounds.[57] Appeal rights are always statutory. The question as to whether certain initial decisions should attract a right of appeal is

[55] *R (Majera) v Secretary of State for the Home Department* [2021] UKSC 46 [43]–[56].

[56] See, eg, 'Woman Told to Leave UK Despite Court Ruling She Has Right to Live with Family' *The Guardian* (15 February 2024): 'a classic example of the Home Office misapplying the law and failing to implement tribunal decisions'.

[57] See, eg, Social Security Act 1998, s 12; School Standards and Framework Act 1998, s 94; Nationality, Immigration and Asylum Act 2002, s 82; and Children and Families Act 2014, s 51.

essentially a policy decision for the relevant government department.[58] Government is not legally required to introduce appeal rights, but has often done so as a result of the social need for them, the political forces in play and the inadequacy of other means of redress. Many tribunals are long-established. Social security tribunals have operated since the early twentieth century, when social welfare schemes were originally introduced. It is always open to government to modify tribunal appeal rights. This occurs when government changes the underlying administrative scheme or for other reasons. Most tribunal systems are relatively secure. The exception are immigration tribunals, which have been repeatedly overhauled in light of the Home Office's concerns that appeals take too long to be finally decided, thereby enabling unmeritorious applicants to abuse the process by spinning out their appeals almost endlessly to prevent them being removed.

The Leggatt Review advanced three pragmatic criteria to inform the decision as to whether to allocate cases to tribunals or the courts.[59] First, there is the ability of unrepresented users to participate in proceedings and, where the legal and factual issues raised in many cases are not so complex, that people can therefore prepare and present their own cases. Second, there is the need for specialist expertise in the particular context, which makes for better decisions. Third, there is the need for expertise in the relevant legislation and rules, and also the mixed issues of fact and law which commonly recur. Leggatt also emphasised that a tribunal route of challenge should be the normal option because of its accessibility compared with judicial review. Other factors are relevant, including cost, timeliness and caseload.

Even when statutory appeal rights are introduced, the government may delay bringing them into effect. For instance, the Care Act 2014 introduced appeal rights against various social care decisions taken by English local authorities concerning the assessment of an adult's needs for care and support.[60] However, while the government recognised the importance of appeals, it has not implemented them.[61] A minority of local authorities have introduced their own informal non-statutory processes, thereby leading to something of a postcode lottery between different councils.[62] In the absence of a formal appeal system, the available remedies comprise local authority's internal complaint processes, complaining to the Local Government and Social Care Ombudsman and judicial review.[63] But these are limited routes of challenge. A legal challenge against the non-implementation of

[58] For instance, the Home Office takes initial asylum and immigration decisions; it also has policy responsibility for immigration and asylum appeals. The administration of that right of appeal is the responsibility of the Ministry of Justice and HM Courts & Tribunals Service.

[59] Leggatt (n 14) [1.10]–[1.13].

[60] Care Act 2014, s 72.

[61] Department of Health and Social Care, *People at the Heart of Care: Adult Social Care Reform White Paper* (CP 560, 2021) [5.18].

[62] Independent Age, *Reviewing the Case: The Right to Appeal in Adult Social Care* (2019); Equality and Human Rights Commission, *Challenging Adult Social Care Decisions in England and Wales* (2023).

[63] Local Authority Social Services and National Health Service Complaints (England) Regulations 2009, SI 2009/309.

appeal rights failed.[64] Many other administrative decisions do not attract any right of appeal.[65]

What of asylum appeals? Given the human rights context, especially the Refugee Convention and the prohibition against torture and inhumane and degrading treatment under Article 3 ECHR, it is accepted that a right of appeal is required in asylum cases. The Home Office has long sought to accelerate the appeals process so as to ensure that it cannot be used as a means by which appellants can avoid removal by lodging abusive challenges. The appeals process has been overhauled many times. Yet, the Home Office has itself, over many years, been responsible for significant amounts of delay because of the build-up of significant backlogs of undecided asylum claims. In 2025, the Home Office announced the creation of a new appeals body staffed not by tribunal judges, but by professionally trained adjudicators to increase capacity to deal with the large backlog of asylum cases.[66] This may expand capacity, but will likely lower the quality of appeal decisions, thereby promoting more onward challenges. There is an inherent tension here between, on the one hand, making and enforcing immigration decisions and, on the other hand, allowing refused claimants to go through multiple levels of onward challenge and judicial review which can potentially frustrate Home Office efforts to remove them. Good decisions are required, but should they be achieved at the cost of enforcing immigration control? Deciding precisely where the balance lies is a political judgement on which different people may reasonably disagree.

Most tribunals are now part of the First-tier and Upper Tribunal structure. The two largest volume tribunals are social security and immigration. Other chambers bring together a number of smaller and quite different tribunals. For instance, the Health, Education and Social Care Chamber is one of the largest First-tier Tribunal chambers. It handles more than 40,000 appeals and applications, lists over 50,000 judicial sitting days, and conducts some 18,000 hearings per year. This chamber comprises various jurisdictions: mental health tribunals; the Special Educational Needs and Disability Tribunal; and Care Standards and Primary Health Lists. The same body – HM Courts and Tribunals Service (HMCTS) – provides administrative support to both courts and tribunals. This structure largely mapped onto pre-existing tribunals. In total, there are over 1,400 tribunal judges and over 3,000 non-legal members. Some tribunal judges work full-time and are salaried; fee-paid judges work part-time. Tribunal judges are appointed by the Judicial Appointments Commission in the same way as court judges. Tribunal hearings are always presided over by a tribunal judge. For instance, immigration appeals are heard by a single judge, whereas social security appeals are usually heard by a judge and one or two non-legal members, including those with a medical and disability expertise. Figure 4.2 shows the structure of the First-tier and Upper Tribunals.

[64] *R (HL) v Secretary of State for Health and Social Care* [2023] EWHC 866 (Admin).

[65] See, eg, Administrative Justice and Tribunals Council Scottish Committee, *Right to Appeal: A Review of Decisions Made by Scottish Public Bodies Where There is No Right of Appeal or Where the Appeal Procedure is Inaccessible or Inappropriate* (Edinburgh, AJTC, 2011).

[66] Home Office, *Restoring Order and Control: A Statement on the Government's Asylum and Returns Policy* (CP 1418, 2025) 22.

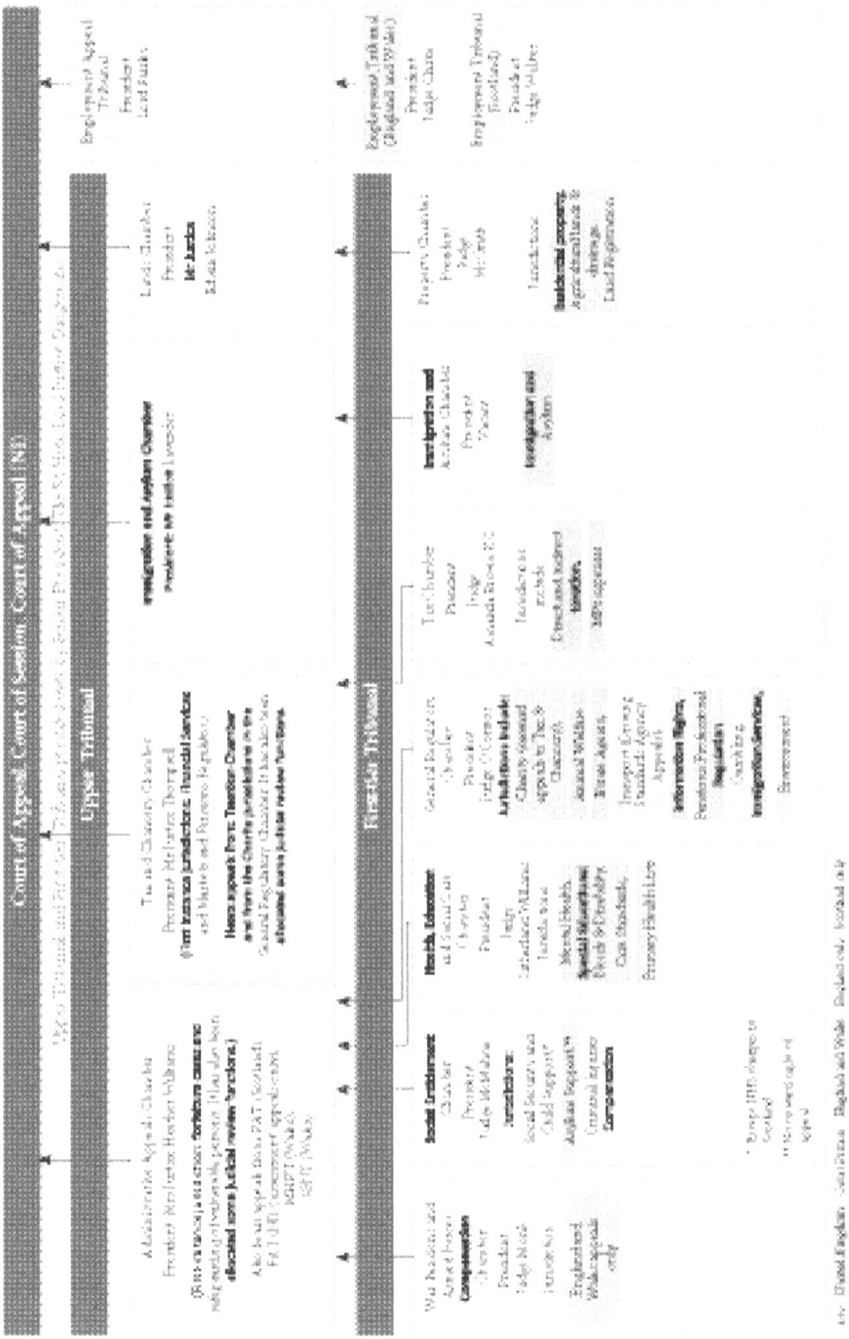

Figure 4.2 Tribunals organisation chart[67]

[67] Judicial Office, 'Courts and Tribunals Judiciary' (2025), www.judiciary.uk/guidance-and-resources/tribunals-organisation-chart.

The unified tribunal structure has provided a significant degree of rationalisation and coherence. Tribunal procedures rules are drafted by the Tribunal Procedure Committee and are consistent across different jurisdictions. Tribunal judges are appointed to either the First-tier Tribunal or the Upper Tribunal and are then assigned to a particular jurisdiction by the relevant Chamber President. They can also be assigned to a different chamber when caseload and business needs require it. For instance, when immigration judicial reviews were transferred from the Administrative Court to the Upper Tribunal (Immigration and Asylum Chamber) in 2013, the caseload was increased significantly. Some judges from the Upper Tribunal (Administrative Appeals Chamber) were trained and then deployed to the Upper Tribunal (Immigration and Asylum Chamber) to hear such cases. Fee-paid judicial appointments enable flexible deployment in the light of variable caseloads. There is more similarity between the lower-level tribunals and court judiciary (eg, district judges in the county court) than between the latter and the higher judiciary. Another benefit of the unified structure is that it has enabled good judicial practice to be shared across tribunals and also highlighted poor practice.[68] This has occurred through both the formal structures and the informal connections made by judges sitting in more than one jurisdiction and benefiting from cross-Chamber experience.

On the other hand, the tribunal structure added little that was really substantively new. Previous tribunals were incorporated into the unified system and carried on operating in their own silos pretty much as before. At the ground level, tribunal hearings proceed the same as before, although bringing tribunals within the formal judiciary has enhanced their constitutional standing. For years, tribunals had something of an inferiority complex compared with the 'proper courts'. For many years, immigration adjudicators repeatedly argued that they should become 'Immigration *Judges*' to recognise the nature of their work.[69] From this perspective, the creation of the unified structure of the First-tier and Upper Tribunals was a success for tribunals as it brought them fully within the established model of the courts. Another aspect of tribunals is their specialist nature; there are no generalist tribunals.[70] This should enable expertise and efficiency.[71] At the same time, repeatedly hearing the same types of repetitive appeals may make some judges become case-hardened. While judges have their home jurisdiction, some also sit in other jurisdictions, often as a break from a relentless diet of the same type of cases.

[68] N Wikeley, 'Justice in the Welfare State: Tribunals in the Modern Era' (2022) 29 *Journal of Social Security Law* 74, 80.

[69] They later became immigration judges: Asylum and Immigration Tribunal (Judicial Titles) Order 2005, SI 227/2005.

[70] Although the First-tier Tribunal (General Regulatory Chamber) handles appeals against regulatory decisions made by a wide range of regulatory bodies relating to: charities; community right to bid; environment; energy and infrastructure; estate agents; exam boards; food safety; gambling; immigration services; information rights; pensions regulation; standards and licensing including secondary ticketing, consultant lobbyists and copyright licensing; transport, including driving instructors; and the welfare of animals, including microchipping dogs.

[71] SH Legomsky, *Specialized Justice: Courts, Administrative Tribunals, and a Cross-national Theory of Specialization* (Oxford, Oxford University Press, 1990).

There are some anomalies with the unified tribunal structure.[72] Various tribunals and appeal panels remain outside of it. For instance, the Valuation Tribunal decides appeals concerning council tax and business rates. It is the responsibility of the Ministry of Housing, Communities and Local Government, not the Ministry of Justice.[73] There are also local authority tribunals, including school admission appeal panels, school exclusion panels and the Traffic Penalty Tribunal.[74] There is no interest from government in moving these tribunals into the unified system. Instead, they exist and operate in their own silos, left to their own devices, with separate procedures and non-uniform rights of appeal. This has created some anomalies, as illustrated by exclusion appeals. Decisions (in England) by a school to exclude a child permanently can be challenged to independent review panels. Previously, these panels exercised an appeal function, but since 2011, they have been restricted to a judicial review function.[75] Wales, Scotland and Northern Ireland have retained appeals. In the absence of a second-tier appellate body, the onward routes of redress in England are either judicial review or complaining to the Local Government and Social Care Ombudsman (LGSCO). However, the LGSCO can only investigate complaints about school admission and exclusion panels relating to local authority-maintained schools, but not those concerning academy and free schools (which are entirely separate from local government and therefore outside the LGSCO's jurisdiction).[76]

Viewed collectively from a horizontal perspective, tribunals comprise a distinct system. At the same time, the tribunal structure functions as more of a federation of different tribunals. Tribunals are also built into the vertical administrative schemes (social security, immigration etc) and only operate within them. The relevant government department decides whether there should be tribunals, whereas the Ministry of Justice administers that right of appeal.

[72] For instance, appeals against safeguarding decisions by the Disclosure and Barring Service (DBS), such as that an individual is banned from working with children or vulnerable adults and therefore put on one of the barred lists under the Safeguarding and Vulnerable Groups Act 2006. Such challenges proceed direct from the DBS to the Upper Tribunal without an initial fact-finding appeal to the First-tier Tribunal, as is the normal appeal structure. Even more remarkable is that this right of appeal can only be exercised with permission of the Upper Tribunal and lies on any material point of law or mistake of fact by the DBS. By contrast, the normal position is that there is no onward appeal on matters of fact, but only errors of law. Furthermore, the question as to whether it is 'appropriate' for a person to be put on the barred list is not a question of fact or law. The normal position is that judicial bodies decide issues of fact and law, but not issues which are neither. The better position would simply be to have appeals on issues of fact to the First-tier Tribunal and onward appeals to the Upper Tribunal on error of law grounds. See Safeguarding Vulnerable Groups Act 2006, s 4(3); N Wikeley, 'Justice in the Welfare State Revisited: Tribunals in the Modern Era' (2022) 29 *Journal of Social Security Law* 74, 80.

[73] Onward appeals from the Valuation Tribunal go to the Upper Tribunal (Lands Chamber).

[74] School admissions and exclusion panels are more informal than the First-tier Tribunal (eg, hearings take place in council offices or now online) and decisions are not issued as 'determinations', but through decision letters. Panel members are volunteers and not paid. There is no appraisal system. The Independent Agricultural Appeals Panel, which considers appeals against decisions of the Rural Payments Agency, is not a formal tribunal, but an advisory non-departmental public body.

[75] Education Act 2011, s 4.

[76] The LGSCO has recommended that it should be able to investigate all such complaints irrespective of the type of school concerned: LGSCO, *Local Government and Social Care in 2024 and Beyond: Time to Rebuild: Triennial Review by the Local Government and Social Care Ombudsman and Commission for Local Administration in England* (Coventry, LGSCO, 2024) 12.

While tribunals are now separate from their parent government departments, there is an inherent relationship between the two, which is often reflected in the management of caseloads. For instance, in the 2010s, the volumes of social security appeal increased dramatically. The DWP had contracted out the medical assessments for disability benefits (which then informed its initial decisions) to a private provider, but the quality of such assessments was poor. The contractor then exited its contract at short notice for reputational reasons. In turn, the tribunals and HM Courts & Tribunals Service (HMCTS) had significantly underestimated the volume of appeals and lacked capacity to hear and decide them.[77] Overall, the system descended into chaos.[78] There were huge delays and backlogs for appellants, many of whom eventually had their appeals allowed. Similar problems have arisen with immigration appeals when, for instance, the Upper Tribunal (Immigration and Asylum Chamber) ruled that a certain category of immigration decisions did not attract a right of appeal, which was later overturned by the Court of Appeal.[79] In the meantime, many appeals had built up, in addition to the ordinary run of other appeals resulting in backlogs. Matters such as caseloads, appeal forecasts and judicial deployment dominate the in-trays of senior judge-managers. Figure 4.3 shows the caseloads of the First-tier Tribunal in 2007–24.

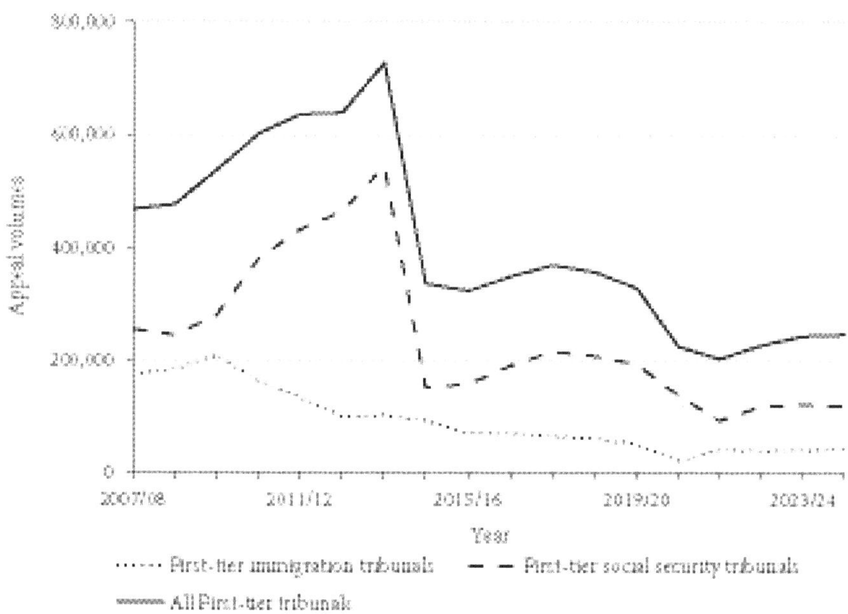

Figure 4.3 The caseloads of the First-tier Tribunal, 2007–24. Source: Ministry of Justice, *Tribunal Statistics* (2024)

[77] HMCTS is responsible for the administration of courts and tribunals.
[78] House of Commons Work and Pensions Committee, *Employment and Support Allowance and Work Capability Assessments* (HC 2014–15, 302).
[79] *Sala v Secretary of State for the Home Department* (EFMs: Right of Appeal: Albania) [2016] UKUT 411 (IAC); *Khan v Secretary of State for the Home Department* [2017] EWCA Civ 1755; [2018] 1 WLR 1256 (CA).

Tribunal procedures vary somewhat from one context to another depending on the nature of appeals. The overriding objective of the tribunal procedure rules is that appeals must be handled and heard justly and fairly.[80] The typical procedure is for tribunals to either hold hearings, decide appeals on the papers or over the phone or online. It has long been recognised that tribunals should not replicate formal legalistic and adversarial judicial procedures, but should instead be 'user-friendly', flexible, informal and accessible. At the same time, some degree of formality is required for what can be some of the most important decisions for the person concerned. A perennial concern has been the need to maintain the distinctiveness of tribunals.[81] Their procedures are simpler than those of the courts. In between the two ends of the adversarial-inquisitorial spectrum, tribunals to occupy a middle ground in which they adopt an enabling approach by asking questions which go to the core of the individual appeal and ensures people receive justice. This partly (although not fully) ameliorates the challenges and barriers that unrepresented people experience.[82]

Procedures are also influenced by the underlying nature of the administrative scheme and the relationship between the individual and the state in that context. For instance, the purpose of social security is to assist people by providing them with the support and benefits to which they are entitled. The process of benefit decision-making and appeals is not a form of adversarial litigation, but an inquisitorial and co-operative fact-gathering exercise to which both claimants and the department must contribute, the latter by undertaking its own inquiries to supplement the information given by claimants.[83] This cooperative shared duty reflects the wider normative relationship between claimants and the welfare state based on a set of reciprocal set of rights and responsibilities. Appellants are almost always unrepresented. DWP presenting officers rarely attend tribunals.[84] The DWP's approach is to hand over decision-making entirely to tribunals. Tribunal procedures are enabling and interventionist.[85] In disability benefit appeals, the tribunal's medical member typically takes the lead by questioning the claimant. Tribunals might hear six or more appeals a day. Procedures are deliberately designed

[80] See, eg, Tribunal Procedure (First-tier Tribunal) (Social Entitlement Chamber) Rules, SI 2008/2685, r 2.

[81] B Hale, 'Courts and Tribunals' (Annual Upper Tribunal Lecture, 14 October 2021).

[82] G McKeever, 'A Ladder of Legal Participation for Tribunal Users' [2013] *PL* 575; G McKeever, 'Comparing Courts and Tribunals through the Lens of Legal Participation' (2020) 39 *Civil Justice Quarterly* 217; G McKeever, L Royal-Dawson, E Kirk and J McCord, *Litigants in Person in Northern Ireland: Barriers to Legal Participation* (Belfast, Ulster University, 2018); G McKeever, 'The Snakes and Ladders of Legal Participation: Litigants in Person and the Right to a Fair Trial under Article 6 of the European Convention on Human Rights' (2022) 49 *Journal of Law and Society* 71.

[83] *R v Medical Appeal Tribunal (North Midland Region) ex p Hubble* [1958] 2 QB 228 (QBD) 240 (Diplock J); [1958] 3 WLR 24; *Kerr v Department for Social Development* [2004] UKHL 23; [2004] 1 WLR 1372 (HL) [15] (Lord Hope) and [62] (Baroness Hale).

[84] In 2009, the attendance rate by presenting officers was 19 per cent: President's Report Social Entitlement Chamber, *Report by the President of the Social Entitlement Chamber of the First-tier Tribunal on the Standards of Decision-Making by the Secretary of State and Child Maintenance and Enforcement Commissioner 2008–09* (London, Appeals Service, 2009) [1.5]. In 2014, 'the attendance rate by presenting officers was 0.5 per cent': House of Commons Work and Pensions Committee, *Oral Evidence: Employment and Support Allowance and Work Capacity Benefits* (HC 2014–15, 1212, 7 May 2014) (HH Judge Robert Martin, President of the First-tier Tribunal (Social Entitlement Chamber)) Q173.

[85] N Wikeley, 'Future Directions for Tribunals: A UK Perspective' in R Creyke (ed) *Tribunals in the Common Law World* (Sydney, Federation Press, 2008) 175, 185–90; R Thomas, 'From "Adversarial v Inquisitorial" to "Active, Enabling, and Investigative": Developments in UK Tribunals' in L Jacobs and S Baglay (eds), *The Nature of Inquisitorial Processes in Administrative Regimes: Global Perspectives* (Farnham, Ashgate, 2013) 51, 62–64.

to be informal, simple, quick and not over-complicated. The tribunal panel will ask the right questions to decide the appeal correctly and to ensure that the appellant has a fair hearing. Decisions are usually issued following the hearing after a short period of deliberation. Appellants can request statements of reasons.[86]

Contrast this with immigration appeals. The Home Office has rejected a person's immigration application which they now appeal against. There is a strong emphasis on the burden of proof being on the appellant to demonstrate that they fulfil the requirements of the immigration rules. The Home Office typically maintains and defends its refusal decisions. Presenting officers attend hearings to defend initial refusal decisions, even when appeals could be conceded. Appellants are often legally represented. Tribunal procedures naturally tend towards the adversarial, although hearings are variable and depend on the presence and quality of representation. Decisions are almost always reserved. The judge will write up a detailed determination. For every hour spent in a hearing, the judge will spend an average of two hours writing up the determination, which can be lengthy. By contrast, to decide low-value appeals against parking tickets, the Traffic Penalty Tribunal has for many years operated an online interactive portal to which people can upload evidence from their smartphone in order to have their appeals decided quickly.

Procedures must be sufficiently flexible to accommodate the background issues and particular needs of appellants. For instance, it was unfair for a tribunal to hold a conventional adversarial hearing in the case of a vulnerable 17-year-old Afghan asylum claimant with learning difficulties when a psychologist expert had recommended informal procedures, such as court dress and seating arrangements, exclusion of the public, modified style of questions and cross-examination.[87] Tribunals must ensure appellants can obtain effective access to justice so that their voice can be heard. Issues like the appellant's age, vulnerability and learning disability should be taken into account as factors relevant to the limitations on the appellant's oral evidence. Likewise, the tribunal's procedures should have been adjusted to ensure the appellant was able to participate effectively. The judiciary's *Equal Treatment Benchbook* gives detailed guidance on how to adjust procedures, for instance, for people with physical or mental health issues or for whom English is not their first language.[88]

A wider question concerns the degree to which tribunals can actually provide effective justice in practice. The Leggatt Review emphasised the ability of tribunals to handle cases concerning unrepresented appellants in areas where the law was not complex. However, areas of law such as social security, immigration and tax are complex.[89] Moreover, the

[86] Tribunal Procedure (First-tier Tribunal) (Social Entitlement Chamber) Rules, SI 2008/2685, r 34(4) and (5).

[87] *AM (Afghanistan) v Secretary of State for the Home Department* [2018] 4 WLR 78; [2017] EWCA Civ 1123 (CA); R Thomas, 'Administrative Justice and Vulnerable People' [2024] *PL* 234.

[88] Judicial College, *Equal Treatment Bench Book* (2024). See also *LC v Secretary of State for Work and Pensions (DLA)* [2015] UKUT 100 (AAC) (Tribunal Procedure and Practice: Fair Hearing) (the tribunal should not have decided an appeal by a woman with severe agoraphobia on the papers, but should have offered her a telephone or online hearing); *WA v Secretary of State for Work and Pensions* [2016] UKUT 86 (AAC) (in a child maintenance appeal, it was wrong to hear the case in the mother's absence as she felt intimidated by the father and unable to be in the same room as him).

[89] See, eg, *Kabir v Secretary of State for the Home Department* (UTIAC, Appeal Number: UI-2022-002538, 3 January 2023): some immigration rules 'are barely comprehensible even to experienced legal professionals, including the Secretary of State's own representatives, who through no fault of their own often seem unable to explain the meaning of the provisions to the Tribunal with any confidence'; the rules are 'so difficult to comprehend that it is at least arguable that they lack the clarity of law'.

procedures used and the marshalling of evidence into arguments can be beyond the ability of many unrepresented appellants. Although there is variation, some tribunals (such as immigration tribunals) are court-like and there is a perception that the tribunal system as a whole may have become too legalistic. Yet, there will be never be sufficient funding for legal representation. Ultimately, much depends upon the ability of tribunal judges to hear and decide appeals as best they can. However, effective justice is not limited to fair procedures. Two values overlooked by Franks were efficiency and timeliness. Claimants can wait months for tribunals to hear an appeal, thereby weakening their usefulness. It takes six months for a social security appeal to be heard. There is a backlog of some 106,000 immigration appeals (including over 50,000 asylum appeals) with a waiting time of at least 53 weeks.[90] The new independent body composed of professional adjudicators is intended to speed up hearings. The body will have statutory powers to prioritise cases from those in asylum accommodation and foreign national offenders, and a legal requirement to decide such appeals within 24 weeks. There is ample scope for reasonable doubts about how this will work in practice. Other tribunals must decide appeals within specified timescales – for example, 40 school days for school admission appeals.

The daily work of first-tier tribunals is to hear the evidence, hold fair hearings, make decisions and give reasons – and then to hear the next appeal. This involves hearing, eliciting and handling the evidence and then evaluating and assessing it to make decisions. Tribunals are not bound by the formal rules of evidence.[91] The issue for fact-finding tribunals is often how much weight to place on the evidence and then to craft an informed and robust decision. Collecting and evaluating the evidence cannot be reduced to a set of prescriptive rules. Instead, it is a form of tacit knowledge acquired through experience and practice. The questioning at the hearing enables the tribunals to fill in the gaps in the evidence and resolve any conflicts in the evidence. Perhaps the biggest practical challenges are handling the evidence, deciding what to make of it and giving reasons.

The jurisdiction of First-tier Tribunals is typically to rehear and redecide appeals afresh on issues of fact and law. It is a 'full merits' and de novo jurisdiction. The Tribunal 'stands in the shoes' of and has the same powers as the initial decision-making body.[92] The Tribunal's jurisdiction is not limited merely to affirming or setting aside the decision under appeal. Tribunals make their own substantive decisions by either allowing or dismissing the appeal. If, having made its own findings of fact, the Tribunal comes to a different outcome from that of the initial decision, it makes its own decision which replaces that of the initial decision-maker. Tribunals are designed to be a superior fact-finding body which is able to hear, investigate and consider the evidence and facts in greater depth than usually occurs before decision-makers. This feature arises because of the membership of tribunals and their procedures.

Tribunals hear the evidence, apply the relevant rules and substitute their own decision. In practice, the focus is not on the correctness of the initial decision, but the tribunal's own assessment. The vast majority of tribunal appeals turn on their own individual facts. In this respect, tribunals undertake the same task as initial decision-makers; they

[90] Home Office, 'Tribunal System Reforms to Speed up Asylum Decisions' (24 August 2025), www.gov.uk/government/news/tribunal-system-reforms-to-speed-up-asylum-decisions.

[91] Tribunal Procedure (First-tier Tribunal) (Social Entitlement Chamber) Rules, SI 2008/2685, r 15(2).

[92] *TR and GD v Secretary of State for Work and Pensions* [2025] UKUT 332 (AAC), [117].

apply the same sets of rules made by government which embody policy choices about immigration, tax and social security and so on. The principal differences are that tribunals are judicial, independent and have different procedures, such as hearings.

Tribunals cannot question the policy choices underpinning the substantive rules they apply. As the Upper Tribunal (Administrative Appeals Chamber) has explained: 'In the field of social security law, it is a matter for Parliament to decide who receives benefits and who does not. This Tribunal will ensure the fair and proper allocation of benefits within the law but will not grant socio-economic benefits that Parliament has decided to withhold.'[93] The same point applies to all of the other areas in which tribunals operate: tax, immigration and so on. Nonetheless, in some contexts, tribunals apply broad standards that involve a balancing test and policy choices. A good example is the right to private and family life under Article 8 ECHR in immigration appeals. Such cases involve balancing the public interest in immigration control against the immigrant's right to family life. Some tribunal decisions have attracted significant controversy and government has legislated to introduce more prescriptive rules.[94] There are wider policy choices for tribunals that lie underneath the formal surface of the rules – for instance, who should qualify for disability benefits or asylum. At the same time, there is a fine line between policy and judgement. Individual judges may be more or less generous than others.

There are then the more technical rules concerning which evidence tribunals can and cannot take into account. Tribunals typically only decide appeals on the basis of the facts in existence at the date of the initial decision, as opposed to facts which come into existence after the initial decision.[95] For instance, if, in a disability benefits appeal, the appellant's health has deteriorated since the initial decision, then this cannot be taken into account. Tribunals decide appeals against decisions already taken; they are not an extension of the initial decision-making process. The longer the delay between initial decisions and tribunal hearings, then the more abstruse and unreal the nature of the tribunal's task can become. The current waiting time from an initial decision to an appeal of around six months arises because of the caseload pressure. From the appellant's position, it may well seem strange and perplexing to have to wait months for a social security tribunal hearing which is typically an hour long but which cannot take account of any subsequent evidence. Nonetheless, tribunals decide appeals on the basis of the facts at the date of the original decision rather than being part of an ongoing decision process. By contrast, in asylum appeals, tribunals can consider post-decision evidence, such as changes in the conditions in the country from which someone is seeking asylum.[96] These appeals involve both an assessment of past events (was the

[93] *AR v Secretary of State for Work and Pensions* [2020] UKUT 165 (AAC) [31]. Similarly, the former Social Security Commissioners – now the Upper Tribunal (Administrative Appeals Chamber – once noted that 'tribunals are part of the adjudication system which is designed to ensure that claimants receive neither more nor less than the amount of social security benefit to which they are properly entitled (as opposed to the benefits to which the parties may be contending that they are entitled). There is a legitimate public interest in ensuring such a result': R (IB) 2/04 [32].

[94] Immigration Act 2014, s 19; J Finnis and S Murray, *Immigration, Strasbourg, and Judicial Overreach* (London, Policy Exchange, 2022).

[95] Social Security Act 1998, s 12(8)(b). To clarify, evidence concerning the claimant's circumstances that comes into existence after the initial decision can be considered. However, changes in those circumstances – such as the deterioration of physical or mental health – following the initial DWP decision cannot be considered by tribunals. Instead, the claimant will have to contact the DWP in order for it to revise its decision.

[96] Nationality, Immigration and Asylum Act 2002, s 85(4).

person persecuted?) and the risk of future events (is there a real risk that they will be persecuted on return to their country of origin?). Given the focus on the prospective risk of persecution that an appellant may face on return to their home country, tribunals can consider facts and evidence arising after the initial refusal decision.

The influence of government over tribunals extends far beyond overarching structural-institutional matters. It also includes the various ways in which government can frustrate the effective operation of tribunals and people's ability to receive authentic and not just formal access to justice. On a practical level, government bodies can informally negate people's right of access through, for instance, delays and by not issuing formal decision notices. The Home Office has a poor reputation for not always cooperating with appellants and tribunals in terms of supplying bundles and documents. In 2018, a First-tier Tribunal criticised the DWP for not complying with the tribunal's directions by failing to produce relevant evidence: 'This non-compliance appears endemic and is taking up significant First-tier Tribunal time which could be used more productively. More pertinently it is having a knock-on effect of causing serious delays and prejudice to appellants.'[97] The DWP responded that it had not intended to ignore instructions and that operational officers had been informed of the concerns. Anyone familiar with tribunals would not be surprised if this problem soon resurfaced.[98]

Tribunals have increasingly become digital, including telephone and online hearings. The leading online tribunal, the Traffic Penalty Tribunal, has for some years operated an online interactive portal to which people can upload evidence from their smartphone in order to have their appeals against parking tickets decided quickly. Before the COVID-19 pandemic, the Ministry of Justice introduced a large tribunals and court reform project to make them more accessible, user-friendly and efficient.[99] During the pandemic, by necessity, tribunals moved online. Digital procedures have since become embedded within tribunals and online case management.[100] Tribunals also have telephone hearings. The big question is whether this enables or hinders access to justice and the degree to which procedures affect outcomes. There has long been a higher success rate for appellants who opt for oral hearings than those who have their appeals decided on the papers.[101] Some evidence suggests that remote hearings in social security tribunals are less suited to the needs of unrepresented appellants.[102] It remains to be seen whether online hearings provide the same access to justice as ordinary oral hearings.[103]

[97] *NW v Secretary of State for Work and Pensions (PIP)* [2019] UKUT 150 (AAC) [2]. Tribunals can take action in the event of non-compliance by referring a case to the Upper Tribunal with a request to punish the party concerned for contempt of court.

[98] The problem often arises in immigration tribunals by both appellants and the Home Office. See, eg, *Maleci v Secretary of State for the Home Department* (Non-admission of Late Evidence) [2024] UKUT 28 (IAC) [47]: 'Non-compliance with directions imposing specified time limits may impact on judicial and administrative resources, on the ability of the other party to participate fully in the proceedings, and could delay the administration of justice. It is also disrespectful of the judicial process and the rule of law'.

[99] Ministry of Justice, *Transforming Our Justice System* (2016), https://assets.publishing.service.gov.uk/media/5a803d9ae5274a2e8ab4f019/joint-vision-statement.pdf.

[100] HMCTS, *Immigration and Asylum Appeals Reformed Service: Evaluation Report* (London, HMCTS, 2025).

[101] R Thomas, 'Immigration Appeals for Family Visitors Refused Entry Clearance' [2004] *PL* 612.

[102] M Burton, 'Remote Hearings in the Social Security Tribunal: Should We Be Worried?' (2021) 28 *Journal of Social Security Law* 36. The proposed introduction of 'continuous online resolution' – interactive online exchanges between tribunal panels and appellants – was later abandoned in 2019.

[103] L Mulcahy and A Tsalapatanis, *Digital Justice: Engineering Disadvantage?* (London, Palgrave Macmillan, 2024).

Online procedures also extend to digital processes for submitting evidence. In 2025, it was reported that the online process used by HMCTS by which claimants uploaded evidence online had been flawed. A bug in the case-management software meant that some claimants' evidence went missing, was overwritten or appeared to have been lost. Consequently, social security tribunals (and other courts) had decided cases without considering appellants' evidence, resulting in possibly wrong decisions.[104] A former senior judge described the situation as scandalous; the missing evidence could have led to miscarriages of justice, such as a vulnerable person missing out on essential benefits. HMCTS then, having undertaken assurance work, reported that 10 social security appeals needed to be reconsidered.[105] Nonetheless, both this and the experience of the Post Office Horizon highlights the risks on relying on IT systems and the unintended consequences.

Tribunal decisions must provide reasons that are proper, adequate and intelligible, and which deal with the substantial points raised.[106] The process of decision-making is an iterative process informed by the evidence but also the tribunal's background, assessment and experience. Some appeals result in clear win-lose outcomes, but many are finely balanced and could easily go either way. One issue here concerns the number of people on the tribunal. Some tribunals have a two or three-person panel (such as social security). By contrast, First-tier Tribunal immigration appeals are heard by a single immigration judge. This raises the prospect that the outcome of an appeal may turn on which judge hears the case.[107] Empirical research into this issue has been limited by the fact that First-tier Tribunal decisions have traditionally not been published.

The proportion of appeals allowed varies from one tribunal and appeal category to another and over time. The following is indicative of the proportion of appeals allowed: immigration appeals 40–50 per cent; disability benefits (Employment and Support Allowance) 50–60 per cent; PIP 60–80 per cent; special educational needs and disability approximately 90 per cent.[108] Tribunals allow appeals for various reasons. Their more inquisitorial approach enables them to elicit additional evidence from claimants at oral hearings, evidence that may not have been collected initially because of the lack of interaction between claimants and decision-makers. Good decision-making also relies

[104] 'Courts Service "Covered up" IT Bug That Caused Evidence to Go Missing' *BBC News* (8 August 2025), www.bbc.com/news/articles/cwye2q00k51o; BBC Radio 4, File on Four, 'The IT Bug That's Caused Chaos in the Courts' (11 November 2025).

[105] 'Hundreds of Thousands of Benefit Cases to Be Checked for Errors after "Potentially Catastrophic"' IT bug' *The Independent* (23 October 2025); Letter from HMCTS to House of Commons Justice Committee (11 November 2025).

[106] *In re Poyser and Mills' Arbitration* [1964] 2 QB 467, 478 (Megaw J); *South Bucks District Council v Porter (No2)* [2004] UKHL 33; *R (Iran) v Secretary of State for the Home Department* [2005] EWCA Civ 982; [2005] Imm AR 535 (CA); Senior President of Tribunals, *Practice Direction Reasons for Decisions* (2024).

[107] R Thomas, 'Refugee Roulette: A UK Perspective' in J Ramji-Nogales, AI Schoenholtz, and PG Schrag (eds), *Refugee Roulette: Disparities in Asylum Adjudication and Proposals for Reform* (New York, New York University Press, 2009); M Ovádek, 'Judicial Diversity and Immigration Appeals: Evidence from the United Kingdom' (2025) *West European Politics*; E Marshall, 'Reconsidering the Asylum Lottery: Refugee Determination and the Structure of Luck' (2025) 34 *Social & Legal Studies* 791.

[108] Ministry of Justice, *Tribunal Statistics Quarterly* (2024), www.gov.uk/government/statistics/tribunals-statistics-quarterly-october-to-december-2024.

heavily on the integrity and good judgement of tribunal judges and members; they are vulnerable to the same emotional responses and cognitive biases as everyone else.[109]

What then is the quality of tribunal decisions? This is another very broad question. At a general level, it is reasonable to assume that tribunals make better-quality decisions than government. Tribunals have more qualified personnel, they decide cases de novo, use better procedures, including hearings, and give better and more considered reasons. They build up their own expertise through their specialisation. Of course, tribunals are not perfect. They make errors, including unfair procedures, poor reason-giving and misapplying the law.[110] Nonetheless, the overall quality of tribunal decision-making is higher than that of government caseworkers. However, this is not quite comparing like with like. Government makes millions of initial and review decisions, whereas the volumes of tribunal decisions are in the hundreds of thousands. Only a small proportion of decisions are ever appealed to tribunals. Tribunals already have challenges managing their caseloads as they are. Tribunals would collapse if appeals volumes doubled, let alone if their caseloads increased to the scale of initial decision-making.

Overall, tribunals enable people to participate in decisions of great importance to them and generally make good decisions. People receive justice in a narrow sense, although they can often feel that they have been failed by the wider shortcomings concerning the initial handling of claims and decisions, administrative reviews, a lack of assistance and procedural challenges.[111]

The Upper Tribunal

An important feature of the tribunal structure is the Upper Tribunal, the second-tier appellate body, which replaced previous appellate bodies.[112] A principal rationale for the Upper Tribunal was that it would provide procedural coherence in the routes of onward challenge, which were previously confused and incoherent.[113] Another rationale was that

[109] Scenarios in immigration appeals involve a judge becoming frustrated with an appellant's representative or judging a case on the performance of the representatives, or the judge forms a theory about the 'truth' of a case and then asks questions of the appellant to confirm that theory.

[110] See, eg, *MM v Secretary of State for the Home Department* (AA/06906/2014) [2017] UKIAT (IAC) (unreported) (serious errors in various decisions by the same immigration judge); *GC v HMRC and DC* [2018] UKUT 223 (AAC) [4] ('The FTT's procedural handling of these appeals has been shambolic. It has also resulted in a prolonged and unacceptable delay'); *Hima v Secretary of State for the Home Department* [2024] EWCA Civ 680 (CA) (First-tier Tribunal judge entered into the arena by undertaking what amounted to a cross-examination); *FA (Iran) v Secretary of State for the Home Department* [2024] EWCA Civ 149 (CA) (numerous errors by FTTIAC judge); *AA (Morocco) v Secretary of State for the Home Department* [2025] EWCA Civ 144 (CA) (same case remitted to the FTTIAC on three occasions owing to a series of errors, thereby taking over five years to be finally concluded).

[111] C Barnard and A Ludlow, 'Administrative (In)Justice? Appellants' Experiences of Accessing Justice in Social Security Tribunals' [2022] *PL* 406.

[112] These were principally: the Social Security and Child Support Commissioners; the Immigration Appeal Tribunal; and the Special and General Commissioners for Tax. While the formal structure of tribunals changed, there was continuity in terms of judicial personnel. Specifically on second-tier appellate tribunals, see: R Micklethwait, *The National Insurance Commissioners* (London, Stevens, 1976); T Buck, D Bonner and R Sainsbury, *Making Social Security Law: The Role and Work of the Social Security and Child Support Commissioners* (Farnham, Ashgate, 2005); Thomas (n 4) ch 8.

[113] H Woolf, 'A Hotchpotch of Appeals: The Need for a Blender' (1988) 7 *Civil Justice Quarterly* 44.

the Upper Tribunal would provide judicial leadership and also undertake some judicial review work.[114] Like the First-tier Tribunal, the Upper Tribunal is divided into chambers, thereby enabling specialisation. All Upper Tribunal Chamber Presidents are High Court judges. Despite the apparent jurisdictional breadth implied by its name, the Upper Tribunal (Administrative Appeals Chamber) is not a generalist appeal tribunal covering the entirety of administration, but a de facto specialist public law court with one very large jurisdiction (social security) and other smaller jurisdictions (special educational needs, information rights, transport, mental health, and criminal injuries compensation). It does much of its work on the papers and has a relatively small number of hearings. This contrasts with the Upper Tribunal (Immigration Appeals Chamber), which holds more hearings. It also undertakes the bulk of the immigration judicial review caseload which the overloaded Administrative Court lacks the appetite and resources to undertake.[115]

The Upper Tribunal has two principal functions: first, to decide routine onward challenges against First-tier Tribunal decisions on error of law grounds; and, second, to use its expertise to issue guidance on important matters of law and practice in order to ensure consistency across First-tier Tribunals. Routine error of law challenges are handled by Upper Tribunal judges who consider applications of permission to appeal on the papers and then (in the Upper Tribunal (Immigration and Asylum Chamber)) through hearings. The rate of onward challenge varies. Only around 1–2 per cent of first-tier social security appeal decisions are challenged to the Upper Tribunal (Administrative Appeals Chamber). There is a much higher rate of challenge by the Home Office against first-tier immigration and asylum appeals.[116]

The Upper Tribunal's jurisdiction is limited to error of law.[117] This includes: misunderstanding or misapplying the law; taking account of irrelevant factors; failing to take relevant factors into account; procedural unfairness; irrationality; and failing to give adequate reasons for a decision. An error of fact is not an error of law unless the First-tier Tribunal's conclusion on the facts is perverse, which is a high threshold.[118] In order for the Upper Tribunal to find an error of law because of a factual error by the First-tier Tribunal, the latter's conclusion must have been irrational or wholly unsupported by the evidence. In the interests of finality, an onward appeal to the Upper Tribunal is not an opportunity to re-argue the case on its merits – otherwise, appeals would circulate endlessly round the system.

Most challenges to the First-tier Tribunal decisions concern the tribunal's reasons regarding the findings of fact, the application of the relevant rules or some other issue of procedure. In practice, there is an inherent elasticity as to what an error of law is and when an appellate tribunal ought to intervene. If an Upper Tribunal judge thinks that the decision under challenge is wrong, then they might be tempted to 'find' an error of

[114] Tribunals, Courts and Enforcement Act 2007, ss 15–21.

[115] The Upper Tribunal also has a non-appellate jurisdiction; principally judicial reviews transferred from the Administrative Court to the Upper Tribunal (Immigration and Asylum Chamber), which are mostly routine, repetitive and sometimes low-quality judicial reviews against non-appealable initial Home Office immigration decisions. See Thomas and Tomlinson (n 49).

[116] This is partly because of the political sensitivity, legal complexity and the poor quality of some FTTIAC decisions.

[117] Tribunals, Courts and Enforcement Act 2007, s 11.

[118] *R (Iran) v Secretary of State for the Home Department* [2005] EWCA Civ 982; [2005] Imm AR 535 (CA) [9]–[13] (Brooke LJ).

law in order to intervene. Appeals vitiated by an error of law will normally be remitted or sent back to be reheard afresh by a different first-tier tribunal, although some findings of fact may be preserved. One notable feature is that the DWP often supports appellants' onward appeals. By contrast, in the immigration context, there is a much higher rate of onward challenge against appeals dismissed by the FTTIAC decisions, which the Home Office will usually resist. Further, the Home Office has, at times, challenged appeals allowed in appellants' favour by First-tier Tribunals on poor-quality grounds. Like claimants' representatives, the Home Office has also been criticised for poor litigation practice.[119] Yet, the Home Office has also rightly challenged some poor FTTIAC decisions in favour of claimants. A notorious case concerned an Albanian man whose appeal on family life grounds (Article 8 ECHR) was allowed by the First-tier Tribunal judge on the basis that the man's son would be unable to 'eat the type of chicken nuggets available abroad'. The Upper Tribunal allowed the Home Office's appeal.[120] There are also various immigration decisions – such as the submission of fresh evidence – which cannot be appealed, but which are challenged through judicial review.

The Upper Tribunal's second function – clarifying recurring or problematic issues of wider importance – involves issuing guidance on often complex matters of statutory interpretation and general points of procedure and practice. In the asylum context, the Upper Tribunal (Immigration and Asylum Chamber) performs a distinctive function of issuing country guidance decisions setting out whether particular categories of asylum claimants will be at risk on return to their country of origin. This involves considering the relevant factual materials and then issuing guidance, which will be applied by First-tier Tribunals unless the position in the relevant country has changed or new evidence has come to light. Most First-tier Tribunal decisions are not published; they are simply individual decisions on issues of fact.[121] By contrast, Upper Tribunal decisions are published.[122]

When the Upper Tribunal was established, it had been suggested that it would perform a wider and distinctive role in the overall tribunal system. Procedural coherence would be complemented by 'jurisprudential coherence'.[123] As a strong and dedicated appellate body, the Upper Tribunal would take the 'lead on developing the law underlying administrative justice'.[124] In addition to rule interpretation, the Upper Tribunal would develop norms and standards of general application to all tribunals, thereby yielding long-term

[119] *MR v Secretary of State for the Home Department* (permission to appeal: Tribunal's approach) Brazil [2015] UKUT 00029 (IAC) (the Home Office's challenge against the appellant's successful appeal was 'manifestly devoid of any substance or merit'); *R (El-Ashkar) v Secretary of State for the Home Department* (JR-2022-LON-002069, 30 January 2024) ('grave' and 'shockingly poor' conduct by the Home Office, including deliberately not notifying the applicant of a decision). It should be noted that the quality of immigration representatives varies enormously; the worst are incompetent, corrupt and/or mendacious.

[120] *Disha v Secretary of State for the Home Department* (UTIAC, UI-2024-004546, 9 January 2025).

[121] Although, in the interests of transparency and open justice, FTTIAC decisions are to be published: Judiciary of England and Wales, *The Lady Chief Justice's Report 2025* (London, HMSO, 2025) 54–55.

[122] See tribunalsdecisions.service.gov.uk/utiac and gov.uk/courts-tribunals/upper-tribunal-administrative-appeals-chamber.

[123] G Hickinbottom, 'Tribunal Reform: A New Coherent System' [2010] *JR* 103, 107–09 (Hickinbottom was then Chamber President of the Upper Tribunal (Administrative Appeals Chamber) and later a Court of Appeal judge and President of Welsh Tribunals).

[124] Tribunals Service, *Transforming Tribunals: Implementing Part 1 of the Tribunals, Courts and Enforcement Act 2007* (CP 30/07, 2007) [131].

and sustained benefits for administrative justice more broadly.[125] The new structure would be more than just a federation of existing tribunals; regular interchange amongst judges would ensure consistency of approach. The authority of the Upper Tribunal would 'derive from its specialist skills, and its status as a superior court of record, with judicial review powers, presided over by the Senior President' that would 'come to play a central, innovative and defining role in the new system, enjoying a position in the judicial hierarchy at least equivalent to that of the Administrative Court'.[126]

To some extent, this has been achieved through guidance issued by the Upper Tribunal to First-tier Tribunals. At the same time, the Upper Tribunal has not, for instance, taken the lead by issuing landmark rulings to develop the legal standards governing tribunals and to take administrative justice into new areas and directions. For the most part, the Upper Tribunal is a relatively conservative judicial body that operates through its respective specialist chambers. It has never, as a corporate entity, issued rulings on wider principles of administrative justice to, for instance, improve the quality of initial decision-making. Most of the Upper Tribunal's work is deciding onward appeals and making sense of often complex rules. In legal-formal terms, the Upper Tribunal is a superior court of record and thereby has an equivalent standing to the Administrative Court, although opinions may differ as to whether this has really occurred as a matter of substantive legal-cultural reality.[127] There are various explanations for this state of affairs: the dominance of a conservative legal culture amongst senior judicial leaders; the perceived dangers of taking an innovative approach; a less conducive governmental context since 2010; and the politics of judicial review prompting the judiciary to take a formal approach to insulate itself from criticism.

However, the Upper Tribunal remains central to the tribunals structure. It is widely seen as an expert, credible and authoritative body. It exerts significant influence through its interpretation of the specialist rules and has produced an extensive body of decisions. Much of this case law is highly formalistic, given the arcane and abstruse nature of, for instance, immigration, tax and benefit regulations. The Upper Tribunal has also made some significant interventions, such as ensuring that social security appellants do not lose their right of appeal to a tribunal when they have applied out of time for an internal administrative review, which is compulsory before an appeal.[128] Similarly, the Upper Tribunal (Immigration and Asylum Chamber) strongly criticised the Home Office for forcing student migrants accused of cheating on their English language tests to use out of country of appeals over the preferable in-country appeals.[129] As regards the relationship between the Upper Tribunal and the higher courts, the Supreme Court has stated that the courts should respect Upper Tribunal decisions unless it is quite clear that it has decided incorrectly. The higher courts should adopt a pragmatic approach to the dividing line between law and fact and should allow tribunals to exercise their expertise

[125] Hickinbottom (n 123) 108; R Carnwath, 'Tribunal Justice: A New Start' (AJTC Conference, 19 November 2008).

[126] Tribunals Service (n 124) [178].

[127] Tribunals, Courts and Enforcement Act 2007, s 3(5).

[128] *R (CJ) v Secretary of State for Work and Pensions* (n 28); *TR and GD v Secretary of State for Work and Pensions* (n 92).

[129] *R (Mohibullah) v Secretary of State for the Home Department* (TOEIC – ETS – judicial review principles) [2016] UKUT 00561 (IAC).

to best effect.[130] The tests here are inherently malleable and the higher courts can and have intervened when they have wished to do so.

A final point is a comparative one. The UK system of tribunals may seem unusual from the perspective of other countries with a more formal separation of powers, such as the US and Australia.[131] It might be queried how tribunals can exercise executive power and yet be staffed by judges. It might also seem unusual that UK courts and tribunals are now more or less equivalent bodies, and that the Upper Tribunal now decides both appeals and judicial reviews. The answers are that in the UK's unwritten constitution, there is no overarching formal separation of powers with an 'executive branch' and a 'judicial branch'. Instead, statute law confers on tribunals the ability to decide appeals against specified administrative decisions. Statute law also made tribunals into judicial bodies. Similarly, statute gave the Upper Tribunal the ability to handle specific types of judicial review claims. Behind the formal legal position, there are many crossovers. High Court judges sitting in the Royal Courts of Justice doing judicial reviews, will, from time to time, also sit in the Upper Tribunal (Immigration Appeal Chamber). Other types of judges sit on tribunals from time to time. The title 'tribunal' is sufficiently long-standing and embedded in legal culture. Furthermore, it captures their distinctive role. For instance, many people who go to social security tribunals might well be dissuaded from doing so if it was a 'court'. For many people, 'going to court' has connotations of a criminal prosecution, of being put on trial and being cross-examined. Such an image is, of course, completely at odds with what happens in practice. Social security appeals involve an inquisitorial and relatively informal hearing by a tribunal of an appeal typically brought by an unrepresented person. The tribunal will understand the appellant's position, that they likely do not know or understand the system and the legal rules, and that they need someone to make sense of their circumstances. The tribunal will then make up for this by asking the right questions to elicit the necessary information to make the right decision. This is the pragmatic ethos of tribunals to ensure ground-level justice.

Improving Decision-Making: Getting it Right

So far, we have considered initial administrative decisions, administrative reviews and also tribunal appeals. Government possesses processing capacity, but the outcomes are of variable quality. Tribunals make better-quality decisions, but the volumes are far lower. How is it possible to improve the quality of initial decisions? How can the experiences of and learning from tribunals be used in this respect? Are there other ways of trying to improve the quality of initial decision-making?

[130] *Cooke v Secretary of State for Social Security* [2001] EWCA Civ 734; [2002] 3 All ER 279 (CA); *AH (Sudan) v Secretary of State for the Home Department* [2007] UKHL 49; [2008] 1 AC 678 (HL) [30] (Baroness Hale); *Jones v First-tier Tribunal and Criminal Injuries Compensation Authority* [2013] UKSC 19 [16] (Lord Hope). See also E Laurie, 'Assessing the Upper Tribunal's Potential to Deliver Administrative Justice' [2012] *PL* 288.

[131] See S Thomson, M Groves and G Weeks (eds), *Administrative Tribunals in the Common Law World* (Oxford, Hart Publishing, 2024); S Thomson, *Administrative Law: A Very Short Introduction* (Oxford, Oxford University Press, 2025) ch 3.

External redress by tribunals is necessary, but insufficient.[132] Better-quality initial decision-making is required. The Franks Report noted that 'nothing can make up for a wrong approach to administrative activity by the administration's servants'.[133] Many people do not appeal even though they might well succeed if they did so. When people do appeal, the delay and costs involved can be frustrating and stressful. During its short existence, the Administrative Justice and Tribunals Council emphasised the need to get decisions 'right first time'.[134] It made a forceful argument that if government could make better initial decisions, this would reduce injustice for claimants and the demand for and costs of redress systems. More could be done to improve the design of government bodies and systems and to invest in training of decision-makers to improve the quality of their decision-making. The Council recognised that embedding a 'right first time' culture would require management, commitment and careful preparation and concerted effort, but the gains would be worthwhile.

The high proportion of allowed appeals has often been highlighted as evidence of the poor decision-making, although it is difficult to extrapolate from this when considering the overall standards of administrative decision-making. Tribunals only decide appeals concerning the comparatively small subset of initial decisions which are appealed. Appeals can be allowed if new evidence is submitted or collected and had not been previously considered. Procedural differences and tribunal procedures can affect substantive outcomes. These is some substance to these points, although the quality of initial decisions is variable.[135] However, government has often defensively argued that there is little correlation between success rates and the quality of initial decisions because appeals are allowed as a result of new evidence being presented for the first time before tribunals rather than because initial decisions are flawed. Yet, this explanation is too broad brush. It is the case that the quality of initial decisions is variable. It is notable that government has adopted this stance in response to criticism of benefit and immigration decisions, areas of central government decision-making. By contrast, a government minister once described high appeal success rates in the Special Educational Needs and Disability Tribunal against decisions by local authorities as 'symptomatic of a system that is failing'.[136] Both responses are self-serving in terms of government shifting the blame elsewhere. The proportion of allowed benefit appeals is high and cannot be attributed solely to new evidence being presented on appeal. Delivery of educational provision for children and young people with special educational needs and disabilities

[132] M Adler, 'A Socio-legal Approach to Administrative Justice' (2003) 25 *Law & Policy* 323, 324.

[133] Franks Committee, *Report of the Committee on Administrative Tribunals and Enquiries* (Cmnd 218, 1957) [405].

[134] AJTC, *Right First Time* (London, AJTC, 2011); AJTC, *Putting it Right: A Strategic Approach to Resolving Administrative Disputes* (London, AJTC, 2012).

[135] In some tribunal contexts, there is no relationship at all between the quality of initial decisions and allowed appeals. For instance, school admission appeal panels decide some 40,000 appeals per year in England by children refused a place at their preferred school, of which 20 per cent are allowed. Panels weigh up, on the one hand, the prejudice to the provision of efficient education to the school caused by having additional children and, on the other hand, the child's case to be admitted, an issue that is not considered initially. Panels hear directly from parents/guardians about their personal situations. Decisions are essentially judgemental. Different panels may decide differently, but, as in all tribunals, there needs to be a decision one way or the other rather than no decision at all. As a result, the overall proportion of allowed appeals is not indicative of the quality of initial decisions in that context.

[136] HC Deb 29 March 2022, vol 711, col 721 (Nadhim Zahawi MP Secretary of State for Education).

(SEND) is undertaken by local government, but the system is not adequately funded by central government. Further, people do not appeal even though they might well have reasonable prospects of success. People may also not appeal because of a lack of advice, vulnerabilities, not understanding the system, not having the confidence to challenge government and the process being too stressful and distressing. There is a significant volume of submerged injustice which remains hidden away as a result of poor initial decisions, the effects of mandatory reconsideration and low appeal rates.

While First-tier Tribunals are not perfect, in light of their membership and procedures, they typically undertake a more intensive consideration of the evidence and informed application of the rules than initial decision-makers. There is extensive evidence about the variable quality of initial decision-making.[137] Tribunals have expressed their concern and bafflement at poor initial procedures and decisions. 'Every working day, the First-tier Tribunal overturns decisions … because the decision maker has omitted to consider all the relevant issues.'[138] 'Yet another case in which the removal of an award of the Personal Independence Payment was not dealt with in any sense adequately.'[139] 'Yet another case in which the putative appellant and the First-tier Tribunal was misled by the DWP and its defective procedures … a sorry state of affairs.'[140] Immigration decisions frequently 'do not sufficiently rely on the law and guidance' relevant to the decision.[141] 'Initial decision-making by government departments is often very inadequate.'[142] While initial decision-making processes work well for some claimants, they also generate significant problems for a sizeable proportion. Problems materialise before tribunals because of the structures and outputs of earlier decisions. There is a real need for initial decision-makers to be better trained not just in the legal rules they apply, but also in the collection and handling of evidence, how to apply standards of proof to make findings of fact and on reason-giving.

How then is it possible to improve the quality of initial decisions? How can the experiences of and learning from tribunals be used in this respect? What is or should be the relationship between government and tribunals in seeking to improve initial decision-making? Does government want to do better? Does it have the capacity to do so? If so, then how?

Before the unified tribunal structure was introduced, social security tribunals had a close but conducive relationship with government. The then Department of Health and Social Security viewed tribunals not as a threat, but as a means of promoting better decision-making.[143] One institutional feature particular to the social security

[137] JUSTICE and AJC, *Reforming Benefits Decision-Making* (London, JUSTICE, 2020); Reading Welfare Rights, *Ten Years of PIP: A Decade-Long Mistake?* (2023), www.rightsnet.org.uk/pdfs/PIP_Project_Report_-_Reading_Welfare_Rights.pdf.

[138] *RR v Secretary of State for Work and Pensions* [2017] UKUT 50 (AAC) [39].

[139] *PM v Secretary of State for Work and Pensions* [2017] UKUT 37 (AAC) [1].

[140] *DG v HMRC and EG* [2016] UKUT 505 (AAC) (TC) [1]–[2]. See also *JW v HMRC* [2015] UKUT 359 (AAC) (TC) [1]: 'yet another case that falls into the litany of cases in which the dreadful quality of HMRC's appeal response to the First-tier Tribunal is a central issue'.

[141] Oral evidence of Sir Ernest Ryder (Senior President of Tribunals) before the House of Lords Constitution Committee, *The Legislative Process* (HL 2015–16, 27) Q44.

[142] CG Blake, 'Judicial Review, Second Tier Tribunals and Legality' in M Partington (eds), *The Leggatt Review of Tribunals: Academic Seminar Papers* (Bristol, University of Bristol Press, 2001) 70.

[143] B Hale, 'Courts and Tribunals' (London, Annual Upper Tribunal Lecture, 14 October 2021) 5–6.

context was that claims were decided by the 'independent statutory authorities': the three tier-system of adjudication officers (initial decision-makers), tribunals and the then Social Security Commissioners (now the Upper Tribunal (Administrative Appeals Chamber)). There was also an 'internal separation of powers' within the Department between policy-making, administration and adjudication. Making decisions on benefit claims – adjudication – involved proactively gathering evidential material, the deliberative weighing of evidence and the independent exercise of judgement.[144] The commitment to improving decision-making was illustrated by the establishment of the Chief Adjudication Officer to provide advice and guidance on decision-making and to monitor standards.[145] This culture of adjudication reached its height in the 1980s. Senior tribunal members trained adjudication officers to help them understand the working of tribunals.[146] There was a sense of cooperation between the Department and the tribunals in the shared endeavour of raising the overall quality of decision-making, both initially and on appeal. Not all of these features would be considered acceptable today. Government departments wrote the procedural rules for 'their' tribunals. Benefits appeals were usually heard in the Department's local offices rather than in separate accommodation as now happens. Nonetheless, there was a culture of adjudication in which initial decision-makers, tribunal members and the Social Security Commissioners formed part of an overall system focused on making good-quality decisions. Tribunals provided feedback to departments as to how they could improve their initial decisions. Presenting officers would also provide feedback to initial decision-makers and there were efforts to avoid appeals being overturned on appeal.

Over time, things changed. Financial and other pressures on the system increased. Decision-making became akin to the straightforward administrative processing of benefit claims.[147] The gathering of evidence by engaging with claimants was replaced by processing data from application forms. The exercise of judgement was replaced by more prescriptive regulations. The position of Chief Adjudication Officer was downgraded and later abolished. Responsibility for initial decisions was transferred from the 'statutory authorities' to the 'Secretary of State' and in practice undertaken by civil servants.[148] Decisions were processed according to key performance indicators. Concerns were raised that the speed and volume of processing were being prioritised over quality.[149] Tribunals became increasingly judicial and separate from the Department.

Other feedback mechanisms were introduced. In the 2000s, the president of social security appeal tribunals produced annual reports on the standards of initial

[144] N Warren, 'The Adjudication Gap: A Discussion Document' (2006) 13 *Journal of Social Security Law* 110; HH Judge Robert Martin (President of the First-tier Tribunal (Social Entitlement Chamber)), Memorandum submitted to the House of Commons Work and Pensions Committee, *Decision Making and Appeals in the Benefits System* (HC 2009–10, 313).

[145] Health and Social Services and Social Security Adjudications Act 1983; AW Bradley, 'Recent Reform of Social Security Adjudication in Great Britain' (1985) 26 *Les Cahiers de Droit* 403; R Sainsbury, 'The Social Security Chief Adjudication Officer: The First Four Years' [1989] *PL* 323.

[146] H Woolf, *Protection of the Public: A New Challenge* (London, Stevens, 1990) 73–76.

[147] J Baldwin, N Wikeley and R Young, *Judging Social Security: The Adjudication of Claims for Benefit in Britain* (Oxford, Clarendon Press, 1992).

[148] Social Security Act 1998, s 1; N Wikeley, 'Decision-Making and Appeals under the Social Security Act 1998' (1998) 5 *Journal of Social Security Law* 104.

[149] N Wikeley, 'Burying Bell: Managing the Judicialisation of Social Security Tribunals' (2000) 63 *MLR* 475.

decision-making, as did the DWP itself.[150] These reports identified various persistent themes. Tribunals frequently overturned decisions because tribunal hearings generated additional evidence, usually in the form of oral evidence provided by the appellant. This suggested the need for more direct engagement by the DWP with claimants. Initial decision-makers felt bound to follow medical evidence or assessment reports (particularly relevant as regards disability benefits) to the exclusion of other evidence, including from appellants. Decision-makers did not explain why they relied on medical evidence in preference to the claimant's evidence. They were often confused by how much evidential weight to give to assessments and how to resolve conflicting evidence.[151] Decisions were not effectively reviewed before they came to tribunals. Despite these problems, no real action was taken to improve matters. By 2005, the president of social security tribunals had lost patience with the DWP's inaction; there was little point in producing reports that were ignored.[152] One weakness was that the reports were generic.[153] In practice, decision-makers never find out whether their decisions are overturned on appeal. Further, the DWP had largely disengaged from tribunals through the low attendance of its presenting officers who might be able to feedback points to decision-makers.[154] This also removed the 'embarrassment' factor when a presenting officer is placed in the position of defending a poor-quality initial decision.

Leggatt had envisaged that the new independent tribunals would enter a dialogue with government to improve decisions.[155] The 2004 White Paper announced that the new tribunals system would have a key role in stimulating improvements and entering into agreements with departments.[156] Scepticism was expressed; this agenda was 'unduly optimistic' and 'unrealistically grandiose.'[157] In the event, unsurprisingly, no real progress was made. The Ministry of Justice and HMCTS became focused solely on creating and operating the new tribunal system. Moreover, they lacked the authority to get much larger departments, such as the DWP and the Home Office, to improve their decisions and procedures. The wider political situation changed with austerity.

Further, tribunals are now part of the formal judiciary. Given the principle of judicial independence, there have been sensitivities within the judiciary about engaging directly with government to try to improve initial administrative decision-making. After all, government bodies are a party to all appeals. If tribunals helped departments to improve

[150] Social Security Act 1998, s 81 and sch 1, para 10; DWP, *Report on the Standards of Decision Making in the Benefits Agency, Child Support Agency and Employment Service 2001–02* (HC 2002-03, 880).

[151] President's Report, *Report by the President of Appeal Tribunals on the Standards of Decision-Making by the Secretary of State 2006–2007* (London, Appeals Service, 2007) [1.8].

[152] President of Appeal Tribunals, *Report on the Standards of Decision-Making by the Secretary of State 2004–05* (Appeals Service, 2005) [1.12]. The 2007–08 report noted that 'there is little evidence of significant change over time in standards of administrative decision-making, as gauged by the cases coming before tribunals'.

[153] ibid [1.3]: 'feedback suggests that the [DWP] finds it difficult to use the empirical data which we provide as a basis for instrumental reform of the decision-making process which has prompted me to question the utility of the current methodology'.

[154] N Wikeley and R Young, 'The Administration of Benefits in Britain: Adjudication Officers and the Influence of Social Security Appeal Tribunals' [1992] *PL* 238.

[155] Leggatt (n 14) [9.11]–[9.21].

[156] Department for Constitutional Affairs, *Transforming Public Services: Complaints, Redress, and Tribunals* (Cm 6243, 2004) [6.32]–[6.34].

[157] N Wikeley, 'Decision Making and the New Tribunals' (2006) 13 *Journal of Social Security Law* 86, 88; P Cane, *Administrative Tribunals and Adjudication* (Oxford, Hart Publishing, 2009) 213.

their decisions, then this could undermine the perception of judicial independence. One response to this is that tribunal feedback would focus not on individual cases, but on general problems, such as how best to collect and assess evidence.[158] Giving feedback could be seen as an indication of tribunal's independence by demonstrating that they hear individual appeals impartially, while also giving general advice on to improve primary decisions. A former Senior President of Tribunals was not unduly worried and saw no difficulty with exchanges between judges and decision-makers or judges giving training, provided that it was undertaken openly and responsibly.[159] In turn, government needed to accept the challenge of learning from feedback and putting the lessons into practice. Unsurprisingly, given the DWP's inaction following the reports concerning social security tribunals and differences of view within the judiciary about the propriety of providing feedback, nothing happened. Responsibility for reporting on the standards of benefit decision-making was transferred to the Senior President of Tribunals – no report was ever issued – and then quietly removed altogether.[160] The declining role of tribunals in providing feedback coincided with them moving into the mainstream judiciary.

Subsequent efforts achieved little. In 2012, the DWP and HMCTS made another effort through tribunals providing 'summary reasons' as feedback to initial decision-makers.[161] The DWP analysed the data to provide insight and learning. Judges were asked to ascribe the reason why an appeal is allowed from a drop-down list of reasons – for example, 'cogent oral evidence' from the appellant. This produced surface-level knowledge about appeals, but it lacked the depth required to attain a more informed understanding. In any event, there was a lack of action by the DWP to take matters forward.[162] In 2023, a select committee recommended that the DWP investigate the reasons for the high rate of allowed appeals and the costs and effectiveness of mandatory reconsideration, and consider practical recommendations for learning from tribunal decisions.[163] In response, the DWP undertook a number of small-scale internal learning exercises to better understand what it could learn from the disputes stage. It also worked to improve feedback loops so that it could continue to learn from tribunals with a view to improving decision-making across all stages of the claim journey. This included improving feedback from DWP presenting officers following tribunal hearings so that the Department could look for further points of learning to feed into internal decision-making and medical assessments. However, this work was still at a very early stage.[164] By contrast, the President of Northern Ireland Appeal Tribunals has repeatedly expressed concern about the quality of initial decisions,

[158] M Partington and E Kirton-Darling, *Research Issues Paper: Feedback* (London, AJTC, 2008) [1.4].

[159] Carnwath (n 125) [26].

[160] Social Security Act 1998, s 15A(2) (inserted by the Transfer of Tribunal Functions Order, SI 2008/2883, sch 3, para 153); Deregulation Act 2015, s 79. The President of Northern Ireland Appeal Tribunals still publishes an annual report: Northern Ireland President of Appeal Tribunals, *Standards of Decision Making by the Department for Communities* (Belfast, Appeals Service, 2024).

[161] DWP, *Social Security and Child Support Tribunal Hearings: Early Analysis of Appeals Allowed from Pilot Data* (London, DWP, 2012).

[162] House of Commons Work and Pensions Committee, *Employment and Support Allowance and Work Capability Assessments* (HC 2014–15, 302) [110]–[113].

[163] House of Commons Work and Pensions Committee, *Health Assessments for Benefits* (HC 2022–23, 128) [92].

[164] House of Commons Work and Pensions Committee, *Health Assessments for Benefits: Government Response to Committee's Fifth Report of Session 2022–23* (HC 2022–23, 1558) 13.

particularly concerning disability benefits, the low attendance of presenting officers and the quality of assessments. Many incorrect initial decisions could be avoided if there was better collection of medical evidence.[165]

Only social security tribunals have ever issued formal feedback on allowed appeals. Other tribunals are typically the end of the process with no formal machinery to feedback their views on decision-making, although some, such as criminal injuries compensation tribunals, previously had regular meetings with the initial decision-making body, the Criminal Injuries Compensation Authority. Immigration tribunals have never produced reports analysing why they allow appeals. This is not just because of concerns about judicial independence; it is also tribunal time and workload. Immigration tribunals issue detailed determinations and it is the Home Office's responsibility to improve its decision-making. The Independent Chief Inspector of Borders and Immigration has also repeatedly scrutinised initial decision-making.[166] In 2018, the Home Office created a Chief Caseworker Unit to provide internal support, guidance and leadership to raise the profile and quality of decision-making and later an ethical decision-making model.[167] In 2024, the Home Office was holding regular forums to feedback common errors and trends to operational staff. Following increased administrative reviews, legal challenges and the lack of a strategic approach to mitigate risks of recurring legal action, it launched a Litigation Strategy Board to address these issues by building a network to improve initial decision-making and make better use of data to improve feedback mechanisms.[168] Such mechanisms doubtless play a role, but improving decision quality will always be a hard grind.

Rulings from the Upper Tribunal can clarify aspects of decision-making and the relevant law. Such guidance is principally directed to the First-tier Tribunal, although representatives also become aware of it. The degree to which such guidance penetrates into the realm of initial decision-making is unclear. Beneath the level of tribunals, the large administrative machinery churns out high volumes of individual decisions of variable quality. The pressure to process large volumes of decisions can mean that government resorts to a default position in which it relies on tribunals to act as a safety net to pick up bad decisions. Making decisions – any decision irrespective of quality – enables government to get such matters out of its hands and offload them onto the tribunals. This incurs costs in terms of avoidable appeals and also for those claimants who receive poor-quality decisions, but do not appeal them.

Another option is a 'polluter pays' principle. The theory is that poor-quality initial decisions 'pollute' the legal system by requiring people to appeal, thereby shifting the costs onto the tribunal system.[169] Over the years 2011–21, social security and immigration

[165] Northern Ireland President of Appeal Tribunals (n 160).

[166] ICIBI (n 9).

[167] Independent Chief Inspector of Borders and Immigration, *An Inspection of the Effectiveness of the UKVI Chief Caseworker Unit's Referral Process* (London, ICIBI, 2022); Home Office, *The Ethical Decision-Making Model* (London, Home Office, 2021).

[168] National Audit Office, *Immigration: Skilled Worker Visas* (HC 2024–25, 745) [3.10].

[169] Law Society, *Access to Justice Review* (London, Law Society, 2010) 20–21; House of Commons Justice Committee, *Government's Proposed Reform of Legal Aid* (HC 681 2010–12) [60]; E Dugan, 'A Senior Judge Has Suggested Charging the Government for Every "No-Brainer" Benefits Case it Loses in Court' *BuzzFeed News* (9 November 2017), www.buzzfeed.com/emilydugan/most-dwp-benefits-cases-which-reach-court-are-based-on-bad.

tribunals each cost over £1 billion.[170] The argument is that the failure of government to invest in good-quality decision-making creates a moral hazard by which departments are insulated from the consequences of their poor decision-making. The solution is then to require government departments and public bodies to bear these costs, which should, in turn, motivate them to improve the quality of its decisions. Unsurprisingly, government has been unwilling to adopt a 'polluter pays' approach or to engage with the Administrative Justice Council on the issue. After all, there may be little direct correlation between the quality of initial decisions and the outcome of appeals given tribunals' exercise of judgement and fresh evidence not previously considered. But a more fundamental problem concerns the likely effects of operating a 'polluter pays' principle in practice. In theory, charging government for successful appeals might induce it to improve the quality of its decisions. However, in practice, it could be counter-productive. Improving the quality of initial decision-making requires more resources, not less. It is difficult to know until a 'polluter pays' approach has been modelled and applied in practice, but even so, there is no enthusiasm from government. Greater professionalisation of casework staff would be welcome, although the general direction has been the other way, with decision-making staff being progressively deskilled.[171] Other options include better training, enhanced quality assurance and organisational learning.[172]

The reality is that improving primary decisions requires real commitment, effort and resources from government, but this does not really exist. To expect the DWP or the Home Office unilaterally to improve their decision-making is simply to restate the endemic and lethargic nature of the problem. Even seemingly basic improvements, such as sending tribunal decisions back to the caseworkers who made the initial decisions or having caseworkers act as presenting officers to defend their initial decisions, would involve considerable organisational upheaval. Improving decision-making will always be a long, hard slog for what government views as diminishing returns. Despite various reports criticising the quality of initial decision-making and urging government to do better, the matter has low political salience. Government departments respond to the agendas of ministers who are largely uninterested in routine operations. There is no political pay-off. Improving decisions would involve additional investment for which

[170] There are other indirect costs: Pro Bono Economics, *The Cost of Not Getting Personal Independence Payment Decisions Right First Time* (London, Pro Bono Economics, 2021).

[171] D Martin, 'Making Tax and Social Security Decisions: Lean and Deskilling in the UK Civil Service' (2017) 32 *New Technology, Work and Employment* 146. In 2022, it was reported that the Home Office was recruiting asylum casework staff from supermarkets and McDonald's and giving them two days of training. See 'Revealed: Supermarket Staff Recruited to Make "Life and Death" Asylum Decisions' *The Guardian* (5 November 2022); 'Tough Asylum Cases Handled by New Home Office Staff, Say Insiders' *BBC News* (23 November 2022), www.bbc.com/news/uk-63720698. See also Ministry of Defence, *Armed Forces Compensation Scheme Quinquennial Review 2022/23* (London, Ministry of Defence, 2023) 46, which found that caseworkers were limited to collecting evidence, based on the belief that the evidence alone provided an objective decision. This conceptualisation of the claims process as objective and formulaic obviated the true significance of caseworkers in exercising judgement and resulted in their disempowerment. Caseworkers needed to be recognised and empowered to interpret the evidence and apply their discretion in complex and borderline cases in order to advance the scheme's objectives. They needed to be recruited, trained and supported in a manner which enabled the Ministry of Defence to have full confidence in their judgements. Caseworkers required structures that afforded them the space and support to confidently exercise the necessary judgement to achieve the objectives of the Armed Forces Compensation Scheme.

[172] R Thomas, 'Administrative Justice, Better Decisions, and Organisational Learning' [2015] *PL* 111.

the resources do not exist and which can be remedied by people appealing to tribunals. Another consideration is that there is no way of knowing for certain whether decisions are right first time because they involve the exercise of judgement, although it is possible to know when things go wrong through errors in decision letters. Tribunals are well placed to do this and identifying avoidable errors hardly seems to undermine judicial independence, although the experience of the annual reports from the president of social security tribunals was discouraging.

A quite different approach is to have deep and systemic scrutiny of decision-making. Decision-making is not just about individual decisions, but also the wider systems, processes and cultures in which they are produced. In 2021, the Northern Ireland Public Services Ombudsman published its own-initiative investigation into PIP, the disability benefit which provides people with physical or mental health conditions who have difficulties undertaking everyday tasks.[173] The process comprises initial assessment, healthcare assessment, substantive decisions, mandatory reconsideration and then tribunals. The Ombudsman found systemic maladministration throughout the decision process. A key problem was that the outsourced assessors rarely requested further evidence from claimants' healthcare professionals despite guidance requiring them to consider whether to collect such information. Assessors and decision-makers were under pressure to process claims quickly. This affected the rest of the decision-making process, leading to many claimants dropping out of the process and potentially losing their entitlements, while others proceeded through the various stages of reviews and then to tribunals. The investigation identified numerous problems, including decision-makers deferring to assessments, poor reason-giving, inadequate mandatory reconsiderations, and poor and misleading communications with claimants.

Crucially, the Ombudsman found that maladministration was built into the system and reinforced by its institutional culture, which made the systemic errors seem unexceptional and indeed necessary to officials. Decision-makers assumed that further evidence from claimants' health professionals would be gathered by claimants, even though they were told not to collect it. Alternatively, such evidence could be gathered and provided 'later on' in the process, thereby placing claimants at a systemic disadvantage. Decision-makers were focused on processing decisions on the basis of whatever information was available, even when it was clearly incomplete, and then moving on to the next claim. The burden was then placed upon claimants to keep challenging decisions throughout the process, despite them not knowing what evidence had been considered. When decisions were later overturned, the Department for Communities rationalised this on the ground that 'new' evidence had been provided that was previously unavailable. However, this 'new' evidence had often been available from the outset, but it had not collected by assessors or decision-makers. The Department argued that the high rate of allowed appeals was not evidence of incorrect initial decisions because tribunals considered 'new' evidence. By contrast, the Ombudsman concluded that this narrative

[173] Northern Ireland Public Services Ombudsman, *PIP and the Value of Further Evidence* (Belfast, NIPSO, 2021). See also R Thomas, 'The Northern Ireland Public Services Ombudsman's Report into Personal Independence Payment and Collective Administrative Justice' (2023) 30 *Journal of Social Security Law* 143 and (2024) 31 *Journal of Social Security Law* 277.

provided an inaccurate assurance to the public that the Department's decision processes were robust when they were not. This assumption had become deeply embedded within the system and accepted as an objective truth. The 'simple narrative' that there was no maladministration in the system was itself 'likely to perpetuate rather than rectify' that maladministration.[174] These assumptions were an illusion of rationality generated by the Department's own culturally determined assumptions, the pressures of its operating environment, the need to project a vision of its legitimacy and its institutional culture. The Ombudsman had exposed the flaws within the Department's purportedly 'rational' approach, which were self-serving myths that enabled it to cope with its workload and deflect criticisms of its decision-making. The Ombudsman issued 33 improvement recommendations, each of which comprised several components, most of which were accepted. It also undertook follow-up scrutiny.[175] It will take some years for the recommendations to be implemented.

No decision process had previously been subject to such deep and thorough scrutiny. The Ombudsman provided the Northern Ireland Department for Communities with something of a wake-up call. The minister concerned had been surprised to learn that such extensive problems existed when officials had assured her that all was well.

This episode suggests two wider points. First, such systemic scrutiny goes far beyond what tribunal-based feedback could ever achieve. There is a fundamental underlying difference of approach. Tribunals operate within a court-based model of autonomous law.[176] This model is based on the separation of law from politics. Law is viewed as a system of rules. Further, the focus is on procedural, not substantive, justice. This is a low-risk and court-based model. Tribunals perform a useful but limited function of deciding one appeal at a time, but they have no wider role in trying to improve decision-making systems. By contrast, the Ombudsman's intervention was a more ambitious exercise in responsive law – that is, an institutional diagnosis of systemic weaknesses accompanied by recommendations to improve administrative performance. A fundamental aspect of responsive law is that the burden of correcting errors should not fall on the individual. Instead, government bodies should be capable of correcting their own errors. The Ombudsmen was explicitly trying to get government to improve the whole process of making benefit decisions. For precisely this reason, such responsive law interventions are more high-risk than routine tribunal hearings and decisions, although they are more ambitious and more likely to identify to the underlying causes of poor decision-making.

The second and related point goes deeper to the core issue of improving decision-making, while also revealing its challenges and difficulties. Administration is not just a technical process; it is also cultural.[177] To cope with their work, officials in government interact with each other and thereby generate institutional cultures which

[174] Northern Ireland Public Services Ombudsman (n 173) 25.

[175] NIPSO, *PIP and the Value of Further Evidence: Own Initiative Follow up* (Belfast, NIPSO, 2023).

[176] P Nonet and P Selznick, *Law & Society in Transition: Toward Responsive Law* (Piscataway, NJ, Transaction Publishers, 2001).

[177] See generally WW Powell and PJ DiMaggio (eds), *The New Institutionalism in Organizational Analysis* (Chicago, University of Chicago Press, 1991); RL Jepperson and JW Meyer, *Institutional Theory: The Cultural Construction of Organizations, States and Identities* (Cambridge, Cambridge University Press, 2021).

can, in some instances, actually create and reinforce systemic maladministration and poor decision-making. Government bodies (and redress mechanisms) are also influenced by the cultures of the sectors they govern. To legitimise themselves and to manage their workloads, organisations produce their own culturally constructed myths and narratives. These myths and narratives come to be seen as a taken-for-granted objective reality, which then affect administrative behaviours. Accordingly, much of what is presented by governmental institutions as rational behaviour is, in reality, a self-interested and post hoc claim of rationality to justify their actions in an acceptable way. The myth identified by the Ombudsman was that decisions were overturned because of 'new' evidence and therefore did not indicate any initial error. However, such evidence had often been available from the outset, but it was not being requested due to caseload pressures. Instead, decision-makers viewed such evidence as something that could be considered later on in the process, even though it should have been requested earlier to get initial decisions right first time.

In short, decision-making is about not just technical procedures, but also the culture of organisations and how government operates and behaves, which is in turn influenced by the wider political, social and economic forces that bear down upon it. In some contexts, good decision-making is part of the culture within government; in other areas, institutional cultures can generate systemic problems and make them appear ordinary and even a necessary feature.

This confirms the importance of the Ombudsman's investigation into not just surface-level problems, but also the institutional culture of a system which simultaneously generates those problems and makes them invisible.[178] It also raises the challenging problem of how to improve not just the operation of the decision process, but also its culture, how officials think and behave, and their implicit assumptions. It is entirely possible for two different departments to administer the same scheme and procedures, but in very different ways, owing to the cultures that inform them. It is also inherently difficult to measure or assess positive changes in culture. Leadership, more resources and better decision-making procedures play a part. Government must also want to improve. This involves more than enhancing technical administrative procedures; it also means transforming the institutional cultures in which such procedures are used. As the Ombudsman noted, 'systemic improvement in public administration is an ongoing process and required continued focus'.[179] Only by identifying the problem can it can be addressed. Systemic scrutiny of initial decision-making has also been undertaken by other bodies, including the National Audit Office and the Chief Inspector of Borders and Immigration, although ombudsmen are more focused on the experiences of claimants as opposed to value for money criteria. The Northern Ireland Ombudsman's investigation into PIP demonstrates the need to go beyond surface-level problems and positively seek to improve decision-making in ways that tribunals cannot. Government must want to improve the quality of its decision-making and also have the capacity to do so.

[178] See also the Windrush scandal considered in ch 7 258–262.
[179] Northern Ireland Public Services Ombudsman (n 173) 19.

Automated Decision-Making

A new development has been the increasing use of artificial intelligence (AI), automation and algorithms to take administrative decisions. Digitisation and automation assume many different forms and are proceeding apace within government.[180] This includes using AI to compile information for use in making decisions and also providing reasons for decisions. AI and automation offer efficiency, speed and reduced costs. They have huge attractions for government in terms of volume-processing and quicker and more consistent decision-making. Along with online virtual hearings by tribunals, AI and automation are part of the new and unstoppable digital wave of change that is affecting and conditioning administrative justice. The big question is whether AI and automation promotes or hinders fair, correct and good-quality decision-making. Of course, government itself has been notably reluctant to open up its use of AI to critical scrutiny .

However, we can consider some instances of the use of AI. In the PIP investigation, the Northern Ireland Public Services Ombudsman found that the reasons for PIP decisions had been compiled by an electronic tool which relied on pre-populated and automated responses. This resulted in long and unwieldly sentences that were difficult to read and comprehend, and lacked personalisation to the individual claimant. The reasons for decisions were poorly recorded and explained to claimants, who were not sufficiently informed as to what evidence existed in their claim and why some pieces of evidence had been preferred over conflicting evidence. Consequently, they were not adequately informed of the reasons for decisions or to identify the evidential areas of dispute. The Ombudsman emphasised the importance of better reason-giving and caseworkers explaining how they had evaluated all relevant evidence. The proposed alternative was an electronic template designed to assist case managers to evaluate the evidence and thereby construct more individualised and comprehensible reasons in decision letters that could be reviewed by other staff for quality purposes. The Ombudsman considered this template to be a useful investment of resources to help get the decision right at the earliest point. However, the Department considered that it would incur significant resources and duplicate other measures; improved reason-giving could be achieved through training and quality checks.

Another episode of the use of AI concerned tax credit compliance checks. In 2015, the then Conservative government wanted to reduce benefit spending by undertaking fraud checks on people in receipt of tax credits.[181] HMRC contracted out tax credit compliance checks to Concentrix Ltd, a private technology company, in a £75 million contract on a payment-by-results basis. Concentrix had to deliver over a billion pounds worth of cuts. One of the main tasks of Concentrix was to uncover whether people claiming tax credits were living with an 'undisclosed partner'. If someone was claiming tax credits as a single person, but actually living with another person, then Concentrix would stop their claims on the ground of fraud. It sought to do so by querying some

[180] B McGurk and J Tomlinson, *Artificial Intelligence and Public Law* (Oxford, Hart Publishing, 2025). For evidence of current use, see the UK government's 'Algorithmic Transparency Recording Standard Hub Repository' and the Public Law Project's 'Tracking Automated Government Register'. At present, the latter appears to be much more detailed and useful. See also JUSTICE, *AI in Our Justice System* (London, JUSTICE, 2025).

[181] On tax credits, see ch 7 240–245.

1.5 million tax credit claims and identifying 100,000 cases of fraud and error. It used a data-matching tool to link up data from different sources. The data used were from third parties and included financial data from credit reference agencies. Predictive AI analytics was also used to assess potential fraud.

However, the data used were in many cases itself incorrect or had been matched improperly, leading to anomalies and flawed decisions. In Scotland, many claimants had their tax credits stopped because Concentrix claimed that they were in a relationship with a Mr RS McColl. In fact, the claimants lived in flats above a RS McColl shop, a well-known convenience shop in Scotland.[182] In England, Concentrix contacted a single mother in receipt of tax credits who it said was cohabiting with Joseph Rowntree, the nineteenth-century Quaker philanthropist who died in 1925. In fact, the woman was living in a property provided by the Joseph Rowntree Housing Trust, a housing association.[183] Claimants had been wrongly linked by Concentrix's flawed data-matching algorithm. The merest hint that a claim contained more than 'zero-risk' of fraud, error or overpayments was sufficient to prompt a compliance check. People who had their tax credits stopped were left in acute financial difficulties.

The flawed data-matching tool was not the sole problem. Concentrix staff were under pressure to open up 40–50 investigations a day and to take 20 decisions a day.[184] HMRC's contract with Concentrix operated on a 'payments by results' basis, which created a perverse financial incentive for Concentrix to terminate as many tax credit awards as possible.[185] Other failures included: official errors in decision-making; poor communications with claimants; unlawfully reversing the burden of proof so that claimants had to prove that they were not committing fraud; and slow and unreliable systems used to consider claimants' evidence. MPs were flooded with constituency cases and there was uproar about the chronic incompetence which resulted in people relying on food banks because their tax credits had been wrongly stopped.[186] Following intense parliamentary criticism and the breakdown of public trust, the government cancelled the whole programme.[187] Overall, the episode was a 'catastrophic failure'.[188] Vulnerable people had lost benefits to which they were entitled, causing hardship and indebtedness.[189]

These episodes caution against heavy reliance on AI. They also illustrate the risk of automation bias. Automation can be used to make decisions. It can also be used as a decision support tool by supplying a prompt which caseworkers then accept, reject or amend. Automation itself may embed biases, be discriminatory and lead to incorrect decisions. When used as a decision support tool, decision-makers risk placing excessive confidence in and reliance on the recommended outcomes. When combined with

[182] HC Deb 26 October 2016, vol 618, col 300 (Mhairi Black MP).
[183] 'Tax Agency Accused Mother of Living with 19th-Century Quaker' *The Times* (20 September 2016).
[184] 'People in Need at Risk of Losing Tax Credits after Being Wrongly Accused of Cheating' *The Independent* (20 February 2015).
[185] Social Security Advisory Committee (n 20) 38–39.
[186] HC Deb 14 September 2016, vol 614, cols 904–17; HC Deb 26 October 2016, vol 618, cols 285–336.
[187] House of Commons Work and Pensions Committee, *Concentrix* (HC 2016–17, 720); National Audit Office, *Investigation into HMRC's Contract with Concentrix* (HC 2016–17, 915).
[188] House of Commons Public Accounts Committee, *HMRC's Contract with Concentrix* (HC 2016–17, 727) 3.
[189] 'Tax Credit Claimants Who Suffered from Botched Concentrix Outsourcing Plan Paid Just £14 Compensation Each' *The Independent* (21 January 2018).

caseload volumes and pressures, the default position is likely to be that the AI recommended outcome becomes the default used by caseworkers.

Perhaps the largest use of AI to date is in relation to benefit fraud checks. The DWP has started using machine learning algorithms to highlight potentially fraudulent benefit claimants.[190] This involves assessing levels of fraud and error throughout the decision-making process. For the DWP, machine learning provides an additional capability in an effort to reduce fraud and error. There is a legitimate public interest here.[191] Data and predictive models are used to identify claims that are at higher risk of being incorrect and therefore require additional consideration through a targeted case review. The machine learning AI then identifies those claims at high risk of fraud. The decision whether to have a targeted case review is then taken by a caseworker. The DWP has stated that caseworkers are expected not to assume that claims flagged by the model are illegitimate; instead, caseworkers are to undertake a manual inspection of the claim history and evidence to decide whether it may contain fraud or error. The actual targeted case review itself involves an in-depth telephone interview by a DWP official who assesses the claim for incorrectness (either an overpayment or an underpayment) by considering the evidence and identifying any inconsistencies. This in itself can involve some detriment, including delay and claimant anxiety. At the same time, there is an important legitimate public interest in reducing benefit fraud. The actual substantive decision is not automated. The machine learning algorithm model is based on historical fraud and error data, which is then fed back into it.

As with all decision-making, there are error costs either way. People might receive more or less than their entitlements, whereas innocent people might be wrongly selected for a review and accused of fraud. There is also a need to reduce administrative costs by using machine learning. Machine learning can get things wrong, but the appropriate comparator is not a utopian vision of decision-making perfection; it is the errors that would otherwise normally arise by having caseworkers do all of the work. Like many issues of administrative decision-making, the assessment depends upon judgement. Nonetheless, errors and biases within automated decision-making are more likely to be systemic. They may also be hidden away with in the coding and algorithms relied upon. The DWP has said that it recognises the need for it to ensure that its system does not result in bias and poor outcomes. It has adopted measures to mitigate the risk of error: pre-launch 'fairness' analyses; a human caseworker to sign off whether to have targeted reviews; governance structures to monitor biases in the models; and adherence to guidelines and quality assurance.[192] The DWP started off with low numbers of reviews, which have since increased. A fairness assessment found minimal concerns of discrimination, unfair treatment or detrimental impact on legitimate claimants arising from the AI 'Advances' model.[193] It remains to be seen what happens with the use of automated decision-making. So far, the UK has avoided the significant systemic AI failures that have occurred elsewhere, such as the Dutch childcare benefits scandal and

[190] DWP, *Fighting Fraud in the Welfare System: Going Further* (CP 1072, 2022).

[191] 'Gang Jailed over £50m Benefit Fraud' *BBC News* (30 May 2024), www.bbc.com/news/articles/c844g4k-pjxdo.

[192] DWP, *Annual Report and Accounts 2024–25* (HC 2024–25, 995) 101–03.

[193] DWP, *Universal Credit Advances Model: Fairness Assessment* (London, DWP, 2025).

the Australian 'Robodebt' fiasco.[194] Nonetheless, there have been problems concerning automated immigration decisions.[195]

A wider overarching matter is the need for transparency and public confidence in the system irrespective of the quality of decisions. The Public Accounts Committee has emphasised the need for the DWP to be more transparent in its use of machine learning in order to support public trust in the fairness of the benefits system.[196] The Committee's view was that the DWP had not done enough to understand the impact of machine learning on benefit claimants or to provide them with confidence that it would not result in unfair decisions. The Department needed to consider explicitly the impact of machine learning on legitimate benefit claims being delayed or reduced, the number of those affected and whether it was affecting specific groups of people.

On the other hand, too much transparency could enable fraudsters to understand how the DWP is tackling fraud and thereby undermine its efforts. The Department has therefore provided some information on its use of machine learning, but has refused to reveal more on the ground that this could compromise its ability to detect fraud and error.[197] Third-sector and civil society bodies have expressed concern that the DWP has not been as transparent as it could be.[198] While an initial review found no evidence that algorithms or similar technologies were harming claimants in the welfare and social care sector, more detailed scrutiny will be required once usage increases and when evidence of injustices emerge.[199]

Overall, there is a growing and indeed unstoppable movement towards automated decision-making. It poses new challenges for administrative justice in terms of testing its quality and making it more transparent. To date, there have been relatively few judicial challenges.[200] Automation has potential gains in terms of efficiency and speed, but it also has risks, in particular poor decisions, biases and harm to affected individuals. The key issue is whether automation actually leads to better-quality decisions than those taken in the ordinary manner by caseworkers. All types of decision-making can produce errors. At the same time, there is a risk that through automation, something is lost in the process – the human nature of people's interactions with government. It is true that caseworkers working under the pressure of high workloads can themselves

[194] M Bouwmeester, 'System Failure in the Digital Welfare State: Exploring Parliamentary and Judicial Control in the Dutch Childcare Benefits Scandal' (2023) 44 *Recht der Werkelijkheid* 13; M Fenger and R Simonse, 'The Implosion of the Dutch Surveillance Welfare State' (2024) 58 *Social Policy & Administration* 264; Royal Commission into the Robodebt Scheme, *Report* (2023), https://robodebt.royalcommission.gov.au/publications/report.

[195] J Maxwell and J Tomlinson, *Experiments in Automating Immigration Systems* (Bristol, Bristol University Press, 2022).

[196] House of Commons Public Accounts Committee, *The Department for Work & Pensions Annual Report and Accounts 2022–23* (HC 2023–24, 290) 7 and 18–19.

[197] National Audit Office, *Report on Accounts: DWP* (2023) [5.8]–[5.14]; DWP, *Annual Report and Accounts 2022–23* (HC 2022–23, 1445) 101; DWP *Annual Report and Accounts 2023–24* (HC 2023–24, 62) 112.

[198] Public Law Project, *Written Evidence Submitted to the House of Commons Public Accounts Committee* (2023), https://committees.parliament.uk/writtenevidence/148287/pdf/

[199] Information Commissioner's Office, 'Blog: Addressing Concerns on the use of AI by Local Authorities' (19 January 2023), https://ico.org.uk/about-the-ico/media-centre/blog-addressing-concerns-on-the-use-of-ai-by-local-authorities.

[200] R Thomas and J Tomlinson, 'Judicial Review of AI in UK Government: Two Emergent Forms of Legal Risk' in Y-F Ng and M Groves (ed), *Automation in Governance: Theory, Practice and Problems* (Oxford, Hart Publishing, 2025).

become case-hardened, deal with people in a brusque manner and mentally slot cases into pre-established patterns without fully considering their individual circumstances. In-person interactions can enable understanding and empathy, but can also mislead decision-makers through knee-jerk reactions and cognitive biases. Automation may fundamentally change the nature of an administrative decision process from one based on personal interactions between humans to a dehumanised, depersonalised and technocratic set of interactions devoid of even the possibility of human understanding and empathy. There is wide scope for debate and scrutiny over the use of AI in decision-making. The task ahead will be for redress and scrutiny mechanisms to examine how AI works in practice and for government to be more open and transparent about its use of automated decision-making.

Conclusion

Individualised decision-making on people's entitlements – whether taken initially, on review or by tribunals – is a core task of administrative justice. The details change, but the issues endure. They comprise: how claims and applications are considered by decision-makers; the quality of initial decisions and the reasons given; whether dissatisfied claimants challenge decisions; the accessibility, effectiveness and procedures of administrative reviews and tribunals; and how to improve initial decision-making. Like much of administrative justice, decision-making is suspended between contradictory impulses. Decisions must get taken. Caseloads must be processed. Most decisions are deemed acceptable, otherwise tribunal systems would collapse. Yet, a fair proportion of decisions are of poor quality. While some people seek redress, many do not. High tribunal success rates and other evidence point to the need for better initial decisions. Government should take efforts to improve matters, but this rarely happens and this in turn reinforces the need for tribunals. While the overall system provides administrative justice for many, significant weaknesses remain. Government needs to make continual efforts to improve the quality of its decision-making. This is a perennial challenge.

5

Complaint-Handling

Another core area of administrative justice is complaints against public bodies. Complaints act as a catch-all redress mechanism for grievances not otherwise covered by tribunals. Beyond the relatively narrow category of initial appealable decisions, there is a far larger and diverse range of administrative actions and interactions people have with public services. When things go wrong and people feel aggrieved, the only practical means of redress is typically through complaints. The premise of complaints is that people are entitled to receive certain standards – in relation to public services, health-care and so on – and when those standards are not met, they can complain to the public body concerned. All complaint-handling starts at this level and the vast majority of it finishes there also. Complaints can then be escalated to either directly to an ombudsman or to an intermediate second-tier complaint-handling body and then to an ombudsman. Ombudsmen themselves only ever consider a tiny proportion of complaints compared with the volumes handled by public bodies themselves. Initial complaint-handling is then an important public service in its own right. To investigate further, this chapter examines the purpose, structure and quality of initial complaint-handling. It also considers the recent role of ombudsmen in developing complaints standards frameworks.

There are challenges in examining initial complaint-handling. The task is distributed across an enormous range of public bodies and there is no system-level data or even baselines for collecting data. The large-scale nature of the complaints landscape makes generalisation both problematic and necessary. Each public service operates its own complaint procedures which are highly conditioned by the nature of that service. It is difficult for anyone to possess complete and wide-ranging knowledge and understanding of initial complaint-handling as it is almost always encased within a protective surrounding wall of governmental impenetrability. Whereas ombudsmen's investigations and increasingly tribunal decisions are published, public bodies' complaint responses are not (like initial and administrative review decisions) published for reasons of privacy, confidentiality and volume. It is possible only to glimpse this large part of administrative justice at one remove through secondary sources, including generic reports and ombudsmen's investigations. Initial complaint-handling is a largely hidden area that is at the bottom of the redress hierarchy.[1] Yet, it is precisely this level that handles the bulk of cases.

[1] L Mulchahy, 'Sliding Scales of Justice at the End of the Century: A Cause for Complaints?' in M Harris and M Partington (eds), *Administrative Justice in the 21st Century* (Oxford, Hart Publishing, 1999) 70 ('legal scholars have paid little serious attention to complaints systems, leaving them … as something of a poor relation in mainstream public law'); J Gulland, 'Current Developments in the UK: Complaints Procedures and Ombudsmen' in M Adler (ed), *Administrative Justice in Context* (Oxford, Hart Publishing, 2010) 457.

It is difficult to know precisely the number of complaints made against public bodies, although a conservative estimate would be well over a million complaints per year.[2] Far more people use internal complaint procedures than use tribunals, the courts and ombudsmen combined. For the vast majority of people, a complaint is their only option of redress. Initial complaint-handling is therefore an aspect of administrative justice that is undertaken by and within government. Ironically, the most highly used redress mechanism – complaints – receives very limited attention in the academic literature compared with tribunals, let alone judicial review. Initial complaint-handling therefore deserves examination.

Complaints: An Overview

A complaint is commonly defined as any expression of dissatisfaction that requires a response. Complaints arise for a wide range of reasons. There is a superabundance of ways in which government bodies and public services can go wrong; virtually every aspect of the governmental process and of public services has the potential to cause injustice and dissatisfaction to people who rely upon and interact with them. Complaints arise in the context of a pre-existing interaction(s) between a person and a public body. They embody an extension and development of that relationship. Having interacted with a public body, a person then experiences a problem and lodges a complaint, thereby asking the same public body to recognise and redress that problem. The notion and culture of complaining carries a range of negative connotations.[3] It implies a degree of fault and blame that lodging an appeal and requesting an administrative review do not. Complaints can generate defensive or complacent responses. The notion of complaining can imply that a person is being difficult, awkward and likely to be a problem. Alternatively, some people may not complain about legitimate concerns precisely because they do not want to be viewed negatively and thereby potentially prejudice future relationships.

Complaint procedures are informed by – and can be evaluated against – the values of administrative justice articulated by John Milton. Complaints should be 'freely heard, deeply considered and speedily reformed'.[4] Complaint procedures should be accessible. The substance of complaints should be properly considered and accompanied by reasoned outcomes. Public bodies should also put things right. Successful complainants should be given a personal remedy for the injustice they have suffered. The underlying causes of complaints should also be remedied. Lessons should be learnt and implemented; improvements should be made for the future. These principles are fleshed out in ombudsmen's principles for remedy and of complaint-handling and, more recently, their complaint standards frameworks, which are considered below.[5]

[2] Calculating the actual figure would involve extensive data collection from an enormous number of public bodies.

[3] J Gulland, 'Taking Complaints Seriously: The Role of Informality in Complaints about Public Services' (2011) 10 *Social Policy & Society* 483, 491.

[4] J Milton, *Areopagitica* (1644).

[5] See the PHSO's *Principles for Remedy* (Appendix B) and *Principles of Good Complaint Handling* (Appendix C).

There are different models of complaint-handling which carry quite different implications. The predominant 'consumerist' model views the individual as a 'consumer' of public services as opposed to a 'citizen'. Public bodies often have standards and charters that set out what people can expect. When things go wrong, the individual is entitled to have their complaint heard and resolved. Complaints are then considered en masse as single-instance transactions to check whether public bodies have followed their service standards. This in turn provides management information within the public body which can be used to monitor its performance.[6] One concern with this model is that people's complaints about government are seen as isolated one-off instances as opposed to highlighting wider lessons for improvement. In the process, the substance of complaints become bureaucratised by being channelled into complaint procedures and processed according to the public body's own standards, thereby preserving the status quo. There is no wider democratic examination or discussion about how such services and their delivery could be fundamentally reconsidered.

An alternative model is 'complaints as systems for disruptive innovation' or as opportunities for a democratic reassessment of public services.[7] On this approach, complaints should not be seen primarily or only as mechanisms for determining whether officials have applied the rules correctly or complied with their service standards. Instead, the notion of complaint assumes a far wider importance in terms of contesting and rethinking how public services are delivered and prompting consideration of alternative and innovative approaches. A single complaint could provide the basis for understanding the perspective of a person using the service and for reassessing how public services are provided and how they could be improved. Rather than serving the narrow purposes of managerial oversight and performance, complaints can be a stimulus to innovative reforms that diagnose and address problems in order to provide an improved service. One concern with this model is that it is optimistic, even idealistic. Complainants may not want to contest the nature of public service delivery, but just secure it for themselves. Further, front-line complaint-handlers may well not possess the capability or status within a public body to use complaints as a means of disruptive improvement; that is a matter for senior staff. Public bodies may just see complaints as mere 'noise', something to be notionally ticked off, but which are in practice overlooked.

In practice, the consumerist-managerialist model of complaint-handling dominates. It has developed in response to various government initiatives, starting with the *Citizen's Charter* (1991), which was introduced to improve the performance and standards of the public sector by adopting a similar approach to complaint-handling as was adopted in the private sector. As a parliamentary committee noted, 'how complaints are handled determines the quality of the relationship between consumers and public services. The best performing organisations welcome complaints as a way of engaging consumers'.[8] One concern is that a consumerist model devalues the notion of citizenship based on the reciprocal rights and duties of the individual and the state, and the importance of

[6] J Allsop and K Jones, 'Withering the Citizen, Managing the Consumer: Complaints in Healthcare Settings' (2007) 7 *Social Policy & Society* 233.

[7] C Gill, 'Re-imaging Public-Sector Complaint Systems' *Essex Constitutional and Administrative Justice Initiative* (2 October 2018), https://essexcaji.org/2018/10/03/re-imagining-public-sector-complaint-systems.

[8] House of Commons Public Administration Select Committee, *More Complaints Please!* (HC 2013–14, 229) 3.

democratic public accountability of government. Moreover, the notion of consumerism implies that people can shop around and go elsewhere, whereas government and public services are often monopolistic and the individual has little, if any, choice. The phrases 'consumer' and 'citizen' reflect quite different conceptions of relationship between the individual and the state and of the role of complaints.

Other models exist. There is a difference between complaint-handling as regards conventional administrative functions and complaints against professionals, such as doctors, where the exercise of expert and professional judgement often arises. Another model is complaints as a means of therapeutic justice – that is, complaints provide the opportunity for positively improving the psychological well-being of complainants as well as their emotional and mental well-being.[9] This is an ambitious goal which might be achievable if there is sufficient investment in terms of resources and professional ability. To the extent that this model operates in practice, it seems to be the exception rather than the norm.

Of course, complaints have a messy reality. Some are valid; some are not. Some cluster on that nebulous borderline. Most complaints are isolated individual matters; other complaints coalesce into political campaigns brought by a whole cohort of people similarly affected. Behind every complaint, there is an individual's story and life. The consequences of some failures can be minor and can be resolved relatively quickly and easily. Other failures are banal in their origin, but have wide-ranging, harmful and sometimes tragic consequences for people. Describing an individual complaint in the bureaucratic language of service fault, maladministration or even as an injustice rarely adequately captures the impact on people.

There are various deep-seated problems with complaint-handling. A key issue concerns how many people with grievances actually complain. There are various reasons why grievances often do not become complaints: barriers to access, fatigue and scepticism about whether government bodies would listen to their complaints or that it would result in any positive difference for them. Some people may think that making a complaint might lead to them being negatively treated by that public body in the future and they fear the repercussions of complaining. Those who do complain can experience difficulties and frustrations in doing so. The complaints system is a maze; it comprises a bewildering variety of different and often relatively informal complaint-handling procedures. Public bodies may view complaints as a criticism of their inadequacies and respond defensively. Alternatively, public bodies can downplay the importance of complaints and not take them seriously. There is also the issue of the quality of complaint processes and substantive outcomes. The consumerist model of complaints has been criticised as narrow and limited. However, the reality is that initial complaint-handling may well often struggle to fulfil even the limited promise of the consumerist model, let alone the more ambitious model of complaints as disruptive innovation. Complainants can feel that they have been 'fobbed off' – that is, legitimate grievances are not properly identified and resolved, but instead closed down. Despite these problems, for most people, a complaint will be their principal, if not only, means of redress.

[9] J Williams, C Gill and C Hirst, 'Towards Therapeutic Complaints Resolution' in M Groves and A Stuhmcke (eds), *The Ombudsman in the Modern State* (Oxford, Hart Publishing, 2022) 276–86.

In 2015, the National Audit Office reported that of the 10.6 million people who had a problem using a public service in 2014, 49 per cent did not complain, whereas 36 per cent of those who did complain spent more than a year trying to resolve their problem with a local authority, care provider or school before complaining to an ombudsman.[10] More recently, a PHSO survey found that while 57 per cent of respondents stated that they would feel confident speaking up about their complaint, just under a third were worried that complaining would lead to the organisation treating them differently.[11] More than two-thirds of people did not think organisations would listen to their complaints and fewer than one-fifth of respondents thought that making a complaint would make a difference. People often lack confidence as regards both their capacity to complain and also whether it would make any difference. Around a third of respondents in recent contact with a public body within the PHSO's jurisdiction were unhappy with the public service they received. The majority of them did not complain, although this differed slightly depending on the organisation. People were more confident in knowing how to complain about the NHS than government organisations. The same factors influence whether people escalate their complaints further. A study of complaints against the DWP found that people frequently gave up on the complaints process despite not having their problem satisfactorily resolved. This reflected a strong sense that they saw no point in continuing with the process as they did not think it would achieve anything. Related concerns were that pursuing their complaints would take up too much time, effort and stress in relation to the likely outcome.[12]

People need persistence, stamina, determination and energy in order to pursue complaints. Officials within public bodies will be aware of these and other behavioural features. They can in turn deploy various tactics, whether intentionally or otherwise, to deter, deflect and close down complaints to prevent them from escalating further.[13] Public bodies may provide poor complaint responses or delay responding to complaints in the expectation that some complainants are likely to fall out of the process because their stamina has been depleted. The problems about complaint fatigue become more acute in relation to vulnerable and marginalised groups of people who lack the social capital and confidence to pursue matters. It is well recognised that vulnerable people are less likely to complain.[14] There is a particular issue concerning the lower rate of complaints made by people in adult social care compared with other types of complaints. Concerns have been raised that some care homes may unfairly (threaten to) evict residents by way of reprisal if their families make complaints – or ban or restrict visitors.[15] Public bodies can also: place formal and informal barriers and conditions on complaints; not inform people how they can complain; discourage complaints by advising potential complainants that their concerns are unlikely to go anywhere and they

[10] National Audit Office, *Public Service Markets: Putting Things Right When They Go Wrong* (HC 2014–15, 84) 4.

[11] PHSO, *PHSO Stakeholder Surveys 2021* (2021) 12.

[12] S Syrett, D Etherington, I Ekanem and P Macaulay, *Understanding the Experiences of PDCS Customers Engaged with the Formal Complaints Process* (London, DWP Research Report No 770, 2011) 34.

[13] N Lewis, M Senerviratne and S Cracknell, *Complaints Procedures in Local Government* (Sheffield, University of Sheffield, 1987) 221.

[14] PHSO, *Breaking Down the Barriers: Older People and Complaints about Health Care* (London, PHSO, 2015).

[15] Competition and Markets Authority, *Care Homes Market Study: Final Report* (London, CMA, 2017) [11.40].

will only end up wasting their time; and delay the handling of complaints so that some people may simply give up.[16]

It is impossible to know how many other people give up because they feel exhausted or because of game-playing tactics by public bodies, but it manifestly happens. People with valid grievances may not complain at all, while others with hopeless complaints may pursue them to extreme lengths, and then see the rejection of their complaints as confirmation that the system is rigged against them. Initial complaint-handling can reinforce the inequality between the individual and government because complaints are handled by the public body responsible for the problem complained of. It can be difficult for officials embedded within a wider institutional culture to consider complaints independently. Yet, it is necessary to guard any presumption that initial complaint-handling is invariably of poor quality. There is a tendency for problems and failures to cast too dark a cloud across the whole sky. There are certainly problems with initial complaint-handling and huge variations, but at the same time many people will feel that their complaints have been properly and adequately considered by a public body. Moreover, a fair proportion of complaints lodged will not be valid.

Government Policies on Complaint-Handling

Successive governments have sought to raise the profile of initial complaint-handling. The purpose of the Citizen's Charter (1991) was to make public services more accountable and responsive to their users by establishing service standards for public services.[17] If these standards were not complied with, then people could complain. Accordingly, complaint mechanisms needed to be: open and accessible; simple, speedy; fair; effective; supported by clearly displayed standards at the point of service; provide readily available information about how to complain; and provide a code of practice for handling complaints.[18] There needed to be targets for resolving complaints and clear information on further procedures if people remained dissatisfied.[19] A Complaints Task Force was established to advise on the establishment of complaint systems. When internal complaints procedures failed, there needed to be independent and external complaint routes, such as the Tax Adjudicator created in 1993, one of the various second-tier complaint-handling bodies.[20]

Some aspects of the Citizen's Charter were criticised. It was seen as introducing consumerism into public services as opposed to enhancing the constitutional and political rights of citizens.[21] Other shortcomings included: an emphasis on individual

[16] See, eg, LGSCO, *Are We Getting the Best from Children's Social Care Complaints? Focus Report: Learning Lessons from Complaints* (2015); Isle of Wight Council (19015597); West Sussex County Council (20001685).

[17] Prime Minister, *The Citizen's Charter: Raising the Standard* (Cm 1599, 1991). For a detailed account of the background, see R Lowe and H Pemberton, *The Official History of the British Civil Service: Reforming the Civil Service, Volume II: The Thatcher and Major Revolutions, 1982–97* (Abingdon, Routledge, 2020) ch 8.

[18] Complaints Task Force, *Effective Complaints Systems: Principles and Checklist* (London, Cabinet Office, 1993).

[19] ibid 42.

[20] PE Morris, 'The Revenue Adjudicator: The First Two Years' [1996] *PL* 309.

[21] A Barron and C Scott, 'The Citizen's Charter Programme' (1992) 55 *MLR* 526; I Taylor, 'Raising the Expectation Interest: New Labour and the Citizen's Charter' (1999) 14 *Public Policy and Administration* 29.

entitlements without simultaneously encouraging collective civil obligations; the absence of a legal basis; and the exposure of under-trained front-line staff to the wrath of empowered consumers.[22] Nonetheless, the programme represented an important shift in the delivery of public services by giving greater prominence to the perspective of users and in defining their entitlements to public services.[23] The Charter was credited with having 'swept away the public's deference towards the providers of public services, and their readiness to accept poor services'.[24] In some respects, the Charter was seen as innovative in terms of expanding the concept of administrative justice beyond a conventional focus on individual redress to include improving systems and standards of administration.[25] Nonetheless, the practical success of the project was limited. There had been some 'clearly identifiable benefits for the public services in handling complaints well', but little evidence that public bodies had calculated the current costs of dealing with complaints or improved their complaint-handling.[26] The Complaints Task Force recognised that it was 'extremely unlikely' that it could come forward with an all-embracing answer as to how to deal with complaints: 'public services are too varied in their nature and scope to allow such a simplistic approach'.[27] While the Citizen's Charter had promised better complaint-handling, successive ombudsman reports revealed the inadequacy of much of the redress offered by government; an unwillingness to admit fault, refusals to apologise, and failures to identify and compensate all those affected by maladministration.[28] The PHSO had sought to persuade government departments to improve their complaint procedures and their compensation to those adversely affected by maladministration, but many departments had not adopted redress practices which adequately reflected the principles of the Citizen's Charter.[29]

During the New Labour years (1997–2010), the Citizen's Charter was rebranded as 'Charter Mark'.[30] This retained the idea of standards and merged it with a culture of performance targets for public services.[31] Initial complaint-handling did not form part of the Labour government's administrative justice reforms. Curiously, the 2004 White Paper *Transforming Public Services* explicitly referenced complaints in its subtitle, but contained nothing of substance concerning complaints other than

[22] G Drewry, 'Citizen's Charters' (2005) 7 *Public Management Review* 321.

[23] House of Commons Public Administration Select Committee, *From Citizen's Charter to Public Service Guarantees: Entitlements to Public Services* (HC 2007–08, 411) [20].

[24] House of Commons Public Services Committee, *The Citizen's Charter* (HC 1996–97, 78) [20].

[25] A Page, 'The Citizen's Charter and Administrative Justice' in Harris and Partington (n 1) 85, 95–98.

[26] Cabinet Office, *The Citizen's Charter Complaints Task Force: Interim Report* (London, Cabinet Office, 1994) 14.

[27] ibid 2. See also M Blackmore, 'Complaints within Constraints: A Critical Review and Analysis of the Citizen's Charter Complaints Task Force' (1997) 12 *Public Policy and Administration* 28.

[28] House of Commons Select Committee on the Parliamentary Commissioner for Administration, *Maladministration and Redress* (HC 1994–95, 112) [1].

[29] ibid.

[30] Cabinet Office, *Service First, the New Charter Programme* (London, Cabinet Office, 1998); Cabinet Office, *How to Deal with Complaints* (London, Cabinet Office, 1999). See also M Bevir and D O'Brien, 'New Labour and the Public Sector in Britain' (2001) 61 *Public Administration Review* 535.

[31] M Barber, *Instruction to Deliver: Tony Blair, Public Services and the Challenge of Achieving Targets* (London, Politico's, 2007).

noting that they were a 'flexible and informal way of dealing with issues'.[32] So, even when administrative justice as a whole was a matter of relatively high-level government policy, initial complaint-handling was overlooked. The obvious explanation is that the Ministry of Justice was leading on tribunal reform, whereas initial complaint-handling is very much a cross-government issue. Again, governmental centrifugal forces were at work.

The NAO subsequently reported on complaints. It found that the overall 'system' of initial complaint-handling procedures was something of a sprawling, confusing, difficult-to-navigate, fragmented and complex set of constantly evolving processes that provided a poor service at a high cost.[33] There was little consistency in terms of standards and benchmarking of complaints across government. Complaint systems had developed piecemeal over time and had been rarely systematically thought about as a whole. There was also little robust data about the volume of complaints, their timeliness and outcomes. The NAO raised concerns about the accessibility of complaints; most central government departments only accepted written complaints and not those received by email or telephone. Few government departments reported trends in complaints to their management board. There were limited processes for learning from complaints and ensuring that the underlying causes of grievances could be addressed or resolved.

The NAO emphasised that government could make savings by reviewing the practices that generated complaints and by improving the quality of services. There could also be closer alignment of complaints and appeals, more systematic collection of data on complaints and greater importance accorded to the views of complainants on the handling of their complaints. Comparatively little real progress was made with any of this.[34] For instance, it would certainly be worthwhile and important for the Cabinet Office to take a strategic lead over complaint-handling across government, and this would help benefit and improve many people's lives. However, the reality is that complaint-handling is one of many low-priority administrative matters with little, if any, political pay-off. Moreover, significant improvements to complaint-handling involve years of work and hard slog to coordinate a hugely disparate set of public sector complaint systems. There are also the typical issues of the intrinsically departmental nature of central government and the risk of a 'one-size-fits-all' approach. However, the Cabinet Office did establish the Cross-Government Complaints Forum, composed of complaints managers from central government, to share experience and good practice. The Forum met three times a year. Little is known about its work and any outcomes or changes that occurred as a result. The Forum's obscurity suggests its relatively limited role and influence.[35]

During the Coalition government (2010–15), there were negligible efforts to improve complaint-handling. The 2011 *Open Public Services* White Paper was

[32] Department for Constitutional Affairs, *Transforming Public Services: Complaints, Redress, and Tribunals* (Cm 6243, 2004) [3.5].

[33] National Audit Office, *Citizen Redress: What Citizens Can Do if Things Go Wrong with Public Services* (HC 2004–05, 21); P Dunleavy, S Bastow, J Tinkler, S Goldchluk and E Towers, 'Joining up Citizen Redress in UK Government' in Adler (n 1).

[34] House of Commons Public Administration Select Committee, *When Citizens Complain* (HC 2007–08, 409).

[35] Public Administration Select Committee (n 8) [51]–[52].

principally concerned with reforming public services by opening them up to competition, although it did also consider complaint-handling. [36] The government had a fundamental responsibility to ensure the provision of high-quality, accessible public services, including healthcare, education and policing, although a new approach to delivering public services was urgently needed. The old centralised approach to public service delivery had broken down. Too many public services were still operated on the basis of top-down prescription and centralisation that elevated bureaucratic imperatives above the needs of service users, while damaging the public service ethos by continually second-guessing highly trained professionals.[37] While many public services were of good quality, in too many places, the quality of services had not kept up with either the expectations of citizens or the aspirations of public sector professionals. Consequently, the answer was to ensure that everyone could access the best public services by opening up such services to competition and increased choice by ensuring fair access to public services provided by a range of different providers. In doing so, public services would be more accountable to their users and taxpayers. Public services needed to be responsive to the people they served and held to account by citizens and their elected representatives. There would be clear mechanisms of accountability to ensure that commissioned services would be held accountable through a combination of mutually reinforcing choice, voice and transparency mechanisms. In addition to setting standards, people could seek redress about the quality of services if a choice of services was unavailable or if standards were not good enough. The government would provide the most appropriate means of redress for each service area and in particular make the most effective use of ombudsmen.

The then PHSO, Julie Mellor, responded by emphasising the need for government to modernise the ombudsman service by adopting a modern legislative framework and making the ombudsman more accessible: 'Open public services must go hand in hand with a more open ombudsman service.'[38] Mellor's enthusiasm contrasted with the more pessimistic view of her predecessor, Ann Abraham. For Abraham, the proposals in the 2011 White Paper had been 'ill-informed and muddled'; the emerging picture was that the government improperly envisaged the ombudsman acting as an advocate for its choice agenda, thereby shifting the PHSO away from its long-established function of being an independent and impartial complaints investigator.[39] In any event, the White Paper's focus on the ombudsman concealed a glaring omission: the relative paucity of any discussion of initial complaint-handling. Complaints can only be escalated to ombudsmen once initial complaint procedures have been exhausted. Indeed, there was an inherent contradiction in the White Paper by advocating improved and open public services, while largely overlooking the role of initial complaint mechanisms as a public service in their own right. Furthermore, the White Paper was entirely lacking in detail as to how improved redress against external providers would be secured and

[36] HM Government, *Open Public Services White Paper* (Cm 8145, 2011).

[37] ibid [1.9].

[38] PHSO, *Responsive and Accountable? The Ombudsman's Review of Complaint Handling by Government Departments and Public Organisations 2011–12* (HC 2010–12, 799) 30.

[39] A Abraham, 'Making Sense of the Muddle: The Ombudsman and Administrative Justice, 2002–2011' (2012) 34 *Journal of Social Welfare and Family Law* 91, 94.

how government would monitor the quality of complaint mechanisms. It is difficult to identify any discernible improvements to initial complaint-handling that occurred as a result. The vague and generalised promise of providing 'for each service area, the most appropriate means of redress' amounted to next to nothing. On the contrary, the 2011 White Paper was issued against the backdrop of austerity, which weakened both public services and also complaint-handling.

Overall, while these high-level government documents are important in terms of framing the wider relationship between the individual and the state, there is little to suggest that they have positively impacted upon initial complaint-handling. It is all too easy for such intent to become deflected when implementation rests with parts of government and public services at the coal-face that lack the resources and energy to improve complaint-handling.

The Complaints Pyramid

Once people do decide to complain, the next issue is then precisely to whom and how. This in turn raises the issue as to how complaint procedures are structured and how complaints can be escalated. One way of trying to understand this is to view the overall complaints systems as a pyramid. Figure 5.1 provides a simplified version of the more complex and intricate reality.

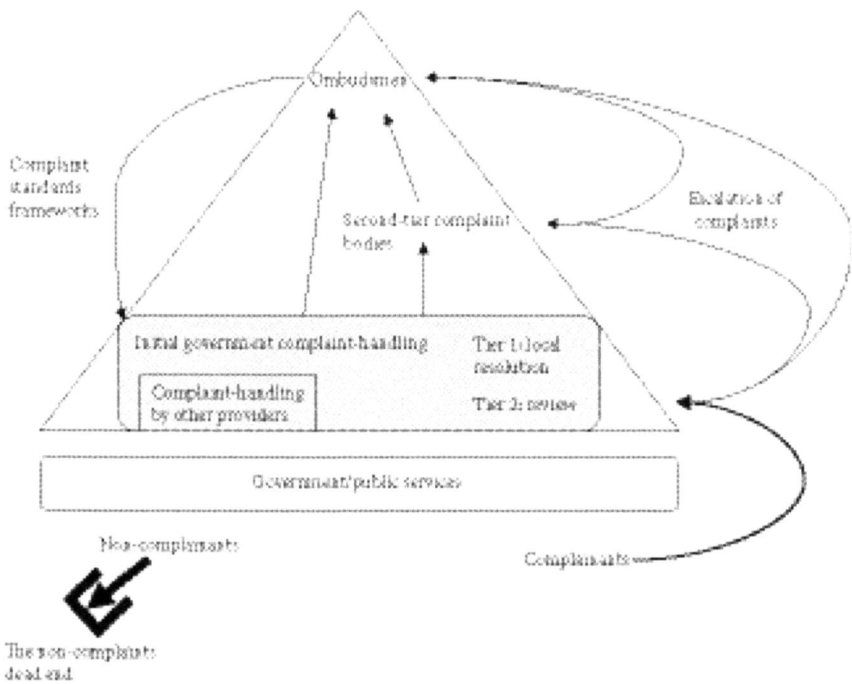

Figure 5.1 The complaints pyramid

The pyramidal structure has both horizontal and vertical differentiation. There is considerable fragmentation within governmental structures. Each public body has its own complaint process and this is often at the level of the specific service concerned. While generalisation is risky, there are nonetheless some common features. Complaints are considered initially by the public body that provided the service and is responsible for generating their grievance. This could be a central government department, a local authority, some other public service delivery body, or a private or voluntary sector body which has been commissioned to provide the particular service. These providers are responsible for managing complaints about their own services – as opposed to the government body that commissions and outsources these services. There is then an enormous multitude of different complaint-handlers located within government and other public bodies which span multiple domains. Large administrative systems – tax, benefits and immigration – have their own back-office complaint-handling. In other bodies, complaints may be considered by a member of front-line non-specialist staff or by a complaints manager. The largest central government complaint systems include: tax (75,000 complaints per year); NHS England (200,000 complaints per year); immigration (39,000 complaints in 2021 and 70,000 pieces of correspondence from MPs); and social security/benefits (20,000 complaints per year). Another large area of complaints is local government services, which have sometimes involved three stages of internal complaint-handling.

A two-stage complaints process is now more widespread. This involves stage 1 – initial complaints are resolved through local resolution by the particular service area responsible – and then stage 2 – a review by another official. However, practice varies though. For instance, complaints against schools are initially considered by the school concerned. Those dissatisfied can then seek a review by the Department for Education.

In most cases, the handling of initial complaints by the relevant public body marks the end of the road; dissatisfied people can then escalate matters to an ombudsman. However, in some areas – mostly central government high-volume contexts – second-tier complaint-handling bodies have been established. They include: the Independent Case Examiner (for social security and child support complaints) and the Tax Adjudicator.[40] There is also the Independent Complaints Reviewer (complaints about HM Land Registry) and the Independent Complaints Assessors (who review complaints made against the Department for Transport). These intermediate second-tier complaint handlers are appointed, staffed and funded by their parent government department, and have been established within particular contexts as and when the perceived need has arisen. They are largely separate from government. In practice, they have relative autonomy to decide complaints, although they are not independent ombudsmen. Following the Windrush scandal, the Home Office established a second-tier independent case examiner for immigration complaints, the Office for the Independent Examiner of Complaints, although, despite its title, it does not investigate complaints in the same way as the Tax Adjudicator or the Independent Case Examiner; it reviews whether the initial handling of complaints has been in line with

[40] R Thomas, 'Benefit Complaints: A Critical Analysis' (2022) 44 *Journal of Social Welfare and Family Law* 258, 264–66; The Adjudicator's Office, *Annual Report* (2023).

procedures and guidance.[41] There is a significant difference between investigating complaints afresh and merely reviewing whether relevant procedures and guidance had been applied properly.

Such second-tier complaint-handling bodies come with both pros and cons. Having an intermediate level of complaint resolution can avoid the costs and lengthy delays associated with the more formal and lengthy investigations by the PHSO. On the other hand, if second-tier bodies do not properly resolve complaints, then they simply add to the length of the process. The risk is that second-tier complaint-handlers may become infected by the same dysfunctions which afflict initial complaint-handling, in particular a processing mentality. This can increase the need for escalating complaints to the PHSO, but that in itself comes with the additional delays involved in exhausting the second-tier complaint stage and the risk of complainants giving up at that stage. Further, access to the PHSO is only through the MP filter. On the other hand, second-tier complaint handlers have, on the whole, demonstrated their independence, competence and effectiveness. As specialist bodies, they have built up their expertise in how the relevant government department operates and its behaviours. They have adopted the position of being an informed observer of the relevant department which can independently handle complaints as well as having a close relationship with the department and thereby being able to recommend service improvements by providing valuable insights from their complaints casework. The Tax Adjudicator and the Independent Case Examiner both have a relatively good reputation for handling complaints and prompting improvements by government.

After someone has received a complaint outcome – whether initially from the public body and/or from a second-tier complaints body – the matter can potentially be escalated to an ombudsman. Ombudsmen sit at the top of the hierarchy and provide the only fully independent means of considering complaints. Ombudsmen can typically be accessed only once the complainant has exhausted all prior avenues and they are the final stage for complaints to be considered. Only a very small proportion of complaints get this far. However, matters are more nuanced than this. For instance, the Local Government and Social Care Ombudsman (LGSCO) investigates more complaints against local government and more quickly than the PHSO does in relation to complaints against central government.

Various points flow from this. The complaints 'system' then is not really an overall system, but a highly diverse dispersed collection of various specific complaint processes. Complaints are at the extreme end of an already strong tendency within administrative justice for a decentralised and fragmented approach. They are not and indeed cannot be organised through an overarching top-down cross-government framework in the same way as tribunals. Instead, they are organised through the specific public service and public body concerned. Complaint procedures are, on the whole, non-statutory and informal. The few exceptions include health, social care, and children and young people's services.[42]

[41] Home Office, 'Make a Complaint to the Independent Examiner of Complaints' (2024), gov.uk/guidance/make-a-complaint-to-the-independent-examiner-of-complaints.

[42] Children Act 1989 Representations Procedure (England) Regulations, SI 2006/1738; Local Authority Social Services and National Health Service Complaints (England) Regulations, SI 2009/309.

Initial complaint-handling is 'owned' – both institutionally and culturally – by the government department or public body concerned. A long-standing and unresolved concern with initial complaint procedures is that they cannot be considered effective unless they are regarded as reliable and fair. The handling of complaints by public bodies can deter many people because they lack confidence and trust in that body and therefore also its complaint procedures. The concern is most acute in sensitive areas. For instance, there is a long-standing concern about immigration complaints against the Home Office being considered by the Home Office and the variable quality of its complaint-handling.[43] The wider sentiment is, to some extent, pervasive in all contexts. Unsurprisingly, no government body has agreed to hand over the entire volume of complaints to an entirely independent body. There are arguments against this in terms of the complaint-handling function becoming detached from service delivery and becoming too formal and time-consuming, and complaint responses becoming less likely to be acted upon. However, there are obvious risks. Of course, this is why ombudsmen and second-tier complaint-handlers have been established.

The complaints landscape is complex and confusing, although people do not need to understand the overall landscape. What they do need is to be signposted directly to an accessible and effective complaint system for their individual grievances. However, from the perspective of complainants, the overall system may seem less like a pyramid and more of a maze which they need to navigate through with care.[44] Certain complaints may fall into gaps in the system. Complainants may go down various dead ends. They may be referred from one body to another and have to go through various procedural hoops. The maze-like structure can itself discourage some people from pursuing matters.

A related feature is that complaint processes are in a seemingly perpetual state of flux. The fragmented and constantly changing structures of initial complaint-handling reflect how government and public services in general are organised and reorganised. Complaint procedures are regularly overhauled across many contexts, including healthcare, immigration and benefits, in response to problems in those areas and as a result of wider systemic failures. Until the early 2010s, the DWP had an internal three-stage complaints structure, which was then reduced to two stages and was then replaced with a single stage in which complaints were triaged with priority given to those most in need.[45] In 2019, the Environment Agency moved to a two-stage complaints process to include an independent review stage for the most complex of cases.[46] Alternatively, complaint procedures will be refreshed, although whether this amounts to be anything more than a cosmetic change is often debateable. A further point is that the operation of complaint systems will vary depending on the pressures within that public body, in

[43] House of Commons Home Affairs Committee, *Immigration and Nationality Department of the Home Office* (HC 1984–85, 277) [8]–[10]; Independent Chief Inspector of Borders and Immigration, *An Inspection of the Handling of Complaints and MP's Correspondence by the Home Office Borders, Immigration and Citizenship System (BICS)* (London, ICIBI, 2020).

[44] LGSCO, 'The Complaints Maze', flickr.com/photos/110744519@N03; PHSO, *Responsive and Accountable? The Ombudsman's Review of Complaint Handling by Government Departments and Public Organisations 2011–12* (HC 2012, 799) 6.

[45] National Audit Office, *Department for Work and Pensions: Handling Customer Complaints* (HC 2007–08, 995).

[46] Environment Agency, *Annual Report and Accounts 2020–21* (HC 2021–22, 768) 52.

particular complaint volumes and caseloads and other pressures. Complaint systems have sometimes developed piecemeal over time in response to external pressures and internal forces within their particular contexts.

There are also various non-institutionalised complaint mechanisms, such as the media. One is 'going to *The Guardian*', a quick means by which individual and wider injustices can get attention and put direct pressure on government to reconsider. Prominent examples include people's immigration problems and Windrush.[47] In 2024, *The Guardian* investigated carer's allowance and the DWP's heavy-handed enforcement action towards unpaid carers looking after elderly or disabled relatives. Many carers had been required to repay large sums of money for minor breaches of the earnings rules, resulting in indebtedness and criminal prosecutions.[48] The DWP had warned those affected that their fines could increase if they appealed to a tribunal.[49] This then prompted scrutiny by the NAO, select committees and an internal review by the DWP itself.[50] Of course, the role of the media depends on the newsworthiness of a particular story, but it has, on occasion, proved to be a quick and effective means of highlighting a particular issue, putting a matter on the news agenda and getting government to respond.

What is the Quality of Complaint-Handling?

The quality of complaint-handling is a crucial determinant of its adequacy. From the perspective of complainants, the quality of complaint-handling is often intrinsically related to outcomes. There are challenges in trying to assess the quality of complaint-handling, given its scale and fragmented nature. The practices of initial complaint-handling are often hidden away and not easily accessible. The quality of complaint-handling varies from one context to another and within each context. Moreover, the poor handling of complaints is more likely to lead to criticism than the good handling of complaints is likely to win praise. This illustrates the general negativity bias of administrative justice.

However, we can consider what evidence there is. Broadly speaking, there are two models of complaint-handling which are relevant here. At one end of the spectrum is a 'quality and learning' model. Complaints are considered by trained and competent staff in a thorough, fair and timely way. Outcomes are evidence-based, fair, acknowledge failings and put things right. Complaints are seen as a valuable source of learning about how people experience public services, what has gone wrong and what needs to

[47] 'Woman Told to Leave UK Despite Court Ruling She Has Right to Live with Family' *The Guardian* (15 February 2024); 'Home Office U-Turn Lets Woman Stay in UK with Husband and Son' *The Guardian* (10 May 2024); A Gentleman, *The Windrush Betrayal: Exposing the Hostile Environment* (London, Faber, 2019); 'HMRC Admits 71% Wrongly Targeted in Child Benefit Fraud Crackdown' *The Guardian* (13 January 2026).

[48] 'Carers Threatened with Prosecution over Minor Breaches of UK Benefit Rules' *The Guardian* (7 April 2024); P Butler and J Halliday, '"Something Has Gone Very Wrong": How the Carers Scandal was Exposed' *The Guardian* (24 May 2025).

[49] 'DWP Warns Carers They Could Face Greater Penalties if They Appeal against Fines' *The Guardian* (17 April 2024).

[50] National Audit Office, *Carer's Allowance* (HC 2024–25, 377); L Sayce, *Independent Review of Carer's Allowance Overpayments* (London, DWP, 2025).

improve. Senior leaders then analyse complaint outcomes to improve services. Effective complaint-handling is part of the wider endeavour to deliver public services that are transparent, responsive, effective, accountable and focused on improvement. At the other end of the spectrum is the 'groundhog day' model.[51] The public body views complaints negatively. A blame culture means that complaints are responded to defensively, thereby preventing them from being seen as a source of learning. Complaint outcomes are of variable or poor quality – for instance, by not properly considering the complainant's concerns or through a failure or an unwillingness to acknowledge mistakes and problems. The public body's understanding of its own handling of complaints is inadequate. Senior leaders do not value the feedback from complaints or from front-line operational staff. This retreatist approach alienates complainants, thereby compounding their concerns and reducing trust in government.

The location of any particular complaint process on this spectrum varies. Given the size and scale of many complaint systems, any particular system is likely to straddle across various gradations of the spectrum. Moreover, complaint-handling is not an isolated task. It reflects wider features of a public body: its vision, culture, political context, behaviours, governance and leadership, The quality of complaint-handling is often a barometer of the public body's wider culture, operations and the nature of the services it provides.

The evidence available on the quality of complaint-handling suggests considerable variation. In 2008, the Public Administration Select Committee was disturbed that second-tier complaint reviewers had raised concerns about the poor standard of initial complaint-handling, which suggested systemic weaknesses.[52] In 2014, the Committee found some 'encouraging signs of increased attention on good complaints handling' within parts of government, but overall it concluded that government as a whole could not 'be said to be complying with best practice in complaints handling or adapting to the needs and expectations of today's citizens'.[53] MPs themselves have a relatively informed position on which to comment about complaint-handing. They are often the last resort for constituents who have a complaint about a public service. They are 'frequently confronted by people in deep distress, suffering intense pain or loss, and who may be at the end of their tether'.[54] The Committee explained that many people who complain do so for most altruistic reasons – not to punish or to gain something for themselves, but to try to ensure that the same experience they have suffered is not experienced by others. They want the system, and the people within it and who lead it, to learn and to benefit from their experience. The Committee further noted that 'all too frequently, complaints are greeted by a management who are defensive, even legalistic, and who see complaints as a hostile criticism, rather than as an opportunity to learn from failure'.[55] To embrace a positive agenda for complaint-handling was both a challenge and an opportunity for every organisation that serves the public, but particularly in public services.

[51] PSOW, *Ending Groundhog Day: Lessons from Poor Complaint Handling* (Pencoed, PSOW, 2016).

[52] House of Commons Public Administration Select Committee, *When Citizens Complain* (HC 2007–08, 409) [48].

[53] Public Administration Select Committee (n 8) 3.

[54] ibid.

[55] ibid.

While ombudsmen only see a small proportion of initial complaints, they have a good vantage point to make informed assessments. The PHSO has often highlighted the variable quality of complaint-handling. In 1994, it noted that 'there are some areas where it is done quite well; there are other areas where complaints are handled abysmally'.[56] A more recent assessment identified various recurrent problems: not adequately involving complainants in the process; delays; not applying complaint guidelines and policies properly; incomplete, unhelpful or confusing responses to complaints; failing to consider all of the issues raised in a complaint; poor record-keeping and decision-making on complaints; public bodies not apologising properly and not doing enough to put things right or providing sufficient financial remedy; and not learning from mistakes.[57] HMCTS and the Home Office have, at times, not considered complaints properly. Following two investigations into delays by the Rural Payments Agency, the PHSO ended up knowing more about the Agency's handling of complaints than it did.[58]

The PHSO's report into the decision-making of the Driver and Vehicle Licensing Agency (DVLA) about whether people with certain medical conditions are safe to drive found that many people were unfairly prevented from driving for several years as a result of flawed decisions.[59] Problems included delays, poor communications, the quality of information provided, flawed decisions and poor complaint-handling, leading to distress and loss of earnings. The DVLA's complaint-handling had been defensive and had failed to recognise when things had gone wrong. It had not properly considered the impact of its actions on affected people, issued very few consolatory or financial loss payments and had not learnt from complaints. Similarly, HS2 has failed properly to engage and communicate with complainants concerning the sale of their family home to make way for the train line. Instead, it has been dishonest, misleading and inconsistent, and has failed to follow its own processes, causing complainants severe stress and worry for years.[60] Tick-box responses to complaints illustrate an attitude of viewing them as a 'nuisance'.[61]

The quality of immigration complaint-handling has long been a matter of concern. The problems reflect the Home Office's long history of dysfunctionality, backlogs and systemic flaws.[62] In 2021, the PHSO found that the Home Office had wrongly decided

[56] House of Commons Select Committee on the Parliamentary Commissioner for Administration, *Report of the Parliamentary Ombudsman for 1994* (HC 1994–95, 394) [12] (William Reid, PHSO 1990–96).

[57] PHSO, *Responsive and Accountable? The Ombudsman's Review of Complaint Handling by Government Departments and Public Organisations* (HC 2011–12, 799); *Complaints about UK Government Departments and Agencies and Other UK Public Organisations 2016–17* (2017).

[58] House of Commons Public Administration Select Committee, *Oral Evidence: Complaints: Do They Make a Difference?* (HC 2013–14, 229) Q115, 11 June 2013 (Julie Mellor, PHSO).

[59] PHSO, *Driven to Despair: How Drivers Have Been Let Down by the Driver and Vehicle Licensing Agency* (HC 2016–17, 660).

[60] PHSO, *Report on an Investigation into Complaints about High Speed Two Limited* (HC 2015–16, 620) and *An Investigation into HS2's Failure to Communicate with a Family about Acquiring Their Home* (HC 2021–22, 211); E Malnick, 'HS2 Showed a Lack of Respect for Residents, Ombudsman Warns' *Sunday Telegraph* (3 April 2022).

[61] T Markson, 'Government Departments "See Complaints as a Nuisance"' *Civil Service World* (30 May 2022), www.civilserviceworld.com/news/article/government-departments-see-complaints-as-nuisance.

[62] R Thomas, *Administrative Law in Action: Immigration Administration* (Oxford, Hart Publishing, 2022).

that a Windrush man who had lived lawfully in the UK for 50 years did not have immigration status in the UK and then told him that he was to be deported.[63] The man had spent years trying to prove his status, which was exacerbated by flawed decision-making, poor record-keeping and missed opportunities to put things right. The Home Office's handling of the man's complaint had suffered from significant and unexplained delays, failed to investigate fully and respond to all of the issues raised in the complaint, and also failed to take account of the widely publicised Windrush scandal caused by the Home Office's own failings. The department has also failed to acknowledge the impact of its errors on the man's life.

The Public Services Ombudsman for Wales has similarly reported on various instances of poor complaint-handling which amount to public bodies 'going through the motions' of considering complaints.[64] Recurrent problems with complaint-handling have included inadequate investigation of complaints and complaint procedures that do not precisely prescribe how investigations should be carried out, with the consequence that important aspects are missed out. There have been delays in considering complaints, such as not responding to a complaint for 18 months. Complaint responses have sometimes been incomplete or contained information for which there was no supporting evidence or was actually contradicted by the documents provided.

The LGSCO has regularly highlighted weaknesses in local government complaint systems, including: not informing people or signposting them to complaint processes; inadequate responses to complaints; responses that do not address all of the concerns raised in a complaint; not providing an effective remedy or apology; and not correctly following prescribed statutory complaint procedures for children's services complaints.[65] Some local authorities have maintained that their complaint-handling processes for children's social care complaints were in line with those of other local authorities when, in fact, they contravened statutory guidance.[66] Delays in handling complaints have been a common problem. One council should have responded to both first-stage and second-stage complaints within 10 working days, but actually took three months to respond to each stage respectively.[67] Another council took more than two years to respond to a children's services complaint, despite assuring the LGSCO three times that it would investigate.[68] In 2015, the LGSCO found that, on average, people spent nine months trying to resolve their complaint with a local authority. Furthermore, 43 per cent of people were not advised by councils that they could refer their complaint to the ombudsman.[69] According to the Equality and Human Rights Commission, some councils have taken up to two years before reaching a resolution on social care complaints; some complaints have only been resolved months after the individual concerned had died. Such timescales undermine the purpose of using formal complaint processes to

[63] PHSO, *An Investigation into UK Visas and Immigration's Handling of Windrush Man's Status* (2021).
[64] PSOW (n 51).
[65] LGSCO, London Borough of Lewisham (16003985); LGSCO, West Sussex County Council (20001685).
[66] LGSCO, Worcestershire County Council (12009203).
[67] LGSCO, Westminster City Council (19018657).
[68] LGSCO, Derbyshire County Council (13001686).
[69] LGSCO, *Review of Local Government Complaints 2014–15* (2015).

resolve urgent issues for people in crisis or at the end of their life. Some legal professionals have advised people not to complain, but to use judicial review instead.[70]

In 2023, the LGSCO uncovered a backlog of 170 unanswered complaints concerning children's services and special educational needs and disabilities provision which had accumulated as a result of low staffing levels and high workloads.[71] The LGSCO expressed concern about the potential for significant ongoing injustice to many other children until the council could address this backlog. Other problems identified by the LGSCO have included poor responses to complaints that do not give any or sufficient analysis or weighing up of the issues or reasons to explain the complaint outcomes reached, and investigations that concentrate on the public body's procedures and processes, but do not examine the impact of failings on complainants or consider the potential remedy in respect of the fault found.[72]

In 2022, the LGSCO reviewed Liverpool City Council's complaint-handling procedures as part of a wider review by government-appointed commissioners brought in to oversee the council's performance. The LGSCO found some good practice and clear intentions to improve, although this was more the result of individual officers taking the initiative as opposed to a coherent, coordinated approach to handling complaints. Senior leaders had limited oversight of complaint-handling. Nonetheless, the council responded positively to the review and demonstrated a willingness and ability to change.[73] In its own-initiative investigation into PIP, the Northern Ireland Public Services Ombudsman found that complaints about the assessments undertaken by the outsourced provider, Capita, were received by the Department for Communities, but were then forwarded to Capita for responses. The Department did not itself undertake any independent investigation of the complaints and relied entirely upon assurances from Capita that complaints had been investigated and addressed. While learning from complaints could, if properly done, be a powerful means of improving public services and building trust, the Ombudsman found that the way in which complaints were handled had the opposite effect of reducing people's trust and prompting them to disengage from the process.[74]

Another major area of complaints is the NHS. There has been a whole series of scandals in which health and care services have collapsed and health bodies have failed to hear and properly consider the complaints of patients and their families. Such scandals have included Mid Staffordshire Hospital, in which systemic failures led to poor patient care and premature deaths.[75] There have been other shocking NHS

[70] Equality and Human Rights Commission, *Challenging Adult Social Care Decisions in England and Wales* (London, EHRC, 2021) 15. See also J Gulland, 'Administrative Justice and Austerity: The Case of Disputes About Adult Social Care' in S Cowan and S Halliday (eds), *Socio-legal Generation: Essays in Honour of Michael Adler* (London, Palgrave Macmillan, 2024).

[71] LGSCO, 'Ombudsman Investigation Reveals 170 Delayed Complaints in Kent' (2023); Kent County Council (22003403).

[72] LGSCO, Dudley Metropolitan Borough Council (17016386) [24]; LGSCO, Sheffield City Council (18004957).

[73] LGSCO, *External Review of Liverpool City Council's Complaints Procedures by the Local Government and Social Care Ombudsman* (2022); LGSCO, 'Ombudsman Encouraged by Liverpool's Response to Complaints Review' (27 July 2023).

[74] NIPSO, *PIP and the Value of Further Evidence* (Belfast, NIPSO, 2021) 23.

[75] Mid Staffordshire NHS Foundation Trust Public Inquiry Chaired by Robert Francis QC, *Report of the Mid Staffordshire NHS Foundation Trust Public Inquiry* (HC 2012–13, 947).

failures in which poor complaint-handling was part of a larger picture of inadequate care for patients. The independent review of maternity services at the Shrewsbury and Telford Hospital NHS Trust uncovered a litany of failures: families experiencing pregnancies ending with stillbirth, newborn brain damage and the deaths of both babies and mothers. The review also identified poor responses to complaints, including inaccurate information, with the Trust justifying its actions or omissions in care, and in some cases including explanations that laid blame on the families themselves. There was both a lack of senior oversight and input into complaint-handling and patient experience and a lack of openness and transparency in the handling of complaints.[76] In 2013, the then PHSO, Julie Mellor, described NHS complaint-handling as a 'toxic cocktail' resulting from the combined combination of reluctance of patients and families to express their concerns or complain, a defensiveness on the part of hospitals and staff to hear and address concerns, and lost opportunities to learn and improve care.[77]

It is important not to assume that initial complaint-handling is invariably of low quality. A large and fragmented complaints system can simultaneously produce both good and poor-quality complaint responses. Ombudsmen have, on occasion, highlighted improvements with initial complaint-handling. In 2012, the PHSO commended various government bodies for adopting a 'mix of hands-on leadership from senior managers, careful planning by staff and hard work to tackle complaints'.[78] The DWP had used specially trained complaints resolution managers to handle complaints.[79] HMRC's reputation for customer service and complaint-handling has improved as a result of an internal focus to raise standards. Nonetheless, there is ample evidence that complaint-handling is highly variable and sometimes, if not often, of low quality.

Poor-quality and defensive complaint-handling has obvious negative consequences. It compounds and exacerbates the sense of injustice that prompted people to complain in the first place. Many complainants may simply give up, become alienated and revert back into the complaints dead end. Some escalate their complaints further, which brings about its own costs in terms of entering and navigating a further part of the complaints maze, with the delay and uncertainty that this involves. Poor handling of complaints means there will be no opportunity for the public body to use the complaint to learn lessons and potentially to improve public services. It also has wider effects by alienating people and reducing public trust in government.

Why does poor complaint-handling happen? Complaint-handling is a form of problem-solving: an individual has a complaint which requires investigation and a response as to whether or not their grievance has merit. If so, then the issue of an appropriate remedy arises – for instance, an apology and financial redress. Effective complaint-handling is often a skilled job that is informed by the wider culture and ethos of an organisation. It depends in part upon the willingness of a public body to be open

[76] *Independent Review of Maternity Services at the Shrewsbury and Telford Hospital NHS Trust* (HC 2021–22, 1219).

[77] Public Administration Select Committee (n 8) [4].

[78] PHSO, *Responsive and Accountable? The Ombudsman's Review of Complaint Handling by Government Departments and Public Organisations 2011–12* (HC 2012–13, 799) 27.

[79] ibid.

to scrutiny and to understand the real-life impacts of its systems and procedures on individuals. Good and effective complaint-handling, like taking good-quality decisions, requires skill, expertise, empathy, and an understanding of administrative operations and public services and the human consequences. A public body can have all the right policies and procedures in place, but without the right culture, support, resources, expertise, leadership and other related factors, it is likely that complaint-handling will be suboptimal.

Individual complaint-handling is principally focused on the immediate concerns raised by the complainant, but it can also raise wider lessons about how services are being delivered. The public's experience of public services provides insights that can then be used to learn and to improve the delivery of services. When policies are being devised and services are being designed, it is virtually impossible to anticipate and cater for all the many variables which influence and determine how front-line operational delivery works in practice. In large administrative systems, it is often very difficult for senior leaders to have a deep understanding about what is happening at the front line, assuming that they are interested in this. Consequently, complaints provide a rich and free source of information about people's experiences, how policies are being implemented and how services are being delivered, and the unintended consequences. They can be used as part of an early warning system to identify problems that might otherwise stay unseen or before they escalate.

In practice, complaint systems are beset with inherent tensions. Complainants want matters resolved quickly and efficiently, but excessive speed can dilute the quality of complaint-handling. On the other hand, more formal procedures take more time and are likely to come across as being fixated on process at the expense of sorting matters out. There are also practical pressures, such as an increase in the number of complaints, which will lead to backlogs and delays, and corresponding moves to speed up the process and/or filtering mechanisms. Public bodies may triage the most serious cases and people most in need, but there is no guarantee that such mechanisms will always work effectively. There is a constant risk of complaints falling through gaps or being met with defensive reactions.

There are many ways in which initial complaint-handling can go wrong and many inter-related reasons why this happens. This question is often inseparable from the underlying generic causes of the faulty administrative behaviours that generate the grievances which then develop into complaints. Initial complaint-handling is likely to be infected by precisely the same tensions that inform the work of public bodies themselves. Casework organisations such as the DWP and the Home Office impose performance targets on complaints staff, thereby leading to a focus on clearing the volume of complaints and an adherence to process. Any complaints process should always have in mind that an individual complaint may be symptomatic of wider systemic problems, but it takes additional time and effort to make these connections and for data to be collated.

Another factor is, at a basic level, the power imbalance between a person and government. It is difficult to overestimate the potential for officials to have knee-jerk reactions against people perceived to be 'difficult'. Wherever there are power imbalances between an individual and an official, there is the potential for abuse and for poor complaint-handling. The LGSCO has criticised councils for allowing complaints to be considered by the same officer responsible for the matter complained of and for only having one stage in their complaints process.[80]

Complaint-handling is typically a low-priority function in terms of the development of its expertise and professionalism. Within large organisations, complaints staff will work within their own silos as well as the wider culture of the public body. Complaint-handling teams are often 'service backwaters with poorly qualified staff and managers, located on the periphery of organisations', which attract little attention from senior management.[81] Such teams may well feel and be poorly equipped to handle complaints. They may receive little training or assistance, despite the nature of the serious and complex issues they have to deal with. The consequence is often that pressure is placed on complaints staff, inevitably resulting in poor experiences for complainants. While complaint-handling should be recognised a distinct professional skill, it is rarely viewed as such in practice. Complaint-handling staff may not possess sufficient authority, respect or status within their organisations to make negative findings against other staff. Complaint-handling can become too process-focused and operate as another bureaucratic procedure that fails to see matters from the perspective of complainants and prioritises process over substance. With little direct contact with complainants, complaints staff will simply see case files and documents, and will lack the insight into how people are affected by administrative behaviours.

The high turnover of staff within public bodies is another factor. From the outside, it might seem that public bodies can build up their experience and expertise in specific tasks, such as complaint-handling, over time. However, the reality is often that staff turnover weakens institutional expertise and memory. There are also the effects of repeated exposure to the same or similar types of complaints. This can, over time, have a numbing effect and make officials case-hardened. Accordingly, the all-important informal and implicit criteria for complaints to succeed can become increasingly elevated over time. In order for a complaint to be upheld, an individual's case may have to demonstrate something above the norm, despite the normal run of cases providing evidence of faulty administration. This 'normalising of maladministration' has been a feature of many areas, such as immigration delays.

The handling of complaints can also be affected or predetermined by higher-level policy decisions. Such ministerial steers and 'lines to take' have occasionally been revealed. For instance, a DWP minister approved the blanket refusal of providing financial compensation in response to complaints from people who had been underpaid benefits as a result of the Department's flawed transfer of disability claimants to a new benefit scheme.[82] The PHSO found that this blanket approach contravened both the PHSO's and the Department's guidance that each complaint be considered on its own merits. It is not known how many other such ministerial policy steers exist.

[80] LGSCO, Calderdale Metropolitan Borough Council (19005195) [67]–[70]: 'the Council is not using the one chance it gives itself to carry out a proper investigation of complaints. Everybody makes mistakes, it is how a council deals with its mistakes that matter'.

[81] Dunleavy et al (n 33) 447.

[82] PHSO, *An Investigation into the Department for Work and Pensions' Handling of the Ms U's Migration to Employment and Support Allowance* (HC 2021–22, 856) [18]. The DWP also incorrectly advised the woman that she could not complain further to the Independent Case Examiner and did not inform her about the PHSO (at [22]). See further ch 7 at 253–254.

There is also scope for muddle and confusion for complainants in terms of which redress route to pursue. For instance, the Independent Case Examiner has often encountered tribunal records which show that the judge had suggested to someone that they need to complain to the DWP (and then potentially the Independent Case Examiner itself) to seek redress for an administrative or service failure as the tribunal is unable to do so. Some cases have required input from both a tribunal and the Independent Case Examiner to be fully resolved. This has resulted in some people being surprised to learn that while a tribunal judge acknowledges that errors have arisen as a result of the claimant being given incorrect advice from the DWP, the tribunal cannot resolve the matter as it can only apply the relevant rules.[83] Conversely, the Independent Case Examiner can investigate complaints, but cannot determine a person's benefit entitlements. Another feature is the need for some people to escalate a problem to the second-tier complaint handler when it could have been properly resolved earlier. For instance, the DWP has recognised that it is at fault, but it denies any injustice has been caused as a result or it offers a small consolatory payment. The claimant then pursues the matter further to the Independent Case Examiner, which then awards a higher payment.

There can be other behaviours. In many instances, the poor handling of complaints will be just one weakness amongst many within the relevant service. If a local authority team is under-resourced for the volume of work it has to deal with, this can lead to fault and injustice for the people concerned. In turn, considering the complaints that arise will generate additional work. Complaints about delays can themselves be delayed and so on. The handling of complaints will often reflect and indeed reinforce wider structural problems. Poor complaint-handling is often an extension of the initial faulty administration or public service, and all administrative systems and public services have their own pathologies.

The financial position of local government has been hit particularly hard and this has clearly affected its services and complaint-handling.[84] In 2021, the LGSCO has expressed concern about the diminished status of council complaints services and the 'general erosion of the visibility, capacity, and status of complaint functions within councils'.[85] Engaging with the public and their complaints needed to be central to running a healthy and effective democratic organisation, but it had 'fallen off the agenda'.[86] Complaints escalated to the LGSCO have increasingly concerned not just one-off errors, but also more systemic and policy issues, reflecting the gap between people's legal entitlements and what councils can deliver. The pandemic exposed pre-existing fault-lines and created additional pressures.[87] The adoption of stringent and harsh policies, in the immigration and benefit contexts, has provided another context in which complaints are made.

[83] Independent Case Examiner, *Annual Report 2024–25* (London, DWP, ICE, 2025) 5, 14–17.

[84] LGSCO (n 69) 1.

[85] LGSCO, *Review of Local Government Complaints 2020–21* (2021) 4.

[86] J Hill, 'Michael King: "Listening to Public Complaints Has Fallen off the Agenda"' *Local Government Chronicle* (20 July 2021).

[87] LGSCO, *Unprecedented Pressure: Learning from Complaints about Council and Care Provider Actions during the COVID-19 Pandemic* (Coventry, LGSCO, 2022).

Similarly, the PHSO has identified various core weaknesses with central government and NHS complaints systems.[88] First, there is no single vision for how complaint-handling staff are expected to undertake their task. Different public bodies have their own view on what constitutes good or best practice. This leads to a lack of clarity about the best way of handling and resolving complaints, and variable experiences for complainants. Second, complaints staff are not given consistent access to training to support them in what is a complex role and which should be recognised as a professional skill. When staff do receive training, its quality and consistency is variable. Third, public bodies often view complaints negatively rather than as a learning tool to improve their services. This often leaves complaints staff feeling that they are not valued or supported by senior leaders in their organisation and lacking the resources to carry out their role effectively. Fourth, there is the influence of organisational culture, which conditions how complaints are handled. Public bodies may lapse into viewing complaints in negative and defensive terms rather than as a learning tool to be used to improve their services. There is a wider trend of government viewing complaints as a nuisance has arisen because of a 'leadership deficit' within government, which erodes public trust.[89]

What then are the experiences of people who do complain? There is limited evidence on this issue, but what information exists suggests that people's satisfaction levels are often low. Many university students who complained to their university and then to the Adjudicator for Higher Education felt disappointed, let down, angry, emotionally drained, exhausted, discriminated against, depressed, sad and victimised.[90] Research into the DWP's complaints found that a major source of dissatisfaction was complaints that remained unresolved or inadequately dealt with.[91] People's views of their experience are, to a large extent, influenced by outcomes. At the same time, complaining is often an inherently negative experience irrespective of the outcome. If a complaint is upheld, then this will confirm that the person had a legitimate grievance and often they will have a concern about the delays involved in resolving it. If a complainant is not upheld, then this may be seen as a refusal by the public body to recognise its error. People's dissatisfaction with complaints and their consequent negative attitudes towards the public body are then carried over into and inform their subsequent dealings with both the specific body as well as other public services.

Concerns about the quality of complaint-handling are reflected and reinforced by the variable quality of complaints data collected by government. It is not just the case that little is known publicly about initial complaint-handling; government bodies themselves often possess only a limited and fragmentary knowledge and oversight of their own complaints systems. Complaints data is important in terms of transparency from government about its operations. Complaints can also be used as part of a wider early warning system to detect structural problems by linking up data on complaints with other data to flag and fix wider systemic issues before they escalate into major problems,

[88] PHSO, *Making Complaints Count: Supporting Complaints Handling in the NHS and UK Government Departments* (HC 2019–21, 390) 8.

[89] Markson (n 61).

[90] D Price and A Laybourne, *Student Satisfaction with the Office of the Independent Adjudicator for Higher Education Report of the OIA Student Survey 2009* (London, King's College London, 2009) 79.

[91] Syrett et al (n 12).

as highlighted by the Windrush Lessons Learned Report.[92] In 2005, the NAO recommended that government collect more data on complaint-handling.[93] However, several years later, it was found that some government bodies do not collect the most basic data on complaints. The DWP and the Home Office only started collecting data on complaint outcomes in 2020. Practice elsewhere within government is variable. The Department for Education (DfE) does not hold any central information about its complaints.[94] No individual or team in the Department has overall responsibility for all complaints received by the Department. Instead, there are at least 16 teams within the DfE that are responsible for reviewing complaints by schools. Each team has its own method for handling complaints and recording data. Complaint-handling is not only fragmented between different government bodies, but also within them. By contrast, HMRC has much better data and understanding of its complaint-handling and has become more responsive to systemic recommendations made by the Tax Adjudicator, the second-tier complaints body.

At the same time, what data that does exist may rebut any presumption that complaint systems are invariably rigged against complainants. Consider two large areas of central government administration: immigration and social security. Over the years 2020–23, the volume of immigration complaints fluctuated from almost 15,000 in 2020 to over 52,000 in 2023. The proportion of immigration complaints upheld/partially upheld was between 28 per cent and 47 per cent.[95] Figure 5.2 shows the number of benefit complaints handled by the DWP and the outcomes. The proportion of complaints fully or partly upheld – ranging from 41 per cent to 55 per cent – indicates that the DWP does not simply reject complaints. However, the complaints landscape is so large and diverse that generalisation is impossible. Both good and poor practice is evident.

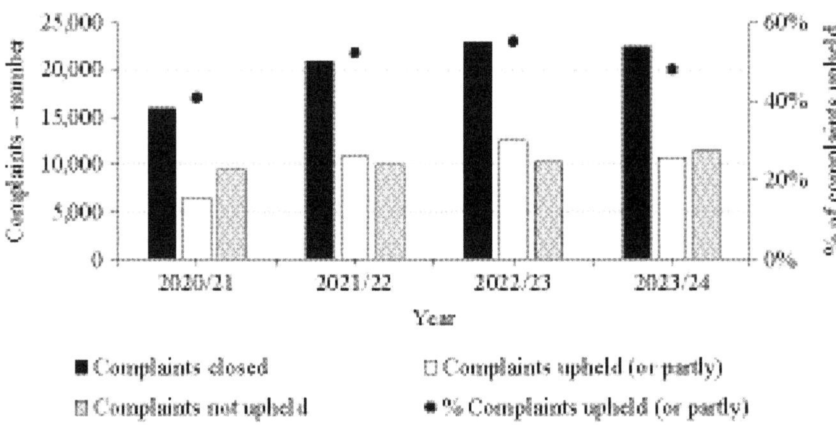

Figure 5.2 The number of benefit complaints handled by the DWP, the outcomes and the percentage of upheld complaints, 2020–24. Source: Freedom of information (FOI) responses from the DWP

[92] W Williams, *Windrush Lessons Learned Review* (HC 2019–21, 93) 147-148.
[93] National Audit Office (n 34) 15.
[94] Department for Education, FOI Response (FOI 2021/0037200, 13 August 2021).
[95] Home Office, FOI Response 1204/05180, 2 July 2024.

We should also consider what remedies people receive and whether complaint-handling is used to improve systems and services. According to cross-government guidance, 'public sector organisations should seek to learn from their complaints. If an internal or external review, or a PHSO investigation, shows there are systemic faults, defective systems or procedures should be overhauled and corrected'.[96] It is a false economy and poor administrative practice to deal with complaints individuals and not to address their underlying cause.

What happens in practice? This is an enormously wide question for which there is limited evidence and on which more research is required, but consider the DWP. In 2022–23, it received over 22,000 complaints and made 11,169 *ex gratia* financial payments totalling £1.2 million.[97] This suggests some recognition of complaints, although no further data were available. The Independent Case Examiner issues service improvement 'observations' to the DWP.[98] For instance, there was a misunderstanding of the difference between 'parental responsibility' and 'legal parentage', particularly in relation to same-sex couples dealing with the DWP's Child Maintenance Service. The DWP then updated its guidance and communicated this to its staff. The DWP has provided some information about its responses to such observations and has noted that learning from complaints is a key priority. Overall, there is a lack of data and understanding about the impact of initial complaint-handling and what happens within government.

A final point – and one that applies to administrative justice redress more broadly – concerns the different perspectives of government and the individual, and the challenges that arise for people when services and redress are fragmented across multiple domains. Both government and redress processes are highly differentiated. There are many different government departments, public bodies and public services, each of which operates its own different redress processes and systems which are separate and isolated from each other. From an administrative perspective, this seems natural and makes sense. However, things are different from the perspective of the individual. The same person or family interacts with a variety of different administrative systems and public services, each of which operates differently and which are, at best, weakly coordinated with each other. They can lack the advice and support needed to navigate this maze. A person may have a number of different problems with various public bodies concerning matters such as benefits, local services and schools. Matters often become more complex for families, such as those with a child with disabilities. They may experience challenges in trying to access services from a range of different public bodies, including special educational needs and disabilities (councils, schools, hospitals, social care, the police etc), school transport (a different part of the same council), disability benefits (the DWP), home adaptations (another part of the same council) and so on. A similar complexity arises for older people concerning adult social care – both funding and the provision of care, mental capacity and so on.

There are real challenges for people when dealing with public bodies, chasing them up and working to their procedures and timescales; it can easily become a full-time

[96] HM Treasury, *Managing Public Money* (London, HM Treasury, 2023) 145.

[97] DWP, *Annual Report and Accounts 2022–23* (HC 2023–24, 1455) 61. This amounted to an average of £93 for each complainant.

[98] Thomas (n 40) 270; Independent Case Examiner (n 83) 35–37.

job for the most able person, parent or carer. The problems are inevitably more significant for people who already experience social and economic disadvantage and/or are in vulnerable circumstances. In such 'clustered injustices', both the legal process and administrative justice redress do not necessarily assist, but can actually create, reinforce and exacerbate the problems that people experience.[99] People can end up juggling a multitude of problems and deal with a number of different public bodies. Inevitably, the stresses and strains will become too much even for the most patient of people, who can then be seen as 'difficult' by the public bodies concerned, thereby prompting indifference or retaliatory action. The end result often seems like a world of organisational dysfunction and deep frustration for individuals and families who struggle to navigate multiple different public services and redress systems.

The chances of public services being entirely reorganised to make them more person-centred are exceedingly remote, although some smaller-scale improvements are possible. These would include more advice and assistance services for people. It is better for people to have more personal interactions with public bodies through help and support services, as opposed to formal online or written interactions. This could help prevent problems from escalating into formal complaints and resolve complaints more effectively when they do arise.

Ombudsmen and Complaint Standards

The preceding discussion suggests the following points. There is no effective cross-government coordination of complaints and, consequently, there is a lack of strategic vision.[100] There is a real need to improve the handling of complaints and this has to be taken forward by government and public services themselves, although external support and assistance would help in this respect. What then of the role of ombudsman in relation to overseeing and improving complaint-handling by public bodies?

The LGSCO has long issued guidance on complaint-handling and also trained local authority officers.[101] It publishes annual reviews of local government complaints and focus reports on specific sectoral areas, and also sends annual letters to each English local authority highlighting the key issues for them to address. By contrast, while the PHSO has published many reports on complaint-handling since 2000, it has typically played little role in informing government thinking on complaint-handling, but has instead focused on its own investigations of complaints, thereby confirming its previously limited role.[102]

In recent years, all ombudsmen have taken a proactive role by developing complaint standards frameworks. This involves ombudsmen setting standards for initial complaint-handling and then encouraging and requiring public bodies to adopt those standards in order to improve and monitor the quality of their complaint-handling.

[99] L Clements, *Clustered Injustice and the Level Green* (London, Legal Action Group, 2020). See also L Clements and AL Aiello, *Unacceptable Delay: Complaints Procedures for Disabled Children and Their Families* (Leeds, University of Leeds, 2019).

[100] National Audit Office (n 33).

[101] LGSCO, *Effective Complaint Handling for Local Authorities* (Coventry, LGSCO, 2020).

[102] Dunleavy et al (n 33) 442.

The purpose is to ensure that initial complaint systems meet the needs of the public and to raise their quality and consistency. This should then produce earlier and better outcomes for complainants and thereby also reduce demands on ombudsmen. Devolved ombudsmen have been at the forefront of the endeavour. The pioneer has been the Scottish Public Services Ombudsman (SPSO), which has the most developed complaint standards framework scheme. All of the devolved ombudsmen now have their own statutory complaint standards frameworks.[103] The PHSO has developed a non-statutory scheme.[104]

Each complaints standards framework broadly works as follows. The ombudsman consults on and then publishes a set of complaints-handling principles and devises a model complaint-handling procedure. Different models are adopted for different purposes. For instance, there are specific complaint-handling procedures as sector-specific complaint standards, such as for higher education, the NHS, social work, and registered social landlords. The ombudsman then monitors how public bodies apply the standards in practice and collects data. The whole endeavour is informed by joint and collaborative working by ombudsmen with public bodies comprising support, training and guidance to encourage good practice. These types of collaborative interactions are typical of the approach of ombudsmen. Devolved ombudsmen can also undertake more formal interventions to address poor performance by a public body, including potentially issuing a declaration of non-compliance, thereby drawing the matter to the attention to the relevant devolved legislature.[105] At the core of complaint standards frameworks is getting public bodies to embed principles and procedures of good complaint-handling.

The complaint standards principles adopted are broadly similar. For the Public Services Ombudsman for Wales (PSOW), complaint procedures should be complainant-focused, simple, fair and objective, timely and effective, accountable, and committed to continuous improvement.[106] For the SPSO, an effective complaint-handling procedure needs to be user-focused, accessible, simple and timely, thorough, proportionate and consistent, objective, impartial and fair, and should seek early resolution and deliver improvement.[107] The Northern Ireland Public Services Ombudsman's principles are: start off right, fix it early, focus on what matters, be fair and honest, and learn and improve.[108] For the PHSO, an effective complaints scheme should promote a learning culture, welcome complaints in a positive way, be thorough and fair, and give fair and accountable responses.[109] The development of complaint standards frameworks represents an extension of the role of ombudsmen beyond their core function of investigating complaints themselves. The whole package is described as the ombudsman's role as a 'Complaints Standards Authority', the purpose of which is to drive improvement in public services and complaint-handling.

[103] Scottish Public Services Ombudsman Act 2002, ss 16A–G; Public Services Ombudsman Act (Northern Ireland) 2016, ss 34–42; Public Services Ombudsman (Wales) Act 2019, ss 36–41.

[104] PHSO, *UK Complaint Standards: Summary of Expectations* (Manchester, PHSO, 2022).

[105] SPSO, *Support and Intervention Policy* (Edinburgh, SPSO, nd).

[106] PSOW, *Complaints Standards Authority – Wales Complaint Handling Processes – Statement of Principles* (Pencoed, PSOW, 2019).

[107] SPSO, *SPSO Statement of Complaints Handling Principles* (Edinburgh, SPSO, 2011).

[108] NIPSO, *Draft Model Complaints Handling Procedure: The Complaints Handling Process* (Belfast, NIPSO, 2022).

[109] PHSO, *UK Central Government Complaint Standards: Summary of Expectations* (Manchester, PHSO, 2022).

Another important aspect is the analysis of complaints data by ombudsmen. The Scottish complaint standards framework requires public bodies to collect and report on a range of key performance indicators: complaints received; the number and proportion of complaints closed within timescales; the average time to provide full responses; and complaint outcomes.[110] The SPSO has a small improvement, standards and engagement unit that works with public service providers to improve standards of complaint-handling.

The complaints standards work of ombudsmen is in its early days. It is widely recognised that the task of improving complaint-handling will be a long-term endeavour. The devolved ombudsmen have more formal and, in some respects, more advanced frameworks than the LGSCO and the PHSO. The LGSCO provides training for council staff. It has also collaborated with the Housing Ombudsman on the Joint Complaint Handling Code as regards complaints concerning social housing providers (which include local councils and other providers).[111] The position as regards the PHSO is different again. Conventionally, the PHSO would only investigate complaints once when they had been escalated to it, although since the late 2000s, the PHSO has published reports on the quality of initial complaint-handling. The PHSO has personally raised such matters with relevant senior staff within government. The draft Public Services Ombudsman Bill 2016 proposed that a reformed single public services ombudsman would have its own statutory complaint standards powers, although the powers proposed were limited to the provision of information, advice and training.[112] By contrast, devolved ombudsmen can monitor compliance by public bodies with complaint standards frameworks, demand information, publicise failings and issue declarations of non-compliance. As the 2016 Bill did not progress, the PHSO adopted its own non-statutory complaint standards scheme.[113]

It is too early to make an authoritative assessment concerning the impact and effectiveness of complaint standards frameworks, although the following points can be made. First, given their accumulated experience, ombudsmen occupy a good position from which to develop complaint standards. There are limits to what can be achieved. Ombudsmen could never seek to redesign initial complaints by, for instance, recommending the establishment of independent statutory complaint systems separate from the public bodies concerned. Ombudsmen are essentially working within the system as it is and are trying to improve what is already there, as opposed to promoting wholesale radical reform. Nonetheless, this is valuable work. Making complaint standards frameworks work in practice involves much more than issuing principles and frameworks; it also involves all the behind-the-scenes work, informal discussions, encouragement and persuasion – the type of soft skills that ombudsmen possess and which can be more effective than strict legal enforcement.

[110] SPSO, *Complaints Indicators Key Performance for the Model Complaints Handling Procedures* (Edinburgh, SPSO, 2022).

[111] Social Housing (Regulation) Act 2023; LGSCO and Housing Ombudsman, *Joint Complaint Handling Code* (Coventry, LGSCO, 2023).

[112] Cabinet Office, *Draft Public Services Ombudsman Bill 2016* (Cm 9374, 2016).

[113] PHSO, *Complaint Standards Framework: Summary of Core Expectations for NHS Organisations and Staff* (Manchester, PHSO, 2022); PHSO, *UK Central Government Complaint Standards: Summary of Expectations* (Manchester, PHSO, 2022).

Second, it remains to be seen how effectively ombudsmen can monitor the operation of complaint standards in practice. The complaint standards function is characterised by the familiar problem of the differentials in power and knowledge that characterise the relationship between those doing the regulating and those being regulated. Ombudsmen are relatively small bodies, whereas public bodies are more numerous, larger and more powerful. The SPSO's Complaints Improvement Framework works on the basis of self-assessment by public bodies of their complaint-handling.[114] The SPSO's support and interventions are focused on auditing an organisation's complaint responses, although this is only likely to occur following the escalation of problems. The other conventional way in which ombudsmen become aware of problems in the handling of initial complaints is through complaints that are escalated to them.

Third, there is evidence about the beneficial effects of complaint standards frameworks. An initial study of the Scottish scheme found that local authorities had fully complied with adopting the new complaint-handling procedures and that their staff recognised that the overall project had definite advantages.[115] There were clear signs of cultural changes, with councils recognising complaints as a source of information to drive improvements. There were also benefits for councils in terms of enabling them to compare their performance and analysing data to better understand how complaints operate and how they could be improved. This tends to confirm that the benefits of complaint standards frameworks far outweigh the relatively minimal costs involved. In 2023, the DWP adopted a new quality framework for its complaint-handling, across the majority of its service delivery areas. This aligned with the PHSO's complaint standards. The DWP also committed to working closely with the PHSO and other government departments to embed those standards.[116] In other respects, there is limited provision by which ombudsmen can examine complaints handled by a public body; instead, they rely on self-assessment by public bodies. The devolved ombudsman can potentially audit an organisation's complaint responses if necessary.

Fourth, complaint standards frameworks will develop and mature over time. Ombudsmen can refine and develop their complaint frameworks and how they are implemented in practice. More detailed data could be collected to analyse how initial complaints are operating in practice. Ombudsman have sought to avoid standardisation. There is a risk that complaint standards frameworks could function as a symbolic validation mechanism that public bodies can use to defend themselves without necessarily fulfilling those standards in practice. Perhaps the most substantial challenge will be for the PHSO in terms of size and scale, as illustrated by problems with healthcare complaints and complaint-handling by the DWP and the Home Office. Ombudsmen have often argued for the need to improve the culture of complaint-handling and leadership. And therein lies the challenge. Publishing complaint standards is one thing; changing the culture of complaint-handling is quite another. While public bodies can formally align their policies and procedures with complaint standards, differences of

[114] SPSO, *SPSO Complaints Improvement Framework* (Edinburgh, SPSO, 2017).

[115] T Mullen, C Gill and N Vivian, *Scotland's Model Complaint Handling Procedures: Exploring Recent Developments and the Usefulness of Complaint Data for Administrative Justice Research* (Glasgow, University of Glasgow, 2017).

[116] DWP, *Quality Framework* (London, DWP, 2023).

substance may remain. The real test of the whole effort will likely come when initial governmental enthusiasm wears off and the hard grind kicks in. The devolved ombudsmen benefit from the relative closeness and smallness of their jurisdictions, as well as their greater capacity to encourage and promote best practice. By contrast, the PHSO is unique in that it deals with UK central government complaints and large systems (immigration, benefits and healthcare). There is a significant challenge seeking to get central government not just on board with complaints standards, but also to implement them effectively. There are endemic problems in health complaint systems which have proved to be quite resistant to change. Overall, the development of complaint standards frameworks is a positive development. It is necessary to see how what now happens in practice.

The development of complaint standards frameworks by ombudsmen raises a wider question. Could this lead to a fundamental shift in the role of ombudsmen, perhaps even supplanting their traditional role of investigating complaints? The Scottish Crerar Report (2007) recommended the development of complaint standards frameworks by ombudsmen. It also recommended that the role of the Scottish ombudsman be refocused away from investigating complaints and towards inspecting or regulating initial complaint-handling by public bodies.[117] On this approach, ombudsmen would either altogether relinquish their own complaint-investigation role or they would only investigate complaints when public bodies could not demonstrate sufficient robustness in their own complaint-handling. Ombudsmen would investigate complaints about complaints rather than undertake their own substantive investigations.

However, this recommendation was rejected and for good reason. It was based on a misconception of the ombudsman institution as being just another part of the wider scrutiny and inspection landscape, as opposed to being a distinct constitutional office grounded in administrative justice redress that investigates complaints and recommends personal remedies and service improvements. This was a dangerous moment for the SPSO, which could have been substantially weakened as an ombudsman.[118]

Just because ombudsmen create and monitor complaint standard frameworks to improve initial complaint-handling, it does mean that their traditional core complaint-investigation function should be abolished or significantly curtailed. Doing so would significantly reduce redress for complainants. Ombudsmen would also inevitably lose the expertise and insight gained from their complaints casework, which in turn enables them to establish and oversee complaints standard frameworks. It is unrealistic to expect

[117] L Crerar, *The Crerar Review: The Report of the Independent Review of Regulation, Audit, Inspection and Complaints Handling of Public Services in Scotland* (Edinburgh, Scottish Government, 2007) [11.18] (which recommended that the SPSO have responsibility for developing and overseeing complaints standards, but should no longer have responsibility for investigating and making final decisions on cases, as complaints would be resolved by public bodies – unless they could not demonstrate sufficient robustness or failed to adhere to complaints standards processes). See also C Harlow, 'Ombudsmen: "Hunting Lions" or "Swatting Flies"' in M Hertogh and R Kirkham (eds) *Research Handbook on the Ombudsman* (Cheltenham, Edward Elgar, 2018) 73, 88–89 (ombudsmen should be limited to investigating complaints about complaints and only retain an investigatory own-initiative function).

[118] *cf* C Gill, 'The Evolving Role of the Ombudsman: A Conceptual and Constitutional Analysis of the "Scottish Solution" to Administrative Justice' [2014] *PL* 662, 672 and 680: 'Had Crerar's recommendations been fulfilled, Scotland would effectively have retained an ombudsman in name only, replaced with what would have become a regulator for public service complaints … This was a near miss for Scotland, which came close to losing its ombudsman.'

government and public services to undertake the same type of thorough investigation of complaints as ombudsmen and thereby to have the final say on individual complaints. Ombudsmen are the only fully independent complaint-handling bodies. Even with complaint standards frameworks, there will always be many instances of maladministration and service failure for ombudsmen to investigate when initial complaints have not been properly considered by public bodies. There is a superabundance of evidence for this to be found in virtually every complaint upheld by ombudsmen. They have an important role to play in developing the standards of maladministration and publicly holding government to account in a way that does not happen with initial complaint-handling. Ombudsmen publish their complaint decisions; public bodies do not. Moreover, it cannot be assumed that the trajectory of initial complaint-handling is necessarily one of continual improvement. On the contrary, the quality of complaint-handling varies considerably both within government and over time.

Even specialist second-tier complaint-handling bodies at best merely reduce the need to escalate complaints to ombudsmen. The point applies to routine complaints and even more so as regards more systemic ombudsmen investigations. The Independent Case Examiner, for instance, lacks the type of institutional independence, strength and capability required to undertake substantial investigations affecting large numbers of people, such as the PHSO's big investigations into the DWP.[119] The Independent Case Examiner does not have the legal powers to access government documents. While the quality of initial complaint-handling should be improved, there will always be a need for ombudsmen to perform their core role of investigating complaints.

Conclusion

For many people with grievances with a public body, initial complaint-handling will, in practice, be their first and often only step on the redress ladder. Complaint-handling procedures handle vastly more grievances than all other redress mechanisms combined. While there are pockets of good practice, it is difficult to be positive about initial complaint-handling. Alongside the considerable volumes of complaints, there is a fragmented and uncoordinated landscape which produces outcomes of variable quality. It is not just the volume that dilutes the quality, but also the pressures on complaints staff. Initial complaint-handling is also a very largely unexplored area. There is a need for more research into complaint-handling and the views and experiences of complaints. It is ironic that complaints – the most frequently used redress mechanism – have received relatively little attention. The work of ombudsmen to establish complaint standards is important and necessary, although it remains to be seen what happens in the longer term. However, ombudsmen also have other core roles – investigating individual complaints and also identifying ways of improving administration and public services – which will be examined in the next chapter.

[119] See ch 6 195–212.

6

Ombudsmen

This chapter examines ombudsmen and their role and contribution to administrative justice. Ombudsmen investigate complaints of maladministration. They evaluate the quality of administration that people experience and recommend ways to improve public services. Since ombudsmen were introduced in the late 1960s, the tasks of government and public services delivery have become much more complex. There have also been changes in the makeup, needs and expectations of society. Ombudsmen likewise have evolved and have assumed related functions, such as own-initiative powers and complaint standards. The ombudsman is something of a 'chameleon' institution that adapts to different changing contexts.[1] To explore their work, this chapter examines: the handling of routine complaints by ombudsmen; the principles of good administration; the big investigations undertaken by the PHSO and its working relationships with government and Parliament; the impact of ombudsmen on government; and own-initiative powers of investigation. The focus is principally on the work of the PHSO and the LGSCO, although the discussion includes coverage of other UK ombudsmen.

Individual Complaint-Handling

The core daily task of ombudsmen is handling individual complaints. An aggrieved person, having exhausted a public body's internal complaint procedures, remains dissatisfied. Ombudsmen provide independent and external investigation, although they cannot accept all complaints for investigation. Whereas tribunals can only hear appeals against specific administrative decisions, ombudsmen have a wider jurisdiction; they investigate complaints concerning all types of administrative (in)actions and public service delivery. At the same time, while tribunals hear all appeals they receive,[2] ombudsmen exercise significant discretion about which complaints they decide to investigate.[3] Managing demand is undertaken through various formal and informal filters: jurisdictional limits; time limits; alternative remedies; the merits of complaints and their substance; whether a complaint is ready for an ombudsman investigation; and whether

[1] R Kirkham, 'The Ombud as a Chameleon' in M Hertogh, R Kirkham, R Thomas and J Tomlinson (eds), *The Oxford Handbook of Administrative Justice* (Oxford, Oxford University Press, 2022) 89.

[2] So long as such appeals are within the tribunal's jurisdiction and lodged within the time limit.

[3] See, eg, Parliamentary Commissioner Act 1967, s 5(1) and 5(5); Public Services Ombudsman Act (Northern Ireland) 2016, s 5. This is analogous to the permission stage in judicial review proceedings.

an investigation would be worthwhile given the resources involved. While ombudsmen should provide an accessible, independent and effective redress, they have never had and will never have the resources and capacity to investigate all the complaints they receive. For instance, the LGSCO has increasingly focused on complaints with the greatest public interest and ability to lead to wider changes to improve services rather than just trying to resolve large volumes of low-level transactional complaints.[4] Similarly, the PHSO undertakes significant filtering of complaints. On a daily basis, ombudsmen make difficult decisions about which complaints to investigate. Their other functions – complaint-standards functions, big investigations and own-initiative investigations – are, in turn, conditioned by how ombudsmen handle and prioritise routine complaints.

There is, of course, an additional hurdle in relation to the PHSO's 'parliamentary' jurisdiction concerning central government: the MP filter. Recommended by the Whyatt Report as a temporary mechanism, the MP filter has persisted despite extensive criticism that it is iniquitous and limits access to the PHSO. Around 10 per cent of MPs do not refer any complaints to the PHSO.[5] Moreover, some complainants do not want to involve their MP. Despite a broad consensus for a dual-track approach – by which people could complain directly or through their MP – successive governments have resisted reform on the ground that, without the filter, MPs would lose touch with their constituents' concerns and increased complaint volumes would require additional resources for the PHSO.[6] Removal of the MP filter would widen access to a larger number of complaints, although it would likely involve more filtering by the PHSO itself.[7] There are additional hurdles in some specific contexts. For instance, the PHSO receives investigates relatively few benefit complaints relative to the scale of the benefits system. This is attributable not just to the low level of initial complaints, but also the intermediate filtering effects of the second-tier complaint-handler, the Independent Case Examiner, the length of time it takes to consider complaints, and then the MP filter.[8] While the requirement to exhaust internal complaint procedures seems reasonable enough, in practice, it can involve tortuous and lengthy processes before being able to access an ombudsman, by which time the original grievance has long been absorbed. Nonetheless, demand for ombudsmen has increased.[9]

There are differences between individual ombudsmen schemes in terms of complaints accepted for investigation and different investigation procedures. While the PHSO is often discussed in terms of its 'parliamentary' jurisdiction of investigating complaints against central government departments, it principally operates as a health ombudsman. Its caseload is 80 per cent health complaints and 20 per cent 'parliamentary'

[4] House of Commons Levelling Up, Housing and Communities Committee, *Oral Evidence: Local Government and Social Care Ombudsman Triennial Review* (HC 2021–22, 960) Q28, 10 January 2022 (Mick King, LGSCO); Letter from LGSCO to PACAC (25 July 2023).

[5] R Thomas, 'The Operation of the MP Filter for Complaining to the Parliamentary and Health Service Ombudsman' *Essex CAJI* (16 February 2023), https://essexcaji.org/2023/02/16/the-operation-of-the-mp-filter-for-complaining-to-the-parliamentary-and-health-service-ombudsman.

[6] PHSO, *Report on the Consultation on Direct Access to the Parliamentary Ombudsman* (London, PHSO, 2011).

[7] The MP filter does not apply to complaints by victims of crime who complain to the PHSO: Victims and Prisoners Act 2024, s 27.

[8] R Thomas, 'Benefit Complaints: A Critical Analysis' (2022) 44 *Journal of Social Welfare and Family Law* 258.

[9] PHSO, *Demand across the Public Service Ombudsman Landscape* (Manchester, PHSO, 2025).

Table 6.1 PHSO parliamentary complaints, 2022–25. Source: data supplied by the PHSO (for more detailed information, see Appendix F)

Year	Complaints concluded at initial checks or primary investigation – parliamentary	Detailed investigations concluded – parliamentary	Complaints fully/ partly upheld – parliamentary
2022–23	6,063	81	44
2023–24	5,957	74	45
2024–25	5,934	45	29

Table 6.2 PHSO health complaints, 2022–25. Source: data supplied by the PHSO (for more detailed information, see Appendix F)

Year	Complaints concluded at initial checks or primary investigation – health	Detailed investigations concluded – health	Complaints fully/ partly upheld – health
2022–23	26,601	531	375
2023–24	27,099	621	449
2024–25	26,951	677	516

complaints.[10] Tables 6.1 and 6.2 show the numbers of health and parliamentary complaints considered by the PHSO. What is notable is the significant filtering out of complaints throughout the process and the relatively small numbers of detailed investigations undertaken, especially in relation to complaints against central government.

The LGSCO investigates around 4,000 complaints per year, of which around 70 percent are upheld (see Figure 6.1). A comparison places the relatively limited role of the PHSO in context. The small number of detailed investigations concerning complaints against central government tends to weaken the usefulness of the 'swatting-flies' metaphor. The PHSO itself would argue that the MP filter is a significant constraint. There are also substantial differences in investigatory procedure and style between the PHSO and the LGSCO. Since its creation, the PHSO has provided a 'Rolls-Royce' service with formal, detailed and protracted investigations, whereas the LGSCO adopts a more informal approach. One upshot is that the PHSO is often limited in terms of what impact it can exert over central government. As O'Brien has noted, 'perched aloft that super-escalated pyramid, too far from the action to make sufficient difference on the ground and too dependent on chance to take a consistently strategic approach to investigation', the PHSO is 'left with an unattractively remote, reactive and retrospective remit'.[11] A related issue is that there are the differing models of ombudsmen across the UK. Scotland, Wales and Northern Ireland have each adopted the model of the single unified public services

[10] PHSO, *Complaints about UK Government Departments and Other Public Organisations 2023–24* (Manchester, PHSO, 2024).

[11] N O'Brien, 'No End of Searching: A Comment on the Draft Public Service Ombudsman Bill 2016' *UKAJI Blog* (2 February 2017), essexcaji.org/2017/02/02/no-end-of-searching-a-comment-on-the-draft-public-service-ombudsman-bill-2016.

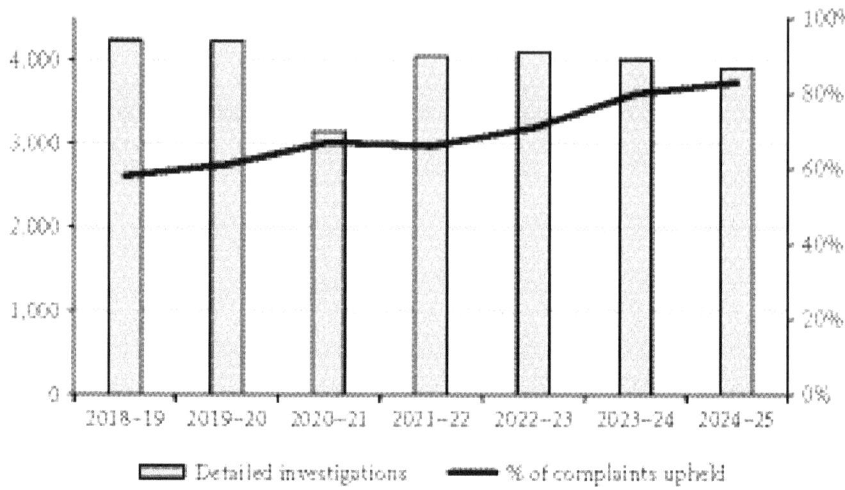

Figure 6.1 The number of detailed investigations by the LGSCO and the percentage of those investigations upheld. Source: LGSCO, *Annual Reviews of Local Government Complaints, 2018–25*

ombudsman that investigates complaints against the devolved government, local government and health. By contrast, in England and the UK (as regards non-devolved policy areas, such as immigration), complaints go to separate ombudsmen: the PHSO for central government and health complaints and the LGSCO for English local government complaints. Further, these two ombudsmen are quite different substantively in terms of how they operate and investigate complaints.

Another distinctive feature of ombudsmen is their anthropomorphic character. Each ombudsman decision is viewed as a personal decision by the office-holder. But, of course, this is not the case. Complaints are considered by caseworkers acting under delegated authority of the office-holder. Yet, criticism of ombudsmen's decisions sometimes focuses upon the individual office-holder. To some extent, this has been ameliorated by the transition from an understanding of the office as a single office-holder to one framed as an 'ombudsman service'.[12] The same problem does not arise in relation to tribunals. No one would ever suppose that the Tribunal Chamber President judge is responsible for defects in an appeal decided by a tribunal judge.

While tribunals are judicial, ombudsmen operate and think of themselves more as a public service, separate and independent from the governmental service complained of, but a public service nonetheless. Tribunal judges are lawyers; there is no equivalent ombudsmen profession. Ombudsmen caseworkers have a more junior status than First-tier Tribunal judges. Ombudsmen also differ from tribunals in that they do not hold public hearings, but investigate complaints on the papers or through speaking with complainants over the telephone or online. By contrast with the judicial process,

[12] In legal terms, each ombudsman is a corporation sole – that is, a legal entity consisting of a single, incorporated office, occupied by a single natural person. This is somewhat archaic and contrary to contemporary norms of accountable governance.

which emphasises the importance of oral hearings for presenting and contesting evidence, the investigatory procedures of ombudsmen are private. Ombudsmen can access documents and papers from public bodies and interview officials. One risk is that ombudsmen themselves come to be seen as impersonal and distanced from the people whose complaints they investigate.

In recent years, ombudsmen have indeed attracted criticism on the following grounds: a lack of robustness and thoroughness of investigations and their fact-finding processes; a lack of transparency and the limited ability of complainants to participate in the process; and the perception that ombudsmen case-handlers side with the public body concerned.[13] Critics have also argued that while complainants must prove their cases, representations from public bodies are seemingly accepted by ombudsmen without much challenge. For instance, the clinical advice commissioned by the ombudsmen was not previously shared with complainants and such advice is anonymised (unlike expert evidence presented before courts and tribunals). More generally, it is difficult to research ombudsmen investigatory procedures precisely because they are private and there are no hearings.

A wider concern arises from the structural position of ombudsmen. All redress institutions inevitably become and operate as a microcosm of the sectors they operate within; they become informed by the same tensions, cultures and issues. One critique of ombudsmen is they share an outlook and perspective with public bodies that results in an implicit alignment with them. Such criticisms are a matter of opinion, although ombudsmen have a general problem which cannot easily be resolved. Many people approach ombudsmen with the expectation that they are an all-purpose redress authority that can resolve their problems, but ombudsmen have a limited role. As a former PHSO once noted, there is inevitably a degree of disappointment built into the system.[14] People's lack of appreciation of the relatively limited role of ombudsmen can then generate additional grievances against ombudsmen themselves. People who have already experienced considerable distress from their experience with a public body can become disillusioned and then approach an ombudsman, only for such feelings to turn into alienation and the perception that the whole system is rigged against them. The criticism is that a culture of denial pervades the entire process from initial complaints to ombudsmen and that the default is to find no wrong and ignore evidence to the contrary.[15] For some, ombudsmen provide an at best second-rate 'pseudo system of administrative justice'.[16] While much of the criticism may go too far, it cannot be dismissed altogether.

The PHSO in particular has been heavily criticised as regards its handling of health complaints.[17] Concerns have included the following: complaints referred to the PHSO not being accepted for investigation and those which are accepted only receiving a very light-touch investigation; the burden of providing evidence being firmly on complainants

[13] C Gill and N Creutzfeldt, 'The "Ombuds Watchers": Collective Dissent and Legal Protest Among Users of Public Services Ombuds' (2018) 27 *Social & Legal Studies* 367, 378–80.

[14] House of Commons Public Administration Select Committee, *Oral Evidence: Review of Public Sector Ombudsmen* (HC 1999–2000, 612), 21 June 2000 (Michael Buckley, Parliamentary Commissioner for Administration, 1997–2002) Q16.

[15] See phsothetruestory.com.

[16] Gill and Creutzfeldt (n 13) 380.

[17] Patients Association, *Parliamentary and Health Service Ombudsman: The 'Peoples' Ombudsman – How it Failed Us* (2014); Patients Association, *PHSO – Labyrinth of Bureaucracy: Follow-up Report* (2015); 'Health Ombudsman: PHSO Useless' *Private Eye* (No 1659, 16 October 2025) 42.

to prove their case; and the PHSO not undertaking its own proper investigations to elicit evidence or ignoring that provided. Another criticism is that lengthy investigations are undertaken by junior staff who lack the required clinical expertise or knowledge. This then requires families to take on the role of 'overseeing' the ombudsman's investigations to ensure accuracy by posing challenging questions to the ombudsman, identifying gaps in investigators' understanding and explaining the significance of evidence to the ombudsman. The loss of confidence in the PHSO's handling of health complaints was such that the then office-holder, Rob Behrens (PHSO, 2017–24), publicly acknowledged that the PHSO faced a challenge in trying to restore trust in its service.[18] The PHSO needed to bring swifter and more consistent closure to complaints.

The PHSO responded in various ways, including: creating an academy with accreditation for its case-handlers, ongoing professional training and staff development, the introduction of quality assurance standards and independent internal reviews of investigations, an expert advisory panel to advise on complex cases and a review of the use of clinical advice in health complaints. Ombudsmen in general have increasingly used complainants' feedback and advisory forum to improve their experiences. They have also increased their transparency by publishing their decisions online. During his time in office, Behrens emphasised that these initiatives were underpinned by the core values of honesty, independence and reciprocal trust, the development of competence and the fostering of a transparent, internal culture.[19]

A comparison with tribunals as regards onward challenges illustrates the differences. First-tier Tribunal decisions are frequently challenged before the Upper Tribunal on error-of-law grounds: fairness of procedures; adequacy of evidence handling; robustness of findings of fact; adequacy of reasons; and so on. First-tier Tribunal judges are well aware that Upper Tribunal judges will scrutinise and potentially criticise their decisions, poring over and criticising decisions, and the consequent need to ensure they are as robust as possible. Tribunal decisions with material errors of law must be reheard. By contrast, ombudsmen's decisions are final. Ombudsmen review their own decisions. Some (such as the LGSCO) have an external reviewer to consider how the ombudsman handles complaints about its service.[20] The only means of external challenge is judicial review. There are concerns about the lack of hearings by ombudsmen and criticisms of their fact-finding. The response from ombudsmen is that they do not adopt a court-based model because that is not how they work. This is a problematic issue which is difficult to resolve. Ombudsmen will never have the resources required to have enhanced procedures and hearings.

Another issue concerns the acceptance of ombudsmen's findings by public bodies and their compliance with ombudsmen's recommended remedies. When upholding complaints, ombudsmen typically recommend personal remedies (an apology, provision of the relevant service and financial payments).[21] Ombudsmen recommendations are not legally binding or enforceable, but are overwhelmingly accepted in practice, although

[18] 'PHSO Open Meeting, Manchester, 30 November 2017. Part 1: Welcome and Key Note Speakers', youtube.com/live/Ta6nsDEMnfM?si=HcgQkqHCGjrHw0T2.

[19] R Behrens, 'Reform of a National Ombudsman Scheme: A Journey' in M Groves and A Stuhmcke (eds), *The Ombudsman in the Modern State* (Oxford, Hart Publishing, 2022) 211, 212.

[20] LGSCO, 'Challenging Our Decisions' and 'External Reviewer', available at www.lgo.org.uk.

[21] Service improvement recommendations are considered below.

compliance rarely hits 100 per cent. Ombudsmen rely on the mobilisation of shame in order for government to accept their findings and maladministration. The public exposure of maladministration, the reaction of public opinion and the reputational damage to a public body are amongst the most effective influences upon government. During the 1980s, non-compliance by local authorities with the LGSCO was common, prompting discussion as to whether remedies should be legally enforceable.[22] However, that type of behaviour has long since been overtaken by a more compliant approach within local government. This coincided with increased oversight of local government and a culture shift in its role since the 1980s; its reduced status and powers, and the increased need to be more responsive to people.[23] Both the PHSO and the LGSCO can issue public or special reports, thereby giving them additional publicity and scrutiny by elected representatives.

The legal status of findings and recommendations differs between different ombudsmen. The LGSCO's findings of maladministration are binding on councils unless challenged through judicial review, although in practice a local authority may simply ignore the LGSCO.[24] By contrast, the PHSO's findings of maladministration against central government are not legally binding, although government ministers must give cogent reasons for rejecting them.[25] In all instances, ombudsmen's recommendations on personal remedy and service improvements are not legally binding.[26] However, there is special statutory provision concerning the Northern Ireland Public Services Ombudsman. When a public body has rejected the Ombudsman's personal remedy, the complainant can seek damages from the County Court.[27] As regards injustice arising from systemic maladministration, the Ombudsman can request the Attorney General for Northern Ireland to apply to the High Court for relief.[28] These powers have rarely been used in practice, although their presence on the statute book likely has some deterrent effect against public bodies engaging in non-compliance.[29]

Ombudsmen do not want their decisions to be legally binding on public bodies. Their relationship with public bodies is based on trust, cooperation and public confidence. It is for government to take ownership of its shortcomings. Ombudsmen urge public bodies to learn from complaints. Legally enforceable remedies would likely signify a

[22] House of Commons Select Committee on the Parliamentary Commissioner for Administration, *Local Government Cases: Enforcement of Remedies* (HC 1985–86, 448); CMG Himsworth, 'Parliamentary Teeth for Local Ombudsmen?' [1986] *PL* 546; JUSTICE-All Souls Review, *Administrative Justice: Some Necessary Reforms* (Oxford, Oxford University Press, 1988) 111–32; G Marshall, 'Ombudsmanaging Local Government' [1990] *PL* 449; R Kirkham, 'Explaining the Lack of Enforcement Powers Possessed by the Ombudsman' (2008) 30 *Journal of Social Welfare and Family Law* 253.

[23] C Copus, M Roberts and R Wall, *Local Government in England: Centralisation, Autonomy and Control* (London, Palgrave Macmillan, 2017).

[24] *R v Local Commissioner for Administration for England ex p Eastleigh Borough Council* [1988] QB 855 (CA) 867 (Lord Donaldson MR); *R (Gallagher) v Basildon District Council* [2010] EWHC 2824 (Admin); [2011] PTSR 731.

[25] *R (Bradley) v Secretary of State for Work and Pensions* [2008] EWCA Civ 36; [2009] QB 114 (CA).

[26] A complainant can judicially review the refusal of a public body to implement recommendations, although this rarely happens. See *R (Nestwood Homes Developments Ltd) v South Holland District Council* [2014] EWHC 8630 (Admin).

[27] Public Services Ombudsman Act (Northern Ireland) 2016, ss 52–53.

[28] ibid ss 54–55.

[29] See C White, 'Enforcing the Decisions of Ombudsmen: The Northern Ireland Local Government Ombudsman's Experience' (1994) 45 *Northern Ireland Legal Quarterly* 395, 397; email from the Office of the Attorney General for Northern Ireland to author (4 September 2023) (no record of such powers being exercised).

shift towards a more confrontational and litigious relationship with government. This would elevate risks, raise costs and undermine the culture of learning, cooperation and improvement which is the hallmark of the more consensual system of administrative justice that ombudsmen embody. Cases of non-compliance can be reported upon again by an ombudsman and then considered by an elected committee to scrutinise why a public body has refused to redress injustice resulting from its maladministration.[30] The experience of non-compliance with regard to the PHSO has been more high-profile and politically sensitive as it involves central government and Parliament; this is considered below in relation to the PHSO's big investigations. Overall, the current position is not perfect; public bodies can be obdurate.[31] However, non-compliance is rare. The consensus is that legal enforcement is not the solution and would only exacerbate matters. In any event, it is highly unlikely that government would change the status quo.

The Principles of Good Administration

Some standard is required against which ombudsmen assess whether a public body has been at fault. That standard is maladministration.[32] It is necessarily a flexible concept.[33] People interact with government in a wide range of situations. The standards of good administration must also keep up to date with contemporary expectations. At the same time, government will, on occasion, have reservations about how the concept of maladministration has been interpreted and applied. Deciding on maladministration can be

[30] See, eg, LGSCO, 'City Council Censured for Complaints Response' (26 May 2021); Bristol City Council (20007914 and 20007915): the council had accepted the LGSCO's recommendations following upheld complaints – missed bin collections and noise nuisances – but, owing to an oversight, it had not evidenced to the LGSCO that they had been implemented. In response, the LGSCO emphasised that the council had needed to be accountable and make every effort to comply. Not doing so was a 'serious breach of trust'.

[31] For instance, Tameside Council had wrongly charged top-up social care fees contrary to guidance. It had accepted the service improvement recommendation to review other similar cases, but rejected the personal remedy to reimburse the complainant's fees. Following the LGSCO's statement of non-compliance, the complainant was left out of pocket and understandably aggrieved. The complainant was not reimbursed the £4,000 he had been wrongly charged in top-up fees and explained: 'The council put us under so much financial and emotional pressure. All I want is an apology': 'Tameside Council "at Fault" for Ignoring Ombudsman's Advice' *BBC News* (20 March 2015), www.bbc.com/news/uk-england-manchester-31970305. It is difficult to underestimate the profound sense of injustice and loss of trust felt by people who have suffered injustice, received an ombudsman report in their favour, only to have its recommendations rejected by the council with no comeback other than publishing a statement of non-compliance. See LGSCO, Tameside Metropolitan Borough Council (12019862). See also LGSCO, 'Leicester Rejects Ombudsman Recommendation for Homeless Family Placed in B&B for Too Long' (6 November 2025); Leicester City Council (24 005 927).

[32] Parliamentary Commissioner Act 1967, s 5. The LGSCO's jurisdiction was initially solely one of maladministration (sometimes termed 'fault'), although this was later supplemented by the inclusion of 'service failure'. This is any failure in a service provided by the public body and any failure to provide a service which it was a function of the public body to provide. The LGSCO's position is that insofar as 'service failure' adds to or clarifies matters, it confirms that there does not need to be any aspect of blame, intent or bad faith involved in a body's actions in order to find fault. Service failure is an objective test of what happened independent of any judgment about the public body's intentions. The jurisdiction of the PSOW and the SPSO includes both maladministration and service failure, whereas that of the Northern Ireland Public Services Ombudsman is maladministration. See: Local Government Act 1974, s 26; Public Services Ombudsman (Wales) Act 2019, s 11; Scottish Public Services Ombudsman Act 2002, s 5; Public Services Ombudsman Act (Northern Ireland) 2016, s 14. The position is different as regards health complaints, as investigations include the exercise of professional judgement.

[33] G Marshall, 'Maladministration' [1973] *PL* 32; R Gregory and P Hutchesson, *The Parliamentary Ombudsman: A Study in the Control of Administrative Action* (London, Allen & Unwin, 1975) ch 8.

sensitive, especially for the PHSO, when it is undertaking a big investigation with potentially significant consequences.[34] Unsurprisingly, attempts to expand the jurisdiction of ombudsmen beyond maladministration to include 'unreasonable, unjust, oppressive or improperly discriminatory' actions have been rejected on the ground that it would lead to ombudsmen intruding into policy matters.[35] At the same time, the now dated Crossman catalogue has long since been overtaken by fundamental structural reforms in public services and the nature of contemporary governance.[36] Likewise, ombudsmen have shifted their focus towards good administration and systemic maladministration.

The idea of a code of principles of good administration was initially rejected by the then Parliamentary Ombudsman in the 1980s on the ground that it would either amount to a list of 'pious generalisations' or 'cause undesirable bureaucratic rigidity'. A code could become the enemy of that 'sensitivity and flexibility which were essential to good administration'.[37] In the early 1990s, another Parliamentary Ombudsman recognised the point that 'to define maladministration is to limit it' and this could work to the disadvantage of individual complainants with justified grievances that did not fit within a given definition.[38] However, the Crossman catalogue was updated to include: rudeness; unwillingness to treat the complainant as a person with rights; refusal to answer reasonable questions; neglecting to inform a complainant on request of his or her rights or entitlement; knowingly giving advice which is misleading or inadequate; ignoring valid advice or overruling considerations which would produce an uncomfortable result for the overruler; offering no redress or manifestly disproportionate redress; showing bias, whether because of colour, sex, or any other grounds; omission to notify those who thereby lose a right of appeal; refusal to inform adequately of the right of appeal; faulty procedures; failure by management to monitor compliance with adequate procedures; cavalier disregard of guidance which is intended to be followed in the interest of equitable treatment of those who use a service; partiality; and failure to mitigate the effects of rigid adherence to the letter of the law where this produces manifestly inequitable treatment. The Parliamentary Ombudsman's list was endorsed by the select committee and the government.[39]

Things have since moved on. In recent decades, ombudsmen have issued principles of good administration in contradistinction to their traditional role of criticising government for maladministration. That approach is now seen as too negative and backward-looking; the concern is that it can potentially produce defensive reactions from government.[40] Instead, it is better to promote good administration. The initiative was taken by the LGSCO. In 1993, it issued a code of good administrative practice comprising some 42 specific principles to provide guidance to local authorities.[41] In 2007, the PHSO issued its more high-level and general principles of good

[34] PHSO, *The Parliamentary Ombudsman: Withstanding the Test of Time* (HC 2006–07, 421) 7.
[35] JUSTICE, *Our Fettered Ombudsman* (London, JUSTICE, 1977) [19].
[36] For the 'Crossman catalogue', see ch 2 57.
[37] JUSTICE-All Souls Review (n 22) 20.
[38] Parliamentary Commissioner for Administration, *Annual Report for 1993* (HC 1993–94, 290) 4.
[39] House of Commons Select Committee on the Parliamentary Commissioner for Administration, *Maladministration and Redress* (HC 1994–95, 112) [10].
[40] A Abraham, 'The Ombudsman and "Paths to Justice": A Just Alternative or Just an Alternative?' [2010] *PL* 1, 7.
[41] Local Government Ombudsman, *Good Administrative Practice* (London, Commission for Local Administration in England, 1993) (Appendix E).

administration.[42] This was part of an effort to reframe the role of ombudsmen as part of a constructive agenda of promoting good administration. The principles denote a more positive understanding of the ombudsmen enterprise through which they work collaboratively with government to secure improvements. Preceded by a public consultation, the PHSO's principles were devised as a blueprint for humanising administration, 'a template for shaping administrative practice to fit the needs of citizens, not the other way around'.[43] As the then PHSO, Ann Abraham, explained, good administration is a critical component of what people valued in public service delivery. It is the space 'where much of our theory collides with practice in situations of most acute concern' to citizens.[44] There is now a common set of principles across the UK ombudsmen.[45] The exception is the SPSO, which has not adopted a set of principles.

The principles were intended to help shape a 'consensus on what modern public service delivery should look like', create expectations against which it can be judged and 'act as a catalyst for reflection and future development'.[46] The advantage of the principles is that they specify a flexible set of standards about how public bodies ought to treat people. It has been argued that the need for good administration has increasingly been viewed as a constitutional imperative which government itself needed to internalise within the delivery of public services and administrative organisation and behaviours.[47] If it has failed to do so, then the Ombudsman will call out such failures.

The principles are necessarily pitched at a high level of abstraction and generality. Examining the principles themselves, what becomes obvious is how reasonable and relatively mundane and ordinary they are. Public bodies should get things right by acting in accordance with the law, follow policy and guidance, take account of established good practice, and provide effective services by trained and competent staff. Being customer-focused requires that public bodies: ensure people can access services easily; inform people what to expect and what public bodies expect of them; keep to their commitments, including public service standards; deal with people helpfully, promptly and sensitively; and respond to people's needs flexibly and, where necessary, coordinate responses with other providers.[48] Public bodies must also be open and accountable about their policies and procedures. They should ensure that any information and advice they provide is clear, accurate and complete. They should state the criteria for their decisions and give reasons, handle information properly, keep proper records and take responsibility for their actions. Public bodies should also act fairly and proportionately by treating people impartially, without unlawful discrimination,

[42] PHSO, *Principles of Good Administration* (London, PHSO, 2007) (Appendix A).

[43] PHSO, *Principles of Good Administration: Response to Consultation* (London, PHSO, 2007); A Abraham, 'Good Administration: Why We Need it More Than Ever' (2009) 80 *Political Quarterly* 25, 26.

[44] Abraham (n 43).

[45] The current principles of the LGSCO and the PSOW are now very similar to those of the PHSO. See LGSCO, *Principles of Good Administrative Practice* (Coventry, LGSCO, 2018) (Appendix D); PSOW, *Principles of Good Administration* (Pencoed, PSOW, 2022). The Northern Ireland Public Services Ombudsman uses the PHSO's principles.

[46] PHSO (n 34) 2.

[47] R Kirkham, T Buck and B Thompson, 'Putting the Ombudsman into Constitutional Context' (2009) 62 *Parliamentary Affairs* 600.

[48] 'Customer-focused' is unfortunate – people who use government services are not customers; they have no choice; they are citizens.

objectively and consistently, and ensure decisions and actions are proportionate, appropriate and fair. When things go wrong, public bodies should put them right by acknowledging mistakes and putting them right quickly and effectively, informing people about how to appeal or complain and by operating an effective and fair complaints procedure. Finally, public bodies should seek continuous improvement by reviewing their policies and procedures regularly to ensure they are effective, asking for feedback and using it to improve services and performance and by learning appropriate lessons from complaints and using them to improve.

The principles embody a model of good service delivery that draws together various strands informing administration and public service delivery. In part, the principles reflect a Weberian model of bureaucracy. Trained and competent staff should know and apply the rules, policies and guidance devised by senior officials. Public bodies should keep proper records and give reasons for decisions. They must liaise and coordinate with each other. Any tendency towards bureaucratic rigidity should be tempered by the need to consider people's individual needs and by treating them sensitively and flexibly. Further, the bureaucratic world must avoid becoming inward-looking. It must be open and accountable. Public bodies must communicate effectively with the people who rely on their services. They must be clear about their policies and procedures, and must provide people with accurate information and advice. They must also be accountable by operating effective complaints procedures. Another strand is treating people with dignity. People must be treated impartially with respect and courtesy. Finally, public bodies should be learning organisations. They should review their policies and procedures, use feedback to improve and learn lessons from complaints as part of the wider process of continuous improvement.

The principles of good administration apply not only to specific interactions and decisions affecting individuals; they also apply more broadly. For instance, the concept of putting things right does not relate solely to an individual complainant; it also involves a public body reviewing and amending its policies and procedures. In this respect, ombudsmen often issue service improvement recommendations concerning what actions public bodies need to undertake to prevent the repetition of the same faults or service failures.

When examined in the abstract, the principles of good administration project an image of public service delivery is desirable, elementary and sensible. However, all public bodies would struggle to fulfil the principles all of the time. The ordinary challenges of day-to-day government and public service delivery are well known. When the principles of good administration were proposed and consulted upon, the government was concerned that the principles should not articulate a set of ideal standards against which public services would always, in some way or other, fall short. Government and public service-delivery operate in a world of bounded rationality.[49] There is always insufficient time, resources, institutional competence and capacity. From the governmental perspective, it was important that the principles of good administration recognise the balance between good administration and affordability. The general response of ombudsmen is that while government bodies are constrained by resource considerations, finite resources should not be used to excuse maladministration, poor service or poor complaint-handling.

[49] HA Simon, *Administrative Behavior*, 4th edn (New York, Free Press, 1997).

The challenges of public service delivery have only become more acute with austerity. Between 2010 and 2019, the funding of local government was halved without any corresponding reduction of its statutory responsibilities; indeed, those responsibilities increased. All public services have had to do more with less. The inevitable outcome is a likely increase in maladministration. Another issue concerns central government in particular. Ministers may make decisions at odds with the requirements of good administration. In such circumstances, it is not the minister who is made responsible but the department. Further, officials cannot justify the failure to follow good administration by saying 'this is what the minister decided to do'. Ombudsmen do not subscribe to the theory implicit within judicial review challenges that all decisions or actions of central government departments are taken by the Secretary of State.

How then do ombudsmen apply the principles? In general terms, ombudsmen compare what actually happened with what should have happened.[50] This involves establishing both the facts and a clear set of standards against which to assess whether or not there has been maladministration. Such standards can be both of general application and specific to the circumstances of the particular complaint or matter. The general standard is the principles of good administration. The specific standards are derived from the particular legal, policy and administrative context and are to be found in the relevant legislation, regulations and guidance. The ombudsman then assesses whether or not the act(s) or omission(s) complained of constitutes a departure from the applicable standards and whether it amounts to maladministration.

How ombudsmen actually go about finding maladministration varies. In routine complaints, it is usually unnecessary to refer to maladministration or the principles of good administration in any great depth or at all. What is more important are the facts and circumstances of the specific complaint, the rules and guidance applicable to the specific service or task and the ombudsman's findings. Ombudsmen have discretion how to investigate a complaint and how to apply the principles of good administration. As with tribunal decisions, outcomes are highly fact- and context-specific. The courts have emphasised that it is for the ombudsman to decide and explain what standard it is going to apply in determining whether there was maladministration, whether there was a failure to adhere to that standard, and what the consequences are. The courts will not intervene with that standard unless it is unreasonable. However, the court *will* interfere if the ombudsman fails to apply the standard that it says it is going to apply.[51] Many routine complaint decisions do not refer to or elaborate upon maladministration or the principles; they do not need to. Such decisions are highly unlikely to be questioned or challenged by government. However, when an ombudsman undertakes a big investigation with potentially wide-ranging implications, there will be a correspondingly greater need for it to justify its findings given the stakes involved and the potential for resistance by government. In such instances, the principles of good administration assume greater importance as a set of standards and expectations through which the ombudsman makes and justifies through its findings and recommendations.

[50] PHSO, *A Breach of Confidence: A Report by the Parliamentary Ombudsman on an Investigation of a Complaint about HM Revenue & Customs, the Child Support Agency and the Department for Work and Pensions* (HC 2010–12, 709) 15.

[51] *R (Rapp) v PHSO and Ofqual* [2015] EWHC 1344 (Admin) [38].

Another important aspect of ombudsmen's findings is the temporal dimension. Ombudsmen investigate matters after they have happened, sometimes years afterwards. They do so in a detached manner, which may be somewhat different from the situation within government at the time. New information may have come to light. The broader position and applicable standards may have changed and evolved. In such circumstances, even if, with the benefit of hindsight, it seems obvious that a public body got something wrong, the ombudsman must still consider the question of maladministration on the basis of the information known and the situation at the relevant time.[52] The purpose is to prevent the ombudsman from using the benefits of hindsight and thereby shifting the goal posts when retrospectively considering whether there was maladministration.

Maladministration, fault and service failure alone are insufficient for a complaint to be held. There must also be injustice in consequence of that maladministration. The maladministration must result in injustice to the complainant. The role of ombudsmen is to put people back into the position in which they would have been had the maladministration not occurred. The question of what, if any, injustice has resulted from maladministration has, on occasion, been controversial. The issue has arisen in some of the PHSO's big investigations concerning claimed financial losses arising from failures to communicate important changes to pensions.[53]

The challenge comes with putting the principles of good administration into practice. This is rarely a problem in relation to routine individual complaint-handling, but it can be contentious in the context of the PHSO's big investigations affecting a large number of people (see below). A related issue concerns the wider impact of the ombudsman's investigations and the principles of good administration (also considered below). However, two general matters are examined first: (i) the relationship between the principles of good administration; and (ii) the application of human rights by ombudsmen.

Good Administration and Legality

There is a division of responsibility between the courts and ombudsmen. The courts review the lawfulness of governmental action; they have the final say on interpreting legislation and on common law principles. Ombudsmen investigate maladministration. Unlawfulness and maladministration are discrete concepts, although there is some overlap. Acting in accordance with the law and guidance is an aspect of 'getting it right'. Ombudsmen are not constrained by the legal principles applied by the courts. Unlawfulness is not a precondition of a finding of maladministration. Further, only the courts make legally binding decisions; ombudsmen do not.

These statements are pitched at a high level of generality, but matters become more nuanced in practice. The concept of legality can be approached from both narrow and wider perspectives. A narrow approach would focus on the minutiae of statutory interpretation and common law principles. Ombudsmen do not perform these functions. However, they adopt a wider approach by considering whether public bodies understand their statutory responsibilities and are exercising them appropriately. Public bodies may

[52] ibid.
[53] See ch 8 288–305.

fall into error when, for instance, they do not understand their statutory responsibilities, misapply them or do not have a policy to guide officers or the policy does not comply with legislation or other statutory guidance. A common ground of maladministration is the failure by public bodies to comply with legal requirements owing to their staff not understanding their statutory responsibilities. Alternatively, public bodies understand their legal duties, but do not fulfil them in particular cases.[54]

These points are illustrated by various LGSCO investigations. For instance, when a council failed to undertake annual reviews of a boy's Education, Health and Care plan, the LGSCO expressed concern that the council fundamentally misunderstood its legal obligations towards children with special educational needs; training was required.[55] The LGSCO has also found that some councils have not known of or understood their statutory responsibilities as regards homeless people.[56] The LGSCO has also criticised councils for not performing their statutory responsibilities. For instance, one council decided not to implement the new system of Deprivation of Liberty Safeguards (DoLS) assessments.[57] Such assessments are undertaken when depriving residents and patients of their liberty because they lack mental capacity to consent to their care and treatment to keep them safe from harm. Some councils had built up significant backlogs of undecided DoLS applications.[58] Owing to financial pressures, some councils had not fully assessed applications triaged as being of low or medium priority within statutory timescales as they should have done. Fully aware that it was unlawful, one council suspended its DoLS assessments. Over 3,000 vulnerable people were then unlawfully deprived of their liberty without being properly assessed or being able to access to the legal process to challenge decisions. The estimated cost of clearing the assessment backlog was £3.5 million. The failure to implement the legislation was maladministration. The LGSCO recommended that the council devise an action plan to address the situation it had caused and the position of people harmed by the unlawful deprivation of their liberty. These are not the types of findings that a court would make, but they are directly concerned with the ability of public bodies to understand and follow the law and their legal responsibilities.

Another overlap between maladministration and legality concerns the application of guidance. Both the courts and ombudsmen require public bodies to follow guidance unless they have good reason for not doing so. This is fairly basic principle and

[54] Local Government Ombudsman (n 41) 5. See also the report of the Australian Commonwealth Ombudsman, *Following the Law is Not Optional* (2026).

[55] LGSCO, Cambridgeshire County Council (20013354); LGSCO, 'Vulnerable Cambridgeshire Boy Left without Education for 14 Months' (28 April 2022).

[56] LGSCO, Shropshire Council (21017512); LGSCO, 'County Man Forced to Live in Car Because of Council Errors' (24 November 2022). See also LGSCO, London Borough of Barking and Dagenham (18018324); LGSCO, 'Council Fails to Investigate Cancer Cluster Concerns' (2021) (council unaware of its statutory responsibilities under the Health and Social Care Act 2012 to improve the health of its population); LGSCO, London Borough of Ealing (23014586); LGSCO, 'Pregnant Women Turned away after Ealing Council Uses Outdated Definition of Definition of Domestic Abuse, Ombudsman Says' (5 December 2024) (the council used a narrow definition of domestic abuse as limited to physical attacks, not the wider definition introduced by the Domestic Violence Act 2021, which includes psychological abuse and coercive and controlling behaviour).

[57] Mental Capacity Act 2005; Mental Capacity (Amendment) Act 2019.

[58] LGSCO, Staffordshire County Council (18004809); LGSCO, 'Thousands of Vulnerable Staffordshire People Deprived of Their Liberty without Proper Assessment' (1 April 2019); P Butler, 'Council Broke Law over Deprivation of Liberty, Ombudsman Rules' *The Guardian* (1 April 2019); LGSCO, Cheshire East Council (19010786); 'Cheshire East "Unlawfully" Deprived People of Liberty' *BBC News* (19 February 2021), www.bbc.com/news/uk-england-manchester-56129513.

the consequences of not following it can be wide-ranging. Consider, for instance, the own-initiative report by the Northern Ireland Public Services Ombudsman into disability benefits.[59] Guidance required assessors and decision-makers to take necessary steps to collect relevant evidence to decide claims for disability benefits, including evidence from claimants' healthcare professionals. However, this rarely happened in practice partly because of caseload pressures and the assumption that such evidence could be considered later on in the process. This was a relatively simple and narrow error. It was also part of a much wider episode of systemic maladministration. The LGSCO has similarly criticised councils for not applying national statutory guidance when, for instance, they had not increased the allowances for special guardians in line with those for foster parents, as required by statutory guidance.[60] Alternatively, councils have adopted their own local policy guidance which contravenes national statutory guidance. This has typically been done for budgetary reasons in order to reduce people's entitlements.

Ombudsmen also apply the principle of non-fettering of discretion. For instance, a council refused a personalised disabled parking bay to a young boy with autism and severe behavioural difficulties who was also in receipt of higher-rate mobility disability benefits. However, the council had not properly considered whether the boy's case was exceptional. Instead, it had rigidly applied its criteria, despite its policy having an exceptions clause into which the boy's case fell, thereby denying a parking space to a family with an obvious and significant need.[61] The council had to review the individual decision, reconsider its parking bay policy for people with hidden disabilities and also contact all those previously refused so that they could re-apply under the new, corrected policy. It also had to retrain its staff on providing services to people with hidden disabilities. In another case, a council had refused to allow a disabled man to use his disability-related expenses to fund the holiday costs for his full-time carer, which the council considered to be an unnecessary expense; without his carer, the man could never go on holiday. The council had adopted blanket approach and thereby fettered its discretion by not considering the man's individual circumstances.[62]

The LGSCO has also emphasised the importance of councils having clear and accessible policies in place about how they intend to deliver services. Having a policy is an important aspect of the requirements of openness and accountability, and enables services to be administered more effectively and consistently.[63] For instance, when a council had granted a disabled facilities grant to fund a home adaptation for people with disabilities

[59] Northern Ireland Public Services Ombudsman, *PIP and the Value of Further Evidence* (Belfast, NIPSO, 2021).

[60] Special Guardianship is a means of providing a permanent home for children who cannot live with their birth parents: Adoption and Children Act 2002, s 115. See LGSCO, Rochdale Metropolitan Borough Council (17010167); 'Rochdale Council's Legal Challenge Rejected and it Must Now Consider Ombudsman's Recommendations' (19 December 2019) (the council's legal challenge to the LGSCO failed and it paid backdated special guardianship allowances at a cost of £900,000); North Tyneside Metropolitan Borough Council (17002928) (a flawed policy on special guardianship allowance resulted in underpayments to the complainant and 171 other families). The LGSCO asked other councils to check whether their policies were in line with the statutory guidance.

[61] LGSCO, London Borough of Tower Hamlets (19006122); LGSCO, 'Autistic Boy Denied Parking Bay by Tower Hamlets' (29 October 2020).

[62] LGSCO, Northumberland County Council (20001819); LGSCO, 'Northumberland Council Asked to Look Again at Man's Disability Expenses' (17 November 2021). See also LGSCO, Derby City Council (23013529); LGSCO, 'Councils Told Not to Make Blanket Decisions on Post-16 School Transport Applications' (2025).

[63] LGSCO, Cotswold District Council (20008553) [52]; LGSCO, 'Cotswold Council Criticised for Poor Tax Relief Response' (26 August 2021).

to help them live in their homes, the matter ran into protracted difficulties. The family had concerns about the quality of the building work undertaken by the council's contractors. Without a formal policy, there was a lack of transparency from the council about its roles and responsibilities and those of the applicant as regards the commissioning and inspecting of building work and resolving disputes when problems arose. The council's record-keeping was poor. All this led to avoidable confusion, uncertainty and distress for the family. The core systemic fault was that the council did not have a formal policy in place to address these and related matters. If it had, then the problems could have been more easily resolved without the difficulties that ensued. The LGSCO made detailed recommendations about the content of the policy to be adopted.[64]

Overall, the courts and ombudsmen approach issues of good administration and legality from different perspectives. Ombudsmen criticise public bodies when, for instance, they do not understand their statutory responsibilities or do not have a formal policy in place. This complements the role of the courts. Moreover, it is very unlikely that the problems identified by ombudsmen would otherwise be scrutinised by the courts; ombudsmen adopt a more flexible approach and are more accessible than the courts.

Good Administration and Human Rights

What then of ombudsmen, good administration and human rights? Some ombudsmen offices elsewhere have been given explicit and wide-ranging roles to oversee and monitor human rights, the rule of law and democratic values.[65] By contrast, UK ombudsmen are 'classic' ombudsmen based on the traditional maladministration function. Nonetheless, given that administrative justice concerns the interactions people have with government, this role can necessarily raise human rights concerns. To what extent have ombudsmen moved into the territory of protecting human rights and also equality rights?

Again, there are different roles here between the courts and ombudsman. Only the courts can decide whether a public body has acted unlawfully by breaching the Human Rights Act 1998 or the Equality Act 2010. Only the higher courts can issue declarations of incompatibility against primary legislation. This type of hard-law enforcement of human rights law can be contrasted with the softer approach towards human rights compliance by non-judicial bodies, such as the Equality and Human Rights Commission and ombudsmen. Ombudsmen cannot decide whether a person's human or equality rights have been breached; however, they can find that a public body has not taken account of a person's human rights. This is an aspect of 'getting it right' by making sure that people's rights are considered by public bodies at all stages of their processes. This is viewed by ombudsmen as a means of informing the public about their legal rights and educating public bodies about their legal responsibilities. Public bodies are obliged to consider the human rights of people who use their services, promote equality and avoid

[64] LGSCO, Birmingham City Council (21000323); LGSCO, 'Councils Warned to Ensure Grant Processes are Transparent Following Ombudsman Complaint' (19 May 2022).

[65] LC Reif, *Ombuds Institutions, Good Governance and the International Human Rights System*, 2nd edn (Leiden, Brill, 2020).

discrimination. The LGSCO has also emphasised that public bodies should take human rights and equality rights into account when they design and deliver their services.[66] They should show how they have done this and keep policies and practices under review. One means of doing this is by producing Equality Impact Assessments. Ombudsmen can also recommend that public bodies educate themselves about such matters.

In recent years, the LGSCO has consciously adopted a more explicit approach when deciding whether public bodies have taken account of an individual's rights. Its findings and recommendations have increasingly referred to the Human Rights Act and the Equality Act. In 2021–22, the Equality Act was a significant feature of 103 LGSCO decisions, most of which concerned public bodies not making reasonable adjustments to accommodate people with disabilities. The LGSCO also made 51 decisions linked to the Human Rights Act, most of which concerned the right to private and family life. These decisions mainly concerned the arrangement of adult residential care services, the failure of councils to provide education for children (especially SEND), deprivation of liberty safeguard assessments and failing to take account of people's right to express themselves freely.[67]

The Northern Ireland Public Services Ombudsman has adopted a human-rights based approach to its work by viewing this role as reflecting the essence of the Ombudsman's historic and fundamental objective of humanising bureaucracy and improving the experiences of people who use public service. A lack of regard for human rights can be maladministration, and human rights can also be an effective way of expressing the injustice suffered by an individual as a consequence of maladministration. In 2016, together with the Northern Ireland Human Rights Commission, the Ombudsman produced a human rights manual for is investigating officers.[68] The Equality and Human Rights Commission has produced its own human rights guide for English ombudsman schemes.[69] The PSOW has published an annual Equality and Human Rights Casebook detailing investigations in which human rights have been engaged.[70] The SPSO has also adopted a rights-based approach to complaint-handling.[71]

The approach of ombudsmen towards human rights and equality issues is illustrated through specific cases. When councils have separated elderly couples by placing one partner in a care home and the other remaining at the family home, leading to distress, the LGSCO held that this engaged the right to family life under Article 8 ECHR.[72] Under the pressure of high caseloads, officials had not considered the couple's family life or whether the interference was proportionate or necessary. The councils were at fault and needed to train their staff.

A man with dementia had been placed in a care home some distance away from his family for five months, thereby preventing his family from visiting him; officers had not

[66] LGSCO, *Equal Justice: Learning Lessons from Complaints about People's Human Rights* (Coventry, LGSCO, 2022) 6.

[67] ibid 5.

[68] Northern Ireland Public Services Ombudsman, *Human Rights Manual* (Belfast, NIPSO, 2016).

[69] Equality and Human Rights Commission, *A Human Rights Guide for Ombudsman Schemes* (London, EHRC, 2019).

[70] PSOW, *Equality and Human Rights Casebook 2023/24* (Pencoed, PSOW, 2024).

[71] SPSO, *Strategic Plan 2024–2028* (2024).

[72] LGSCO, Royal Borough of Windsor and Maidenhead (18015872); Kent County Council (19015406).

considered his family life.[73] A homeless family of seven was given a one-bedroom flat to live in for over a year. Council officers had not considered how the family's housing conditions had affected their family life.[74] Officers should have considered whether the accommodation provided might cause physical or psychological harm and whether it interfered with their private and family life. Another example concerns a catalogue of failures in a SEND case in which a young boy had been left without education for 14 months. The council had not considered the boy's right to education.[75] These investigations suggest that councils may not always be properly embedding human rights law into their training, behaviours and practices or those of their contractors. Consequently, the LGSCO has adopted a more rights-based approach, drawing upon the Human Rights and Equality Acts, something which it considers needs to be cultivated.[76] The PHSO's work has also occasionally raised human rights matters, such as the treatment of disabled people and serious failings in NHS mental health services.[77] There have also been specific investigations including the British academic who had been detained and tortured in the United Arab Emirates for six months. The PHSO concluded that the Foreign Office had failed to recognise that he might have been tortured.[78]

Overall, ombudsmen now refer to human rights more frequently, but usually as a supplementary ground of not taking such rights into account. Further, this is the limit to which they can go, given that only the courts can rule on whether a person's human rights have been breached.

Should a separate human rights ombudsman be established? There are already dedicated human rights bodies, such as the Equality and Human Rights Commission and the Northern Ireland Human Rights Commission, although they do not deal with individual complaints. In 2023, Parliament's Joint Committee on Human Rights considered whether a separate human rights ombudsman should be created. Given that ombudsmen can already consider human rights during their investigations, the Committee concluded that creating a new ombudsman would create jurisdictional overlap, add to what was already at times a confusing and complex landscape, and risk duplication of work. It therefore rejected the idea of separate human rights ombudsman. However, the Committee did recommend that the existing ombudsmen schemes be modified and expanded.[79] The current framework could be changed to make it easier for people to bring complaints, including those involving their human rights. There was also a need for ombudsmen to do more, particularly in relation to traditionally harder-to-reach groups of people who were likely to be less aware of their human rights and the complaint processes available. It was also necessary for the government to consider legislative change to give ombudsmen a more explicit human rights mandate. Furthermore,

[73] LGSCO, Nottinghamshire County Council (19015363).

[74] LGSCO, London Borough of Bromley (20012225).

[75] LGSCO, 'Vulnerable Cambridgeshire Boy Left without Education for 14 Months' (2022); LGSCO, Cambridgeshire County Council (20013354); European Convention on Human Rights, Protocol 1, art 2.

[76] L Marsons, 'The Greenshoots of a Human Rights Ombudsprudence in the Local Government and Social Care Ombudsman' (2024) 46 *Journal of Social Welfare and Family Law* 104.

[77] PHSO and LGSCO, *Six Lives: The Provision of Public Services to People with Learning Disabilities* (HC 2008–09, 203); PHSO, *Maintaining Momentum: Driving Improvements in Mental Health Care* (HC 2018, 906).

[78] PHSO, Foreign, Commonwealth and Development Office (P-002064, 2023); PHSO, 'Foreign Office Missed Signs of Potential Torture of British Academic' (2023).

[79] JCHR, *Human Rights Ombudsperson* (2022–23 HL 175 HC 222).

reform of the MP filter and the introduction of own-initiative powers were both needed. However, the Committee's recommendations were rejected by the government.[80] This has been a perennial theme of ombudsmen reform.

The PHSO's Big Investigations

We now consider the recent history of the PHSO, in particular its working relationships with the UK government and Parliament. Such working political relationships are both formal and informal. Ultimately, it is these relationships which determine the effectiveness of the PHSO and the degree to which government is made accountable. These relationships shift and mutate over time as fresh developments and challenges arise, thereby affecting the relative authority of the PHSO vis-à-vis government and the wider enterprise of administrative justice.

To explore these relationships, this section examines the PHSO's big investigations. They are of a quite different character from routine individual complaints. Such investigations also distinguish the PHSO from other ombudsmen because it deals with UK central government. Central government is uniquely capable of generating large-scale maladministration affecting large numbers of people. Central government can also be obdurate and resist the PHSO's investigations in ways that other public bodies do not.

The PHSO's big investigations typically proceed as follows. Campaign groups complain that they have suffered financial loss from maladministration. The PHSO then undertakes a lengthy, complex and large investigation, often taking years, which finds maladministration and recommends financial payments, running into millions and sometimes billions (see Table 6.3). While each investigation is unique, they also fall into a wider pattern of interactions between the respective institutions and they often have significant consequences. They are also landmarks in the evolution of the PHSO because of their importance, the number of people affected, the involvement of ministers and the nature of the remedies recommended by the PHSO. Looked at over a prolonged period of time, these big investigations also highlight the changing nature of the relationships between the PHSO, the government and Parliament. The government has typically resisted big investigations, which have then been resolved through protracted scrutiny by the select committee, and sometimes litigation, resulting in grudging and/or partial acceptance by the government. All of this involves a series of complex and prolonged interactions, tensions and complications between the PHSO and government. Moreover, while the select committee's purpose was originally to scrutinise the government's rejection of the PHSO's reports and to undertake follow-up scrutiny of government, its role has diminished over time.[81]

[80] JCHR, *Human Rights Ombudsperson: Government Response to the Committee's Eleventh Report* (HC 2022–23, 1489).

[81] R Gregory, 'The Select Committee on the Parliamentary Commissioner for Administration, 1967–1980' [1982] *PL* 49. The Committee has been through various iterations: the House of Commons Select Committee on the Parliamentary Commissioner for Administration (1969–97); the House of Commons Public Administration Select Committee (PASC) (1997–2015); and the House of Commons Public Administration and Constitutional Affairs Committee (PACAC) (2015–).

Table 6.3 The PHSO's big investigations

Investigation	**Context**	**PHSO's findings**	**Government response**
Barlow Clowes (1989)	Regulation of financial services. Investors in Barlow Clowes had sustained losses from financial fraud.	The Ombudsman made five significant findings of maladministration by the Department of Trade and Industry in not regulating Barlow Clowes effectively.	The Department rejected findings of maladministration, but offered a financial remedy (£150 million) without admission of fault or liability.
Channel Tunnel Rail Link (1995)	Blight to homes caused by construction of the Channel Tunnel Rail Link.	The Department of Transport did not consider the effects of its policy on those affected. It should have considered the position of people suffering exceptional or extreme hardship and provided redress.	The Department initially rejected the findings of maladministration, but following committee scrutiny, accepted the Ombudsman's report.
SERPS (2000)[82]	The inheritance rules for the State-Earnings Related Pension Scheme (SERPS) were halved in 1986, with the change coming into effect in 2000. Some 1.5 million of people were affected.	The DWP did not publicise the change and misled people. DWP staff were not informed of the change. There was a lack of end-to-end accountability within the department's operations.	The DWP introduced a redress package in which SERPS inheritance entitlements gradually reduced to half over a 10-year period. The cost was £12 billion.
Debt of Honour (2005)	*Ex gratia* compensation scheme for British people detained by the Japanese during the Second World War.	The compensation scheme was announced before the eligibility criteria had been worked out. New criteria were added afterwards. The scheme was not administered correctly.	The Ministry of Defence initially rejected the findings of maladministration, but following committee scrutiny, later accepted the PHSO's report.

[82] See ch 8 288–293.

Investigation	Context	PHSO's findings	Government response
Occupational pensions (2006)	125,000 people lost their occupational pensions when their pensions schemes were wound up.	The DWP misled people into believing that their pensions were entirely safe. They did not have the opportunity to save in other ways and suffered heavy losses.	The DWP rejected the report and the financial remedy (costing £15 billion), but, following committee scrutiny and litigation, agreed to a limited financial assistance scheme.
Equitable Life (2008)	Financial regulation of Equitable Life. One million policyholders had sustained financial losses following the collapse of Equitable Life.	Multiple findings of maladministration by regulators and the Government Actuary's Department in the regulation of Equitable Life.	HM Treasury accepted some findings of maladministration, but rejected others and the resultant injustice (costing £4.1 billion), although a less expensive compensation scheme was later established.
Women's state pension age (2024)[83]	The communication of the increase to the women's state pension age. Some 3.6 million women were affected.	The DWP did not act on feedback that many women did not know their state pension age. It also failed to act promptly in sending notification letters. There was also poor complaint-handling.	The DWP largely accepted the findings of maladministration, but rejected those concerning injustice. It also rejected financial redress (costing £11 billion) as impractical and too costly.

The 1990s: Barlow Clowes and the Channel Tunnel

We can start with Barlow Clowes, a highly complex investigation concerning investors who had been the victims of financial fraud, known as 'bond-washing' by the financial firm Barlow Clowes. The investors then complained to the PHSO that the then Department of Trade and Industry had not properly regulated the firm or protected the investors. Following a lengthy investigation, the PHSO found 'significant maladministration' by the Department in five areas and recommended that investors who had suffered as a result should receive financial payments.[84] As a regulatory agency, the Department should have adopted a rigorous and inquiring approach as regards

[83] See ch 8 298–304.
[84] Parliamentary Commissioner for Administration, *The Barlow Clowes Affair* (HC 1989–90, 76).

material coming into its possession concerning an undertaking about which suspicions have been aroused, and also representations made to it as regards the firm in question.[85] It was that lack of a sufficiently rigorous and enquiring approach which had then led to the losses suffered by the investors. The investigation had also highlighted a distinct advantage of the PHSO. Given its time, resources and the right of unrestricted access to persons and papers, the PHSO had been able 'to mount a fact-finding exercise far more formidable than MPs or the media could possibly have undertaken. Rarely, if ever, can any record of administration have been so closely scrutinised, and reconstructed in such detail'.[86] In response, the government rejected the findings of maladministration. The purpose of regulation was 'not to provide any sort of warranty in a particular case to a particular investor but to establish reasonable standards in the sector which provide a framework within which investors can take their own judgements about risk and reward'.[87] Nonetheless, the government decided to provide financial redress to the investors (totalling £150 million), without admission of fault or liability, 'out of respect' for the Ombudsman and without setting a precedent.[88]

Why would the government disagree with the Ombudsman's findings, but then also accept its recommended financial payments? There were clearly political considerations in play for the then Conservative government. The case had stirred up a degree of hostility amongst investors, who were natural Conservative voters. Aware of this, the government had been 'loath to tangle further with a resourceful and well organised pressure group, fighting for what was on the whole a popular cause and anxious not to add to its problems by prolonging a parliamentary row' over the case.[89] Discretion was the better part of valour. There was nothing unusual or surprising about this behaviour by the government. The notion of 'parliamentary control' over government is based on the principle of trouble avoidance. However, the episode illustrated how securing redress against government is first and foremost a function of the political process and how political calculations naturally enter into the government's thinking. Nonetheless, the Ombudsman had operated 'very much as its architects originally envisaged, providing MPs with "a new and powerful weapon" when taking up the cudgels against the government on behalf of aggrieved constituents'.[90]

In the Channel Tunnel Rail Link investigation, the PHSO found exceptional hardship to homeowners caused by blight to their homes from the construction of the Channel Tunnel Rail Link project, which was overseen by the Department of Transport.[91] The Ombudsman found maladministration by the Department. It should have considered the need to provide redress for people suffering extreme or exceptional hardship who were not covered by existing compensation schemes. Good administration included having due regard at all times to the position of the citizen, not just to the position of

[85] ibid [8.13].

[86] R Gregory and G Drewry, 'Barlow Clowes and the Ombudsman, Part 2' [1991] *PL* 408, 439.

[87] Department of Trade and Industry, *Observations by the Government on the Report of the Parliamentary Commissioner for Administration on Barlow Clowes* (HC 1989–90, 99) [5].

[88] ibid [43]–[44].

[89] Gregory and Drewry (n 86) 441.

[90] ibid 442.

[91] Parliamentary Commissioner for Administration, *The Channel Tunnel Rail Link and Blight: Investigation of complaints against the Department for Transport* (HC 1994–95, 193).

the government and the taxpayer. While it was not government policy to compensate those affected by generalised blight, the Department had a responsibility to consider the circumstances of individuals who had suffered exceptional hardship and to make recompense in exceptional cases on an *ex gratia* basis. However, the government rejected the Ombudsman's report, which was published under section 10(3).[92] The matter was then considered by the Select Committee to decide whether or not to support the Ombudsman.[93] When considering a section 10(3) report, the Committee would not automatically assume that the Ombudsman was right, but would itself consider the arguments from the Ombudsman and from the relevant government department and do so objectively and dispassionately, and then come to its own conclusion.[94]

The Committee decided to support the Ombudsman. The Department for Transport should have considered whether any *ex gratia* payments were appropriate. It was desirable to provide redress to those affected to an extreme and exceptional degree by generalised blight. This was in accordance with the principle that maladministration included a failure to mitigate the effects of rigid adherence to the letter of the law where that produces manifestly inequitable treatment. The Department therefore needed to reconsider: 'There would be no point in having an Ombudsman if the government were to show disregard for his Office, his standing as an impartial referee, and for the thoroughness of his investigation.'[95] At the heart of the matter was how to define one aspect of maladministration – namely, the failure to mitigate the effects of rigid adherence to the letter of the law where that produced manifestly inequitable treatment. The Committee supported the Ombudsman's approach: when an individual is faced with extraordinary hardship as a result of the strict application of law or policy, then government needed to consider whether help could be given.[96] The Committee was arguing for the exercise of discretion, not an open-ended duty to compensate.

The Department responded by accepting the need to make financial payments in the specific case – as per Barlow Clowes – 'out of respect' for the Ombudsman, albeit without admission of fault.[97] A key factor was that the homeowners were property owners and likely supporters of the then Conservative government. Nonetheless, the Department resisted the Ombudsman's findings of maladministration and the 'fundamental new principle of administration', which implied that 'if a new policy is adopted, or new circumstances arose which affected an existing policy, then the Government was under a *duty* to identify those individuals who would be particularly adversely affected

[92] Under s 10(3) of the Parliamentary Commissioner Act 1967, when it appears to the PHSO that injustice has been caused to the person aggrieved as a consequence of maladministration and has not or will not be remedied, then it can lay before Parliament a special report on the case. Under s 10(4), the PHSO may lay other reports before Parliament. The first s 10(3) report was: Parliamentary Commissioner for Administration, *Rochester Way, Bexley: Refusal to Meet Late Claims for Compensation* (HC 598 1977–78); House of Commons Select Committee on the Parliamentary Commissioner for Administration, *The Land Compensation Act 1973* (HC 1978-79, 91); C Harlow, 'Comment' [1977] *PL* 301.

[93] House of Commons Select Committee on the Parliamentary Commissioner for Administration, *The Channel Tunnel Rail Link and Exceptional Hardship* (HC 1994–95, 270).

[94] ibid [5].

[95] ibid [1].

[96] ibid [20].

[97] House of Commons Select Committee on the Parliamentary Commissioner for Administration, *Fifth Special Report: The Channel Tunnel Rail Link and Exceptional Hardship – The Government Response* (HC 1994–95, 819) iv.

and to provide financial redress'.[98] Such a principle 'would make government unworkable'.[99] However, the 'duty' rejected by the Department was a misconstruction of the discretion proposed.[100] In short, the Department had either deliberately rejected the Committee's recommendation or its thinking was too obtuse to appreciate the difference being drawn – in other words, a brush-off rejection by the Department as a result of 'thin-end-of-the-wedge' concerns about financial payments.

Both the Barlow Clowes and Channel Tunnel investigations had concerned financial payments for relatively specific cohorts of people who had experienced injustice, as opposed to the overall performance of an administrative system used by a wider population. In the early 1990s, the PHSO produced two special reports on large-scale systems that affected large numbers of people; the flawed introduction of a new disability benefit, Disability Living Allowance (DLA), which led to delays and backlogs, and the troubled Child Support Agency.[101] The PHSO was extending its role by recognising that investigations should benefit not just individual complainants, but a whole cohort of people at risk of injustice.[102] Both reports revealed systemic weakness in the handling of a high volume of routine individual cases of acute and sensitive importance to the people concerned. As regards DLA, the Ombudsman warned that maladministration leading to injustice was likely to arise whenever a new administrative task had not been piloted; when new staff, perhaps inadequately trained, formed a substantial proportion of the workforce; where procedures and technology supporting them had not been tried and tested and where quality of service was subordinated to sheer throughput.

These reports represented a new departure by the PHSO focused not on expensive financial remedies, but on improving government systems. Government needed to take great care when devising a new administrative task or system affecting large numbers of the public. The PHSO had only been able to undertake the investigations because it had received sufficient complaints to produce a special report. This is a valuable strand of work for ombudsmen to undertake, although it has not featured in the PHSO's work as much as it should. Government later sought to contest and weaken the PHSO's approach to maladministration. For instance, the Home Office argued that delays in handling immigration applications occurred so routinely because of the pressure of work that they should not therefore be viewed as maladministration – an evident attempt to dilute the standards of good administration that was rejected as such by both the PHSO and the Committee.[103]

[98] ibid (emphasis added).
[99] ibid.
[100] R James and D Longley, 'The Channel Tunnel Rail Link, the Ombudsman and the Select Committee' [1996] *PL* 38, 45. Financial redress was finally made after a further four years of debate and a change of government: HL Deb 17 December 1998, vol 595, col WA166 (Lord Whitty, Parliamentary Under-Secretary of State, Department of the Environment, Transport and the Regions). Some 28 people each received £10,000 for extreme and exceptional hardship. See also House of Commons Select Committee on the Parliamentary Commissioner for Administration, *The Channel Tunnel Rail Link and Exceptional Hardship – Government Proposals for Redress* (HC 1996–97, 453).
[101] Parliamentary Commissioner for Administration, *Delays in Handling Disability Living Allowance Claims* (HC 1992–93, 652); Parliamentary Commissioner for Administration, *Investigation of Complaints against the Child Support Agency* (HC 1994–95, 135); *Investigation of Complaints Against the Child Support Agency* (HC 1994–95, 135).
[102] Parliamentary Commissioner for Administration, *Annual Report for 1993* (HC 1993–94, 290) 2.
[103] PASC, *Ombudsman Issues* (HC 2002–03, 448) [27].

The 2000s: Abraham and Wright

Prior to 2002, successive ombudsmen had usually been traditional establishment figures, including former senior civil servants.[104] The appointment of Ann Abraham in 2002 signalled a change. Abraham wanted the PHSO to become a much more significant player by taking on big issues, making wide-ranging findings of maladministration, recommending systemic improvements and drawing them to Parliament's attention.[105] A unique function of ombudsmen was their ability to get beyond the individual case and to identify patterns of deficiency and to make recommendations for systemic change that went beyond securing redress in the individual case. The PHSO had an important role at the centre of the constitution by holding government to account as regards its day-to-day encounters with citizens. The office was to be understood by both the public and government as a partner in the broader agenda of improving public services and therefore in tune with the then Labour government's policy drive.

There then followed a number of big investigations by the PHSO into high-profile problems which proved irksome to the Labour government. In 2005 and 2007, the PHSO produced two reports into a flagship government policy, tax credits, which had led to substantial injustice for hundreds of thousands of people and families because of how the system operated.[106] Implicit within these reports was that the PHSO was investigating and criticising not just the maladministration of tax credits, but also the design of the policy and legislation underpinning them. As Abraham later recognised, the complaints raised 'fundamental questions which are not administrative or service issues as such, but policy considerations related to the design of the tax credits system which only government and Parliament' could address.[107] This report fell into the pattern of the two previous reports on disability benefits and the Child Support Agency. However, the PHSO was going further. As Abraham later acknowledged, the PHSO had been investigating grievances that 'brought into doubt the viability of government policy, not just its implementation', which then informed public debate. Abraham did not think that this had involved the Ombudsman 'usurping the legitimate function of the executive'. It was instead 'acting in its proper constitutional capacity, as Parliament's ombudsman, in helping to keep the executive in check'.[108] However, there was a fine balancing act here, which, if pushed further, could lead the ombudsman into potential difficulties. Importantly, Abraham received much support from the Committee and its chair, now Tony Wright MP (2001–10), a former academic political scientist and independent-minded Labour backbencher closely interested in political and constitutional reform.[109]

[104] See generally R Gregory and P Giddings, *The Ombudsman, The Citizen, and Parliament: A History of the Office of the Parliamentary Commissioner for Administration and Health Service Commissioners* (London, Politico's, 2002).

[105] A Abraham, *The Parliamentary Ombudsman and Administrative Justice: Shaping the Next 50 Years* (London, JUSTICE, 2011) 11.

[106] PHSO, *Tax Credits: Putting Things Right* (HC 2005–06, 124); PHSO, *Tax Credits: Getting it Wrong?* (HC 2006–07, 1010). See further ch 7 240–245.

[107] ibid [4.2].

[108] A Abraham, 'Making Sense of the Muddle: The Ombudsman and Administrative Justice, 2002–2011' (2012) 34 *Journal of Social Welfare and Family Law* 91, 95.

[109] PASC, *Tax Credits: Putting Things Right* (HC 2005–06, 577); T Wright, *Citizens and Subjects: An Essay on British Politics* (Abingdon, Routledge, 1994).

The PHSO then switched away from a systemic improvement role back to big investigations finding maladministration and recommending high-value financial remedies for cohorts of people. This involved a series of battles with the government.

The first, the 'Debt of Honour' report, concerned the compensation scheme established by the Ministry of Defence for British civilians detained by Japanese forces during the Second World War. The key flaw had been a hurried ministerial announcement of the compensation scheme, which had raised people's hopes that they would be compensated. However, such hopes had been undermined by the publication of the detailed rules and eligibility criteria, which meant that many people concerned did not in fact qualify for compensation and who therefore felt they had been misled and betrayed. The criteria included the requirement that only internees who were British subjects and had been born in the UK or their parent or grandparent had born in the UK would be compensated. Yet, this 'blood link' criterion had not been disclosed to those who had been encouraged to apply. Moreover, many applicants did not fall within the criteria, despite being the intended recipients of compensation.

An unsuccessful judicial review confirmed the legality of the scheme, whereas the PHSO found maladministration.[110] The rushed manner in which the scheme had been devised had caused avoidable confusion. The Minister's announcement of the scheme had been unclear and imprecise, and had given rise to misunderstanding. When the Ministry had settled upon the 'blood link' criterion, it had failed to ensure that this did not lead to unequal treatment. For ministers to have expedited the announcement for political purposes may perhaps have been expected. However, the Ministry then resisted the PHSO's report arguing that because the courts had upheld the legality of the compensation scheme, there was no basis for the PHSO to criticise it. Institutional defensiveness had set in. However, the Ministry's approach collapsed under committee scrutiny. The Committee considered it shameful that the Ministry of Defence had remained steadfastly opposed to any change of approach for over a year, only to then be forced by the PHSO to undertake a review and compensate those internees who had fallen outside of the narrowly framed compensation scheme.[111] The Committee's support for the PHSO's report had brought 'a degree of moral and political clout' that would otherwise have been absent.[112]

In 2006, the PHSO published its substantial 'pensions promise' report, which concerned the DWP's regulation of occupational pension schemes.[113] Some 125,000 people had lost their occupational pensions when their pension schemes had been wound up. They complained that the DWP had failed to communicate important changes concerning the regulation of their pensions and that the information provided had been misleading. This was a highly complex investigation. The PHSO upheld the complaints and found maladministration. It also recommended that the government

[110] *R (Association of British Civilian Internees – Far Eastern Region) v Secretary of State for Defence* [2003] EWCA Civ 473; [2003] QB 1397 (CA); PHSO, *'A Debt of Honour': The Ex Gratia Scheme for British Groups Interned by the Japanese during the Second World War* (HC 2005–06, 324) (a section 10(3) report).

[111] PASC, *A Debt of Honour* (HC 2005–06, 735).

[112] R Kirkham, 'Challenging the Authority of the Ombudsman: The Parliamentary Ombudsman's Special Report on Wartime Detainees' (2006) 69 *MLR* 792, 815.

[113] PHSO, *Trusting in the Pensions Promise: Government Bodies and the Security of Final Salary Occupational Pensions* (HC 2005–06, 984) (a section 10(3) report).

consider restoring the pension entitlements, at some cost, despite other factors having contributed to the financial losses.

This investigation is considered in more detail elsewhere.[114] The key points at present are as follows. The PHSO found large-scale maladministration and recommended a costly financial remedy (£15 billion). The government rejected the report and its findings. It was concerned that the PHSO had exceeded its jurisdiction by recommending a financial remedy for losses which arose from causes other than maladministration, whereas the PHSO's role is only to redress injustice in consequence of maladministration.

The Committee considered the case. As before, the Committee noted that it would not automatically accept the PHSO's findings, but would test both them and the government's response.[115] The Committee again supported the PHSO and also warned the government. Tensions between the government and the PHSO had become increasingly acute. Abraham considered there to be 'an emerging attitude amongst government departments that they can properly, and with impunity, reject my independent assessment of their actions, and my findings of maladministration'.[116] The Committee noted that 'the government's relationship with the Ombudsman was changing'.[117] The series of rejections by the government and its wider attitude towards the PHSO was 'deeply troubling'.[118] The ombudsman system would only work if there was a common understanding between the PHSO, Parliament and the government as to what constituted maladministration and who had the authority to identify it. The government had too readily dismissed the PHSO's findings of maladministration. It was 'unprecedented for there to be so many problems, in such a short space of time'.[119] The Committee's view was that the fault lay with the government, not the Ombudsman. If the government routinely rejected the PHSO's findings without good reason, then this would 'raise fundamental constitutional issues about the position of the Ombudsman and the relationship between Parliament and the Executive'.[120] The Committee would monitor the government's responses to the report and, if necessary, seek a debate to re-establish the PHSO's role. The Parliamentary Ombudsman was 'Parliament's Ombudsman: Government must respect her'.[121] In a more emollient tone, the Committee noted that it did not want the government to be defensive, but to engage constructively with both the PHSO and the Committee, and to focus on putting things right.

All this occurred during the New Labour government (1997–2010). The economic context was then relatively benign and there was a favourable governmental attitude towards administrative justice, although it was principally focused on tribunals reform and emanated from the Ministry of Justice. Other departments, such as the DWP, were clearly more willing to be resistant. Nonetheless, there were some concessions made on

[114] See ch 8 294–296.
[115] House of Commons Public Administration Select Committee, *The Ombudsman in Question: The Ombudsman's Report on Pensions and its Constitutional Implications* (HC 2005–06, 1081) [61].
[116] ibid [66].
[117] ibid [63].
[118] ibid [67].
[119] ibid [70].
[120] ibid [78].
[121] ibid [79].

occupational pensions, prompting the Committee to note that the ombudsman system had 'proved to be effective even in the face of Government resistance'.[122]

Matters then escalated to the courts. Could the government's rejection of the PHSO's findings of maladministration be judicially reviewed? In *Bradley*, the Court of Appeal held that a minister, acting rationally, was entitled to reject the PHSO's findings of maladministration and to prefer his own view.[123] However, it was insufficient for the Minister simply to reject those findings or to reach his own view on rational grounds. The Minister also had to give cogent reasons to demonstrate that the rejection of the PHSO's findings was not irrational, having regard to the underlying purpose of the 1967 Act. This test inverted the standard irrationality test. On the particular facts, the court concluded that the Minister's rejection of the PHSO's findings of maladministration had been irrational.

The *Bradley* ruling has been criticised on the ground that it makes the PHSO's findings de facto legally binding on the government by placing the burden on the minister to justify their rejection, which is then subject to judicial review and to the court's assessment.[124] The implication is that judicial scrutiny of a ministerial decision to reject the PHSO's findings of maladministration is being elevated above ministerial responsibility to Parliament. If so, then this position sits oddly with the parliamentary nature of the PHSO scheme and the fact that it was established to enhance parliamentary scrutiny of government. It has therefore argued that *Bradley* should be reversed to limit judicial involvement in what is a principally political matter.[125] This matter is likely to resurface at some future stage.

Two subsequent reports reinforced the tensions between the PHSO and the government. In 2009, the PHSO criticised the Rural Payments Agency for its delays in issuing subsidy payments to farmers.[126] However, the government resisted the report and the modest compensation payments recommended. A committee hearing revealed that the Agency's parent department, the Department for Environment, Food and Rural Affairs (DEFRA), and the PHSO had been speaking at cross-purposes and that DEFRA had not properly understood the PHSO's approach and its role.[127] The Committee chair, Tony Wright MP, had been 'mystified' as to why the Department had been obstructive; it had taken 'an adversarial rather than a common-sense, compassionate approach to people' who had undoubtedly suffered injustice as a result of its administrative failings.[128] The Minister then accepted the PHSO's report in full.[129]

[122] PASC, *Pensions Bill: Government Undertakings Relating to the Financial Assistance Scheme* (HC 2006–07, 523) [11].

[123] *Bradley* (n 25).

[124] JNE Varuhas, 'Governmental Rejections of Ombudsman Findings: What Role for the Courts?' (2009) 72 *MLR* 102.

[125] JNE Varuhas, *Judicial Capture of Political Accountability* (London, Policy Exchange, 2016); Policy Exchange, *What Do We Want from the King's Speech?* (London, Policy Exchange, 2023) 46; *Re Application for Judicial Review by JR55 (Northern Ireland)* [2016] UKSC 22 [20]: 'The decision in *Bradley* raises delicate questions about the relationship between judicial and Parliamentary scrutiny of a minister's rejection of the recommendations of the Parliamentary Commissioner for Administration' (Lord Sumption).

[126] PHSO, *Cold Comfort: The Administration of the 2005 Single Payment Scheme by the Rural Payments Agency* (HC 2009–10, 81) (a section 10(3) report); PHSO, *More Cold Comfort: How the Rural Payments Agency Handled Claims to the Single Payment Scheme in 2005–06* (HC 2010–12, 1662) (a section 10(4) report).

[127] PASC, *Defra's Response to the Ombudsman's Report on the Single Payment Scheme* (HC 2009–10, 331).

[128] Letter from Tony Wright MP, PASC Chair to Hilary Benn MP, Secretary of State for Environment, Food and Rural Affairs (4 February 2010).

[129] Letter from Hilary Benn MP, Secretary of State for Environment, Food and Rural Affairs, to Tony Wright MP, PASC Chair (5 March 2010).

The next big report concerned the PHSO's decade-long investigation and very lengthy report into the regulation of Equitable Life, a pensioner provider.[130] Having encountered difficulties, Equitable Life had collapsed in 2000. Consequently, many of its members had their pension payments substantially reduced. In essence, the PHSO found serial regulatory failure and maladministration by the regulators. It recommended that the government establish a compensation scheme for the one million people affected. Coming during the midst of the global financial crisis of 2008–09, the report prompted deep concern within government – namely HM Treasury – about the financial implications and the costs to the taxpayer, estimated at £4.1 billion.

The Committee again supported the PHSO: 'if the government chose to act as judge on its own behalf by refusing to accept that maladministration took place', then that would seriously undermine the PHSO and the ability to learn lessons from the affair.[131] If the government rejected the PHSO's report, then the matter should be debated on the floor of the House of Commons to allow MPs to discuss the issues and their constitutional nature and to re-establish the PHSO's constitutional role. The government, unsurprisingly, resisted the PHSO's report.[132] While accepting some of the findings of maladministration and injustice, it also rejected a number of them, including the recommendation for a compensation scheme. For the government, the question of compensation raised difficult and complex questions. The PHSO could only investigate the role of the regulator, not that of Equitable Life which itself had been responsible for a series of failings. The government also had a responsibility to taxpayers generally to balance competing demands on the public purse. The government therefore rejected the recommended compensation scheme, while recognising that there had been maladministration which would be addressed through some *ex gratia* payments.

The Committee expressed disappointment at this.[133] The government had acted as a judge on its own behalf when rejecting and qualifying a number of the PHSO's findings – and it had done so for reasons that were not well explained and were difficult to assess. The government may not have been legally obliged to put things right, but it was morally responsible for the losses that had arisen.[134] The PHSO itself was unpersuaded by the government's position.[135] The Committee also reflected on the role and effectiveness of the PHSO in undertaking such a large, extensive and complex investigation. The PHSO secured satisfactory remedies in the vast majority of the complaints investigated. Nonetheless, it inevitably faced greater obstacles in its big investigations, which were very expensive to put right. On the one hand, the government's record in

[130] PHSO, *Equitable Life: A Decade of Regulatory Failure* (HC 2007–08, 815).

[131] PASC, *Justice Delayed: The Ombudsman's Report on Equitable Life* (HC 2008–09, 41) 3.

[132] HM Treasury, *The Prudential Regulation of the Equitable Life Assurance Society: The Government's Response to the Report of the Parliamentary Ombudsman's Investigation* (Cm 7538, 2008).

[133] PASC, *Justice Denied? The Government's Response to the Ombudsman's Report on Equitable Life* (HC 2008–09, 219).

[134] ibid 3: 'We are disappointed that the Government has decided that compensation is not warranted, arguing that it is under no duty to put right, even in part, wrongs that it admits the State has caused … The only potentially valid reason that the Government provides, namely that Parliament has considered that financial regulators should not normally be held liable in the courts for financial loss, was introduced late in the day in a way that we find to be shabby, constitutionally dubious and procedurally improper.'

[135] PHSO, *Injustice Unremedied: The Government's Response on Equitable Life* (HC 2008–09, 435).

such cases and the PHSO's lack of enforcement powers prompted the question as to whether it was even worth the PHSO conducting such lengthy and costly investigations which could raise false hopes amongst complainants and which might ultimately be fruitless. On the other hand, it was unrealistic to expect the government itself to establish truly independent and wide-ranging investigations of this kind, which may find that the government itself was, at least partly, to blame. There were weaknesses with the PHSO in that it could only ever consider a part of the wider picture. Nonetheless, it was the best option for holding public bodies to account for their administrative failings. Accordingly, so long as there was no better alternative for dealing with grievances of this kind, 'the Ombudsman should continue to consider investigating cases such as this, irrespective of the likelihood of a remedy being provided'.[136]

The government was clearly unhappy with the PHSO. Behind the scenes, senior ministers vented their frustrations with Abraham, who had unexpectedly landed fresh and large demands on the public purse during the financial crisis. It is possible that the government itself could have thought that, by undertaking such big investigations, the PHSO was exceeding its established traditional role as originally envisaged when the Ombudsman had been established in 1967. From a different perspective, it could be said that the government had not properly acclimatised itself or adjusted its habits of thought to accommodate the changing nature of external scrutiny provided by the PHSO. The tensions here between governmental power and accountability through the PHSO are self-evident and baked into the nature of the PHSO scheme. Nonetheless, the government clearly considered that Abraham had overstepped the mark.

The Committee chair, Tony Wright MP, then attempted to abolish the MP filter and to have the PHSO's section 10(3) reports routinely debated and voted upon on the floor of the House of Commons.[137] Given the governmental control over timetabling in the Commons, such debates could only take place if the government itself found the parliamentary time, which was highly unlikely for obvious reasons. The Committee therefore considered that it was constitutionally inappropriate for Parliament, which exists to scrutinise government, to have to rely on the government to provide debating time to scrutinise the government's rejection of the PHSO's reports.[138] The alternative was for section 10(3) reports always to be debated in the Commons or at least for the Commons itself to decide whether or not to do so and to therefore not rely upon the government. None of the proposals found favour with the government.[139] The Equitable Members Action Group then sought judicial review of the government's position and succeeded on various grounds.[140] Ultimately, the issue was resolved by the 2010 general election. The Conservative manifesto pledged to implement the PHSO's recommendation to make fair and transparent payments to Equitable Life policy holders, through an independent

[136] PASC (n 133) [85].

[137] Wright had also led efforts to enhance scrutiny procedures in the House of Commons, following the MPs' expenses scandal: House of Commons Reform Committee, *Rebuilding the House* (HC 2008–09, 1117).

[138] PASC, *Parliament and the Ombudsman* (HC 2009–10, 107).

[139] PASC, *Parliament and the Ombudsman: Further Report* (HC 2009–10, 471), Appendix: Government Response.

[140] *R (Equitable Life Members Group) v HM Treasury* [2009] EWHC 2495 (Admin).

payment scheme, for their relative loss as a consequence of regulatory failure.[141] This was motivated by political factors. A compensation scheme was then introduced.[142]

However, the money allocated to the compensation scheme (£1.5 billion) was significantly less than that requested by the Equitable Members Action Group (£4–5 billion) and the government's own estimation of the losses (£4.1 billion). The vast majority of those affected received only 22 per cent of the money they had lost.[143] There were also failures in the design and administration of the compensation scheme, delays in making payments and poor customer service.[144] Many years later, there were complaints of widespread errors in the calculation of compensation and serious doubts were expressed over the accuracy and reliability of the Treasury's methodology used to calculate awards. A Commons debate sharply criticised the government.[145]

Equitable Life also cast a long shadow over and within the PHSO for many years. The episode marked the limits of the government's patience with the PHSO undertaking big investigations that landed the government with a large and unexpected financial bill. Abraham's term of office ended. The PHSO absorbed the message and became much more cautious. It did not undertake another big investigation for many years until the women's state pension report published in 2021.[146] By this time, all the PHSO's staff had changed and it had reformulated its approach to financial remedies. The PHSO now viewed itself as 'an organisation that is not primarily about financial compensation', but with identifying maladministration and learning points for government.[147] The longer-term effect of Equitable Life was then to prompt the PHSO to limit its general approach towards recommending significant financial remedies to large cohorts of people. The PHSO did not undertake a big investigation for many years.

This period was the high-water mark for big investigations and for positive relations between the PHSO and the Committee. Overall, Abraham had made a major push for systemic investigations involving complex and sensitive policy and delivery issues with substantial consequences for government. In some instances, the government accepted the PHSO's reports, but in other instances, government rejected the reports. There was then protracted scrutiny by the Committee and litigation in the higher courts. The relationship between Abraham and Wright was an effective and conducive one. Both of them wanted to secure wider systemic change – not just in relation to the specific reports, but also wider cultural change and improvement within government by making it more accountable. However, there had been a perception that Abraham had been

[141] Conservative Party, *Invitation to Join the Government of Britain: The Conservative Manifesto 2010* (2010) 12; *The Coalition: Our Programme for Government* (May 2010) 26.

[142] Equitable Life (Payments) Act 2010.

[143] House of Commons Library, *Errors in Payments Made to Victims of the Equitable Life Scandal* (CDP-2021-0012, 2021).

[144] House of Commons Committee of Public Accounts, *Administering the Equitable Life Payment Scheme* (HC 2013–14, 111).

[145] House of Commons Library (n 143); HC Deb 21 January 2021, vol 687, cols 1167–97.

[146] See ch 8 298–304.

[147] House of Commons Work and Pensions Committee, *Oral Evidence: PHSO Report on Women's State Pension Age* (HC 2023–24, 740) 7 May 2024, Q47 (Rebecca Hilsenrath, interim PHSO): 'Most people who come to us are motivated by the fact that they want an apology and they want the system to change to ensure that other people don't suffer the same experience that they had … we are not a tribunal or a court and we will not award the kind of very high levels of compensation that you see in negligence cases.'

pursuing something of a personal crusade and had been over-reaching the limits of the PHSO's role. Both occupational pensions and Equitable Life were rightly criticised by the government on the ground that the PHSO had recommended financial redress for losses not arising from maladministration. If the PHSO had continued to pursue this, then there really would be huge problems. However, the global financial crisis ushered in a new age. Following the 2010 general election, the wider political mood changed sharply with the introduction of austerity policies.

2010–25: Mellor and Behrens

The appointment of Julie Mellor as PHSO in 2012 marked a clear shift of focus away from big investigations back to individual redress and routine complaint-handling. Mellor had previously been a chair of the Equal Opportunities Commission and there was a perception that her leadership style was to run the PHSO as another quango. The PHSO had been criticised for not investigating a significant number of complaints. In response, Mellor committed the PHSO to investigating every individual complaint where there was any indication of someone having been let down by a public service and experienced injustice. This change of strategic direction coincided with and was prompted by wider political changes, in particular austerity. The government would likely have had little, if any, sympathy with the PHSO undertaking detailed, protracted and expensive investigations recommending high-value financial payments. The consequent shift towards individual complaints would, Mellor argued, produce better outcomes and remedies for individuals and also learning for public bodies to prompt them to improve.[148] But this was hardly problem-free. An obvious difficulty was that an increased caseload would pose real challenges for the PHSO, given its reduced budget and decreased staff numbers. Indeed, a fivefold increase in the number of investigations was unprecedented in the office's history and would require extensive and efficient case management. There was also the potential for unleashing a pent-up demand of complaints from the public, thereby leading to increased complaint volumes and backlogs and delays.

Ombudsman reform was also on the agenda. The Conservative MP, Bernard Jenkin MP, now Committee chair (2010–19), was in favour of enhancing the PHSO's powers, mission, profile and effectiveness by bringing it into line with international best practice. This meant abolishing the MP filter and own-initiative powers.[149] A draft Bill proposed to bring together the PHSO and the LGSCO to create a new public service ombudsman and enhance the office in various respects.[150] The Bill was viewed as a positive, albeit modest step forward, but in need of greater ambition.[151] However, the Bill stalled and nothing

[148] PHSO, *Our Strategic Plan 2013–2018* (2013).
[149] PASC, *Time for a People's Ombudsman Service* (HC 2013–14, 655).
[150] R Gordon, *Better to Serve the Public: Proposals to Restructure, Reform, Renew and Reinvigorate Public Services Ombudsmen* (London, Cabinet Office, 2014); Cabinet Office, *Draft Public Service Ombudsman Bill* (Cm 9374, 2016).
[151] R Kirkham and C Gill (eds), *A Manifesto for Ombudsman Reform* (London, Palgrave Macmillan, 2020).

happened. The Committee (now the Public Administration and Constitutional Affairs Committee (PACAC)) also undertook follow-up scrutiny on various PHSO reports.[152]

However, the PHSO was itself now heading into difficulties, especially with regard to its poor handling of health complaints.[153] A critical report by the Committee identified 'serious questions about the capacity and capability of the Ombudsman', the 'considerable anguish and disquiet' for complainants when investigations had failed to uncover the truth' and the PHSO's own 'defensiveness and reluctance to admit mistakes' – precisely the same criticism made by the PHSO of government.[154] There was a 'need for improved competence and culture change'.[155] Ombudsmen watchers became increasingly vocal critics. The significant loss of public confidence culminated in Mellor's resignation in 2016.[156]

The PHSO had lost its way and was in crisis. Turning matters around – almost saving it from potential abolition – comprised the bulk of the work for the new office-holder Rob Behrens and his leadership team.[157] The Committee's focus also shifted. Its new chair, William Wragg MP (2019–24), had no interest in using the PHSO's reports to undertake follow-up scrutiny of government. Instead, the Committee focused on holding the PHSO itself to account through annual scrutiny sessions.[158] The shift of attention highlighted a hitherto neglected tension in the Committee's role between, on the one hand, supporting the PHSO and using its reports to scrutinise government and challenge non-compliance, and, on the other hand, holding the PHSO itself to account. The Committee also missed opportunities to undertake follow-up scrutiny of important PHSO reports finding significant maladministration by government. A section 10(3) report on the Environment Agency was, contrary to long-established practice, ignored by the Committee.[159] In Wragg's view, the Environment Agency needed to be answerable to Parliament for its non-compliance or to the relevant departmental select committee.[160] Either way, the Committee had no interest in scrutinising government when it rejected PHSO reports. Behrens doubted that departmental select committees were better placed than the Committee to undertake follow-up scrutiny and was right

[152] PACAC, *Follow-up to PHSO Report on Unsafe Discharge from Hospital* (HC 2016–17, 97); PACAC, *Will the NHS Never Learn? Follow-up to PHSO Report 'Learning from Mistakes' on the NHS in England* (HC 2016–17, 743); PACAC, *PHSO review: Quality of NHS Complaints Investigations* (HC 2016–17, 94); PACAC, *Follow up to PHSO Report of an Investigation into a Complaint about HS2 Ltd* (HC 2015–16, 793).

[153] Patients Association, *Parliamentary and Health Service Ombudsman* (n 17); Patients Association, *PHSO – Labyrinth of Bureaucracy* (n 17).

[154] PASC, *Investigating Clinical Incidents in the NHS* (HC 2014-15, 886) [75].

[155] ibid.

[156] S Brecknell, 'Julie Mellor Resigns as Parliamentary and Health Services Ombudsman' *Civil Service World* (5 July 2016).

[157] Behrens (n 19).

[158] See, eg, PACAC, *PHSO Scrutiny 2021–22* (HC 2022–23, 745).

[159] PHSO, *The Earl Report: An Investigation into a Complaint about the Environment Agency* (HC 2021–22, 1233) (a section 10(3) report). Previously, the Ombudsman's threat of issuing a section 10(3) report had been sufficient to get government to fall into line; it was 'a nuclear deterrent rather than a conventional weapon' as excessive use would diminish its effect. See C Clothier 'Fact-Finding Inquiries: The PCA's perspective' [1996] *PL* 384, 388.

[160] Letter from William Wragg MP, PACAC Chair, to Thérèse Coffey, Secretary of State for Environment, Food and Rural Affairs (12 December 2022).

to do so.[161] The Committee's change of approach confirmed a distinct indifference to the PHSO's investigations and the standards of public administration, the principal reason for the Committee's creation in 1969. This opened up a constitutional gap in parliamentary scrutiny of government, which had arisen not from conscious deliberation, but from omission and disinterest by the Committee.

The Committee missed other opportunities for follow-up scrutiny. These included the DWP's flawed migration of disability benefit claimants to a new benefit scheme, resulting in hardship for 118,000 people and the failure by HS2 to communicate properly with a family about acquiring their home for the purpose of building the high-speed rail line.[162] In the latter case, HS2 had taken issue with the PHSO's approach to 'maladministration' because it had not been used to describe a departure from policy/process, but rather to describe a situation where no policy/process existed – despite this being long-established aspect of maladministration.[163]

The Committee's responsibilities had expanded in 2015 to include constitutional matters and this now provided the bulk of its scrutiny work.[164] Of course, the remit and focus of select committees change, although when they do so, it is preferable to ensure that there is no reduction in the scrutiny of government. The Committee's lack of interest in undertaking follow-up scrutiny confirms a substantial weakening of the ombudsman system. It also sends a wider message to government that it can reject ombudsman reports without critical challenge, an undesirable outcome given that the PHSO was in part established to strengthen parliamentary scrutiny of government. Despite this, there is a degree of continuity here. Since its creation, MPs have typically shown little interest in the PHSO's work – unless it can be used for political purposes, such as to criticise the government or to support a campaign group. To its credit, the Committee again supported ombudsman reform, although this was again rejected by the government.[165]

Towards the end of his term of office, Behrens became more vocal by publicly raising serious concerns about the NHS, namely unsafe care, poor complaint-handling, failure to learn appropriate lessons, the burying of evidence, undermining whistleblowing staff and a 'cover-up' culture.[166] The government also rejected the women's state pension age report.[167] In 2024, the Conservative government vetoed the preferred

[161] Letter from Rob Behrens, PHSO, to William Wragg MP, PACAC Chair (29 June 2022). A similar proposal had been rejected by the Ombudsman in 1978 on the ground that the Committee's follow-up scrutiny work would not be adequately performed if it were fragmented amongst different select committees: Gregory (n 81) 50. Wragg had also argued that the government's rejection of the PHSO's report be published as a command paper laid before Parliament, which the government rejected.

[162] PHSO, *An Investigation into the Department for Work and Pensions' Handling of Ms U's Migration to Employment and Support Allowance* (HC 2021–22, 956). See ch 7 253–254 (the DWP's reasons for rejecting the PHSO's recommendations only came to light through an FOI request); PHSO, *An Investigation into HS2's Failure to Communicate with a Family about Acquiring Their Home* (HC 2021–22, 211).

[163] Letter from HS2 Ltd to PHSO (28 May 2021).

[164] When it became the House of Commons Public Administration and Constitutional Affairs Committee.

[165] PACAC, *Parliamentary and Health Service Ombudsman Scrutiny 2022–23* (HC 2023–24, 198); PACAC, *Parliamentary and Health Service Ombudsman Scrutiny 2022–23: Government and PHSO Response* (HC 2023–24, 774); PACAC, 'Government Still "Not Convinced" by Case for Reform of the Parliamentary and Health Service Ombudsman' (23 May 2024);

[166] 'NHS Ombudsman Rob Behrens: "There are Serious Issues of Concern"' *The Guardian* (17 March 2024).

[167] See ch 8 298–304.

candidate to be the new office-holder despite the PHSO being an officer of the House of Commons appointed by the Crown and independent of the government.[168] Further, the PHSO's credibility in investigating health complaints was weakened by the establishment of the Health Services Safety Investigations Body and its 'safe space' under which medical professionals could disclose information which the PHSO could not then easily access.[169] All of this confirmed the sense of decline in the PHSO's constitutional standing.

***

The working political relationships between the PHSO, the government and the Committee are complex and have evolved over time. The preceding account suggests various points. Big investigations arise by circumstance. They can enhance the PHSO's impact. Limited by the MP filter, the PHSO's complaints caseload overwhelmingly comprises repetitive and routine complaints – of great importance for complainants, but of no wider public interest, thereby reinforcing its relatively obscure position. By contrast, big investigations are high-profile and more likely to increase the PHSO's impact upon government and bring it to wider public attention.[170] Another motivation cannot be discounted: the desire of the individual office-holder to undertake a big investigation and thereby make their mark.

While big investigations carry the potential for greater impact, they have their risks. There have been controversial reports which have caused tensions with government. Government has tended to be obdurate rather than view big investigations as a learning process. When the PHSO had the Committee's support, it was more likely that matters could be successfully resolved. Yet, the Committee's relationship with the PHSO has shifted from one of strong interest and support to indifference. This has weakened the PHSO's constitutional standing and also parliamentary scrutiny of government. The PHSO has also had some missteps. The occupational pensions and Equitable Life reports were seen by government and others as the PHSO overreaching itself and being used as a surrogate political process by campaigners.[171] Moreover, the resources involved in undertaking a big investigation can hinder routine complaint-handling. The Barlow Clowes investigation had 'a wider impact on the Office which was not wholly beneficial … the investigation put a brake on the

[168] HC Deb 25 March 2024, vol 747, cols 1356–59; 'No 10 Accused of Blocking Nick Hardwick to Be Health Ombudsman' *The Guardian* (27 March 2024); Cabinet Office, *Cabinet Manual* (London, Cabinet Office, 2011) [5.40]. Nick Hardwick had previously led the Independent Police Complaints Commission and HM Inspectorate of Prisons before being forced to resign as chair of the Parole Board during the Worboys case. See J Roberts, 'The Parole Board and the Worboys case' [2018] *Criminal Law Review* 808.

[169] Health and Care Act 2022, ss 109–35; European Commission for Democracy (Venice Commission) (Opinion No.1044/2021 CDL-AD(2021)041, 18 October 2021). In 2025, the government announced that the Health Services Safety Investigations Body – along with many other health bodies – would be abolished: 'Hundreds of NHS Agencies to Be Scrapped' *BBC News* (28 June 2025), www.bbc.com/news/articles/c3w4xl8gyyqo.

[170] AW Bradley, 'Sachsenhausen, Barlow Clowes – and Then?' [1992] *PL* 353; WK Reid 'What's the Good of Law in a Case o' the Kind?' [1993] *PL* 221.

[171] C Harlow and R Rawlings, *Law and Administration*, 4th edn (Cambridge, Cambridge University Press, 2022) 576–78.

efforts of the Office to increase its output of cases and to bring down the time taken for individual investigations'.[172] Similarly, the women's pension age investigation took six years during a period in which the PHSO was criticised for delays in handling routine complaints.[173]

It can be queried whether the PHSO should undertake big investigations.[174] Such investigations had not been envisaged when the PHSO was established. In one sense, the question whether it should undertake such investigations is little different from whether it should investigate individual complaints. Everyone who complains has their own personal campaign. The scale of big investigations and the financial remedies involved reflect the reality that central government administers policy on a large scale affecting millions of people. Refusing to undertake big investigations would undermine the rationale for the PHSO's existence. Yet, there are dangers for the PHSO when it is being used to fight what are essentially political battles. Overall, big investigations are an efficient means of addressing a large volume of grievances. They are a practice that has evolved over time and have been implicitly accepted by both the government and Parliament. The government has strongly contested some specific investigations, but has not challenged the general practice or sought to confine the PHSO to individual complaints. However, there are limits as to how far the PHSO should go in its big investigations, as highlighted by both occupational pensions and Equitable Life. Moreover, the Committee's lack of interest has weakened the PHSO's constitutional standing.

Nonetheless, the PHSO has had more successes than failures. It has subjected government to close scrutiny and secured redress that would otherwise not have been forthcoming. The PHSO's ability to function, as originally envisaged, as an 'extremely sharp and piercing instrument of investigation' places it above judicial mechanisms when it comes to scrutinising central government.[175] At the same time, there have been few big investigations all told. Governmental compliance has not usually been motivated by some deeper governmental commitment to good administration, but more so by political forces bearing down upon government. The PHSO will likely be most effective when there are tensions with government and when political factors push government towards providing redress. To this end, the PHSO's investigations should receive more detailed follow-up scrutiny by the Committee or it should make arrangements with departmental select committees. The PHSO is now less of a key player than it once was. The office's low public profile, the MP filter, its jurisdictional limits, the small number of complaints against central government investigated and its formal and lengthy investigations all constrain its role. Office-holders have done what they can, but only within a limited statutory framework. Reform is required, although that depends on the willingness of government and Parliament.

[172] House of Commons Select Committee on the Parliamentary Commissioner for Administration, *Report of the Parliamentary Commissioner for Administration 1989* (HC 1990–91, 129) [3].

[173] PACAC, *Parliamentary and Health Service Ombudsman scrutiny 2021–22* (HC 2022–23, 745) [26]–[30].

[174] Harlow and Rawlings (n 171) 578.

[175] HC Deb 18 October 1966, vol 734, col 60 (Richard Crossman MP, Leader of the House of Commons).

The Impact of Ombudsmen

Traditionally, ombudsmen were principally focused on investigating and correcting wrongs, and only secondarily concerned with improving administration. However, over time, the improvement function of ombudsman has become more prominent. What then is the impact and influence of ombudsmen upon government and public services beyond resolving individual complaints? What difference do ombudsmen make in terms of improving public services to prevent the same and similar problems from happening again? How do different ombudsmen compare?

These are big questions to which there are few simple answers. There are inherent problems and challenges for an ombudsman, as an external body, in seeking to get the same government body responsible for maladministration and injustice to then learn for the future and to improve. There are also challenges in assessing the impact of ombudsmen because of the range of variables in play. It is necessary to be cautious and to guard against any assumption that ombudsmen invariably exert influence and impact on government or, conversely, that they have little, if any, impact upon government and public services. Nonetheless, we can consider the general issues that have been raised.

Unlike tribunals, ombudsmen cannot substitute their own decisions for those of government, but also unlike tribunals, ombudsmen can examine and criticise the decision-making processes and other behaviours of government. Ombudsmen also recommend improvements to public services. This is particularly useful given that many people do not complain at all, let alone to an ombudsman. A single complaint can uncover a problem affecting not only the complainant but also other people. Complaints can identify wider dysfunctions, gaps and omissions within public bodies. Ombudsmen can then issue service improvement recommendations to address those problems and to promote better administration. In turn, such improvements will then benefit a wider population beyond the individual complainant.

The ability of ombudsmen to prompt service improvements depends on a range of variables. Ombudsmen must correctly diagnose the underlying problem and craft appropriate service improvement recommendations. Those recommendations must then be formally accepted and be substantively implemented in practice by the public body. This in turn depends on factors such as the leadership of the public body, its culture and resources, its willingness to learn and improve, and its capacity to deliver those improvements and to embed them with its practices. Public bodies may be sceptical of an outsider, an ombudsman, providing advice and improvement recommendations when the ombudsman is not itself responsible for delivering public services. On the other hand, the ombudsman brings a fresh external perspective unencumbered by an established attitude of 'this is how we do things here'. Further, recommendations are based on the ombudsman's investigations of specific cases in which a public body's maladministration has caused injustice. The adverse publicity from such cases often reinforces the need for the public body to improve its services. Ombudsmen work within a consensual system of administrative justice. They rely upon public bodies wanting to improve. There is often public and media interest and potential follow-up scrutiny by elected committees.

Of course, the impact of ombudsmen on government – along with that of tribunals and the courts – competes with other forces, including political, financial, organisational and cultural factors.[176] At the same time, there is a strong normative argument that government should take greater account of the lessons identified by ombudsmen and use them to improve. Further, ombudsmen themselves have sought to enhance their impact on government by issuing more service improvement recommendations and engaging directly with public bodies. To explore this further, we can consider the work of the LGSCO and the PHSO.

The LGSCO

The LGSCO investigates some 4,000 complaints per year from across the range of English local services. Prominent areas include: education and children's services; adult social care; housing; and planning. Until 2014, the LGSCO principally focused on individual complaint-handling, but it then consciously started to use complaints to prompt councils to improve their service delivery by issuing more service improvement recommendations. Figure 6.2 shows the number of complaints upheld and service improvement recommendations issued by the LGSCO.[177] What is striking here is the significant increase in service improvement recommendations.

This change of approach was prompted by a significant reduction in the LGSCO's funding and an effort to make more of individual complaints to generate wider public

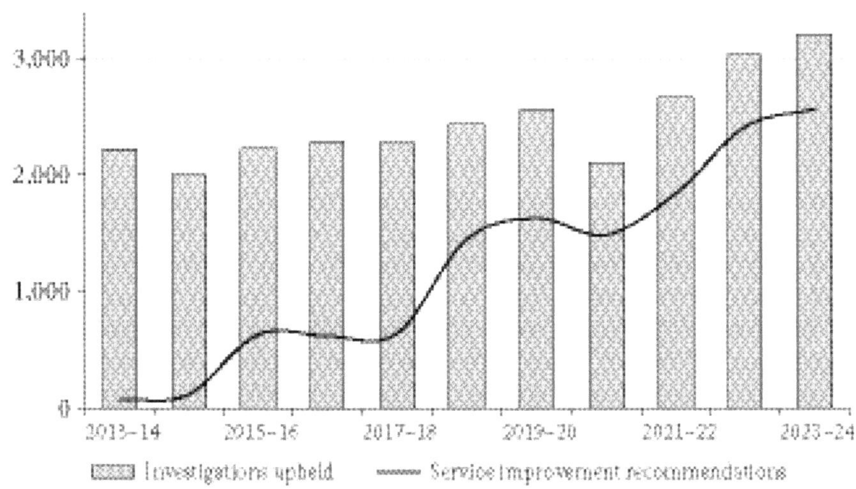

Figure 6.2 LGSCO investigations upheld and service improvement recommendations, 2013–24. Source: LGSCO, *Annual Reviews of Complaints, 2013–24*

[176] C Gill, 'Right First Time: The Role of Ombudsmen in Influencing Administrative Decision-Making' (2011) 33 *Journal of Social Welfare and Family Law* 181.

[177] The LGSCO's annual *Reviews of Local Government Complaints 2013–2024.*

benefits.[178] Being the lowest-cost ombudsman and having a high caseload has presented challenges for the LGSCO. One of the LGSCO's key organisational risks concerns its ability to adapt to changes in demand for its service, given the operational difficulties arising from its significantly reduced budget.[179] This has forced the LGSCO to think carefully about how to best use its limited resources to achieve as much impact as possible.[180] The LGSCO has therefore increasingly sought to use individual complaints as a vehicle for identifying wider systemic failures and their underlying structural causes and then issuing improvement recommendations. Such recommendations include councils: adopting and reviewing their policies; devising and reviewing systems and processes to keep track of people's cases and entitlements; introducing better coordination and joint working between different council departments; developing action plans to address problems identified, such as a backlog of decisions; staff training; reviewing whole services characterised by ongoing problems; and so on. Some examples from the LGSCO's casework help to illustrate this.

Consider those faults which arise because of inadequate coordination and cooperation between different departments within councils. A lack of coordination and cooperation between different services and departments can lead to gaps into which people fall, thereby resulting in injustice. For instance, an elderly homeless man with dementia had been placed by his council in temporary accommodation while it decided what could be done for him. Under the Care Act 2014, councils are required to undertake an assessment for any adult who may have needs for care and support.[181] Such assessments must be carried out over a suitable and reasonable timescale, given the urgency of a person's needs. Councils should make arrangements to ensure cooperation between, for instance, their social care and housing departments.[182] In the specific case, the man had been placed in unsuitable accommodation by the council's housing department. This prevented him from accessing community health services to medicate his dementia. Given his growing needs, the man had been sectioned under the Mental Health Act 1983 and later died. The LGSCO criticised the council's handling of his case.[183] The council had failed to: undertake an assessment of the man's needs and best interests; offer advocacy support for him; include his sister in meetings and decision-making concerning his situation; and finalise a Care Act assessment. The council had shown a lack of initiative when trying to help him. The fundamental problem was that the council's housing service had refused to act until a social care assessment had

[178] House of Commons Levelling Up, Housing and Communities Committee, *Oral Evidence: LGSCO Triennial Review* (HC 2021–22, 960) Q17, 10 January 2022 (Mick King, LGSCO). Between 2011 and 2019, the LGSCO's funding was reduced by 41 per cent. The LGSCO is funded by the Department for Levelling Up, Housing and Communities. Since 2010, the LGSCO's budget has been artificially linked to reduced funding of local government; it is significantly underfunded and operates with elevated risk and a lack of resilience. The LGSCO receives lower pro rata funding compared with the PHSO (which is funded directly by HM Treasury), even though both perform essentially the same function. The LGSCO has 185 full-time staff, including nine assistant ombudsmen and 90 investigators.

[179] LGSCO, *Adapting and Innovating: Annual Report* (HC 2020–21, 900) 52–53.

[180] House of Commons Levelling Up, Housing and Communities Committee, *Oral Evidence: LGSCO Triennial Review* (HC 2021–22, 960) Q28, 10 January 2022 (Mick King, LGSCO).

[181] Care Act 2014, s 9.

[182] ibid s 6(4)(b).

[183] LGSCO, 'Yorkshire Man with Dementia Left Unsupported in Hotel for Too Long' (8 September 2023); LGSCO, Calderdale Metropolitan Borough Council (22008699).

been undertaken, while the council's social care department would not act until the man had been placed in appropriate housing by the housing department. There was a lack of joined-up and collaborative planning between different departments within the council. The man had thereby suffered the injustice of being left in unsuitable accommodation for too long without proper support. The LGSCO recommended that the council train its social care and housing officers about their statutory duty to ensure cooperative working between different services.

Similar problems have arisen with councils installing home adaptations for children with disabilities.[184] Haringey Council had taken so long to install agreed home adaptations for a boy with severe disabilities that he had outgrown them by the time they were finally completed.[185] Over several years, the council had: only partially undertaken and then delayed the building work; not kept in contact with the family; and not properly considered the family's request for alternative adaptations.[186] The underlying problem was that the council's service, its contractors and the input of occupational therapy had not been effectively managed.[187] The LGSCO recommended that the council review how its home adaptations service could be delivered more effectively and report back on its progress. Council services require coordination and cross-working between different teams and external bodies and professionals. A lack of joined-up working in the delivery of services can result in people falling through the gaps and thereby experiencing injustice. The LGSCO emphasised the need for more coordination and monitoring by managers and councillors.

Another issue concerns council officers not understanding councils' statutory responsibilities. This is bound to lead to problems. A homeless man had been failed by his council because council officers did not understand their statutory responsibilities towards him. The LGSCO recommended that the Council provide training or guidance to its housing team to ensure they understand the Council's duties to provide accommodation under the Housing Act 1996.[188] There have been many similar recommendations from the LGSCO that councils provide training to their staff, issue guidance to junior officers, and that senior officers review the work of junior officers or develop an action plan to improve the particular service.

Another type of situation arises when a whole service is failing as a result of delays and backlogs, such as Deprivation of Liberty Safeguards assessments or the processing of social housing applications. In such situations, the LGSCO has typically recommended that the council review the service and devise an action plan to address the backlogs.[189] Of course, there will be wider constraints that limit how councils respond

[184] Housing Grants, Constructions and Regeneration Act 1996, ss 19–24.

[185] LGSCO, London Borough of Haringey (19020651).

[186] Under s 34(1) of the Housing Grants, Constructions and Regeneration Act 1996, councils should decide applications as soon as reasonably practicable and no later than six months after the date of the application. Work should be completed within 12 months of approval.

[187] Haringey Council, Cabinet minutes 8 March 2022.

[188] LGSCO, Shropshire Council (21 017 512); LGSCO, 'County Man Forced to Live in Car Because of Council Errors' (24 November 2022).

[189] LGSCO, Staffordshire County Council (n 60); LGSCO, Birmingham City Council (20 007 658); LGSCO, 'Ombudsman Investigation Highlights Housing Delays in Birmingham' (13 October 2021) (a significant backlog of social housing applications affecting thousands of people; the LGSCO recommended that an action plan be devised).

to such recommendations. For instance, in one Deprivation of Liberty Safeguard complaint, the LGSCO had recommended that the council review all previous cases in which deprivation of liberty safeguards assessments had not been completed. However, the council was unable to action this recommendation owing to a national shortage of trained assessors.[190]

Another cause of problems concerns the lack of policies or guidance adopted by councils to guide how their deliver their services. Without such policies and guidance, there is a risk that informal and ad hoc practices will prevail and that people reliant upon services will be failed in some way or other. The principle of being open and accountable requires councils to have clear and accessible policies in place about how they will deliver their services. For instance, a man experiencing financial difficulties in paying his council tax bill had fallen into arrears with his payments and sought assistance from his council. Councils can apply a discretionary council tax relief to a person's council tax bill.[191] Such decisions are appealable to the Valuation Tribunal. The council knew that the man was in financial difficulties, but despite several interactions with him, officers had not at any stage advised him to apply for discretionary relief. Further, the council did not have any formal process or policy in place for considering such applications. It had not adopted a formal policy with criteria for considering requests for discretionary relief, as other councils had done so. The LGSCO considered this to be significant fault.[192] Local people had been left unaware that the discretionary council tax relief scheme existed and how the council would consider their applications. There was a risk of injustice in such circumstances. When the man had asked the council to write off his arrears, this was rejected without reasons. The LGSCO concluded that the combined lack of published criteria and reasons created a risk that those refused tax relief would be prevented from appealing to the Valuation Tribunal. The council responded by adopting a policy about discretionary council tax relief containing the eligibility criteria.

The LGSCO has emphasised that its ability to scrutinise defective council policies is central to its work. It has repeatedly criticised councils for adopting local policies that contravene national statutory guidance issued by central government. Such local policies have typically been adopted by councils to reduce people's entitlements or services. In response, the LGSCO has recommended that councils adopt valid policies and provide redress to everyone who has lost out by, for instance, making backdated payments. For instance, councils have adopted flawed policies resulting in the underpayment of special guardianship allowances to families. In response, the LGSCO has recommended that councils bring their policies back into line with statutory guidance and that underpaid allowances be paid to all families concerned.[193] Another area in which councils have acted contrary to statutory guidance is adult social care charging. Under financial pressures, some councils have wrongly required people to pay

[190] LGSCO, Kent County Council (19015406); Kent County Council, Adult Social Care Cabinet Committee (29 September 2021).
[191] Local Government Finance Act 1992, s 13A(1)(c).
[192] LGSCO, Cotswold District Council (20008553); LGSCO, 'Cotswold Council Criticised for Poor Tax Relief Response' (26 August 2021).
[193] LGSCO, Rochdale Metropolitan Borough Council (n 60).

unnecessary charges and 'top-up' fees for social care.[194] The LGSCO has criticised councils for abdicating their responsibilities.[195] In various cases, families have been placed in financially and personally difficult situations by both councils and care providers.[196] In response, the LGSCO has issued wide-ranging recommendations, including that: councils review their care charging policies and procedures, retrospectively apply new policies to all those adversely affected and refund backdated fees wrongly paid by families. It has also recommended that councils reorganise their payment and IT systems to ensure that families do not pay higher fees than they should and that elderly relatives are not threatened with eviction by social care providers. Adult social care charging is an area that has required repeated interventions by the LGSCO.

Another situation arises when a council performs a decision-making function, which it then discharges in a flawed way by, for instance, incorrectly interpreting or applying the relevant rules or policy, or by using a flawed assessment process. Such errors will affect not just the individual complainant, but also a wider population. In such circumstances, the LGSCO has recommended that the council correct its approach and also audit and reconsider previous decisions to ensure that other people have not lost out on their entitlements. This is another useful and practical means of ensuring that other people who have not complained do not experience the same fault and consequent injustice. For instance, Birmingham City Council refused to fund school transport for two children with SEND, issued them with bus passes and expected them to be accompanied by a parent. This contravened statutory guidance. The LGSCO recommended a revised school transport policy and that the council review its previous other school transport decisions.[197] Similarly, Bexley's school transport team had applied the school transport guidance incorrectly.[198] The council had misunderstood the legal test to be applied and consequently applications were wrongly refused. The LGSCO recommended that the council audit all such decisions. Finally, a London council had wrongly rejected applications for freedom passes (which entitle people to free public transport in London). Its process had been out of line with the statutory guidance, lacked transparency and officers had not offered the applicant an independent medical assessment. The LGSCO recommended that the council adopt a new policy that complied with statutory guidance and reconsider the applications of more than 200 other people who had been rejected.[199]

[194] LGSCO, Southampton City Council (11021923); LGSCO, *Counting the Cost of Care: The Council's Role in Informing Public Choices about Care Homes* (2015); LGSCO, Solihull Metropolitan Borough Council (14014177); LGSCO, Stockport Metropolitan Borough Council (21004194).

[195] LGSCO, Walsall Metropolitan Borough Council (10018968); LGSCO, Dudley Metropolitan Borough Council (16002186, 2017); LGSCO, Further Report (2019) and (20003362).

[196] LGSCO, London Borough of Barking & Dagenham and Moreland House Care Home (18002772 & 17012203).

[197] LGSCO, Birmingham City Council (19016798 & 19019859). See also LGSCO, Coventry City Council (19008896).

[198] LGSCO, London Borough of Bexley (19003689 & others).

[199] LGSCO, London Borough of Newham (22006753); LGSCO, 'Hundreds of Rejected Freedom Pass Applications to Be Reviewed by London Borough of Newham' (7 September 2023). See also LGSCO, 'Devon to Review Benefits Calculations for Nearly 300 Carers Following Ombudsman's Investigation' (22 February 2024); LGSCO, Devon County Council (23000973); LGSCO, 'Hackney to Review Rejected Blue Badge Applications from Past 16 Months Following Ombudsman Investigation' (10 April 2025); LGSCO, London Borough of Hackney (24003887); LGSCO, South Gloucestershire Council (23005373); LGSCO, 'Families in South Gloucestershire Being Denied the Respite Support They Need – Ombudsman' (7 November 2023).

Sometimes a number of problems coalesce, resulting in significant 'clustered injustice'. A London council had sought to recover housing benefit overpayments of £8,000 from a young single mother of three children (one of whom was disabled) living in rented accommodation.[200] However, the council had miscalculated the alleged overpayment; it had misapplied the housing benefit rules because it did not understand them.[201] The mother wanted to appeal the housing benefit decision, but the council had failed to forward her case to the First-tier Tribunal, thereby depriving her of the right of appeal. The council had also wrongly informed her landlord about the overpayment. The family was then unlawfully evicted, became homeless and ended up in unsuitable accommodation, causing considerable hardship. When the woman applied to the council as a homeless person with children, the council should have recognised the family as being in priority need and offered accommodation immediately. Instead, officers closed the case without notifying the mother that her application had been refused, thereby unlawfully depriving her of review and appeal rights. When the council later reduced the overpayment, the woman 'was baffled that with no new evidence the claim that I was once written to and told I owed £8,000 for has now reduced to £4,000. This was a huge mistake and that cost my family my home. The stress and hardship this has placed on myself and my family is inconceivable'.[202] Overall, the family sustained serious injustice as a result of the council's multiple and avoidable failures. In addition to a financial payment, the LGSCO recommended that the council investigate and report on its housing benefit calculation errors and audit all other decisions to ensure that other residents were not adversely affected by the Council's overpayment miscalculations.

Many other examples could be given.[203] The LGSCO publishes all of its ordinary 'statements' and also some 40 public reports per year, which must be considered by a council committee.[204] Councils must confirm publicly and to the LGSCO what action it will take as a result. Public reports are issued when there are: recurrent and/or significant faults; non-compliance with previous recommendations; repeated complaints on the same issue; or significant topical issues or systemic problems. The LGSCO's ability to require council committees to consider its public reports ensures senior leaders and elected members become aware of the service failures of their council.[205]

In general, councillors want their councils to deliver good-quality services.[206] They are often concerned about what has gone wrong and what is being done to put things right. They seek reassurance from Cabinet members whether the proposed actions will

[200] LGSCO, London Borough of Haringey (18015518); LGSCO, 'Young Family Left Homeless by Haringey Benefits Blunder' (7 January 2020).

[201] The DWP had previously expressed concern that many local authorities have incorrectly applied housing benefit regulations and wrongly calculated overpayments. See also Milton Keynes Council (18004072) (the council's contractor miscalculated a housing benefit overpayment by not carrying out appropriate checks; the claimant was wrongly required to repay more than £20,000; following the LGSCO's report, the council agreed that a senior officer would check and approve substantial overpayment demands before issuing them).

[202] ibid [72]–[73].

[203] R Thomas, 'The English Local Government and Social Care Ombudsman: Systemic Administrative Justice and Bureaucratisation, Parts 1 & 2' [2023] *PL* 240, 424.

[204] Local Government Act 1974, s 31(2).

[205] Local Government Act 1974, ss 26(1) and 31(2B) and (2BA). Service improvement recommendations are also issued through ordinary statements. Such recommendations can also be made following a finding of fault to prevent its recurrence to others, despite there being no injustice caused to the individual complainant.

[206] C Copus, *In Defence of Councillors* (Manchester, Manchester University Press, 2022) ch 5.

resolve the problems identified. Committee discussions concentrate on the specific details of the particular service concerned, how it can be improved and what is being done. In this respect, the LGSCO performs an important role in supporting councillors and enabling them to undertake scrutiny; its reports provide an independent evidence base for this purpose. In many cases, committee meetings have an air of contrition and willingness to learn and put things right.[207] Committees invariably accept the LGSCO's recommendations. Occasionally, there are internal tussles between council officers and councillors. Officers either disagree with the LGSCO or think that implementing recommendations is too expensive. In response, councillors have argued that it would be wrong in principle to ignore the LGSCO.[208] Council committees can have a ritualistic character with hand-wringing and promises to do better, although councils are under significant financial pressures. Nonetheless, such episodes illustrate how the LGSCO's public reports enable councillors to scrutinise council services and how, in turn, the LGSCO relies upon councillors asserting political control over officers for its recommendations to be actioned. Another feature of complaints concerning services that are significantly underfunded, such as SEND, is that council officers can actually welcome criticism from the LGSCO, which they can then use as a political lever within the council to argue for more resources.

The LGSCO also issues advice and guidance on good administrative practice based on its casework.[209] It is the most proactive ombudsmen in this respect.[210] Its thematic 'focus reports' bring together learning from its complaint decisions and provide guidance to councils and scrutiny questions for councillors. As of 2024, there were 37 focus reports on: housing benefit; homelessness; adult social care and funding; SEND; and equal access to services for disabled people.[211] While being on the receiving end of a complaint likely has more impact, these focus reports are intended to provide useful guidance for councils.

Overall, the LGSCO has made significant efforts to enhance its impact. Its service improvement recommendations carry weight, as evidenced by councils adopting new policies, staff training and introducing new systems and procedures. Councils would prefer to avoid being criticised. They take the LGSCO seriously. The same point applies to other ombudsmen.[212] There are inevitably challenges, especially given the financial pressures. While compliance with recommendations is high, the LGSCO lacks

[207] Commenting on a public report, Croydon's Chief Executive explained: 'We have a council that is not properly customer focused. We have got a way to go to get our customer culture right, we really have': Croydon Council Audit and Governance Committee (7 July 2022).

[208] R Whitehouse, 'Council Officers Told Not to Ignore Ombudsman Recommendations Due to Cost' *Cornwall Live* (28 April 2021) www.cornwalllive.com/news/cornwall-news/councillors-tell-officers-not-ignore-5347823; V Munro, 'Redbridge Councillors "Uncomfortable" about Administration's Plan to Ignore Ombudsman' *Yellow Advertiser* (15 June 2021).

[209] Local Government Act 1972, s 23(12A); Public Services Ombudsman (Wales) Act 2019, s 34.

[210] R Kirkham, 'Prevention is Better Than Litigation: The Importance of Good Administration' (2004) 26 *Journal of Social Welfare and Family Law* 301.

[211] See, eg, LGSCO, *Counting the Cost of Care: The Council's Role in Informing Public Choices about Care Homes* (Coventry, LGSCO, 2015); *Not Going to Plan? – Education, Health and Care Plans Two Years on* (Coventry, LGSCO, 2019); *Focus on Housing Benefit* (Coventry, LGSCO, 2020); *Home Truths: How Well are Councils Implementing the Homelessness Reduction Act?* (Coventry, LGSCO, 2020); *Equal Access: Getting it Right for People with Disabilities* (Coventry, LGSCO, 2022).

[212] See, eg, PSOW, *Complaint against Welsh Government* (202206003) (recommendations made to the Welsh government to review the process for gypsy and traveller accommodation assessments and to monitor arrangements).

the resources to follow up with councils whether recommendations are successfully implemented and effective in addressing the faults identified. Instead, it undertakes a desk-based check that is reliant upon councils' statements that they have actioned recommendations. The LGSCO can only undertake further scrutiny if other complaints arise.[213] Follow-up scrutiny is for council committees. This reflects the division of responsibility between councils and the LGSCO. The LGSCO investigates complaints and makes recommendations, whereas it is for councils to provide local services and improve their delivery.

The PHSO

The position with regard to the PHSO is different. It is not as active with regard to central government in the same way as the LGSCO is in relation to local government. There are significant differences between the PHSO and the LGSCO which reflect structural and political differences between central and local government. Councils principally deliver policies devised by central government; they have no policy function. By contrast, central government makes and implements policy on a large scale and views itself as a set of autonomous institutions subject to political direction by ministers. Inevitably, the PHSO faces more acute challenges than the LGSCO in promoting good administration. Central government is an altogether different beast compared with local government. Moreover, the PHSO's parliamentary jurisdiction simply does not generate the same volume of reported investigations. It had been originally envisaged that the PHSO would assist central government in improving administrative standards and efficiency.[214] Unlike the LGSCO, the PHSO has no explicit statutory power to issue guidance on good administration, although it has occasionally done so through its reports.[215] If the PHSO issued guidance concerning, for instance, how DWP officials should handle benefit claims, then the risk is that this could be seen as an unwarranted intrusion and/or simply be ignored.

What then of the PHSO's role in improving administration and service delivery? For many years, the principal instance of the PHSO's wider impact concerned 'legal entitlements and administrative practices' (LEAP). An investigation concerning war pensioners not paid their full pension entitlements raised a wider question: what is the obligation of government towards people who have been denied their full legal entitlements as a result of flawed administrative practices?[216] A review led to the cross-government LEAP guidance. If people had been deprived of their legal

[213] See, eg, Kent County Council (22003403) (the LGSCO identified a recurrent fault by the council's SEND service – 'The fault in this case indicates lessons are not being learnt, issues are not being addressed appropriately and service improvements are not being fully or adequately embedded' – and issued a public report to draw attention to past failings and highlight issues that required improvement as a priority); Essex County Council (23003950) (previous LGSCO recommendations had not been implemented successfully; the council had to review).

[214] Prime Minister, *The Parliamentary Commissioner for Administration* (Cmnd 2767, 1965) [15].

[215] For instance, the PHSO has issued guidance on setting up a compensation scheme: PHSO, *Put Together in Haste: 'Cod Wars' Trawlermen's Compensation Scheme* (HC 2006–07, 313).

[216] Parliamentary Commissioner for Administration, *A War Pensions Injustice Remedied* (HC 1977–78, 312); House of Commons Select Committee on the Parliamentary Commissioner for Administration, *Reports of the Parliamentary Commissioner for Administration* (HC 1977–78, 544).

entitlements as a result of flawed administrative practices or a different interpretation of the rules through judicial decision, then the government is obliged to proactively correct the position by undertaking a corrective LEAP exercise to ensure that people receive their full entitlements.[217] Such exercises involve reviewing past decisions and correcting them to ensure that they are lawful and that people receive their full statutory entitlements. This was held up by the Ombudsman as 'an excellent example' of the office's ability to prompt 'a major re-examination by the civil service of a particular area of administrative practice', thereby improving the quality of administration in the public interest.[218] This was indeed an important development. The LEAP policy is a significant aspect of administrative law, as demonstrated by various LEAP exercises undertaken in recent years, especially in the benefits context.[219] This has been a substantial and long-lasting extension of good administration to ensure that people do not lose out on their legal entitlements as a result of flawed administrative practices.

In other respects, the record of the PHSO has been more modest. Its tax credits reports contained some improvement recommendations, but resulted in few real tangible changes.[220] The anticipated era of the PHSO 'auditing by stealth' did not really materialise, although there have been some advances.[221] In 2007, the PHSO recommended that the Department of Health develop and distribute properly considered national guidance for the NHS on redress for people wrongly refused denied Continuing Health Care funding.[222] In an investigation concerning a Windrush man wrongly subject to immigration enforcement action, the PHSO recommended that the Home Office explore the lessons learnt, given its failure, and consider how learning from complaints could be part of developing a culture of learning.[223] On occasion, the PHSO has recommended improvements and has been ignored, thereby revealing real failures by government. In 2011, the PHSO criticised the Foreign and Commonwealth Office and its Embassy in Cairo for its poor response to a British woman travelling abroad who had been sexually assaulted.[224] The PHSO recommended a review of procedures and the provision of empathetic support in such circumstances, but little seemingly improved. Years later, the PHSO upheld a very similar complaint, suggesting that its prior recommendation had made little difference. The department then devised an action plan.[225] The role of ombudsmen in improving administration relies heavily upon government itself wanting to improve and prioritising such improvements and then ensuring they are implemented in practice.

We can look at the numbers of service improvement recommendations. Figure 6.3 shows the overall number of service improvement recommendations (both parliamentary and health) issued by the PHSO in 2012–25.[226] Figure 6.4 shows the breakdown of such

[217] Civil Service Department, *Legal Entitlements and Administrative Practices: A Report by Officials* (HMSO, 1979).
[218] Parliamentary Commissioner for Administration, *Annual Report for 1979* (HC 1978–79, 402) [15].
[219] R Thomas, 'Legal Entitlements and Administrative Practices: LEAP Exercises and Benefits Administration' (2022) 29 *Journal of Social Security Law* 49.
[220] PHSO, *Tax Credits: Putting Things Right* (n 106); PHSO, *Tax Credits: Getting it Wrong?* (n 106).
[221] R Kirkham, 'Auditing by Stealth? Special Reports and the Ombudsman' [2005] *PL* 740.
[222] PHSO, *Retrospective Continuing Care Funding and Redress* (HC 2006–07, 386).
[223] PHSO, *An Investigation into UK Visas and Immigration's Handling of Windrush Man's Status* (2021).
[224] PHSO, *Sexual Assault Abroad* (HC 2013–14, 837).
[225] PHSO, 'Woman Assaulted Overseas Told: "Carry on with Your Holiday and Enjoy it" by Foreign Office' (29 April 2022); Foreign, Commonwealth and Development Office, *FCDO Consular Network: Rape and Sexual Assault Action Plan* (London, FCDO, 2022).
[226] These data are taken from the PHSO's Annual Reports 2012–24. There are no available data for 2013–14.

recommendations between parliamentary and health complaints in 2020–25.[227] Figures 6.5 and 6.6 respectively show the nature of the service improvement recommendations for parliamentary and health complaints (eg, action plan, changes to policy or procedure, other service improvements, staff training and other systemic remedies) for the years 2020–25.[228]

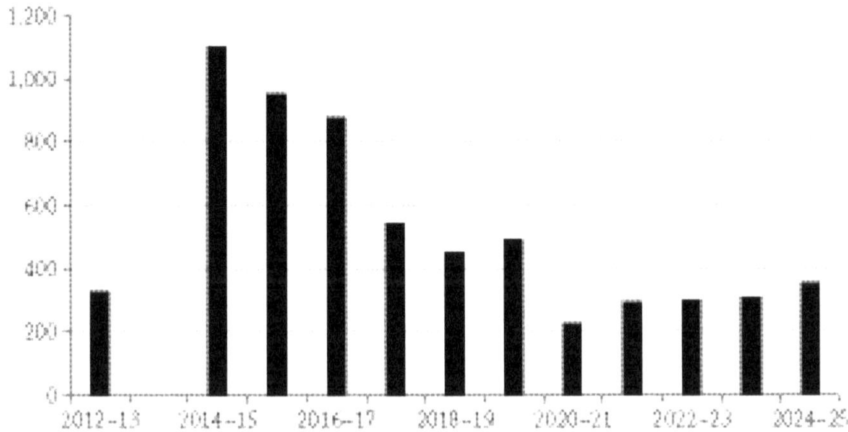

Figure 6.3 PHSO service improvement recommendations (parliamentary and health complaints combined), 2012–25. Source: PHSO Annual Reports, 2012–25 (no data are available for 2013–14)

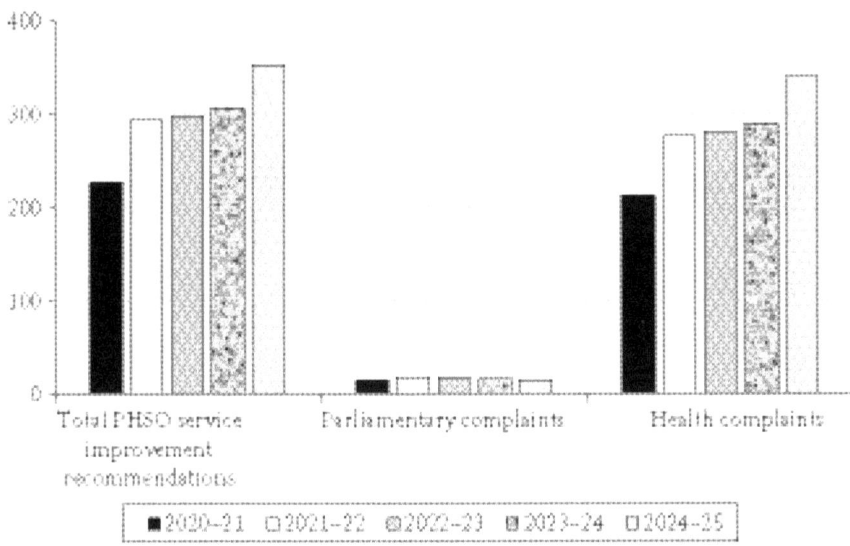

Figure 6.4 PHSO service improvement recommendations (broken down between parliamentary and health complaints), 2020–25. Source: information supplied by the PHSO

[227] FOI requests (2024 and 2025). The PHSO did not break down the data between health and parliamentary recommendations before 2020. As such, it is difficult to account for the overall decline in recommendations since 2014–15, although it seems reasonable to assume that this is largely a reduction in health rather than parliamentary recommendations, which have been consistently low in number.

[228] ibid.

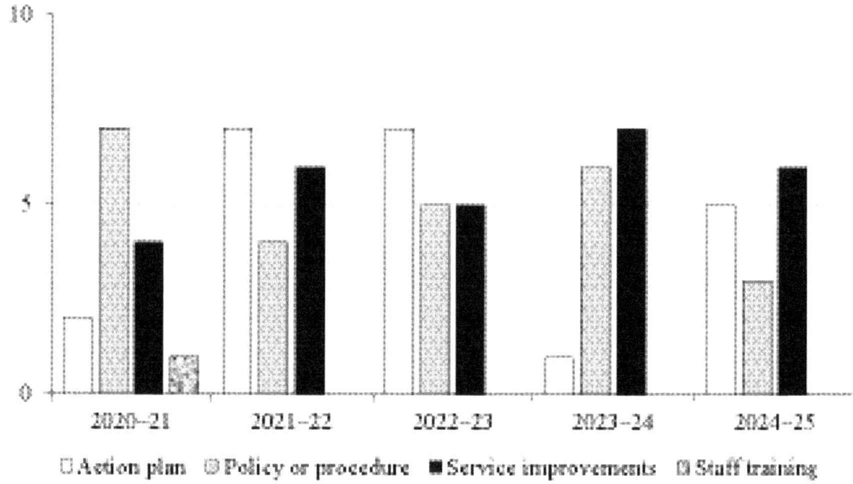

Figure 6.5 The nature of PHSO service improvement recommendations: parliamentary/central government complaints, 2020–25. Source: information supplied by the PHSO.

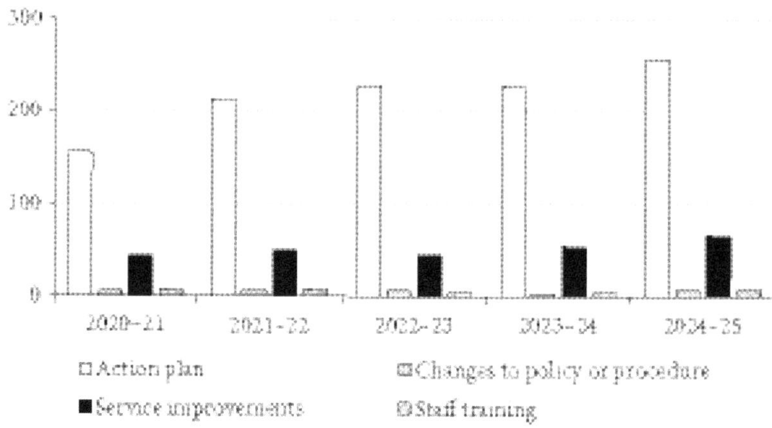

Figure 6.6 The nature of PHSO service improvement recommendations: health complaints, 2020–25. Source: Information supplied by the PHSO

From these data, it is apparent that the PHSO issues relatively few service improvement recommendations to central government departments compared with improvement recommendations concerning health and also the LGSCO's recommendations to local government (see Figure 6.2, page 214 above). However, the following points need to be borne in mind.

First, the PHSO's work is heavily skewed towards health complaints. It investigates far fewer complaints concerning central government than the LGSCO does as regards local government. Beneath the small number of big investigations, the PHSO's parliamentary caseload soon flattens out to a relatively low number of individual routine complaints against central government. The PHSO investigates only around one per cent of the parliamentary complaints it receives. Its investigations are protracted and lengthy. Of this already low number, some 40 or so complaints against central government are fully or partly upheld each year.[229] Unlike the LGSCO, the PHSO's 'parliamentary' caseload is affected by both the MP filter and second-tier complaint-handling bodies, such as the Independent Case Examiner, which themselves issue some service improvement recommendations. What is largely absent from the PHSO's 'parliamentary' casework are mid-level reports – akin to the LGSCO's public reports – that can provide a vehicle for substantive service improvement recommendations. The PHSO has issued some such reports, but they have been rare and intermittent.[230] It does not receive sufficient repeat complaints into routine areas of administration by central government in the same way that the LGSCO does.

Second, the differences between central and local government are highly relevant. The LGSCO issues many service improvement recommendations to the 317 English local authorities, which, broadly speaking, deliver the same services. The same point applies to health bodies that fall within the PHSO's jurisdiction. By contrast, in its parliamentary jurisdiction, the PHSO deals with a smaller number of large central government departments, each of which has a unique set of functions and which operate on a national rather than a local basis. For instance, the LGSCO has issued many repetitive service improvements to a large number of different councils concerning the delivery of special educational needs, which is a real problem area. The problems that arise are, in part, faulty administration by councils, but they are also, in part, the downstream consequences of central government policy and inadequate funding. However, the PHSO receives very few complaints against the Department for Education precisely because it is not responsible for the front-line delivery of services. Instead, councils do the administration and receive the accompanying complaints (and blame).

Conversely, when the PHSO does issue service improvement recommendations to central government, they can have a much wider impact that those of the LGSCO precisely because of the scale of central government. Consider the PHSO's investigation into the women's state pension age. Having found that the DWP had failed to communicate important changes to the women's state pension age, the PHSO recommended that the DWP take steps to improve its communications and to take more account of feedback and research.[231] In response, the DWP agreed to work with the PHSO to develop a detailed action plan in order to ensure that all lessons were learnt and actioned.[232] This counted as only one recommendation, although it would involve a significant piece of work for both the DWP and the PHSO, affect tens of millions of people and would, if implemented properly, positively improve the DWP's communications to them. Despite being only a

[229] See Appendix F.

[230] See, eg, PHSO, *Investigation into Delays in Making Payments under the Arable Area Payments Scheme* (HC 1999–2000, 635); PHSO (n 223); PHSO, *An Investigation into the Department for Work and Pensions' Handling of Ms U's Migration to Employment and Support Allowance* (n 162).

[231] PHSO, *Women's State Pension Age: Our Findings on Injustice and Associated Issues* (HC 2023–24, 638) 92. See further ch 8 at 298–305.

[232] DWP, *Government Response to the Parliamentary and Health Service Ombudsman's Investigation into Women's State Pension Age and Associated Issues* (London, DWP, 2024) 31–33.

single improvement recommendation, it was on an altogether different scale in terms of its substantive reach and effect. By contrast, a recommendation from the LGSCO that a council remind staff to follow guidance can be actioned simply by sending an email.

Despite these points, it can still be concluded that the number of service improvements recommended by the PHSO in its parliamentary jurisdiction is lower than it should be. The PHSO's parliamentary casework falls into the two extremes of a small number of big investigations and a somewhat larger, although still quite small, number of individual complaints. Further, knowing the number of service improvement recommendations only gets us so far. What is not really known is the degree to which such recommendations are not just formally accepted but also substantively acted upon by public bodies and their wider impact and longevity. That would require detailed empirical research.

What then of the PHSO's health jurisdiction? It issues more service improvement recommendations in its healthcare casework (see Figures 6.4 and 6.6 above). When investigating complaints that patients have received poor-quality care from the NHS, the PHSO has frequently recommended that the relevant health body produce an action plan to ensure that the failings identified are not repeated.[233] This places the responsibility on the health body to improve and learn from complaints. The PHSO has seen both good and less robust action plans. In one instance, the PHSO followed up multiple times with the health trust to ensure that the proposed action plan was satisfactory. The trust's action plan had not explained how it would audit its proposed new processes; consequently, there was no means of knowing whether they were effective.[234]

The PHSO has also published thematic reports concerning national problems in the NHS. Its *Ignoring the Alarms* report investigated poor NHS treatment of patients with eating disorders, resulting in avoidable deaths.[235] Concerns were raised about a lack of awareness of eating disorders amongst medical professionals, problems in the transition from child to adolescent eating disorder services, poor coordination, scarcity of specialists and poor coordination between different services to investigate avoidable deaths. The report identified serious matters affecting some 750,000 people which required national attention. The PHSO's recommendations concerned: the training of medical professionals; the quality and availability of adult services; coordination of services; and improving investigation and learning, in particular from serious incident investigations. The select committee later found that insufficient action had been undertaken; greater urgency and leadership from the Department for Health and Social Care was required.[236] Familiar themes in the PHSO's healthcare reports have included calls for meaningful change, raising awareness amongst medical professionals and the need for NHS leaders to embed a culture of learning from mistakes, improving care and responding to mistakes with compassion. The government's response detailed various actions that had been put in place, including an NHS PHSO delivery group to bring together the various arm's-length bodies to oversee and coordinate delivery of the

[233] PHSO, 'Writing Action Plans', ombudsman.org.uk/organisations-we-investigate/putting-things-right/writing-action-plans. The PHSO might also require that the action plan is shared with the complainants and regulators, eg, NHS Improvement and the Care Quality Commission.

[234] PHSO, *Broken Trust: Making Patient Safety More Than Just a Promise* (HC 2022–23, 1444) 35.

[235] PHSO, *Ignoring the Alarms: How NHS Eating Disorder Services are Failing Patients* (HC 2017–19, 634).

[236] PACAC, *Ignoring the Alarms Follow-up: Too Many Avoidable Deaths from Eating Disorders* (HC 2017–19, 855).

recommendations.[237] A few years later, the PHSO later warned that people with eating disorders were still being failed; radical changes were needed to prevent further tragedies.[238] A parliamentary debate highlighted concerns about the need for progress in effectuating real change.[239] Small steps in improvements had taken place, such as scaling up early intervention services to support children and young people, but overall progress had been slow. A much bigger scale of change was required.

The episode reveals variable progress by the NHS, but also the scale and complexity involved: improved professional training and stakeholder engagement; issuing guidelines, revised frameworks and protocols; changing medical professional cultures; raising awareness; and improved coordination between many different responsible owners, different NHS bodies, professional bodies, and regulation and oversight. These are all long-term and hard-slog issues. The same point arises in relation to the PHSO's other health reports.

In its *Broken Trust* report on patient safety including avoidable deaths, the PHSO broke new ground by the explicitness of its recommendations.[240] The report focused on patient safety and followed in the wake of many other reports criticising poor-quality health services.[241] Government had made significant efforts to improve patient safety, but there was still a significant gap between best practice and reality. The biggest threat to patient safety was a healthcare system at breaking point. The NHS itself could only go so far in terms of improving patient safety. Concerted and sustained action was required to ensure that NHS leaders had the tools to prioritise the safety of patients and were made accountable for doing so. This meant 'getting past politics to put patient safety at the very top of the agenda'.[242] Amongst other recommendations, government needed to ensure that patient safety was a priority for the NHS and seek cross-party support to embed patient safety into the NHS's culture and leadership. The report illustrates wider concerns about repetitive cycles of healthcare complaints with seemingly little corresponding action being taken to address the underlying causes.

Such reports highlight wider issues of culture in the NHS and attitudes towards accountability, the need for compassionate handling of complaints, and learning and improvement. These are complex matters that are not conducive quick fixes. There are limits as to what the PHSO can recommend. The organisation and resourcing of the NHS are big issues. The PHSO's reports have clearly been important in terms of highlighting such matters. At the same time, it is now only one of a multitude of bodies that comprise the wider, confusing and uncoordinated landscape of health oversight, regulation and inspection.[243] Moreover, the NHS has become overwhelmed by so many

[237] Department of Health and Social Care, *Government Response to the Recommendations of the Public Administration and Constitutional Affairs Committee's Seventeenth Report of Session 2017–19: Ignoring the Alarms Follow-up: Too Many Avoidable Deaths from Eating Disorders* (CP 105, 2019).

[238] PHSO, 'Urgent Action Needed to Prevent Eating Disorder Deaths' (27 February 2023).

[239] HL Deb 29 June 2023, vol 831, cols 843–54.

[240] PHSO (n 234).

[241] See, eg, B Kirkup, *The Report of the Morecambe Bay Investigation* (2015); *Independent Review of Maternity Services at the Shrewsbury and Telford Hospital NHS Trust* (HC 2021–22, 1219); *Maternity and Neonatal Services in East Kent: 'Reading the Signals' Report* (HC 2021–22, 681).

[242] PHSO (n 234) 7.

[243] E Oikonomou, J Carthey, C Macrae and C Vincent, 'Patient Safety Regulation in the NHS: Mapping the Regulatory Landscape of Healthcare' (2019) *British Medical Journal Open* 9:e028663.

safety and improvement recommendations that it struggles to action them. Despite its commitment to improve patient safety and reduce harm, the NHS has not outlined any specific measures to achieve it.[244]

Overall, ombudsmen have sought to enhance their impact, although the results are inevitably mixed. The LGSCO has been the most proactive ombudsman in this respect. It has been able to exert more influence on local government than the PHSO has in relation to central government. As regards its parliamentary jurisdiction, the PHSO's role and influence is far weaker than it should be. What is largely missing from the PHSO's repertoire is mid-level reports akin to the LGSCO's public reports that identify systemic failures within government. The PHSO also compares unfavourably with the NAO, which regularly issues wide-ranging recommendations that are then followed up by the House of Commons Public Accounts Committee.[245] As noted above, the House of Commons Public Administration and Constitutional Affairs Committee now has little interest in using the PHSO's reports to undertake follow-up scrutiny. That this no longer happens in the way it once did reinforces the sense that the PHSO's model of ombudsmanry is long out of date moribund and urgently in need of reform.

In any event, the impact of ombudsmen does not just concern ombudsmen, but also governmental behaviours and the organisation, funding and cultures of public services. Government can resist or ignore ombudsmen reports and recommendations when it should accept them. The influence that ombudsmen can exert is largely beyond their own control. They can issue recommendations, but ultimately it is for government and public services to take appropriate action. Improving public services is very challenging. Trying to improve complex public services such as health can run into numerous complex obstacles. There is also the consideration that if government accepts all service improvement recommendations made by ombudsmen, then those recommendations are too timorous and are not doing enough to push government to do more. There is also a difference in perspectives here. A cynic might argue that all the reports of ombudsmen achieve little and are not worthwhile. By contrast, suppose that ombudsmen did not exist. If so, then public service failures would not be investigated at all or criticised. Overall, ombudsmen have achieved some success, but more could be done. This is the perennial challenge. How then could their role be enhanced?

Own-Initiative Powers of Investigation

Ombudsmen want to exert more impact upon government. There is a justifiable need for this. Administrative systems and public services can fail and result in avoidable injustice. These concerns are reinforced by the unwillingness of many people to complain. There is an unquantifiable, although large, volume of unremedied injustice which exceeds the relatively small number of ombudsmen investigations. There is only so much ombudsmen can achieve when they are based on a limited and reactive model of individual complaint-handling. The small number of complaints against central government is a

[244] House of Commons Public Accounts Committee, *Costs of Clinical Negligence* (HC 2024–25, 1234) 4.

[245] HC Midgley, L Ferry and AD Murphie, *Holding Government to Account: Democracy and the National Audit Office* (Abingdon, Routledge, 2024).

largely inadequate basis upon which the PHSO can investigate systemic failures that affect a wider population. What more could be done?

The principal option is for ombudsmen to undertake own-initiative investigations into potential systemic maladministration. The basic idea is that rather than waiting for a complaint, the ombudsman identifies an area of potential systemic maladministration for investigation. Own-initiative powers reflect a conceptual shift from a reactive model of individualised redress to a more proactive model of prospective investigation and scrutiny based on systemic improvement.

With own-initiative powers, ombudsmen investigate how systems work, how well they serve individuals and whether they fulfil the principles of good administration. Such powers are particularly valuable when those affected include people who are marginalised or in vulnerable circumstances who will be less likely to complain and who may experience high levels of hidden injustice. If an important function of ombudsman is to protect the rights and interests of cohorts of people against inefficient and oppressive administration, then own-initiative powers are a valuable part of their toolkit.[246] They enable ombudsman to 'hunt lions' without being tied to and limited by the circumstances of individual complaints. There is no good reason why an ombudsman should be a powerless bystander when it is apparent that a group of people are likely experiencing injustice caused by systemic maladministration.

The following issues arise. Which ombudsmen have own-initiative powers? What use have they made of them? Why do other ombudsmen not have them? Should they similarly be given own-initiative powers? And, if so, what are the prospects for this actually happening?

At present, only the Northern Ireland Public Services Ombudsman and the PSOW have full own-initiative powers to investigate systemic maladministration.[247] The LGSCO has a power somewhat approaching an own-initiative power. Neither the PHSO nor the Scottish Ombudsman has own-initiative powers.

Own-initiative powers represent a step-change in the role of ombudsmen, especially the proactive ability to investigate systemic maladministration. This touches directly upon their relationship with government. Inevitably, there is a degree of apprehension within government about enhancing the role of ombudsmen. The concern is that the ombudsman will start probing into sensitive areas, thereby uncovering problems that government would prefer were best left alone. Own-initiative powers generate more

[246] See H Street, *Justice in the Welfare State* (London, Stevens, 1968) 121–22 ('Experts agree that the Ombudsman should have power to proceed on his own initiative without waiting for a complaint – that is how much of the best work is done'); AW Bradley, 'The Role of the Ombudsman in Relation to the Protection of Citizens' Rights' (1980) 39 *CLJ* 304; N Lewis and P Birkinshaw, *When Citizens Complain: Reforming Justice and Administration* (Buckingham, Open University Press, 1993) 123 and 129 ('one of the primary functions of an ombudsman is to seek out the causes of injustice at the systemic level in the way that a court of law could never do … The normal justification [for own-initiative powers] is that the weak and oppressed may be unable to protest in their own interests … If alerted by press stories, an ombudsman with his traditional authority would be ideally placed to conduct an enquiry … We have no doubt that British ombudsmen should possess such powers'); N O'Brien, 'Ombudsmen and Public Authorities: A Modest Proposal' and C Harlow, 'Ombudsmen: "Hunting Lions" or "Swatting Flies"' both in M Hertogh and R Kirkham (eds), *Research Handbook on the Ombudsman* (Cheltenham, Edward Elgar, 2018); C Gill, 'The Ombud and Own-Initiative Investigation Powers' in Kirkham and Gill (n 151).

[247] Public Services Ombudsman Act (Northern Ireland) 2016, s 8; Public Services Ombudsman (Wales) Act 2019, ss 4–5.

scrutiny of and work for government. It has a vested interest in confining ombudsmen to individual complaint-handling. In this way, problems can be characterised as single-instance isolated problems – regrettable no doubt, but one-off cases that do not cast any wider light on governmental performance. The decision to give ombudsmen own-initiative powers is therefore a relatively bold and enlightened one by government. It reflects the recognition that systemic problems can exist which would otherwise likely remain undetected but for the ombudsman's ability to investigate on its own initiative. Such powers exhibit a willingness and openness by government to be held accountable and that ombudsmen have a wider inspectorial-improvement function.

Ombudsmen have themselves lobbied government to have own-initiative powers. Much depends on how the argument is framed. In Northern Ireland, the argument was simply that own-initiative powers would enable the ombudsman proactively to investigate matters of concern, especially those affecting a wide number of people unlikely or unable to complain.[248] In Wales, own-initiative powers were seen as a means of strengthening social justice. The Ombudsman argued that without them, Wales would be left behind compared with ombudsmen schemes in Europe.[249] By contrast, the Scottish government has clearly rejected requests by the SPSO for own-initiative powers, although the debates rumbles on.[250]

The LGSCO has a degree of own-initiative capacity. If, when investigating a complaint, the LGSCO becomes aware of a matter causing actual or potential injustice to other people, then it can investigate even though those affected have not complained.[251] The power was introduced to clarify the LGSCO's role and to enhance its effectiveness and accessibility.[252] The LGSCO has used this power in relation to councils overcharging care home fees and delays in Deprivation of Liberty Safeguards assessments, important legal protections for individuals living in care homes who lack mental capacity to consent to care or treatment.[253] When investigating why a child with SEND who had not received an updated Education, Health and Care plan, the LGSCO uncovered a backlog of 1,500 such plans. It then issued a public report recommending that the

[248] Committee for the Office of the First Minister and Deputy First Minister, *Report on the Committee's Proposals for a Northern Ireland Public Services Ombudsman Bill Volume One* (Seventh Report, 2013) [187]–[195] and [219]; Northern Ireland Assembly, *Research and Information Service Briefing Paper: Own-Motion Investigations by Ombudsmen* (Paper 80/15, 2014).

[249] 'Public Services Ombudsman for Wales "Needs Greater Power"' *BBC News* (28 October 2016), www.bbc.com/news/uk-wales-mid-wales-37789875; N Bennett, 'The New Public Services Ombudsman for Wales Act 2019: The Story, 2014–2020' (2020) 42 *Journal of Social Welfare and Family Law* 391.

[250] Letter from Scottish Government Cabinet Secretary for Justice to Convenor of the Scottish Parliament Local Government and Communities Committee (25 September 2019); Scottish Parliament Local Government, Housing and Planning Committee, *Oral Evidence of the Scottish Public Services Ombudsman*, 6 December 2022, cols 13–15.

[251] Local Government Act 1974, s 26D (as inserted by the Local Government and Public Involvement in Health Act 2007, s 174(1)).

[252] Department for Communities and Local Government, *Strong and Prosperous Communities: The Local Government White Paper* (Cm 6939, 2006) [2.35]. In 1986, the Widdicombe Report on local government had recommended that the then Local Government Ombudsman be given an own-initiative power, but this was rejected by the then government: D Widdicombe, *The Conduct of Local Authority Business* (Cmnd 9797, 1986) [9.74].

[253] See, eg, LGSCO, Lincolnshire County Council (19006248) (overcharging of residential care home fees); Staffordshire County Council (18004809), Cheshire East Council (19 010 786) and Surrey County Council (22 014808) (delays in deprivation of liberty safeguards assessments); Thomas (n 203) 260–62.

council devise an action plan to resolve matters, which would then be overseen by a council committee.[254] This significant fault would not otherwise have come to light. In such cases, the people concerned are in vulnerable circumstances and are unlikely to complain. Overall, the LGSCO has a valuable power, although it could be more widely exercised. At the same time, the LGSCO's section 26D power falls into the wider pattern by which central government increases the scrutiny and oversight of local government but not itself.

It has then been the PHSO which has faced the greatest difficulty in seeking to acquire own-initiative powers. The matter was initially raised during parliamentary debates on the 1967 Bill.[255] Since then, the issue has bounced back and forth between the Committee and the government over many decades, but with little progress.[256] The government has consistently refused to give the PHSO own-initiative powers on various grounds. The power would detract from and undermine the PHSO's handling of individual complaints, place a heavy burden on it, undermine its impartiality and complicate or interfere with the role of regulators. In 2014, the Committee concluded that if the PHSO was to work effectively to identify systemic defects, then it needed to see more than the relatively small number of complaints that reached the office.[257] The PHSO is one of the few ombudsmen in Europe without own-initiative powers. Such a power would give the PHSO a much greater ability to act on emerging trends. The PHSO could investigate issues of immediate concern to Parliament and citizens, and respond to potential systemic failures before they escalated, thereby maximising its proactive and preventative role – as opposed to the institution's default reactive approach. This would extend access to justice to those least likely to complain, including vulnerable and marginalised people, prevent initial complaints systems from becoming over-burdened with similar complaints, enable trends across a particular sector to be addressed in a single investigation and gain insight into service failures which would be used to recommend systemic remedies. In 2014, a government-sponsored review argued that own-initiative powers would enable a reformed PHSO to play 'a full and enhanced role in driving up public delivery standards'.[258] On both occasions, the government rejected the idea. Own-initiative powers would detract from the PHSO's task of putting things

[254] LGSCO, Rochdale Metropolitan Borough Council (24010066); LGSCO, 'Rochdale's Systemic SEND Issues Highlighted in Ombudsman Report' (13 March 2025).

[255] HC Deb 18 October 1966, vol 734, cols 78, 145 and 167; HL Deb 8 February 1967, vol 279, col 1399.

[256] House of Commons Select Committee on the Parliamentary Commissioner for Administration, *Parliamentary Commissioner for Administration (Review of Access and Jurisdiction)* (HC 1977–78, 615) [31]; Cabinet Office, *Fourth Report from the Select Committee on the Parliamentary Commissioner for Administration (Review of Access and Jurisdiction) Session 1977–78: Observations by the Government* (Cmnd 7449, 1979) [18]–[19]; House of Commons Select Committee on the Parliamentary Commissioner for Administration, *Report of the Parliamentary Commissioner for Administration 1989* (HC 1990–91, 129) [21]–[22]; House of Commons Select Committee on the Parliamentary Commissioner for Administration, *The Powers, Work and Jurisdiction of the Ombudsman* (HC 1993–94, 33) [39] and [44]; House of Commons Select Committee on the Parliamentary Commissioner for Administration, *Government Reply to the First Report from the Select Committee on the Parliamentary Commissioner for Administration, Session 1993–94, The Powers, Work and Jurisdiction of the Ombudsman* (HC 1993–94, 619) [18]; Cabinet Office, *Review of the Public Sector Ombudsmen in England: A Report by the Cabinet Office* (London, Cabinet Office, 2000) [6.15]–[6.16]; PASC, *Review of Public Sector Ombudsman in England* (HC 1999–2000, 612) [11]; JCHR (n 80) 3-4.

[257] PASC (n 149) [65]–[72].

[258] Gordon (n 150) [134]–[138].

right for individuals – a formalistic surface reason under which lay a deep civil service resistance to the interference of own-initiative powers.[259]

After more than half a century of back and forth between the Committee and the government, there has been no formal change. The attitude of successive ombudsmen has varied. William Reid (PHSO, 1990–96) did not think it was for him to 'go out and look for trouble' or to operate as 'an inspector-general of the public service'.[260] Michael Buckley (PHSO, 1997–2002) thought that in order for the Ombudsman to identify systemic defects, it needed to see more than the relatively small numbers of cases than reached it received.[261] Ann Abraham (PHSO, 2002–11) was initially sceptical of own-initiative powers on the ground that it risked the PHSO being captured by the media and pressure groups, although she later changed her mind in favour of them because of the need to investigate problems affecting vulnerable and socially disadvantaged people unlikely to complain.[262] Rob Behrens (PHSO, 2017–24) strongly urged the government to give the PHSO own-initiative powers on the grounds that it would strengthen the PHSO's effectiveness and ability to provide an early warning system. A 2021 survey of MPs found that 48 per cent of supported the PHSO having own-initiative powers.[263]

Like the original rejection of the Whyatt Report's proposal on ombudsmen in 1962, the surface arguments of successive governments against own-initiative powers barely conceal the real reason: central government simply does not want systemic weaknesses being uncovered as that would be inconvenient, intrusive and create difficulties. The resistance here is more likely to be senior officials than ministers. Own-initiative powers involve government being made more accountable and for that reason they are resisted. An own-initiative power in the draft Public Service Ombudsman Bill 2016 was vetoed by a single Cabinet minister.[264] The reservations of government reflect a deep unease and lack of confidence about its own administrative systems, although they may be, to some degree, understandable. Central government administers on a large scale and there will always be problems in areas such as benefits and immigration. There is also the inherently blurred line between policy and administration within central government. Perhaps a future enlightened and far-sighted government may confer own-initiative powers on the PHSO, although all governments quickly become bogged down in the hard grind of administration and become defensive. The problem is a mindset that is apprehensive of scrutiny. Ultimately, the determinant of whether the PHSO ever gets own-initiative powers will not be just the balance of rational arguments either way, but also the strength of political forces demanding enhanced scrutiny of government. More recently, the Committee on Standards in Public Life – now the Ethics and Integrity Commission – has emphasised the need for

[259] Cabinet Office, *A Public Service Ombudsman: Government Response to Consultation* (London, Cabinet Office, 2015) 18.
[260] House of Commons Select Committee on the Parliamentary Commissioner for Administration, *Oral Evidence: The Powers, Work and Jurisdiction of the Ombudsman* (HC 1992–93, 650) 5 May 1993, col 17 (William Reid).
[261] PASC (n 149) [66].
[262] Abraham (n 105) 28.
[263] PHSO, *PHSO Stakeholder Survey* (Manchester, PHSO, 2021) 39–40.
[264] Behrens (n 19) 241.

public bodies to recognise and respond to early warning signs of problems. It is also considering whether the ombudsmen system should play a greater role in examining systemic issues.[265]

In the absence of own-initiative powers, the scrutiny space has become increasingly occupied by others; the NAO,[266] select committees,[267] bespoke government-sponsored reviews[268] and non-governmental reviews.[269] The NAO has increasingly reported on systemic administrative justice problems.[270] There is some overlap between the NAO's value for money reports and own-initiatives into systemic maladministration. What sets ombudsmen apart from auditors is their focus on the position of individuals and how they are affected by systemic maladministration. The PHSO could not itself undertake all of this work, although its exclusion from this scrutiny space is anomalous. There is a real need for the PHSO to have own-initiative powers. Government should accept the need for it to be held accountable and the wider public benefits that arise from systemic scrutiny.

The utility of own-initiative powers is illustrated by the own-initiative investigations undertaken. The Welsh Ombudsman (PSOW) has undertaken two own-initiative investigations finding systemic maladministration in relation to homelessness services and carers' needs assessments.[271] In its homelessness investigation, the PSOW found as follows: councils were not always informing claimants of their right to an administrative review; there were variable communications with claimants; councils not taking account of human rights and equality duties–in addition to delays, important matters being overlooked during the assessment process, and councils not considering the suitability of accommodation or providing support to vulnerable claimants. The investigation resulted in some improvements, although further work was required.[272] The PSOW's recommendation that a regulator oversee the administration of homelessness legislation found favour with the Welsh Parliament and government.[273]

The pioneer of hard-hitting own-initiative investigations has been the Northern Ireland Public Service Ombudsman, which has published two large own-initiative reports into personal independence payments and communications to patients

[265] Committee on Standards in Public Life, *Recognising and Responding to Early Warning Signs in Public Sector Bodies* (London, CSPL, 2025); 'Ethics and Integrity Commission Reveals Topic for First Review' *Civil Service World* (11 February 2026).

[266] See, eg, the NAO's reports on disability benefit assessments, Windrush, the flawed transfer of Employment and Support Allowance, state pension underpayments and Concentrix.

[267] The House of Commons Public Accounts Committee routinely follows up on NAO reports.

[268] See, eg, W Williams, *Windrush Lessons Learned Review* (HC 2019–20, 93); L Sayce, *Independent Review of Carer's Allowance Overpayments* (London, DWP, 2025).

[269] See, eg, JUSTICE, *Reforming the Windrush Compensation Scheme* (London, JUSTICE, 2021); Child Poverty Action Group, *You Reap What You Code: Universal Credit, Digitisation and the Rule of Law* (London, CPAG, 2023).

[270] See generally ch 7.

[271] Public Service Ombudsman for Wales, *Homelessness Reviewed: An Open Door to Positive Change* (Pencoed, PSOW, 2021); Public Services Ombudsman for Wales, *Are We Caring for Our Carers? An Own Initiative Investigation into the Administration of Carers' Needs Assessments in Wales* (Pencoed, PSOW, 2024).

[272] Public Service Ombudsman for Wales, *Homelessness Reviewed: Revisited* (Pencoed, PSOW, 2023).

[273] Welsh Senedd, Local Government and Housing Committee, *Homelessness* (Cardiff, Welsh Senedd, Government, 2023); Welsh Government, *Response* (Cardiff, Welsh Government, 2023).

on waiting lists.[274] It has also issued three shorter 'overview' reports.[275] The two large own-initiative investigations provided in-depth studies of how two major public services – benefits and health – operated in practice. The reports made multiple and detailed findings of systemic maladministration and issued various improvement recommendations. Such investigations reflect an important shift from individual to collective administrative justice by trying to get government to improve services used by almost all or at least a significant proportion of the population. The scale of the ambition is matched by the challenges in getting government to improve.[276] Addressing systemic maladministration requires systemic change and this is again inevitably challenging as it goes to the core of how public services are organised and the institutional cultures which inform them. Yet, the Northern Ireland Public Services Ombudsman has provided added value in terms of its focus on people's experiences and interactions with government. Own-initiative investigations also enable ombudsmen to investigate matters which are less traditional 'individual and the state' fare, but more concerned with, for instance, the provision of communal services, as illustrated by the Northern Ireland Public Services Ombudsman's report into tree protection orders.[277] At the same time, there are limits on the exercise of own-initiative powers. If an ombudsman receives increased routine complaints, then this will condition how it uses its own-initiative powers.

In summary, own-initiative powers are an important means by which ombudsmen can investigate systemic maladministration which causes people avoidable injustice and which would otherwise not receive scrutiny. The use of such powers reflects the shift from the confining limits of autonomous law towards a more responsive law approach. In this model, the focus is on diagnosing systemic problems, proposing improved ways of accomplishing public goals, enabling government to become more effective and responsive to people's needs and to redesign institutional arrangements. This is an innovative agenda that should be pursued. However, the debate around own-initiative powers has often been a cautious one, with concerns being raised about time, cost and some governments being defensive. Different approaches have emerged. Some ombudsmen (the Northern Ireland Public Services Ombudsman and the PSOW) have moved ahead, whereas others (the PHSO and the SPSO) remain behind. Underlying this is the influence of government over the design and role of ombudsmen. The unwillingness to allow independent scrutiny of its inner workings itself suggests governmental

[274] Northern Ireland Public Services Ombudsman, *PIP and the Value of Further Evidence: An Investigation into Personal Independence Payment* (Belfast, NIPSO, 2021); Northern Ireland Public Services Ombudsman, *'Forgotten': An Investigation into Healthcare Waiting List Communications* (Belfast, NIPSO, 2023).

[275] Northern Ireland Public Services Ombudsman, *Overview Report: The Use of Restrictive Practices in Northern Ireland Schools* (Belfast, NIPSO, 2021); Northern Ireland Public Services Ombudsman, *Strengthening Our Roots: An Overview Report on Tree Protection in the Planning System* (Belfast, NIPSO, 2023); Northern Ireland Public Services Ombudsman, *Lost in Translation: An Overview Report by the Northern Ireland Public Services Ombudsman on General Practitioner Use of Interpreting Services* (Belfast, NIPSO, 2025). 'Overview' reports are issued when the criteria for a full own-initiative investigation have not been met, but it would still be useful to provide learning for the public body concerned.

[276] In own-initiative investigations, the specific issues of the injustice caused by maladministration and personal remedies do not arise because there are no complainants. The ombudsman is thereby freed from the circumstances of complaints and able to focus upon systemic matters.

[277] Northern Ireland Public Services Ombudsman, *Strengthening Our Roots* (n 275).

resistance to scrutiny and a lack of confidence in its operations. Ideally, government should welcome external scrutiny as a means of improvement, although realistically this attitude is unlikely to change.

Conclusion

Ombudsmen are a principal institution of administrative justice. They perform an important role in investigating complaints and recommending service improvements. They achieve a great deal beyond what tribunals and courts can do. They operate within the wider context of a deep tension between how government should operate and the realities of how government actually operates. This involves a relentless challenge of ombudsmen calling out public service failure – not by blaming public bodies, but in a manner that promotes organisational learning and improvement in a transparent way. There will always be tensions. However, there is scope to enhance the role and impact of ombudsmen. A significant aspect of this concerns the working relationships between ombudsmen and government and the degree to which government bodies respond positively to ombudsmen's reports. Ombudsmen are part of the political process and work most effectively when elected committees take a strong interest in their work. All ombudsmen should have own-initiative powers.

7

Systemic Administrative Justice

Administrative justice is often understood principally in terms of individualised interactions and redress. However, while the topic of remedies is itself quite large, it is a small part of a larger inquiry: how to promote good government.[1] Administrative justice extends far beyond individualised interactions and redress to include the design and operation of public services and governmental behaviours. Many of the problems people experience with administration and public services are not one-off or idiosyncratic errors. They fall into wider patterns that affect many other similarly situated people and stem from the design and operation of the overarching systems and processes which frame and underpin specific decisions and actions.[2] These systemic errors often reveal and reflect deeper institutional, behavioural and cultural dysfunctions within government. We must therefore consider administrative justice as a composite whole. It is necessary to look beyond the downstream individualised decisions and actions, and consider the upstream design and operation of administrative systems. The micro-level of individual interactions via operational delivery must be understood alongside the macro-level of policy and system design and the meso-level of organisation and implementation.

The model that emerges is one of systemic administrative justice. Its structural character reflects and is predicated upon the organisational nature of administration. The concept of administration – the process of managing an organisation – has a pronounced systemic character. Accordingly, when things go wrong with public services, the root causes may well lie in these wider systems and processes, and the cultures which inform them. The solution is to improve administration by addressing these upstream structural problems, although this is much easier said than done.

Given the scale of systemic failures, it is important to understand why they arise and what could potentially be done to avoid them. The chapter proceeds by undertaking a 'thick' detailed analysis of various systemic failures, often affecting large groups of people, that have occurred over the last few decades. The purpose is not primarily to expose and to castigate government for its errors, but to understand and analyse systemic failures and their causes. In doing so, we can seek to acquire a better understanding of how government actually operates in practice, the challenges involved and what it needs to do to promote just and effective administration.

[1] KC Wheare, *Maladministration and its Remedies* (London, Stevens, 1973) 2.

[2] R Thomas, 'Analysing Systemic Administrative Justice Failures: Explanatory Factors and Prospects for Future Research' (2021) 43 *Journal of Social Welfare and Family Law* 339.

Government and Good Administration

To frame the discussion, it is necessary to highlight some key aspects of governmental structures and processes. The activity of governing is political, legal and administrative. Government can be seen as comprising three core aspects: political demand and direction from ministers; policy and system design by mid-level policy staff; and front-line operational delivery. In political terms, government is responsible for articulating the policy goals and ends to be pursued. Such decisions involve political choices by ministers, which must then be implemented. This involves enacting laws and regulations, and establishing administrative systems and processes and operational delivery. The processes of administrative implementation are fundamental. Front-line delivery is where most people interact with government and experience it at first hand, but this interface is only the public aspect of government. Front-line staff are at the bottom of a huge institutional pyramid. There are also intermediate organisational levels and functions being performed within government such as management and system-design, which are often hidden away from public view. The intermediate level deals with the fine print of policy. It also designs, maintains, and constantly monitors the systems and processes of operational delivery. Problems, gaps and weaknesses within these systems and processes will often directly feed into front-line decisions and services with potential adverse consequences for those affected.

Effective governance depends upon a wide range of factors including institutional competence, resources, robust systems and processes and end-to-end accountability throughout governmental structures to deliver policy goals. Stating that government should implement policy effectively and deliver good-quality public services is simple enough, but given the scale of what government does, it is extremely difficult to achieve in practice.[3] Intricate and large-scale administrative systems are often genuinely challenging to coordinate and administer correctly, especially given the dynamic nature of social, economic and political contexts. Consequently, systemic administrative justice problems often result from and reflect wider structural dysfunctions within government. There is a wide range of issues here: policy design; whether systems and processes are designed in light of the needs of users; how those systems and processes work in practice; administrative knowledge; institutional cultures and behaviours within government; workforce and staffing issues; and political interventions by ministers. Systemic problems can reflect ongoing and sometimes intractable policy problems and tensions. They can also reveal deep-seated structural weaknesses in how administration operates.

It is precisely at this point that the need for administrative justice and the principles of good administration come in. Public service delivery is challenging and difficult, but millions of people depend on it for their lives and well-being. It is precisely because government is monolithic and prone to error that it needs to treat people fairly. Consequently, the principles of good administration should be embedded within the design and operation of administrative systems. These principles define what effective and fair service delivery

[3] JL Pressman and A Widavsky, *Implementation*, 3rd edn (Berkeley, University of California Press, 1992); A Dunsire, *Implementation in a Bureaucracy* (London, Martin Robertson, 1978); C Scott, 'Implementation: Facilitating and Overseeing Public Services at Street Level' in P Cane, H Hoffman, E Ip and PL Lindseth (eds) *The Oxford Handbook of Comparative Administrative Law* (Oxford, Oxford University Press, 2020).

looks like and how people should experience government. When government fails to live up to these standards, then injustice often arises. Individual redress is needed, but this places the burden upon people to challenge government. Government should itself accept responsibility to improve its practices and the quality of public services. At the normative level, the concept of administrative justice therefore provides a set of standards that prescribes how government ought to behave and a set of expectations for citizens.

How government operates and how public services are delivered in practice are just as important as the substantive policies underpinning them. Operational delivery influences people's views and experiences of those services. Implementing policy is not a solely technocratic bureaucratic exercise; it is also concerned with embedding values into public service delivery, in particular, the principles of good administration and the need for ethical, humane and professional public services.[4] If government can treat people better and act in accordance with these principles and values, then this should, in turn, lead to better outcomes and improved experiences and public trust in government.

There are obvious challenges in this respect. The standards of administrative justice and effective operational delivery are important, but government works within a world of competing norms and pressures. It needs to ensure value for money. Politicians work according to electoral cycles. There are pressures from Parliament, the media and public opinion. There are also deep organisational and institutional challenges. Each administrative system is path-dependent and has its own processes and cultures which shape how it operates. By its nature, administrative justice contends with many other counter-pressures. Yet, people are entitled to fair treatment.

Systemic scrutiny is typically undertaken by ombudsmen and other non-judicial scrutiny mechanisms, the NAO, select committees and other reviews. By its nature, systemic scrutiny reflects the character of responsive law by diagnosing institutional, policy and implementation failings and seeking to secure improvements. In this respect, it is important to highlight the role of the NAO. It examines governmental effectiveness in terms of value for money and has a particular focus on how overarching systems and processes work and operate and improving operational delivery. For many decades, the provision of public services by government has, at times, fallen short, sometimes significantly so.[5] Recognising the need for government to improve its capabilities and process management, the NAO has developed a model for improving operational delivery. This is based on senior officials adopting a whole-system approach: aligning policy objectives, funding, governance and accountability; and ensuring the reality of services reflects their policy intent. It also involves managing operations effectively: building technical and leadership capability; meeting the diversity of users' needs; and taking an end-to-end service perspective.[6] All of this may seem banal, but it is essential to the effective operation of government and public services.

[4] A Abraham, 'Good Administration: Why We Need it More Than Ever' (2009) 80 *Political Quarterly* 25. See more widely MH Moore, *Creating Public Value: Strategic Management in Government* (Cambridge, MA, Harvard University Press, 1997).

[5] J Bourn, *Public Sector Auditing: Is it Value for Money?* (Chichester, Wiley, 2007); K Jenkins, *Politicians and Public Services: Implementing Change in a Clash of Cultures* (Cheltenham, Edward Elgar, 2008).

[6] National Audit Office, *Managing Business Operations: What Government Needs to Get Right* (2015) and *Improving Operational Delivery in Government* (London, NAO, 2021).

So far, we have highlighted the core tensions embodied within the concept of 'systemic administrative justice'. We now need to make progress in understanding and analysing it in practice. This involves investigating specific systemic failures in order to understand their causes, the problems and challenges facing government, and the lessons that can be drawn from them.

Tax Credits: Not Understanding the Position and Circumstances of People Who Use Public Services

To provide public services effectively, government should understand the needs and circumstances of the people who use them. Society is not a single mass, but a diverse collection of people with a range of different needs and circumstances. Government should try to understand the citizen's perspective when it designs and operates public services, and the needs and circumstances of the general sector of society concerned. But does it? We can consider the experience of tax credits introduced by the Labour government in the early 2000s.

The purpose of tax credits was to support working households on low incomes, to reduce child poverty and to encourage people into work by providing them with income-related support.[7] Although called 'tax credits', they were a form of welfare benefit.[8] Social security benefits are administered by the DWP, which possesses accumulated institutional experience and knowledge in this respect. However, tax credits were delivered through the tax system and were therefore owned, designed and administered by HMRC, the UK's tax authority.[9] Which government department is responsible for a particular policy area might seem like a minor technical detail; after all, both the DWP and HMRC are government departments. However, it turned out to be a crucial determinant of how the tax credits system worked and the quality of service which claimants received.

Claimants applied for tax credits by completing forms about their circumstances and earnings. Tax credit awards would then be issued through HMRC's automated IT system. People then received tax credit payments into their bank accounts. In practice, many claimants experienced considerable difficulties with their tax credits and the whole system. There were various reasons for this.

First, there was the inherent design of the system. Tax credit awards were calculated on an annual basis. Awards were calculated on the basis of a person's earnings and income, which vary over time. If an individual's income increased, then they would be entitled to a lower tax credit award. However, awards were calculated over and lasted for the whole tax year. If someone's earnings increased, they would receive a higher than necessary tax credit award and be required to repay back the difference. Overpayments were an inherent part of the system. Claimants would receive their tax credits for the whole tax year and any overpayments would then be clawed back the next tax year

[7] Tax Credits Act 2002.

[8] Tax credits have now been replaced by Universal Credit.

[9] There was later a turf war between HMRC and the DWP over the ownership of tax credits. See D Freud, *Clashing Agendas: Inside the Welfare Trap* (London, Nine Elms Books, 2021) 90–91.

through an adjustment to the claimant's tax credit award. This would not necessarily matter if the affected cohort of people were relatively well-off, could manage their financial affairs on a relatively stable basis and budgeted on an annual basis. But none of this applied to the cohort of people for which tax credits were introduced to help. Claimants were overwhelmingly families on low incomes who typically budgeted on a week-by-week basis. They did not have the financial stability to budget on an annual basis. Accordingly, being overpaid tax credits in one tax year and then having to find the money to repay what were often significant sums of money in the next tax year caused real practical difficulties for many people.

A fundamental issue here was that HMRC had simply assumed that claimants would have a financial buffer to smooth out any overpayments or underpayments from one tax year to the next. After all, this was the basis on which most people who interacted with HMRC managed their financial arrangements and tax liabilities. HMRC was accustomed to dealing with businesses and the well-off, people with relatively high incomes and earnings who were used to paying off a tax bill at the end of the tax year because of their additional income. HMRC simply assumed that the same approach would apply to tax credit claimants. However, people claiming tax credits were a very different customer base – they were typically people in precarious financial circumstances living week-by-week and without the savings needed to pay off overpayments. When they received their tax credits money, they spent it on their essential needs. Yet, under the annualised assessment awards adopted by the tax credits system, many claimants were given more money than they were strictly entitled to and which they were often unable to repay at a later date. This might not have been too much of a problem if HMRC had written off the overpayments or amended people's awards immediately, but it did neither. Instead, it sought to claw back the overpayments at the start of the next tax year. This posed problems for many claimants, many of whom ended up in real financial difficulty.

Second, unlike other benefits at the time, tax credits were administered through a wholly automated IT-based system designed in the early 2000s. In practice, this system suffered from numerous technical errors and problems which led to overpayments. The automated system made it very difficult for claimants to understand, let alone resolve any errors or problems. The automated decision notices and award letters posted out to claimants by HMRC were often entirely unintelligible and incomprehensible for virtually everyone concerned. Despite this, claimants were expected to take responsibility for managing own claims. A related problem concerned the sheer complexity of the relevant legislation and the lack of clear and straightforward information provided by HMRC. The governing legislation was extremely complex and obscurely drafted. It was not just the case that claimants did not understand the law and rules; HMRC often did not understand them either. These features made it virtually impossible for most people to understand the system or to know what they had to do or when an error had been made. These problems were compounded by HMRC's poor customer phone lines; claimants experienced considerable difficulty in trying to talk to someone about their tax credit awards.

In 2003–04, a third of all tax credit payments (1.8 million) included overpayments to the value of £1.9 billion. Claimants were required to repay their overpayments, but many were unable to. The problems were intensified because HMRC took no account of claimants' ability to repay the overpayments. This imposed substantial hardships on families struggling on low incomes – precisely the group of people that the tax credits system was intended to help. Complaints ballooned and there was extensive and critical scrutiny by select committees and the PHSO.[10] HMRC received many complaints about large reductions to tax credit awards in subsequent years to recover overpayments in the previous year, which claimants said had been created by HMRC's own official error and had caused people financial hardship. There was in fact a litany of problems: harsh consequences for vulnerable people; unintelligible and often multiple tax credit award notices that made it virtually impossible for claimants to work out their entitlements without assistance; poor communication by HMRC with claimants; claimants experiencing real difficulties in contacting HMRC to answer queries and to sort out their tax credit awards; and delays by HMRC in dealing with complaints and appeals. Many claimants did not know that they had been overpaid and so it came as a shock to them that they would have to repay substantial sums of money to HMRC that they did not have. People would call the helpline, but there were often insufficient HMRC staff to answer the phones. Claimants either experienced long delays or simply could not get through to speak with an adviser.

A third problem was that the automated nature of the system itself caused difficulties. For instance, application forms completed by claimants were then scanned into the IT system, but there were scanning errors. Claimants who had provided correct information, albeit not in the exact prescribed manner, ended up receiving incorrect awards. To compound matters, HMRC deemed such 'errors' to have been the responsibility of the claimants concerned and not that of HMRC. Unless claimants carefully checked their award statement, the errors would remain undetected for long periods of time and huge overpayments would arise, thereby creating intense worry and difficulties for claimants. Yet, claimants had provided all of the relevant information; it was the automated system that was at fault. From the perspective of claimants, it was incomprehensible why HMRC had been unable to identify such problems.

Matters were then made worse by extensive errors by HMRC. In many cases, HMRC miscalculated claimants' awards and then commenced the automatic recovery of overpayments contrary to its own Code of Practice. In a significant number of cases, claimants on low incomes had been unfairly required to pay back sometimes large overpayments – which they could not afford – but which had been caused by HMRC's own official errors. Another problem was that HMRC often unlawfully adjusted claims without asking claimants and then recovered overpayments from claimants which had arisen from its own errors. If HMRC could not follow its own legislation, then it was very difficult to understand how it could expect ordinary people to do so. All of this meant that disadvantaged families often suffered unnecessary distress and hardship. Some claimants responded to all of these problems by cancelling their tax credits claims entirely, despite being entitled to them. At the same

[10] House of Commons Treasury Committee, *The Administration of Tax Credits* (HC 2005–06, 811); PHSO, *Tax Credits: Putting Things Right* (HC 2005–06, 124); House of Commons Committee of Public Accounts, *Inland Revenue Standard Report: New Tax Credits* (HC 2005–06, 782); House of Commons Public Administration Select Committee, *Tax Credits: Putting Things Right* (HC 2005–06, 577); PHSO, *Tax Credits: Getting it Wrong?* (HC 2006–07, 1010); House of Commons Public Accounts Committee, *HM Revenue and Customs: Tax Credits and Income Tax* (HC 2008–09, 311).

time, there were also high levels of fraud by people claiming tax credits to which they were not entitled. Over time, some of the problems were somewhat ameliorated, but the difficulties caused for many claimants were severe and other problems persisted with tax credits for many years.

What were the underlying causes of this systemic failure? There were three key interlocking problems. The first was the design of the tax credits system. Many of the problems caused by overpayments were a direct consequence of the inherent defects in the design of the system, in particular annual awards and the automatic recovery of overpayments. A second problem was poor customer service. In essence, HMRC had expected claimants to think and act like bureaucrats who understood the system and how it worked, but it had provided them with very little assistance when trying to interact with and navigate the system.

A third problem was institutional and concerned the government department responsible for administering tax credits and its cultural viewpoint. The core government department responsible for welfare benefits is the DWP. Many benefit claimants experience problems with the DWP, although it has established knowledge about its customer base. Tax credits had been given to HMRC to administer. Its core mission was and remains collecting taxes. As a tax collection department, HMRC was simply culturally ill-equipped to administer a system of welfare benefits. Its expertise was in dealing with taxpayers, often high-earning individuals and companies. It had no institutional experience of administering welfare benefits and providing a service for claimants on low incomes. It simply did not understand how this group of people would react. The consequence was that HMRC entirely failed to appreciate the lifestyles and circumstances of tax credit claimants, the difficulties they would encounter, and how they would respond and behave. It overestimated the ability of tax credit claimants to cope with and manage overpayments, which were an inherent feature of the system. HMRC officials had simply assumed that people would know that they had been overpaid tax credits and that they would then deposit the overpayments in a separate interest-bearing savings account so that they could earn the interest and then repay the money to HMRC at the end of the tax year. But these assumptions were deeply flawed and reflected the depth of HMRC's lack of cultural understanding.

The underlying problem was that the scheme had been designed by mid-level policy officials, well-off middle-class people who did not appreciate the position and behaviours of people in precarious financial circumstances and the challenges they face. There was a profound cultural disconnect between those who designed the tax credits scheme and the claimants who were using it and who the government had intended to help by introducing it.[11] The Public Administration Select Committee expressed concern that HMRC had lacked any understanding of the needs of tax credit claimants 'for whom regular and reliable payment is not a desirable budgeting convenience but a real necessity'.[12] The scheme reflected 'a failure of imagination and sociological competence' by

[11] A King and I Crewe, *The Blunders of Our Governments* (London, Oneworld, 2013) 248–49.

[12] House of Commons Public Administration Select Committee, *Tax Credits: Putting Things Right* (HC 2005–06, 577) [27].

government.[13] It overpaid people on low incomes who often experienced difficulty in managing their money. The subsequent demands for repayments then caused a great deal of anguish. Ann Abraham, the then PHSO, highlighted HMRC's 'total lack of understanding about the customer base'.[14]

Despite the scrutiny of the PHSO and select committees in the mid-2000s, problems with tax credits continued. Years later, the Upper Tribunal raised a number of concerns with how tax credits worked in practice: IT systems that did not send decision letters to claimants;[15] poor-quality reasons for decisions;[16] poor-quality responses to appeals by HMRC; [17] and confusion amongst HMRC officials about the scope of their powers and their ignorance of the basic statutory structure of decision-making.[18] In one appeal, an Upper Tribunal judge criticised HMRC for 'yet another sorry tale of institutional incompetence and inefficiency which could well have led to injustice, were it not for the persistence of the appellant':

> In the parallel universe that is tax credits adjudication, the file does not actually include something as elementary or fundamental as the actual decision notice. As HMRC's original response to the FTT appeal explained, the HMRC computer cannot provide a copy of a decision notice – only the claimant can do that. So, in a classic Orwellian doublespeak, the response continues: 'HMRC has not omitted to include the decision notices from the bundle; it is simply unable to provide copies'. How are we supposed to respond to this? 'Oh well, that's all right then.' Who designed this computer system? Did anyone think to check it was compatible with basic tenets of good public administration, let alone the principles of administrative justice?[19]

In another appeal, a first-tier tribunal had been erroneously lured by HMRC into deciding against the claimant on the basis that he had allegedly failed to respond adequately to a letter sent to him by the department. In fact, HMRC had only sent its letter to the

[13] M Godwin and C Lawson, 'The Working Tax Credit and Child Tax Credit 2003–08: A Critical Analysis' (2009) 17 *Benefits* 3, 7. See also House of Commons Public Administration Select Committee, *Good Government* (HC 2008–09, 97-II) Oral Evidence 8 (John Bourn, former Comptroller and Auditor General): 'If you take the tax credit case, it is an interesting one where, in some ways, you can say, "How crazy to set up a system where you're going to pay people more money than they really deserve and you're going to get it back from them!" Now, we might say that most middle-class people that you find in the Civil Service would be prepared to pay it back and able to pay it back, but, when you think of who gets the tax credits, they are often very poor people without very much experience in handling money and budgets, so they get tax credits over the odds and they spend it and then the money is not there to pay it back. Therefore, of course you do not get the money back. But you leave the evidence of a failed project and disappointment all round.'

[14] ibid Oral Evidence 67 (Ann Abraham, PHSO).

[15] *VO v HMRC (TC)* [2017] UKUT 343 (AAC).

[16] *HO v HMRC* (TC) [2018] UKUT 105 (AAC) [3]: a case which revealed 'yet again the inadequacy of first instance decision making conducted by HMRC under the Tax Credits Act 2002 and the inadequacy of HMRC's explanation for its decision making in its decisions and appeal responses provided to the First-tier Tribunal. That has been the subject of commentary in, regrettably, too many Upper Tribunal decisions. HMRC's own submission writer in his submissions to the Upper Tribunal described HMRC's decision making process in this case as "somewhat perplexing" and that its "administration of its decisions and the appeal in this case has been entirely inept, and it is HMRC's submissions that led the [First-tier Tribunal] down an incorrect path"'.

[17] *JW v HMRC (TC)* [2015] UKUT 369 (AAC) [1]: 'Yet another case that falls into the litany of cases in which the dreadful quality of HMRC's appeal response to the First-tier Tribunal is a central issue.'

[18] *GC v HMRC and DC (CHB)* [2018] UKUT 223 (AAC) [24]–[26]: 'Where did HMRC go wrong? It is difficult to know where to start in answering this question … errors in decision-making, in the absence of proper scrutiny, can infect appellate adjudication in the tribunal system … there appears to be a systemic ignorance within HMRC of the basic architecture of decision-making under the Social Security Act 1998.'

[19] *VO v HMRC (TC)* (n 15) [2].

claimant *after* he had lodged his appeal; an instance of 'sentence first, verdict afterwards'. As the judge noted: 'This is the stuff of Kafka.'[20]

The PHSO emphasised that there were wider lessons to be learned from the episode that were relevant for all government bodies implementing new policies and systems. When designing new systems, government needed to start by understanding the perspective of the people who would use that system. Government needed to maintain its customer focus throughout the development of the programme. There were dangers of adopting a 'one-size-fits-all' approach. Such an approach could superficially provide a fair, consistent and efficient service for all customers, but it would risk failing to pay sufficient regard to the different circumstances and needs of the different groups of people. It could also have unintended and unfair consequences for people in vulnerable circumstances. When designing large systems, government needed to recognise the importance of understanding the perspective of claimants, keeping people informed, good communication and having effective redress mechanisms when things go wrong. The PHSO emphasised that these considerations 'should not be afterthoughts, but central and built into system design'.[21]

A wider point is that a well-meaning policy goal – helping people on low incomes – can be undermined by poor policy design, complex implementation, excessively rule-based administration, poor customer service and not understanding the needs of the people affected. More specifically, if a government department is to deliver a new policy for a different set of customers with whom it has not worked before, then it seems like a good idea to find out about the position and circumstances of those people. This enables government to think through how these people are likely to experience the service being delivered and respond to it. Government needs to pay considerable attention when planning how to deliver services and what the possible effects will be on the people concerned. It is precisely because of this lack of awareness and planning that tax credits resulted in failed delivery, disappointment and frustration. There should also be sufficient scope for people to have some direct personal interactions with officials in order to address hard and problematic circumstances not envisaged when the system was created. It can be a false economy to pretend otherwise, as illustrated by the experience of tax credits.

The 'Cod Wars' Compensation Scheme: The Problems That Arise When Administrators Lack Relevant Knowledge

The tax credits fiasco suggests a wider problem. Systemic failures are blunders, mistakes that happen because of ignorance, carelessness or incompetence. In other words, when government lacks knowledge, then problems are likely to arise. It is elementary that officials who design policies should possess relevant knowledge to ensure that those policies can work and be implemented effectively. In 1918, the Haldane Committee emphasised the need for policy to be formulated on the basis of the 'organised acquisition of facts and

[20] *ZB v HMRC* [2015] UKUT 198 (AAC) [8]. See also *SA v HMRC (TC)* [2016] UKUT 0063 (AAC).
[21] PHSO, *Tax Credits: Putting Things Right* (n 10) 8.

information, and for the systematic application of thought, as preliminary to the settlement of policy and its subsequent administration'.[22] These requirements are reflected in various models of policy-making. According to one such model, the policy-making process involves the following steps: first, define the problem to be addressed; second, consider the range of alternative solutions to achieve the desired goal; third, analyse each of those solutions and their likely consequences; and then, fourth, choose the solution that seems most suited to achieving the desired policy goal.[23]

Each of these stages presuppose that administrators possess a developed understanding of the socio-economic reality is being bureaucratised. An essential component is that policy goals and the means of achieving them have to be integrated or aligned. To do this, officials require knowledge and understanding of the policy and operational context and detail. This is necessary so that they can assess whether the relevant mechanisms and means selected are likely to be appropriate to the task. Of course, this is an ideal model; reality is often otherwise. Administrators operate in a complex and changing world and have limited time and resources. They satisfice rather than optimise.[24] The knowledge they work with is socially constructed. There are also political pressures. Moreover, within UK central government, officials frequently move from one department for another for career purposes. All of this is accepted. This is why policy-makers should be required to demonstrate that the ways or means they have chosen possess at least a reasonable chance of success. Requiring certainty would be too high a standard given the social complexity, contingencies and uncertainties involved.

For the present purposes, the key point is that this process of aligning policy goals with the means of implementation presupposes administrative knowledge and understanding of the relevant social context so that officials can make sensible choices when selecting the best way of achieving the desired policy goal. If this is not the case, then there is considerable potential that policy-makers may choose inappropriate means, which would then lead to systemic administrative justice failures.

One context in which such challenges arise is when government establishes a compensation scheme to compensate people who have, for one reason or another, experienced some form of loss or harm. A fundamental aspect of any compensation scheme concerns the eligibility criteria. These criteria determine who qualifies for compensation and who does not. This makes demands on officials' knowledge and their understanding of the particular context concerned, and how the aims of any such scheme are to be achieved. As in much of administrative justice, the detailed fine print really matters. If policy-makers understand the social facts, then they can devise appropriate eligibility criteria. Conversely, if officials lack knowledge and understanding of the relevant social context, then the risk is that the eligibility criteria may end up excluding people for whom the compensation scheme was intended to cater. A good illustration of the problems caused by a lack of knowledge and understanding is provided by the compensation scheme devised in the early 2000s for British trawlermen who had fished in Icelandic waters until the mid-1970s.

[22] Ministry of Reconstruction, *Report of the Machinery of Government Committee* (Cd 9230, 1918) [12].
[23] E Stokey and R Zeckhauser, *A Primer for Policy Analysis* (New York, Norton, 1979) 5–6.
[24] HA Simon, *Administrative Behaviour*, 4th edn (New York, Free Press, 1997).

Some background is required. In the 1950s and then again in the 1970s, there were three 'cod wars' between Iceland and the UK over fishing rights.[25] For many decades, British trawlermen had fished within Icelandic territorial waters. Iceland then decided to limit what it viewed as the intrusion of British fishing in its waters. It did so by extending its territorial fishing limits to 200 miles from the coast of Iceland to prevent British fishermen from entering its waters. The consequence was that the British Icelandic fishing industry collapsed. British fishermen working out of ports such as Hull, Grimsby and Fleetwood were in effect made redundant, although they were not entitled to any redundancy payments. This clearly affected the fishermen themselves and their families and communities. Throughout the 1980s and 1990s, the fishermen and their representatives lobbied the government to compensate them for the loss of their industry and jobs. Eventually, in 2000, the then Labour government announced a compensation scheme that would be established and administered by the then Department for Trade and Industry.[26]

There were some inherent challenges for the Department in setting up the scheme. It concerned events that occurred more than two decades previously. It was necessary to distinguish between those trawlermen whose livelihoods had been adversely affected by the cod wars – the fishermen who were to receive compensation – and those who had lost their jobs as a result of the wider decline in the fishing industry. The aim of the scheme was to compensate the former. The administrative challenge was to devise appropriate eligibility criteria and to ensure that the compensation scheme operated effectively. In practice, the compensation scheme that was set up was flawed. Some fishermen complained to the PHSO, which found the following forms of maladministration.[27]

First, the Department had set up the scheme quickly, in haste and before it was ready. Officials had not sufficiently acquainted themselves with all of the relevant facts about the decline of the fishing industry some decades earlier. Second, the compensation scheme did not in practice compensate those trawlermen who were its intended beneficiaries. The eligibility criteria to determine entitlement to compensation did not align with the policy intention behind the scheme. There was a mismatch between what the scheme was intended to deliver and how it actually worked. Officials had devised the eligibility criteria and launched the compensation scheme before several important critically important factors had been properly considered and resolved. The eligibility criteria lacked clear definitions and sufficient flexibility to take account of individual circumstances. For instance, a key criterion of the scheme was that a trawlerman must have fished within 200 miles of Iceland. However, it was unclear whether this referred to

[25] H Jónsson, *Friends in Conflict: The Anglo-Icelandic Cod Wars and the Law of the Sea* (London, Hurst, 1982); S Steinsson, 'The Cod Wars: A Re-analysis' (2016) 25 *European Security* 256.

[26] Now the Department for Business and Trade.

[27] PHSO, *Put Together in Haste: 'Cod Wars' Trawlermen's Compensation Scheme* (HC 2006–07, 313). Following the PHSO's report, the Department consulted on a new compensation scheme which was then the subject of a second investigation also resulting in findings of maladministration: PHSO, *Ombudsman's Report on the Icelandic Water Trawlermen Compensation Scheme 2009* (London, PHSO, 2012); Department for Business, Innovation and Skills, *Apology from the Department for Business, Innovation and Skills: Icelandic Water Trawlermen Compensation Scheme 2009* (London, DBIS, 2012).

imperial or nautical miles.[28] Furthermore, the scheme did not take account of specific working practices of the industry in the 1970s. The PHSO concluded that the eligibility criteria had been 'devised in the absence of a fully developed understanding of the industry in which those who were eligible to claim compensation had worked'.[29] Consequently, the scheme, as it had been set up, did not and could not deliver its policy goal. Many of the intended beneficiaries of the scheme did not in practice qualify for compensation. There were also differing interpretations of the scheme's rules as to which type of fishing work attracted compensation and which did not. This led to inconsistent decisions.

Another major problem was that officials had not considered how to verify claimants' applications. This was especially important given the difficulties in locating reliable records of fishermen's working arrangements from decades ago. For instance, the National Insurance records of fishermen dating back three decades were not available. Officials had not come to an agreed position on how to verify claims when fishing records were unavailable, given the inability to access such records. This made the compensation scheme virtually unworkable in practice. Stakeholders had warned officials about the weaknesses within the scheme, but their warnings had been ignored. Even when officials knew that the compensation scheme was deficient and had led to unintended consequences, they had failed to undertake a comprehensive review to understand fully its problems and to develop practical solutions. Another weakness was that officials had not monitored or evaluated the scheme's effectiveness.

Overall, the PHSO concluded that there had been significant flaws with the design of the compensation scheme. The eligibility criteria did not properly reflect the scheme's policy intention. The Department had not known enough about the Icelandic fishing industry, its structure or working practices to enable it to draw up workable rules.[30] It had not checked the availability and robustness of the evidence required to verify individual compensation claims or to establish how the compensation rules would work in practice with applicants from different UK ports. Given the circumstances – devising a compensation scheme about an industry that had ended two decades previously – the Department was never going to find a perfect solution. Nonetheless, a better understanding of the social context and more thorough preparation would have placed the Department in a stronger position from which to manage the uncertainties it faced.

The flawed compensation scheme highlights an important point. Establishing and designing administrative schemes and systems makes demands on administrative knowledge. Officials need to be fully informed as possible about the relevant social facts and contexts when devising an administrative system. Any lack of understanding and knowledge is almost certainly going to lead to a poorly designed scheme and cause injustice to those concerned. There are other ways in which a compensation scheme can go wrong, as the flawed compensation scheme established after the Windrush scandal

[28] A nautical mile is slightly longer than an imperial mile; the former is based on the Earth's longitude and latitude coordinates.

[29] PHSO, *Put Together in Haste* (n 27) [149].

[30] National Audit Office, *The Compensation Scheme for Former Icelandic Water Trawlermen* (HC 2006–07, 530); House of Commons Public Accounts Committee, *The Compensation Scheme for Former Icelandic Water Trawlermen* (HC 2007–08, 71).

illustrates.[31] Nonetheless, as far as the cod wars compensation scheme is concerned, the lack of knowledge by the officials concerned and the speed with which the compensation scheme was set up meant that it was almost guaranteed to generate problems.

In its report, the PHSO laid down its expectations as to how a compensation scheme ought to be designed. First, those who set the policy intention behind a compensation scheme – which general class of people are to be compensated – should formulate and articulate that intention clearly, set defined objectives that are workable and can reasonably be delivered by those who will implement the detail of the scheme in practice. Second, officials who write the detailed rules should possess sufficient knowledge of the background of the issues involved so that they can devise rules that work effectively. They should research the context to establish all the relevant factual considerations. They should consult, seek advice and pilot the scheme. Third, those who operate the scheme should fully understand its rules, make informed and reasoned decisions on individual cases, and apply the rules consistently and fairly having regard to the relevant circumstances of each case. Fourth, those officials who manage and oversee the operation of the scheme in practice should put in place systems to enable them to monitor how it operates in practice. This should enable them to learn whether the scheme is operating as intended. And if any aspect of the scheme is found to be ineffective, unworkable or unfair, then prompt action should be taken to review the scheme and to rectify any problems identified.

What is notable is that this guidance from the PHSO reflects much of the model of policy-making outlined above. Officials need to think clearly about integrating ends and means. They need to devise systems and processes based on a full awareness of the social context. They need to consult with stakeholders, seek advice, undertake pilot projects and assess them, and then feed back the learning into the operation of the scheme in practice and also monitor and review how the scheme works in practice. Following these precepts does not mean that no problems will arise, but it will at least ameliorate some of them.

The cod wars compensation scheme is only one compensation scheme of many that have led to problems and been criticised. Other recent schemes concern the Windrush scandal and the infected blood scandal and Post Office Horizon scandals, all of which have been criticised.[32] Inevitably, people who have already experienced injustice can be retraumatised by complex and lengthy delays when seeking compensation, thereby further weakening or eliminating trust altogether. Such compensation schemes vary widely in terms of key features. They have typically been established ad hoc and without any sense of wider coordination across government or a central point within government for accumulating knowledge and experience about how best to design and

[31] JUSTICE, *Reforming the Windrush Compensation Scheme* (London, JUSTICE, 2022); House of Commons Home Affairs Committee, *The Windrush Compensation Scheme* (HC 2021–22, 204).

[32] 'Windrush Scandal Victims Got Less Compensation Due to Lack of Legal Advice Funding, Review Finds' *The Guardian* (16 June 2025) (claimants who challenged their awards after taking legal advice significantly increased the amounts offered, in one case from £300 to £170,000); 'Call for Urgent Windrush Payouts as Survivors Say Home Office "Waiting for Us to Die"' *The Guardian* (5 September 2025); *Post Office Horizon IT Inquiry Report Volume 1* (HC 2025, 1119); 'Post Office Victims tell BBC of "Cruel and Never-Ending" Compensation Schemes' *BBC News* (9 July 2025), www.bbc.co.uk/news/live/cglzg8rnje7t; Infected Blood Inquiry, *Additional Report on Compensation* (HC 2025, HC 1167); 'Blood Scandal Victims "Harmed Further" by Compensation Delays' *BBC News* (9 July 2025), www.bbc.co.uk/news/articles/cd78zgj0wwdo.

operate compensation schemes.[33] In some instances, the same or similar mistakes have been repeated. The NAO has identified a long list of lessons from such schemes covering various themes, including: the principles of scheme design; understanding stakeholder perspectives and building trust; the trade-offs between speed of payments and other factors; claims processing and administration; engagement with claimants; and monitoring scheme performance. The PHSO's principles for remedy were particularly relevant in this respect.[34] The NAO has also highlighted matters of wider importance for systemic administrative justice within government: the need to learn appropriate lessons; the sharing experience of best practice within government; and embedding the principles of good administration into system design and operations. What is required is a central repository of knowledge and experience within government about how best to establish and administer compensation schemes effectively and fairly.

Transferring Benefit Claimants: The Importance of Effective Managerial Controls

The previous section considered the problems that can occur when government introduces a new administrative scheme. Another situation is when government replaces an established scheme with a new one. This occurs from time to time in the benefits system. Many people are in receipt of one type of benefit for years. Government then decides to overhaul the system and introduce a new benefit scheme, often with different eligibility criteria and conditions. This is something of a cyclical event. Social security policy evolves over time and in response to the wider social and economic circumstances. The decision whether to replace one benefit scheme with another is clearly a policy choice. However, the processes by such changes are implemented can lead to administrative injustice if they are not handled effectively.

One feature of replacing one benefit scheme with another is that people in receipt of the old benefit scheme will need to be moved – or transferred or converted – to the new benefit and be reassessed. The issue then is how smoothly the process of converting or transferring claimants to the new benefit scheme is managed in practice. The task of transferring or converting claimants to a new benefit sounds simple enough. However, in reality, there are significant risks, given the number of claimants, the complexity of specific cases and the need for the correct handling of not just many individual cases, but also the effective management of the whole system. The number of claimants can potentially include millions of people. Each person's case will need to be reconsidered carefully during the transfer process. If claimants are not properly transferred, then they will not receive their full entitlements under the new benefit and this will then have to be corrected. Consequently, the process of transferring claimants makes demands on both administrative knowledge and the internal management and oversight of the transfer process to ensure that claimants do not lose out on their entitlements when they are transferred.

[33] NAO, *Lessons Learned: Government Compensation Scheme* (HC 2024–25, 121).
[34] See Appendix B.

In the early 1990s, the then Conservative government had introduced the Disability Living Allowance to replace previous disability benefits.[35] On that occasion, the then Department of Social Security (now the DWP) significantly underestimated the workload and the logistical challenges involved. The higher-than-expected workloads, the use of inexperienced staff and an over-estimation of staff productivity meant that the Department simply could not cope with the volume. This resulted in large delays, backlogs and people in need not receiving their benefit entitlements. The then PHSO had trenchantly criticised the Department for its delays, poor planning and inadequate service.[36] For a time, chaos reigned and many claimants did not receive their benefit entitlements. Accordingly, government needed to manage such processes carefully and effectively. A key aspect of this concerns the degree to which the government department responsible has effective internal managerial controls over its processes. Such internal controls are an essential aspect of managing any large system. Their importance is well illustrated by the next case study, which concerned the process of transferring benefit claimants over the period from 2008 to 2013.

One of the UK's principal benefits is for people with disabilities who are either unable to work or have limited capacity to do so. From the mid-1990s until the late 2000s/early 2010s, people unfit for work could claim Incapacity Benefit, the old legacy benefit.[37] In light of the burgeoning number of claimants and costs, the Labour government in 2008 replaced Incapacity Benefit with Employment and Support Allowance (ESA).[38] Like all benefits, ESA has its detailed eligibility criteria and assessment process. For the present purposes, it is important to note that there are two principal types of ESA: contribution-based ESA, which is based on a person's National Insurance contributions; and income-related ESA, which is means-tested. Income-related ESA attracts extra payments called premiums. Claimants who were entitled to these premiums could also be entitled to 'passported' benefits, such as medical prescriptions, dentistry costs and free school meals.

In 2011, the DWP started the process of reassessing around 1.5 million Incapacity Benefit claimants and transferring or 'converting' them to ESA. As with much of benefits administration, this was a high-volume mass-transactional process. However, the transfer process had been badly designed and deeply flawed in various respects. Many claimants were placed on contribution-based ESA alone when they were, in fact, also entitled to income-related ESA. Consequently, many people missed out on the payment of premiums and also their 'passported' benefits – in other words, they were underpaid their full statutory entitlements.

In 2013, the DWP became aware that many claimants had been incorrectly converted to ESA, but it did not then explore the systemic nature of its error.[39] In 2017, it was reported that an estimated 75,000 people transferred to ESA had been underpaid their premiums because they had been placed on contribution-based ESA only when they

[35] Disability Living Allowance and Disability Working Allowance Act 1991.

[36] Parliamentary Commissioner for Administration, *Delays in Handling Disability Living Allowance Claims* (HC 1992–93, 562).

[37] Social Security (Incapacity for Work) Act 1994.

[38] Welfare Reform Act 2007.

[39] HC Deb 14 December 2017, vol 633, col 35WS (David Gauke MP, Secretary of State for Work and Pensions).

might also have been entitled to income-related ESA.[40] An NAO investigation found serious flaws with the transfer process. Its design had been delegated to inexperienced junior staff. The responsible team had not sought legal advice to ensure that the process complied with the DWP's own regulations. Furthermore, the DWP's senior managers had failed to oversee and scrutinise the process to ensure that it was robust, lawful and would be administered properly.[41] Indeed, even when both some front-line staff and external stakeholders had alerted senior managers to the systemic nature of the error, those warnings were ignored by senior DWP managers.

The result was that over 100,000 people had been significantly underpaid their full benefit entitlements for several years and thereby experienced avoidable hardship. Frank Field MP, then Chair of the Commons Work and Pensions Committee, highlighted that the 'historic proportions' of the DWP's errors had 'wrongly impoverished' many people.[42] The Public Accounts Committee found that this 'unacceptable and entirely avoidable situation' that had stemmed from 'multiple failures'.[43] The DWP's transfer process had been fundamentally flawed and implemented without basic checks. The DWP had failed to design a lawful transfer process, had not properly scrutinised it and had not listened to its front-line staff, claimants, the DWP's own Social Security Advisory Committee or external stakeholders – all of whom had warned the DWP that there was a major problem. The Committee criticised the DWP's management for not proactively and systematically acting on intelligence from front-line officials and for not addressing mistakes when they occurred.[44] Compounding matters, the DWP had also failed to act even when it had been 'painfully obvious' that a significant number of people had been underpaid their benefit entitlements. In all, the DWP took six years to take the necessary corrective action.[45] Its lack of urgency in addressing the systemic errors reflected a 'culture of indifference to underpayments' as opposed to its more proactive approach towards clawing back overpayments made to benefit claimants.[46] The DWP had a management culture which did not proactively and systematically act on intelligence from its own front-line officers or fully address mistakes when they first occurred.

To resolve the situation, the DWP then undertook a corrective LEAP exercise ('Legal Entitlements and Administrative Practices').[47] This involved reviewing the cases of some 600,000 affected people, contacting them to gather information, and then repaying them arrears for the benefit entitlements they should have received, but which they had not actually been paid.[48] Given the scale of the task, it took the DWP some time to undertake the reviews. Some 5,000 people died before being paid their full benefit entitlements.[49]

[40] 'Up to 75,000 Benefit Claimants were Underpaid for Years' *The Guardian* (17 November 2017).
[41] National Audit Office, *Investigation into Errors in Employment and Support Allowance* (HC 2017–19, 837).
[42] 'Frank Field MP "Gobsmacked" by ESA Pay-out Errors' *BBC News* (17 November 2017), www.bbc.co.uk/news/av/uk-42028942.
[43] House of Commons Public Accounts Committee, *Employment and Support Allowance* (HC 2017–19, 975) 3.
[44] ibid 5.
[45] ibid.
[46] ibid.
[47] Civil Service Department, *Legal Entitlements and Administrative Practices: A Report by Officials* (London, HMSO, 1979).
[48] HC Deb 17 October 2018, vol 647, col 46WS (Sarah Newton MP, Minister for Disabled People, Health and Work).
[49] '5,000 People Died before Being Repaid over Benefits Error' *The Guardian* (16 January 2020).

Overall, the episode revealed a major gap in the DWP's knowledge and institutional competence. The transfer process had been flawed. Managerial controls had been inadequate. External experts and stakeholders had been ignored. There were deep organisational weaknesses within the department reflected in the failure to follow its own regulations. Frank Field MP criticised the DWP for its 'serially botched operation' that had led to the underpayments as well as the avoidable expense – £40 million – of 'fixing its own catastrophic incompetence'.[50] The DWP's errors had been both foreseen and avoidable, yet it proceeded to make them anyway. The lack of internal managerial oversight of the transfer process suggested a degree of administrative incompetence verging upon an almost blatant negligent disregard for claimants and ignorance of the principles of good administration.

However, that was not the end of the matter. The claimants concerned had been underpaid their entitlements. This had been largely corrected by the LEAP exercise. But what of the hardships many people had experienced during the years in which they been underpaid? As a result of the DWP's flawed transfer process, many vulnerable and disabled people had spent years living in extreme poverty and below the minimum income levels required for living an ordinary basic existence. These hardships could have been avoided if the DWP had managed the transfer process properly and correctly. The established principle is that when a government body has caused injustice or hardship because of maladministration, it should then restore people to the position they would have been in had things been done correctly.[51] However, in 2018, the DWP's Minister for Disabled People ruled out compensation for any of the affected claimants. In essence, anyone who sought compensation would be refused by the DWP without any consideration of their individual circumstances and the degree and duration of the impact of them not receiving their full benefit entitlements. The DWP justified this blanket refusal of compensation on the ground that paying compensation would set an unwelcome precedent for future LEAP exercises and would involve additional costs.

One claimant who asked for compensation was Ms U, a vulnerable woman who had been significantly underpaid her entitled benefits and had lived in extreme hardship for five years at considerable cost to her physical and mental health. In response, the DWP acknowledged its initial maladministration and the flawed transfer process, and repaid Ms U her benefit arrears (without interest); however, it refused compensation to her for the hardship she had experienced during the five-year period. Ms U then escalated her complaint to the PHSO, which found that the DWP's blanket refusal of compensation to both her and the other 118,000 affected people without considering their individual circumstances contravened two basic principles of good administration.[52] First, individuals should not be disadvantaged by maladministration; instead, they should be put back into the position they would have been in had it not occurred. Second, each case of injustice arising from maladministration should be considered on an individual basis. These principles are recognised by both the PHSO's principles for

[50] Quoted in S Sandhu, 'DWP Expected to Pay out £1bn to Fix Underpayment Issues for Claimants of Disability Benefits' *INews* (19 April 2019).

[51] HM Treasury, *Managing Public Money* (2021) [A4.14.4].

[52] PHSO, *An Investigation into the Department for Work and Pensions' Handling of Ms U's Migration to Employment and Support Allowance* (HC 2021–22, 956).

remedy and indeed also the DWP's own internal guidance on financial redress.[53] The PHSO recommended that the DWP review Ms U's case and pay her compensation, which it then did. The PHSO also recommended that the DWP proactively compensate the other 118,000 people who had suffered injustice. However, the DWP rejected this; the burden was on the people concerned to complain.[54] Despite parliamentary criticism of the DWP, it refused to compensate other people.[55] This was clearly motivated by financial considerations.

This episode illustrates the importance of effective internal managerial controls within government when seeking to correct a systemic error. It also exemplifies the secondary failures caused by government when it adopts a defensive approach towards remedying injustices caused by its initial maladministration. The principal failure of the flawed transfer process had arisen in part because of a lack of knowledge and internal controls within the DWP and the disinterest of senior managers in what both junior officials and external stakeholders were telling them. The DWP's subsequent decision not to proactively compensate people who had not complained was motivated by a deliberate unwillingness to do so. After all, the DWP could say that it would consider individual complaints, but it was also implicitly relying upon the lack of knowledge of those concerned and the unwillingness or inability of people in vulnerable circumstances to complain. As Rob Behrens, the then PHSO, noted, 'it is human to make mistakes, but not acting to right wrongs is a matter of policy choice'.[56]

COVID Grants and the Windrush Scandal: Collecting and Using Information and Legibility

Another way in which government relies upon knowledge is when it generates information itself in order to understand and control society. To govern society, administrators first need to make it 'legible' or readable. The ability of government to make effective interventions in society – to govern and provide public services – crucially depends on its understanding of society. This in turn depends on the administrative data that government collects and how it is used. This type of data typically takes the form of large-scale quantitative datasets and the associated standardised categories which administrators devise and use to understand and manage society.[57] From a wider perspective, the growth of administrative governance since the early nineteenth century has proceeded alongside the huge increase in the capacity of government to collect and analyse data and information about society in order to make it legible and therefore more governable. This has now been accelerated by the industrial-scale collection of mass digital data.

[53] PHSO, *Principles for Remedy* (2009) (Appendix B). The DWP's guidance on financial redress has gone through several iterations. The current version is: DWP, *Financial Redress for Maladministration: Staff Guide* (London, DWP, 2020).

[54] Letter from Peter Schofield CB, Permanent Secretary, DWP to PHSO (11 April 2022).

[55] HC Deb 13 January 2022, vol 706, cols 647–55; HL Deb 18 January 2022, vol 817, cols 1545–48.

[56] PHSO, 'Over 118,000 People Denied Compensation from DWP after Benefits Error Cut Payments' (13 January 2022), www.ombudsman.org.uk/dwp-esa.

[57] JC Scott, *Seeing Like a State: How Certain Schemes to Improve the Human Condition Have Failed* (New Haven, Yale University Press, 1998) 76–83.

To collect such data, government necessarily relies upon simplifications, standardisations and abstractions from the much more messy and complex reality of society. As the political scientist James Scott has explained, 'no administrative system is capable of representing *any* existing social community except through a heroic and greatly schematized process of abstraction and simplification'.[58] Government is always limited as to the depth and granularity of information it can collect because of the size and complexity of society. Another constraint is that officials are only interested in collecting information relevant to the particular task at hand, whether that is administering benefits or taxation. The types of simplifications include quantitative data and also official documents, such as national insurance and tax records.

Accordingly, officials are always at least one step, and sometimes several steps, removed from the society they are responsible for governing. They only 'see' society largely through the simplified approximations of standardised documents and data. By its nature, the data and information collected by government in order to make society legible and hence governable cannot fully capture and reflect the detailed, shifting and complex reality of society. On the other hand, standardised and simplified facts have real advantages. By simplifying mass society, they make it legible and hence governable, thereby increasing administrative effectiveness. Standardised facts enable large systems to process huge volumes of cases quickly and efficiently; people's circumstances can be managed so that they can be slotted into pre-determined categories.

The processes by which government seeks to make society legible involve an extension of its administrative power. It is government that decides upon the categories through which complex social phenomena become standardised facts. The more standardised and uniform society is made through this process, the more legible it becomes for the purposes of government. Government looks at society as an aggregate whole, as this is the most efficient way of understanding it. Officials are not particularly concerned with nuance, but with bulk facts slotted into uniform categories. Another feature is that the social facts collected are typically more static than the changeable social phenomena they purport to represent and therefore become out of date.

So far, so good. But what happens when the governmental mechanisms for making society legible – its standardised facts and information records and databases – are incorrect, incomplete, become out of date or when unidentified gaps in the data emerge over time? What happens to particular cohorts of people who fall outside of the typifications and standardised categories created and used by government?

These methods of making society legible have their uses, but there are potential unforeseen and serious unintended consequences. Administrators can make their categories stick and impose their simplifications. The resulting data can take on a life of their own. Officials can rely heavily on such data as if they are correct and reliable, irrespective of their objective accuracy or otherwise. The risk is that for officials, such data become the reality of the world as they understand it. Indeed, the standardised social facts collected by government can end up over-riding actual social reality. As Scott notes, the habitual reliance by government on its data will often mean that 'there are virtually no other facts for the state than those that are contained in documents

[58] ibid 22.

standardised for that purpose'.[59] *Quod non est in actis, non est in mundo.*[60] An omission or an error in official data or documents can have far more power – and for far longer – than an unreported truth. Standardised facts collected and organised by officials can help make society legible, but there is a risk that they can also authoritatively rewrite reality for those officials despite protestations to the contrary from the people concerned. The process of making society legibility risks becoming dysfunctional when administrators rely solely on official data records, even when there is good reason for doubting their accuracy. And this can result in administrative injustice.

Consider how Camden London Borough Council administered a grant scheme introduced during COVID-19 to support small local businesses during the economic difficulties caused by the pandemic. The scheme was designed by central government and administered by local authorities. A business was eligible for a grant if, amongst other things, it paid local business rates (taxes). When considering applications, councils had to check whether a business was registered as the ratepayer in its local area by using their database of ratepayers. Of course, there was a risk of fraudulent applications; some people might falsely claim that they had a legitimate business. There was a genuine need for a check. But there was also the risk that legitimate businesses may not have been registered as the ratepayer in the business premises. To consider such borderline cases, there was a proviso in the guidance that if councils' information about ratepayers was inaccurate, then the council could exercise its discretion when considering individual cases.

Councils administered the grants by using the information available, which included their database of ratepayers. Two local businessmen applied to Camden Council for a grant to help them through the pandemic. However, their applications were refused because neither of the two businessmen was the registered ratepayer of their business premises. In fact, the businesses had changed names, but the ratepayer details had not been updated on the Council's database. The two businessmen had therefore been operating valid businesses from their premises. Nonetheless, their applications were refused. The Council had considered the two applications by relying solely on the information contained in its database of ratepayers and therefore rejected the applications. Despite the guidance stating that the Council could exercise its discretion in individual cases as to whether the business owner had valid reasons why he was not registered as the ratepayer, the Council refused the applications. The Council officer had misinterpreted the relevant guidance as not conferring any discretion to consider individual circumstances when, in fact, the guidance did confer such discretion. Furthermore, the two businessmen were not been given the opportunity to clarify the position or to make representations.

As we have seen throughout this book, an important way of correcting poor-quality decisions is to have some sort of appeal or review process by which another officer or an independent body can listen to what the person concerned has to say and then arrive at a fresh decision. When the government introduced the grant schemes, it had not – quite understandably, given the circumstances of the pandemic – required councils to set up an appeals mechanism. Nonetheless, the principle of putting things

[59] ibid 83.

[60] 'What is not in the records, is not in the world.'

right requires that public bodies must be open to the idea that their decision-makers can get something wrong and therefore some redress process should be available. During the early stages of the pandemic, the LGSCO had issued guidance on the importance of councils acting in accordance with good administration despite the challenges presented by COVID.[61] The guidance recognised that although councils were working under pressure, they were still expected them to adhere to established standards of good administration, such as undertaking proper, reasoned and evidence-based decision-making. Further, while complaint-handling capacity might well be reduced, councils still needed to consider complaints properly. At a minimum, the LGSCO expected the Council to offer the two businessmen access to its complaint procedure with input from officers not involved in the decision complained about. Nonetheless, Camden Council failed properly to consider the complaints of the two businessmen, who then escalated their grievances to the LGSCO, which investigated and upheld their complaints.

The LGSCO concluded that the Council should have exercised its discretion to consider the individual cases when it had been informed that a change of ratepayer had taken place. The Council officer had not allowed the businessmen to clarify whether or not that they were indeed ratepayers and whether the Council's database was out of date.[62] The officer could have taken steps to identify the correct ratepayer before paying a grant, but did not do so. Indeed, the Council had good reason to believe that the information it held about the identities of ratepayers was wrong, but it did not take reasonable steps to identify the correct ratepayer. That was fault. Further, the problem was not limited to the two businessmen concerned. As with many other systemic problems, the Council had adopted the same blanket approach with regard to a few hundred other cases which it had similarly refused. The LGSCO concluded that the Council had engaged in maladministration causing injustice. [63]

The wider point is that standardised official information – whether council rating list databases or other forms – can assume canonical and decisive importance in the minds of officials despite it being out of date or objectively incorrect. The problems are then compounded when officials ignore the representations of those affected and refuse to exercise discretion in individual cases. As Nonet has noted, it is 'a natural pathology of administration' to reduce the scope for official discretion and judgement by hardening them into rigid rules, even though judgement has been explicitly conferred. It takes time and 'energy to preserve and exercise discretion; deciding by rules is generally easier and safer, more conservative'.[64] Administrators can adopt a rule-bound approach that operates as a self-denying ordinance, thereby preventing them from exercising the discretion they quite legitimately and properly possess to consider individual cases. There are other motivating factors. Rule-boundedness can also serve as a useful device

[61] LGSCO, *Good Administrative Practice During the Response to Covid-19* (Coventry, LGSCO, 2020).

[62] LGSCO, London Borough of Camden (20006485 and 20009015); LGSCO, 'London Council Set to Learn from How it Handled COVID Business Grants' (13 January 2022), www.lgo.org.uk/information-centre/news/2022/jan/london-council-set-to-learn-from-how-it-handled-covid-business-grants.

[63] 'Local Government Watchdog Slams Camden's Handling of Covid Grants after Complaints from Two Businesses' *Camden Citizen* (13 January 2022). Other councils might have taken the same approach.

[64] P Nonet, *Administrative Justice: Advocacy and Change in a Government Agency* (New York, Russell Sage Foundation, 1969) 247.

for officials who fear being blamed if things go wrong: 'I was only following the rules'. The tendency of such officials to prefer rules over discretion illustrates the difference between administration and adjudication. The latter involves thinking, investigating, asking for information, exercising discretion carefully and reasoning. In many instances, officials may lack the confidence and time for this, and fear the repercussions if it subsequently turns out that their decisions were wrong.

The reliance of administrators solely upon official sources of information and data can be inconvenient. It was clearly frustrating and financially difficult for the two businessmen that the officer at Camden Council had relied on the Council's database, which showed that the applicants were not registered as the ratepayers for those businesses, even though the businessmen could have explained the matter. However, in other instances, relying on standardised data can have tragic consequences for those concerned.

* * *

One of the most acute systemic administrative justice failures over recent decades has been the Windrush scandal. The Home Office engaged in extensive immigration enforcement action against thousands of people who had, for many years, lived entirely lawfully in the UK and had the right to remain. To understand how and why this happened, we first need to consider some of the structural features of immigration administration.

The immigration system depends almost entirely on binary classifications that determine people's immigration status. A person either has immigration status to enter or remain in the UK or they do not. They are either in the country legally or they are an irregular migrant and therefore potentially subject to enforcement action. Given its scale and the millions of individual interactions required, the immigration system can only function by relying on standardised facts to check a person's immigration status and thereby make the relevant population 'legible' or readable. This is done by checking a person's passport and immigration documents. People with valid immigration documents have immigration status, whereas those without valid immigration documents are irregular migrants. Having valid immigration documents is the only operative fact. All of this is deeply embedded within the immigration system and the assumptions of immigration officials. The coverage of this method is extensive and it works well in the large majority of cases, but not universally so. People can fall into the gaps that emerge. A person may have a valid immigration status but not have the documentation to prove it. Such people are likely, if not virtually guaranteed at some stage, to experience problems. Indeed, the robustness of the entire immigration system is undermined when immigration controls are enforced to the detriment of people who have a valid immigration status, but not the documents to evidence it. In such circumstances, the instinctive response of immigration officials is often to suspect that the person concerned is pulling a fast one and trying to abuse the system, a response which reinforces the view that they are not credible and therefore do not have a valid immigration status. However, such people may in fact have the right to remain, but not the documents to evidence it.

Precisely this situation occurred in the Windrush scandal.[65] Between the late 1940s and early 1970s, around half a million people from Commonwealth countries lawfully entered the UK and were given the statutory right of abode.[66] Many entered on their parents' passports. At the time, the Home Office did not issue them with any formal documentation concerning their immigration status. In legal terms, these people had a right of abode in the UK. However, they did not have the documents to prove this status because the Home Office had not given them any such documents when they had entered. For decades, members of the Windrush generation lived in the UK. Many of them worked in public services such as the NHS and public transport. Over the years, the Home Office's institutional memory of the distinctive immigration position of the Windrush generation faded entirely as it became focused increasingly on asylum cases.

In the 2010s, the Home Office introduced a hostile immigration environment. The aim of the policy was to make life uncomfortable for irregular migrants by preventing them from accessing essential rights and services, such as healthcare, employment, renting a property, having a driving licence and bank account, and so on. The Home Office's logic was that people who could evidence their immigration status would not be caught by the hostile environment policies; the only people who would be affected would be those without any right to remain in the country. People who could not evidence their immigration status had no right to remain. However, many thousands of Windrush people were caught out by the hostile environment. They received letters from the Home Office that they had no legal right to remain in the UK, that their lives would become increasingly difficult, that they would lose their rights to benefits, NHS healthcare, driving licences, and access to bank accounts and pensions, and that they would be removed or deported. Yet, such people were in the country lawfully. They could not evidence their immigration status because the Home Office had not issued them with any immigration documentation when they had arrived decades earlier.

The scandal involved thousands of individual cases of profound injustice. Some Windrush people were detained and removed from the UK. Many lost their jobs, benefits and homes, and could not access healthcare.[67] Some Windrush people who had travelled to visit relatives overseas were then unable to return back to the UK, which had been their lawful home for decades.[68] One man, Mr Winston Knight, was wrongly deported from the UK to Jamaica, where he spent a decade living homeless in horrific conditions. The Home Office eventually agreed to arrange his return back to the UK. As Mr Knight said: 'I'm doing much better now I know I have won my case and will be returning to the UK. But I am coming from hell. I have been living in a war zone in Kingston and I've had some very tough days.'[69]

[65] W Williams, *Windrush Lessons Learned Review* (HC 2019–20, 93); R Thomas, *Administrative Law in Action: Immigration Administration* (Oxford, Hart Publishing, 2022) ch 3.

[66] Immigration Act 1971, s 2.

[67] A Gentleman, *The Windrush Betrayal: Exposing the Hostile Environment* (London, Faber, 2019).

[68] A Gentleman, 'A 975-Day Nightmare: How the Home Office Forced a British Citizen into Destitution Abroad' *The Guardian* (2 December 2021); '"Nothing is the Same": Windrush Victim Allowed to Return to UK after 28 Years' *The Guardian* (18 August 2025).

[69] 'UK Agrees to Fly Home Wrongly Deported Windrush Generation Man from Jamaica' *The Guardian* (16 May 2025).

The fundamental problem was that the immigration system did not make any allowance for the distinctive position of the Windrush generation. Instead, officials continued using the standard method to check a person's immigration status: requiring the person to evidence their immigration status by presenting a passport or other immigration document. A significant part of the systemic failures of the Windrush scandal had been caused by the Home Office's institutional culture, and its deeply embedded and flawed assumption that it possessed full and reliable knowledge about people's immigration status. By relying solely upon the thin surface knowledge of whether or not someone had evidence of their immigration status, officials had entirely overlooked the fact that the Home Office did not give Windrush people such documents in the first place. The standardised facts that the Home Office relied upon were incomplete. The Home Office's failure to recognise the limitations of its approach enabled the Windrush scandal to happen.

The Windrush scandal was an appalling episode of bureaucratic oppression. However, it had been avoidable. Government departments are established institutions; they build up their knowledge over time through their institutional memory. It was the Home Office that in 1971 legislated to give Commonwealth citizens a statutory right to live in the UK. The department should have known this and that the fact that people were not at that time issued with formal immigration documents. However, there was a distinct lack of knowledge within the Home Office department about not only the immigration status of the Windrush generation, but also the department's own administration of immigration policy and how it had developed over the years. When combined with the high turnover of staff and the political drive for a hostile environment, the position of the Windrush generation ended up being entirely forgotten about. External stakeholders had warned the Home Office that the hostile environment policies would wrongly harm people who had the legal right to live in the UK. These warnings were explicitly made in publications and in parliamentary debates, but they were ignored. Given that Home Office's internal culture and hardline approach, any engagement or collaboration by officials with stakeholders was actively discouraged. The Home Office was defensive, lacked awareness, and was unwilling to listen to and learn from external stakeholders.

Yet, there was another means by which the Home Office could have avoided the full-scale impact of the Windrush scandal. When government takes action against a cohort of people, it can adopt a blanket approach by treating all of the people concerned in the same way. Alternatively, government caseworkers can consider individual cases on their own individual merits, give the individuals concerned the opportunity to explain their situation and then make appropriate decisions, which can then be appealed to a tribunal. This can enable the circumstances of individuals with complex personal situations to be investigated and considered. However, a common feature of administrative systems that rely heavily on standardised facts is that an implicit '(il)logic of legibility' can arise.[70] Officials may fall into the trap of assuming that the standardised 'facts' used by government to make society legible are objectively correct and determinative, even though they are just simplified abstractions that do not necessarily reflect reality or may

[70] T Snow, 'The (il)logic of Legibility: Why Governments Should stop Simplifying Complex Systems' *London School of Economics Impact Blog* (12 February 2021), https://blogs.lse.ac.uk/impactofsocialsciences/2021/02/12/the-illogic-of-legibility-why-governments-should-stop-simplifying-complex-systems.

well be incorrect. Again, the risk is that there are no other facts for administrative bodies apart from those contained in its own standardised systems of documents and records. These 'facts' and systems then assume decisive importance, even when they are objectively wrong or incomplete and despite the protestations of the individuals concerned. This was reinforced by the Home Office's focus on enforcing the hostile environment to crack down on people perceived to be abusing the system. Once the process had decided that someone did not have a valid status, it became virtually impossible for their case to be considered impartially and fairly, despite the fact that the system was itself at fault.

Members of the Windrush generation could apply to the Home Office to confirm their immigration status. They were required to present copious amounts of personal evidence – such as years of school attendance and employment records going back decades – to prove they had lived in the UK. These unreasonable evidential requirements were virtually impossible for anyone to fulfil. Caseworkers should have assessed this evidence against the normal civil standard of proof – the balance of probabilities – in order to make factual findings. But, in practice, officials applied the criminal standard of proof – beyond reasonable doubt. This was completely inappropriate and unlawful. The criminal standard of proof never applies in administrative-legal decision-making. Further, Home Office caseworkers assessed individuals' applications by applying a checklist of required documents. Windrush people were not interviewed by caseworkers in person. They were not given the opportunity to explain their circumstances and personal history. Consequently, caseworkers could not appreciate the challenges and problems experienced by Windrush people and their circumstances. Caseworkers were unable to understand how the underlying problem was with the system itself and how Windrush people had been placed in an impossible situation. Instead, caseworkers had made decisions on the basis of thin surface knowledge. Furthermore, people who had their applications refused could not appeal to the immigration tribunal because the right of appeal had been withdrawn in 2014.[71]

The upshot of this flawed process was that many people's applications were wrongly refused. Consider the case of a man from Jamaica who entered the UK in 1962 aged 19 and had indefinite leave to remain. In the 2010s, he experienced considerable and protracted difficulties in trying to prove that he had been granted indefinite leave to remain.[72] The lack of proper records combined with the Home Office's culture of disbelief and multiple errors amounted to significant maladministration, resulting in significant harm and distress to the man and his family. The man was threatened with enforcement action by the Home Office. He became depressed and anxious, withdrawn and immobile during what were the last years of his life. The PHSO recommended that the Home Office take systemic action to improve the quality of its complaints process to ensure that it was central to developing a learning culture focused on continuous improvement and providing fair outcomes for people affected by the Windrush scandal.

Some wider points can be extracted. Administrative institutions require data and information to regulate society. Administration can be seen as a system for collecting

[71] Immigration Act 2014, s 15.

[72] PHSO, *An Investigation into UK Visas and Immigration's Handling of Windrush Man's Status* (Manchester, PHSO, 2021). See also PHSO, *Final Investigation Report of a Complaint about UK Visas and Immigration* (Manchester, PHSO, 2020).

and analysing information and data. However, the necessarily simplistic nature of these abstractions can never reflect the full granular complexity of society. A bureaucratic machine that relies almost entirely on thin, formulaic standardised facts will lack the thick and in-depth knowledge required to guard against such errors and mistakes. By their nature, such large-scale machine organisations prioritise form over substance.

Governing by means of context-free standardised facts can lead to people being incorrectly misclassified, with harmful consequences. The processes of making society legible becomes dysfunctional when administrators rely solely upon official data, despite good reason for doubting their accuracy. The risks are heightened when the whole political drive of government is focused upon hardline and restrictive policies, the administrative procedures used are unfair and there is limited or no external redress.[73] In these circumstances, the burden is really upon government to recognise the limits of its own standardised knowledge and to supplement it with a deep understanding of the social contexts subject to administrative control.

What then can government do? Part of the answer is for government to embrace complexity and messiness. It needs to think more deeply about what it does not know, what data are missing and the untested assumptions that lie deep within its organisational cultures and standard operating routines. Another approach concerns the types of data relied upon. Standardised facts typically take the form of simplified, binary and context-free quantitative information. Government should take account of other types of data, including more qualitative information, such as people's stories about their lives and their individual circumstances.[74] Government also needs to become more curious about the consequences of its actions and the impacts upon people. Monitoring and evaluation is important to understand whether the chosen means of implementation are working in practice. As the Windrush scandal illustrates, failing to take these and other actions can lead to deep-seated systemic failures and injustice for people subjected to incompetent and oppressive administration.

Remarkably, these points are nothing new. They have been previously recognised and acted upon, albeit in a now largely forgotten administrative history of the implementation of the Old Age Pensions 1908. This Act provided an old age pension to people of seventy years of age. The administration of the Act was based on the assumption that people actually possessed written evidence of their date of birth and that such evidence even existed. However, this was often not the case. The problem of limited records was most acute in Ireland, where there were then no official records of people's date of birth. Many people in rural subsistence farming communities did not even know their date of birth, let alone have evidence of it. Some people only knew their date of birth from an inscription in the family Bible. It was recognised that proof of age would be the crux of

[73] Another systemic immigration failure concerned overseas student English-language tests. See R Thomas and J Tomlinson, *Immigration Judicial Reviews: An Empirical Study* (London, Palgrave Macmillan, 2021) 176–86. The common feature with Windrush was the difficulties that the students experienced in rebutting allegations that they had cheated in their language tests, which were treated as objectively correct. Note also the Post Office Horizon scandal, in which subpostmasters convicted of theft and fraud had great difficulty in rebutting computer evidence that they had committed fraud. It was assumed that the computer records were correct when they were in fact incorrect. See *Post Office Horizon IT Inquiry Report* (n 32).

[74] Snow (n 70).

the evidential challenge when administering the scheme in Ireland. It was hoped that the legislation would be administered in order not to defeat its objectives so that people legally entitled to a pension would not be deprived of that right by any unfair reliance on a technicality or too strict an interpretation of the letter of the law, regardless of its spirit: 'We should hope justice will not be defeated by a quibble and rights strangled by a technicality.'[75] This hope seems to have been largely fulfilled in the practical administration of the Act in Ireland. Pension officers carefully investigated and researched individual cases to inform their exercise of judgement. They also worked closely with postmasters in tight-knit rural communities to understand individual cases and people's histories. On the whole, there seems to have been fair deliberation on appeals by local committees and the Local Government Board, which often gave people the benefit of the doubt. Overall, precautions were taken to ensure that the lack of records and evidence concerning people's date of birth were not used to deny people a pension on a blanket basis.[76] The general point is that officials should avoid falling into error by processing decisions by relying solely upon standardised information – or the lack of it. Officials making decisions also need to think carefully about the position of the individual and the nuances of human and social life.

State Pension Underpayments: The Importance of Effective Quality Assurance within Government

Another type of knowledge that government needs concerns the quality of its own internal operations. Administrative control within large organisations, such as government departments, relies heavily upon management information systems and quality assurance processes. Large casework departments that make millions of decisions, such as the DWP and the Home Office, need to understand whether their caseworkers are applying the rules properly and how administrative processes are operating in practice. There are inherent challenges in this respect because of the sheer number of decisions involved, the complexity of the rules being administered, the operation of legacy IT systems, the competence of staff, the risk of errors and the adequacy or otherwise of quality assurance system used to monitor initial administration. Government can seek to mitigate the risk of error by operating effective internal control and quality assurance systems. They can be used to identify and correct errors. However, the robustness of such systems depends on the extent of their coverage in proportion to the scale of the underlying administrative system.

A good illustration of the importance of quality assurance systems is provided by the underpayment of the state pension to several thousands of pensioners. Millions of people rely upon the state person in their retirement. In 2020, it came to light that an estimated 375,000 pensioners, mostly female, had been underpaid their state pension

[75] RJ Kelly, *Old Age Pensions Act 1908* (Dublin, Sealey, Bryers and Walker, 1908) 4-5.

[76] C Breathnach, '"The Night of the Big Wind": Reticent Subjects and the Introduction of Old Age Pensions in Ireland' (2025) 99 *History Workshop Journal* 29.

entitlements by the DWP.[77] The total estimated value of the underpayments was over £2.5 billion and the average underpayment was £5,000, although in some cases it was far higher. Some of the errors dated back to 1985. Despite the systemic and long-standing nature of the problem, it had not been identified by the DWP. The errors had only come to light through the work of external pension experts. How did the Department fail to pay pensioners their full state pension entitlements over so many years and why did it not identify its own error earlier?

The state pension is paid to pensioners who meet the relevant entitlement conditions based on their qualifying National Insurance contributions. There are different categories of the state pension which relate to different cohorts of people depending on their circumstances. The relevant rules are complex and been amended on many occasions. Since 1989, 14 Acts of Parliament and multiple sets of regulations have affected precisely which type of state pension a person is entitled to. Pensions law is therefore a highly complex and recondite area of law. By 2020, only a small number of DWP staff understood the relevant legal rules and possessed the expertise to know how to apply them correctly.

Some 13 million people are in receipt of the state pension. People pay National Insurance contributions to build up their state pension entitlement. The only way of administering so many individual National Insurance records is through a computerised system. However, the DWP's IT systems are old and antiquated. The core legacy IT system dates from 1988. Additional IT systems had been introduced on top of the elderly core IT system. Given their age, these IT systems have limited automation. They rely heavily upon records being manually updated by caseworkers. Given the millions of records and the complexity and risks of upgrading, the DWP has preferred to retain the various IT multiple systems that had developed piecemeal rather than replace them altogether with a new, single fully automated modern system. Accordingly, caseworkers had to use the old 'not fit for purpose' multiple IT systems to process awards. To calculate a pensioner's state pension entitlement, caseworkers had to set prompts on the system and copy information across manually from one IT system to another. The information was not transferred automatically. The upshot was that the process of calculating awards – people's state pensions entitlements – was inherently vulnerable to human error.

Repeated human errors did indeed occur over many years. In many instances, caseworkers had not manually set prompts on the system so that a person's record would be reviewed at a later date. The process of reviewing cases had been necessary because a person's state pension entitlement would be affected by key life events, such as when the person reached age 80 or when their spouse reached pension age. Caseworkers had also sometimes failed to action prompts that had previously been set on the system. The work of caseworkers had also been affected by pressures within the DWP. The priority had been on processing new claims rather than reviewing existing ones. Consequently, many prompts on the IT systems had not been actioned when they should have been.

[77] 'Woman Who Got 86p a Week State Pension Finds She is Owed £42,000' *The Guardian* (6 February 2021); 'Pension Scandal: "I've Lost 14 years of Payments"' *BBC News* (2 June 2021), www.bbc.co.uk/news/business-57314686; National Audit Office, *Investigation into the Underpayment of the State Pension* (HC 2021–22, 665).

These errors were reinforced and compounded by wider weaknesses. Caseworkers found their instructions difficult to use. They had not been properly trained on how to process complex cases. The DWP's internal organisation had also affected matters. Its pension services had been centralised into a small number of specialist centres. Consequently, the accuracy of a pensioner's overall state pension award relied on multiple teams correctly handling different elements of each case. No single officer was responsible for checking the overall accuracy of a person's state pension award. Given the complexity of the rules, the inadequacy of IT systems and the lack of overall checking of awards, some level of error was inevitable. Indeed, multiple errors occurred over many years.

All administrative systems are intrinsically susceptible to error. This is well known. However, government can – and often does – take steps to mitigate the risk of such vulnerabilities. This can be done by having quality assurance systems to identify and correct errors. Quality assurance involves setting quality assurance standards which managers then use to check a sample of administrative decisions or actions. The purpose of quality assurance systems is to enable senior staff to check for errors and to decide whether they are simply one-off errors or whether they are part of a wider pattern or trend that might indicate systemic problems. If this occurs, then – in theory – senior officials can investigate to decide whether there is in fact a wider systemic error that needs to be rectified.

A crucial issue is then the robustness and adequacy of quality assurance systems to detect, correct and prevent errors. A particularly important matter is their breadth of coverage – that is, the size of the sample of decisions that are checked for quality assurance purposes. There is an obvious balance to be achieved in this respect. Increasing the sample size of decisions increases the capacity to detect errors, but requires a corresponding increase in administrative resources. Reducing the sample size can save costs and time, but increases the risk of errors not being detected. This tension is particularly relevant in the context of very large administrative systems, such as the state pension, in which a small sample size will nevertheless amount to a large number of decisions that need to be checked. This will amount to a significant volume of work. However, when placed within the truly enormous scale of the entire volume, even these sample sizes can likely be insufficient to identify systemic errors.

The DWP's state pension systems had a three-tier quality assurance process. This comprised: a tier 1 check by a local team leader; tier 2 checks by a centralised national team; and tier 3 checks as part of the DWP's fraud and error and analytics checks. This is the familiar 'three lines of defence' model of quality assurance. These mechanisms may seem like a thorough monitoring system. However, in practice, none of them was able to be identify, correct or prevent the systemic errors that led to thousands of pensioners not receiving their full state pension entitlements. The DWP's tier 1 checks only involved reviewing 0.2 per cent of cases per month, a very small sample of all state pension awards. Moreover, the team leaders who undertook these checks lacked the technical expertise to assure the accuracy of awards. Tier 2 and 3 checks similarly involved small sample sizes. The underpayment errors were identified at tier 3. However, there was a further weakness in the quality assurance process. The DWP did not then investigate and assess whether the errors had a wider systemic cause. Overall, there were deep inherent weaknesses in the DWP's quality assurance systems because of the small sample sizes in proportion to the overall volume.

The consequence of this was that the quality assurance checks were largely unable to detect systemic errors in the calculation of people's state pension awards or to prevent such errors from arising. It was precisely these vulnerabilities that led to over 134,000 pensioners being underpaid their state pension entitlements. As the Public Accounts Committee noted: 'The lack of effective measures to mitigate against the system's intrinsic vulnerability to error constituted a fundamental control failure in a critical part of the department's responsibilities.'[78] Moreover, the errors continued undetected for many years. They were only investigated properly by the DWP after they had been identified by external pension experts.

The weaknesses of the DWP quality assurance systems were in part intrinsic and in other respects reflected its long-standing approach to fraud and error. The DWP had focused on tackling the largest sources of fraud and error. For instance, Universal Credit has some of the highest overpayments and disability benefits have some of the largest underpayments. By contrast, the error rate in state pension calculations has historically been relatively low. This was reflected in the proportional size of the samples to be checked for quality assurance purposes. This approach towards tackling error in the state pension meant that errors that had small financial impacts upon the Department's budget were overlooked, despite having quite large financial impacts for the individuals affected. The Public Accounts Committee expressed concern that the DWP did not attach equal importance to correcting underpayments as it did to overpayments. The problem was also partly attributable to the DWP's complacency and lack of action. It knew that its IT systems were antiquated, heavily reliant on manual checks and vulnerable to error, but it did not then strengthen its quality assurance systems accordingly.[79] The end result of these factors was a systemic error in which over a few hundred thousand people were underpaid their state pension entitlements, which they needed to live on. The Committee concluded that the DWP had been complacent by failing properly to monitor its calculations of people's state pension awards.

The problem of error is a particular issue for the DWP, given its massive scale as an organisation and the needs of people who rely on it for their living costs. During the Public Accounts Committee hearing, the DWP's Permanent Secretary, the Department's most senior civil servant, sought to reassure MPs that, from the perspective of operational delivery, the Department had been getting much better at making sure that its systems could respond to the reality people's lives – as opposed to a Whitehall view of people's lives. In response, the Committee Chair cynically wondered whether that would ever really happen and invited officials to attend MPs' constituency surgeries to see the reality of people's lives: 'If you see some of the letters that your Department sends out … they are impossible to understand.'[80] It was therefore important for officials to be able to access and understand the reality of people's lives, and to appreciate the real impact that a couple of bad bureaucratic mistakes made across two government departments could have, thereby resulting in someone becoming caught up in 'a vortex

[78] House of Commons Public Accounts Committee, *Underpayments of the State Pension* (HC 2021–22, 654) 5.
[79] ibid.
[80] House of Commons Public Accounts Committee, *Oral Evidence: Underpayments of the State Pension* (HC 2021–22, 654) 28 October 2021, Q33 (Meg Hillier MP, Committee Chair).

of Whitehall bureaucratic impossibility'.[81] If it is hard enough for experienced MPs to address such problems, then the average person will be easily defeated, especially when trying to interact with a large impersonal bureaucracy, such as the DWP.

To correct its systemic errors, the DWP undertook a large corrective LEAP exercise that involved reviewing over 800,600 people's pension records to identify underpayments. Experienced staff were transferred from processing state pension awards to correcting the underpayments, thereby leading to delays in awards for new pensioners. While the purpose of corrective LEAP exercises is to address past errors, the NAO found that the LEAP exercise had itself been affected by the same underlying issues that caused the underpayments: weaknesses with staff training, their instructions and quality assurance. Some 13 per cent of decisions ostensibly corrected during the LEAP exercise had themselves incorrectly assessed pensioners' entitlements. The DWP responded by then strengthening its controls, although the NAO cautioned that some errors would likely continue to arise, particularly in complex cases. Further, some pensioners who had contacted the Department had been falsely reassured that their payments were correct when they were not. Given the scale of the underpayments, the Committee later expressed serious doubts about the DWP's ability to make accurate and complete payments.[82] A further problem was that some people who had been repaid their underpayments by way of a lump sum then had their other benefits cut by their local authority as a result, including their housing and council tax benefit. This was because the lump sum exceeded the relevant savings limit for those benefits.[83] Many people affected found interacting with the DWP to resolve their situations to be problematic.[84]

Overall, the episode illustrates how complex, overloaded and outdated systems and processes can become infected by deep and widespread errors which then remain dormant and undetected for years. Quality assurance systems are required, but when they are themselves inadequate, they provide false assurance. Further, the DWP had been institutionally complacent. It knew the systems were vulnerable to error, but it just assumed that its quality assurance processes were sufficient, which was not the case. All three of its quality assurance tiers failed to detect a large-scale widespread systemic error. Reflecting on the systemic failure, one member of the Public Accounts Committee noted that in a huge complex administrative machine such as the DWP, it was all too easy for officials to lose sight of the human beings whose lives had been severely impaired by the Department's errors. The Committee was concerned that the DWP's organisational complacency meant that it had not fully appreciated the human costs of its failings.[85]

[81] ibid.

[82] House of Commons Public Accounts Committee, *The Department for Work & Pensions Annual Report and Accounts 2022–23* (HC 2023–24, 290).

[83] 'Help! My Mum was Underpaid State Pension by the DWP for 12 Years, and Now the Council is Coming after Her Backpayment' *Thisismoney.co.uk* (6 April 2021), www.thisismoney.co.uk/money/pensions/article-9419063/My-mum-underpaid-state-pension-years-penalised-council.html.

[84] 'Chaotic DWP Response to State Pension Scandal under Attack, as Five More Women Receive a Total of £53k after String of Errors and Delays' *Thisismoney.co.uk* (19 November 2020), www.thisismoney.co.uk/money/pensions/article-8961701/Chaotic-DWP-handling-state-pension-scandal-attack.html.

[85] P Grant, 'A Complacent DWP Failed Pensioners, Says MP, as his Watchdog Committee Issues "Blistering" Report on State Pension "Fiasco"' *Thisismoney.co.uk* (21 January 2022), www.thisismoney.co.uk/money/comment/article-10422365/A-complacent-DWP-failed-people-state-pension-fiasco-says-MP.html.

The episode of state pension underpayments also demonstrates both the inherent legal-administrative challenges and the avoidable problems that government itself creates. As regards the former, the sheer complexity of the legal framework involved some 70 legislative changes introduced since 1995 being incorporated into both upgraded systems and the understanding of caseworkers. Another aspect concerns the ongoing enterprise of improving systems as illustrated by the LEAP exercise itself repeating initial errors. The wider challenge is improving quality assurance throughout every level of the DWP, something which needs to be revisited time and again with cycles of feedback and then improvements to reduce error. Nonetheless, as the DWP's Permanent Secretary noted, 'the harsh fact is that we will not eliminate all official error anywhere across DWP'.[86] These are the inherent and never-ending challenges of government and of administrative justice: the hard ongoing slog of grinding casework and mass administration; the need to ensure that people are treated fairly and properly; ensuring systemic errors are exposed, corrected, and provide learning to improve.

Analysing and Understanding Systemic Administrative Justice

It is time to consider the broader picture. Table 7.1 pulls together the above case studies.

Table 7.1 Systemic administrative justice failures

Context	Nature of systemic failure	Causes
Tax credits	The administration of tax credits through the tax system by HMRC as opposed to the DWP; overpayments were built into the tax credits system, generating widespread problems for claimants	Flawed policy design Lack of knowledge and understanding of the affected cohort of people Legal complexity and administrative error Poor-quality systems and processes
The cod wars compensation scheme	Compensation scheme did not compensate its intended recipients	Inadequate integration of implementation with the policy goal Lack of knowledge and understanding of affected people and industry Compensation scheme designed too quickly

[86] House of Commons Public Accounts Committee (n 80) Q100, 28 October 2021 (Peter Schofield, Permanent Secretary, DWP).

Context	Nature of systemic failure	Causes
Transfer of benefit claimants to Employment and Support Allowance	Transfer process badly designed and contrary to the DWP's own regulations	Lack of effective internal controls and oversight Ignorance of regulations Failure to listen to stakeholders A culture of indifference to people being underpaid their benefit entitlements
COVID grants	Applicants for COVID grants were wrongly refused because they did not appear on the council's ratepayer database	The '(il)logic of legibility' Relying on the ratepayer database and not investigating the individual cases by exercising the discretion and judgement that officials had
The Windrush scandal	Windrush people were wrongly subject to hostile immigration policies and treated as though they did not have the right to remain in the UK	The '(il)logic' of legibility Institutional amnesia Ignorance of legislation Failure to listen to stakeholders Inadequate decision procedures Wrong burden of proof applied Poor-quality decision-making
State pension underpayments	State pensioners were underpaid their state pension entitlements	Legal complexity and administrative error Limited and inadequate nature of quality assurance systems which failed to identify systemic underpayment of pensions

The preceding analysis has focused on systemic failures by central government that have been subject to extensive scrutiny. It is far from exhaustive.[87] Systemic failures also occur within local government and elsewhere. There are many ways in which government can go wrong. It is also important to recognise that many administrative systems operate reasonably well and effectively. Nonetheless, the analysis presented here illustrates the type of structural shortcomings that occur. It demonstrates the importance of systemic administrative justice and how the problems people experience with administration and public services arise not because of isolated errors, but as a result of structural causes buried deep within the systems, processes, policies and governmental behaviours. This model of systemic administrative justice has a significantly

[87] See also the own-initiative investigation into PIP by the Northern Ireland Public Services Ombudsman (ch 4 137–139) and the DWP's systemic communication failures (ch 8). There have been systemic failures elsewhere. In 2021, the Dutch government resigned over a scandal relating to child benefits in which more than 20,000 families were wrongly accused of fraud by the tax authority and a highly critical report from a parliamentary committee. See J Henley, 'Dutch Government Resigns over Child Benefits Scandal' *The Guardian* (15 January 2021). Following the 'Robodebt' scandal, the Australian government established a public inquiry. See P Whiteford, 'Debt by Design: The Anatomy of a Social Policy Fiasco – or Was it Something Worse?' (2021) 80 *Australian Journal of Public Administration* 340; M Groves, 'Systemic Failure and Systemic Unfairness' (2023) 30 *Australian Journal of Administrative Law* 151.

different structure from the established model of individualised decisions and redress. Systemic administrative justice is not focused just on the downstream retail end, but also upstream, the substance of public policies and how they are designed, administered and implemented. There is, of course, a point at which these two models overlap and a degree of gradation between them, but they comprise distinct models of administrative justice. It also needs to be borne in mind that those officials responsible for a problem may have a vested interest in it being labelled as systemic in order to deflect blame away from them individually.

The above systemic failures arose from a range of quite different policy and administrative contexts, but there share some common features. These include weaknesses in the quality of the policy-making and implementation processes used by government, the lack of knowledge and understanding of the social contexts and social facts that are being subject to administrative regulation, and the institutional behaviours of administrative bodies. When government lacks knowledge, does not think through the consequences of its policies, or creates administrative systems without adequate managerial oversight and controls, then the scope for systemic problems increases. Large systems of mass administration such as benefits, pensions and immigration are particularly susceptible to systemic errors because of their scale, complexity and the effects of 'legacy'. Systems and processes are developed piecemeal and overlay established structures. A single error repeated in hundreds of thousands or millions of cases over many years can have significant repercussions. Some of the state pension underpayments dated back to 1985. The resulting errors can be similarly long-lasting. A Windrush man was stuck in Poland for 28 years.[88]

A common theme running throughout all of the case studies is the inherent tension between the imperatives of policy and administration on the one hand, and the need to understand and consider the position of people on the other hand. In all instances, the harms caused to people were embedded within the policies and their implementation. Government might have thought that it had considered the needs of the people concerned. However, in all of the case studies, government had failed to design services that catered properly for people. The problem is often inherent within the nature of government. Officials want to provide to public services that meet people's needs. Yet, the scale and complexity of the systems and processes required often means that officials act at a distance and simply may not understand how public services operate from the perspective of the citizens who use and experience them.[89] Tax credits were motivated by the benevolent desire to help people on low incomes, but ultimately ended up alienating many of them as they got caught up in a complex bureaucratic-legal web that failed to understand how they lived their lives and made many of these people worse off. Officials simply lacked the ability to step outside of their own cultural frames and to see and understand the world from a different perspective. As the tax credits fiasco illustrates, when government does consider the possible human costs, it can be more of a self-delusion by officials rather than a credible attempt to understand how policies work on the ground level and from the perspective of the people concerned. Instead,

[88] '"Nothing is the Same": Windrush Victim Allowed to Return to UK after 28 Years' *The Guardian* (18 August 2025).

[89] Bourn (n 5) 189.

government can expect ordinary people to act, think and behave like bureaucrats. By contrast, Windrush occurred because government was deliberately pursuing a hostile environment towards immigrants.

There are huge challenges inherent in organising and delivering effective public services. Government is a large collection of large organisations. Its sheer size and scale mean that it is difficult to get things done. This requires skill, tenacity, political leadership and effective administrative implementation. Problems will always arise because of the scale of the activity and the scope for error. The more complex public service delivery becomes and the more demands placed upon government, the greater the scope for error and injustice. The instances examined in this chapter illustrate the significant harms that arise when government gets things wrong. Yet, some of this could have been avoided. It is entirely possible that officials know what is going wrong, but correcting the direction of such a large endeavour is incredibly difficult. Government is both the problem and the solution. The principal means of preventing systemic failures and promoting administrative justice within government is through more effective administrative action.

Systemic administrative justice failures are a subset of wider governmental blunders.[90] A number of factors are relevant here: the constitutional set-up within which central government operates; the relative lack of scrutiny and accountability of government departments; and the relationships between ministers and civil servants. There are also human errors and biases. The cultural disconnect between senior officials and the population concerned was evident in the case of tax credits. There are also organisational and operational errors. This is illustrated by the DWP's lack of management information and effective oversight which allowed underpayments of the state pension to go undetected for several years. Another organisational error has been the reliance by officials upon standardised information – databases, immigration documents or the lack of them – as being objectively correct, despite the protests of affected people that such information is incorrect and incomplete.

In addition to illustrating the systemic harms imposed on people, each episode considered here can also be mined to extract discrete principles of systemic good administration. When government is designing and implementing a policy or public service, it needs to understand the position, needs and circumstances of the general cohort of people affected (for example, tax credits and the Windrush scandal). When government is designing an administrative scheme, it should possess sufficient knowledge and understanding so that the detailed rules align with the policy goals for which the scheme was established to advance (for example, cod wars compensation). When an administrative system is operational, the internal monitoring and quality assurance processes should be able to detect errors and listen to both front-line officers and external stakeholders (for example, the flawed ESA transfer and state pension underpayments). When government operates systems which are administered on the basis of its own information, government should not assume such information is always reliable

[90] P Dunleavey, 'Policy Disasters: Explaining the UK's Record' (1995) 10 *Public Policy and Administration* 52; King and Crewe (n 11); B Hudson, D Hunter, and S Peckham, 'Policy Failure and the Policy-Implementation Gap: Can Policy Support Programs Help?' (2019) 2 *Policy Design and Practice* 1; S Freedman, *Failed State: Why Nothing Works and How We Fix It* (London, Macmillan, 2024).

and objectively correct (for example, COVID grant schemes and the Windrush scandal). Government should be receptive to other sources of information and knowledge. Finally, government should be aware that the institutional cultures embedded within administrative systems can both generate maladministration while making it seem an ordinary part of the process to the officials working within that system. Consequently, government should positively welcome external engagement and challenge from people with different views.

How can such failures be prevented or, at least, how can the risk of them be reduced? Government should learn lessons for the future. This is the essence of organisational learning.[91] It requires a deep commitment and willingness by government to learn and improve rather than adopting a grudging defensiveness. Each systemic failure could potentially be used as the basis for avoiding future failures. Yet, organisational learning often appears to be more of an aspiration than reality. Instead, government commits errors only to later repeat them or for new errors to arise. Even if government is more receptive and open to challenge, there will always be blind spots, wilful blindness and groupthink. There are genuine 'unknown unknowns' that often arise owing to the complexity of governing and the social, political and organisational nature of what government is trying to do. There will also be those 'don't go there' problem areas of which officials are painfully aware, but which are too difficult and troublesome to address.

The opposite of organisational learning is organisational forgetting or institutional amnesia.[92] This occurs when rather than learning from lessons and past failures, government forgets about them. The impetus to do so is obvious. Government does not like to admit or think about its failures. These are often met with a defensive response, or explanations that the matter was an isolated issue or a one-off event such as a ministerial resignation. But of course, such responses do nothing to address the underlying issues of systemic maladministration and the cultures underpinning them. There are various causes of institutional amnesia.[93] With organisational churn, the quick turnover of ministers and officials, institutional memory is quickly lost. Government is inherently political. Ultimately, ministers decide. This was particularly evident in the case of tax credits and the Windrush scandal. Ministers at the time had clear views as to both policy and how it should be implemented. There is also the limited absorptive capacity of an institution – that is, its ability quickly to hardwire new reforms into its pre-existing systems and process and thereby to institutionalise change. Some changes are easier than others. Changing guidance and staff instructions is relatively easy, whereas legislative changes and costly system redesigns are far more difficult. Once a given design has been agreed upon, government will be reluctant to depart from it, let alone introduce an entirely new system. The fast pace of change within politics and government means that one issue is quickly buried by others; the focus is always on present and immediate concerns as opposed to long-term matters. In this context, remembering

[91] C Argyris and DA Schön, *Organizational Learning II: Theory, Method and Practice* (Reading, Addison-Wesley, 1996); C Argyris, *On Organizational Learning*, 2nd edn (Oxford, Blackwell, 1999); R Thomas, 'Administrative Justice, Better Decisions, and Organisational Learning' [2015] *PL* 111; A Edmondson, *Right Kind of Wrong: How the Best Teams Use Failure to Succeed* (London, Penguin, 2024).

[92] C Pollitt, 'Institutional Amnesia: A Paradox of the "Information Age"' (2000) 19 Prometheus 5.

[93] A Stark, 'Explaining Institutional Amnesia in Government' (2019) 32 *Governance* 143; A Stark and B Head, 'Institutional Amnesia and Public Policy' (2019) 26 *Journal of European Public Policy* 1521.

a systemic failure from a decade ago is unlikely to be a priority. There are then many reasons why organisational learning rarely prevails over institutional amnesia. On the other hand, thorough scrutiny of ministers and officials before committees is likely the most effective means of exposing failures and getting government to do better. NAO and committee reports provide *ex post* analysis of failures, although there is the risk that they become forgotten about.

The discussion here has had the benefit of hindsight. It is all very well undertaking a retrospective analysis, but quite another thing to identify what might be going wrong in real time. It is also difficult to predict future systemic problems, especially when they will be unforeseen and potentially unforeseeable. The next systemic failure might be something altogether unexpected. Further, while government is rightly blamed for its failures, it has also had its successes.

The general conclusion is then that while government should promote good administration, systemic failures are inevitable; given its size and scale, there are many different ways in which government can go wrong. The preceding analysis has presented a range of problems, but new and unexpected problems will arise. The activities of government are too large, complex, intricate and fragmented to expect otherwise. The people at the top of government can never fully understand what is and is not happening. Furthermore, officials can become so acclimatised to the institutional culture that it becomes difficult to perceive what is going wrong. Ultimately, government should take the demands of systemic administrative justice seriously to ensure that people are not harmed by faulty administration. The scrutiny provided by ombudsmen, the NAO and select committees also needs to be enhanced and taken more seriously by government. Nonetheless, it is only realistic to expect the cycle of systemic errors to continue and for unexpected and unforeseen systemic errors to arise – and this will in turn generate and reinforce the need for administrative justice.

8

Government Communications

An important aspect of people's interactions with government concerns the provision of information by government and its communications with people. Government generates and stores an enormous amount of information about its policies and services. When people need to access public services or claim their legal entitlements, they usually need clear and accurate information from government about such services and what they need to do in order to access and use them. The need for government to communicate effectively and to supply people with accurate, complete and timely information seems like a relatively simple requirement. However, inevitably, problems arise. Government may not give people the information they need. It may give them incorrect and misleading information. It may give them the right information, but at the wrong time. It may also give people a surfeit of complex, unnecessarily detailed or incomprehensible information. All of this can have significant consequences for people using public services and can cause harm and injustice. Indeed, poor communications are at the root of many problems and grievances.

This chapter explores communications and the provision of information as a key aspect of the individual–government relationship and its importance as an issue of administrative justice. It examines the principles concerning good communication and how they are applied by redress mechanisms. It then considers a series of big PHSO investigations into flawed communications by the DWP concerning changes to pensions. These investigations have concerned the communication of important changes that affected millions of people, which came into effect over long periods of time and which reduced people's entitlements. Such investigations deserve in-depth consideration given their complexity, the consequences that arise when things go wrong and the underlying causes.

Communication, Information and Administrative Justice

Communication and the provision of information is a central aspect of the relationship and interactions between the individual and the state – and hence of administrative justice. The importance of effective communication reflects and reinforces key themes of administrative justice: the inequality of power inherent within individual–government relations; the individual's lack of choice; the injustice and practical challenges that arise as a result of the behavioural dysfunctions of government; and the resulting need for improved administration. Virtually all interactions people have with government and public services involve communications and the mutual exchange of information.

They range from single-instance transactions to government communicating complex messages to millions of people over many years. Government takes many forms: an official, a health professional, an online service and so on. Government knows – or should know – the system. It possesses expertise in whatever area of responsibility is concerned. On the other hand, there is the individual: benefit claimants, patients, pensioners, taxpayers and so on. They know about their own circumstances, but they do not know about the system, its procedures, eligibility criteria, and how it works etc. Communication problems in this relationship inevitably lead to misunderstandings and often have significant adverse consequences for people.

A substantial part of the power that bureaucracies exercise is through the information they possess and what information they decide to communicate to people and how. Indeed, government as a whole can be understood as a system for collecting and distributing information. People typically have no choice but to rely on government information. Given government's unique role, its scale and authority, people should be able to have confidence in the accuracy and completeness of information provided by government. Without reliable information, people cannot take well-informed personal decisions in their best interests. Unclear, inaccurate and incomplete information can result in confusion and potentially significant human and financial consequences for people. Given the huge scale on which government operates, communication problems can generate considerable injustice. Many such problems could be prevented.

Communications occur on a number of levels, ranging from the one-to-one interactions reaching up to the higher levels of overarching systems. The scale on which government administers policies and also its own organisation creates practical challenges to communicating with people effectively. Good communication makes demands on the knowledge and institutional competence of government bodies. They must understand the law and their legal responsibilities, their policies and procedures. This knowledge must be shared internally. Large administrative institutions also need to have robust internal systems in place to disseminate information throughout their organisational structures. Effective external communication by government to the public requires effective internal communication within the relevant government body. There is plenty of scope for both human and system error.

In addition to practical challenges, there are also the behavioural pathologies of government. To communicate effectively, public bodies need to appreciate and understand the position of the people concerned. For officials working within government who know the system, it can seem obvious what the relevant law and policies are. A principal *déformation professionnelle* of officialdom is the 'illusion of similarity'. Officials can unwittingly assume that people understand the system in the way they do and then expect them to behave like bureaucrats in attending to their own needs.[1] However, the system is typically highly complex, arcane, inaccessible and continually changing. It often requires considerable time and mental energy to understand how administrative systems work – and also the difference between how they should operate and how they in fact operate in practice and their unwritten rules. No one encountering these and the many other systems can be expected to understand them. Accordingly, public bodies must communicate effectively

[1] Behavioural Insights Team, *Behavioural Government: Using Behavioural Science to Improve How Governments Make Decisions* (London, BIT, 2018).

with people in ways that reach them and that they understand. This in turn requires a deeper appreciation by government of society and the needs of different cohorts of people.

Communications from public bodies take many forms: the provision of generic information about policies, services and entitlements; specific advice and communications to individuals on their personal situation; giving reasons for decisions; communications as part of initial complaint-handling; and so on. There are various ways in which government communications can go wrong: not communicating at all; delayed communication; and providing ambiguous or incorrect and misleading information. Not communicating at all and delayed and ambiguous communications can generate uncertainty. Incorrect and misleading information can generate false certainty. One type of communication failure can reinforce another. Providing incorrect information and then seeking to correct it can lead to muddle and confusion. There are endless multiple permutations, especially when communications problems intermingle with other types of maladministration.

As an illustration, consider delayed communication. In one instance, a council towed away a woman's car for contravening temporary parking restrictions, but it did not inform her of this until a year later. The women wrongly assumed that her car had been stolen and claimed on her car insurance.[2] The council had informed the police that the car had been removed in case it was reported missing. However, the police then failed to inform the woman of this when she reported her car as stolen. The council then later demanded a year's storage fees from the woman. When she complained to the council about its year-long delay, it attributed this to staffing issues and 'changes in processes'. The council only waived the fines and fees when a newspaper intervened. There is also giving people misleading advice. For instance, the Marine Management Organisation, which issues marine licences, wrongly advised two fishermen that the boats they intended to buy could be used to fish for sea bass, only for them later to find out this was not the case, thereby leading to stress, frustration and loss of income.[3] The Independent Case Examiner has upheld complaints in which the DWP has issued incorrect advice to benefit claimants about their position. In one case, three different requests for information resulted in three different and inconsistent pieces of advice from the DWP.[4]

There is also the issue of not providing information in an accessible way, given a person's individual circumstances. For instance, a council repeatedly failed to give a woman with poor eyesight letters in large print, which she needed to access information about her council tax. Under the Equality Act 2010, public bodies should make anticipatory reasonable adjustments to remove or prevent obstacles that people with disabilities would otherwise experience when accessing public services.[5] The LGSCO emphasised

[2] 'Council Forgets to Tell Driver it Towed Car Away – Then Demands Year's Storage Fees' *The Guardian* (5 June 2024).

[3] PHSO, *The Ombudsman's Casework Report 2019* (HC 2020, 63) 16.

[4] Independent Case Examiner, *Annual Report 2024–25* (London, DWP, 2025) 8–11 and 18–20.

[5] LGSCO, London Borough of Lambeth (23017707). This followed two previous complaints; (21006085) and (22012376). See also: 'I Brought a Judicial Review Against the DWP and Won £7,000' *BBC News* (23 August 2023), www.bbc.com/news/uk-england-london-66547199; *R (Osman) v Secretary of State for Work and Pensions* (Consent Order, CO/2101/2022, 18 July 2023) (a blind man requested the DWP to send him benefit letters in braille or accessible PDFs, which it then failed to do); LGSCO, Worcestershire County Council (24020635) (the council sent a blind man multiple invoices for his social care costs despite having carried out a care assessment finding he was visually impaired; consequently, the man accrued a significant financial debt).

that service providers cannot wait until a disabled person wanted to use their services; they must think in advance about what disabled people with a range of impairments might reasonably need and how to meet those needs.

Not fully communicating important information to people can lead to avoidable problems. For instance, the DWP had published advertisements with the intention of ensuring people on legacy benefits did not claim Universal Credit too late. However, this led to a person claiming too early and thereby losing her entitlements. The claimant had contacted the DWP to migrate from tax credits to Universal Credit, but the call-handler did not explain that it was necessary to wait for the migration notification to be eligible for transitional protection; instead, the call-handler helped the claimant to apply afresh for Universal Credit. The claimant was left significantly financially worse off as a result. The Independent Case Examiner concluded that the DWP's advertisement did not make clear to claimants the importance of waiting for the migration notification and the difference this made to a person's entitlements. The financial remedy included a small consolatory payment and a larger payment for the loss of statutory entitlement.[6]

Another aspect to be considered is initial complaint-handling. Between 2020 and 2024, the DWP handled some 18,875 complaints solely in relation to Universal Credit on the theme of communication, of which 48 per cent were upheld.[7] These were complaints about one benefit (out of over 30) and on one theme, communication (out of seven themes). The theme of communication was then broken down into some 20 different root causes, including: 'you told me the wrong thing (misdirection)', 'what you told me was confusing/contradictory', 'you haven't answered my questions', 'I don't understand your system letter or manual letter', 'you didn't tell me about your decision', 'you didn't keep me informed', 'I didn't understand the process', 'I didn't understand – your English/ Welsh is poor', 'you have asked for the same information again', 'you failed to reply to correspondence', 'you didn't listen to me', 'you were rude/threatening/abusive towards me' and so on.

Then there are the really tragic cases that arise as a result of communication failures. A young woman took her own life after her disability benefits had been incorrectly reduced. The DWP had communicated the decision by sending her a standard letter, without attempting to reduce the impact the decision could cause. The coroner concluded that this had been inappropriate, given the woman's vulnerabilities, and it had significantly contributed to her declining mental health.[8]

Communication is a huge challenge for the NHS, given its size. The NHS has failed to send thousands of letters to patients owing to widespread errors on its IT systems, resulting in delays, muddle and confusion.[9] People have received appointment invitations after the date of the appointment. Poor communication within the NHS has led to

[6] Independent Case Examiner (n 4) 20–22.

[7] DWP, FOI response (FOI2024/62269, 23 August 2024).

[8] 'Woman Took Her Own Life after Benefits Cut in Error' *BBC News* (28 January 2026), www.bbc.com/news/articles/cz0p2jp5d77o.

[9] 'Newcastle Hospitals Says Computer Error Lost Patient Letters' *BBC News* (26 September 2023), https://www.bbc.com/news/health-66917025; 'Nottingham University Hospitals Trust Failed to Send 400,000 letters' *BBC News* (29 September 2023), https://www.bbc.com/news/health-66950204.

avoidable harm to patients, including deaths and insensitive treatment.[10] An NHS trust did not tell a man that his cancer diagnosis was terminal. Consequently, he did not have the time to come to terms with his condition and did not see his son before dying.[11] A woman was called by her health board to attend a pregnancy scan days after having a miscarriage, which the IT system had not flagged.[12] Poor communication by and within the NHS arises in three principal ways: people have difficulty accessing or navigating the system because it is unclear what communication to expect or who to communicate with at different points; administrative errors creating inaccurate or erroneous communications, leading to problems with care, treatment or experience; and NHS staff not being able to communicate internally or to advise on next steps to patients because they do not know or understand enough about patients' medical histories.[13] Such problems cause harmful delays, endanger patients' health and undermine trust in the NHS by negatively impacting people's experiences and in turn generate perceptions of an organisation that wastes money, time and staff resources. All of this reflects a wider structural problem: the scale and complexity of NHS administration, bureaucracy and systems which often do not meet the needs of patients.

The ways in which government communicates – or seeks to do so – can be just as important as what it is trying to communicate. The means of communication can affect who receives the intended message and also at which point of time, which can often be critically important. There can also be difficulties concerning both the volume and content of communications. Both insufficient and excessive communications can be problematic. While communications should be accurate, complete and understandable, there are real challenges for government in seeking to provide understandable and accessible information on arcane, detailed and complex areas, such as pensions and benefits, while ensuring that it is also accurate and complete.

In addition to poor-quality communications from government, it can also be difficult for people to make contact and communicate with government when they need information and advice to fulfil the obligations and requirements placed upon them by government. Consider contacting HMRC about a tax query. Millions of people do this each year. With the closure of local HMRC offices, the only way to contact HMRC is over the phone. In 2022–23, HMRC spent £881 million on its customer services and had 21,000 tax advisers. Nonetheless, many people experienced long delays waiting on the phone to speak to an adviser.[14] Callers spent a total of 798 years (seven million hours) on hold. Moreover, HMRC estimated that 73 per cent of those calls arose from 'failure demand' – that is, increased demand caused by HMRC's own process failures or delays, customers chasing progress and customers' errors when interacting online with HMRC.

[10] 'NHS Computer Issues Linked to Patient Harm' *BBC News* (30 May 2024), https://www.bbc.com/news/articles/c4nn0vl2e78o.

[11] PHSO (n 3) 51.

[12] 'Pregnancy Loss: Woman Distressed by Scan Reminder after Miscarriage' *BBC News* (18 November 2023), https://www.bbc.com/news/uk-wales-67416870.

[13] Demos, *'I Love the NHS, But …': Preventing Needless Harms Caused by Poor Communications in the NHS* (London, Demos, 2023); The King's Fund, *Lost in the System: The Need for Better Admin* (17 February 2025), www.kingsfund.org.uk/insight-and-analysis/long-reads/lost-in-system-need-for-better-admin.

[14] National Audit Office, *Customer Service: HM Revenue & Customs* (HC 2023–24, 726).

Principles and Redress Mechanisms

We will now consider the principles concerning good communications and their application by redress institutions. Take first the principle that government provides the public with accurate and complete information about legislation and its policies. This seems like a basic, simple and unexceptional principle of good administration. People are entitled to know where they stand in relation to legislation and governmental policies. When a major policy change is introduced, government should communicate the change effectively to the affected population thereby enabling people to make informed decisions about how they can respond and make appropriate alternative arrangements. It is generally recognised that laws affecting people should be published and clearly expressed.[15] Yet, while legislation is formally enacted and published, few people read it. Even if they did, many of them (including some lawyers) would struggle to understand its implications, given the complexity and abstruseness of statutory language and the frequency with which legislation is amended. Instead, people learn about changes in legislation through government guidance and information; leaflets, advertisements, advice from officials and online information.

Despite the importance of people being able to understand the law, there is no legal duty on government to provide information on changes to the law.[16] In 1971, JUSTICE noted that one of the most remarkable gaps in the law was the absence of any remedy for the 'irresponsibility' of a government body carelessly providing people with incorrect information.[17] There are some specific (albeit limited) statutory duties on government to communicate information. For instance, English local authorities must provide information and advice about care and support for adults and carers.[18] Such information and advice must be accessible to and proportionate to the needs of those for whom it is being provided. However, this and the few other statutory duties on public bodies to communicate information to people are only specific and limited exceptions to the general principle that government is not legally required to provide such information. If government does issue provide information – for instance, on people's statutory entitlements – then it is under a common law duty to ensure that the information provided is both accurate and complete.[19] People should be able to rely on information and guidance provided by government and assume that it is accurate and presents a complete picture of the law. This approach clearly has limits. The duty only arises when government issues such information to people. Paradoxically, if government provided no information in the first place, it would not then be under a legal duty to provide accurate information.

A more encompassing and substantial set of standards is provided by the principles of good administration, which explicitly recognise the importance of effective communications by government to individuals.[20] 'Being customer-focused' requires public bodies to communicate effectively by providing clear, accurate, complete and

[15] LL Fuller, *The Morality of Law* (New Haven, Yale University Press, 1969) 49–51 and 63–65.

[16] *R (Delve) v Secretary of State for Work and Pensions* [2020] EWCA Civ 1199; [2021] 3 All ER 115 (CA).

[17] JUSTICE, *Administration under Law* (London, Stevens, 1971) 20.

[18] Care Act 2014, s 4.

[19] National Audit Office, *State Earnings-Related Pension Scheme: The Failure to Inform the Public of Reduced Pension Rights for Widows and Widowers* (HC 1999–2000, 320) 3.

[20] PHSO, *Principles of Good Administration* (2009) (Appendix A).

understandable information about their services. Public bodies should ensure that people are clear about their entitlements and what they can and cannot expect. 'Being open and accountable' requires that public bodies provide services that are easily accessible. They should be clear and open about their policies and procedures. They should provide accurate and complete information about the relevant service. They should also state their criteria for decision-making and give reasons for their decisions.

The principle of 'seeking continuous improvement' requires public bodies to review their policies and procedures to ensure they are effective, and then use that feedback to improve services and performance. This seemingly innocuous principle can have significant consequences as regards the efforts of public bodies to communicate to people. Suppose, for instance, that a public body has sought to inform people of an important change of policy or legislation. It then reviews whether its efforts have been effective in reaching those people affected who need to know of the change. If such efforts have not or have only partially succeeded, then the principle of seeking continuous improvement requires the public body to use the lessons learnt to improve its services. If a public body does not then act on such feedback, then that could be maladministration. Such a finding of maladministration was made by the PHSO in relation to the communication of changes to the women's state pension age (see below).

What then of good communication and redress mechanisms, including tribunals and ombudsmen? Effective communication is central to the operation of tribunals and indeed the entire judicial process.[21] Given that people often appear before tribunals without legal representation, they need to understand the role of the tribunal, its procedure and what it can and cannot do. Similarly, tribunals need to understand the evidence given by people. A communication error in the hearing room or online can have significant consequences in terms of the handling and assessment of the evidence and of appeal outcomes. Tribunal judges must ensure that appeals are heard fairly. Communication is an important aspect of this. Tribunal procedures must take account of appellants' wider background circumstances to ensure that they can have fair hearings and that there is effective two-way communication. In some types of appeals, in particular asylum appeals, appellants often give evidence through an interpreter. Interpretation involves considerable skill and is not just a matter of straightforward linguistic translation of words; it also raises subtle matters of cultural meaning.

Another form of communication – by both initial decision-makers and tribunals – occurs through reason-giving. When government bodies and tribunals make decisions, a crucial aspect of their communications concerns the quality and adequacy of their reasons and whether decision letters are comprehensible. The most frequent ground for challenging tribunal decisions concerns reason-giving. Moreover, problems in initial decision-making can infect tribunal appeals. Courts and tribunals have repeatedly emphasised to government departments the importance of claimants being able to understand the reasons for decisions. In one case, the claimant had been informed by the DWP that his benefit entitlements had been terminated because 'the law says we cannot pay you'. In fact, DWP caseworkers had muddled up two different benefit schemes. The Upper Tribunal concluded that this was 'an entirely inadequate

[21] Judicial College, *Equal Treatment Bench Book* (London, Judicial College, 2022) 6.

communication, and was part of a series of inadequate communications and gaps in communication', which left the claimant in complete ignorance of what was happening.[22] In its own-initiative report into Personal Independence Payments, the Northern Ireland Public Services Ombudsman criticised the use of pre-populated and automated production of reasons introduced to enhance efficiency. However, the IT system limited the number of characters that caseworkers could input. The result was decision letters that lacked personalisation and customisation to individual decisions, were difficult to read and understand, and were often simply incomprehensible.

Tribunals are not themselves otherwise concerned with the quality of government communications. Instead, ombudsmen and other non-judicial forms of scrutiny have taken the lead in this respect. Since their early days, ombudsmen have recognised that giving misleading advice and information is maladministration.[23] Over the years, ombudsmen have repeatedly found maladministration because of poor communications and have recommended that government bodies improve the quality of their advice, information and communications to people.[24] Successive ombudsmen have emphasised that communication is a perennial issue that public bodies often do not get right and is at the root of many complaints.[25] For instance, the LGSCO criticised Transport for London for not communicating important policy changes concerning a vehicle scrappage scheme to the public.[26] The changes had been introduced by way of unpublished instructions to staff; they had not been made public. The people affected had spent time fruitlessly applying to the scheme, unaware that their vehicles were no longer eligible. The policy change was legitimate, but the failure to communicate the changes had clearly misled people and contravened core principles of fair, transparent and honest public service. Such changes needed to be published online.

A theme of this book is that while some administrative justice failures result from one-off errors, other problems arise from deeper, structural and behavioural dysfunctions. Consider poor-quality communications that arise as a result of internal organisational weaknesses and disconnects within a public body. The external world that administrators deal with is more complex than their internal siloed world. A person's case or problem may straddle different units within the same public body. If those units are fragmented and not adequately coordinated, then problems will often arise. Take the case of a homeowner who had experienced years of distress when her

[22] *SM v Secretary of State for Work and Pensions (JSA) (Contributions and Credits, Jobseeker's Allowance)* [2021] UKUT 179 (AAC) [26]–[27].

[23] B Schwartz and HWR Wade, *Legal Control of Government* (Oxford, Clarendon Press, 1972) 66; R Gregory and P Hutchesson, *The Parliamentary Ombudsman: A Study in the Control of Administrative Action* (London, Allen & Unwin, 1975) 289–93; AW Bradley, 'The Role of the Ombudsman in Relation to the Protection of Citizens' Rights' (1980) 39 *CLJ* 304, 311; C Clothier, 'The Value of an Ombudsman' [1986] *PL* 204, 206.

[24] AR Mowbray, 'A Right to Official Advice: The Parliamentary Commissioner's Perspective' [1990] *PL* 68; P Brown, 'The Ombudsman: Remedies for Misinformation' in G Richardson and H Genn (eds), *Administrative Law & Government Action: The Courts and Alternative Mechanisms of Review* (Oxford, Oxford University Press, 1994).

[25] W Reid, *Resolving Complaints and Promoting Openness: Can the Ombudsman Help?* (London, Nuffield Trust, 1998) 10 and 56 (William Reid, PHSO (1990–96)); House of Commons Work and Pensions Committee, *Oral Evidence: PHSO Report on Women's State Pension Age* (HC 2023–24, 740) 7 May 2024, Q44 (Rebecca Hilsenrath, interim PHSO).

[26] LGSCO, 'Ombudsman Criticises Way TfL Changed its ULEZ Scrappage Schemes' (6 November 2025); LGSCO, Transport for London (24021232).

council did not properly investigate a range of noise, licence and planning permission concerns about the restaurant next door. These matters were considered separately by the council's planning, licensing and environmental health teams; the council did not consider the woman's concerns as a whole in a coordinated way. Instead, she had to raise the same concerns repeatedly with each team and was often passed from one team to another, with no one taking overall responsibility. The LGSCO found communication failures by the council owing to the lack of internal coordination between its different teams.[27] The Ombudsman emphasised that the burden should not be on a complainant to navigate the council's processes; instead, council teams should properly liaise and communicate with each other to provide a coordinated response to residents' concerns. Different teams or units within a public body need to liaise and coordinate with each other effectively if they are to provide joined-up services for the public.

The same problem has arisen in relation to a lack of coordination between different bodies. For instance, the DVLA makes around 800,000 decisions a year about whether people with certain medical conditions are safe to drive.[28] The PHSO has upheld several complaints from people with complex medical conditions who have been unfairly prevented from driving, sometimes for several years, as a result of flawed decisions by the DVLA, significant delays, and poor communication and complaint-handling.[29] This has impacted on people's lives, causing some to lose their jobs, being unable to see friends and family, and suffering significant stress and frustration. The various failures included poor communications to drivers whose licences had been revoked. They also included the lack of communication and information from the DVLA to medical professionals, who struggled to understand what the DVLA required from them in order to make quick and informed decisions about how drivers' medical conditions affected their ability to drive. Overall, there had been flawed decisions, significant delays, poor communication and complaint-handling.

Another issue to consider is poor communications arising from routine casework administration. Caseworkers have to deal with many different individual cases. In some contexts, decision-making is a 'once and done' task. In other contexts, there are repeat cycles of assessments and decisions and timescales within which officials must interact with claimants and manage their cases so that they receive their entitlements. However, because there are so many cases, the public body must have proper and effective case management systems and processes in place to keep track of cases and to ensure that timescales are met. Such systems are mundane and taken for granted, but without them, matters can quickly descend into chaos.

Precisely this problem has arisen in the SEND system.[30] A child may have an Education, Health and Care Plan (EHCP) which sets out their needs. Councils are responsible for ensuring that the educational and other provisions specified are put in

[27] LGSCO, 'Council Fails to Respond to Restaurant Nuisance Complaints' (21 September 2023); LGSCO, Brentwood Borough Council (22008221).

[28] 'DVLA Makes Record Number of Medical Decisions as Elderly Motorists Face £1,000 Driving Licence Fine' *GB News* (18 March 2024), https://www.gbnews.com/lifestyle/cars/dvla-medical-decisions-driving-licence-fine.

[29] PHSO, *Driven to Despair: How Drivers Have Been Let Down by the Driver and Vehicle Licensing Agency* (HC 2016, 660).

[30] See ch 9 316–32.

place. EHCPs should be reviewed at least every 12 months. The council must notify the parent/guardian of its decisions to maintain, amend or discontinue the EHCP. This involves councils consulting with schools, health and educational professionals and others. The statutory timescale for EHCP assessments is 20 weeks, but in practice, it often takes much longer, resulting in significant delays. This is partly because councils must liaise and collaborate with other bodies, but also the under-resourced nature of the system and staff shortages. When parents/carers contact councils for updates, they often do not receive any response. Councils' responses to complaints are also delayed, resulting in distress and frustration.[31] The communication problems and delays often mean that many children do not receive the educational provision they should. An underlying problem is that some councils have not had adequate case management systems so that officers can systematically keep track of SEND cases.[32] Without such systems, councils do not know the status of each case and whether the required provision has in fact been secured for the child. Consequently, officials have been unable to communicate effectively with parents/carers. Many children have not received the educational provision to which they are entitled and which they need. The LGSCO has therefore recommended that councils introduce effective record-keeping systems to track all SEND cases to ensure that timescales are complied with and that they also improve their management of cases and also communication with parents.

Poor communications can also arise from dysfunctional institutional cultures distinguished by indifference or hostility towards people. The nature of a public body's communications with people and their content can reveal its implicit institutional priorities and attitudes towards of cohorts of people. We can return to the DWP's flawed transfer of benefit claimants to ESA, which resulted in over 100,000 people being underpaid their entitlements for some years.[33] The scale and impact of the DWP's systemic errors had been exacerbated by its 'abysmal communication with claimants'.[34] The letters sent by the DWP to claimants did not clarify the precise details of the transfer or the advantages to claimants of them providing the Department with additional information in order to claim the higher-rate benefit. A senior MP has noted that some of the letters sent to people by the DWP 'are impossible to understand'.[35] Such communication failures were of a piece with the Department's culture of indifference towards people being underpaid their benefits compared with its tough pursuit of overpayments. The DWP had also been unwilling to listen to external experts and stakeholders. Its management culture did not value acting proactively and systematically on intelligence from its own front-line staff or addressing mistakes when they first occurred.

[31] J Pennington, 'The Cheshire Parents Left "Broken" as They are Made to Fight for Their Children's Education' *Cheshire Live* (30 April 2024), https://www.cheshire-live.co.uk/news/chester-cheshire-news/cheshire-parents-left-broken-made-29082837; 'Parents Protest over Special Needs Education' *BBC News* (1 May 2024), https://www.bbc.co.uk/news/articles/crggzkk3pvmo; 'EHCP: Councils Missing Education Plan Deadlines for Children with Complex Needs' *BBC News* (15 May 2024), https://www.bbc.co.uk/news/education-68668602.

[32] LGSCO, Dorset Council (21002722); Suffolk County Council (21003011); Kent County Council (22003403).

[33] See ch 7 250–254.

[34] House of Commons Public Accounts Committee, *Employment and Support Allowance* (HC 2017–19, 975) 6.

[35] House of Commons Public Accounts Committee, *Oral Evidence: Underpayments of the State Pension* (HC 2021–22, 654) 28 October 2021, Q33 (Meg Hillier MP, Committee Chair).

A similar problem is evident in the handling of complaints by homeowners whose properties had been adversely affected by the construction of the HS2 train line. HS2 Ltd had failed to communicate properly with a complainant concerning the sale of their family home to make way for the new train line. HS2 had been dishonest, misleading and inconsistent when negotiating compensation for the loss of the family's home.[36] The investigation had exposed fundamental cultural problems, leading to defensive communications and disregard for the public.[37] The select committee was not convinced that the necessary fundamental changes had taken place. Senior leaders needed to understand that they served the public and this had to be reflected through improved communications and complaint-handling.

Poor communication by public bodies can also stem from the financial, political and other pressures placed upon government and the resultant toxic cultures. Croydon Council had agreed to pay a grant to a family as part of a special guardianship arrangement. Under intense financial pressure, it then failed to pay the grant, forcing the family to live in unsuitable accommodation for many months. The council had repeatedly asked the family for the same information they had already given. The LGSCO concluded that these communications and repeated requests for information already provided were, in essence, an underhand tactic by the council to delay the payment.[38]

Perhaps the extreme case of a toxic and defensive institutional culture generating communication failures is the Home Office, as illustrated by the Windrush scandal.[39] At the macro-level, the Home Office failed to engage meaningfully with stakeholders and communities when devising the hostile environment policy. At the micro-level of individual interactions with the department, it was – and remains – virtually impossible for someone to contact the caseworker dealing with their case or to seek advice or guidance about what are often quite legally complex matters.[40] When Windrush people sought to provide evidence of their immigration history, they were unable to attend personal interviews with caseworkers. This is the exemplar of the defensive administrative bureaucracy sealed off from society and which makes it as difficult as possible for people with complex cases to interact with it.

In other contexts, a particular public service experiences increased demand, which weakens its capacity to communicate effectively, which is then progressively downgraded. There are distinct traces of this in the health context. The NHS has long focused on reducing waiting times for patients. This places considerable pressure on health staff, administrative staff, managers and healthcare professionals, diverting them away from communicating with patients on waiting lists and keeping them updated. In 2023, the Northern Ireland Public Services Ombudsman published its own-initiative investigation concerning communications to patients on healthcare

[36] PHSO, *Report on an Investigation into Complaints about High Speed Two Limited* (HC 2014–15, 620); PHSO, *An Investigation into HS2's Failure to Communicate with a Family about Acquiring their Home* (HC 2021–22, 211).

[37] House of Commons Public Administration and Constitutional Affairs Committee, *Follow up to PHSO Report of an Investigation into a Complaint about HS2 Ltd* (HC 2015–16, 793).

[38] LGSCO, 'Council's Failure to Pay Agreed Grant Leaves Family Living on Building Site' (12 May 2022); LGSCO, London Borough of Croydon (20009101).

[39] See ch 7 258–262

[40] W Williams, *Windrush Lessons Learned Review* (HC 2020, 93) 98 and 141.

waiting lists.[41] While communicating with patients had previously been a priority, the Northern Ireland Health Service had focused on waiting lists processes instead of being patient-centred. Patients on long waiting lists had too often been provided with little, if any, communications, sometimes for years. This led to many patients feeling they had been forgotten about. There was long-standing non-compliance with guidance requiring communication with patients, and a failure to monitor this and to address matters. The Ombudsman found a fractured and complex waiting list system that was in disarray and verging upon chaos. Information was held on multiple IT systems. There was variable practice within and between different health trusts. Patients found it difficult to access information about waiting lists, leading to stress and frustration, and, in some cases, mismanagement of their healthcare needs. Many doctors could not fully access the system or keep up to date with their patients' positions on waiting lists. There was a lack of coherence between different parts of the system, a lack of clear communication and no agreed plan for improvement. The Ombudsman recommended that the Department of Health work more cohesively with health trusts, doctors and patient stakeholder groups to improve matters. At the same time, there were funding and financial challenges. The extensive backlogs and waiting lists in Northern Ireland had been built up over years and would take years to be fully addressed. The Department had taken some steps to improve the level of information available to patients, although implementing the Ombudsman's recommendations would require additional resources, both financial and staffing, at a time of severe budgetary pressures.[42]

In addition to the many individual instances of poor communications, there have also been a number of big PHSO investigations concerning large-scale communication failures by central government concerning changes to pensions affecting thousands and sometimes millions of people. These investigations deserve detailed examination, given the nature, causes and consequences of the underlying communication failures. Such episodes also raise another wider issue: the PHSO's changing approach to injustice as a result of maladministration.

The DWP's Communication of Pension Changes and the PHSO

In many areas, government operates and funds large-scale systems: tax; social security benefits; and the state pension. These systems are fundamental to the structure of people's lives and are deeply embedded both within government and society. People have multiple and ongoing interactions with these systems that stretch out over years and decades. At the same time, social, economic and political contexts evolve, government policy changes and these systems are adjusted accordingly. Some of these changes

[41] Northern Ireland Public Services Ombudsman, *'Forgotten': An Investigation into Healthcare Waiting List Communications* (Belfast, NIPSO, 2023).

[42] 'Northern Ireland's Healthcare Waiting Lists Having "Adverse Impact" on Patients, Says Ombudsman' *ITV News* (15 June 2023), https://www.itv.com/news/utv/2023-06-15/waiting-list-failures-amount-to-systemic-maladministration-says-ombudsman.

are long-term endeavours and only come into effect many years after government has legislated for them. While much governmental action typically focuses on immediate and short-term concerns, government also has to think, plan and act on much longer-term timescales.

Accordingly, the temporal dimension of both government and administrative justice assumes considerable importance. This in turn implicates how government communicates with large numbers of people about changes that will come into effect many years down the line. It also raises matters relating to the behaviours and organisation of government itself, its knowledge about its own operations, its institutional memory and how policy can be effectively implemented in practice. All of this is important because some large-scale systemic failures have their roots in the development of areas of law and policy, such as changes to pensions laid many years, sometimes decades, previously.

Since 1908, the UK state has provided pensions to people in their old age.[43] The state pension is one of the principal foundations of the welfare state. In 1948, the basic state pension was introduced. It was paid to men when they reached the age of 65 and to women when they reached 60.[44] The state pension has changed over time. There is an inherent tension between increased life expectancy and the increasing costs of providing publicly funded pensions to millions of people. In 2000–01, the state pension cost around £40 billion. By 2024–25, some 12.9 million people were in receipt of the state pension at a cost of £146 billion – 11.4 per cent of total UK government spending and 45 per cent of social security expenditure. The state pension is important. Many pensioners could not live without it. In addition to the state pension, which is administered by the DWP, there are also personal pensions. Unlike the state pension, private pensions are funded by individuals, whereas government is responsible for the legal, regulatory and administrative framework. A very technical and complex area, pensions have also been subject to many changes for a variety of reasons, not least the increasing pensions and savings gap.

Given the long-term nature of pension reforms and the millions of people affected, the quality and timing of government communications assume great importance. It is recognised that any changes to people's pension entitlements made by government should not come into effect for many years. People need a significant pre-warning notice period – at least 15 years – to give them certainty and sufficient time to make alternative arrangements.[45] Information provided by government must be clear and accurate. Government must also communicate such information to millions of people and many years before such changes come into effect. One risk of such a long time horizon is that government may not adequately and effectively communicate such changes. When government does communicate changes, a whole range of practical issues arise about the best ways and means of communicating with millions of people. Another issue is that there are many different government institutions communicating with the

[43] Old Age Pensions Act 1908; J Macnicol, *The Politics of Retirement in Britain, 1878–1948* (Cambridge, Cambridge University Press, 1998).

[44] Old Age and Widows' Pension Act 1940 s 1; National Insurance Act 1946.

[45] Pensions Commission, *A New Pension Settlement for the Twenty-First Century: The Second Report of the Pensions Commission* (London, Stationery Office, 2005) 406.

public and there is a risk of people receiving many different messages from government and/or missing some of them.

Communication failures can provide the basis for a complaint to the PHSO. Yet, redress is potentially problematic, given the wider implications. If past governmental failures have adversely affected many people's pension entitlements, then the costs of financial redress can be considerable. Whatever failures or problems there may have been in the past, government has to work within existing available resources. Any additional liabilities resulting from payments to compensate people for past failures will have to be met within current budgets. Inevitably, administrative justice becomes entangled and embroiled within a problematic and complex set of wider forces and factors, including public spending, the financial pressures on government and the capacity, behaviours and organisation of government departments. We can now consider in detail specific instances of communication failures by government concerning pensions.

The State Earnings-Related Pension Scheme (SERPS)

In 1978, the then Labour government introduced the State Earnings-Related Pension Scheme (SERPS) alongside the state pension.[46] This provided people with a second pension, related to their earnings. The measure was enacted with cross-party support in Parliament. An important aspect of SERPS concerned the inheritance rule that widows (and widowers) would inherit the whole of their late spouse's SERPS entitlement. Given the structure of society at the time, this meant that many people, mostly women who had not built up a sufficient state pension for themselves, would inherit their husband's full SERPS pension.

By the mid-1980s, matters have moved on. The then Conservative government was concerned about the costs of SERPS. It had initially proposed phasing out SERPS altogether because of the high anticipated future costs in light of increasing life expectancy and a projected decline in the ratio of working-age people to pensioners.[47] However, the government later watered down its proposals. SERPS would be modified rather than abolished.[48] One of the principal changes concerned the inheritance rules; widows (and widowers) would no longer inherit their spouse's full SERPS entitlement, but only half of it. The government justified this change on the ground that it would bring SERPS into line with private occupational pension schemes. The change would correct what had widely been seen as a generous position as regards the inheritance of pensions by widows (and widowers) compared with private pensions. The change to the inheritance rules was enacted by the Social Security Act 1986. A crucial feature was that the 50 per cent reduction in the inheritance provisions would not come into effect until 2000.[49]

At the time, the length of the transition period – 15 years – was unprecedented. Government had never previously introduced a major policy change that would not

[46] Social Security Pensions Act 1975.
[47] Department of Health and Social Security, *Reform of Social Security* (Cmnd 9517, 1985) ch 1.
[48] Department of Health and Social Security, *Reform of Social Security: Programme for Action* (Cmnd 9691, 1985).
[49] ibid 13.

come into effect until so many years in the future. The reason for the long transition period was obvious: to give the people affected by the change the opportunity to make and build up alternative pension contributions before the change came into effect. The then Social Security Minister, John Major MP, told Parliament that the protected position of widows (and widowers) would continue until 2000. People would have plenty of time and ample warning. There would be no sudden, overnight, dramatic change in their position and they would have plenty of time during which they could make alternative provision for the remaining spouse.[50] Another Minister, Tony Newton MP, assured Parliament that the government had 'every intention of mounting a major publicity campaign to herald the pension changes'.[51] The Labour Party had resisted the change on the basis that there would be no 'smooth' transition between full inheritance and half-inheritance. Instead, there would be an abrupt 'cliff-edge' between those people widowed on 5 April 2000 and those on the day after. The latter would only be entitled to the half-inheritance. Despite the concerns raised, the changes were enacted into legislation.[52]

If everything had gone to plan, in accordance with ministers' intentions, the then Department of Health and Social Security (now the DWP) would have mounted the major publicity campaign that had been promised. But this did not happen. The Social Security Act 1986 had been extensively debated in Parliament, although the detail of the changes was not otherwise publicly announced. There was never any publicity campaign as promised by ministers and, indeed, many officials within the Department were unaware of the change. At the time, people received information about their state pension entitlements through leaflets produced by the Department. Apart from one leaflet produced in 1986, none of the DWP's successive leaflets contained any information about the planned future changes to the SERPS inheritance rule. Leaflets continued to advise people that a widow (or widower) would receive all of their partner's SERPS. People were misled. Even after the Department recognised the need to amend its incorrect leaflets in 1996, it did not also accept that its leaflets up to that point had been incorrect and misleading. Nor did it appreciate or accept that its misleading leaflets would have wider implications that would need to be addressed. A further problem was that front-line operational staff in local Benefit Agency offices had been entirely unaware of the planned change. They had not themselves been informed of the impending change. They had therefore proceeded inadvertently to give people misleading and incorrect information. This remained the case for many years. When people went to their local Benefit Agency office for advice on the SERPS inheritance rules, the staff then gave out incorrect advice. People were wrongly informed told that widowed spouse would be entitled to all of their partners' SERPS pension, whereas in fact the SERPS entitlement for widowers was to be halved in 2000.

[50] House of Commons Social Security Bill Standing Committee B 25 February 1986, cols 463–64 (John Major MP, then Parliamentary Under-Secretary of State for Social Security and later Prime Minister (1990–97)).

[51] House of Commons Social Security Bill Standing Committee B 25 February 1986, col 451 (Tony Newton MP, Minister of State, Department of Social Security). In the 2000s, Lord Newton chaired the Council on Tribunals and then the Administrative Justice and Tribunals Council. See T Newton, 'The Role of the Administrative Justice Council' (2006) 13 *Journal of Social Security Law* 98.

[52] Social Security Act 1986, s 19.

Overall, the DWP had 'forgotten' about an important change introduced by its own legislation. People affected by the change were not properly informed and were therefore unaware. Consequently, many affected people did not understand their pension entitlements and had not made alternative appropriate pension arrangements. Some 1.5 million people were affected. The lack of information influenced people's behaviour. Many decided to stay with the SERPS scheme and make contributions on the understanding that their surviving spouse would receive a full pension. Given the lack of information from the DWP about the change to the scheme, people quite reasonably assumed that the inheritance rules remained unchanged.

Matters came to a head in the late 1990s. Newspapers reported on the change to the inheritance rules. People raised concerns with MPs, who then wrote letters to the DWP highlighting that their constituents who had been given incorrect information by the Benefits Agency about their SERPS entitlements. The charity Age Concern also raised the matter with the government. MPs took up the issue in parliamentary questions and debates. Given the media coverage, many people became deeply concerned about the adequacy of their pensions and the uncertainty surrounding exactly what their pension entitlements were. Over the same period of time, the Department realised, through checks of its IT systems, that the required changes had not been made. Front-line staff still remained unaware of the change. They had continued to give people advice about the old inheritance rules without knowing that this had been incorrect. For many years, the DWP had given incorrect and incomplete information about the SERPS inheritance rules – an 'inexcusable' state of affairs.[53]

The government's failure received extensive scrutiny. Select committees noted that the episode had been 'an appalling administrative blunder', 'a political and administrative failure' that had caused confusion, distress, and injustice for many people and cost the taxpayer billions.[54] One minister described the affair as 'probably the single greatest example of public maladministration since the war'.[55] The NAO concluded that the episode revealed 'a very worrying lapse of normal administrative standards' that raised a number of questions about the way in which the Department dealt with people.[56]

Having received 344 complaints, the then PHSO, Michael Buckley, investigated four of them and found maladministration.[57] The Ombudsman strongly criticised the Department's to ensure that its leaflets were accurate and sufficiently comprehensive. This had been compounded by its failure to ensure that front-line staff at local Benefit Agency offices and staff at its pension directorate were properly informed and aware of the impending change, and had been given appropriate guidance on how to respond to enquiries from the public.

[53] HC Deb 15 March 2000, vol 346, col 307 (Alastair Darling MP, Secretary of State for Social Security).

[54] House of Commons Public Accounts Committee, *State Earnings-Related Pension Scheme: The Failure to Inform the Public about Reduced Pension Rights for Widows and Widowers* (HC 1999–2000, 401) [6]; House of Commons Public Administration Select Committee, *Administrative Failure: Inherited SERPS* (HC 1999–2000, 433) [45].

[55] HC Deb 24 July 2000, vol 354, col 803 (Jeff Rooker MP, Minister of State, Department of Social Security).

[56] National Audit Office (n 19) 1.

[57] Parliamentary Commissioner for Administration, *State Earnings-Related Provision (SERPS) Inheritance Provisions* (HC 1999–2000, 305).

The underlying causes of the systemic failure could be traced back to significant internal organisational weaknesses within the Department throughout the 1980s and 1990s. According to the then Secretary of State for Social Security, 'the crux of the problem was that there was no clear line of accountability in the Department for ensuring that the policy changes were properly implemented or that information provided to the public was accurate and complete'.[58] This state of affairs was symptomatic of a wider problem, namely that the Department was not focused on the people whom it was meant to serve. The public relied on government information and were entitled to be reassured that such information was both accurate and comprehensive. The PHSO concluded that the failure had arisen because of a 'simple oversight' with very far-reaching consequences. That oversight had not been identified because of the lack of 'adequate management arrangements of a coherent and systematic kind' to ensure that 'all the necessary administrative actions had been taken to secure the full and timely dissemination of the provisions in the highly complex 1986 Act'.[59]

Similarly, the NAO concluded that the failure had arisen because of the lack of end-to-end responsibility and weaknesses in the accountability within the Department, a lack of customer focus, and fundamental weaknesses in the Department's systems and process. The NAO has frequently emphasised the importance of a whole-system approach; effective delivery requires a clear alignment embedded throughout the organisation so that strategic priorities are reflected in ground-level operations.[60] Policy decisions taken by ministers at the top should fully cascade down to front-line operational staff and be implemented in practice on the ground. This was absent in the case of SERPS. There was no effective internal accountability and responsibility within the Department. This meant that the commitments made by ministers to Parliament that people affected by the change to the inheritance rules would be informed of the change were not fulfilled in practice.[61] This had been compounded by a lack of customer focus and fundamental weaknesses within the Department's systems and processes – in particular, poor internal communications and poor-quality IT systems. The handling and implementation of state pension policy involved coordination between different units within the Department which were located at different geographical locations, such as directorates in Leeds and Newcastle, front-line staff in local Benefit Agency officers and staff in the Department's headquarters in London. This had created difficulties in terms of internal communications. The Department should have ensured that front-line staff were kept up to date with changes in legislation, but there were deep-seated and serious internal communication problems stemming from its limited and outdated IT systems. At the time, the Benefits Agency relied solely upon paper-based communications and weekly briefing meetings to update its staff. Indeed, the Department's IT systems in the 1980s and 1990s were so poor that it was actually quicker for it to put out information through the press or on the television than it was to communicate with its own staff.[62] These problems had been further compounded by the Department's 'byzantine' structure

[58] HC Deb 15 March 2000, vol 346, cols 308–09 (Alastair Darling MP, Secretary of State for Social Security).

[59] Parliamentary Commissioner for Administration (n 57) [35].

[60] National Audit Office, *Improving Operational Delivery in Government: A Good Practice Guide for Senior Leaders* (London, NAO, 2021).

[61] National Audit Office (n 19) 9.

[62] Public Accounts Committee (n 54) [31].

and its culture.[63] During the 1980s and 1990s, the Department had been too large to manage and there had been ongoing chaos and crisis in its many local Benefit Agency offices, which had become close to collapse owing to the lack of modern IT systems and very low staff morale. This contributed to a culture of dealing with immediate problems and issues at the expense of longer-term planning.[64] The change to the SERPS inheritance rules was simply far beyond the time horizon of officials who were focused on addressing immediate tasks.

The DWP had also lacked the necessary systems by which it could manage risks effectively and properly. This was particularly relevant given that the change to SERPS had a lead-in time of 15 years. It was obvious that much would happen in the meantime: a change of government, new ministers, staff turnover, and changes in the internal structure of the Department. Consequently, the Department should have put in place appropriate arrangements to ensure that, whatever changes might happen, people affected by the inheritance rules would nevertheless be properly informed of them. However, no single official had overall responsibility for ensuring that the changes were publicised or implemented correctly. Instead, important decisions had been taken by relatively junior staff who did not appreciate the importance of the issues and adopted a narrow view of their responsibilities. The Department's internal systems were insufficiently robust to withstand, identify and correct a simple error, which then had very wide-ranging and significant consequences for a large number of people. Further, the error remained undetected and uncorrected for many years and was later compounded. When civil servants responsible for the Pensions Bill 1995 became aware of the problem, nothing was done to communicate the problem to others within the Department for three years.[65] A simple administrative error cast considerable light on the Department's poor communications and treatment of its customers, as well as its major institutional weaknesses. It did not have in place systems to identify and become aware of important issues raised by MPs in Parliament or through correspondence. In 1997 and 1998, two MPs had written to the relevant minister on behalf of constituents who had been given misleading and incorrect advice by the Department. These letters could have been picked up by the Department and used as an opportunity by which it could have investigated the matter, corrected its failures and taken appropriate action. But this did not happen. Instead, one DWP letter had reassured an MP that 'we … make every effort to publicise significant legislative changes and, of course, we give advice on individual circumstances when asked to do so'.[66]

Again, we encounter organisational disconnects between different levels of the administrative hierarchy within government. One feature of UK government is that policy officials are located centrally in Whitehall, whereas operational staff work in local offices throughout the country. The policy–operations divide is inevitable, but it generates problems when the two do not communicate effectively with each other. Policy officials may simply expect operational staff to implement policy without much appreciation of the practical challenges involved. The conditions in which operational

[63] HC Deb 15 March 2000, vol 346, col 317 (Alastair Darling MP, Secretary of State for Social Security).
[64] Public Administration Select Committee (n 54) [13].
[65] ibid [10]–[21].
[66] Quoted in National Audit Office (n 19) 60.

staff work may often be far from ideal, especially if they face intense pressures and the systems they use, such as IT and other systems, are inadequate. Front-line staff will require direction and assistance from policy staff as to what needs to be done and how.

What redress did the government provide? The PHSO had emphasised that government needed to provide redress on a global rather than an individual basis, but did not recommend a specific financial remedy. The government's final redress package involved a graduated scheme under which the inheritance rule was progressively reduced in accordance with people's retirement age. Widows (and widowers) reaching retirement age inherited all of their late spouse's SERPS entitlement up to 2002. The inheritance rules then progressively reduced by 10 per cent over each successive two-year period, until they reached the 50 per cent inheritance rule in 2010.[67] This provided full protection for those at or very near to retirement age while providing transitional arrangements for those retiring over the next 10 years, thereby enabling them to make appropriate arrangements. The effect was to put many people into a better position than if the original legislation – the 1986 Act – had been implemented as intended. The inheritance rule was not reduced to 50 per cent for surviving widows (an widowers) until a decade later than originally intended. The redress package provided protection for over 1.5 million pensioners over a 10-year period at a cost of £12 billion over 50 years. In other words, a measure designed to save money ended up costing more due to a systemic administrative failure.

Despite the cost, this was seen as an appropriate response, given the public outrage at the DWP's incompetence. Moreover, the redress package had been led and designed by the government. Nonetheless, the government had ended up providing a more generous and costly set of arrangements than what Parliament had legislated for. This was in response to the shock and scale of the failure. However, the reduction to people's SERPS entitlements had not been caused by poor communication. It had been caused by statutory changes to entitlement enacted by Parliament. The maladministration had been the DWP's failure to notify people of those changes in a proper and timely way. That failure had resulted in injustice and difficulties for people, but it had not resulted in the loss or reduction of their substantive SERPS entitlements. This raised a wider issue concerning the role of the PHSO. Its role is to investigate and remedy injustice in consequence of maladministration. The precise point at which injustice arises from maladministration in such cases would later resurface in subsequent PHSO investigations.

The DWP's 'Public Information Policy Statement'

Following SERPS, the DWP adopted a 'Public Information Policy Statement' (2002). This set out the DWP's position on the standards of information it provided to the public. All information provided by the DWP had to be 'appropriate, relevant, correct, up-to-date, clear, concise and to the point, helpful and targeted'.[68] It was widely accepted that

[67] HC Debs 29 November 2000, vol 357, col 966 (Alistair Darling MP, Secretary of State for Social Security); Social Security (Inherited SERPS) Regulations, SI 2001/1085. See also Parliamentary Commissioner for Administration, *State Earnings Related Pension Scheme (SERPS) Inheritance Provisions: Redress for Maladministration* (HC 2000–01, 271); House of Commons Library, *Reductions in Inherited SERPS* (SN-00706, 2016).

[68] DWP, *Public Information Policy Statement* (2002) reproduced in PHSO, *Trusting in the Pensions Promise: Government Bodies and the Security of Final Salary Occupational Pensions* (HC 2005–06, 984) [5.22]–[5.28].

the DWP had a duty to give information or advice to inform the public about any new policies and developments that might affect them and, crucially, to keep them informed on a continuing basis of their rights and responsibilities. It would be unreasonable for the DWP not to do this and it was clearly necessary. The statement also recognised that the DWP needed to take care to achieve the necessary balance of resource and effort between announcing changes and new policies and its duty to provide routine information. The common law duty of care meant that any information it provided to the public had to be timely, complete and correct. The DWP could also be responsible if it gave incorrect advice and someone relied on it to their detriment. The Public Information Policy Statement is internal government guidance. In the PHSO's view, the statement was consistent with the principles of good administration. The 'duty' is not therefore a legal duty, but reflects the requirements of good administration. Further, the 'widely accepted' duty pre-dated the statement, as opposed to it introducing a new duty.[69] The statement was never published by the DWP, although it was reproduced in two PHSO reports. The statement was complemented by various administrative improvements. By 2003, the DWP had made some progress in improving its systems for dealing with the public, although more needed to be done.[70] The effectiveness of improvements to the Department's systems for communicating with the public would, to a large extent, depend on the degree to which its staff were both aware of, and complied with, the new standards, guidance and procedures. Internal assurance work suggested that awareness of these developments among front-line staff was patchy and variable. Given the scale of the SERPS failure, it was necessary for the DWP to learn from that experience and to improve the quality of its communications. As it happens, the quality and accuracy of information provided by the DWP was shortly to be examined by the PHSO in the context of the Department's regulation of occupational pension schemes.

Occupational Pensions: The Pensions Promise

The PHSO's next big investigation concerned privately provided occupational pension schemes.[71] These pension schemes are not, like the state pension, funded by the state; instead, they are provided by private sector companies and funded by employers on behalf of their employees. The DWP is responsible for the legal and regulatory framework. Many people had been members of various occupational pension schemes that had been wound up between 1997 and 2004. The schemes had been wound up without sufficient funds to ensure that their members would receive the full pension entitlements that had previously been promised. Some 125,000 people had been affected and many complained to the PHSO. One of the principal issues for the PHSO's investigation was whether the DWP had given policy-holders correct and accurate information, and, if not, whether this constituted maladministration that had caused injustice. The general impression from

[69] PHSO, *Women's State Pension Age: Our Findings on the Department for Work and Pensions' Communication of Changes* (HC 2019–21, 444) [53]–[54].

[70] National Audit Office, *Improving Service Quality: Action in Response to the Inherited SERPS Problem* (HC 2002–03, 497).

[71] PHSO (n 68).

DWP official statements was that the occupational pensions were safe. People then relied on these statements to their detriment when schemes were wound up, and they did not receive the pensions they had been promised. This was the 'pensions promise'.

Examining a mass of detailed information, the then PHSO, Ann Abraham, found that the information given by the DWP and other public bodies to the public about the degree of security provided by pension schemes had been misleading, incomplete and inaccurate. This information had led pension scheme members to believe that their pensions were completely safe when they were not. Consequently, they suffered significant losses to their pensions when the schemes were wound up and they had not made alternative and additional provision for their retirement. The PHSO found that the information provided by the DWP did not conform with the standards that it had set for itself. Official information about the security of people's pensions had been inaccurate, often incomplete, largely inconsistent and therefore potentially misleading. This was maladministration. The PHSO found that this had caused injustice, namely financial losses for those affected. However, it recognised that the maladministration had not been the sole cause of that injustice. Other factors had contributed to the financial losses suffered, including the winding-up of pensions schemes by providers. The maladministration alone had not caused the financial losses, although it had been a significant factor. Abraham then boldly recommended that the government *consider* restoring the core pension benefits it had promised (at a cost of £15 billion), even though other factors had contributed to the losses.[72] In doing so, the PHSO referenced the SERPS episode. This was a controversial recommendation because the PHSO's role is to redress injustice as a consequence of maladministration, not to compensate people for the other losses that might arise with regard to financial investments.[73]

In this respect, Abraham had been chancing her arm. After all, why should the government and the taxpayer bear the cost of injustice when governmental maladministration had not been the sole cause? The PHSO was established to remedy injustice as a result of maladministration, not injustice arising from other causes. Unsurprisingly, the DWP rejected the PHSO's findings of maladministration and responsibility for the losses suffered.[74] Instead, the DWP argued that the pension schemes had been responsible. Further, the PHSO had stepped beyond its established accepted principle of putting people back into the position they would have been in had the maladministration not occurred.[75] It would be inappropriate for the DWP to use public money to compensate people for losses which reflected the risks inherent in financial and investment decisions, unless those losses had been caused by government maladministration. Clearly, a major issue concerned the amount of public money involved in providing redress, although the DWP argued that affordability was not the sole issue. Distinguishing this case from SERPS, the DWP argued that if it had been responsible for these losses, or if the schemes in question had been government schemes (as had been the case in SERPS), then there would be a powerful argument that it should put things right. The core issue for the

[72] ibid.
[73] Parliamentary Commissioner Act 1967, s 5(1).
[74] DWP, *Response to the Report by the Parliamentary Ombudsman 'Trusting in the Pensions Promise'* (London, DWP, 2006).
[75] ibid 30–31.

DWP was then how to strike the balance between those who had suffered losses and the government's obligation to taxpayers.[76] Accepting the PHSO's recommendations in full would set a dangerous precedent for the future.

The Public Administration Select Committee supported the PHSO.[77] There was then a judicial review challenge against the DWP's rejection of the findings of maladministration. The Court of Appeal held that while the PHSO's findings were not legally binding, it was not enough for a minister simply to reject the PHSO's findings; the minister had to give rational and cogent reasons for rejecting those findings, which had not been the case.[78] The eventual outcome was that pensioners could access some financial support from the financial assistance scheme, although this was less than the PHSO's recommended financial remedy.[79]

Both SERPS and occupational pensions had been notable episodes of poor communications. There was another aspect to them: the PHSO's role in recommending costly financial remedies to large cohorts of people. From one perspective, both investigations appeared to suggest that the PHSO could now potentially be used to secure financial redress for entitlements withdrawn by legislation (as in SERPS) and/or for financial losses that had not resulted from maladministration (as in occupational pensions). However, this was never the purpose of the PHSO. Its jurisdiction is one of 'injustice in consequence of maladministration'.[80] There must be a causal link between the maladministration and the injustice to affected people. The PHSO was not intended to operate as a wide-ranging mechanism for compensating people's losses arising from changes in legislation, government policy or factors other than maladministration. Over time, the sense of over-reach by Abraham and governmental displeasure with the PHSO became evident. Years later, the PHSO itself recognised the issue and responded by adopting its current financial remedy guidance.[81] This comprises six levels of injustice of increasing severity which correspond to graduated levels of financial payments. This had significant consequences for which financial remedies that the PHSO would then recommend, although this did not become apparent until many years later.

Guaranteed Minimum Pensions

Another type of state pension scheme was the Guaranteed Minimum Pension. This was a form of the second state pension that had been 'contracted out'. This meant that the both the employer and employee paid lower National Insurance contributions. When

[76] DWP, *The Government Response to the Public Administration Select Committee's Sixth Report of Session 2005–06 The Ombudsman in Question: The Ombudsman's Report on Pensions and its Constitutional Implications* (Cm 6961, 2006).

[77] House of Commons Public Administration Select Committee, *The Ombudsman in Question: The Ombudsman's Report on Pensions and its Constitutional Implications* (HC 2005–06, 1081) [34].

[78] *R (Bradley) v Secretary of State for Work and Pensions* [2008] EWCA Civ 36; [2009] QB 114 (CA).

[79] House of Commons Public Administration Select Committee, *Pensions Bill: Government Undertakings relating to the Financial Assistance Scheme* (HC 2006–07, 523); HC Deb 17 December 2007, vol 469, col 100WS. See also R Kirkham, B Thompson and T Buck, 'When Putting Things Right Goes Wrong: Enforcing the Recommendations of the Ombudsman' [2008] *PL* 510.

[80] Parliamentary Commissioner Act 1967, s 5(1).

[81] PHSO, *Our Guidance on Financial Remedy* (Manchester, PHSO, nd).

people with Guaranteed Minimum Pensions reached the state pension age, the DWP would carry out an annual comparison to check whether they would receive the same amount of pension that they would have received if they had not been contracted out. The purpose was to ensure that people with Guaranteed Minimum Pensions received roughly the same amount after they reached the state pension age. Such payments included inflationary increases, known as 'indexation'. However, this was changed by the Pensions Act 2014. This Act replaced the old basic state pension and the second state pension by introducing the new State Pension, a new flat-rate state pension for everyone reaching state pension age after 2016. The 2014 Act also removed indexation of the Guaranteed Minimum Pension. In other words, people with Guaranteed Minimum Pensions who reached state pension age after 2016 would no longer benefit from inflationary increases (indexation). The effect was that people with Guaranteed Minimum Pensions would receive much less over the course of their retirement than if they had not contracted out.

The change affected some 900,000 people. Several people with Guaranteed Minimum Pensions contacted the NAO to raise concerns that they would be worse off and that the DWP had not given sufficient warning and information to those who would be adversely affected. The NAO found that the impact of new state pension reforms on people with Guaranteed Minimum Pensions would vary widely.[82] The uprating of Guaranteed Minimum Pensions was complex. The impact of the changes on individuals depended on a range of factors, including their age, employment history, earnings and future inflation. Some people who were likely to lose out had been unable to find the information they needed to understand how the changes affected them personally and what action they could take. In this respect, the NAO recognised that communicating the impact of technical pension reforms was far from straightforward, owing to the complexity of pension rules and the fact that it was difficult to generalise about the impact of policy changes on individuals, given the number of factors affecting their entitlements. The DWP had issued factsheets on the new state pension, but these only included limited details. The DWP believed it could be misleading to show people how they might be affected by one aspect of pension reforms in isolation, without considering the combined impact of changes. The NAO concluded that the DWP had not provided people with clear and sufficient information. In response, the DWP sought to improve its communications so that people could make informed decisions, although this was complex, given that the effects of the changes depended on people's individual circumstances, which varied. Matters were then escalated to the PHSO. Two people complained that the DWP had failed to communicate that the introduction of the new state pension system could have a negative long-term impact on people with Guaranteed Minimum Pensions. The PHSO concluded that the DWP had not properly communicated the change to those affected.[83] It had not explained that people with long periods of contracting out would be significantly worse off as a result of the changes. Instead, the DWP had focused only on the benefits of the new State Pension. The DWP had not acted on warnings from the NAO and the Work and Pensions Select Committee that

[82] National Audit Office, *The Impact of State Pension Reforms on People with Guaranteed Minimum Pensions* (HC 2015–16, 907).

[83] PHSO (n 3) 14–15.

better communications were needed for those with long periods of contracting out. The DWP had also failed to make clear that some people could be worse off and that they needed to seek independent financial advice and make alternative provision for their retirement. That was maladministration.

A notable feature of the case was the PHSO's approach to injustice as a consequence of maladministration. The PHSO adopted a narrower approach than that adopted in both SERPS and occupational pensions. The PHSO found that there had not been any financial loss as a result of the DWP's poor communications. It did not therefore recommend the restoration of lost pension entitlements or a substantial financial remedy to compensate for the reduced pensions. The substantive policy changes introduced by the 2014 Act were always going to affect people irrespective of whether they had been communicated properly. Nonetheless, the two complainants had suffered frustration and inconvenience, and therefore the PHSO recommended relatively modest financial payments (£500 and £750). This was a significant difference compared with the SERPS and occupational pensions cases.

Another aspect of the case was that the PHSO recommended financial payments only in relation to the two complainants, whereas the change affected a much larger number of people in total, although the circumstances of individual cases varied. Other people affected therefore needed to complain to the DWP for a remedy. By contrast, in another investigation, the PHSO had (unsuccessfully) recommended that the DWP proactively make payments to all those affected rather than simply wait and see who complained.[84] It is difficult to discern any principled approach by the PHSO in this respect as to the circumstances in which either other people affected must complain or the government body should itself proactively identify those concerned and pay them a financial remedy. In terms of service improvements, the PHSO recommended that the DWP ensure that its literature clearly and appropriately pointed out that some individuals with large Guaranteed Minimum Pensions reaching state pension age might be negatively affected by the changes. The DWP needed to tell people explicitly to check their circumstances. The DWP accepted the PHSO's report and paid the financial remedy to the two complainants. The key learning point was that the DWP recognised it should have provided timely, well-signposted and accessible information to people about the change. Concerns were later raised by the House of Commons Work and Pensions Committee about the DWP's delay in issuing a factsheet to inform people about the change and its contents.[85]

The Women's State Pension Age: The WASPI Case

The next big investigation concerned the communication of changes to the women's state pension age. Since 1940, the state pension age had been 65 for men and 60 for women. This position reflected social attitudes at the time and the position of women in

[84] PHSO, *An Investigation into the Department for Work and Pensions' Handling of Ms U's Migration to Employment and Support Allowance* (HC 2021–22, 956), ch 7 253–254.

[85] Correspondence between the House of Commons Work and Pensions Committee and the DWP, 12 August 2021, 29 June 2022 and 9 January 2024.

the labour market. Women typically had lower state pension entitlements than men.[86] They had also accrued lower occupational pensions owing to part-time work and the gender pay gap. In 2004, a senior minister described women's pensions as a 'national scandal'.[87] On the other hand, the growing movement for gender equality made the women's pension age seem increasingly anomalous.[88] In 1995, the then Conservative government equalised the state pension age by increasing it to age 65 for both men and women.[89] The rationale was that women were increasingly playing an equal role to men in the economy and then made up nearly half of those in employment. Given longer life expectancy, the cost of the state pension was going to increase, thereby imposing a greater burden on those in work. A common state pension age of 65 would save money and strike a fair balance between different generations.

As with SERPS, the government had recognised that a long lead-in period was required. The change would be phased in between 2010 and 2020. Two further changes followed. In 2007, the state pension age was increased for both men and women to 66 between 2024 and 2026, 67 by 2036 and 68 by 2046.[90] In 2011, the timetable for raising the state pension age for both men and women was accelerated.[91] Accordingly, the increase in women's state pension age would reach 65 by late 2018 instead of 2020.

A large number of women were always going to lose out from the change. They therefore needed to be properly informed in good time so that they could make alternative arrangements. From 1995 onwards, the DWP issued generic information through the print media, online and in Jobcentres to notify women of the changes. In 2009–13, the DWP sent out millions of individually tailored letters to those affected.[92] However, these letters had been significantly delayed. Many women did not receive the recommended 15 years' notice of the increase to their state pension age. Women received the letters, on average, one year and four months before they turned 60.[93] Consequently, they were unable to adjust their retirement plans. The change came as a shock to many of the women affected. They either did not know about the change to their state pension age or, if they did, they did not understand how it applied to them personally. In 2015, a campaigning organisation – WASPI (Women Against State Pension Inequality) – was founded. It strongly criticised the lack of notification. A legal challenge failed.[94] There was no legal obligation on the DWP to communicate the changes. However, the requirements of good administration go beyond what is required by law. The PHSO then undertook a large investigation lasting some six years.

The PHSO found that between 1995 and 2004, the DWP had used generic communications to provide people with accurate information about the change to the women's

[86] P Thane, 'The "Scandal" of Women's Pensions in Britain: How Did it Come about?' in H Pemberton, P Thane and N Whiteside (eds), *Britain's Pensions Crisis: History and Policy* (Oxford, Oxford University Press, 2006).

[87] House of Commons Work and Pensions Committee, 20 October 2004, oral evidence (HC 2003–04, 1171) Q 35 (Alan Johnson MP, Secretary of State for Work and Pensions).

[88] H Pemberton, 'WASPI's is (Mostly) a Campaign for Inequality' (2017) 88 *Political Quarterly* 510.

[89] Department for Social Security, *Equality in State Pension Age* (Cm 2420, 1993); Pensions Act 1995.

[90] Pensions Act 2007.

[91] Pensions Act 2011.

[92] DWP, *State Pensions Reform: Detailed Communications Plan* (2008).

[93] House of Commons Work and Pensions Committee, *Communication of State Pension Age Changes* (HC 2015–16, 899) [14] (evidence of Paul Lewis, a financial journalist).

[94] *Delve* (n 16).

state pension age.[95] Based on what the DWP knew at the time about the effectiveness of those methods of communication, this was sufficient and reflected the applicable standards of good administration. However, in 2004, research by the DWP found that only 43 per cent of women affected by the change actually knew what their state pension age was.[96] The research concluded that the generic information provided was not reaching the women affected. The DWP needed to send out individually tailored letters to notify the women. The DWP did not then act on this. The PHSO found that this was maladministration. It also found that when the DWP decided to send out individual letters, it had delayed acting on this on that proposal for over a year. The DWP later sent out individual letters, but there had been a 28-month delay. That was also maladministration. The millions of letters sent out by the DWP over the years 2009–13 had been delayed by 28 months.[97] Consequently, the women affected were unable to adjust their retirement plans.

The next crucial issue concerned what injustice had been caused by the maladministration. The WASPI campaign had wanted the restoration of their pension benefits and relied on the precedents of the SERPS and occupational pensions investigations. They argued that the DWP's maladministration had caused them significant financial loss, including their lost state pension payments (at a cost of approximately £50 billion). Alternatively, it was argued that the women had lost the earnings from employment which they would otherwise have continued with had they been properly notified of their pension age. However, the PHSO held that the women had not suffered a direct financial loss as a result of the DWP's maladministration. Their lost state pension entitlements had resulted from legislation, not maladministration. The PHSO could not recommend a financial remedy for losses arising from legislation. It also concluded that it would not recommend a financial remedy for any loss that depended on the choices someone would have made if the maladministration had not occurred, such as staying in work. This was because there had been intervening events between the maladministration and the loss experienced; the choices made, for instance, to seek or stay in work or spend time with family. The PHSO considered that it was inappropriate for it to quantify losses arising from lost opportunities to make different choices. Overall, this reflected a significant change of approach towards injustice by the PHSO compared with its previously more expansive approach adopted in SERPS and occupational pensions. However, while the PHSO departed from its approach adopted in those earlier investigations, it did not explain the reasons for doing so; instead, it merely cited case law. It is for the PHSO to decide and explain what standard it is going to apply and what the consequences are; the courts will only interfere if the PHSO acts unreasonably or fails to apply its own standard.[98] There was a certain degree of intellectual fudging here. After all, the courts explain why a precedent was wrong and should no longer be followed. If the PHSO had provided a more substantive reason for distinguishing the precedents

[95] PHSO (n 69); PHSO, *Women's State Pension Age: Our Findings on Injustice and Associated Issues* (HC 2023–24, 638).
[96] C Murphy, *Public Awareness of State Pension Age Equalisation* (London, DWP Research Report No 221, 2004).
[97] DWP, *State Pensions Reform: Detailed Communications Plan* (London, DWP, 2008) (not published; acquired through FOI request).
[98] *R (Rapp) v Parliamentary and Health Service Ombudsman and Ofqual* [2015] EWHC 1344 (Admin) [38].

of SERPS and occupational pensions, then that would have involved explaining why its prior approach adopted in those investigations had been wrong. But it did not do this.

Despite these points, the PHSO concluded that the women had suffered a degree of injustice. They had lost opportunities to make informed decisions about their futures, thereby diminishing their personal autonomy and financial control over their lives. They had been unable to make informed decisions concerning their future, such as whether to seek or stay in employment, or to retire and spend time with family. The loss arising from such decisions was not a direct financial loss. Therefore, the recommended financial remedies did not include the restoration of pensions or lost earnings. Instead, the PHSO suggested a payment of level 4 within its injustice scale (£1,000–2,950 for each woman). This was far less than what the WASPI campaigners had sought. Nonetheless, it was still a significant amount of money given the number of women affected. The total amount was estimated at between £3.5 billion and £10.5 billion. This shift of approach by the PHSO was appropriate, given the somewhat excessive approach previously taken in occupational pensions. The PHSO also suggested that any redress package could be administered either by way of an individual assessment of each woman's personal circumstances or a more efficient flat-rate payment. Both options had their respective pros and cons. Individually assessing each woman's case would be very costly, whereas a flat-rate payment would overpay some and underpay others. In any event, the PHSO had concerns that the DWP would reject its report. Therefore, the PHSO did not formally recommend a financial remedy, but instead took the rare step of asking Parliament to intervene by identifying an appropriate remedy.

The WASPI case divided public opinion. The argument for financial redress was that the women had suffered an injustice. There was an organised campaign and lobbying of MPs. By contrast, others argued that the increase to the pension age had been debated in Parliament and widely publicised. There had to be some personal responsibility on people to acquaint themselves with important matters affecting them.[99] There were also concerns that the cost of redress was too high and would lead to generational unfairness.

Responding to the PHSO's report posed a political challenge for the Labour government. Throughout the investigation (undertaken during the previous Conservative government), the DWP had made it quite clear that it would also reject the PHSO's report.[100] In opposition, Labour politicians had strongly supported the WASPI campaign.[101] Having come into government in 2024, Labour ministers had inherited considerable financial challenges. No money had been set aside for the £11 billion compensation bill.[102] Paying out such a large sum was not viable, although there was

[99] D Gauke, 'The Government is Right to Refuse to Pay Compensation to the WASPI Women' *Conservative Home* (25 March 2024), https://conservativehome.com/2024/03/25/david-gauke-the-government-is-right-to-refuse-to-pay-compensation-to-the-waspi-women; W Hague, 'Sorry, WASPI Women, We Gave You Fair Warning' *The Times* (26 March 2024), https://www.thetimes.com/uk/politics/article/sorry-waspi-women-we-gave-you-fair-warning-3sqml7x6t.

[100] House of Commons Work and Pensions Committee, *Oral Evidence: PHSO Report on Women's State Pension Age* (HC 2023–24, 740), 7 May 2024, Qs 84, 88–89 (Karl Banister, Director of Legal and Casework, PHSO).

[101] 'All the Labour Ministers Who Backed WASPI Campaign' *The I Paper* (18 December 2024), https://inews.co.uk/news/politics/labour-shadow-minister-refuse-waspi-support-2970844?srsltid=AfmBOooOoE61s-7fODcG7uLwcWcf3rghSRSheCQnMSsxZvyJWrPJTp-C4.

[102] 'Reeves: No Cash Available for WASPI Campaigners' *Daily Business* (4 June 2024), https://dailybusiness-group.co.uk/2024/06/reeves-no-tax-relief-changes-no-cash-for-waspi/.

evidently a need for careful handling of the case by trying to present the least politically unpalatable response.

How then did the DWP respond? It accepted the PHSO's principal findings of maladministration – its poor communications and not notifying the women sooner. It also accepted the need to improve its future communications.[103] However, the DWP rejected the PHSO's finding that there had been injustice as a result of maladministration. The DWP's position was that there had not been any causal link between the sending out of individually tailored letters and any injustice. The PHSO had assumed that if the individually tailored letters had been sent out to the women earlier, then they would have read them. However, the DWP emphasised that only a minority of people recall receiving letters sent out by the DWP. The majority of the women would likely not have read the letters or recalled their contents. Receiving a letter earlier would have likely made little, if any, difference to what the majority of women knew about their state pension age. Accordingly, the PHSO's conclusion that the delay in sending out the letters had led to an injustice had been logically flawed. The PHSO had assumed that the letters would have made a difference to the women, whereas the evidence pointed in the opposite direction. There was also evidence that the majority of the women knew that their state pension age was changing, although they may not have known their exact pension age. In such circumstances, it was therefore reasonable to expect the women to seek out information to understand their own position.

The DWP was also concerned that the administration of a large financial redress scheme – either by way of a flat-rate payment to all of the women irrespective of their particular circumstances or an individualised assessment – was impractical and represented poor value for money. A flat-rate scheme would cost over £10 billion and would involve making payments to some, possibly many, women who had been aware of the increase to their state pension age and who had therefore not suffered any injustice. The alternative would be to invite applications for compensation and then consider them on an individual basis. However, this option also had its problems. It would involve establishing a decision process that could reliably verify the individual circumstances of millions of women, including whether someone genuinely did not know that their state pension age was changing and whether they would have read and remembered a letter from many years ago and acted differently. The DWP concluded that it would be impractical to set up a compensation scheme to try to assess applications and to decide such matters conclusively. It would involve administrative costs and delay. It would also involve assessing past events that might or might not have happened many years earlier; who did or did not receive a letter, who could remember receiving a letter and what they would have done differently as a result. This involved clear evidential challenges and there were also great practical difficulties in trying to undertake individual assessments for some 3.6 million women at a reasonable cost. The DWP therefore rejected any financial redress. All this occurred against the background of extensive parliamentary discussion of the case and strong support by backbench MPs for the WASPI

[103] HC Deb 17 December 2024, vol 759, cols 167–87; DWP, *Government Response to the Parliamentary and Health Service Ombudsman's Investigation into Women's State Pension Age and Associated Issues* (London, DWP, 2024).

campaign.[104] Nonetheless, the DWP resisted a financial remedy on the ground that the women affected were unlikely to have read the letters had they been sent out earlier.[105]

The DWP could have simply rejected the PHSO's report on the grounds of financial cost alone. This was, of course, the real reason for rejecting the report. The real decision-making body was not the DWP, but the Treasury. However, despite all the tensions between the government and the PHSO over the years, especially in big investigations, the government has typically been loath simply to reject PHSO reports on the ground of cost alone. The explanation is that the government ultimately recognises that there is a political price to be paid for not remedying injustice caused by maladministration. It therefore needs to find a more plausible ground or cover with which to reject a PHSO report, that recommends an expensive financial remedy.

While the DWP had resisted the PHSO's report, it had nonetheless been made accountable. It had accepted the PHSO's findings of maladministration and recognised the need to improve its future communications, although the PHSO later expressed 'serious concerns about the DWP's significant delays in the implementation of the actions that the DWP had committed to undertake'.[106] Given the number of PHSO reports on flawed DWP communications, such improvements are important and necessary. The PHSO had emphasised that poor communications damage people's trust in public services. There will be future changes to the state pension and other benefits. If effectively implemented, better communications will benefit the public as a whole. At the same time, this does not involve just the DWP; there is a need for more cross-government coordination and guidance on this and all other administrative justice problems.

The WASPI case also highlighted that the PHSO's approach to remedying injustice as a result of maladministration had come full circle. In SERPS, the maladministration had been the failure to communicate, but the DWP had adopted a high-value redress package that went beyond people's entitlements as legislated by Parliament. In occupational pensions, the PHSO had recommended that the government consider restoring the core pension benefits it had promised, despite factors other than maladministration having contributed to the losses. This caused distinct concern within government that the PHSO was exceeding its statutory role and over-reaching itself. The PHSO has since reverted to the proper approach towards injustice as a consequence of maladministration in both the guaranteed minimum pensions and the WASPI case. In any event, this did little to induce the DWP to pay the PHSO's suggested financial remedy.

Another PHSO investigation reinforced its approach to injustice. This investigation concerned the DWP's failure to inform overseas recipients of the withdrawal of

[104] HC Deb 25 March 2024, vol 747, cols 1280–301; HC Deb 16 May 2024, vol 750, cols 463–523; HC Deb 15 January 2025, vol 760, cols 135–61WH; House of Commons Work and Pensions Committee, 7 May 2024, *Oral Evidence: PHSO Report on Women's State Pension Age* (HC 2023–24, 740); House of Commons Work and Pensions Committee, 22 January 2025, *Oral Evidence: Pensioner Poverty: Challenges and Mitigations* (HC 2024–25, 165); Scottish Parliament, *Official Record*, 21 January 2025, cols 9–61; HC Deb 17 March 2025, vol 764, cols 1–40WH; HC Deb 3 July 2025, vol 770, cols 486–516.

[105] A judicial review against the DWP's initial rejection of the PHSO's report prompted a reconsideration and the DWP later reissued a modified decision. See *R (WASPI) v Secretary of State for Work and Pensions* (AC-2025-LON-000811); HC Deb 11 November 2025, vol 775, cols 44–48; DWP, *Government's New Decision: Women's State Pension Age Communications Response to the Parliamentary and Health Service Ombudsman's Investigation* (London, DWP, 2026); HC Deb 29 January 2026, vol 779, cols 1071–83.

[106] Letter from PHSO to the Chair of the House of Commons Work and Pensions Committee (8 January 2026).

the Adult Dependency Increase (ADI) to their state pension. ADI had supplemented the state pension for single-income households where the main earner (typically the husband) had reached state pension age while the other partner (typically the wife) had not and was without any independent income. ADI had been removed by the Pensions Act 2007 with transitional arrangements. The DWP had notified recipients of ADI living in the UK of this change, but it had seemingly entirely forgotten about those living overseas, thereby leaving the complainant some £3,000 a year worse off. Further, the DWP had not provided the same transitional period as that for UK-based recipients. To compound matters, when the man complained to the DWP, it had then taken some 11 months to respond to his complaint. The PHSO noted that the change in legislation would always have affected the complainant irrespective of whether or not he had been informed. Nonetheless, finding out about the change to ADI some eight years late had been traumatic. Without the right information, the complainant had lost the opportunity to prepare for his retirement, thereby causing financial worry. The PHSO recommended a financial payment of £800. As the PHSO noted, the DWP had 'a history of failing to communicate pension policy changes clearly and failing to learn from its mistakes'.[107]

* * *

The preceding episodes illustrate the awkward and difficult situations that government gets itself into and its different responses to its administrative failures. Comparing these investigations, important differences arise in terms of the nature of communication problems, the injustice caused by maladministration and government responses to the PHSO's interventions. In SERPS, the DWP had not communicated the change at all, contrary to ministerial assurances made to Parliament. Instead, it had continued providing people with outdated and misleading information, even when it had been informed of this. The underlying cause was the lack of internal end-to-end responsibility within the DWP; its inability to ensure that ministerial intentions were embedded within front-line operational delivery. In the women's state pension age case, the issue was the effectiveness of different means of communication – that is, individually tailored letters rather than generic information. The DWP had made efforts to communicate the change. It had also reviewed what it was doing and had sought feedback on its approach. However, when it became aware that its efforts were not working, it had then delayed changing its approach. A core lesson from the women's state pension age case is that it is insufficient for government just to collect feedback and evidence about its delivery of services; it also needs to act on that feedback to improve its services. This represented an important extension to the previously understood principle that government communicate clearly and provide correct and accurate information. Government should also communicate in an effective and timely way to ensure that this properly reaches the intended audience. The journey from SERPS to the women's state pension age highlights how the standards of good administration are dynamic, not static. This applies

[107] PHSO, *Investigation into the DWP* (21 August 2024); PHSO, 'DWP Failings Left Ex-pat in the Dark about £3,000 a Year Pension Cut' (15 January 2025).

particularly to the demands of seeking continuous improvement; government should seek out feedback and then act upon it.

The following questions arise. To what extent should people take personal responsibility to acquaint themselves of changes to matters of some importance to them (such as their pension)? Do people have a duty to keep themselves abreast of changes in the law that affect them? If people do not understand how pension changes affect them, then they can always contact the DWP for advice and further information. There was a difference here between SERPS and women's state pension age in this respect. In SERPS, the DWP had failed to mount a major publicity campaign. It had also given people incorrect and misleading information when they had approached it for advice. By contrast, in the women's state pension age case, the DWP had issued generic information, but then delayed acting on its own research which found that individually tailored information was required. In response to the PHSO's report, the DWP considered it is reasonable to expect people to plan for their retirement by taking personal responsibility for their pensions.

If fully accepted, such an argument would have potentially moderated the findings of maladministration or mitigated the injustice occasioned as a result. In response, the PHSO did not deny an element of personal responsibility for people to find out about their position, although it made three countervailing points. First, government needed to be user-focused. This involves working with people and acting on feedback to ensure that information is actually reaching the target audience.[108] Second, people may not realise that they have reason to take action to establish their circumstances, as a result of flawed communications. If people do not know they have not been properly informed, then they are unlikely to seek out information to clarify their position. Third, the DWP's own 'Public Information Policy Statement' (2002) required it to inform people about new policies and on a continuing basis. All the PHSO had done was to ask the DWP to adhere to its own policy statement as to how it would communicate with people. Whether or not people keep themselves informed, this does not absolve government of its responsibility to communicate important changes effectively to people. However, it remains to be seen whether this position is sustainable. If applied too broadly, it could open the floodgates to many complaints. After all, there are many legislative changes that affect people, who bear some personal responsibility for keeping themselves informed. Finally, time will tell whether or not the WASPI case marks the end of the road for the PHSO undertaking big investigations that result in recommendations for expensive financial remedies. There seems little point in the PHSO issuing such recommendations if the government will almost certainly reject them.

Improving Government Communications

How then can government and public services improve their communications? As with much of administrative justice, poor communications by government mostly occur as a result of a lack of institutional competence and inadequate administration. The capacity

[108] House of Commons Work and Pensions Committee, 7 May 2024, *Oral Evidence: PHSO Report on Women's State Pension Age* (HC 2023–24, 740) Qs 51–52 (Rebecca Hilsenrath, interim PHSO).

and capabilities of government depend critically upon the competence and effectiveness of its administrative institutions. This is directly relevant to people who depend on government and public services so that they can order their lives and expectations with reasonable certainty and receive their entitlements. The point is well illustrated by the communication failures considered above. In the case of SERPS, the fundamental underlying problem was the lack of internal end-to-end responsibility within the DWP. Without this internal alignment within the Department's structures and organisational behaviours, it was unable to ensure that the wishes of ministers became embedded within front-line operational delivery. It then made some efforts to improve its communications. In the case of the women's state pension age, the DWP's failures had included not acting upon the findings of its own research that individually tailored information was required and then a delay of over a year before writing directly to affected women. These failures can be attributed to dither and delay, poor internal communications, a lack of internal understanding about the Department's responsibility to communicate the change effectively and a failure within the Department to give the matter the importance it manifestly deserved, and then a failure to act in a decisive and timely manner to address the issue. The matter was likely not viewed as a priority and was not given the importance it required.

The underlying issues concern and illustrate various organisational, behavioural and cultural dysfunctions: the division between policy and operational staff; civil servants frequently moving around from one post to another and a consequent lack of continuity and institutional memory; groupthink; a top-down style of governing; a lack of sufficient internal organisational coordination; a lack of engagement with stakeholders; and a focus on the latest immediate pressures at the expense of important longer-term tasks. In essence, good administration involves effective organisation and behaviours from officials. A substantial part of this depends on technical processes, but the wider challenge concerns the institutional cultures which inform governmental behaviours and how administrative procedures are operated in practice.

As a way forward, we can highlight some general principles to help improve government improve matters. A first point is ensuring that services are user-focused. This requires government to understand the perspectives of people who use public services, work with them and to recognise that they are not a homogeneous group of people, but have a wide range of different needs. This involves public engagement and piloting communications. Increasingly, communications are digital, although to be more effective, communications should not be limited to one-way communications, but should become more interactive and responsive.[109] A second point is the need to proactively monitor and evaluate the effectiveness of the communications used and then acting on this learning to address the weaknesses identified. This involves working with people with lived experience and also stakeholders. Third, there should be external scrutiny of government communications. This has been undertaken by the NAO, parliamentary committees and the PHSO. This has been of value and therefore this scrutiny should continue and be enhanced. There is no good reason why the administrative failures

[109] See generally M-J Canel and V Luoma-aho, *Public Sector Communication: Closing Gaps between Citizens and Public Organizations* (Chichester, Wiley, 2018); V Luoma-aho and M-J Canel (eds), *The Handbook of Public Sector Communication* (Chichester, Wiley, 2020).

of the past should be repeated, especially when the consequences can be so severe. Government has a responsibility to communicate important changes to the public and this should be built into administrative practices and cultures. Yet, even if government ensured that all bases were covered, the complexities of social and administrative life mean that something may go awry or that some unanticipated event or development will arise. Past failures of communication may not be repeated in precisely the same way; instead, new problems will arise. Accordingly, it seems likely that ombudsmen will scrutinise future complaints. Government must be willing to learn from ombudsmen investigations. Overall, as with so much of administrative justice in practice, it is important to get the basics of administration right and to learn the lessons from scrutiny.

9

Pathological Administrative Justice

Administrative justice is inevitably imperfect, although much of the time it possesses a serviceable functionality. Many people receive a reasonable degree of fair and just administration. However, in certain contexts, inherent dysfunction is the norm. 'Pathological administrative justice' refers to deep weaknesses and shortcomings within administrative justice that are not merely problematic, but often chronic, persistent, hardened and highly resistant to improvement. This category of administrative justice is far from a universal phenomenon, although it occurs with sufficient regularity across a range of different contexts to justify examination. The principal feature is that people interact with a public body, but the attainment of genuine and authentic administrative justice is often rendered very difficult, if not impossible, to achieve in any meaningful sense. This is because the public body has been given a set of intractable tasks permeated by competing and conflicting pressures. These tensions arise from the wider social, economic, political and organisational forces which bear down upon what government is trying to do in a specific area. Such pressures are endemic and full of deep-seated conflict. They cannot be satisfactorily resolved, but only managed and, even then, with considerable difficulty.

In such situations, people who interact with government often come off worse for it. The effectiveness of redress mechanisms is often variable and sometimes highly limited, because they are informed by precisely the same intractable tensions that bear down on the relevant public body. Redress institutions function as a microcosm of the sectors within which they work. The outcome is typically a weak and hollow form of administrative justice from which it is often difficult, if not impossible, to escape. This is not to say that the attainment of some degree of justice is completely hopeless. There are victories for some people, although typically only after a time-consuming and stressful battle. Yet, even then, such successes can serve a ritualistic purpose of re-asserting the symbolic importance of administrative justice, but without its full substantive force. Moreover, such victories can come at the expense of others who lose out. There is also the perennial problem that many people do not seek redress at all. Indeed, public bodies often consciously rely on people not seeking redress. They also engage in some dubious and underhand tactics to prevent people from both accessing services and seeking redress. These include people being 'fobbed off' and officials erecting additional procedural and other barriers for people to overcome and denying or delaying redress rights. Even when people do seek redress, the wider effects can be limited. Further, at a structural level, government can consciously weaken redress mechanisms. There are also some problems – such as administrative delay – which are highly resistant to correction.

To explore these matters, this chapter examines three different generic cross-cutting problems: entitlement decisions with a rationing aspect; decision processes underpinned by a punitive or disciplinary orientation; and administrative delay. While each problem exists across a range of contexts, the unifying thread is that underlying structural factors simultaneously generate a real need for administrative justice and often severely weaken it in practice. The result is often a seemingly permanent condition of compromised administrative justice to which there are few, if any viable solutions, other than wide-ranging – and often unrealistic – changes in government policy and resourcing.

Entitlement Decisions with a Rationing Aspect

In decision-making contexts, such as social security and immigration, people's applications are considered under the eligibility criteria. Claimants who meet those criteria must be granted. There is no limit on the number of claims that can be granted. Each claim is considered individually and the outcome is unaffected by the position of other claimants. If government has concerns, for instance, that too many claims are being allowed, then it must change its policy and the applicable rules. By contrast, in a variety of other contexts, public bodies assess people's eligibility for services that are resource-dependent. These services often concern crucially important human needs: housing for homeless people; Continuing Health Care (CHC), that is, publicly funded health and personal care for people with long-term and complex health needs; educational provision for children and young people with special educational needs and disabilities (SEND); and adult social care. The public body concerned has a dual role: it both assesses individuals' entitlements to services and provides or commissions those services. The number of applications received will often exceed, and sometimes far exceed, the resources available to provide the relevant service. The public body concerned inevitably has to balance one individual's needs against those of other people and the overall resources that are available.[1]

The need to ration when making resource-dependent assessments is a major structural factor that shapes the substance of administrative justice. People do not have a legal right to access services; their only legal 'right' is to have their applications considered. The decision processes share some common features. Assessments are often taken by local public bodies. The eligibility criteria are highly discretionary and can therefore vary in accordance with demand. Redress mechanisms are typically informal and limited. Instead of appeals to the First-tier Tribunal, there are administrative reviews, informal appeal panels and limited onward rights of challenge through judicial review. Another feature is the frequent use of dubious and improper informal practices by

[1] G Richardson and H Genn, 'Tribunals in Transition: Resolution or Adjudication?' [2007] *PL* 116, 138–40 label this situation as 'entitlements to an assessment or to a consideration' which fall short of the assertion of a private law right, but which involve the assertion of a resource-dependent social right and are therefore highly conditional and have to be balanced with wider interests.

officials, in particular 'gatekeeping' – that is, controlling access to services. The basic problem is that the public bodies concerned are faced with perennial and intense difficulties precisely because these services are resource-dependent and therefore necessitate a strong rationing aspect. This creates challenges in terms of how they seek to discharge their responsibilities. It also results in real injustices for many people concerned who have acute personal needs and turn to the state for help and assistance. They are entitled to be treated fairly. However, the pressures bearing down on the public body inevitably lead to a fair degree of slippage, compromise and sometimes harsh treatment. This raises difficult questions about what administrative justice can be reasonably expected from such areas.

Homelessness

A principal area of resource-dependent assessments is homelessness. Local authorities are under a statutory duty to provide temporary accommodation to people who are unintentionally homeless and in priority need.[2] At the core of homelessness law is the assessment duty. Councils must make inquiries and decide whether someone is unintentionally homeless. Homelessness law in practice can only be understood within its wider social-economic context: the housing crisis and the inadequate funding of local government, exacerbated by austerity. Some (often urban) councils are under enormous pressure. There are insufficient housing resources and emergency accommodation is costly. In addition to budgetary pressures, there have been increased numbers of people presenting to themselves councils as homeless.[3] Homeless applicants are often vulnerable, in real need and facing a range of acute challenges.

Initial homelessness assessments and also the suitability of accommodation offered can be challenged through internal administrative review and then an appeal to the County Court on a point of law and/or judicial review. There has never been a full right of appeal in homelessness cases. As regards internal reviews, a senior or another officer will make inquiries and review the initial assessment.[4] Some councils have contracted out the review function to private contractors.[5] The courts have resisted efforts to judicialise the review process because, in essence, this would divert valuable resources away from providing housing and would only exacerbate the problem of limited resources.[6] Many claimants will not seek redress for reasons of scepticism, lack of faith and fatigue.[7]

[2] Housing Act 1996; Homelessness Reduction Act 2017.

[3] R Loopstra, A Reeves, B Barr, D Taylor-Robinson, M McKee and D Stuckler, 'The Impact of Economic Downturns and Budget Cuts on Homelessness Claim Rates across 323 Local Authorities in England, 2004–12' (2016) 38 *Journal of Public Health* 417.

[4] Housing Act 1996, s 202; Homelessness (Review Procedure etc) Regulations 2018, SI 2018/223.

[5] Local Authorities (Contracting out of Allocation of Housing and Homelessness Functions) Order, SI 1996/3205; *De-Winter Heald v Brent London Borough Council* [2009] EWCA Civ 930; [2010] 1 WLR 990.

[6] *Begum v Tower Hamlets London Borough Council* [2003] UKHL 5; *Ali v Birmingham City Council* [2010] UKSC 8; *Poshteh v Kensington and Chelsea Royal London Borough Council* [2017] UKSC 36; E Laurie, 'Homelessness and the "Over-judicialisation" of Welfare' (2020) 21 *Legal Studies* 39.

[7] D Cowan and S Halliday, *The Appeal of Internal Review: Law, Administrative Justice and the (Non-)emergence of Disputes* (Oxford, Hart Publishing, 2003).

It is not known how many pursue their case to the County Court, but the numbers seem low and this reflects the wider trend of the low rates of challenge made by welfare claimants.[8] In some areas, review decisions have become increasingly legalistic in order to insulate councils against legal challenge.[9]

Given the pressure of applications and limited housing stock, many councils inevitably resort to various gatekeeping tactics to limit or prevent people from accessing what is a highly resource-conditioned service. This involves reducing demand by putting barriers in people's way. Informal practices are used to deflect or delay claims, or to refuse them by default. This is a coping mechanism for officials – an essentially retreatist tactic by which councils try to manage their statutory duties.[10] For instance, a council does not accept a person's homeless application or it does not undertake the necessary inquiries to decide whether the applicant meets the criteria. It is then down to the applicant to decide whether or not to challenge it. The barriers to administrative justice then enable gatekeeping because typically only the most determined, well-resourced and supported claimants are likely to seek redress. Alternatively, people who present themselves to councils as homeless and requiring emergency accommodation are turned away. Another tactic has been for councils to impose additional requirements and criteria above those in the legislation and guidance in order to ration access.[11]

Gatekeeping is the response to high pressures, a lack of temporary housing, limited staff resources and the target-driven environment in which housing officers often work. This happens on a daily basis. Gatekeeping practices are either unlawful and/or bad practice. But more than this, gatekeeping represents the failure of local authorities to assist people in need. Council officers will be fully aware of this. They would publicly deny that such practices are adopted, but resort to them in any case.[12] Some claimants seek judicial review. However, the ability of external legal norms to

[8] R Atkinson, T Buck, D Pollard, and N Smith, *A Regional Study of Local Authority and Court Processes in Homelessness Cases* (London, Lord Chancellor's Department, 1999). Central government does not collect any official statistics on the numbers of internal reviews or County Court homelessness decisions, although see D Cowan, A Dymond, S Halliday and C Hunter, 'Reconsidering Mandatory Reconsideration' [2017] *PL* 215.

[9] D Cowan, 'Reducing Homelessness or Re-ordering the Deckchairs?' (2019) 82 *MLR* 105, 110.

[10] P Lidstone, 'Rationing Housing to the Homeless Applicant' (1994) 9 *Housing Studies* 459; P Carlen, 'The Governance of Homelessness: Legality, Lore and Lexicon in the Agency-Maintenance of Youth Homelessness' (1994) 41 *Critical Social Policy* 18; G Peaker, 'Gatekeeping in Times of Austerity' (2012) 15 *Journal of Housing Law* 107; Z Nabi, 'Gatekeeping: Lessons from the Birmingham Cases' (2012) 15 *Journal of Housing Law* 109; D Cowan, S Halliday and C Hunter, 'Gatekeeping Administrative Justice: Homelessness Internal Reviews' (2012) 15 *Journal of Housing Law* 122; A Arden and C Cullen, 'No Surprises: Gatekeeping' *Legal Action* (November 2014); S Alden, 'Discretion on the Frontline: The Street Level Bureaucrat in English Statutory Homelessness Services' (2015) 14 *Social Policy and Society* 63; S Alden, 'On the Frontline: The Gatekeeper in Statutory Homelessness Services' (2015) 30 *Housing Studies* 924.

[11] Hansen Palomares, 'The London Borough of Southwark Ordered to Stop "Gatekeeping" Vulnerable Homeless Families' (20 February 2015); 'Council Ordered to Stop Gatekeeping Practices' *Housing Rights* (8 April 2015); H Fearn, 'The Scandal of Councils Turning Away the Homeless is Finally Being Exposed' *The Guardian* (27 February 2015); LGSCO, 'Ombudsman Investigation Finds Brentwood Gatekeeping Homelessness Applications' (9 January 2025); LGSCO, Brentwood Borough Council (23018930).

[12] S Dobie, B Sanders and L Teixeira, *Turned Away: The Treatment of Single Homeless People by Local Authority Homelessness Services in England* (London, Crisis, 2014).

penetrate into and become embedded within the practices of local authorities is notoriously weak.[13]

The LGSCO has identified gatekeeping by councils delaying or not taking homelessness decisions. Councils have not provided claimants with interim accommodation when there was good reason to believe that an applicant was homeless.[14] They have engaged in extensive delays and bad practice.[15] Another tactic has been for councils to refuse applicants without issuing formal refusal letters, thereby leaving people in limbo and denying them an administrative review and an appeal to the County Court.[16] Without a refusal letter, there is no formal decision to challenge. In one case, a young homeless woman had approached her council's homelessness unit on five occasions over a 15-month period for housing support.[17] Each approach had triggered a legal duty on the council to investigate her circumstances. However, instead of investigating whether she was homeless, the council had only provided her with advice and referred her to a charity. For every grievance that becomes visible, many others remain invisible.

Gatekeeping cannot be precisely quantified. It is also the case that there is often no correct single outcome of individual assessments. However, there is a substantial difference between, on the one hand, careful and sensitive exercises of discretion and, on the other hand, refusing claims on the basis of financial and resource factors and/or engaging in poor practices. Using delay and other tactics to manage down demand relies on people lacking the energy to pursue matters. Claimants can become so frustrated and worn out by the process that they simply give up. Behind the scenes, officials will seek to stem the flow of applications, claims, reviews and appeals, in the hope that claimants go away. Another consequence of rationing is inconsistency of decision-making over time. When demand increases, the eligibility criteria are raised in response. Claims that would previously have been granted are now refused. Even when people do challenge, redress mechanisms such as internal reviews can be used to close down grievances. These practices can be employed intentionally or emerge over time as part of the public body's culture and assessment practices in light of the pressures placed upon it. Officers will often feel they have no alternative.

[13] I Loveland, *Housing Homeless Persons: Administrative Law and the Administrative Process* (Oxford, Oxford University Press, 1995); S Halliday, *Judicial Review and Compliance with Administrative Law* (Oxford, Hart Publishing, 2003).

[14] LGSCO, *Homelessness: How Councils Can Ensure Justice for Homeless People* (Coventry, LGSCO, 2011); LGSCO, *Home Truths: How Well are Councils Implementing the Homelessness Reduction Act?* (Coventry, LGSCO, 2020) 20.

[15] LGSCO, London Borough of Hounslow (13014921) (the council took 62 weeks to reach a final decision when it was should not have taken longer than 15 weeks); LGSCO, 'Manchester Mum had to live in Unsafe Accommodation for 18 Months Longer Than Necessary, Ombudsman Says' (5 December 2024); Manchester City Council (23017649).

[16] LGSCO, 'Bristol City Council Denying People Their Right to Appeal' (2013); Bristol City Council (12015826); Basingstoke & Deane Borough Council (17012432); 'Family Left in Unaffordable Flat after Council Denies Right to Appeal Homelessness Decision' (2019); London Borough of Waltham Forest (22012789) (the council's delay in issuing decisions delayed the right to review that decision); 'Halton Did Not Do Enough to Help Homeless Domestic Abuse Survivor' (2025); Halton Borough Council (23005581).

[17] LGSCO, London Borough of Barnet (16002971).

Continuing Healthcare

Continuing Healthcare (CHC) is a package of NHS-funded health and social care for adults with complex, long-term health needs. It covers the costs for health and personal care in settings such as a person's home or a care home, provided that the person's primary need is health-related. CHC operates on the borderline between publicly funded NHS healthcare and privately funded and expensive social care. Those who qualify for CHC will have their health and personal care needs paid for by the NHS. Those who do not qualify will have to fund themselves, often at considerable expense. Unsurprisingly, securing CHC is difficult. A person with serious disabilities will represent a long-term resource commitment for the NHS. This can result in health bodies and local authorities in dispute with each other, with both seeking to avoid responsibility for a person's care.

The principal eligibility criterion is whether a person's primary need is a health need.[18] This involves evaluation and judgement. After initial assessments are taken by local NHS bodies, there is a system of onward reviews through local resolution processes and then to independent review panels, which make advisory recommendations. An inescapable aspect of CHC is the increasing demands and costs. This inevitably means raising eligibility thresholds and refusing claims.[19] While some people are eligible, many experience difficulties with the assessment process, prompting repeated concerns that people do not receive the care packages to which they are entitled. Assessments must be conducted by a multi-disciplinary team of health and social care professionals. However, these teams have often not been assembled, or minimally constituted, or team members have not possessed knowledge of the patient or specialist understanding of their health condition.[20] The quality of assessment decisions has been criticised.[21] There has been limited central monitoring and poor quality assurance of assessments.[22] Assessments have often been driven by budgetary concerns rather than patient need, and clinical assessments are overturned without explanation.[23]

Health bodies can resort to a range of gatekeeping tactics and behaviours. For claimants and their families, the assessment process is often 'intimidating, humiliating, unfriendly, exhausting, degrading, aggressive, frustrating and adversarial':[24] 'A closed, opaque and frustrating chase around an NHS maze where the rules change around every corner and

[18] Department of Health and Social Care, *National Framework for NHS Continuing Healthcare and NHS-Funded Nursing Care* (London, DHSC, 2018).

[19] The 2018 target from NHS England was for Clinical Commissioning Groups (now Integrated Care Boards) to make £855 million of efficiency savings in CHC and NHS-funded nursing care by 2020–21.

[20] National Health Service Commissioning Board and Clinical Commissioning Groups (Responsibilities and Standing Rules) Regulations, SI 2012/2996, reg 21(5); Continuing Healthcare Alliance, *Continuing to Care? Is NHS Continuing Healthcare Supporting the People Who Need it in England?* (London, Continuing Healthcare Alliance, 2016) 8–10.

[21] R Burley-Stower, 'Poor Decision-Making in NHS Continuing Healthcare' *Legal Action* (May 2019), www.lag.org.uk/article/206434/poor-decision-making-in-nhs-continuing-healthcare. Clinical Commissioning Groups were replaced by Integrated Care Boards in 2022, which now undertake assessments.

[22] House of Commons Public Accounts Committee, *NHS Continuing Healthcare Funding* (HC 2017–19, 455) 8.

[23] House of Commons Health Committee, *NHS Continuing Care* (HC 2004–05, 399) [148].

[24] Karen Guy, Parkinson's Disease Nurse Specialist quoted in All Party Parliamentary Group on Parkinson's, *Failing to Care: NHS Continuing Care in England* (2013) 15.

even when there are clear rules, they are routinely disregarded by NHS decision-makers.'[25] The criteria governing assessments are always open to interpretation and it is often a real battle for families.[26] Delayed assessments are common. Those refused can make a challenge through a local resolution process and then to panels. Most cases should proceed to an independent review panel within six months, but many people have waited years.[27] Some claimants have died waiting to hear about their eligibility. Alternatively, many claimants do not challenge refusal decisions because they feel that the redress process would be too distressing and exhausting to endure.[28] Significant variations in assessment outcomes between different health bodies have been attributed in part to the assessment criteria being interpreted and applied inconsistently.[29] In 2018, the Equality and Human Rights Commission commenced legal action against blanket policies that imposed arbitrary caps at the expense of the specific needs of individual patients.[30]

One man who applied on behalf of his mother, a dementia sufferer, experienced a catalogue of mistakes and delays throughout the process alongside his mother's worsening condition. It was a difficult experience; fighting a bureaucracy while supporting his mother. He suggested that the health body had adopted a very obvious tactic: 'refuse as many as you can, and then make it as difficult as you can to appeal, on the basis that most people are not as stupidly determined as me to pursue it and will just give up'.[31] Claimants will feel they have been treated unjustly. By contrast, health bodies will struggle to balance budgets and may feel that some claimants may seek CHC funding to avoid costly social care.

In 2003, the PHSO found that NHS bodies had been using overly restrictive local criteria and had therefore wrongly refused many applications.[32] The Department of Health then repaid £180 million to people who had unnecessarily funded their own care.[33] In 2020, the PHSO found a range of assessment failures by health bodies.[34] Failings in care and support planning included not accurately identifying a person's needs in full, inappropriately withdrawing care and poor communications. Nonetheless, these are relatively small inroads into the underlying problem. In addition to the usual low-level muddle and incompetence, CHC is dominated by the overwhelming and fundamental problem of not just limited but also reduced resources to fund care packages in the face of rising demand. The PHSO has advocated the mantra of getting it right first time

[25] Burley-Stower (n 21). See also E Peel and R Harding, '"It's a Huge Maze, the System, it's a Terrible Maze": Dementia Carers' Constructions of Navigating Health and Social Care Services" (2014) 13 *Dementia* 642.

[26] House of Commons Health and Social Care Committee, *Oral Evidence: Supporting Those with Dementia and Their Carers* (HC 2020–21, 96) Q20 (Sarah Pickup, Deputy Chief Executive, Local Government Association) (18 May 2021).

[27] National Audit Office, *Investigation into NHS Continuing Healthcare Funding* (HC 2017–19, 239) [2.7].

[28] Continuing Healthcare Alliance, *Continuing to Care? Is NHS Continuing Healthcare Supporting the People who Need it in England?* (Continuing Healthcare Alliance, 2017) 17.

[29] National Audit Office (n 27) [5.2].

[30] Equality and Human Rights Commission, 'NHS Facing Court Action over Unlawful Policies' (19 March 2018); Equality and Human Rights Commission, 'NHS U-Turns on Discriminatory Policies' (31 May 2018).

[31] House of Commons Health and Social Care Committee, *Oral Evidence: Supporting Those with Dementia and Their Carers* (HC 2020–21, 96) 18 May 2021, Q2 (Jonathan).

[32] Health Service Ombudsman, *NHS Funding for Long Term Care* (HC 2002-03, 399).

[33] HC Deb 16 January 2008, vol 470, col 1366W. See also PHSO, *Retrospective Continuing Care Funding and Redress* (HC 2006–07, 386).

[34] PHSO, *Continuing Healthcare: Getting it Right First Time* (HC 2019–21, 872); PHSO, *Continuing Healthcare: An Investigation into Hounslow Clinical Commissioning Group* (2022).

and has encouraged NHS bodies to learn and improve, although it is doubtful whether this has made any difference, given the fundamental intractable problem of insufficient resources. Like all redress institutions, the PHSO has to stay away from issues of policy and resources. Beneath a few symbolic victories, there are a large number of people who have been disappointed by the process.

Special Educational Needs and Disability

In 2024, around 1.9 million English children and young people had special educational needs and/or a disability (SEND). Under the Children and Families Act 2014, Education, Health, and Care Plans (EHCPs) were introduced to ensure that children received the best support and outcomes in light of their needs. An EHCP identifies the educational, health and social needs for children and young people up to the age of 25, and sets out the additional support to meet these needs. These plans should ensure that children and young people receive the provision and support that they require. The SEND process is administered by local authorities. The process involves an assessment of a child's educational needs and, if necessary, an EHCP detailing how such needs are to be met. The provision of support also involves collaboration and partnership working between councils, schools, and health and care and other providers. Children with an EHCP should have an annual review of their needs. Children with SEND but without an EHCP may well miss out on the support they need, especially if they are in mainstream schools under significant financial pressure. While SEND provision is crucially important to children and young people, it can also be very expensive. There has been a 'significant funding shortfall' as regards SEND which has contributed to the failure to deliver the 2014 Act reforms and to meet children's needs.[35]

Making good-quality assessments about the needs of young people with SEND is complex. The process works reasonably well for many.[36] However, a significant proportion do not receive the support they need.[37] There have been delays, poor-quality assessments and unlawful practices. There are substantial and unexplained variations in the proportion of pupils identified as needing support between different geographical areas.[38] In 2019, the Education Select Committee concluded that the implementation of the 2014 Act had been badly hampered by poor administration and the funding environment: 'the system is not working … fundamental problems need fixing now … Families are in crisis, local authorities are under pressure, schools are struggling'.[39] There was confusion, bureaucratic problems, unlawful practices,

[35] House of Commons Education Committee, *Special Educational Needs and Disabilities* (HC 2019, 20) 3.

[36] L Adams, A Tindle, S Basran, S Dobie, D Thomson, D Robinson, and C Shepherd, *Experiences of Education, Health and Care Plans: A Survey of Parents and Young People* (London, DfE, 2017); L Adams, A Tindle, S Basran, S Dobie, D Thomson, D Robinson, and G Codin, *Education, Health and Care Plans: A Qualitative Investigation into Service User Experience of the Planning Process* (London, DfE, 2018).

[37] House of Commons Public Accounts Committee, *Support for Children with Special Educational Needs and Disabilities* (HC 2019–21, 85).

[38] National Audit Office, *Support for Pupils with Special Educational Needs and Disabilities in England* (HC 2017–19, 2636) [1.10]–[1.12]; National Audit Office, *Support for Children and Young People with Special Educational Needs* (HC 2024–25, 299).

[39] House of Commons Education Committee (n 35) [232].

buck-passing, a lack of effective accountability, limited resources and adversarial experiences.

Local authorities, schools, and health and care and other providers should cooperate and engage in partnership in terms of working to provide special needs schooling. In reality, unlawful practices and poor coordination and communication are common. The practical interdependencies across education, health and care sectors are challenging, given varying pressures, thresholds and statutory assessment timeframes. For instance, the Children and Families Act 2014 Act imposes a duty to make joint commissioning arrangements by a local authority and its partner commissioning bodies to secure provision for SEND children.[40] However, there is a lack of clarity about who in practice is responsible for commissioning and which budgets are to be used.[41]

The question then is to how to hold the system to account so that children get the support that they need. The inspection regime (OFSTED and the Care Quality Commission) lacks rigour and does not tackle unlawful practice. For their part, local authorities have complained about being held accountable for health and social care services, matters that are beyond their control. The upshot is that in the SEND system, 'no one appears to be asking anyone to take responsibility for their actions. There appears to be an absence of responsibility for driving any change or holding anyone accountable when changes do not happen.'[42]

The Department for Education has taken a 'hands-off' approach towards delivery. Instead, it has been left to local authorities, inspectorates, the LGSCO, and – ultimately parents and carers – to police the system. This provides little effective means of countering unlawful practices, failures to adhere to statutory timescales and to meet children's needs, and the very variable coordination and communication between agencies. The Education Committee's assessment was that the Department for Education had not been taking enough responsibility for ensuring that its reforms were overseen; it needed to do more than 'preside serenely over chaos'.[43] The Committee therefore recommended that the Department introduce a mechanism by which parents can report unlawful local practices directly to the Department and also produce an annual scorecard for local authorities and health bodies to measure their performance.[44] Unsurprisingly, the Department disagreed: current accountability measures were sufficient.[45]

SEND differs from other contexts in that children and young people have legal rights to receive the support and provision they require. Local authorities are under a legal duty to ensure that the contents of EHCPs are delivered. However, this does not resolve the underlying issue of limited resources, but instead exacerbates it. In this context, parents and carers have to self-police the system to ensure that their children get the support they need. This is undertaken by parents/guardians using appeals and

[40] Children and Families 2014 Act, s 26.
[41] OFSTED, *SEND: Old Issues, New Issues, Next Steps* (2021).
[42] House of Commons Education Committee (n 35) [27].
[43] ibid 3 and [33].
[44] ibid [34].
[45] Department for Education, *Government Response to the Committee's First Report of Session 2019*, published by the House of Commons Education Committee as: *Special Educational Needs and Disabilities* (HC 2019–21, 668).

complaints when local authorities do not meet their statutory duties.[46] This often erodes trust in the system. Furthermore, increasing volumes of complaints and appeals reinforce an adversarial culture.[47] The Education Committee has described the experiences of parents and carers as having to 'wade through a treacle of bureaucracy, full of conflict, missed appointments and despair'.[48] The result is 'a bureaucratic nightmare' that requires 'significant levels of legal knowledge and personal resilience', a 'complex, awful and often unnecessarily antagonistic experience for parents' which 'can prevent them from accessing their entitlements'.[49] This often disadvantages those who lack the necessary personal or social resources. 'For some, Parliament might as well not have bothered to legislate.'[50]

The underlying problem is inadequate funding to meet increased demand. The significant shortfall in funding has been a serious contributory factor to the failure on the part of all concerned to deliver the SEND reforms and meet children's needs.[51] The tension is inherent in the role of local authorities. They both assess children's SEND needs and commission and fund provision. This mean that local authorities focus more on what they are able to provide and what is affordable rather than what provision children need. School funding has increased, particularly for children with high needs, but has not kept pace with the rise in the number of pupils. The degree of rationing and gatekeeping varies across local authorities, but is significant and inevitable. Councils themselves feel that they have been set up to fail by central government. Other problems include the poor coordination and communications between education, health and social care sectors. Overall, there has been rationing and gatekeeping, and children and young people's needs being unidentified and unmet.[52]

The LGSCO has reported that the SEND system has been beset with problems and bordering on crisis as illustrated by the high number of upheld complaints.[53] Common problems include delays by local authorities in undertaking assessments and annual reviews. Severe delays of up to 90 weeks, but regularly more than a year, have been common. Delay has been seen by parents as attempts by councils to limit the number of EHCPs in order to save money. Other problems include: poor planning and anticipation of needs, such as council areas simply lacking any specialist provision; poor communication and preparation for meetings with parents including frequent non-attendance and no (or insufficient) paperwork submitted; inadequate partnership working; EHCPs regularly being issued without advice from health or social care services; and a lack of oversight from senior managers with cases 'drifting' needlessly. The LGSCO has found that some local authorities had put up additional barriers to services in efforts to ration

[46] M-A Cullen and G Lindsay, 'Special Educational Needs: Understanding Drivers of Complaints and Disagreements in the English System' (2019) 4 *Frontiers in Education* 1.

[47] During the passage of the 2014 Act, Robert Buckland MP warned: 'if we rely on parents to self-police available services … [then] … the age-old battle that families often face will not be reduced and the adversarial nature of the complaints process will remain'. The Education Committee (n 35) [121] noted: 'Events have proven [Buckland] and others right, not just in relation to parents holding local authorities to account, but in other areas too. Parliament and Government were warned about many of the risks in the proposed system, and both Parliament and Government failed to heed those warnings.'

[48] ibid 3.

[49] ibid [51] and [54].

[50] ibid [54].

[51] ibid 3 and [8]–[10].

[52] ibid [35]. See also House of Commons Education Committee, *Solving the SEND Crisis* (HC 2024–25, 492).

[53] LGSCO, *Not Going to Plan? Education, Health and Care Plans Two Years on* (Coventry, LGSCO, 2019).

scarce resources: 'while sympathetic to the severe financial constraints which councils tell us they are working under, we can never accept this as an excuse for failing to meet the statutory rights of children'.[54] Parents and carers commonly view the process as a battleground in which they have to fight the system established to support them, resulting in 'heartbreaking stories of children failing to meet their potential'.[55]

In some investigations, the LGSCO has found that local authorities have not responded to a request from parents for an assessment for their child. Councils have also introduced additional requirements to trigger an assessment decision, a tactic used to manage down demand.[56] Other investigations illustrate the typical failures that arise. A boy with special educational needs had not been provided with suitable alternative education by his local authority and consequently missed out on much of his secondary education.[57] In another case, the local authority's consistently poor administration of a teenager's case involved multiple delays in reviewing and updating her EHCP. The girl's college was then unable to support her learning properly.[58]

While the LGSCO provides redress, there are important gaps. It does not have the statutory jurisdiction to investigate complaints concerning the actions of a school in fulfilling an EHCP or concerns regarding SEND provision for children without an EHCP. The LGSCO has therefore argued that it should have the ability to investigate and remedy all aspects of non-appealable matters about the provision of services and support for children and young people with SEND.[59]

Parents and young people can also appeal to the First-tier Tribunal (SEND) against the refusal by a local authority not to secure an EHC assessment, reassess their EHC needs, or issue, change or maintain an EHCP.[60] The number of appeals has increased significantly. Some 90 per cent of appeals are allowed or settled. Parents have argued that relentlessly unlawful decisions by local authorities have damaged children and have forced the Tribunal into crisis.[61] Predictably, many families need legal assistance;

[54] ibid 2.

[55] ibid.

[56] See, eg, LGSCO, London Borough of Hackney (17001811).

[57] LGSCO, Sheffield City Council (18004957) (multiple failures by the council, which included placing a boy in a disused chip shop; he missed 43 months of educational provision; the LGSCO recommended a financial remedy of £19,950).

[58] LGSCO, Staffordshire County Council (20000770) (a girl lost access to speech and language therapy and occupational therapy, causing distress). See also LGSCO, Royal Borough of Greenwich (20013834) (delay by the council in completing an EHC assessment, which delayed the parent's right to appeal the EHCP by nine months; the child missed out on special educational provision; the council also failed to assess social care needs which delayed provision by 14 months; there was then a further delay in securing therapy for the child following a SEND Tribunal decision).

[59] LGSCO, *Review, Refresh, Renew: Triennial Review of Local Government and Social Care Complaints and Public Accountability Arrangements* (Coventry, LGSCO, 2021) 16.

[60] Children and Families Act 2014, s 51.

[61] M Keer, 'Relentlessly Unlawful LA Decisions are Damaging Children and Forcing the SEND Tribunal into Crisis' *Special Educational Needs Jungle Blog* (18 December 2019), www.specialneedsjungle.com/.well-known/sgcaptcha/?r=%2Frelentlessly-unlawful-la-decisions-damaging-children-forcing-send-tribunal-into-crisis%2F&y=ipr:43.225.189.121:1776942157.908. On the user experience of tribunal appeals, see: K Runswick-Cole, '"The Tribunal was the Most Stressful Thing: More Stressful than My Son's Diagnosis or Behaviour": The Experiences of Families Who Go to the Special Educational Needs and Disability Tribunal (SENDisT)' (2007) 22 *Disability & Society* 315; MA Cullen and S Cullen, 'Young People's Right to Appeal to the English First-tier Tribunal (Special Educational Needs and Disability): Learning from the First Two Years' (2021) 43 *Journal of Social Welfare and Family Law* 60.

legal aid restrictions create obvious problems. In some instances, parents have been denied access to the Tribunal because of bureaucratic delays and mistakes by local authorities.[62]

There are also significant variations in the use of the Tribunal across different local authorities and regions. Those with lower socio-economic status are less likely to appeal.[63] 'The people who go to tribunal are white and middle-class and educated, so there is in-built unfairness in the system.'[64] People from less well-off backgrounds may not understand the system and lack the confidence to challenge.[65] More generally, this self-selecting use of redress mechanisms has been described as the 'Matthew effect'– that is, well-resourced individuals are more likely to secure their entitlements than others, thereby reinforcing pre-existing social disadvantages.[66] In any event, it has been argued that the proportion of allowed appeals should not be seen as 'wins' for children and their families: 'no family who has sunk their time, savings, mental health, relationships, and their child's future into the tribunal process has "won" anything. What they've "won" is the same right to an appropriate education that other families rightly take for granted'.[67] Lawyers have criticised local authorities that cynically refuse applications for gatekeeping and issue poor-quality EHCPs, thereby forcing some parents into the expensive tribunal process.[68]

SEND is one of the few areas of administrative justice that use mediation. The rationale is to avoid costly, lengthy and stressful proceedings in the Tribunal. Despite initial scepticism about mediation, its use has increased.[69] Analysis suggests that mediation can be a promising method of resolving disagreements that reduces appeals and enhances well-being for people.[70] Families who take up mediation are significantly less likely to appeal to the Tribunal. There has been no analysis to date comparing the quality of mediation and tribunal outcomes. Increasingly, some parents have sought judicial review to secure provision specified in EHCPs and/or or failures to comply with statutory timescales.[71] This has prompted local authorities to raise concerns about

[62] See, eg, LGSCO, Staffordshire County Council (n 58) (frequent delays by the council meant the family lost opportunity to appeal to the Tribunal).

[63] AJ Marsh, 'Special Educational Needs and Disability Tribunals in England, 1994–2019' (2022) 37 *Research Papers in Education* 797.

[64] House of Commons Education Committee, *Oral Evidence: Special Educational Needs and Disabilities* (HC 2017–19, 968) Q149 (20 November 2018) (Dame Christine Lenehan, Director, Council for Disabled Children).

[65] O Drummond, *The Access to Justice Barriers for Tribunal Users: A Comparative Case Study on Special Educational Needs Tribunals* (Belfast, Northern Ireland Assembly, Knowledge Exchange Seminar Series, 2015) 2.

[66] B Hubeau, 'The Profile of Complainants: How to Overcome the Matthew Effect?' in M Hertogh and R Kirkham (eds), *Research Handbook on the Ombudsman* (Cheltenham, Edward Elgar, 2018).

[67] Keer (n 61).

[68] G Langdon-Down, 'Special Education Needs: Learning to Fight' *Law Society Gazette* (26 February 2018).

[69] S Riddell, N Harris, E Smith and E Weedon, 'Dispute Resolution in Additional and Special Educational Needs: Local Authority Perspectives' (2010) 25 *Journal of Education Policy* 55; N Harris, 'Mediation, Lawyers and Special Educational Needs: Ensuring a Balanced Approach to Dispute Resolution' (2021) 32 *King's Law Journal* 1.

[70] G Lindsay, G Conlonb, V Totsikaa, G Graya and MA Cullen, 'The Impact of Mediation on Resolution of Disagreements around Special Educational Needs: Effectiveness and Cost Effectiveness' (2021) 26 *Research Papers in Education* 275.

[71] Council for Disabled Children, *Survey Results: Legal Action Threatened Against Local Authorities in Relation to EHC Plans* (2020). There have also been complaints to the ombudsman. See, eg, LGSCO, Suffolk County Council (20012908) (the council was told to pay £8,000 after it failed to implement an EHC plan).

having to spend significant time and resources on legal action which then eats into their budgets.[72]

For their part, local authorities emphasise that they have not been given sufficient resources to deliver SEND services and the increased demand. Local authorities are under statutory legal duties that they often cannot fulfil because of a lack of resource. A real problem for local authorities concerns their statutory duty to secure the special educational provision specified in an EHCP.[73] This is an absolute duty; there is no 'best endeavours' defence. However, there is inevitably a tension between the way in which one child or young person's needs are to be provided and those of all other children and the resources available. For instance, the local authority concludes that the child's needs can be met in one way, but the parents prefer an alternative and more expensive school place or provision. Alternatively, a school fails a child, for which the local authority is responsible, but it lacks the levers to compel the school to act.

There are also concerns from councils that the SEND Tribunal gives excessive weight to the chosen placement at a particular school without considering the efficient use of resources. The Tribunal's decisions have an inevitable knock-on impact of this on the many other children that the council deals with – many of whom do not appeal. The Tribunal is, in essence, often allocating the limited resources of councils, although the Tribunal itself has no responsibility to balance those finite budgets. The Tribunal has been criticised for prioritising the needs of the individual child and not the wider needs of all children and young people. This is contentious and inherently problematic. The Local Government Association has argued that the SEND Tribunal should be abolished and replaced with non-judicial redress through complaints and the LGSCO.[74]

Overall, the policy goals underpinning SEND provision are well intentioned, but its delivery has been highly problematic. Local authorities were unprepared and under-resourced for the reforms and the increased demand, and have struggled as a result. The system is in crisis. There is a deep tension between limited resources and increased demand on the one hand and compliance with the law on the other hand. The resource-dependent social welfare schemes considered above operate principally as discretionary schemes with limited judicial control. By contrast, the SEND Tribunal makes decisions which bind councils, but without considering the financial pressures that councils are under. There is a fundamental disconnect between the resources available to councils and the legal position. From the perspective of families, the real problem is councils' non-compliance with the law, and councils that delay assessments and provision in order to save money. From the perspective of councils, the system is under-resourced, but they cannot use insufficient resources as a reason for not providing provision. The result is an ongoing crisis.

* * *

[72] See, eg, Letter from Councillor James McInnes, Cabinet Member for Children Services and Schools, Devon County Council to the Secretary of State for Education (11 August 2020).

[73] Children and Families Act 2014, s 42.

[74] Local Government Association, *Towards an Effective and Financially Sustainable Approach to SEND in England: An Independent Report by ISOS Partnership Commissioned by the County Council Network and Local Government Association* (2024).

Rationing and gatekeeping also occur in adult social care[75] and school transport.[76] In the 2010s, central government devolved various discretionary-based local welfare schemes to local government while also significantly reducing the funding available at a time of increased demand. This was a means of shifting the accompanying blame and fallout.[77] These areas illustrate the strain between the needs of individuals and limited resources, often verging into crisis. Further, in such areas, the weaknesses of administrative justice are often the downstream manifestations of wider intractable social problems: the housing crisis and the funding problems of the NHS, SEND and adult social care. Central government either cannot or will not address these huge challenges. The problems of administration and the accompanying blame games are then delegated down to the front line. Officials do not want to gatekeep and ration, but are compelled by circumstance to do so. The experience is typically an unhappy and frustrating one for claimants. Redress institutions exert little effect and cannot resolve the underlying resource problems. Whenever demand exceeds resources, a pinch point arises somewhere in the process; for some people to succeed, others must lose. The overall effect is one of ongoing and deep-seated dysfunction.

One exception is school admissions. Children refused a place at their preferred school can appeal to a school admission appeal panel. Panels decide appeals by examining whether the school could admit additional children without prejudicing the provision of efficient education. They then balance the prejudice to the school against the child's case to be admitted.[78] This is a judgemental assessment based on the facts of individual cases and involves considering matters including travel distances, routes to school and personal circumstances. Given the limited nature of school places, appeals are compared with each other to determine which are the most deserving. Panels have far less discretion in reception class appeals (children aged five to seven). The

[75] House of Lords Adult Social Care Committee, *A 'Gloriously Ordinary Life': Spotlight on Adult Social Care* (HL 2022–23, 99) [101] and [107]: 'social care assessments are too often a "tickbox" exercise … local authorities facing reduced budgets are likely to act as "gatekeepers" to keep people out of the system … Local authorities and social workers face significant challenges in the provision of social care … the difficulty of accessing care and support is such that they are often seen as rationing services for older adults and disabled people. The need to stretch inadequate budgets across as many people as possible can lead to the codifying of a penny-pinching approach to assessment, which is at odds with the purpose of adult social care'. See also LGSCO, 'Disabled Boy Missed out on Education and Support Because of Poor Council Practice' (2021); West Sussex County Council (20001685); (extensive failures by the council, which refused to assess parents for respite care as regards their disabled boy; the LGSCO expressed concern that the council was gatekeeping by placing a barrier in front of people claiming respite care); 'Croydon Council Fails to Provide Respite for Disabled Teen's Mum' (8 December 2022); LGSCO, London Borough of Croydon (21013878) (the council's approach to deciding upon respite care was fundamentally flawed as it placed budgetary considerations above meeting individual needs); London Borough of Croydon (24009003) (undue emphasis on cost and funding arrangements); 'Nearly 100,000 Adults in England Denied State-Funded Social Care Due to Cuts' *The Guardian* (25 June 2025).

[76] LGSCO, 'Wirral Council Asked to Reconsider School Transport Decisions for Children with Special Educational Needs' (2017); LGSCO, Wirral Metropolitan Borough Council (15018169); LGSCO, *All on Board? Navigating School Transport Issues* (Coventry, LGSCO, 2017); LGSCO, 'Mum Left in Debt after Council Stopped Autistic Son's School Transport' (2020); LGSCO, Nottingham City Council (18018188); LGSCO, 'Stockton-on-Tees to Improve its Education Transport Policy for Young Adults Following Ombudsman Investigation' (14 June 2023); LGSCO, Stockton-on-Tees Borough Council (22010732); LGSCO, 'Councils Told Not to Make Blanket Decisions on Post-16 School Transport Applications (2025); LGSCO, Derby City Council (23013529).

[77] J Meers, 'Discretion as Blame Avoidance: Passing the Buck to Local Authorities in "Welfare Reform"' (2019) 27 *Journal of Poverty and Social Justice* 41; F Cole Norton, '"This is Counterproductive': The Design of Local Welfare Assistance Schemes in England" (2024) 46 *Journal of Social Welfare and Family Law* 413.

[78] Department for Education, *School Admission Appeals Code* (London, DfE, 2022).

government has limited reception class sizes to 30 children per teacher.[79] Panels can only admit an additional child to a reception class if the refusal decision was irrational, a deliberately high hurdle. There are some 40,000 appeals per year in England with an overall success rate of around 20 per cent. School admissions differ from the contexts considered above in one key respect: the limited resource being allocated is not whether a child gets a place at a school, but whether they get a place at their preferred school. This can still be a significant issue, given school distances, transport, parental preferences and differences between schools and so on. Nonetheless, school admissions are quite different from homelessness, CHC and SEND, in which a substantive resource is being rationed as opposed to its type and location (as in school admissions). Children refused a place at their preferred school will get a school place elsewhere. Yet, it is not apparent that the policy of promoting school choice has succeeded as originally envisaged. It was intended to empower parents/guardians.[80] However, parents and guardians are often left feeling cynical, fatalistic and disempowered about how such choice works in practice.[81] This may, in part, be because the language of 'choice' is itself misleading. A familiar comment made at panel hearings is that parents do not have a choice of school, but only the right to express a preference, which must be balanced up against the preferences of other children. The 'choice' of school is limited by which school places are available, the admissions criteria and how appeal panels exercise their discretion. Moreover, some parents try to game the system.[82] School admissions may not exhibit the dysfunctions present elsewhere, although it leaves many parents/carers feeling fatalistic.

Disciplinary Administrative Justice

Across a range of contexts, government exercises disciplinary powers over people to penalise them and to induce them to change their behaviour: prison discipline, benefit sanctions, school exclusions, and the hostile immigration environment. These contexts reveal the punitive aspect of administration and generate a direct clash with the individual. The exercise of disciplinary power requires people to be treated fairly. Procedural fairness will likely lead to better decisions and ensure respect for human dignity. However, such demands are often at some distance from what actually happens. There is always the risk that disciplinary processes – both formally and informally – weaken the ability of people to participate in important decisions. Anyone with experience of disciplinary power will know the pervasive social and cognitive pressures that can insidiously come into play: the knee-jerk emotional response to a person's conduct; the rush to judgement; confirmation bias; and the bending of procedural and substantive norms to reach the desired result. Beyond the skills and competencies of individual

[79] School Standards and Framework Act 1998, s 1.

[80] N Harris, Education, *Law and Diversity: Schooling for One and All?*, 2nd edn (Oxford, Hart Publishing, 2021) ch 5.

[81] A Bhattacharya, 'How Much Choice is Enough? Parental Satisfaction with Secondary School Choice in England and Scotland' (2023) 52 *Journal of Social Policy* 661.

[82] 'Parents Using "Dubious Tactics" to Beat School Admissions Criteria' *The Guardian* (13 September 2018); 'How the Middle Classes are Gaming the School System' *Daily Telegraph* (1 November 2022).

decision-makers and the inherent disciplinary pressures, a wider structural factor comes into play: the ability of government both formally and informally to weaken process and redress rights. Procedure and substance are closely connected. Just as scrupulously fair procedures can mask substantive unfairness, reduced process rights can load the dice against people. There is a perennial risk that the overall framework and disciplinary ethos can erode both procedural and substantive fairness for the individuals concerned.

It is not the case that such disciplinary administrative justice is invariably harsh, heavy-handed or unfair. The Traffic Penalty Tribunal is widely acknowledged as an innovative tribunal, given its extensive use of online dispute resolution.[83] People can contest parking fines through the Tribunal's online procedure. A parking adjudicator interacts with appellants online, who can upload pictures and documents through their phone. Cases are heard quickly and without hearings, and satisfaction rates are high. This performance surpasses all other tribunals. However, parking fines are relatively simple and low-value matters compared with, for instance, immigration, asylum or tax appeals.[84]

Matters are different elsewhere. Consider the prison disciplinary system. Prisoners are subject to the prison disciplinary regime, a system notorious for its unfairness and punitive ethos. Prisons are violent, unsafe and overcrowded, with many inmates restricted, isolated or experiencing long periods of segregation.[85] Common problems include suicide, self-harm, persistently high levels of violence, drugs, under-staffing and disturbances within prisons. The number of disciplinary adjudications has also increased. Since the 1970s, the courts have opened up this previously closed system in order to inject the norms of procedural fairness, although there are also many complaints of unfairness by prisoners.[86] In this context, the disciplinary system has been stretched beyond its original purpose of punishing unacceptable behaviour; it is also used as a routine means of managing prisoner behaviour. Increased use of discipline has led to a negative cycle of ever-greater restriction, with counter-productive consequences.[87] The use of punitive adjudications has been associated with an increased risk of reoffending.[88]

In other punitive contexts, government has, to varying degrees, adopted hardline policies that penalise certain groups of people and reduced procedural rights. Two contexts in particular illustrate the problems of disciplinary administrative justice: school exclusions and benefit sanctions.

[83] L Mulcahy, 'Modernisation or Transformation? User Led Design and the Facilitation of Systemic Change in the Traffic Penalty Tribunal' (2024) 43 *Civil Justice Quarterly* 120.

[84] A Penalty Charge Notice is around £70.

[85] Council of Europe, *Report to the United Kingdom Government on the Visit to the United Kingdom Carried Out by the European Committee for the Prevention of Torture and Inhuman or Degrading Treatment or Punishment (CPT) from 13 to 23 May 2019* (Strasbourg, CoE, 2020) 5.

[86] *Leech v Deputy Governor of Parkhurst Prison* [1988] AC 533; Prisons and Probation Ombudsman, *Adjudication Complaints* (London, PPO, 2013); M Butler and S Maruna, 'Rethinking Prison Disciplinary Processes: A Potential Future for Restorative Justice' (2016) 11 *Victims & Offenders* 126; Howard League for Penal Reform, *Justice Does Not Stop at the Prison Gate: Justice and Fairness in Prisons* (2020).

[87] HM Inspectorate of Prisons, *Incentivising and Promoting Good Behaviour* (London, HMIP, 2018).

[88] B Fortescue, FF Howard, P Howard, G Kelly and M Elwan, *Examining the Impact of Sanctions on Custodial Misconduct following Disciplinary Adjudications* (London, Ministry of Justice, 2021).

School Exclusions

A school can permanently exclude a child if there has been a serious or persistent breach of its behaviour policy and keeping the child in school would seriously harm the education or welfare of others.[89] Such decisions are taken by the headteacher and then reviewed by the school's governing body. A child's behaviour can be highly disruptive to others. On the other hand, permanent exclusion can impact upon a child and their prospects. As a result, there needs to be a fair and independent means of challenging exclusions so that schools can be held to account. Previously, there was a full right of appeal to an independent panel.[90] Panels could remake exclusion decisions by rejecting appeals or reinstating an excluded child back to the school. These arrangements were imperfect. There were concerns that some parents and children struggled to participate in the process. Better-qualified panels were needed.[91] On the other hand, teaching unions criticised appeal panels for undermining the authority of teachers.[92] In 2011, exclusion panels were downgraded to Independent Review Panels. These panels can only review exclusion decisions on judicial review principles.[93] The rationale was that there was the need to ensure schools could discipline pupils and to stop appeal panels undermining the authority of headteachers.[94] If an independent review panel finds a legal error, then it can send the case back to the school's governing board to reconsider the case and order an adjustment to the school's budget if the child is not reinstated. The exercise of a judicial review jurisdiction by panels composed of voluntary lay members, not legal experts, results in a somewhat unusual state of affairs.[95]

In practice, exclusion panels involve hearing from the school and then the family/parent of the excluded child. The parties cannot be expected to appreciate that the review panel is limited to judicial review principles. Unrepresented families/parent(s) will likely know nothing about judicial review and will be more concerned with the evidence, the facts and circumstances of the individual case, especially when there are differing versions of the events. The challenge in the hearing is then to ensure that the focus remains on the legality of the decision to exclude and not to re-decide on the merits or merely rubber stamp the exclusion. The limited role of panels inevitably

[89] Department for Education, *Exclusion from Maintained Schools, Academies and Pupil Referral Units in England: Statutory Guidance for those with Legal Responsibilities in Relation to Exclusion* (London, DfE, 2017) [16].

[90] Education Act 2002, s 52. For an overview, see L Ferguson and N Webber, *School Exclusion and the Law: A Literature Review and Scoping Survey of Practice* (University of Oxford, 2015). Education is a devolved function. The focus here is on England. Children permanently excluded in Scotland, Wales and Northern Ireland retain a full right of appeal. On the position in Wales, see S Nason, A Sherlock, H Taylor and H Pritchard, *Public Administration and a Just Wales: Education* (Bangor, University of Bangor, 2020) 59–64.

[91] N Harris, K Eden and A Blair, *Challenges to School Exclusion: Exclusion, Appeals and the Law* (Abingdon, Routledge, 2000); Council on Tribunals, *School Admission and Exclusion Appeal Panels: Special Report* (Cm 5788, 2003).

[92] N Harris, 'The Developing Role and Structure of the Education Appeal System in England and Wales' in M Harris and M Partington (eds), *Administrative Justice in the 21st Century* (Oxford, Hart Publishing, 1999) 315–16.

[93] Education Act 2002, s 51A(4) (as inserted by Education Act 2011, s 4); School Discipline (Pupil Exclusions and Reviews) (England) Regulations, SI 2012/1033.

[94] Department for Education, *The Importance of Teaching* (2010, Cm 7980) [3.28]–[3.29].

[95] *R (CR) v Independent Review Panel of the London Borough of Lambeth* [2014] EWHC 2461 (Admin) [32] (Collins J).

constrains what they can do compared with an appeal. It is a rare case in which a school has exceeded its statutory power to exclude or decided irrationally. The most likely flaws will be a procedural error by the governing body or a failure to follow the exclusion guidance. Another possible ground to intervene arises if the child had special educational needs, which the governing body has not properly considered. At the same time, panels will be influenced by the merits and the behaviours of the school. Governing bodies often uphold the decisions of their headteachers to exclude. There can also be local, social and internalised pressures to make an example of bad behaviour. Further, it cannot be assumed that governors will always act lawfully or follow the exclusions guidance. Panels may then be tempted to 'find' an error of law if they think the decision to exclude was wrong or disproportionate. Of course, this does not guarantee that the exclusion decision will be reversed, as panels can only order a reconsideration.

Parents' experiences of Independent Review Panels have been variable. Some have found panels to be empathetic, whereas other parents have found the process to impose a heavy cost emotionally, physically and financially. Some have felt marginalised and disadvantaged because of the lack of legal support and the power imbalance. A related wider concern is that the views of children in general and in particular those with SEND may not be properly taken into account and may be over-ridden by the imperative to discipline children.[96]

Schools undoubtedly face challenges with discipline. Conversely, there is the risk that resorting to exclusion becomes the dominant and disproportionate response and thereby disadvantages a child's future. Children may be excluded to make an example out of them. The number of exclusions has increased in recent years, prompting concerns that exclusion has increasingly become a tool by which schools manage disruptive behaviours rather than trying to address pupil behaviours within the school.[97] The proportion of SEND children excluded from school has been disproportionately high.[98] Poor behaviour by pupils can arise from a failure to identify or support a child's special needs. Further, a disproportionate number of black and ethnic minority children have been excluded.[99]

In addition to formal exclusions, some schools have engaged in the unlawful practice of 'off-rolling'.[100] This involves schools informally removing pupils to maintain the school's league table position.[101] The Children's Commissioner has emphasised that the

[96] N Hodge and C Wolstenholme, '"I Didn't Stand a Chance": How Parents Experience the Exclusions Appeal Tribunal' (2016) 20 *International Journal of Inclusive Education* 1297.

[97] B Graham, C White, A Edwards, S Potter and C Street, *School Exclusion: A Literature Review on the Continued Disproportionate Exclusion of Certain Children* (London, DfE, 2019) 88–95.

[98] B Lamb, 'Statutory Assessment for Special Educational Needs and the Warnock Report: The First 40 Years' (2019) 4 *Frontiers in Education: Policy and Practice Reviews* 1, 9.

[99] A Carlile, 'An Ethnography of Permanent Exclusion from School: Revealing and Untangling the Threads of Institutionalised Racism' (2011) 15 *Race Ethnicity and Education* 175; F Demie, 'The Experience of Black Caribbean Pupils in School Exclusion in England' (2021) 73 *Educational Review* 55.

[100] EJ Done and H Knowler, '"Off-Rolling" and Foucault's Art of Visibility/Invisibility: An Exploratory Study of Senior Leaders' Views of "Strategic" School Exclusion in Southwest England' (2021) 47 *British Educational Research Journal* 1039; EJ Done, H Knowler and D Armstrong, '"Grey" Exclusions Matter: Mapping Illegal Exclusionary Practices and the Implications for Children with Disabilities in England and Australia' (2021) 21 *Journal of Research in Special Educational Needs* 36.

[101] Children's Commissioner, *'Always Someone Else's Problem': Office of the Children's Commissioner's Report on Illegal Exclusions* (London, Children's Commissioner, 2013); R Adams, 'One in Four Teachers Say Pupils are Being Forced out to Boost School Rankings' *The Guardian* (10 May 2019); N Titheradge, 'Schools Admit Informally Excluding Pupils' *BBC News* (16 November 2018), www.bbc.co.uk/news/uk-46044400; House of Commons Library, *Off-rolling in English Schools* (Briefing Paper No 08444, 2020).

interests of excluded children should be prominent and that the system must ensure equality of opportunity for all young people and their families and prevent discrimination. However, calls for full appeals to be restored have been rejected.[102] Overall, the experience of school exclusions illustrates how the weakening of redress mechanisms accompanies the weakening of substantive rights.

Benefit Sanctions

Over the last few decades, conditionality and sanctions have become prominent and routine features of the benefits system.[103] The intended purpose of sanctions is to motivate claimants to take active steps towards employment. Claimants are expected to comply with various conditions and requirements, including meeting work coaches and attending a work-focused interview. Non-compliance can result in sanctions, such as benefits being suspended for varying durations of time and severity. There are different sanction regimes for different benefits. For instance, claimants in receipt of Employment and Support Allowance, the principal incapacity benefit for people of working age, can be sanctioned, or disqualified from benefits, if they have limited capability for work through their own misconduct, have limited capability for work by not following medical advice for no good reason or have failed to observe any prescribed rules of behaviour.[104]

The introduction of Universal Credit as the principal means-tested benefit for working people on low incomes was accompanied by a tougher approach to sanctions in general.[105] One aspect of Universal Credit is the 'claimant commitment'. Claimants must agree to, for instance, attend and take part in appointments with an adviser. This was justified as part of reducing welfare dependency, the 'something for nothing culture' of people living on benefits. Higher-level sanctions were also introduced. For instance, if a claimant leaves a job voluntarily without good reason or because of misconduct, does not applying for a job that they can be expected to apply for or take up an offered job, then higher level sanctions can be imposed.[106] These sanctions will last for 91 days in the first instance and then 182 days for a second high-level sanction. In 2016, conditionality was introduced for parents of young children to, for instance, be available for and actively seek work or attend work-focused interviews and be subject to a work preparation requirement.[107] Many people previously exempt from sanctions – disabled people, lone parents and low-paid workers – have been brought within the regime.

The overall result has been the imposition of more sanctions of greater severity for longer periods of time to a larger number of people than was previously the case. The period of 2012–16 saw the levels of sanctions and their severity reach unprecedented

[102] Children's Commissioner, '*They Never Give up on You*' (London, Children's Commissioner, 2012).

[103] Jobseekers Act 1995; Social Security Advisory Committee, *Sanctions in the Benefit System* (London, SSAC Occasional Paper 1, 2006).

[104] Welfare Reform Act 2007, s 18.

[105] Welfare Reform Act 2012.

[106] Welfare Reform Act 2021, s 26.

[107] Welfare Reform and Work Act 2016, s 17.

levels.[108] Sanctions obviously significantly affect a person's financial circumstances.[109] Individual decisions to impose sanctions are important for both the DWP, in terms of its policy intent, and for claimants as regards the correctness of decisions and their impacts. We can consider individual sanction decision-making and their policy effectiveness.

DWP Work Coaches decide whether to refer someone for a sanction and then a DWP decision-maker will decide whether to impose one. These decision-makers must often assess whether a claimant's failure to comply with a condition was reasonable. For instance, did someone not attend a job interview for good reason? Conditionality can also be reduced or switched off for a period of time in response to personal circumstances affecting a claimant (for example, someone becomes a victim of domestic violence) or where it would be unreasonable to expect a claimant to complete their requirements (for example, because of homelessness, illness or childcare). There is an inevitable tension between exercising discretion to allow flexibility or using rules to achieve consistency. Work Coaches should exercise reasonable discretion to enable them to tailor sanction decisions appropriately to the personal circumstances of individual claimants. However, there have been concerns of inconsistent decisions between individual Work Coaches and across different regional areas. The DWP has recognised the need to invest the capability of Work Coaches to ensure they understand the policy and can feel confident about exercising discretion.[110]

Stakeholders and benefit advisors have complained about poor-quality decisions and inappropriate sanctions being imposed. Individual cases can be both factually and legally complex. It is doubtful whether decision-makers fully appreciate all of the intricacies and there have been some harsh decisions. For instance, a man with epilepsy was sanctioned for failing to attend a work-focused interview despite being hospitalised following multiple seizures. The decision was upheld on mandatory reconsideration, despite the evidence he had provided.[111] In another case, a man on Universal Credit was sanctioned without taking his illness into account. The DWP should refer claimants who have been ill for more than 28 days for a Work Capability Assessment; but, in this instance, the referral took four months.[112]

While there is legitimate scope for some conditionality, it has been argued that sanctions are often 'ineffective, inappropriate and potentially deeply harmful'.[113] The DWP intended that sanction decisions would involve a personally tailored process, but this has not materialised. Instead, decisions are taken by decision-makers who have no interactions with claimants and therefore are unlikely to possess sufficient insight into

[108] D Webster, 'Explaining the Rise and Fall of JSA and ESA Sanctions, 2010–16' (London, Child Poverty Action Group, 17 August 2016), cpag.org.uk/policy-and-research/policy-briefings-reports/david-webster-briefings; M Adler, *Cruel, Inhuman or Degrading Treatment? Benefit Sanctions in the UK* (London, Palgrave Macmillan, 2018) ch 4.

[109] Sanctioned claimants can apply for hardship payments, which are capped and must be repaid.

[110] House of Commons Work and Pensions Committee, *Benefit Sanctions: Government Response to the Committee's Nineteenth Report of Session 2017–19* (HC 2017–19, 1949) 10.

[111] '"It's Callous and Cold-Hearted": A Man with Epilepsy was Sanctioned after Missing His Universal Credit Appointment Due to Seizures' *The Independent* (22 March 2018). The DWP then reversed its decision following media coverage: 'DWP Reverses Sanctions Decision for Epileptic Man who Missed Benefits Appointment due to Seizure' *The Independent* (6 April 2018).

[112] Independent Case Examiner, *Annual Report 2019–2020* (London, DWP, 2020) 14.

[113] House of Commons Work and Pensions Committee, *Benefit Sanctions* (HC 2017–19, 955) [97].

claimants' personal circumstances. Another aspect is a 'presumption of guilt'. Claimants are required to prove why they should not be sanctioned rather than the decision-maker having to prove why a sanction should be imposed.[114] Claimants are not notified in advance of alleged non-compliance with their benefits conditions and then afforded a reasonable opportunity to respond and explain. Instead, sanctions can only be challenged after they have been imposed. There is no process of issuing warning notices to claimants before a decision.[115]

Redress comprises mandatory reconsideration and then tribunal appeals. Between 2013 and 2018, there were 473,000 sanctions for Universal Credit claimants, and 80,000 mandatory reconsiderations of which 30 per cent reversed the sanction. However, there were only 1,352 First-tier Tribunal appeals, of which 84 per cent were allowed.[116] The low appeal volumes tend to confirm the filtering effects of mandatory reconsideration and the limited role of appeals.

The Upper Tribunal has emphasised that, given the consequences for claimants, 'tribunals need to scrutinise sanctions decisions with considerable care' and strictly construe the legal framework.[117] Tribunals should consider not just whether there was a good reason for the claimant failing to comply with a condition, but also whether the sanction had been validly imposed in the first place. Claimants should be properly notified of both the conditions imposed on them and the adverse consequences of non-compliance. The Upper Tribunal emphasised that 'public law principles of fairness apply to ensure that sanctions are only lawful where the claimant has been given adequate notice of the work-related requirement, and also the consequences of failure to comply with it'.[118] Tribunals can consider whether claimants were adequately notified of a condition and whether the means of communicating that condition were adequate.[119] It is for the DWP to establish that a requirement has been validly imposed and that the claimant has failed to comply. If these points have been demonstrated, then a claimant can only avoid a sanction if they have a good reason for not complying with a condition.

This is laudable and indicates an attempt to mitigate the worst effects of sanctions, although there are practical limitations. Many sanctioned claimants do not appeal. Further, the time taken for appeals to be heard and decided by First-tier Tribunals often exceeds the duration of the sanctions imposed. Sanctions remain in force until they expire or are overturned. It typically takes at least six months for appeals to come before tribunals. There is then a further four weeks before the claimant's benefits are reinstated and arrears repaid. Consequently, a sanctioned claimant can typically wait months for their appeal to be heard by a tribunal, which may then overturn the sanction – but by which

[114] Public Law Project, *Benefit Sanctions: A Presumption of Guilt* (London, PLP, 2022).

[115] House of Commons Work and Pensions Committee (n 113) [114]–[117]; S Sandhu, 'Benefits: "Yellow-Card" System for DWP Sanctions Could Help Ensure People are Not Pushed into Poverty' *The Independent* (23 July 2020).

[116] Department for Work and Pensions, *Benefit Sanctions Statistics* (2018). See also House of Commons Work and Pensions Committee (n 113) [100].

[117] *RR v Secretary of State for Work and Pensions* [2017] UKUT 459 (AAC) [45]. The Tribunal Judge noted (at [44]) that it had been 'unfortunate (putting it mildly) that the Secretary of State's original response to the appeal, as submitted to the First-tier Tribunal, was less than comprehensive in terms of its coverage of the relevant law. The response included a somewhat garbled version' of the relevant regulations.

[118] *JB v Secretary of State for Work and Pensions* [2018] UKUT 360 (AAC) [18].

[119] For an example, see *KG v Secretary of State for Work and Pensions* [2020] UKUT 307 (AAC).

time the sanction will likely have expired.[120] Even if the tribunal allows an appeal, it will make little, if any, practical difference because the claimant has already been sanctioned.

The Upper Tribunal's decision illustrates the point. In the specific case, it had taken the appellant a year to get from the initial sanction decision via mandatory reconsideration to the First-tier Tribunal and then to the Upper Tribunal. As the judge noted, during that time the appellant had endured very difficult financial circumstances, although she had been 'an articulate and determined individual who has persisted when many others might have given up'.[121] Few other claimants will possess the same degree of tenacity. After all, there is little point in appealing against a sanction when the appeal will only be decided sometime after the sanction has expired. In formal terms, claimants can access justice, but they can also be exposed to destitution, stress and uncertainty.

There is little substantive difference between benefit sanctions and criminal fines. Moreover, there is little, if any, sense here of fair procedures being used to ensure due respect to benefit claimants and ensuring their ability to participate in decisions that affect them. On the contrary, in addition to poor-quality decisions, other features include: the lack of advance notice and opportunity to comment before sanctions decisions are taken; the ability to challenge sanctions only after they have been imposed; the reversal of the burden of proof; the low take-up of appeals; and evident problems with their timeliness. As a result, benefit claimants should be entitled to a fairer process before an independent decision-maker when sanctions are initially decided rather than only on appeal.[122] There are ways of ameliorating the problems. Mandatory reconsiderations and appeals against sanctions could be fast-tracked. There could also a system of warnings and provisional decisions before claimants are sanctioned. However, the DWP has rejected these proposals.

There is a direct connection here between process and substantive policy. The reluctance to improve procedures is a direct consequence of the fact that the tougher sanction regime has very much been a politically driven project to reduce benefit spending. Since the introduction of the tougher sanctions regime in 2012, ministers have asserted that sanctions are justified because they will increase claimants' engagement with paid work. The degree of ministerial commitment has also been illustrated by the rare use of retrospective legislation to validate sanction regulations struck down by the courts.[123]

A wider policy question arises: have sanctions been effective in motivating claimants to fulfil the conditions and requirements imposed on them? This question can only be assessed through empirical investigation of how sanctions affect claimant behaviour, but ministers have steadfastly refused to go down this road. When the tougher sanction regime was introduced, the DWP had little understanding of its likely effects, although an ongoing review was promised.[124] However, the DWP has refused to investigate the impact and effectiveness of sanctions – a position described as 'unacceptable' by the Select

[120] Law Society of Scotland, *Benefit Sanctions Inquiry* (21 May 2018).

[121] *RR v Secretary of State for Work and Pensions* [2017] UKUT 459 (AAC) [43].

[122] A Pickup, 'Benefit Sanctions and Procedural Fairness' *Legal Action Group* (March 2020), www.lag.org.uk/article/207664/benefit-sanctions-and-procedural-fairness.

[123] *R (Reilly and Wilson) v Secretary of State for Work and Pensions* [2013] EWCA Civ 66; Jobseekers (Back to Work Schemes) Act 2013.

[124] National Audit Office, *Benefit Sanctions* (HC 2016–17, 628); House of Commons Work and Pensions Committee (n 113) [23].

Committee.[125] The gap has been filled by various studies.[126] These have found that, in many instances, sanctions have little, if any, effect, in motivating claimants to find employment. On the contrary, sanctions can adversely impact people's physical and mental health, thereby making future employment less likely. For a substantial minority of claimants, conditionality and sanctions generate a range of negative behaviours: counter-productive compliance; disengagement from the benefits system; increased poverty and destitution; resorting to survival crime; and ill health. Sanctions are particularly ineffective when applied to vulnerable people who either disengage from the benefit system and rely on charities or resort to crime to meet basic needs.[127] Moreover, it is not just claimants but also their family members and children who are adversely affected. In the view of the Select Committee, without evidence to justify tougher sanctions or data to understand their behavioural impacts, the tougher sanction policy has been 'nothing other than arbitrarily punitive'.[128] When government research on sanctions was finally published, its finding was that sanctions were ineffective in getting people into employment.[129]

Overall, disciplinary schemes tend to be loaded against the people concerned. The macro- and micro-pressures to discipline people are embedded deep within these schemes, with obvious negative implications. The very nature of disciplinary regimes will always embody inherent tensions. However, the weakness of redress mechanisms confirms the often pathological character of this aspect of administrative justice.

Administrative Delay

One of the most pressing problems of administrative justice is not administrative action, but inaction. People who interact with government are almost entirely reliant upon it to make decisions and provide services with a reasonable period of time. The principle of being customer-focused requires public bodies to deal with people promptly and within reasonable timescales and any published time limits. If matters take longer, then people should be informed. However, administrative delay is, in fact, a pervasive, extensive and recurrent problem. Everyone has experience of it. The effects of delayed decisions, entitlements and services are often significant. When viewed as a whole, the aggregate volume of delay experienced by millions of people is colossal. If we add to this

[125] ibid. See also 'Report on Effectiveness of Benefit Sanctions Blocked by DWP' *The Guardian* (27 January 2022); 'Benefit Sanctions Slow People's Progress into Work, Says Report Coffey Suppressed' *The Guardian* (6 April 2023).

[126] Welfare Conditionality Project, *Final Findings Report 2013–18* (York, University of York, 2018); PJ Dwyer, 'Punitive and Ineffective: Benefit Sanctions within Social Security' (2018) 25 *Journal of Social Security Law* 142; B Watts and S Fitzpatrick, *Welfare Conditionality* (Abingdon, Routledge, 2018); P Dwyer, L Scullion, K Jones, J McNeil and ABR Stewart, 'Work, Welfare and Well-Being: The Impacts of Welfare Conditionality on People with Mental Health Impairments in the UK' (2020) 54 *Social Policy and Administration* 311; E Williams, 'Punitive Welfare Reform and Claimant Mental Health: The Impact of Benefit Sanctions on Anxiety and Depression' (2021) 55 *Social Policy and Administration* 157; S Pattaro, N Bailey, E Williams, M Gibson, V Wells, M Tranmer and C Dibben, 'The Impacts of Benefit Sanctions: A Scoping Review of the Quantitative Research Evidence' (2022) *Journal of Social Policy* 1.

[127] E Batty and D Fletcher, *Offenders: Final Findings from the Welfare Conditionality Project* (York, University of York, 2018).

[128] House of Commons Work and Pensions Committee (n 113) [23].

[129] 'Benefit Sanctions Slow People's Progress into Work, Says Report Coffey Suppressed' *The Guardian* (6 April 2023).

the various adverse consequences of such delays, then, in terms of volume and impact, delay emerges as one of the principal problems of administrative justice. Delay therefore deserves examination. The discussion here considers the nature and consequences of administrative delay, its causes, what can be done about it, and the role of redress and scrutiny bodies.

All administrative decisions and actions involve some amount of time. People may think that their case has taken too long, but whether there has actually been a 'delay' requires some standard or yardstick as to what amounts to a reasonable period of time in the circumstances. In many contexts, public bodies have service standards which specify the amount of time that decisions and actions will take. If the time taken has been unreasonable, it may amount to delay and maladministration. Deciding whether delay has occurred also requires knowledge of the relevant administrative system, the pressures it labours under and also an assessment of whether the amount of time has been unreasonable in the circumstances. There can be no uniform standard across all administrative contexts, although there is a point at which delay goes beyond being unreasonable and becomes a substantive denial.[130]

Delay can then be understood as a function of fluctuating variables: the demands placed upon government; its resources and capacity; and the needs of individuals affected. The demands on government change over time, leading to more applicants than the system is able to cope with. Alternatively, the demands remain the same, but resources are reduced. Either way, delays will likely arise. Other variables can come into play. For instance, certain people within the same broad cohort may have good reason to be considered more quickly than others. Alternatively, the nature of individuals' cases can change. It is easier for government to make decisions on straightforward applications, but more complex cases can take longer.

Delay can be specific to an individual or it can be systemic by affecting a whole cohort of people or a significant proportion of them. If a prolonged period of time is taken in one case, then pushing just that person's case to the front of the queue will likely have little effect on the timeliness of incoming cases. However, wide-ranging systemic delays raise problems of different orders of magnitude, which in turn conditions both the assessment of whether it amounts to maladministration and its resolution. Further, while demand and resources are key determinants of timeliness and delay, there are other causes. Delay can become so deeply embedded in a particular administrative system that it just becomes a normalised part of its institutional culture and therefore all the more difficult to address.

The amount of time taken to make decisions and provide services raise operational and management challenges. Indeed, delay goes deep into the core of how government functions. This is especially the case for large high-volume process-based systems such as immigration and benefits. A significant albeit minor delay can soon spiral into major delays for incoming applications. Public bodies often operate on tight margins. They might want to retain some slack in the system to allow for exceptional and unexpected demands and circumstances. Matters can become complex in practice. Governmental decision-making processes often have different segments within them. For instance,

[130] 2 Co Inst 56 ('quia dilatio est quaedam negatio').

disability benefits involve: an assessment by a healthcare professional, an entitlement decision, a mandatory reconsideration, review upon receipt of an appeal and then a tribunal appeal. An increase in claims can cause delays in the assessment stage, which becomes overloaded, whereas the later decision-making stage has insufficient workload. In some systems, it will be possible to move staff around from one workstream to another or appoint new staff. In other contexts, this is not possible. In any event, simply shifting staff around may cause delays elsewhere. Further, appointing and training new staff takes time. For instance, when tribunals experience delays, the solution is to appoint more judges, but it takes a year to appoint and train tribunal judges. There is also the risk that new staff will make variable quality decisions, thereby generating onward challenges and thus increasing delays.

Delay has a range of negative consequences for those concerned. Indeed, delay emerges as a distinct form of governmental power which exists over and above government's formal powers to make decisions and deliver services. By keeping people waiting, government prevents them from continuing with their lives. People are left feeling powerless, thereby reinforcing and exacerbating the structural power asymmetries and the individual's lack of choice. People can spend considerable amounts of time – many months or years – with their lives placed on hold waiting for a government body to decide or act. This is often deeply frustrating because it involves the loss of time, 'the most valuable commodity of all'.[131] Such delays inevitably have wider substantive effects. People will be unable to access the services and entitlements to which they are entitled. Delays in issuing passports and driving tests have obvious consequences. Delays by councils have meant that children and young people with SEND have not received the educational provision and support they require. Delays in processing benefit decisions have meant that people have been placed in financial difficulty. Delays by Mental Health Tribunals have caused many patients to have negative experiences; a significant amount of distress occurs when patients are not informed about likely timescales.[132] NHS delays impact people's lives and health conditions. Many people experience two or more delays to their planned healthcare with little or no notice. Such delays can exacerbate the health issue for which someone was originally referred. Those who experience multiple delays are most likely to face health inequalities, including disabled people and those on lower incomes.[133] In 2023, it was reported that patient deaths arising directly from care delays had increased more than fivefold over the preceding three years. People had been removed from health waiting lists without being told why or without being told at all.[134] Reducing NHS waiting lists is an enormously complex issue raising wider issues of workforce, resources and preventive measures.

A common situation occurs when demand on a service increases and capacity is reduced. Delays in making decisions can lead to complaints and then delays in the handling of complaints and the build-up of backlogs of both assessments and

[131] Seneca, 'On the Shortness of Life' in Seneca, *Dialogues and Essays* (Oxford, Oxford University Press, 2007) 147.

[132] Administrative Justice and Tribunals Council and the Care Quality Commission, *Patients' Experiences of the First-tier Tribunal (Mental Health)* (London, AJTC, 2011).

[133] Healthwatch, *Cancelled Care Research* (2023).

[134] 'NHS Care Delays in England Harmed 8,000 People and Caused 112 Deaths Last Year' *The Guardian* (27 November 2023).

complaints. The dilemma is then whether to prioritise making decisions or resolving complaints. Backlogs and delays can take a lot of time and effort to clear. Indeed, backlogs have become an endemic feature of some decision systems. Delay can be the first administrative justice problem someone experiences before other problems then potentially arise, such as the quality of decisions and then the provision of entitlements. The problems increase when the handling of complaints about the initial delays is delayed.

One of the worst areas of government for delay is immigration. For decades, the Home Office has struggled to process huge repetitive cycles of immigration and asylum delays. Many people have been left in state of 'immigration limbo'. In Dante's *Inferno*, limbo is the first circle of hell, the place where souls who had never sinned were condemned to suffer harm through living in desire, but without hope.[135] Similarly, many asylum claimants and immigrants have waited months, years and sometimes decades for their status to be resolved.[136] Living in a constant state of limbo and uncertainty for years on end has a profound impact on people's mental health. Living a 'frozen life' in limbo means that people's control or agency over their own lives is replaced by an overwhelming uncertainty about their future and how long they have to wait for a decision, thereby leading to high levels of distress.[137] Asylum claimants in limbo have higher rates of post-traumatic stress disorder (PTSD), depression and anxiety than those given refugee status.[138] The lives of many asylum claimants have become so completely intertwined with and indeed emasculated by a faceless bureaucracy, which then becomes the defining, oppressive and pervasive form of control over them. People can become afraid of interacting with the Home Office for fear of arbitrary treatment, but remain entirely dependent upon it. This is a bleak and alienating world in which some people become almost permanently trapped within a complex bureaucratic system of rules, procedures and decisions, unable to communicate with or escape from the Home Office or to progress with their lives. Such limbo exceeds the delays arising from inadequate resourcing and itself becomes a means of immigration control to deter, control and punish irregular

[135] Dante, *Inferno* (London, Penguin, 2006) canto 4.

[136] 'Revealed: Asylum Seekers' 20-Year Wait for Home Office Ruling' *The Guardian* (17 August 2018); Refugee Council, *Living in Limbo: A Decade of Delays in the UK Asylum System* (London, Refugee Council, 2021); 'Sri Lankan Man Left in Immigration Limbo for Decades Can Stay in UK' *The Guardian* (30 January 2022). A Sri Lankan Tamil man, Mr Jothibala, spent nearly 40 years in immigration limbo. During a lengthy immigration history, he had at one point won his deportation appeal, only for the Home Office to have mistakenly recorded on his file that he had lost rather than won his appeal, although it then took no action to remove him. His lawyer noted that 'this case is a sobering reminder of how a historic injustice can devastate a person's life'. Mr Jothibala said he was overjoyed his case had finally been resolved, even though he was now 'an old man'. See also 'Home Office Refuses to Speed up Visa Case of Woman with Terminal Cancer' *The Guardian* (19 September 2022); Greater Manchester Immigration Aid Unit, *'We Lost Our Lives When We Arrived Here': Children in the UK's Asylum System* (Manchester, GMIAU, 2023).

[137] A Cortvriend, 'Coping with Vulnerability: The Limbo Created by the UK Asylum System' (2020) 9 *International Journal for Crime, Justice and Social Democracy* 61; C Hvidtfeldt, J Holm Petersen and M Norredam, 'Prolonged Periods of Waiting for an Asylum Decision and the Risk of Psychiatric Diagnoses: A 22-Year Longitudinal Cohort Study from Denmark' (2020) 49 *International Journal of Epidemiology* 400; C van Eggermont Arwidson et al, 'Living a Frozen Life: A Qualitative Study of Asylum Seekers' Experiences and Care Practices at Accommodation Centers in Sweden' (2022) 16 *Conflict and Health* 47.

[138] M Côté-Olijnyk, J Christopher Perry, M-È Paré and R Kronick, 'The Mental Health of Migrants Living in Limbo: A Mixed-Methods Systematic Review with Meta-analysis' (2024) 337 *Psychiatry Research* 115931.

migration.[139] At the same time, asylum delays and backlogs also increase the costs to the taxpayer of providing asylum support and accommodation. The Home Office has also been criticised for its delays in enforcing immigration control and for not removing those with no right to remain.

The COVID-19 pandemic caused significant pressure upheaval on many government systems. The NHS was already struggling with delays, but the pandemic presented an immediate new pressure which exacerbated those pre-existing delays. The pandemic also caused delays in the criminal courts, children's and mental health services, adoption and family support services, benefits and asylum.[140] In other areas, the pandemic reduced routines pressures, but with the ending of lockdowns, increased demands returned. For instance, following the removal of travel restrictions in 2022, the Passport Office received a record number of applications, which it had anticipated. Nonetheless, hundreds of thousands of people experienced delays and some were unable to travel for family emergencies, lost money on holidays and had difficulties proving their identities.

Delays also arise when government introduces a new system or replaces an old system, but also under-estimates the demand and work involved owing to poor planning.[141] In 2000, a new scheme of farm payments ran into significant delays as a result of poor planning, under-resourcing, inadequate information and the failure to administer the scheme correctly.[142] Five years later, another scheme ran into similar problems thereby creating acute hardship and financial difficulties for farmers. The Rural Payments Agency had also failed to communicate properly with farmers and organise its work appropriately.[143] The PHSO eventually secured compensation payments for a small number of farmers, although its investigation took two years to complete.[144] The underlying causes here included ministerial pressures to roll out new schemes before they were ready, optimism bias within government and a good news culture.

Another case to consider here is the introduction of PIP from 2012 onwards, which was marked by extensive delays. The DWP had expected to assess almost three million claims (from existing Disability Living Allowance claimants and new claims). It had planned to decide claims within 12–15 weeks. In fact, there were widespread delays of six months and more. Many people affected had nothing to live on resulting in stress and uncertainty. Complaints to MPs were passed back and forth between the DWP and

[139] J Lelliott, 'Unaccompanied Children in Limbo: The Causes and Consequences of Uncertain Legal Status' (2022) 34 *International Journal of Refugee Law* 1.

[140] 'Backlog Britain: How Public Sector Delays Spiralled to Record Levels' *Financial Times* (22 November 2022).

[141] Parliamentary Commissioner for Administration, *Delays in Handling Disability Living Allowance Claims* (HC 1992–93, 652); Parliamentary Commissioner for Administration, *Investigation of Complaints against the Child Support Agency* (HC 1994–95, 135).

[142] PHSO, *Investigation into Delays in Making Payments under the Arable Area Payments Scheme* (HC 1999–2000, 635).

[143] National Audit Office, *The Delays in Administering the 2005 Single Payment Scheme in England* (HC 2005–06, 1631); House of Commons Environment, Food and Rural Affairs Committee, *The Rural Payments Agency and the Implementation of the Single Payment Scheme* (HC 2006–07, 107).

[144] PHSO, *Cold Comfort: The Administration of the 2005 Single Payment Scheme by the Rural Payments Agency* (HC 2009–10, 81); PHSO, *More Cold Comfort: How the Rural Payments Agency Handled Claims to the Single Payment Scheme in 2005–06* (HC 2010–12, 1662).

the contracted-out assessment providers, with neither accepting responsibility for the delays or for providing an update on progress on claims. There was scrutiny by the NAO and the Public Accounts Committee.[145] The High Court also heard a test case concerning two claimants who had waited many months for initial decisions – far longer than the DWP's intended timescale of 15 weeks. The court issued a declaration that the claimant's delays were unreasonable, but refused a wider remedy.[146]

The DWP had significantly under-estimated the number of assessments required and the amount of time they would take. To secure contracts from the DWP, contractors had exaggerated their capacity to undertake the assessments. They had then failed to provide a timely acceptable service to claimants. Ministers had also decided to accelerate the roll-out of PIP, thereby overriding the Department's plans. The purpose was, no doubt, to realise the intended financial savings of introducing PIP by re-assessing claimants and stopping their benefits. There had also been administrative errors for claimants in arranging medical assessment appointments, leading to backlogs at every stage of the process. The DWP responded by hiring more staff and requiring its contractors to hire more medical assessors. The delays later reduced somewhat, although concern shifted to the variable quality of medical assessments. The DWP later introduced a fast-track process for terminally ill claimants.

The episode illustrates the complexity and huge logistical challenges of managing large-scale operations, the difficulties of moving from one benefit system to another and the coordination challenges that arise when government contracts out a key part of a service. Even so, government should be able to mitigate these risks by having contingency plans. In this instance, the DWP had to contend with two variables: the behaviours of the private contractors and the political intervention of ministers to accelerate the roll-out of PIP. Both were major destabilising factors. The DWP was eventually able to recover the situation, although only after many claimants had experienced significant distress. The episode again illustrates the importance of the NAO and the Public Accounts Committee in providing direct scrutiny of government and their role in the administrative justice arena. Delays with PIP assessments later resurfaced. In 2022, some 327,000 claimants were waiting five months for an assessment.[147] In 2023–24, only 52 per cent of PIP claims were processed within the 75-day standard, although this was a considerable improvement.[148] The DWP appointed more caseworkers to undertake reviews of claimants' PIP awards without assessments where possible, although this can weaken the quality of decisions. Other efficiency measures included telephone

[145] House of Commons Work and Pensions Committee, *Monitoring the Performance of the Department for Work and Pensions in 2012–13* (HC 2013–14, 1153); National Audit Office, *Personal Independence Payment: Early Progress* (HC 2013–14, 1070); House of Commons Public Accounts Committee, *Personal Independence Payment* (HC 2014–15, 280); M Hodge, *Called to Account: How Corporate Bad Behaviour and Government Waste Combine to Cost Us Millions* (London, Little Brown, 2016) 321–31.

[146] *R (C and W) v Secretary of State for Work and Pensions* [2015] EWHC 1607 (Admin); P Butler, 'Disabled Payment Delay Unlawful, Judge Rules' *The Guardian* (5 June 2015).

[147] Citizens Advice, 'PIP Delays Leave Disabled People Hundreds of Millions of Pounds out of Pocket' (6 July 2022); P Butler, 'Five-Month Disability Benefits Delay Causing Hardship, Says Citizens Advice' *The Guardian* (6 July 2022).

[148] National Audit Office, *DWP Customer Service* (HC 2024–25, 127) [20]. See also House of Commons Accounts Committee, *DWP Follow-up: Autumn 2025* (HC 2024–25, 1447).

assessments and light-touch 10-year reviews for those with the most severe conditions, on the highest level of support.[149]

What then of redress against administrative delay? Mere delay alone is insufficient to justify intervention by the courts. There must be some additional feature(s) which makes the delay unlawful. The reason for judicial caution is that pushing one person up the queue will only have the effect of pushing others down, thereby encouraging others to seek judicial review, which could generate more judicial review claims and delays in the courts. Another reason is that delays often arise because of inadequate resourcing, which the courts are, generally speaking, unwilling to consider. The general tenor of the case law is while delay may be maladministration, additional features are required for it to be unlawful. The courts have intervened on systemic delays when personal liberty was concerned. For instance, delays by mental health tribunals led to detainees being denied timely access to justice concerning the deprivation of their liberty.[150] Further, if someone has an established right to an important benefit (for example, refugee status) and all that is required is its formal grant, then the courts have held that government should act without unreasonable delay.[151] By contrast, asylum applicants who experience delay are unlikely to succeed unless the delay is manifestly unreasonable.[152] Delay alone without some additional legal dimensions or heightened factors is highly unlikely to succeed through judicial review. The result is a Balkanised fact-specific case law.[153]

Tribunals are similarly unable to address delays. They only become seized of a case once a person has appealed. Delays in making initial decisions cannot be appealed because there is no initial decision to appeal against. Moreover, tribunals cannot inquire into maladministration preceding a decision. Consequently, initial administrative delays can infect tribunals by delaying or preventing access to them. This enables government to exert indirect influence over tribunals, thereby weakening their structural independence. Indeed, there has sometimes been a ratcheting-up effect, as illustrated by the use of one redress mechanism (for example, an ombudsman) to investigate delays by

[149] B Smith, 'DWP Hiring More Caseworkers to Tackle PIP Review Delays, Minister Says' *Civil Service World* (3 October 2024), www.civilserviceworld.com/professions/article/pip-review-delay-dwp-hiring-more-caseworkers-stephen-timms.

[150] *R (KB) v Mental Health Review Tribunal* [2002] EWHC 639 (Admin); [2003] EWHC 193 (Admin); [2004] QB 936.

[151] *R v Secretary of State for the Home Department ex p Phansopkar* [1976] 1 QB 606 (CA); *R v Secretary of State for the Home Department ex p Mersin* [2000] INLR 51 (HC).

[152] *R (FH) v Secretary of State for the Home Department* [2007] EWHC 1571 (Admin).

[153] See, eg, *MJ v Secretary of State for the Home Department* [2010] EWHC (Admin) 1800; *R (AO) v Secretary of State for the Home Department* [2011] EWHC 110 (Admin); *R (RSM (A Child)) v Secretary of State for the Home Department* [2018] EWCA Civ 18; [2018] Imm AR 759 (CA); *R (TM (A Minor) by His Litigation Friend, the Official Solicitor) v Secretary of State for the Home Department* (Minor – asylum – delay) [2018] UKUT 00299 (IAC). The JUSTICE-All Souls Review, *Administrative Justice: Some Necessary Reforms* (Oxford, Oxford University Press, 1988) 362 recommended a legal right to compensation for losses arising from unreasonable or excessive delay, but this did not find favour. A key issue is how financial remedies would affect governmental behaviour; would they really induce government to improve or (more likely) just exacerbate its difficulties by 'robbing Peter to pay Paul'? In any event, the debate over the whole issue of monetary remedies was effectively killed off by the Treasury: see R Percival, 'The Challenge of Public Law Law Reform: Reflections on a Failed Law Commission Project' (2019) 41 *Journal of Social Welfare and Family Law* 372. The LGSCO has recommended substantial financial remedies, especially in SEND cases (eg, £10,000 for missed provision), although this may change and matters would likely be different if the total costs fell directly on central government(?).

a public body which have resulted in the denied or delayed access to another redress mechanism (for example, a tribunal). For instance, the LGSCO has criticised councils for their delays in forwarding certain appeals (for example, housing benefit and council tax reduction) to tribunals, with the result that access to a tribunal is then delayed.[154] People have then complained to the LGSCO about the delay incurred in trying to access tribunals. In the SEND context, some families have lost their appeal rights to the First-tier Tribunal (SEND) because of delays by councils.[155] It is a bizarre and dysfunctional situation in which a person denied access to a tribunal is then compelled to complain to the ombudsman to resolve matters.

Some systems do make specific provision for delay. Planning applications must be accompanied by a fee. If the application is not resolved within 26 weeks, then the fee must be refunded to the applicant, unless a longer period has been agreed.[156] Some councils have both delayed considering planning applications and then failed, through ignorance of the law, to refund the fees paid.[157] There is also the 'deemed refusal'. If an applicant does not receive a decision within a stated timescale (for example, three months), then it is deemed to have been refused, thereby generating a right of appeal. For obvious reasons, neither the DWP nor the Home Office has displayed any interest in this.

Delay has been principally scrutinised by ombudsmen and other non-judicial mechanisms. Delay is maladministration.[158] Thousands of LGSCO decisions have criticised council delays in making decisions, considering complaints and providing services. When delays have afflicted entire services (for example, SEND, social housing or Deprivation of Liberty Safeguards), the LGSCO has recommended that the

[154] LGSCO, 'More Than 500 Bradford Benefit Claimants to Have Their Appeal Rights Acknowledged Following Ombudsman Investigation' (2017); LGSCO, City of Bradford Metropolitan District Council (16016522); LGSCO, 'Luton Told to Fix Benefits Backlog by Ombudsman' (2024); LGSCO, Luton Borough Council (23016145) (six years to forward housing benefit appeals to the tribunal when it should have taken four weeks); LGSCO, London Borough of Lewisham (15019725) (the council did not forward a housing benefit appeal to tribunal, but rejected it as being out of time; enforcement agents were then sent to the woman's home to collect the outstanding amounts, generating a further LGSCO investigation); LGSCO, Birmingham City Council (23007528) (the council failed to acknowledge or accept a woman's appeal to the Valuation Tribunal against its decision on council tax reduction, thereby delaying her appeal rights).

[155] LGSCO, 'Oxfordshire Fails to Provide Alternative Education for a Year' (2022); LGSCO, Oxfordshire County Council (21009723); LGSCO, Royal Borough of Greenwich (20013834) (a delay by the council in completing an EHCP assessment delayed the parent's right to appeal by nine months; the child missed out on educational provision; the council also failed to assess social care needs which delayed provision by 14 months; further delay in securing therapy after a Tribunal decision); LGSCO, 'Devon Teen Missed out on Education Because of Council Delays' (3 March 2022); Devon County Council (20008832); LGSCO, 'Vulnerable Cambridgeshire Boy Left without Education for 14 Months' (28 April 2022); LGSCO, Cambridgeshire County Council (20013354); LGSCO, 'Suffolk Girl with Special Educational Needs Left without Vital Therapy' (30 June 2022); LGSCO, Suffolk County Council (21003011); LGSCO, 'Hampshire Council did not Arrange Transport for Boy with Special Needs in Time' (11 August 2022); LGSCO, Hampshire County Council (21004383).

[156] Town and Country Planning Act 1990, s 303(5); Town and Country Planning (Fees for Applications, Deemed Applications, Requests and Site Visits) (England) Regulations, SI 2012/2920, reg 16(2).

[157] 'Bolton Council Faces £100k Pay-out over Planning Blunder' *BBC News* (23 November 2023), www.bbc.co.uk/news/uk-england-manchester-67500497. By contrast, there are long delays in planning enforcement: LGSCO, 'Ombudsman Warns Councils are "Losing Control" of Planning Enforcement as Complaints Increasingly Reveal Years-Long Delays' (17 February 2026).

[158] Delay was included within the Crossman catalogue.

council devise an action plan setting out how it will reduce processing times downwards.[159] The PHSO has criticised large-scale delays concerning benefits, immigration and farm payments, amongst others.[160] Ombudsmen have highlighted the impact of delay and raised its profile as a public issue. There are differences of approach between different ombudsmen. The PHSO will not usually consider a delay to be maladministration if it has arisen as a result of increased or unprecedented demand on a service or if that service has been oversubscribed. If something has gone wrong or if the delay was unnecessary, then that will be maladministration.[161] By contrast, the LGSCO takes a tougher line towards councils, especially in the SEND context where timescales are mandatory.

The NAO and select committees have also examined systemic delays by evaluating efforts to reduce delays,[162] delays in implementing new digital architecture systems (for example, the pensions dashboards) and passport and driving licence delays.[163] The Public Accounts Committee has criticised immigration delays which have cost billions in terms of providing support and accommodation to asylum claimants. It also raised concerns about the Home Office's plan to reduce the backlog by introducing poorly designed questionnaires and assuming that claims would be withdrawn, which meant that genuine claimants might not have their claims properly considered. Further, the Home Office did not understand how making more asylum decisions would impact upon other parts of the system, thereby likely shifting the backlogs elsewhere.[164] The implementation of the HMCTS court reform programme has experienced delays because it consistently under-estimated the scale and complexity of the reforms and multiple technical and design problems.[165] The principal effects of non-judicial scrutiny of delay are to highlight the issue and to flag it up as a matter that government needs to address. Reports from the NAO and the Public Accounts Committee have an immediacy which others, including ombudsmen, typically lack. Ombudsmen undertake retrospective scrutiny of past delays with the intention of highlighting this for the purpose of future improvements. By contrast, the NAO and the Public Accounts

[159] See, eg, LGSCO, Birmingham City Council (20007658); LGSCO, Surrey County Council (22014808); LGSCO, Kent County Council (22004403); LGSCO, 'Family of Disabled Boy Left without Housing Adaptations Because of Council Delay' (2021); LGSCO, London Borough of Haringey (19020651); LGSCO, 'Man Denied Human Rights Because of Council Delay' (2021); LGSCO, Nottinghamshire County Council (19015363); LGSCO, 'Staffordshire Council Missed Multiple Deadlines Reviewing Girl's Special Needs Plans' (2021); LGSCO, Staffordshire County Council (20000770); LGSCO, 'Nearly 60% of Eligible Tameside Children Waited More Than Eight Months for Education Support Plan Update, Ombudsman Reports' (2025); LGSCO, Tameside Metropolitan Borough Council (24000621).

[160] Parliamentary Commissioner for Administration (n 141); PHSO (n 142 and 144); PHSO, *'Fast and Fair?' A Report by the Parliamentary Ombudsman on the UK Border Agency* HC 329 (2009–10); SN McMurtie, 'The Waiting Game: The Parliamentary Commissioner's Response to Delay in Administrative Procedures' [1997] *PL* 159.

[161] PHSO, *Investigation into UK Visas and Immigration* (31 October 2024).

[162] National Audit Office, *Reducing the Backlog in the Crown Court* (HC 2023–24, 728); 'Court Delays "Driving Innocent Prisoners to Please Guilty" in England and Wales' *The Guardian* (9 December 2024).

[163] National Audit Office, *Investigation into the Pensions Dashboards Programme* (HC 2023–24, 732); House of Commons Public Accounts Committee, *Driving Licence Backlogs at the DVLA* (HC 2022–23, 735).

[164] House of Commons Public Accounts Committee, *The Asylum Transformation Programme* (HC 2022–23, 1334).

[165] House of Commons Public Accounts Committee, *Progress on the Courts and Tribunals Reform Programme* (HC 2022–23, 1002).

Committee can highlight systemic delays as they occur and not merely as a result of individual complaints.

Delay also afflicts redress institutions. At various times, there have been extensive delays with administrative reviews, complaint-handling, tribunals, ombudsmen and the courts. There have been occasions in which increased appeal volumes have overwhelmed social security and immigration tribunals, leading to delays.[166] There have been many occasions across tribunals in which appeal volumes have built up, with high numbers of cases waiting to be heard by too few tribunal judges.[167] Delay has been a cause of dissatisfaction with tax tribunals. There have been long delays in the listing of appeals for hearings and delays of up to a year in tribunal judges issuing their decisions.[168] There is also the familiar low-level problem of procedural non-compliance by government, creating delays for tribunals and appellants.[169] In some respects, tribunals can take account of initial delays when deciding appeals. Home Office delays when deciding whether removal would breach a person's right to private and family life may be relevant in reducing the weight to be attached to immigration control if the delay results from 'a dysfunctional system which yields unpredictable, inconsistent and unfair outcomes'.[170] By contrast, the Upper Tribunal has held that the Home Office's delay of a decade in deciding to deprive a person of their citizenship, acquired through fraud and deception, did not enable the appellant to succeed because of the requirements of immigration control and ensuring that people did not gain citizenship fraudulently.[171]

The poor handling of complaints by government can create avoidable and necessary delay. In the 1990s, many people complained about the Child Support Agency, with onward complaints being considered by the second-tier complaints body, the Independent Case Examiner (ICE). However, the Child Support Agency often provided

[166] J Tomlinson and E Kasoulide, 'Delays and Backlogs as an Administrative Justice Problem: Reflections on the Case of the UK's Immigration and Asylum Tribunal' in S Thomson, M Groves and G Weeks (eds) *Administrative Tribunals in the Common Law World* (Oxford, Hart Publishing, 2024).

[167] For instance, in *MA (Somalia) v Secretary of State for the Home Department* (UTIAC) (PA/04147/2016, 2023), a First-tier Tribunal judge promulgated his decision some 11 months after the hearing. Consequently, the decision failed to engage with significant parts of the evidence and was remitted to be re-heard afresh. In *SM v Secretary of State for Work and Pensions* [2017] UKUT 336 (AAC), an Upper Tribunal judge noted that it was 'simply inexcusable' for HMCTS admin staff to take two months to issue a judge's directions to the parties: 'there will always be pressures of work and staff shortages within HMCTS but a system should have been in place to prioritise directions such as these'.

[168] Tax Law Review Committee of the Institute for Fiscal Studies, *The Tax Tribunals: The Next 10 Years* (London, IFS, 2021).

[169] In 2019, a First-tier Tribunal (Social Entitlement Chamber) judge criticised the DWP for non-compliance with tribunal directions by failing to produce relevant evidence: 'This non-compliance appears endemic and is taking up significant First-tier Tribunal time which could be used more productively. More pertinently it is having a knock-on effect of causing serious delays and prejudice to appellants.' The DWP responded that it had not intended to ignore instructions and that operational officers had been informed of the concerns. Compliance with directions by the Upper Tribunal or the First-tier Tribunal is mandatory, but the situation and attendant problems will be familiar to anyone aware of the realities of tribunal practice. Why not refer every instance of non-compliance to the Upper Tribunal? As the judge explained: 'I have had to issue a summons with a penal notice in two appeals in order to get the DWP to issue the documentation … The summons achieved its aim but non-compliance caused satellite litigation and took up valuable time and resources. If I were to issue a summons in each and every case where there was non-compliance, I would cease hearing substantive appeals': *NW v Secretary of State for Work and Pensions* [2019] UKUT 150 (AAC).

[170] *EB (Kosovo) v Secretary of State for the Home Department* [2008] UKHL 41; [2009] 1 AC 1159 (HL) [16].

[171] *Hysaj v Secretary of State for the Home Department* (Deprivation of Citizenship: Delay) [2020] UKUT 00128 (IAC).

the ICE with incorrect and incomplete information about complainants' cases.[172] The effect was to delay the ICE's investigation of those complaints. More recently, the ICE developed its own backlogs so that complaints accepted for investigation would remain lying around within the ICE for some 18 months before being properly opened for investigation.[173] The effect is that redress bodies become tainted and infected by the delays of public bodies. In 2024, the current wait times for complaints to be looked at by the PHSO were up to seven months for NHS complaints and four months for complaints against central government.

What can realistically be done about delay? The responses to delay are as varied as its causes and will differ from one context to another. A common assumption is that delays arise because government bodies are under-resourced. If public bodies were better resourced, then existing delays could be addressed and new backlogs prevented. Indeed, being criticised for delay can potentially strengthen the hand of public bodies in their requests for additional resources. For instance, the Home Office built up a large backlog of modern slavery cases concerning victims of trafficking and abuse who then experienced prolonged uncertainty and anguish as a result of long delays by the Home Office in considering their cases.[174]

However, additional resources may not be forthcoming. Other responses can be highly controversial, such as reducing delays by limiting or curtailing substantive and process rights, such as jury trials.[175] Alternative responses include better communication with people about the timescales involved. Most people will tolerate some degree of delay, but may feel aggrieved about unexplained and unjustifiable delays. Something as simple as sending people text messages can keep them informed about progress. Another response is redesigning systems through technological solutions and automation. This can make systems more efficient by increasing their productivity and capacity. This has worked successfully in many mundane systems, such as passports. There is a long history of delays in people renewing their passports, leading to some being unable to travel.[176] Paper applications have now been replaced with an online application process and a resolution hub to improve the customer experience by reducing the number of contacts a customer query passes through before being resolved, thereby improving the customer experience.

Overall, delay is a stubborn and persistent problem. The prospects for reducing it seem very small. Delays arise. They are criticised. Government scrambles to rectify matters. Then delays occur elsewhere – and so on. The nature, scale and causes of administrative delay impede and confound most attempts to deal with it. Ombudsmen and select committees can highlight delays and possibly induce government to take action. They have some, albeit limited, impact, but the effects are usually short-term and

[172] Independent Case Examiner, *Annual Report 2012–13* (London, DWP, 2013) 12.

[173] '"Obscene" 18-Month Delay for DWP Complaints' *BBC News* (1 February 2020), www.bbc.co.uk/news/business-51326471.

[174] 'Home Office Hires 200 Staff to Clear Huge Backlog of UK Modern Slavery Cases' *The Guardian* (18 October 2024).

[175] 'Starmer Faces Rebellion over Plan to Cut Jury Trials' *BBC News* (18 December 2025), www.bbc.co.uk/news/articles/c93w771g14go; 'Slashing Jury Trials Could Clear Courts Backlog within a Decade, says Lammy' *The Guardian* (11 January 2026).

[176] House of Commons Public Accounts Committee, *Investigation into the UK Passport Office* (HC 2022–23, 738).

mixed. As with almost all problems of administrative justice, addressing delay requires more effective action by government itself.

Conclusion

The pathologies examined in this chapter highlight some disheartening and uncomfortable realities of administrative justice. Across many significant areas of government, administrative justice largely fails – or, at the very minimum, its effectiveness is deeply compromised. This is in large part because of the inherent nature of the tasks it has to grapple with. The difficulties are caused by the wider social, economic, political and organisational forces and the merciless realities of insufficient resources. These factors condition and determine the institutional behaviours of government. They also constrain the effectiveness of external redress mechanisms. The nature of determining eligibility for resource-dependent services often prompts officials to resort to underhand tactics – fobbing off, gatekeeping and delay – to ration services, limit demand and weaken access to redress mechanisms, and to reduce their impact. The disciplinary imperatives and mindset that underpin contexts concerning prisons, school exclusions and benefit sanctions have been accompanied by weakened procedural rights. Administrative delay is a pervasive and endemic source of administrative injustice. The nature and scale of such delay defeats most attempts to address it. The role of redress mechanisms is highly constrained. The next best thing has been for ombudsmen, the NAO and the media to highlight matters and thereby try to prompt government into corrective action. However, the problem of delay often resurfaces elsewhere. Overall, the reality is that, in many contexts, administrative justice is limited in terms of what it can achieve precisely because the capacity of government is itself constrained by the nature of the tasks for which it is responsible. Moreover, while these trends and pressures are a permanent rather than temporary feature of administrative justice, they have become more acute in recent years.

10

Conclusion

Administrative Justice Overall

It is time to consider administrative justice as a whole and its prospects. The principal argument for having administrative justice is that people are entitled to be treated fairly when they interact with government. Administrative justice covers a wide range of different areas of government activity and it affects millions of people. Each of us interacts with multiple administrative systems and public services. It is impossible not to do so. Everyone will have experience of some sort of avoidable administrative error or problem. Such problems will always arise. Everyone will appreciate that the inequality of power between the individual and government can reinforce the difficulties of trying to resolve matters.

From a higher level, administrative justice can be understood as one aspect of the wider relationship between the state and society. The state exercises power over people's lives to protect society and to provide public services. The expansion of such power comes with both benefits and risks. The benefits are that the state can become more effective and thereby enable people to have fulfilling lives. The risks are that government may exceed its powers, treat people unfairly or not fulfil its responsibilities. With the expansion of state power, there is a corresponding need for the state to be made accountable. One way of achieving this is through administrative justice. This means having redress institutions through which people can challenge government and make it accountable. It also means government itself acting fairly. The notion of administrative justice is deeply embedded in our social expectations as to how people should be treated when they interact with government.

This dynamic between the state and society motivated the growth and development of administrative justice. It was particularly pronounced during the formative period of the 1950s and 1970s. Following the creation of the post-war welfare state, there were widespread social concerns about the exercise of administrative power. Traditional parliamentary methods of scrutiny were unsuited to the task of checking the voluminous decisions and actions of the expanded welfare state. Whereas tribunals had existed for some time, they had been viewed as aberrations and suspect. However, tribunals were brought into the constitutional fold by the Franks Report, which recognised them to be essential. Redress also expanded during this period. New tribunals were created. An entirely new type of institution, the ombudsman, was established to investigate maladministration that had caused injustice. The ombudsman is one of the few examples of a successful exercise in comparative administrative law in which an institution from elsewhere was transplanted into UK public law. Moreover, the argument for and the push behind it came not from government, but from civil society. There was also explicit recognition that while redress after the event was important, nothing could make up for a wrong approach to administrative activity by officials. It was just as important for government to internalise the notion of administrative justice within its own procedures and methods. The fundamental aspects remain in place today. The whole episode embedded the notion of administrative justice within the post-war welfare state. It was a period of state-building in which the relationship between the state and society was adjusted in response to social concerns.

Administrative justice ebbs and flows. The 'Franks spirit' lasted for a few decades. It was very much a creature of its time. Things have long since moved on. Since 1979, successive governments have introduced new policies and ways of working: neoliberalism; the new public management; privatisation and outsourcing; and, since 2010, austerity policies. There have been both positive and negative developments. The creation of the First-tier and Upper Tribunals has been a successful and positive reform. Yet, administrative justice has also been weakened through austerity policies and reduced legal aid funding. There has been a preference for enhanced use of administrative review at the expense of tribunals and much criticism of the variable quality of initial decision-making. The Windrush scandal occurred as a result of the hostile immigration environment. Funding pressures in general have affected how public bodies deliver services and administer systems. The problem of rationing services has become more acute.

On the whole, many people within government would like to do better, although they are limited in terms of what they can do. Officials are aware of the weaknesses of their departments and public bodies. Yet, there are other indications that administrative justice is often a low priority. Two challenges are capacity and scale. Government is rarely the all-powerful entity it might appear to be from the outside. The reality of administrative justice within government is that an ever-changing body of junior caseworkers and officials are under pressure to churn out high volumes of decisions and actions irrespective of their quality. Many of the challenges of administrative justice are inherent. Problems such as poor decision-making, poor communications and systemic failures can never be fully and finally resolved. Getting the basics of administration right sometimes seems like an afterthought, although however hard government tries to improve, there will often be oversights and missed opportunities to do better. The contribution of administrative staff and professionals may be overlooked within government. Their views and voices may not be heard by senior officials. The degree of overload within government can generate a culture of 'if someone disagrees with a refusal decision, then they can always challenge it'. This attitude rationalises the variable quality of initial decisions. This may seem complacent and it is, but government bodies are not sufficiently funded and resourced to achieve the most effective and optimum levels of administrative performance. It would require considerable additional resources for the DWP to raise the quality of its initial decisions to the same standard as that of tribunals. A degree of poor decisions and maladministration are, to some extent, inevitable. Government may outsource delivery to the private sector because it is forced to do so by circumstances and a lack of sufficient resources, although this may simply exacerbate the problems and enable government to shift the blame elsewhere.[1]

[1] R Thomas, 'Does Outsourcing Improve or Weaken Administrative Justice? A Review of the Evidence' [2021] *PL* 542.

Administrative injustice is rarely the consequence of the deliberate abuse of power. Much more often, it arises because government lacks the institutional competence and capacity to do better. There are acute challenges in delivery complex public services. Inevitably, things go wrong. The public can rightly expect government to be competent, although viewed from the governmental perspective, such expectations are sometimes unrealistic. The demands placed on government can exceed its capacity to deliver services effectively and justly. Government is a function of the changing contexts in which it operates, the tensions within society, the appropriate balance between taxation and public spending, and how public services are organised and the cultures they embody.

There is a distinct negativity bias within the culture of administrative justice in which administrative injustice looms larger and has more of an impact than when government gets things right and people are treated justly. People feel aggrieved and criticise and blame government when things go wrong, but government often gets many things right for which it typically receives relatively little recognition. Most people are treated fairly and justly much of the time. In any event, the notion of getting things right is often ambiguous and indeterminant. Many individualised decisions involve the handling of evidence and the exercise of judgement. There is seldom a single objectively correct outcome. Furthermore, government sometimes finds itself in some challenging situations in which making a positive decision in favour of one person inevitably means making a negative decision for someone else. Such zero-sum situations are obviously unwelcome for those concerned. They can also be difficult, but necessary, decisions for officials to take.

Another feature (and inherent tension) of administrative justice is reflected in the distinction between autonomous and responsive law.[2] Autonomous law is the familiar model of rule-based and procedure-based model of court-centred adjudication. The focus is on handling and resolving each appeal or complaint on its own individual merits and by using fair procedures, and then turning to the next one. Autonomous law is based on the separation of law from politics. It gives legal institutions (such as tribunals) procedural autonomy at the expense of substantive subordination. Government makes the rules and tribunals decide appeals by applying those rules. The model of autonomous law has both strengths and weaknesses. Much administrative justice redress, such as tribunals and routine complaints, need to operate on the basis of stable low-risk procedures, which are separate from politics and which can deal with the vast bulk of the caseload. Most people just want their individual dispute to be resolved fairly, correctly and quickly. Keeping the show on the road is more than enough of a challenge for tribunals, given the unpredictability of their caseloads and the build-up of backlogs. On the other hand, the focus on individual routine dispute resolution means that wider matters, such as the underlying systemic patterns of poor decision-making and the wider injustices that arise, are not addressed.

The constraints of autonomous law generate pressures for more responsive law-style interventions. This involves being responsive to social needs, having a purposive orientation and diagnosing systemic and institutional failures. One principle of responsive law is that the burden of correcting of unlawfulness or injustice should not fall on the

[2] P Nonet and P Selznick, *Toward Responsive Law: Law & Society in Transition* (New Brunswick, NJ, Transaction Publishers, 1978).

individuals concerned; government should be capable of correcting itself. Individual errors should be understood not just as a prompting the need for individual resolution, but also for understanding and analysing their underlying systemic causes and the most appropriate means of correcting them. Government is responsible for implementing its policies and it should take responsibility to reduce and learn from its failures and from redress institutions. Responsive law involves diagnosing institutional problems and designing more effective institutional arrangements. Such an approach is entirely beyond the useful but limited role of tribunals. However, it has been reflected in some interventions by ombudsmen and the NAO. This is evident from various episodes of systemic administrative justice, such as the own-initiative investigations by the Northern Ireland Public Services Ombudsman, the Windrush Lessons Learned Review, and other ombudsmen and NAO reports into various systemic problems. These investigations examined the deeper causes of poor decisions and services by identifying weaknesses within the wider systems and processes, and the institutional cultures informing them. They resulted in wide-ranging recommendations that a court or tribunal could never have produced. Such responsive law interventions occur when the nature of administrative failings and the underlying social and political forces generate the need to move beyond the confines of a court-centred model of autonomous law into investigating systemic and institutional problems, which then opens government up to wider public accountability. Ombudsmen and other forms of non-judicial scrutiny are far more able than tribunals to pursue this type of scrutiny.

Nonetheless, such responsive law style interventions are very much the exception and their impact is highly variable. Such interventions are more ambitious in scale and scope because of their systemic character. Precisely for the same reasons, such responsive law interventions are also high-risk, precarious and contingent on the circumstances concerned. The success of responsive law depends on the political context and the degree to which government is compelled by social and political forces to recognise the systemic character of its failings and to improve the quality of its administration. The notion of systemic administrative justice has been recognised. At the same, there have been cycles of one systemic failure being scrutinised, only for new systemic failures to arise. The world of administrative justice is predominantly that of autonomous law interspersed with occasional responsive law interventions. Autonomous law has its benefits. In the vast majority of cases, it provides people with an adequate remedy. Autonomous law is also safe, conservative and low-risk because of its limited scope.

Despite the criticisms levelled against it, government is committed to administrative justice. Every year, government spends large amounts of money, time and effort on redress mechanisms and ensuring that they operate effectively. Tribunals are long-established. They are not perfect; no mechanism of governance is. However, they are independent and must deal with cases fairly and justly, and make reasoned decisions. Similar points can be made in relation to ombudsmen. By contrast, the quality of initial complaint-handling within government is much more variable. Public bodies overwhelmingly accept the findings and recommendations of ombudsmen. Non-compliance is not unknown, but it is rare and exceptional. The PHSO has undertaken a number of large investigations. The resolution of some of them has been protracted, but ultimately ombudsmen have been largely successful in securing redress for large numbers of people who had suffered injustice as a result of maladministration. While the DWP rejected financial compensation for women affected by the increase in their state pension age, it accepted the findings of maladministration and agreed to work with the PHSO to improve its communications. Similarly, other ombudsmen have made various recommendations to public bodies to improve their services, which have largely been accepted. Government also invests considerable effort, time and money in initial decision-making and administration. Austerity and funding reductions have affected the capacity of government to administer policy schemes effectively. Many people in government would like to improve the quality of initial decisions and public service delivery. However, it is often genuinely difficult to get the basics right within large and complex systems and processes which operate under funding pressures.

Reforms

How could administrative justice be enhanced? It is necessary to avoid advocating reforms that are either unrealistically ambitious or too modest. Proposals for the radical remodelling of current redress institutions are unlikely to win support. There is no prospect of tribunals and ombudsmen being amalgamated into a single all-purpose institution that would decide appeals, identify maladministration and recommend improvements. There is no developed model of what such an institution would look like and how it would operate – let alone the political will for it. The path-dependent nature of administrative justice needs to be recognised.

Nonetheless, some incremental reforms are possible. One area in need of urgent reform is the PHSO, a particularly rusty and out-of-date piece of machinery which has not been thoroughly reconsidered since it was established in the late 1960s. Ombudsman reform has been repeatedly delayed and kicked into the long grass. Access to the PHSO remains constrained by the MP filter. It lacks own-initiative powers. There is also the jurisdictional division of complaints against UK central government and English local government. The PHSO's constitutional standing has declined and stagnated over the years, as illustrated by the lack of interest shown by the House of Commons Public Administration and Constitutional Affairs Committee. By contrast ombudsmen in Wales, Northern Ireland and Scotland have been reformed along the lines of the single public services ombudsman. The idea of merging the PHSO and the LGSCO has been shelved. This would be a big project that would have significant risks in terms of ensuring the smooth and efficient operation of the day-to-day work of investigating complaints against both central government and English local authorities. The PHSO and the LGSCO are quite different types of ombudsmen. Nonetheless, such a merger would be achievable and should be considered as a long-term goal.

But if this is too ambitious, there remains a compelling case for enhancing the role of the PHSO. People's access to a national ombudsman should not be limited by the discredited MP filter. This should be replaced by a twin-track approach through which people could complain directly to the PHSO or go through their MP. The PHSO needs own-initiative powers. The lack of such powers restricts the ability of both the PHSO and the Scottish Public Services Ombudsman to investigate systemic maladministration.

Parliament and select committees should also take a greater interest in the PHSO's work, as was previously the case. The PHSO has been at its most effective when its reports have been used by the select committee to scrutinise government. These three simple reforms – abolition of the MP filter, own-initiative powers, and greater parliamentary and select committee interest in the PHSO's reports – would enhance administrative justice by enabling the PHSO to undertake more through investigations of systemic and other maladministration, and to identify improvements to administration and public services. Without reform, the PHSO will linger on, but it risks becoming increasingly marginal and moribund.

However, institutional reforms can only go so far. Just as important is the glue that binds together the formal structures and keeps it working in practice; the ethos of administrative justice and its attitude of mind. In this respect, the greatest area of need concerns the largest and most fragmented institutional machinery: government. It needs to take administrative justice more seriously. The requirements of administrative justice should be better incorporated into the training, socialisation and culture of public servants. Administrative justice needs to be better embedded within policy design and implementation and public service delivery. All public servants should be familiar with the principles of good administration. These principles should be part of the mindset and routines of government. Rather than viewing operational delivery as mundane, government needs to do more to raise the quality of initial decision-making. The high volumes of successful appeals in some contexts incur avoidable and unnecessary costs – to the individuals concerned, the taxpayer and government. Government should seek out and understand the causes of poor decision-making and take action to raise the quality of initial decision-making. Tribunals should be able to contribute such discussions without being concerned that this would somehow undermine the principle of judicial independence. Some senior presidents of tribunals have been willing to countenance this – provided that there are safeguards to protect judicial independence. Tribunals can usefully flag up problems with initial decision-making to government without undermining their independence. What is also required is a real commitment by government to take action to improve its decision-making. Similarly, government could make more efforts to improve the quality of initial complaint-handling.

Of course, all of this is a huge challenge. Trying to raise the quality of administrative justice within government depends heavily upon governmental willingness to improve systems, processes and institutional cultures. Indeed, institutional culture may well be the most pervasive feature. There is no neat and easy technocratic solution to the problems of administrative justice. Institutional cultures within government can generate systemic maladministration and make it appear unexceptional. Officials working within government can become so accustomed to their work practices and the assumptions underpinning them that systemic maladministration can become normalised. They can become so habituated to how things are done and labour under organisational pressures that they often lack the ability to detach themselves from it by adopting a fresh vantage point from which to understand the scale of the systemic maladministration. Identifying a dysfunctional institutional culture is one thing; changing it is quite another. Institutional culture deeply influences administrative behaviour. Culture is intangible, yet pervasive. It can change, but cannot be designed. The enveloping nature of institutional culture may be resistant to change. The complexity of the issues illustrates how many of the problems of administrative justice are inherent and permanent rather than temporary features. At the same time, there is little real alternative but to press on. Reports that call out public service failures provide a starting point for systemic and cultural changes, although the real work must necessarily be undertaken by government itself and this is a relentless challenge.

Another matter concerns the greater use of technology, in particular online hearings before tribunals and the use of AI and automated decision-making. This trend is unstoppable. AI and automation generate scope for a more effective and efficient administration and administrative justice. Changes in technology will affect how people interact with government and redress institutions. Technology has significant benefits in terms of making those interactions more efficient, less burdensome and accessible. It is natural that technology will be harnessed in these ways, although it also has its downsides and creates new risks and opportunities for injustice. It is also likely that the use of AI and automation will, by its very nature, generate systemic problems in large-scale decision-making contexts. The approach of government has sometimes been to resist scrutiny of its increasing use of AI. It is much more realistic for government to recognise the risks and to welcome informed scrutiny and criticism. What is required is a range of research projects to examine how effectively and fairly such technology is being used, and the degree to which it advances or hinders administrative justice. Government should support such research and carefully consider its findings. This needs to be accompanied by another shift of mindset within government towards greater recognition of systemic administrative justice. It is unlikely that government will ever welcome such scrutiny, although this is undoubtedly important. This reinforces the need for the PHSO to have own-initiative powers.

Finally, there is also the oversight of administrative justice. The Council on Tribunals (1958–2007) was reformed into the short-lived Administrative Justice and Tribunals Council (AJTC) (2007–13). It had an enhanced and wider remit to keep the administrative justice system under review to ensure that it was accessible, fair and efficient. The AJTC also had a role in promoting good quality administrative decision-making. It made efforts to fulfil its wider remit, although, given its short lifespan, it was unable to achieve its potential. It is still early days for the Administrative Justice Council (AJC). It has not to date challenged the government on a key issue of administrative justice in the same way in which the old Council on Tribunals occasionally did. One feature of the AJC is that it has always been chaired by a senior Court of Appeal judge, the Senior President of Tribunals. This likely cautions the AJC against speaking out on administrative justice issues and criticising government. It can also focus the AJC's attention upon procedure rather than substance and upon tribunals rather than ombudsmen and the wider realm of administrative justice. Furthermore, both the old Council on Tribunals and the AJTC were statutory and publicly funded bodies and could formally report on matters of concern to Parliament. The AJTC's oversight went beyond tribunals to include governmental decision-making and actions. It is certainly the case that the AJC is preferable to no oversight body at all, but it would clearly be better to re-establish the AJTC as an inexpensive and formal statutory body with a wider remit.

Envoi

The preceding suggested reforms could enhance administrative justice if the political will exists. However, such reforms can be jeopardised not just by governmental inertia and self-interest, but also by the wider forces which condition and limit government. What then are the prospects for administrative justice? Predicting the future is a hazardous occupation. Nonetheless, the current position offers diminishing scope for optimism. People's expectations of government and public services have grown to unrealistically high levels. On the other hand, there is the fiscal crisis, persistent low economic growth, high government debt and a pervasive sense of governmental malaise and failure. Government is now saddled with a large number of responsibilities which it struggles to perform or deliver adequately. It has reduced some entitlements to various public goods. Public spending pressures and reductions will likely affect substantive social programmes and redress institutions. Some contexts, such as immigration, are more vulnerable than others to the weakening of administrative justice. The already pathological character of many contexts of administrative justice may likely become more severe. At some stage, government may abandon some of its current responsibilities and, with them, the need for redress mechanisms.

The sense of malaise extends to redress and scrutiny institutions. Having gone through the motions of hearings and investigations, the decisions and reports of tribunals, complaint-handlers, ombudsmen, the NAO and select committees pile up on top of each other. It can reasonably be asked what real difference it all makes. Government may seek to patch and repair the problems, only for the same or new unforeseen problems to arise. The repetitive mantras of 'getting it right' and 'lessons must be learned' have become banal and empty clichés. People may receive some degree of justice from redress institutions – but only if they are sufficiently confident, supported and persistent enough to access them. Redress processes can themselves be dehumanising, alienating, suffer from delay and go wrong. Furthermore, because administrative justice is so intertwined with government, it can be afflicted by the same dysfunctions as government. Indeed, administrative justice can potentially exacerbate the problems. Consider, for instance, asylum claimants whose appeals and judicial review challenges are ultimately refused. How many are then actually removed from or leave the UK? Comparatively few. The Home Office's legitimate concern is that the tribunal system and legal challenges are often used to impede the legitimate enforcement of immigration control against people who are not in need of asylum. It is also worth considering SEND. The SEND Tribunal is both a judicial body and a mechanism for allocating resources from limited council budgets, but without itself having the responsibility for balancing those budgets. Some people have the confidence, resources and persistence to use the Tribunal to secure educational provision. By contrast, those who do not appeal (typically families experiencing socio-economic disadvantage) will likely lose out. The Local Government Association has criticised the Tribunal for prioritising the needs of the individual appellant rather than the wider needs of other children and young people who do not appeal. The consequence is a two-tier system. For this reason, there have been calls for the role of the SEND Tribunal to be replaced altogether with a non-judicial and non-legally binding redress mechanism.

The preceding points, all the compromises and difficulties of administrative justice and its unstable nature, confirm that it is not a 'problem' with a 'solution'. Administrative justice is not a puzzle that can be solved once and for all. Instead, it is a predicament, a dilemma that evolves over time. Administrative justice has its benefits and disadvantages. Justice for individuals is important, but it can only be secured by some cost to the taxpayer and delay for government. Moreover, it is impossible to prevent or to redress all injustices that occur. It is impossible for all refusal decisions to be appealed to tribunals or for all complaints to be investigated. There are distinct limits to the levels of financial redress that government can pay out following a big ombudsman investigation. A fair proportion of the resources devoted to administrative justice is spent by tribunals confirming decisions already taken and by ombudsmen and public bodies finding that there were no valid grounds for complaint.

If administrative justice is a predicament, then it follows that it cannot have a fixed destination. Buffeted around by political and other forces, there is no reason to assume that the path of administrative justice is necessarily one of continual progression and improvement. It is entirely possible that a future government may further weaken administrative justice in one way or another or that its current gradual downgrading will hollow it out. Indeed, given the wider pressures on government, positive reforms to administrative justice may seem an unrealistic goal. Simply hanging on to what currently exists might be considered to be a success. Government has in the past reformed and improved administrative justice as a result of social and political pressures and circumstances to do so. Yet, the threshold of public demands required to force the hand of government has since been elevated. The Crichel Down affair is from an entirely different age and now seems distinctly quaint compared with the range of contemporary systemic failures. Even so, no recent systemic failures have resulted in any significant changes to administrative justice equivalent to the establishment of ombudsmen following Crichel Down. Indeed, there have been so many large-scale systemic failures that they often compete with each other for attention and reinforce the sense of governmental incompetence and overload. Beneath this level, there remains a large body of hidden individual grievances, both genuine and misconceived.

Nonetheless, despite the political headwinds, systemic and other administrative justice failures still possess some ability to shock people. Public opinion is the most effective force that drives the development of and reinforces the need for administrative justice. It is also internalised by officials themselves. No government can afford to ignore administrative failures that have damaged people's trust and faith in public services. This provides some hope for the future.

Overall, administrative justice is well established and deeply embedded within governmental routines and operations and also society's expectations. Its most obvious manifestations are redress institutions, in particular tribunals and ombudsmen, although the largest part of it occurs within government and public services. The above reforms may seem somewhat modest, but if properly implemented, they could result in benefits in terms of improving and enhancing administrative justice. However, the tensions within the concept and practices of administrative justice are inherent and can never be fully resolved. The governmental need to implement policy and the need for fairness for individuals generate tensions which in turn drive the growth and development of administrative justice. When future large-scale failures arise, they provide an opportunity to push for some of the reforms outlined above. In the meantime, the work of and struggle for administrative justice will continue.

APPENDIX A

Parliamentary and Health Service Ombudsman, *Principles of Good Administration* (2007)

Good administration by public bodies means:

1. **Getting it right**
   - All public bodies must comply with the law and have regard for the rights of those concerned. They should act according to their statutory powers and duties and any other rules governing the service they provide. They should follow their own policy and procedural guidance, whether published or internal.
   - Public bodies must act in accordance with recognised quality standards, established good practice or both, for example about clinical care.
   - In some cases, a novel approach will bring a better result or service, and public bodies should be alert to this possibility. When they decide to depart from their own guidance, recognised quality standards or established good practice, they should record why.
   - Public bodies should provide effective services with appropriately trained and competent staff. They should plan carefully when introducing new policies and procedures. Where public bodies are subject to statutory duties, published service standards or both, they should plan and prioritise their resources to meet them.
   - In their decision making, public bodies should have regard to the relevant legislation. Decision making should take account of all relevant considerations, ignore irrelevant ones and balance the evidence appropriately.
   - Public bodies necessarily assess risks as part of taking decisions. They should, of course, spend public money with care and propriety. At the same time, when assessing risk, public bodies should ensure that they operate fairly and reasonably.
2. **Being customer focused**
   - Public bodies should provide services that are easily accessible to their customers. Policies and procedures should be clear and there must be accurate, complete and understandable information about the service.
   - Public bodies should aim to ensure that customers are clear about their entitlements; about what they can and cannot expect from the public body; and about their own responsibilities.
   - Public bodies should do what they say they are going to do. If they make a commitment to do something, they should keep to it, or explain why they cannot.

They should meet their published service standards, or let customers know if they cannot.
- Public bodies should behave helpfully, dealing with people promptly, within reasonable timescales and within any published time limits. They should tell people if things take longer than the public body has stated, or than people can reasonably expect them to take.
- Public bodies should communicate effectively, using clear language that people can understand and that is appropriate to them and their circumstances.
- Public bodies should treat people with sensitivity, bearing in mind their individual needs, and respond flexibly to the circumstances of the case. Where appropriate, they should deal with customers in a co-ordinated way with other providers to ensure their needs.

3. **Being open and accountable**
   - Public administration should be transparent and information should be handled as openly as the law allows. Public bodies should give people information and, if appropriate, advice that is clear, accurate, complete, relevant and timely.
   - Public bodies should be open and truthful when accounting for their decisions and actions. They should state their criteria for decision making and give reasons for their decisions.
   - Public bodies should handle and process information properly and appropriately in line with the law. So while their policies and procedures should be transparent, public bodies should, as the law requires, also respect the privacy of personal and confidential information.
   - Public bodies should create and maintain reliable and usable records as evidence of their activities. They should manage records in line with recognised standards to ensure that they can be retrieved and that they are kept for as long as there is a statutory duty or business need.
   - Public bodies should take responsibility for the actions of their staff.
4. **Acting fairly and proportionately**
   - Public bodies should always deal with people fairly and with respect. They should be prepared to listen to their customers and avoid being defensive when things go wrong.
   - Public bodies should treat people equally and impartially. They should understand and respect the diversity of their customers and ensure equal access to services and treatment regardless of background or circumstance.
   - The actions and decisions of a public body should be free from any personal bias or interests that could prejudice those actions and decisions, and any conflict of interests should be declared. Public bodies should not act in a way that unlawfully discriminates against or unjustifiably favours particular individuals or interests.
   - People should be treated fairly and consistently, so that those in similar circumstances are dealt with in a similar way. Any difference in treatment should be justified by the individual circumstances of the case.
   - When taking decisions, and particularly when imposing penalties, public bodies should behave reasonably and ensure that the measures taken are proportionate to the objectives pursued, appropriate in the circumstances and fair to the individuals concerned.

- If applying the law, regulations or procedures strictly would lead to an unfair result for an individual, the public body should seek to address the unfairness. In doing so public bodies must, of course, bear in mind the proper protection of public funds and ensure they do not exceed their legal powers.

5. **Putting things right**
   - When mistakes happen, public bodies should acknowledge them, apologise, explain what went wrong and put things right quickly and effectively.
   - Putting things right may include reviewing any decisions found to be incorrect; and reviewing and amending any policies and procedures found to be ineffective, unworkable or unfair, giving appropriate notice before changing the rules.
   - The actions of a well-run public body can sometimes bear more heavily on an individual because of their particular circumstances, even though statutory duties, service standards or both have been met. Public bodies should be alert to this and respond flexibly to avoid or, where appropriate, put right any such undue effect.
   - Public bodies should provide clear and timely information about methods by which people can appeal or complain. They should provide information about appropriate organisational or independent ways of resolving complaints. They should also consider providing information about possible sources of help for the customer, particularly for people who may find the complaints process daunting.
   - Public bodies should operate effective complaints procedures which investigate complaints thoroughly, quickly and impartially; and which can provide an appropriate range of remedies to the complainant and any others similarly affected when a complaint is upheld. As a minimum, an appropriate range of remedies should include an explanation and apology from the public body to the complainant, remedial action by the public body, financial compensation for the complainant or a combination of these. The remedy offered should seek to put the complainant back in the position they would have been in if nothing had gone wrong. Where this is not possible – as will often be the case – the remedy offered should fairly reflect the harm the complainant has suffered.
6. **Seeking continuous improvement**
   - Public bodies should review their policies and procedures regularly to ensure they are effective; actively seek and welcome all feedback, both compliments and complaints; use feedback to improve their public service delivery and performance; and capture and review lessons learned from complaints so that they contribute to developing services.

APPENDIX B

Parliamentary and Health Service Ombudsman, *Principles for Remedy* (2009)

Good practice with regard to remedies means:

1. **Getting it right**
   - Quickly acknowledging and putting right cases of maladministration or poor service that have led to injustice or hardship.
   - Considering all relevant factors when deciding the appropriate remedy, ensuring fairness for the complainant and, where appropriate, for others who have suffered injustice or hardship as a result of the same maladministration or poor service.
2. **Being customer focused**
   - Apologising for and explaining the maladministration or poor service.
   - Understanding and managing people's expectations and needs.
   - Dealing with people professionally and sensitively.
   - Providing remedies that take account of people's individual circumstances.
3. **Being open and accountable**
   - Being open and clear about how public bodies decide remedies.
   - Operating a proper system of accountability and delegation in providing remedies.
   - Keeping a clear record of what public bodies have decided on remedies and why.
4. **Acting fairly and proportionately**
   - Offering remedies that are fair and proportionate to the complainant's injustice or hardship.
   - Providing remedies to others who have suffered injustice or hardship as a result of the same maladministration or poor service, where appropriate.
   - Treating people without bias, unlawful discrimination or prejudice.
5. **Putting things right**
   - If possible, returning the complainant and, where appropriate, others who have suffered similar injustice or hardship, to the position they would have been in if the maladministration or poor service had not occurred.
   - If that is not possible, compensating the complainant and such others appropriately.
   - Considering fully and seriously all forms of remedy (such as an apology, an explanation, remedial action, or financial compensation).
   - Providing the appropriate remedy in each case.

6. **Seeking continuous improvement**
   - Using the lessons learned from complaints to ensure that maladministration or poor service is not repeated.
   - Recording and using information on the outcome of complaints to improve services.

APPENDIX C

Parliamentary and Health Service Ombudsman, *Principles of Good Complaint Handling* (2009)

Good complaint handling by public bodies means:

1. **Getting it right**
   - Acting in accordance with the law and relevant guidance, and with regard for the rights of those concerned.
   - Ensuring that those at the top of the public body provide leadership to support good complaint management and develop an organisational culture that values complaints.
   - Having clear governance arrangements, which set out roles and responsibilities, and ensure lessons are learnt from complaints.
   - Including complaint management as an integral part of service design.
   - Ensuring that staff are equipped and empowered to act decisively to resolve complaints.
   - Focusing on the outcomes for the complainant and the public body.
   - Signposting to the next stage of the complaints procedure, in the right way and at the right time.
2. **Being customer focused**
   - Having clear and simple procedures.
   - Ensuring that complainants can easily access the service dealing with complaints, and informing them about advice and advocacy services where appropriate.
   - Dealing with complainants promptly and sensitively, bearing in mind their individual circumstances.
   - Listening to complainants to understand the complaint and the outcome they are seeking.
   - Responding flexibly, including co-ordinating responses with any other bodies involved in the same complaint, where appropriate.
3. **Being open and accountable**
   - Publishing clear, accurate and complete information about how to complain, and how and when to take complaints further.
   - Publishing service standards for handling complaints.
   - Providing honest, evidence-based explanations and giving reasons for decisions.
   - Keeping full and accurate records.

4. **Acting fairly and proportionately**
    - Treating the complainant impartially, and without unlawful discrimination or prejudice.
    - Ensuring that complaints are investigated thoroughly and fairly to establish the facts of the case.
    - Ensuring that decisions are proportionate, appropriate and fair.
    - Ensuring that complaints are reviewed by someone not involved in the events leading to the complaint.
    - Acting fairly towards staff complained about as well as towards complainants.
5. **Putting things right**
    - Acknowledging mistakes and apologising where appropriate.
    - Providing prompt, appropriate and proportionate remedies.
    - Considering all the relevant factors of the case when offering remedies.
    - Taking account of any injustice or hardship that results from pursuing the complaint as well as from the original dispute.
6. **Seeking continuous improvement**
    - Using all feedback and the lessons learnt from complaints to improve service design and delivery.
    - Having systems in place to record, analyse and report on the learning from complaints.
    - Regularly reviewing the lessons to be learnt from complaints.
    - Where appropriate, telling the complainant about the lessons learnt and changes made to services, guidance or policy.

APPENDIX D

Local Government and Social Care Ombudsman, *Principles of Good Administrative Practice* (2018)

1. **Getting it right**
   - Following the law and taking the rights of those concerned into account.
   - Following the organisation's policy and guidance.
   - Taking proper account of established good practice.
   - Providing effective services, using appropriately trained and competent staff.
   - Taking reasonable, timely decisions, based on all relevant considerations.

Examples:
   - Complying with service timescales with a statutory basis by planning and prioritising resources.
   - Explaining and responding to any delays proactively.
   - Giving staff free rein to use their professional judgement to meet properly assessed service needs.
   - Ensuring organisations working on a council's behalf adhere to that council's policies, guidance, good practice and legislation.

2. **Being service-user focused**
   - Ensuring people can access services easily, including those needing reasonable adjustments.
   - Informing service users what they can expect and what the organisation expects of them.
   - Keeping to commitments, including any published service standards.
   - Dealing with people helpfully, promptly and sensitively, taking account of their individual circumstances.
   - Responding to service users' needs flexibly and, where appropriate, coordinating a response with other service providers.
   - Recognising and respecting the diversity of service users and adopting an inclusive approach.

Examples:
   - Retaining continuity for service users when services are changed.
   - Setting expectations for service users by having and communicating appropriate guidance.

- Understanding the individual circumstances of a case – not falling back on 'blanket policies'.
- Having appropriate skills and capacity to effectively contract manage third party suppliers delivering services on behalf of the council.
- Implementing contractual arrangements with suppliers to maintain service standards and provide clarity on the responsibility for managing concerns and complaints.

3. Being open and accountable

- Being open and clear about policies and procedures and ensuring information, and any advice provided, is clear, accurate and complete.
- Stating the criteria for decision making and giving reasons for decisions.
- Handling information properly and appropriately.
- Keeping proper and appropriate records.
- Taking responsibility for actions.

Examples:

- Consulting with stakeholders and service users prior to changing service arrangements.
- Ensuring frontline staff are fully briefed and equipped to support service users to make informed decisions, particularly when there are changes to eligibility criteria.
- Maintaining transparency in the light of complex service delivery arrangements.

4. Acting fairly and proportionately

- Being impartial and treating people with respect and courtesy.
- Treating people without unlawful discrimination or prejudice, and ensuring no conflict of interests.
- Dealing with people and issues objectively and consistently.
- Ensuring decisions and actions are proportionate, appropriate and fair.

Examples:

- Explaining clearly the rationale for decisions and recording them – ensuring any contractors mirror this behaviour.
- Having clear and accessible appeal routes.
- Being alive to the need for reasonable adjustments to ensure no person is placed at a disadvantage in using a service due to a disability.

5. Putting things right

- Acknowledging mistakes and apologising where appropriate.
- Putting mistakes right quickly and effectively.
- Providing clear and timely information on how and when to appeal or complain.
- Operating an effective complaints procedure, which includes offering a fair and appropriate remedy when a complaint is upheld.

Examples:

- Making complaints procedures clear and visible.
- Ensuring the quality of complaint investigation is the same whether it's handled by the council or a contractor.

6. Seeking continuous improvement

- Reviewing policies and procedures regularly to ensure they are effective.
- Asking for feedback and using it to improve services and performance.
- Ensuring the organisation learns lessons from complaints and uses them to improve services and performance.

Examples:

- Building into third party contracts the opportunities for review and learning from feedback.
- Disseminating and embedding relevant learning from feedback and lessons learned from complaints within the organisation.
- Being proactive in sharing complaints information with scrutiny functions.

APPENDIX E

The Local Government Ombudsman, *Good Administrative Practice* (1993)

[Excerpts from this document are provided below. In the document, each principle is accompanied by a detailed explanation.]

The Local Government Ombudsman in England welcomes the current emphasis on customer care, quality assurance and the quest for excellence. Those concepts are now being expressed more strongly than ever before in local government and in the public service generally. They are reflected in the Citizen's Charter.

Striving to serve the customer well and seeking to achieve excellent standards within the constraints of available resources are not new concepts in local government. The Ombudsman does not believe that councils and individual members of staff have failed over the years to achieve significant quality. But there may be a need for a greater consistency of high achievement. The investigations by the Local Government Ombudsmen do show that failings sometimes occur and the accent on quality promotion is timely.

If faults are identified in an investigation the outcome can often be that advice is given to the council concerned by the Ombudsman about measures which the council could consider in order to provide a better service. However, it may be useful that the lessons learnt from individual investigations should be made more widely known so that similar mistakes can be avoided.

The experience of the Ombudsmen in investigating allegations of maladministration has built up a significant body of knowledge about good and bad practice. This guidance note therefore sets out some of the important conclusions which can be drawn from the Ombudsmen's investigations and observations. Following consultation with the local authority associations the Ombudsman is offering this guidance note to councils with the hope that it will be helpful for staff at all levels and for councillors too. In particular the objectives of the note are:

(a) to assist councils in the promotion of good administrative practice for all services and functions and the achievement of high standards for their customers.
(b) to endorse and publicise relevant recommendations of the Committee of Ministers of the Council of Europe.
(c) to provide a checklist of points which could be useful to councils for the review and audit of their administrative arrangements or any part of them.
(d) to provide material and ideas to assist with the briefing and training of staff.
(e) to contribute to the briefing of councillors about how they discharge certain of their responsibilities.

(f) to disseminate information about findings by the Local Government Ombudsmen which illustrate useful points about administrative practice.
(g) to assist councils generally in their understanding of what the Local Government Ombudsmen expect by way of good practice, and conversely why the Ombudsmen make criticisms when they do.
(h) to contribute to the prevention of maladministration and secure a reduction in the volume of complaints to the Ombudsman.

The 42 principles of good administration:

The law

1. Understand what the law requires the council to do and fulfil those requirements.
2. Ensure that all staff working in any particular area of activity understand and fulfil the legal requirements relevant to that area of activity.

Policy

3. Formulate policies which set out the general approach for each area of activity and the criteria which are used in decision making.
4. Ensure that criteria are clear and relevant and can be applied objectively so that decisions are not made on an inconsistent ad hoc or subjective basis.
5. Communicate relevant policies and rules to customers.
6. Ensure that all staff understand council policies relevant to their area of work.

Decisions

7. Ensure that the council does what its own policy or established practice requires.
8. Consider any special circumstances of each case as well as the council's policy so as to determine whether there are exceptional reasons which justify a decision more favourable to the individual customer than what the policy would normally provide.
9. Ensure that decisions are not taken which are inconsistent with established policies of the council or other relevant plans or guidelines unless there are adequate and relevant grounds for doing so.
10. Have regard to relevant codes of practice and government circulars; and follow the advice contained in them unless there are justifiable reasons not to do so.
11. Ensure that irrelevant considerations are not taken into account in making a decision.
12. Ensure that adequate consideration is given to all relevant and material factors in making a decision.
13. Give proper consideration to the views of relevant parties in making a decision.
14. Use the powers of the council only for their proper purpose and not in order to achieve some other purpose.
15. Ensure that decisions are not made or action taken prematurely.
16. Give reasons for an adverse decision and record them in writing for the customer concerned.
17. Ensure that any necessary decisions or actions are taken as circumstances require and within a reasonable time.

18. If a decision is being taken under delegated powers, ensure that there is proper and sufficient authority for this to be done and that use of delegated powers is appropriate in the circumstances.

Action prior to decision taking

19. Carry out a sufficient investigation so as to establish all the relevant and material facts.
20. Seek appropriate specialist advice as necessary.
21. Consult any individuals or organisations who might reasonably consider that they would be adversely and significantly affected by a proposed action.
22. Detect major errors which materially affect an issue under consideration.
23. Give adequate consideration to the reasonable courses of action which are open to the council in any particular circumstances.
24. Ensure that a committee is provided with a report when circumstances require and that the report is materially accurate and covers all the relevant points.

Administrative processes

25. Ensure that the correct action is taken both to implement decisions when they are made and generally in the conduct of the council's business.
26. Have adequate systems and written procedures for staff to follow in dealing with particular areas of activity.
27. Have a system for ensuring proper liaison and cooperation between different departments, different sections of a Department or different areas in the authority.
28. Compile and maintain adequate records.
29. Monitor progress and carry out regular appraisals of how an issue or problem is being dealt with.
30. Seek to resolve difficulties or disagreements by negotiations in the first instance but take formal action when it is clear that informal attempts at resolution are not working.

Customer relations

31. Avoid making misleading or inaccurate statements to customers.
32. Formulate undertakings with care and discharge any responsibilities towards customers which arise from them.
33. Reply to letters and other enquiries and do so courteously and within a reasonable period; and have a system for ensuring that appropriate action is taken on every occasion.
34. Keep customers regularly informed about the progress of matters which are of concern to them.
35. Provide adequate and accurate information, explanation and advice to customers on issues of concern to them.

Impartiality and fairness

36. Ensure that the body taking a decision on a formal appeal from a dissatisfied customer does not include any person previously concerned with the case or who has a personal or otherwise significant interest in the outcome.

37. Avoid unfair discrimination against particular individuals, groups or sections of society.
38. Maintain a proper balance between any adverse effects which a decision may have on the rights or interests of individuals and the purpose which the council is pursuing.
39. Where an individual is adversely affected by a decision, or the decision is otherwise one which the individual potentially might wish to challenge, inform him or her of any rights of appeal or avenues for pursuing a complaint.
40. Ensure that councillors and officers are fully aware of the requirements for declaring an interest where appropriate and the reasons for doing so.

Complaints

41. Have a simple well-publicised complaints system and operate it effectively.
42. Take remedial action when faults are identified, both to provide redress for the individuals concerned and to prevent recurrence of the problem in the future.

APPENDIX F

PHSO complaints, 2022–25

	2022–23			***2023–24***			***2024–25***		
	Health	***Parliamentary***	***No jurisdiction established***	***Health***	***Parliamentary***	***No jurisdiction established***	***Health***	***Parliamentary***	***No jurisdiction established***
Complaints concluded at initial checks or primary investigation	26,601	6,063	2,386	27,099	5,957	3,231	26,951	5,934	3,847
Does not warrant further consideration	1,024	5		1,128	3		1,391	2	
Failings or injustice identified but already corrected	346	163		324	200		286	184	
No failings or injustice identified	1,218	527		1,291	568		1,210	507	
Not ready for PHSO	19,680	4,590	714	20,263	4,366	527	19,814	4,503	308
Other reason to close complaint	2,306	419	22	2,213	427	11	2,256	311	5
Out of jurisdiction	307	182	1,649	323	238	2,693	360	263	3,531
Out of time	929	73		827	63		793	70	

	2022–23			**2023–24**			**2024–25**		
	Health	***Parliamentary***	***No jurisdiction established***	***Health***	***Parliamentary***	***No jurisdiction established***	***Health***	***Parliamentary***	***No jurisdiction established***
Resolved with agreement of complainant	481	58		384	51		416	45	
Withdrawn/ discontinued	310	46	1	346	41		425	49	2
Detailed investigations concluded	531	81		621	74		677	45	
Fully/partly upheld	375	44		449	45		516	29	
Not upheld	133	32		154	26		148	14	
Resolved without a finding	4	1		1			3		
Discontinued	19	4		17	3		10	2	
Service and decision reviews	*Health and parliamentary*								
Service review requests (and upheld)	43 (24 – 59%)			74 (42 – 57%)			104 (47 – 45%)		
Decision review requests (and upheld)	255 (48 – 19%)			339 (35 – 10%)			294 (26 – 9%)		

Source: FOI request and PHSO annual reports.
Note: service and decision requests are considered through the PHSO's own internal (service and decision) review mechanisms.

BIBLIOGRAPHY

Books and Articles

Abel-Smith, B and Stevens, R, *Lawyers and the Courts: A Sociological Study of the English Legal System 1750-1965* (London, Heinemann, 1967).
Abraham, A, 'Good Administration: Why We Need it More Than Ever' (2009) 80 *Political Quarterly* 25.
——. 'The Ombudsman and Individual Rights' (2008) 61 *Parliamentary Affairs* 370.
——. 'The Ombudsman and "Paths to Justice": A Just Alternative or Just an Alternative?' [2010] *PL* 1.
——. 'The Parliamentary Ombudsman and Administrative Justice: Shaping the Next 50 Years' (London, JUSTICE, 2011).
——. 'Making Sense of the Muddle: The Ombudsman and Administrative Justice, 2002-2011' (2012) 34 *Journal of Social Welfare and Family Law* 91.
Acemoglu, D and Robinson, JA, *The Narrow Corridor: States, Societies, and the Fate of Liberty* (New York, Penguin, 2019).
Adler, M and Bradley, AW (eds), *Justice, Discretion and Poverty: Supplementary Benefit Appeal Tribunals in Britain* (Abingdon, Professional Books, 1975).
——. 'The Case for Systematic Reform and the Establishment of a Unified Administrative Tribunal' in Partington, M (ed), *The Leggatt Review of Tribunals: Academic Seminar Papers* (Bristol, Bristol Centre for the Study of Administrative Justice, 2001).
Adler, M, 'Decision-Making and Appeals in Social Security: In Need of Reform?' (1997) 68 *Political Quarterly* 338.
——. 'Who is Afraid of Sir Andrew Leggatt?' (2002) 9 *Journal of Social Security Law* 177.
——. 'A Socio-legal Approach to Administrative Justice' (2003) *Law & Policy* 323.
——. 'Tribunal Reform: Proportionate Dispute Resolution and the Pursuit of Administrative Justice' (2006) 69 *MLR* 958.
——. 'Waiting in the Wings: The Leggatt Report and the Reform of Tribunals' (2006) 13 *Journal of Social Security Law* 73.
——. 'Understanding and Analysing Administrative Justice' in M Adler (ed), *Administrative Justice in Context* (Oxford, Hart Publishing, 2010).
——. 'The Rise and Fall of Administrative Justice: A Cautionary Tale' (2012) 8 *Socio-Legal Review* 28.
——. *Cruel, Inhuman or Degrading Treatment? Benefit Sanctions in the UK* (London, Palgrave Macmillan, 2018).
Alden, S, 'Discretion on the Frontline: The Street Level Bureaucrat in English Statutory Homelessness Services' (2015) 14 *Social Policy and Society* 63.
——. 'On the Frontline: The Gatekeeper in Statutory Homelessness Services' (2015) 30 *Housing Studies* 924.
All-Party Parliamentary Group on Parkinson's, *Failing to Care: NHS Continuing Care in England* (2013).
Allen, CK, *Administrative Jurisdiction* (London, Stevens, 1956).
Allsop, J and Jones, K, 'Withering the Citizen, Managing the Consumer: Complaints in Healthcare Settings' (2007) 7 *Social Policy & Society* 233.
Ambrose, WJL, 'The New Judiciary' (1910) 26 *LQR* 203.
Anderson, J, Hollaus, J, Lindsay A and Williamson, C, *The Culture of Disbelief* (Refugee Studies Centre, 2014).
Arden, A and Cullen, C, 'No Surprises: Gatekeeping' *Legal Action* (November 2014).
Argyris, C and Schön, DA, *Organizational Learning II: Theory, Method and Practice* (Reading, Addison-Wesley, 1996).
Argyris, C, *On Organizational Learning*, 2nd edn (Oxford, Blackwell, 1999).
Arvind, TT and Stirton, L, 'The Curious Origins of Judicial Review' (2017) 133 *LQR* 91.

Arvind, TT, Halliday, S and Stirton, L, 'Judicial Review and Administrative Justice' in M Hertogh, R Kirkham, R Thomas and J Tomlinson (eds), *The Oxford Handbook of Administrative Justice* (Oxford, Oxford University Press, 2022).

Bach Commission on Access to Justice, *The Crisis in the Justice System in England & Wales* (London, Fabian Policy Report, 2016).

Baldwin, J, Wikeley N and Young, R, *Judging Social Security: The Adjudication of Claims for Benefit in Britain* (Oxford, Clarendon Press, 1992).

Barber, M, *Instruction to Deliver* (London, Politico's, 2007).

Barker, E, *Church, State and Society* (London, Methuen, 1930).

Barnard, C and Ludlow, A, 'Administrative (In)justice? Appellants' Experiences of Accessing Justice in Social Security Tribunals' [2022] *PL* 406.

Barron, A and Scott, C, 'The Citizen's Charter Programme' (1992) 55 *MLR* 526.

Bartels, KPR, 'Public Encounters: The History and Future of Face-to-Face Contact between Public Professionals and Citizens' (2013) 91 *Public Administration* 469.

Batty, E and Fletcher, D, *Offenders: Final Findings from the Welfare Conditionality Project* (York, University of York, 2018).

Behrens, R, 'Reform of a National Ombudsman Scheme: A Journey' in M Groves and A Stuhmcke (eds), *The Ombudsman in the Modern State* (Oxford, Hart Publishing, 2022).

Bell, K, *Tribunals in the Social Services* (London, Routledge & Kegan Paul, 1969).

Bell, K, Collison, P, Turner S and Webber, S, 'National Insurance Local Tribunals: A Research Study' (1974) 3 *Journal of Social Policy* 289.

Bennett, N, 'The New Public Services Ombudsman for Wales Act 2019: The Story, 2014–2020' (2020) 42 *Journal of Social Welfare and Family Law* 391.

Bevir, M and O'Brien, D, 'New Labour and the Public Sector in Britain' (2001) 61 *Public Administration Review* 535.

Bhattacharya, A, 'How Much Choice is Enough? Parental Satisfaction with Secondary School Choice in England and Scotland' (2023) 52 *Journal of Social Policy* 661.

Birkinshaw, P, *Grievances, Remedies and the State*, 2nd edn (London, Sweet & Maxwell, 1994).

Blackmore, M, 'Complaints Within Constraints: A Critical Review and Analysis of the Citizen's Charter Complaints Task Force' (1997) 12 *Public Policy and Administration* 28.

Blake, CG, 'Judicial Review, Second Tier Tribunals and Legality' in M Partington (eds, *The Leggatt Review of Tribunals: Academic Seminar Papers* (Bristol, University of Bristol, 2001).

Blom-Cooper, L, 'An Ombudsman in Britain' [1960] *PL* 145.

Bondy, V and Le Sueur, A, *Designing Redress: A Study about Grievances Against Public Bodies in England and Wales* (London, Public Law Project, 2012).

Borrie, G, *Justice and the Administration* (London, Fabian Research Series, No 185, 1957).

Bourn, J, *Public Sector Auditing: Is it Value for Money?* (Chichester, Wiley, 2007).

Bouwmeester, M, 'System Failure in the Digital Welfare State: Exploring Parliamentary and Judicial Control in the Dutch Childcare Benefits Scandal' (2023) 44 *Recht der Werkelijkheid* 13.

Bradley, AW, 'The Redress of Grievances' (1962) 20 *CLJ* 82.

——. 'The Role of the Ombudsman in Relation to the Protection of Citizens' Rights' (1980) 39 *CLJ* 304.

——. 'Recent Reform of Social Security Adjudication in Great Britain' (1985) 26 *Les Cahiers de Droit* 403

——. 'The Council on Tribunals: Time for a Broader Role?' [1991] *PL* 6.

——. 'Sachsenhausen, Barlow Clowes – and Then?' [1992] *PL* 353.

Breathnach, C, '"The Night of the Big Wind": Reticent Subjects and the Introduction of Old Age Pensions in Ireland' (2025) 99 *History Workshop Journal* 29.

Brecknell, S, 'Julie Mellor Resigns as Parliamentary and Health Services Ombudsman' *Civil Service World* (5 July 2016).

Brown, P, 'The Ombudsman: Remedies for Misinformation' in G Richardson and H Genn (eds), *Administrative Law & Government Action: The Courts and Alternative Mechanisms of Review* (Oxford, Oxford University Press, 1994).

Burley-Stower, R, 'Poor Decision-Making in NHS Continuing Healthcare' *Legal Action* (May 2019).

Buck, T, 'Precedent in Tribunals and the Development of Principles' (2006) 25 *Civil Justice Quarterly* 458.

Buck, T, Bonner, D and Sainsbury, R, *Making Social Security Law: The Role and Work of the Social Security and Child Support Commissioners* (Farnham, Ashgate, 2005).

Buck, T, Kirkham, R and Thompson, B, 'Time for a "Leggatt-Style" Review of the Ombudsman System?' [2011] *PL* 20.
——. *The Ombudsman Enterprise and Administrative Justice* (Abingdon, Routledge, 2016).
Burke, E, 'Thoughts on the Present Discontents' (1770) in I Kramnick (ed), *The Portable Burke* (London, Penguin, 1999).
Burton, M, 'Remote Hearings in the Social Security Tribunal: Should We Be Worried?' (2021) 28 *Journal of Social Security Law* 36.
Butler, P, 'Council Broke Law over Deprivation of Liberty, Ombudsman Rules' *The Guardian* (1 April 2019).
Butler, M and Maruna, S, 'Rethinking Prison Disciplinary Processes: A Potential Future for Restorative Justice' (2016) 11 *Victims & Offenders* 126.
Calvert, H, 'Appeal Structures of the Future' in M Adler and AW Bradley (eds), *Justice, Discretion and Poverty: Supplementary Benefit Appeal Tribunals in Britain* (Abingdon, Professional Books, 1975).
Cane, P, *Administrative Tribunals and Adjudication* (Oxford, Hart Publishing, 2009).
Canel, M-J and Luoma-aho, V, *Public Sector Communication: Closing Gaps Between Citizens and Public Organizations* (Chichester, Wiley, 2018).
Carlen, P, 'The Governance of Homelessness: Legality, Lore and Lexicon in the Agency-Maintenance of Youth Homelessness' (1994) 41 *Critical Social Policy* 18.
Carlile, A, 'An Ethnography of Permanent Exclusion from School: Revealing and Untangling the Threads of Institutionalised Racism' (2011) 15 *Race Ethnicity and Education* 175.
Carnwath, R, 'Tribunal Justice: A Quiet Revolution' (Presidential Address of the Holdsworth Club, Birmingham, University of Birmingham Law School, 2005).
——. 'Tribunal Justice: A New Start' (AJTC Conference, 19 November 2008).
——. 'Tribunals Justice: A New Start' [2009] *PL* 48.
——. 'Tribunals Reform: Five Years on' (AJTC, 12 November 2009).
Carr, CT, *Concerning English Administrative Law* (New York, Columbia University Press, 1941).
Cavenagh, WE and Newston, D, 'The Membership of Two Administrative Tribunals' (1970) 48 *Public Administration* 449.
——. 'Administrative Tribunals: How People Become Members' (1971) 49 *Public Administration* 197.
Chapman, B, 'The Ombudsman' (1960) 38 *Public Administration* 303.
Chernaik, W, 'Civil Liberty in Milton, the Levellers, and Winstanley' (1999) 22 *Prose Studies* 102.
Chester, DN, 'The Crichel Down Case' (1954) 32 *Public Administration* 389.
Chester, DN and Wilson, FMG, *The Organization of British Central Government 1914-1956* (London, Allen & Unwin, 1957).
Child Poverty Action Group, *You Reap What You Code: Universal Credit, Digitisation and the Rule of Law* (London, CPAG, 2023).
——. *Mandatory Reconsideration in 2024: A Briefing* (London, CPAG, 2024).
Clements L, and Aiello, AL, *Unacceptable Delay: Complaints Procedures for Disabled Children and their Families* (Leeds, University of Leeds, 2019).
Clements, L, *Clustered Injustice and the Level Green* (London, Legal Action Group, 2020).
Clothier, C, 'The Value of an Ombudsman' [1986] *PL* 204.
——. 'Fact-Finding Inquiries: The PCA's Perspective' [1996] *PL* 384.
Cogswell, T, 'A Low Road to Extinction? Supply and Redress of Grievances in the Parliaments of the 1620s' (1990) 33 *The Historical Journal* 283.
Cole Norton, F, '"This is Counterproductive": The Design of Local Welfare Assistance Schemes in England" (2024) 46 *Journal of Social Welfare and Family Law* 413.
Conservative Party, *Election Manifesto* (1955).
——. *1964 General Election Manifesto: 'Prosperity with a Purpose'* (1964).
——. *Invitation to Join the Government of Britain: The Conservative Manifesto 2010* (2010).
Continuing Healthcare Alliance, *Continuing to Care? Is NHS Continuing Healthcare Supporting the People Who Need it in England?* (Continuing Healthcare Alliance, 2016).
——. *Continuing to Care? Is NHS Continuing Healthcare Supporting the People Who Need it in England?* (Continuing Healthcare Alliance, 2017).
Cooper, Lord TM, 'Administrative Justice' (1954) 32 *Public Administration* 165.
Copus, C, Roberts, M and Wall, R, *Local Government in England: Centralisation, Autonomy and Control* (London, Palgrave Macmillan, 2017).

Copus, C, *In Defence of Councillors* (Manchester, Manchester University Press, 2022).
Cortvriend, A, 'Coping with Vulnerability: The Limbo Created by the UK Asylum System' (2020) 9 *International Journal for Crime, Justice and Social Democracy* 61.
Council for Disabled Children, *Survey Results: Legal Action Threatened against Local Authorities in Relation to EHC Plans* (2020).
Cowan, D and Halliday, S, *The Appeal of Internal Review: Law, Administrative Justice and the (Non-)emergence of Disputes* (Oxford, Hart Publishing, 2003).
Cowan, D, Halliday, S and Hunter, C, 'Gatekeeping Administrative Justice: Homelessness Internal Reviews' (2012) 15 *Journal of Housing Law* 122.
Cowan, D, Dymond, A, Halliday, S and Hunter, C, 'Reconsidering Mandatory Reconsideration' [2017] *PL* 215.
Cowan, D, 'Reducing Homelessness or Re-ordering the Deckchairs?' (2019) 82 *MLR* 105.
Cornford, FM, *Microcosmographia Academica: Being a Guide for the Young Academic Politician* (London, Bowes & Bowes, 1908).
Côté-Olijnyk, M, Christopher Perry, J, Paré, M-È and Kronick, R, 'The Mental Health of Migrants Living in Limbo: A Mixed-Methods Systematic Review with Meta-analysis' (2024) 337 *Psychiatry Research* 115931.
Cox, P, Lamont, R and Sunkin, M, 'Constitutionalising Regulatory Governance: The Case of the Victims' Commissioner' [2025] *PL* 283.
Creutzfeldt, N and Kirkham, R, 'Understanding How and When Change Occurs in the Administrative Justice System: The Ombudsman/Tribunal Partnership as a Catalyst for Reform?' (2020) 42 *Journal of Social Welfare and Family Law* 253.
Creutzfeldt, N, Gill, C, Cornelis, M and McPherson, R, *Access to Justice for Vulnerable and Energy-Poor Consumers Just Energy?* (Oxford, Hart Publishing, 2021).
Crick, B, *The Reform of Parliament* (London, Weidenfeld & Nicolson, 1964).
Cross, C, *The Liberals in Power (1905-1914)* (London, Pall Mall Press, 1963).
Crossman, RHS, *Socialism and the New Despotism* (London, Fabian Tract No 298, 1956).
——. *The Diaries of a Cabinet Minister: Volume Two* (London, Cape, 1976).
Cullen, M-A and Lindsay, G, 'Special Educational Needs: Understanding Drivers of Complaints and Disagreements in the English System' (2019) 4 *Frontiers in Education* 1.
——. 'Young People's Right to Appeal to the English First-tier Tribunal (Special Educational Needs and Disability): Learning from the First Two Years' (2021) 43 *Journal of Social Welfare and Family Law* 60.
Daintith, T and Page, A, *Executive Self-Government and the Constitution* (Oxford, Oxford University Press, 2025).
Dante, *Inferno* (London, Penguin, 2006).
Davis, J, 'Macmillan's Martyr: The Pilgrim Case, the "Land Grab", and the Tory Housing Drive, 1951–9' (2008) 23 *Planning Perspectives* 125.
De Smith, SA, 'Anglo-Saxon Ombudsman?' (1962) 33 *Political Quarterly* 9.
Delafons, J, 'Working in Whitehall: Changes in Public Administration, 1952–1982' (1982) 60 *Public Administration* 253.
Demie, F, 'The Experience of Black Caribbean Pupils in School Exclusion in England' (2021) 73 *Educational Review* 55.
Demos, *'I Love the NHS, But …': Preventing Needless Harms Caused by Poor Communications in the NHS* (London, Demos, 2023).
Denning, A, *Freedom and the Law* (London, Stevens, 1949).
——. 'Law in a Developing Community' (1955) 33 *Public Administration* 1.
Dicey, AV, *Introduction to the Study of the Law of the Constitution*, 8th edn (London, Macmillan, 1915).
Dietz, K, 'Need to Complain? Here's How Renaissance-Era Venetians Did it' *National Geographic* (31 December 2020).
Dobie, S, Sanders, B and Teixeira, L, *Turned Away: The Treatment of Single Homeless People by Local Authority Homelessness Services in England* (London, Crisis, 2014).
Done, EJ, and Knowler, H, '"Off-Rolling" and Foucault's Art of Visibility/invisibility: An Exploratory Study of Senior Leaders' Views of "Strategic" School Exclusion in Southwest England' (2021) 47 *British Educational Research Journal* 1039.
Done, EJ, Knowler, H and Armstrong, D, '"Grey" Exclusions Matter: Mapping Illegal Exclusionary Practices and the Implications for Children with Disabilities in England and Australia' (2021) 21 *Journal of Research in Special Educational Needs* 36.

Donson, F and O'Donovan, D, 'Public Inquiries and Administrative Justice' in M Hertogh, R Kirkham, R Thomas and J Tomlinson (eds), *The Oxford Handbook of Administrative Justice* (Oxford, Oxford University Press, 2022).
Drewry, G and Harlow, C, 'A "Cutting Edge"? The Parliamentary Commissioner and MPs' (1990) 53 *MLR* 745.
Drewry, G, 'Citizen's Charters' (2005) 7 *Public Management Review* 321.
——. 'The Judicialisation of "Administrative" Tribunals in the UK: From Hewart to Leggatt' (2009) 28 *Transylvanian Review of Administrative Sciences* 45.
——. 'Ombudsmen and Administrative Law: Bright Stars in a Parallel Universe?' (2009) 17 *Asia Pacific Law Review* 3.
Drummond, O, *The Access to Justice Barriers for Tribunal Users: A Comparative Case Study on Special Educational Needs Tribunals* (Belfast, Northern Ireland Assembly, Knowledge Exchange Seminar Series, 2015).
Du, J and Zhu, X 'Bureaucratic Encounter, Voice Behaviour and Citizen Satisfaction' (2024) *Public Management Review* 1.
Dunleavy, P, Bastow, S, Tinkler, J, Goldchluk, S and Towers, E, 'Joining up Citizen Redress in UK Central Government' in M Adler (ed), *Administrative Justice in Context* (Oxford, Hart Publishing, 2010).
Dunleavey, P, 'Policy Disasters: Explaining the UK's Record' (1995) 10 *Public Policy and Administration* 52.
Dunsire, A, *Implementation in a Bureaucracy* (London, Martin Robertson, 1978).
Dwyer, PJ, 'Punitive and Ineffective: Benefit Sanctions within Social Security' (2018) 25 *Journal of Social Security Law* 142.
Dwyer, PJ, Scullion, L Jones, K, McNeil J, and Stewart, ABR, 'Work, Welfare and Well-Being: The Impacts of Welfare Conditionality on People with Mental Health Impairments in the UK' (2020) 54 *Social Policy and Administration* 31.
Eardley T, and Sainsbury, R, 'Managing Appeals: The Control of Housing Benefit Internal Reviews by Local Authority Officers' (1993) 22 *Journal of Social Policy* 461.
Edmondson, A, *Right Kind of Wrong: How the Best Teams Use Failure to Succeed* (London, Penguin, 2024).
Edwards, L and Nason, S, 'Judicial Review and Administrative Justice within and Across the UK Nations: A Tale of Divergence and Convergence' in M Aronson and G Weeks (eds), *Controlling the Administrative State: Essays in Honour of Matthew Groves* (Oxford, Hart Publishing, 2025).
Elcock, HJ, *Administrative Justice* (London, Longmans, 1969).
——. 'Opportunity for Ombudsman: The Northern Ireland Commissioner for Complaints' (1972) 50 *Public Administration* 87.
Elliott, M and Thomas, R, *Public Law*, 5th edn (Oxford, Oxford University Press, 2024).
Farmer, JA, *Tribunals and Government* (London, Weidenfeld & Nicolson, 1974).
Feldman, D, 'Changing Boundaries: Crime, Punishment and Public Law' in JNE Varuhas and S Wilson Stark (eds), *The Frontiers of Public Law* (Oxford, Hart Publishing, 2020).
Fenger, M and Simonse, R, 'The Implosion of the Dutch Surveillance Welfare State' (2024) 58 *Social Policy & Administration* 264.
Ferguson, L and Webber, N, *School Exclusion and the Law: A Literature Review and Scoping Survey of Practice* (University of Oxford, 2015).
Finnis, J and Murray, S, *Immigration, Strasbourg, and Judicial Overreach* (London, Policy Exchange, 2022).
Forsyth, C (ed), *Judicial Review and the Constitution* (Oxford, Hart Publishing, 2000).
Freedom from Torture, *Lessons Not Learned: The Failures of Asylum Decision-Making in the UK* (London, Freedom From Torture, 2019).
Freedman, S, *Failed State: Why Nothing Works and How We Fix it* (London, Macmillan, 2024).
Freud, D, *Clashing Agendas: Inside the Welfare Trap* (London, Nine Elms Books, 2021).
Frost, A and Howard, C, *Representation and Administrative Tribunals* (Abingdon, Routledge, 1977).
Fry, GK, 'The Sachsenhausen Concentration Camp Case and the Convention of Ministerial Responsibility' [1970] *PL* 336.
Fulbrook, J, *Administrative Justice and the Unemployed* (London, Mansell, 1978).
Fuller, LL, *The Morality of Law* (Yale University Press, 1969).
Garner, JF, 'The Council on Tribunals' [1965] *PL* 321.
Genn, H, 'Informal Justice and Tribunals' (1993) 56 *MLR* 393.
——. 'Tribunal Review of Administrative Decision-Making' in G Richardson and H Genn (eds), *Administrative Law & Government Action: The Courts and Alternative Mechanisms of Review* (Oxford, Oxford University Press, 1994).

Gentleman, A, *The Windrush Betrayal: Exposing the Hostile Environment* (London, Faber, 2019).
Gibb, F, 'Administrative Justice and Tribunals Service Comes out of the Shadows' *The Times* (10 February 2010).
Giddings, P, 'Whither the Ombudsman?' (2001) 16 *Public Policy and Administration* 1.
Gill, C, 'Right First Time: The Role of Ombudsmen in Influencing Administrative Decision-Making' (2011) 33 *Journal of Social Welfare and Family Law* 181.
——. 'The Evolving Role of the Ombudsman: A Conceptual and Constitutional Analysis of the "Scottish Solution" to Administrative Justice' [2014] *PL* 662.
Gill, C, 'Re-imagining Public-Sector Complaint Systems' *Essex CAJI* (2 October 2018).
——. 'The Ombud and "Complaint Standards Authority" Powers' in R Kirkham and C Gill (eds), *A Manifesto for Ombudsman Reform* (London, Palgrave Macmillan, 2020).
——. 'The Ombud and Own-Initiative Investigation Powers' in R Kirkham and C Gill (eds), *A Manifesto for Ombudsman Reform* (London, Palgrave Macmillan, 2020).
Gill, C and Creutzfeldt, N, 'The "Ombuds Watchers": Collective Dissent and Legal Protest Among Users of Public Services Ombuds' (2018) 27 *Social & Legal Studies* 367.
Godwin, M and Lawson, C, 'The Working Tax Credit and Child Tax Credit 2003-08: A Critical Analysis' (2009) 17 *Benefits* 3.
Greater Manchester Immigration Aid Unit, *'We Lost Our Lives When We Arrived Here': Children in the UK's Asylum System* (Manchester, GMIAU, 2023).
Gregory, R, 'Court Line, Mr Benn and the Ombudsman' (1977) 30 *Parliamentary Affairs* 269.
——. 'The Select Committee on the Parliamentary Commissioner for Administration, 1967-1980' [1982] *PL* 49.
Gregory, R and Alexander, A, 'Our Parliamentary Ombudsman' (1972) 50 *Public Administration*; (1973) 51 *Public Administration* 51.
Gregory, R and Drewry, G, 'Barlow Clowes and the Ombudsman' [1991] *PL* 192; 408.
Gregory, R and Giddings, P, *The Ombudsman, The Citizen, and Parliament: A History of the Office of the Parliamentary Commissioner for Administration and Health Service Commissioners* (London, Politico's, 2002).
Gregory, R and Hutchesson, P, *The Parliamentary Ombudsman: A Study in the Control of Administrative Action* (London, Allen & Unwin, 1975).
Gregory, R and Pearson, J, 'The Parliamentary Ombudsman after Twenty-Five Years' (1992) 70 *Public Administration* 469.
Greenleaf, WH, *The British Political Tradition: Volume Three. A Much Governed Nation Part 2* (London, Methuen, 1987).
Griffith, JAG, 'The Crichel Down Affair' (1955) 18 *MLR* 557.
——. 'Tribunals and Inquiries' (1959) 22 *MLR* 125.
——. 'Comment' [1962] *PL* 1.
——. 'Comment' [1962] *PL* 391.
Groves, M, 'Systemic Failure and Systemic Unfairness' (2023) 30 *Australian Journal of Administrative Law* 151.
Gulland, J, 'Current Developments in the UK: Complaints Procedures and Ombudsmen' in M Adler (ed), *Administrative Justice in Context* (Oxford, Hart Publishing, 2010).
——. 'Taking Complaints Seriously: The Role of Informality in Complaints about Public Services (2011) 10 *Social Policy & Society* 483.
——. 'Administrative Justice and Austerity: The Case of Disputes about Adult Social Care' in S Cowan and S Halliday (eds), *Socio-legal Generation: Essays in Honour of Michael Adler* (London, Palgrave Macmillan, 2024).
Gwyn, WB, 'The Labour Party and the Threat of Bureaucracy' (1971) 19 *Political Studies* 383.
——. 'The British PCA: "Ombudsman or Ombudsmouse?"' (1973) 35 *Journal of Politics* 45.
——. 'The Ombudsman in Britain: A Qualified Success in Government Reform' (1982) 60 *Public Administration* 177.
Hale, B, 'Courts and Tribunals' (London, Annual Upper Tribunal (UTAAC/UTIAC) Lecture, 14 October 2021.
Halliday, S, *Judicial Review and Compliance with Administrative Law* (Oxford, Hart Publishing, 2004).
——. 'Administrative Justice and Street-Level Emotions: Cultures of Denial in Entitlement Decision-Making' [2021] *PL* 727.
Hamson, CJ, 'The Real Lesson of Crichel Down' (1954) 32 *Public Administration* 383.

Hansen Palomares, 'The London Borough of Southwark Ordered to Stop "Gatekeeping" Vulnerable Homeless Families' (20 February 2015).
Harlow, C, Comment [1977] *PL* 301.
——. 'Ombudsmen: In Search of a Role' (1978) 41 *MLR* 446.
——. 'Ombudsmen: "Hunting Lions" or "Swatting Flies"' in M Hertogh and R Kirkham (eds), *Research Handbook on the Ombudsman* (Cheltenham, Edward Elgar, 2018).
Harlow C, and Rawlings, R, *Law and Administration*, 4th edn (Cambridge, Cambridge University Press, 2022).
Harris, N, 'The Reform of the Supplementary Benefit Appeals System' (1983) 5 *Journal of Social Welfare Law* 212.
——. 'The Developing Role and Structure of the Education Appeal System in England and Wales' in M Harris and M Partington (eds), *Administrative Justice in the 21st Century* (Oxford, Hart Publishing, 1999).
——. Education, *Law and Diversity: Schooling for One and All?*, 2nd edn (Oxford, Hart Publishing, 2021).
——. 'Mediation, Lawyers and Special Educational Needs: Ensuring a Balanced Approach to Dispute Resolution' (2021) 32 *King's Law Journal* 1.
Harris, N, Eden, K and Blair, A, *Challenges to School Exclusion: Exclusion, Appeals and the Law* (Abingdon, Routledge, 2000).
Hay, JR, *Origins of the Liberal Welfare Reforms, 1906–14* (London, Macmillan, 1975).
Hayek, FA, *The Road to Serfdom* (London, Routledge, 1944).
Healthwatch, *Cancelled Care Research* (2023).
Heap, D, 'New Developments in British Land Planning Law: 1954 and after' (1955) 20 *Law and Contemporary Problems* 493.
Helliwell, JF and Huang, H, 'How's Your Government? International Evidence Linking Good Government and Well-Being' (2008) 38 *British Journal of Political Science* 595.
Herman, M, *Administrative Justice and Supplementary Benefits: A Study of Supplementary Benefits Appeal Tribunals* (London, Bell, 1971).
Hertogh, M and Halliday, S (eds), *Judicial Review and Bureaucratic Impact: International and Interdisciplinary Perspectives* (Cambridge, Cambridge University Press, 2004).
Hewart, G, *The New Despotism* (London, Benn, 1929).
Hennessy, P, *Never Again: Britain 1945–51* (London, Penguin, 2006).
Hickinbottom, G, 'Tribunal Reform: A New Coherent System' [2010] *Judicial Review* 103.
Hickman, T, 'Public Law's Disgrace' *UK Constitutional Law Blog* (9 February 2017).
Hill, LB, *The Model Ombudsman: Institutionalizing New Zealand's Democratic Experiment* (Princeton, Princeton University Press, 1976).
Himsworth, CMG, 'Parliamentary Teeth for Local Ombudsmen?' [1986] *PL* 546.
——. 'A Cuckoo in the Nest of the Scottish Ombudsman' [2020] *PL* 14.
Hodge, M, *Called to Account: How Corporate Bad Behaviour and Government Waste Combine to Cost us Millions* (London, Little Brown, 2016).
Hodge, N and Wolstenholme, C, '"I Didn't Stand a Chance": How Parents Experience the Exclusions Appeal Tribunal' (2016) 20 *International Journal of Inclusive Education* 1297.
Hodges, C, *Delivering Dispute Resolution: A Holistic Review of Models in England and Wales* (Oxford, Hart Publishing, 2019).
Hodges, C and Voet, S, *Delivering Collective Redress: New Technologies* (Oxford, Hart Publishing, 2018).
Holmberg, S and Rothstein, B, *Good Government: The Relevance of Political Science* (Cheltenham, Edward Elgar, 2012).
Howard League for Penal Reform, *Justice Does Not Stop at the Prison Gate: Justice and Fairness in Prisons* (2020).
Hubeau, B, 'The Profile of Complainants: How to Overcome the Matthew Effect?' in M Hertogh and R Kirkham (eds), *Research Handbook on the Ombudsman* (Cheltenham, Edward Elgar, 2018).
Hudson, B, Hunter, D, and Peckham, S, 'Policy Failure and the Policy-Implementation Gap: Can Policy Support Programs Help?' (2019) 2 *Policy Design and Practice* 1.
Hurwitz, S, 'The Danish Parliamentary Commissioner for Civil and Military Government Administration' [1958] *PL* 236.
——. 'The Folketingets Ombudsmand' (1958) 12 *Parliamentary Affairs* 199.
Hvidtfeldt, C, Holm Petersen, J, Norredam, M, 'Prolonged Periods of Waiting for an Asylum Decision and the Risk of Psychiatric Diagnoses: A 22-Year Longitudinal Cohort Study from Denmark' (2020) 49 *International Journal of Epidemiology* 400.
Hynes, S, *Austerity Justice* (London, Legal Action Group, 2012).

Independent Age, *Reviewing the Case: The Right to Appeal in Adult Social Care* (2019).
Inns of Court Conservative and Unionist Society, *Rule of Law* (London, Conservative Political Centre, 1955).
James, R and Longley, D, 'The Channel Tunnel Rail Link, the Ombudsman and the Select Committee' [1996] *PL* 38.
Jay, D, *The Socialist Case* (London, Faber & Faber, 1937).
Jenkins, K, *Politicians and Public Services: Implementing Change in a Clash of Cultures* (Cheltenham, Edward Elgar, 2008).
Jepperson, RL and Meyer, JW, *Institutional Theory: The Cultural Construction of Organizations, States and Identities* (Cambridge, Cambridge University Press, 2021).
Johnson, J, *Venice Incognito: Masks in the Serene Republic Unmasked* (Berkeley, University of California Press, 2011).
Jónsson, H, *Friends in Conflict: The Anglo-Icelandic Cod Wars and the Law of the Sea* (London, Hurst, 1982).
JUSTICE, *The Citizen and the Administration: The Redress of Grievances* (London, Stevens, 1961).
——. *Administration under Law* (London, Stevens, 1971).
——. *The Citizen and His Council: Ombudsmen for Local Government?* (London, JUSTICE, 1971).
——. *Our Fettered Ombudsman* (London, JUSTICE, 1977).
——. *Delivering Justice in an Age of Austerity: A Report by JUSTICE* (London, JUSTICE, 2015).
——. *Reforming the Windrush Compensation Scheme* (London, JUSTICE, 2021).
——. *AI in Our Justice System* (London, JUSTICE, 2025).
JUSTICE and Administrative Justice Council, *Reforming Benefits Decision-Making* (London, JUSTICE, 2020).
JUSTICE-All Souls Review, *Administrative Justice: Some Necessary Reforms* (Oxford, Oxford University Press, 1988).
Kagan, RA, 'Varieties of Bureaucratic Justice' in NR Parillo (ed), *Administrative Law from the Inside out* (Cambridge, Cambridge University Press, 2017).
Kahneman, D, *Thinking, Fast and Slow* (London, Penguin, 2012).
Keith-Lucas, B, 'Mr Pilgrim and Crichel Down' (1962) 69 *Queen's Quarterly* 135.
Kelly, RJ, *Old Age Pensions Act 1908* (Dublin, Sealey, Bryers and Walker, 1908).
Kim, S and Kim, D, 'Does Government Make People Happy? Exploring New Research Directions for Government's Roles in Happiness' (2012) 13 *Journal of Happiness Studies* 875.
King, A and Crewe, I, *The Blunders of our Governments* (London, Oneworld, 2013).
King's Fund, *Lost in the System: The Need for Better Admin* (17 February 2025).
Kirkham, R, 'Prevention is Better Than Litigation: The Importance of Good Administration' (2004) 26 *Journal of Social Welfare and Family Law* 301.
——. 'Auditing by Stealth? Special Reports and the Ombudsman' [2005] *PL* 740.
——. 'Challenging the Authority of the Ombudsman: The Parliamentary Ombudsman's Special Report on Wartime Detainees' (2006) 69 *MLR* 792.
——. 'Explaining the Lack of Enforcement Powers Possessed by the Ombudsman' (2008) 30 *Journal of Social Welfare and Family Law* 253.
——. 'A 2020 Vision for the Ombudsman Sector' (2016) 38 *Journal of Social Welfare & Family Law* 103
——. 'The Ombud as a Chameleon' in M Hertogh, R Kirkham, R Thomas and J Tomlinson (eds), *The Oxford Handbook of Administrative Justice* (Oxford, Oxford University Press, 2022).
Kirkham, R and Gill, C (eds), *A Manifesto for Ombudsman Reform* (London, Palgrave Macmillan, 2020).
Kirkham, R, Buck T and Thompson, B, 'Putting the Ombudsman into Constitutional Context' (2009) 62 *Parliamentary Affairs* 600.
Kirkham, R, Thompson, B and Buck, T, 'When Putting Things Right Goes Wrong: Enforcing the Recommendations of the Ombudsman' [2008] *PL* 510.
Kirwan, S (ed), *Advising in Austerity: Reflections on Challenging Times for Advice Agencies* (Bristol, Policy Press, 2017).
Knights, M, '"The Lowest Degree of Freedom": The Right to Petition Parliament, 1640–1800' (2018) 37 *Parliamentary History* 18.
Kynaston, D, *Austerity Britain 1945–51* (London, Bloomsbury, 2007).
——. *Family Britain, 1951–57* (London, Bloomsbury, 2009).
Labour Party, *Personal Freedom: Labour's Policy for the Individual and Society* (London, Labour Party, 1956).
——. *Labour Party Election Manifesto 1964: 'The New Britain'* (1964).
Lamb, B, 'Statutory Assessment for Special Educational Needs and the Warnock Report: The First 40 Years' (2019) 4 *Frontiers in Education: Policy and Practice Reviews* 1.

Langdon-Down, G, 'Special Education Needs: Learning to Fight' *Law Society Gazette* (26 February 2018).

Laurie, E, 'Assessing the Upper Tribunal's Potential to Deliver Administrative Justice' [2012] *PL* 288.

——. 'Homelessness and the "Over-judicialisation" of Welfare' (2020) 21 *Legal Studies* 39.

Law Society, *Access to Justice Review* (London, Law Society, 2010).

Law Society of Scotland, *Benefit Sanctions Inquiry* (21 May 2018).

Lawson, FH, 'An Inspector-General of Administration' [1957] *PL* 92.

Le Sueur, A, 'Designing Redress: Who Does it, How and Why' (2012) 20 *Asia Pacific Law Review* 1.

Leathes, S, 'The Alleged "New Despotism". Reply to the Lord Chief Justice: The Civil Service View' *The Daily Telegraph* (10 October 1929).

Legomsky, SH, *Specialized Justice: Courts, Administrative Tribunals, and a Cross-national Theory of Specialization* (Oxford, Oxford University Press, 1990).

Lelliott, J, 'Unaccompanied Children in Limbo: The Causes and Consequences of Uncertain Legal Status' (2022) 34 *International Journal of Refugee Law* 1.

Lewis, N, 'Supplementary Benefits Appeal Tribunals' [1973] *PL* 257.

Lewis, N, 'Filling in the Gaps: A Standing Administrative Conference for the United Kingdom' in M Harris and M Partington (eds), *Administrative Justice in the 21st Century* (Oxford, Hart Publishing, 1999).

Lewis, N and Birkinshaw, P, *When Citizens Complain: Reforming Justice and Administration* (Buckingham, Open University Press, 1993).

Lewis, N, Senerviratne, M and Cracknell, S, *Complaints Procedures in Local Government* (Sheffield, University of Sheffield, 1987).

Lidstone, P, 'Rationing Housing to the Homeless Applicant' (1994) 9 *Housing Studies* 459.

Lindsay, G, Conlonb, G, Totsikaa, V, Graya, G and Cullen, MA, 'The Impact of Mediation on Resolution of Disagreements around Special Educational Needs: Effectiveness and Cost Effectiveness' (2021) 26 *Research Papers in Education* 275.

Lomas, O, 'The 25th Annual Report of the Council on Tribunals: An Opportunity Sadly Missed' (1985) 48 *MLR* 694.

Loopstra, R, Reeves, A, Barr, B, Taylor-Robinson, D, McKee, M, and Stuckler, D, 'The Impact of Economic Downturns and Budget Cuts on Homelessness Claim Rates across 323 Local Authorities in England, 2004–12' (2016) 38 *Journal of Public Health* 417.

Loveland, I, *Housing Homeless Persons: Administrative Law and the Administrative Process* (Oxford, Oxford University Press, 1995).

Lowe, R, *The Official History of the British Civil Service: Reforming the Civil Service, Volume 1: The Fulton Years, 1966–81* (Abingdon, Routledge, 2011).

Lowe, R and Pemberton, H, *The Official History of the British Civil Service: Reforming the Civil Service, Volume II: The Thatcher and Major Revolutions, 1982–97* (Abingdon, Routledge, 2020).

Luoma-aho, V and Canel, M-J (eds), *The Handbook of Public Sector Communication* (Chichester, Wiley, 2020).

MacKenzie, WJM and Grove, JW, *Central Administration in Britain* (London, Longmans, 1957).

Macnicol, J, *The Politics of Retirement in Britain, 1878–1948* (Cambridge, Cambridge University Press, 1998).

Marsh, AJ, 'Special Educational Needs and Disability Tribunals in England, 1994–2019' (2022) 37 *Research Papers in Education* 797.

Marshall, E, 'Reconsidering the Asylum Lottery: Refugee Determination and the Structure of Luck' (2025) 34 *Social & Legal Studies* 791.

Marshall, G, 'The British Parliamentary Commissioner for Administration' (1968) 377 *The Annals* 87.

——. 'Maladministration' [1973] *PL* 32.

Marshall, G, 'Ombudsmanaging Local Government' [1990] *PL* 449.

Marshall, G and Moodie, GC, *Some Problems of the Constitution* (London, Hutchinson, 1971).

Marsons, L, 'The Greenshoots of a Human Rights Ombudsprudence in the Local Government and Social Care Ombudsman' (2024) 46 *Journal of Social Welfare and Family Law* 104.

Martin, D, 'Making Tax and Social Security Decisions: Lean and Deskilling in the UK Civil Service' (2017) 32 *New Technology, Work and Employment* 146.

Mashaw, JL, *Bureaucratic Justice: Managing Social Security Disability Claims* (New Haven, Yale University Press, 1983).

——. 'Models of Administrative Justice' in M Hertogh, R Kirkham, R Thomas and J Tomlinson (eds), *The Oxford Handbook of Administrative Justice* (Oxford, Oxford University Press, 2022).

Maxwell, J and Tomlinson, J, *Experiments in Automating Immigration Systems* (Bristol, Bristol University Press, 2022).

McCorquodale, S, 'The Composition of Administrative Tribunals' [1962] *PL* 298.
McGurk, B and Tomlinson, J, *Artificial Intelligence and Public Law* (Oxford, Hart Publishing, 2025).
McKeever, G, 'A Ladder of Legal Participation for Tribunal Users' [2013] *PL* 575.
——. 'Comparing Courts and Tribunals through the Lens of Legal Participation' (2020) 39 *Civil Justice Quarterly* 217.
McKeever, G, Royal-Dawson, G, Kirk, E and McCord, J, *Litigants in Person in Northern Ireland: Barriers to Legal Participation* (Belfast, Ulster University, 2018).
——. 'The Snakes and Ladders of Legal Participation: Litigants in Person and the Right to a Fair Trial under Article 6 of the European Convention on Human Rights' (2022) 49 *Journal of Law and Society* 71.
McMurtie, SN, 'The Waiting Game: The Parliamentary Commissioner's Response to Delay in Administrative Procedures' [1997] *PL* 159.
Meers, J, 'Discretion as Blame Avoidance: Passing the Buck to Local Authorities in "Welfare Reform"' (2019) 27 *Journal of Poverty and Social Justice* 41.
——. 'Forms of Fettering: Application Forms and the Exercise of Discretion in the Welfare State' (2020) 42 *Journal of Social Welfare & Family Law* 221.
Micklethwait, R, *The National Insurance Commissioners* (London, Stevens, 1976).
Midgley, HC, Ferry, L and Murphie, AD, *Holding Government to Account: Democracy and the National Audit Office* (Abingdon, Routledge, 2024).
Milton, J, *Areopagitica* (1644).
Mitchell, JDB, 'The Ombudsman Fallacy' [1962] *PL* 24.
——. 'Administrative Law and Parliamentary Control' (1967) 38 *Political Quarterly* 360.
——. 'The Irrelevance of the Ombudsman Proposals' in DC Rowat (ed), *The Ombudsman: Citizen's Defender*, 2nd edn (London, Allen & Unwin, 1968).
Mitrany, D, 'Protecting the Citizen. I: The Swedish System' *Manchester Guardian* (6 August 1957).
——. 'Protecting the Citizen. II: A Warden of Rights' *Manchester Guardian* (7 August 1957).
Molavi, M, *Collective Access to Justice: Assessing the Potential of Class Actions in England and Wales* (Bristol, Bristol University Press, 2021).
Moore, MH, *Creating Public Value: Strategic Management in Government* (Cambridge, Harvard University Press, 1997).
Moore, R and Wallace, T, *Slamming the Door: The Administration of Immigration Control* (London, Martin Robertson, 1975).
Morin, D and Hazgui, M, 'We are Much More Than Watchdogs: The Dual Identity of Auditors at the UK National Audit Office' (2016) 12 *Journal of Accounting & Organizational Change* 568.
Morris, PE, 'The Revenue Adjudicator: The First Two Years' [1996] *PL* 309.
Mowbray, AR, 'A Right to Official Advice: The Parliamentary Commissioner's Perspective' [1990] *PL* 68.
Mulchahy, L, 'Sliding Scales of Justice at the End of the Century: A Cause for Complaints?' in M Harris and M Partington (eds), *Administrative Justice in the 21st Century* (Oxford, Hart Publishing, 1999).
——. 'Modernisation or Transformation? User-Led Design and the Facilitation of Systemic Change in the Traffic Penalty Tribunal' (2024) 43 *Civil Justice Quarterly* 120.
Mulcahy, L and Tsalapatanis, A, *Digital Justice: Engineering Disadvantage?* (London, Palgrave Macmillan, 2024).
Mullen, T, Gill, C and Vivian, N, *Scotland's Model Complaint Handling Procedures: Exploring Recent Developments and the Usefulness of Complaint Data for Administrative Justice Research* (Glasgow, University of Glasgow, 2017).
Nabi, Z, 'Gatekeeping: Lessons from the Birmingham Cases' (2012) 15 *Journal of Housing Law* 109.
Nason, S, *Understanding Administrative Justice in Wales* (Bangor, University of Bangor, 2015).
Nason, S, Sherlock, A, Taylor, H and Pritchard, H, *Public Administration and a Just Wales: Education* (Bangor, University of Bangor, 2020).
Nason, S, 'The Impact of Pan-European General Principles of Good Administration on United Kingdom Administrative Law: Shared Principles in a Strained Relationship' in U Stelkens and A Andrijauskaite (eds), *Good Administration and the Council of Europe: Law, Principles, and Effectiveness* (Oxford, Oxford University Press, 2020).
Newark, FH, Book review (1955) 71 *LQR* 571.
Newton, T, 'The Role of the Administrative Justice Council' (2006) 13 *Journal of Social Security Law* 98.
Nicolson, IF, *The Mystery of Crichel Down* (Oxford, Oxford University Press, 1986).
Nonet, P, *Administrative Justice: Advocacy and Change in a Government Agency* (New York, Russell Sage Foundation, 1969).

Nonet, P and Selznick, P, *Law & Society in Transition: Toward Responsive Law* (Piscataway, NJ, Transaction Publishers, 2001).

O'Brien, N, 'Administrative Justice: A Libertarian Cinderella in Search of an Egalitarian Prince' (2012) 83 *Political Quarterly* 494.

——. 'Ombudsmen and Public Authorities: A Modest Proposal' in M Hertogh and R Kirkham (eds), *Research Handbook on the Ombudsman* (Cheltenham, Edward Elgar, 2018).

O'Hara, G, 'The Parliamentary Commissioner for Administration, the Foreign Office, and the Sachsenhausen Case, 1964–68' (2010) 53 *Historical Journal* 771.

——. 'Parties, People, and Parliament: Britain's "Ombuds" and the Politics of the 1960s' (2011) 50 *Journal of British Studies* 690.

Oikonomou, E, Carthey, J, Macrae, C, and Vincent, C, 'Patient Safety Regulation in the NHS: Mapping the Regulatory Landscape of Healthcare' (2019) *British Medical Journal Open* 9:e028663.

Ott, JC, 'Government and Happiness in 130 Nations: Good Governance Fosters Higher Level and More Equality of Happiness' (2011) 102 *Social Indications Research* 3.

Ovádek, M, 'Judicial Diversity and Immigration Appeals: Evidence from the United Kingdom' (2025) *West European Politics*.

Packer, I, *Liberal Government and Politics, 1905–15* (London, Palgrave Macmillan, 2006).

Page, A, 'The Citizen's Charter and Administrative Justice' in M Harris and M Partington (eds), *Administrative Justice in the 21st Century* (Oxford, Hart Publishing, 1999).

Palmer, E, Cornford, T, Guinchard, A and Marique, Y (eds), *Access to Justice: Beyond the Policies and Politics of Austerity* (Oxford, Hart Publishing, 2016).

Partington, M, 'Restructuring Administrative Justice? The Redress of Citizens' Grievances' (1999) 52 *Current Legal Problems* 173.

——. 'The Status of Administrative Judges in the UK: Recruitment, Tenure, Training and Appraisal' (2001) 21 *Journal of the National Association of Administrative Law Judges* 315.

Patients Association, *Parliamentary and Health Service Ombudsman: The 'Peoples' Ombudsman: How it Failed Us* (2014).

Pattaro, S, Bailey, N, Williams, E, Gibson, M, Wells, A, Tranmer, M and Dibben, C, 'The Impacts of Benefit Sanctions: A Scoping Review of the Quantitative Research Evidence' (2022) *Journal of Social Policy* 1.

Paul, S, 'Administrative Empathy: A New Value in Administrative Justice' [2025] *PL* 670.

Peaker, G, 'Gatekeeping in Times of Austerity' (2012) 15 *Journal of Housing Law* 107.

Pedersen, IM, 'The Danish Parliamentary Commissioner in Action' [1960] *PL* 115.

——. 'The Parliamentary Commissioner: A Danish View' [1962] *PL* 15.

Peel, E and Harding, E, '"It's a Huge Maze, the System, it's a Terrible Maze": Dementia Carers' Constructions of Navigating Health and Social Care Services" (2014) 13 *Dementia* 642.

Pemberton, H, 'WASPI's is (Mostly) a Campaign for Inequality' (2017) 88 *Political Quarterly* 510.

Percival, R, 'The Challenge of Public Law Law Reform: Reflections on a Failed Law Commission Project' (2019) 41 *Journal of Social Welfare and Family Law* 372.

Pickup, A, 'Benefit Sanctions and Procedural Fairness' *Legal Action Group* (March 2020).

Policy Exchange, *What Do We Want from the King's Speech?* (London, Policy Exchange, 2023).

Pollard, RSW (ed), *Administrative Tribunals at Work: A Symposium* (London, Stevens, 1950).

Pollitt, C, 'Institutional Amnesia: A Paradox of the "Information Age"' (2000) 19 *Prometheus* 5.

Power, M, 'The Theory of the Audit Explosion' in E Ferlie, LE Lynn and C Pollitt (eds), *The Oxford Handbook of Public Management* (Oxford, Oxford University Press, 2005).

Powell, WW and DiMaggio, PJ (eds), *The New Institutionalism in Organizational Analysis* (Chicago, University of Chicago Press, 1991).

Pressman, JL and Widavsky, A, *Implementation*, 3rd edn (Berkeley, University of California Press, 1992).

Price, D and Laybourne, A, *Student Satisfaction with the Office of the Independent Adjudicator for Higher Education Report of the OIA Student Survey 2009* (London, King's College London, 2009).

Pritchard, H, 'Building a Welsh Jurisdiction through Administrative Justice' in S Nason (ed), *Administrative Justice in Wales and Comparative Perspectives* (Cardiff, University of Wales Press, 2017).

Pro Bono Economics, *The Cost of Not Getting Personal Independence Payment Decisions Right First Time* (London, Pro Bono Economics, 2021).

Prosser, T, 'Poverty, Ideology and Legality: Supplementary Benefit Appeal Tribunals and Their Predecessors' (1977) 4 *British Journal of Law and Society* 39.

Public Law Project, *Benefit Sanctions: A Presumption of Guilt* (London, PLP, 2022).

——. *Written Evidence Submitted to the House of Commons Public Accounts Committee* (2023).
Rawlings, R, 'Review, Revenge and Retreat' (2005) 68 *MLR* 378.
Reading Welfare Rights, *Ten Years of PIP: A Decade-Long Mistake?* (2023).
Refugee Council, *Living in Limbo: A Decade of Delays in the UK Asylum System* (London, Refugee Council, 2021).
Reid, WK, 'What's the Good of Law in a Case o' the Kind?' [1993] *PL* 221.
——. *Resolving Complaints and Promoting Openness: Can the Ombudsman Help?* (London, Nuffield Trust, 1998).
Reif, LC, *Ombuds Institutions, Good Governance and the International Human Rights System*, 2nd edn (Leiden, Brill, 2020).
Richardson, G and Genn, H, 'Tribunals in Transition: Resolution or Adjudication?' [2007] *PL* 116.
Riddell, S, Harris, N, Smith, E and Weedon, E, 'Dispute Resolution in Additional and Special Educational Needs: Local Authority Perspectives' (2010) 25 *Journal of Education Policy* 55.
Ridley, FF, 'The Citizen Against Authority: British Approaches to the Redress of Grievances' (1984) 37 *Parliamentary Affairs* 1.
Roberts, J, 'The Parole Board and the Worboys Case' [2018] *Crim LR* 808.
Robson, WA, 'The Report of the Committee on Ministers' Powers' (1932) 3 *Political Quarterly* 346.
——. *Justice and Administrative Law: A Study of the British Constitution*, 3rd edn (London, Stevens, 1951).
——. 'Administrative Justice and Injustice: A Commentary on the Franks Report' [1958] *PL* 12.
——. *The Governors and the Governed* (Baton Rouge, Louisiana State University Press, 1964).
——. '*Justice and Administrative Law* Reconsidered' (1979) 32 *Current Legal Problems* 107.
Rose, H, 'Who Can De-label the Claimant?' in M Adler and AW Bradley (eds), *Justice, Discretion and Poverty: Supplementary Benefit Appeal Tribunals in Britain* (Abingdon, Professional Books, 1975).
Runswick-Cole, K, '"The Tribunal was the Most Stressful Thing: More Stressful than My Son's Diagnosis or Behaviour": The Experiences of Families Who Go to the Special Educational Needs and Disability Tribunal (SENDisT)' (2007) 22 *Disability & Society* 315.
Ryan, A, 'The Form of Forms: Everyday Enablers of Access to Justice' (2023) 32 *Social & Legal Studies* 690.
Ryan, F, 'DWP Accused of Offering Disabled People "Take it or Leave it" Benefits: Lower Value "Deals" Allegedly Offered to Vulnerable People Appealing Against Decisions' *The Guardian* (2 March 2020).
Ryder, E, 'Driving Improvements: Collaboration and Peer Learning' (Belfast, Ombudsman Association Conference, 2019).
Sainsbury, R, 'The Social Security Chief Adjudication Officer: The First Four Years' [1989] *PL* 323.
——. 'Administrative Justice: Discretion and Procedure in Social Security Decision-Making' in K Hawkins (ed), *The Uses of Discretion* (Oxford, Oxford University Press, 1992).
——. 'Internal Reviews and the Weakening of Social Security Claimants' Rights of Appeal' in G Richardson and H Genn (eds), *Administrative Law & Government Action* (Oxford, Oxford University Press, 1994).
——. 'The Reform of Social Security Adjudication' in M Harris and M Partington (eds), *Administrative Justice in the 21st Century* (Oxford, Hart Publishing, 1999).
Schuster, L, 'Fatal Flaws in the UK Asylum Decision-Making System: An Analysis of Home Office Refusal Letters' (2020) 46 *Journal of Ethnic and Migration Studies* 1371.
Schwartz, B and Wade, HWR, *Legal Control of Government* (Oxford, Clarendon Press, 1972).
Scott, JC, *Seeing Like a State: How Certain Schemes to Improve the Human Condition Have Failed* (New Haven, Yale University Press, 1998).
Scott, C, 'Implementation: Facilitating and Overseeing Public Services at Street Level' in P Cane, H Hoffman, E Ip and PL Lindseth (eds) *The Oxford Handbook of Comparative Administrative Law* (Oxford, Oxford University Press, 2020).
Seneca, 'On the Shortness of Life' in Seneca, *Dialogues and Essays* (Oxford, Oxford University Press, 2007).
Seneviratne, M, '"Joining up" the Ombudsmen: The Review of the Public Sector Ombudsmen in England' [2000] *PL* 582.
Sennett, R, *The Culture of the New Capitalism* (New Haven, Yale University Press, 2005).
Simon, HA, *Administrative Behavior*, 4th edn (New York, Free Press, 1997).
Skelcher, C, 'Reforming the Oversight of Administrative Justice 2010–2014: Does the UK Need a New Leggatt Report?' [2015] *PL* 215.
Smellie, KB, 'Some Aspects of English Administrative Law' (1927) 5 *Public Administration* 276.
Snow, T, 'The (Il)Logic of Legibility: Why Governments Should Stop Simplifying Complex Systems' *London School of Economics Impact Blog* (12 February 2021).

Sparling, RA, 'Corruption and Whistleblowing: Beccaria and Montesquieu on Secret Crimes and Secret Accusations' (2020) 61 *The Eighteenth Century* 413.
Stacey, F, *The British Ombudsman* (Oxford, Oxford University Press, 1971).
Stark, A, 'Explaining Institutional Amnesia in Government' (2019) 32 *Governance* 143.
Stark, A and Head, B, 'Institutional Amnesia and Public Policy' (2019) 26 *Journal of European Public Policy* 1521.
Steinsson, S, 'The Cod Wars: A Re-analysis' (2016) 25 *European Security* 256.
Stockton, P, 'Proportionate Dispute Resolution: What are the Options?' (Nuffield Foundation, Administrative Justice Seminar, 23 January 2006).
Stokey, E and Zeckhauser, R, *A Primer for Policy Analysis* (New York, Norton, 1979).
Street, H, *Justice in the Welfare State* (London, Stevens, 1968).
——. 'Access to the Legal System and the Modern Welfare State: A European Report from the Standpoint of an Administrative Lawyer' in M Cappelletti (ed), *Access to Justice and the Modern Welfare State* (Florence, European University Institute, 1981).
Sunkin, M, 'What is Happening to Applications for Judicial Review?' (1987) 50 *MLR* 432.
Summerskill, E, 'The Functions of Tribunals Within the Modern State' (1954) 1 *British Journal of Administrative Law* 93.
Taylor, H, *The Statesman* (New York, Mentor Books, 1958 [1836]).
Taylor, I, 'Raising the Expectation Interest: New Labour and the Citizen's Charter' (1999) 14 *Public Policy and Administration* 29.
Tax Law Review Committee of the Institute for Fiscal Studies, *The Tax Tribunals: The Next 10 Years* (London, IFS, 2021).
Thane, P, 'The "Scandal" of Women's Pensions in Britain: How Did it Come about?' in H Pemberton, P Thane and N Whiteside (eds), *Britain's Pensions Crisis: History and Policy* (Oxford, Oxford University Press, 2006).
Thomas, R, 'Immigration Appeals for Family Visitors Refused Entry Clearance' [2004] *PL* 612.
——. 'Evaluating Tribunal Adjudication: Administrative Justice and Asylum Appeals' (2005) 25 *Legal Studies* 462.
——. 'After the Ouster: Review and Reconsideration in a Single Tier Tribunal' [2006] *PL* 674.
——. 'Refugee Roulette: A UK Perspective' in J Ramji-Nogales, AI Schoenholtz and PG Schrag (eds), *Refugee Roulette: Disparities in Asylum Adjudication and Proposals for Reform* (New York, New York University Press, 2009).
——. *Administrative Justice and Asylum Appeals: A Study of Tribunal Adjudication* (Oxford, Hart Publishing, 2011).
——. 'From "Adversarial v Inquisitorial" to "Active, Enabling and Investigative": Developments in UK Tribunals' in L Jacobs and S Baglay (eds), *The Nature of Inquisitorial Processes in Administrative Regimes: Global Perspectives* (Farnham, Ashgate Publishing, 2013).
——. 'Administrative Justice, Better Decisions and Organisational Learning' [2015] *PL* 111.
——. 'Immigration and Access to Justice: A Critical Analysis of Recent Restrictions' in E Palmer, T Cornford, Y Marique and A Guinchard (eds), *Access to Justice: Beyond the Policies and Politics of Austerity* (Oxford, Hart Publishing, 2016).
Thomas, R and Tomlinson, J, 'Mapping Current Issues in Administrative Justice: Austerity and the "More Bureaucratic Rationality" Approach' (2017) 39 *Journal of Social Welfare and Family Law* 380.
——. 'A Different Tale of Judicial Power: Administrative Review as a Problematic Response to the Judicialisation of Tribunals' [2019] *PL* 537.
Thomas, R, 'Analysing Systemic Administrative Justice Failures: Explanatory Factors and Prospects for Future Research' (2021) 43 *Journal of Social Welfare and Family Law* 339.
——. 'Does Outsourcing Improve or Weaken Administrative Justice? A Review of the Evidence' [2021] *PL* 542.
——. '*Ridge v Baldwin*: Executive and Judicial Approaches to Administrative Law Before and During the Quartet Years' in TT Arvind, R Kirkham, D Mac Síthigh and L Stirton (eds), *Executive Decision-Making and the Courts: Revisiting the Origins of Modern Judicial Review* (Oxford, Hart Publishing, 2021).
——. *Administrative Law in Action: Immigration Administration* (Oxford, Hart Publishing, 2022).
——. 'Benefit Complaints: A Critical Analysis' (2022) 44 *Journal of Social Welfare and Family Law* 258.
——. 'Legal Entitlements and Administrative Practices: LEAP Exercises and Benefits Administration' (2022) 29 *Journal of Social Security Law* 49.

——. 'The English Local Government and Social Care Ombudsman: Systemic Administrative Justice and Bureaucratisation' [2023] *PL* 240; 424.
——. 'The Northern Ireland Public Services Ombudsman's Report into Personal Independence Payment and Collective Administrative Justice' (2023) 30 *Journal of Social Security Law* 143; (2024) 31 *Journal of Social Security Law* 277.
——. 'The Operation of the MP Filter for Complaining to the Parliamentary and Health Service Ombudsman' *Essex CAJI Blog* (16 February 2023).
——. 'Administrative Justice and Vulnerable People' [2024] *PL* 234.
——. 'UK Tribunals: Structure, History, Constitutional Status and Practice' in M Groves, G Weeks and S Thomson (eds), *Administrative Tribunals in the Common Law World* (Oxford, Hart Publishing, 2024).
Thomas, R and Tomlinson, J, *Immigration Judicial Reviews: An Empirical Study* (London, Palgrave Macmillan, 2021).
——. 'Judicial Review of AI in UK Government: *Two Emergent Forms of Legal Risk* in Y-F Ng and M Groves (ed), *Automation in Governance: Theory, Practice and Problems* (Oxford, Hart Publishing, 2025).
Thompson, B, 'Administrative Justice: Towards the Millennium, Towards Integration?' in M Harris and M Partington (eds) *Administrative Justice in the 21st Century* (Oxford, Hart Publishing, 1999).
——. 'Integrated Ombudsmanry: Joined-up to a Point' (2001) 64 *MLR* 459.
——. 'Current Developments in the UK: System Building: From Tribunals to Administrative Justice' in M Adler (ed), *Administrative Justice in Context* (Oxford, Hart Publishing, 2010).
——. 'Opportunities and Constraints: Reflections on Reforming Administrative Justice Within and Across the United Kingdom' in S Nason (ed), *Administrative Justice in Wales and Comparative Perspectives* (Cardiff, University of Wales Press, 2017).
Thomson, S, *Administrative Law: A Very Short Introduction* (Oxford, Oxford University Press, 2025).
Thomson, S, Groves, M and Weeks, G (eds), *Administrative Tribunals in the Common Law World* (Oxford, Hart Publishing, 2024).
Thornberry, C, 'Non-British Justice' *The Guardian* (11 August 1965).
Tomlinson, J and Kasoulide, E, 'Delays and Backlogs as an Administrative Justice Problem: Reflections on the Case of the UK's Immigration and Asylum Tribunal' in S Thomson, M Groves and G Weeks (eds) *Administrative Tribunals in the Common Law World* (Oxford, Hart Publishing, 2024).
Tomlinson, J and Kirkham, R, 'Revisiting the Administrative Justice Legacy of New Labour' in M Gordon and A Tucker (eds), *The New Labour Constitution: Twenty Years On* (Oxford, Hart Publishing, 2022).
Toye, P, '"The Gentleman in Whitehall" Reconsidered: The Evolution of Douglas Jay's Views on Economic Planning and Consumer Choice, 1937–47' (2002) 67 *Labour History Review* 187.
Utley, TE, *Occasion for Ombudsman* (London, Johnson, 1961).
Van Eggermont Arwidson, C, Holmgren, J and Gottberg, 'Living a Frozen Life: A Qualitative Study of Asylum Seekers' Experiences and Care Practices at Accommodation Centers in Sweden' (2022) 16 *Conflict and Health* 47.
Van Gelder, M and de Vivo, F, 'Papering over Protest: Contentious Politics and Archival Suppression in Early Modern Venice' (2023) 258 *Past & Present* 44.
Varuhas, JNE, 'Governmental Rejections of Ombudsman Findings: What Role for the Courts?' (2009) 72 *MLR* 102.
——. *Judicial Capture of Political Accountability* (London, Policy Exchange, 2016).
Wade, HWR, 'Tribunal and Inquiries Act 1958' (1958) 16 *CLJ* 129.
——. *Towards Administrative Justice* (Ann Arbor, University of Michigan Press, 1963);
——. 'Administrative Tribunals and Administrative Justice' (1981) 55 *Australian Law Journal* 374.
Walwyn, W, 'The Compassionate Samaritane' (1644) in JR McMichael and B Taft (eds), *The Writings of William Walwyn* (Athens, GA, University of Georgia Press, 1989).
Warren, N, 'The Adjudication Gap: A Discussion Document' (2006) 13 *Journal of Social Security Law* 110.
Watts, B and Fitzpatrick, S, *Welfare Conditionality* (Abingdon, Routledge, 2018).
Webster, D, 'Explaining the Rise and Fall of JSA and ESA Sanctions, 2010–16' (London, Child Poverty Action Group, 17 August 2016).
Weiler, P, 'Labour and the Land: From Municipalization to the Land Commission, 1951–71' (2008) 19 *Twentieth Century British History* 314.
Welfare Conditionality Project, *Final Findings Report 2013–18* (York, University of York, 2018).

Wheare, KC, 'The Redress of Grievances' (1962) 40 *Public Administration* 125.
——. *Maladministration and its Remedies* (London, Stevens, 1973).
White, C, 'Enforcing the Decisions of Ombudsmen: The Northern Ireland Local Government Ombudsman's Experience' (1994) 45 *Northern Ireland Legal Quarterly* 395.
Whiteford, P, 'Debt by Design: The Anatomy of a Social Policy Fiasco – or was it Something Worse?' (2021) 80 *Australian Journal of Public Administration* 340.
Whitehouse, R, 'Council Officers Told Not to Ignore Ombudsman Recommendations due to Cost' *Cornwall Live* (28 April 2021).
Wikeley, N, 'Decision-Making and Appeals under the Social Security Act 1998' (1998) 5 *Journal of Social Security Law* 104.
——. 'Burying Bell: Managing the Judicialisation of Social Security Tribunals' (2000) 63 *MLR* 475.
——. 'Decision Making and the New Tribunals' (2006) 13 *Journal of Social Security Law* 86.
——. 'Future Directions for Tribunals: A UK Perspective' in R Creyke (ed), *Tribunals in the Common Law World* (Sydney, Federation Press, 2008).
——. 'Justice in the Welfare State: Tribunals in the Modern Era' (2022) 29 *Journal of Social Security Law* 74.
——. 'Tribunals and Judicial Independence in the Post-war Welfare State: GL Haggen and the "Practical Man's" Approach to "Good Cause"' (2024) 31 *Journal of Social Security Law* 19.
Wikeley, N and Young, R, 'The Administration of Benefits in Britain: Adjudication Officers and the Influence of Social Security Appeal Tribunals' [1992] *PL* 238.
Wilson, H, *Liberty and the Law* (London, Labour Party, 1964).
Williams, DGT, 'The Council on Tribunals: The First 25 Years' [1984] *PL* 73.
Williams, J, Gill, C and Hirst, C, 'Towards Therapeutic Complaints Resolution' in M Groves and A Stuhmcke (eds), *The Ombudsman in the Modern State* (Oxford, Hart Publishing, 2022).
Williams, E, 'Punitive Welfare Reform and Claimant Mental Health: The Impact of Benefit Sanctions on Anxiety and Depression' (2021) 55 *Social Policy and Administration* 157.
Wiltshire, FHC, 'The Appellate Jurisdiction of Central Government Departments' (1924) 2 *Public Administration* 370.
Woolf, H, 'A Hotchpotch of Appeals: The Need for a Blender' (1988) 7 *Civil Justice Quarterly* 44.
——. *Protection of the Public: A New Challenge* (London, Stevens, 1990).
Wraith, RE and Hutchesson, PG, *Administrative Tribunals* (London, Allen & Unwin, 1974).
Wright, T, *Citizens and Subjects: An Essay on British Politics* (Abingdon, Routledge, 1994).
Yardley, DCM, 'The Functions of the Council on Tribunals' (1980) 2 *Journal of Social Welfare Law* 270.
Zorzi, A, *Venice 697–1797: City, Republic, Empire* (London, Sidgwick & Jackson, 1983).

Official Publications

Adams, L, Tindle, A, Basran, S, Dobie, S, Thomson, D, Robinson, D and Shepherd, C, *Experiences of Education, Health and Care Plans: A Survey of Parents and Young People* (London, DfE, 2017).
Adjudicator's Office, *Annual Report* (2023).
Administrative Justice and Tribunals Council, *Principles for Administrative Justice* (London, AJTC, 2010).
——. *Right First Time* (London, AJTC, 2011).
——. *Securing Fairness and Redress: Administrative Justice at Risk?* (London, AJTC, 2011).
——. *Putting it Right: A Strategic Approach to Resolving Administrative Disputes* (London, AJTC, 2012).
——. *Future Oversight of Administrative Justice: The AJTC's Response to the Justice Committee Report* (London, AJTC, 2013).
Administrative Justice and Tribunals Council and the Care Quality Commission, *Patients' Experiences of the First-tier Tribunal (Mental Health)* (London, AJTC, 2011).
Administrative Justice and Tribunals Council Scottish Committee, *Right to Appeal: A Review of Decisions Made by Scottish Public Bodies Where There is No Right of Appeal or Where the Appeal Procedure is Inaccessible or Inappropriate* (London, AJTC, 2011).
Anderson, M, McIlroy, A and McAleer, M, *Mapping the Administrative Justice Landscape in Northern Ireland: Report on Research Undertaken on the Administrative Justice System in Northern Ireland* (Belfast, Northern Ireland Ombudsman's Office, 2014).

Atkinson, R, Buck, T, Pollard, D and Smith, N, *A Regional Study of Local Authority and Court Processes in Homelessness Cases* (London, Lord Chancellor's Department, 1999).
Australian Commonwealth Ombudsman, *Following the Law is Not Optional* (2026).
Australian Royal Commission into the Robodebt Scheme, *Report* (Canberra, Commonwealth of Australia, 2023).
Behavioural Insights Team, *Behavioural Government: Using Behavioural Science to Improve How Governments Make Decisions* (London, BIT, 2018).
Bell, K, *Research Study on Supplementary Benefit Appeal Tribunals. Review of Main Findings: Conclusions; Recommendations* (London, HMSO, 1975).
Beveridge, W, *Social Insurance and Allied Services: Report by Sir William Beveridge* (Cmnd 6404, 1942).
Cabinet Office, *Fourth Report from the Select Committee on the Parliamentary Commissioner for Administration (Review of Access and Jurisdiction) Session 1977-78: Observations by the Government* (Cmnd 7449, 1979).
——. *Complaints Task Force: Effective Complaints Systems: Principles and Checklist* (London, Cabinet Office, 1993).
——. *The Citizen's Charter Complaints Task Force: Interim Report* (London, Cabinet Office, 1994).
——. *The Ombudsman in Your Files* (London, Cabinet Office, 1997).
——. *Service First, the New Charter Programme* (London, Cabinet Office, 1998).
——. *How to Deal with Complaints* (London, Cabinet Office, 1999).
——. *Review of the Public Sector Ombudsmen in England: A Report by the Cabinet Office* (London, Cabinet Office, 2000).
——. *Cabinet Manual* (London, Cabinet Office, 2011).
——. *A Public Service Ombudsman: Government Response to Consultation* (London, Cabinet Office, 2015).
——. *Draft Public Services Ombudsman Bill 2016 Bill* (Cm 9374, 2016).
Children's Commissioner, *'They Never Give up on You'* (London, Children's Commissioner, 2012).
——. *'Always Someone Else's Problem': Office of the Children's Commissioner's Report on Illegal Exclusions* (London, Children's Commissioner, 2013).
Civil Service Department, *Legal Entitlements and Administrative Practices: A Report by Officials* (London, HMSO, 1979).
Competition and Markets Authority, *Care Homes Market Study: Final Report* (London, CMA, 2017).
Coalition Government, *The Coalition: Our Programme for Government* (May 2010).
Committee for the Office of the First Minister and Deputy First Minister, *Report on the Committee's Proposals for a Northern Ireland Public Services Ombudsman Bill Volume One* (Belfast, Northern Ireland Government, Seventh Report, 2013).
Committee on Standards in Public Life, *Recognising and Responding to Early Warning Signs in Public Sector Bodies* (London, CSPL, 2025).
Council of Europe, *Recommendation on the Protection of the Individual in Relation the Acts of Administrative Authorities*, 28 September 1977, R(77)31.
——. *Recommendation of the Committee of Ministers Concerning the Exercise of Discretionary Powers by Administrative Authorities*, 11 March 1980, R(80)2.
——. *Report to the United Kingdom Government on the Visit to the United Kingdom Carried out by the European Committee for the Prevention of Torture and Inhuman or Degrading Treatment or Punishment (CPT) from 13 to 23 May 2019* (Strasbourg, CoE, 2020).
Council on Tribunals, *The Functions of the Council on Tribunals: Special Report by the Council* (Cmnd 7805, 1980).
——. *Social Security: Abolition of Independent Appeals under the Proposed Social Fund* (Cmnd 9722, 1986).
——. *Annual Report 1989/90* (HC 1990–91, 64).
——. *School Admission and Exclusion Appeal Panels: Special Report* (Cm 5788, 2003).
Crerar, L, *The Crerar Review: The Report of the Independent Review of Regulation, Audit, Inspection and Complaints Handling of Public Services in Scotland* (Edinburgh, Scottish Government, 2007).
Department for Business, Innovation and Skills, *Apology from the Department for Business, Innovation and Skills: Icelandic Water Trawlermen Compensation Scheme 2009* (London, DBIS, 2012).
Department for Communities and Local Government, *Strong and Prosperous Communities: The Local Government White Paper* (Cm 6939, 2006).
Department for Constitutional Affairs, *Transforming Public Services: Complaints, Redress and Tribunals* (Cm 6243, 2004).
Department for Education, *The Importance of Teaching* (Cm 7980, 2010).

——. *Exclusion from Maintained Schools, Academies and Pupil Referral Units in England: Statutory Guidance for Those with Legal Responsibilities in Relation to Exclusion* (London, DfE, 2017).
——. *Government Response to the Committee's First Report of Session 2019*, published by the House of Commons Education Committee as: *Special Educational Needs and Disabilities* (HC 2019–21, 668).
——. *School Admission Appeals Code* (London, DfE, 2022).
Department for Work and Pensions, *Report on the Standards of Decision Making in the Benefits Agency, Child Support Agency and Employment Service 2001–02* (HC 2002–03, 880).
——. *The Government Response to the Public Administration Select Committee's Sixth Report of Session 2005–06 The Ombudsman in Question: The Ombudsman's Report on Pensions and its Constitutional Implications* (Cm 6961, 2006).
——. *Response to the Report by the Parliamentary Ombudsman 'Trusting in the Pensions Promise'* (London, DWP, 2006).
——. *State Pensions Reform: Detailed Communications Plan* (London, DWP, 2008) (not published; acquired through FOI request).
——. *Social Security and Child Support Tribunal Hearings: Early Analysis of Appeals Allowed from Pilot Data* (London, DWP, 2012).
——. *Mandatory Consideration of Revision before Appeal* (TSO, 2012).
——. *Benefit Sanctions Statistics* (2018).
——. *Personal Independence Payment Claimant Research: Final Report Summary* (DWP, 2018).
——. *Fighting Fraud in the Welfare System: Going Further* (CP 1072, 2022).
——. *Financial Redress for Maladministration: Staff Guide* (2020).
——. *Quality Framework* (London, DWP, 2023).
——. *Government Response to the Parliamentary and Health Service Ombudsman's Investigation into Women's State Pension Age and Associated Issues* (London, DWP, 2024).
——. *Annual Report and Accounts 2022–23* (HC 2023–24, 1455).
——. *Annual Report and Accounts 2023–24* (HC 2023–24, 62).
——. *Government Response to the Parliamentary and Health Service Ombudsman's Investigation into Women's State Pension Age and Associated Issues* (DWP, 2024).
——. *Annual Report and Accounts 2024–25* (HC 2024–25, 995).
——. *Universal Credit Advances Model: Fairness Assessment* (London, DWP, 2025).
Department of Health and Social Care, *National Framework for NHS Continuing Healthcare and NHS-Funded Nursing Care* (London, DHSC, 2018).
——. *Government Response to the Recommendations of the Public Administration and Constitutional Affairs Committee's Seventeenth Report of Session 2017–19: Ignoring the Alarms Follow-up: Too Many Avoidable Deaths from Eating Disorders* (CP 105, 2019).
——. *People at the Heart of Care: Adult Social Care Reform White Paper* (CP 560, 2021).
——. *Review into the Operational Effectiveness of the Care Quality Commission: Full Report* (London, DHSC, 2024).
Department of Health and Social Security, *Reform of Social Security* (Cmnd 9517, 1985).
——. *Reform of Social Security: Programme for Action* (Cmnd 9691, 1985).
Department for Social Security, *Equality in State Pension Age* (Cm 2420, 1993).
——. *Improving Decision-Making and Appeals in Social Security* (Cm 3328, 1996).
Department of Trade and Industry, *Observations by the Government on the Report of the Parliamentary Commissioner for Administration on Barlow Clowes* (HC 1989–90, 99).
Donoughmore Committee, *Committee on Ministers' Powers* (Cmd 4060, 1932).
Environment Agency, *Annual Report and Accounts 2020–21* (HC 2021–22, 768).
Equality and Human Rights Commission, 'NHS Facing Court Action over Unlawful Policies' (19 March 2018).
——. EHRC, 'NHS U-Turns on Discriminatory Policies' (31 May 2018).
——. *A Human Rights Guide for Ombudsman Schemes* (London, EHRC, 2019).
——. *Challenging Adult Social Care Decisions in England and Wales* (2023).
European Commission for Democracy (Venice Commission) (Opinion No 1044/2021 CDL-AD(2021)041, 18 October 2021).
European Ombudsman, *The European Code of Good Administrative Behaviour* (2001).
Foreign, Commonwealth and Development Office, *FCDO Consular Network: Rape and Sexual Assault Action Plan* (London, FCDO, 2022).

Fortescue, B, Howard, FF, Howard, P, Kelly, G and Elwan, M, *Examining the Impact of Sanctions on Custodial Misconduct following Disciplinary Adjudications* (London, Ministry of Justice, 2021).
Franks Committee, *Report of the Committee on Administrative Tribunals and Enquiries* (Cmnd 218, 1957).
Gordon, R, *Better to Serve the Public: Proposals to Restructure, Reform, Renew and Reinvigorate Public Services Ombudsmen* (London, Cabinet Office, 2014).
Graham, B, White, C, Edwards, A, Potter, S and Street, C, *School Exclusion: A Literature Review on the Continued Disproportionate Exclusion of Certain Children* (London, DfE, 2019).
Hay, C, McKenna, K and Buck, T, *Evaluation of Early Neutral Evaluation: Alternative Dispute Resolution in the Social Security and Child Support Tribunal* (London, Ministry of Justice, Research Series 2/10, 2010).
Health Service Ombudsman, *NHS Funding for Long Term Care* (HC 2002–03, 399).
Home Office, *Report of the Committee on Immigration Appeals* (Cmnd 3387, 1967).
——. *Immigration Bill Factsheet: Appeals* (London, Home Office, 2013).
——. *Government Response to the Joint Committee on Human Rights, Eighth Report of Session 2013–14* (2014).
——. *The Ethical Decision-Making Model* (London, Home Office, 2021).
——. *Restoring Order and Control: A Statement on the Government's Asylum and Returns Policy* (CP 1418, 2025).
House of Commons Communities and Local Government Committee, *The Work of the Local Government Ombudsman* (HC 2012–13, 431).
House of Commons Education Committee, *Oral Evidence: Special Educational Needs and Disabilities* (HC 2017–19, 968).
——. *Special Educational Needs and Disabilities* (HC 2019, 20).
——. *Solving the SEND Crisis* (HC 2024–25, 492).
House of Commons Environment, Food and Rural Affairs Committee, *The Rural Payments Agency and the Implementation of the Single Payment Scheme* (HC 2006–07, 107).
House of Commons Health Committee, *NHS Continuing Care* (HC 2004–05, 399).
House of Commons Home Affairs Committee, *Immigration and Nationality Department of the Home Office* (HC 1984-85, 277).
——. *The Windrush Compensation Scheme* (HC 2021–22, 204).
House of Commons Justice Committee, *Government's Proposed Reform of Legal Aid* (HC 2010–12, 681).
——. *Impact of Changes to Civil Legal Aid under Part 1 of the Legal Aid, Sentencing and Punishment of Offenders Act 2012* (HC 2014–15, 311).
——. *Courts and Tribunals Fees* (HC 2015–16, 167).
——. *Court and Tribunal Reforms* (HC 2019, 190).
House of Commons Levelling Up, Housing and Communities Committee, *Oral Evidence: LGSCO Triennial Review* (HC 2021–22, 960).
House of Commons Library, *Reductions in Inherited SERPS* (SN-00706, 2016).
——. *Off-rolling in English Schools* (Briefing Paper No 08444, 2020).
——. *Errors in Payments Made to Victims of the Equitable Life Scandal* (CDP-2021-0012, 2021).
House of Commons Public Accounts Committee, *State Earnings-Related Pension Scheme: The Failure to Inform the Public about Reduced Pension Rights for Widows and Widowers* (HC 1999–2000, 401).
——. *Inland Revenue Standard Report: New Tax Credits* (HC 2005–06, 782).
——. *The Compensation Scheme for Former Icelandic Water Trawlermen* (HC 2007–08, 71).
——. *HM Revenue and Customs: Tax Credits and Income Tax* (HC 2008–09, 311).
——. *Administering the Equitable Life Payment Scheme* (HC 2013–14, 111).
——. *Personal Independence Payment* (HC 2014–15, 280).
——. *HMRC's Contract with Concentrix* (HC 2016–17, 727).
——. *Employment and Support Allowance* (HC 2017–19, 975).
——. *NHS Continuing Healthcare Funding* (HC 2017–19, 455).
——. *Support for Children with Special Educational Needs and Disabilities* (HC 2019–21, 85).
——. *Underpayments of the State Pension* (HC 2021–22, 654).
——. *The Department for Work & Pensions Annual Report and Accounts 2022–23* (HC 2023–24, 290).
——. *The Asylum Transformation Programme* (HC 2022–23, 1334).
——. *Driving Licence Backlogs at the DVLA* (HC 2022–23, 735).
——. *Investigation into the UK Passport Office* (HC 2022–23, 738).

——. *Progress on the Courts and Tribunals Reform Programme* (HC 2022–23, 1002).
——. *DWP Follow-up: Autumn 2025* (HC 2024–25, 1447).
House of Commons Public Administration Select Committee, *Administrative Failure: Inherited SERPS* (HC 1999–2000, 433).
——. *Review of Public Sector Ombudsman in England* (HC 1999–2000, 612).
——. *Ombudsman Issues* (HC 2002–03, 448).
——. *Tax Credits: Putting Things Right* (HC 2005–06, 577).
——. *A Debt of Honour* (HC 2005–06, 735).
——. *Pensions Bill: Government Undertakings Relating to the Financial Assistance Scheme* (HC 2006–07, 523).
——. *The Ombudsman in Question: The Ombudsman's Report on Pensions and its Constitutional Implications* (HC 2005–06, 1081).
——. *When Citizens Complain* (HC 2007–08, 409).
——. *From Citizen's Charter to Public Service Guarantees: Entitlements to Public Services* (HC 2007–08, 411).
——. *Good Government* (HC 2008–09, 97).
——. *Justice Delayed: The Ombudsman's Report on Equitable Life* (HC 2008–09, 41).
——. *Justice Denied? The Government's Response to the Ombudsman's Report on Equitable Life* (HC 2008–09, 219).
——. *Defra's Response to the Ombudsman's Report on the Single Payment Scheme* (HC 2009–10, 331).
——. *Parliament and the Ombudsman* (HC 2009–10, 107).
——. *Parliament and the Ombudsman: Further Report* (HC 2009–10, 471).
——. *Future Oversight of Administrative Justice: The Proposed Abolition of the Administrative Justice and Tribunals Council* (HC 2010–12, 1621).
——. *More Complaints Please!* (HC 2013–14, 229).
——. *Time for a People's Ombudsman Service* (HC 2013–14, 655).
——. *Investigating Clinical Incidents in the NHS* (HC 2014–15, 886).
——. *Follow up to PHSO Report of an Investigation into a Complaint about HS2 Ltd* (HC 2015–16, 793).
House of Commons Public Administration and Constitutional Affairs Committee, *Follow up to PHSO Report of an Investigation into a Complaint about HS2 Ltd* (HC 2015–16, 793).
——. *Follow-up to PHSO Report on Unsafe Discharge from Hospital* (HC 2016–17, 97).
——. *PHSO Review: Quality of NHS Complaints Investigations* (HC 2016–17, 94)
——. *Will the NHS Never Learn? Follow-up to PHSO Report 'Learning from Mistakes' on the NHS in England* (HC 2016–17, 743).
——. *Ignoring the Alarms Follow-up: Too Many Avoidable Deaths from Eating Disorders* (HC 2017–19, 855).
——. *Parliamentary and Health Service Ombudsman Scrutiny 2021–22* (HC 2022–23, 745).
——. *Parliamentary and Health Service Ombudsman Scrutiny 2022–23* (HC 2023–24, 198).
——. *Parliamentary and Health Service Ombudsman Scrutiny 2022–23: Government and PHSO response* (HC 2023–24, 774).
——. 'Government Still "Not Convinced" by Case for Reform of the Parliamentary and Health Service Ombudsman' (23 May 2024).
House of Commons Public Services Committee, *The Citizen's Charter* (HC 1996–97, 78).
House of Commons Reform Committee, *Rebuilding the House* (HC 2008–09, 1117).
House of Commons Select Committee on the Parliamentary Commissioner for Administration, *Reports of the Parliamentary Commissioner for Administration* (HC 1977–78, 544).
——. *Parliamentary Commissioner for Administration (Review of Access and Jurisdiction)* (HC 1977–78, 615 and 444).
——. *The Land Compensation Act 1973* (HC 1978–79, 91).
——. *Local Government Cases: Enforcement of Remedies* (HC 1985–86, 448).
——. *Report of the Parliamentary Commissioner for Administration for 1989* (HC 1989–90, 129).
——. *Report of the Parliamentary Commissioner for Administration 1989* (HC 1990–91, 129).
——. *Oral Evidence: The Powers, Work and Jurisdiction of the Ombudsman* (HC 1992–93, 650).
——. *Government Reply to the First Report from the Select Committee on the Parliamentary Commissioner for Administration, Session 1993–94, the Powers, Work and Jurisdiction of the Ombudsman* (HC 1993–94, 619).
——. *The Powers, Work and Jurisdiction of the Ombudsman* (HC 1993–94, 33).

——. *The Channel Tunnel Rail Link and Exceptional Hardship* (HC 1994–95, 270).
——. *Fifth Special Report: The Channel Tunnel Rail Link and Exceptional Hardship: The Government Response* (HC 1994–95, 819).
——. *Maladministration and Redress* (HC 1994–95, 112).
——. *Report of the Parliamentary Ombudsman for 1994* (HC 1994–95, 394).
——. *The Channel Tunnel Rail Link and Exceptional Hardship: Government Proposals for Redress* (HC 1996–97, 453).
House of Commons Select Committee on Procedure, *Third Report* (HC 1945–46, 189).
House of Commons Treasury Committee, *The Administration of Tax Credits* (HC 2005–06, 811).
House of Commons Work and Pensions Committee, *Decision Making and Appeals in the Benefits System* (HC 2009–10, 313).
——. *Monitoring the Performance of the Department for Work and Pensions in 2012–13* (HC 2013–14, 1153).
——. *Employment and Support Allowance and Work Capability Assessments* (HC 2014–15, 302).
——. *Oral Evidence: Employment and Support Allowance and Work Capacity Benefits* (HC 2014–15, 1212).
——. *Communication of State Pension Age Changes* (HC 2015–16, 899).
——. *Concentrix* (HC 2016–17, 720).
——. *Benefit Sanctions* (HC 2017–19, 955).
——. *Benefit Sanctions: Government Response to the Committee's Nineteenth Report of Session 2017–19* (HC 2017–19, 1949).
——. *Health Assessments for Benefits* (HC 2022–23, 128).
——. *Health Assessments for Benefits: Government Response to Committee's Fifth Report of Session 2022–23* (HC 2022–23, 1558).
——. *Oral Evidence: PHSO Report on Women's State Pension Age* (HC 2023–24, 740).
——. *Oral Evidence: Pensioner Poverty: Challenges and Mitigations* (HC 2024–25, 465).
House of Lords Adult Social Care Committee, *A 'Gloriously Ordinary Life': Spotlight on Adult Social Care* (HL 2022–23, 99).
House of Lords Constitution Committee, *The Legislative Process* (HL 2015–16, 27).
HM Courts and Tribunals Service, *Immigration and Asylum Appeals Reformed Service: Evaluation Report* (London, HMCTS, 2025).
HM Government, *Open Public Services White Paper* (Cm 8145, 2011).
HM Inspectorate of Prisons, *Incentivising and Promoting Good Behaviour* (London, HMIP, 2018).
HMRC, *Statutory Review Process: Quantitative Research to Understand Customers' Experience and Perception of the Statutory Review Process* (London, HMRC, 2014).
HM Treasury, *The Prudential Regulation of the Equitable Life Assurance Society: The Government's Response to the Report of the Parliamentary Ombudsman's Investigation* (Cm 7538, 2008).
——. *Managing Public Money* (London, HM Treasury, 2023).
Independent Case Examiner, *Annual Report 2019–2020* (London, DWP, 2020).
——. *Annual Report 2024–25* (London, DWP, 2025).
Independent Chief Inspector of Borders and Immigration, *An Inspection of the Administrative Review Processes Introduced Following the 2014 Immigration Act* (London, ICIBI, 2016).
——. *A Re-inspection of the Administrative Review Process* (London, ICIBI, 2017).
——. *An Inspection of Administrative Reviews* (London, ICIBI, 2020).
——. *An Inspection of the Handling of Complaints and MP's Correspondence by the Home Office Borders, Immigration and Citizenship System (BICS)* (London, ICIBI, 2020).
——. *An Inspection of Asylum Casework* (London, ICIBI, 2021).
——. *An Inspection of the Effectiveness of the UKVI Chief Caseworker Unit's Referral Process* (London, ICIBI, 2022).
——. *An Inspection of Asylum Casework* (London, ICIBI, 2024).
Independent Review of Administrative Law (CP 407, 2021).
Independent Review of Maternity Services at the Shrewsbury and Telford Hospital NHS Trust (HC 2021–22, 1219).
Infected Blood Inquiry, *Additional Report on Compensation* (HC 2025, 1167).
Information Commissioner's Office, *Addressing Concerns on the Use of AI by Local Authorities* (19 January 2023).
Joint Committee on Human Rights, *Legislative Scrutiny: Immigration Bill* (2013–14 HL 102 HC 935).
——. *Human Rights Ombudsperson* (2022–23 HL 175 HC 222).

——. *Human Rights Ombudsperson: Government Response to the Committee's Eleventh Report* (HC 2022–23, 1489).
Judicial College, *Equal Treatment Bench Book* (2024).
Judiciary of England and Wales, *The Lady Chief Justice's Report 2025* (London, HMSO, 2025).
Kirkup, B, *The Report of the Morecambe Bay Investigation* (London, The Stationery Office, 2015).
Law Commission, *Public Services Ombudsmen* (Law Com No 329, 2011).
——. *Thirteenth Programme of Law Reform* (Law Com No 377, 2017).
——. *Devolved Tribunals in Wales Report* (Law Com No 403, 2021).
Leggatt, A, *Tribunals for Users: One System, One Service: Report of the Review of Tribunals by Sir Andrew Leggatt* (London, Lord Chancellor's Department, 2001).
Local Government Association, *Towards an Effective and Financially Sustainable Approach to SEND in England: An Independent Report by ISOS Partnership Commissioned by the County Council Network and Local Government Association* (2024).
Local Government Ombudsman, *Good Administrative Practice* (London, Commission for Local Administration in England, 1993).
Local Government and Social Care Ombudsman, *Homelessness: How Councils Can Ensure Justice for Homeless People* (Coventry, LGSCO, 2011).
——. *Are We Getting the Best from Children's Social Care Complaints? Focus Report: Learning Lessons from Complaints* (Coventry, LGSCO, 2015).
——. *Counting the Cost of Care: The Council's Role in Informing Public Choices about Care Homes* (Coventry, LGSCO, 2015).
——. *Review of Local Government Complaints 2014–15* (Coventry, LGSCO, 2015).
——. *All on Board? Navigating School Transport Issues* (Coventry, LGSCO, 2017).
——. *Effective Complaint Handling for Local Authorities* (Coventry, LGSCO, 2020).
——. *Adapting and Innovating: Annual Report* (HC 2020–21, 900).
——. *Not Going to Plan? Education, Health and Care Plans Two Years on* (Coventry, LGSCO, 2019).
——. *Focus on Housing Benefit* (Coventry, LGSCO, 2020).
——. *Home Truths: How Well are Councils Implementing the Homelessness Reduction Act?* (Coventry, LGSCO, 2020).
——. *Good Administrative Practice during the Response to Covid-19* (Coventry, LGSCO, 2020).
——. *Review of Local Government Complaints 2020–21* (Coventry, LGSCO 2021).
——. *Review, Refresh, Renew: Triennial Review of Local Government and Social Care Complaints and Public Accountability Arrangements* (Coventry, LGSCO, 2021).
——. *External Review of Liverpool City Council's Complaints Procedures by the Local Government and Social Care Ombudsman* (Coventry, LGSCO 2022).
——. *Equal Access: Getting it Right for People with Disabilities* (Coventry, LGSCO, 2022).
——. *Unprecedented Pressure: Learning from Complaints about Council and Care Provider Actions during the COVID-19 Pandemic* (Coventry, LGSCO, 2022).
——. *Equal Justice: Learning Lessons from Complaints about People's Human Rights* (Coventry, LGSCO, 2022).
——. *Joint Complaint Handling Code* (Coventry, LGSCO, 2023).
——. *Local Government and Social Care in 2024 and Beyond: Time to Rebuild: Triennial Review by the Local Government and Social Care Ombudsman and Commission for Local Administration in England* (Coventry, LGSCO, 2024).
Maternity and Neonatal Services in East Kent: 'Reading the Signals' Report (HC 2021–22, 681).
Mid Staffordshire NHS Foundation Trust Public Inquiry Chaired by Robert Francis QC, *Report of the Mid Staffordshire NHS Foundation Trust Public Inquiry* (HC 2012–13, 947).
Ministry of Defence, *Armed Forces Compensation Scheme Quinquennial Review 2022/23* (London, Ministry of Defence, 2023).
Ministry of Justice, *Court and Tribunal Fees* (Cm 9181, 2015).
——. *Transforming Our Justice System* (2016).
——. *Tribunal Statistics Quarterly* (2024).
Ministry of Labour, *Unemployment Insurance Acts 1920–1929: Selected Decisions Given by the Umpire from 19th April 1920, to 12th March 1930 Respecting Claims to Benefit* (London, HMSO, 1930).
Ministry of Reconstruction, *Report of the Machinery of Government Committee* (Cd 9230, 1918).

Murphy, C, *Public Awareness of State Pension Age Equalisation* (London, DWP Research Report No 221, 2004).
National Audit Office, *State Earnings-Related Pension Scheme: The Failure to Inform the Public of Reduced Pension Rights for Widows and Widowers* (HC 1999–2000, 320).
——. *Getting it Right, Putting it Right: Improving Decision-Making and Appeals in Social Security Benefits* (HC 2002–03, 1142)
——. *Improving Service Quality: Action in Response to the Inherited SERPS Problem* (HC 2002–03, 497).
——. *Improving the Speed and Quality of Asylum Decisions* (HC 2003–04, 535).
——. *Citizen Redress: What Citizens Can Do if Things Go Wrong with Public Services* (HC 2004–05, 21).
——. *Helping Those in Financial Hardship: The Running of the Social Fund* (HC 2004–05, 179).
——. *The Delays in Administering the 2005 Single Payment Scheme in England* (HC 2005–06, 1631).
——. *The Compensation Scheme for Former Icelandic Water Trawlermen* (HC 2006–07, 530).
——. *Compensating Victims of Violent Crime* (HC 2007–08, 100).
——. *Department for Work and Pensions: Handling Customer Complaints* (HC 2007–08, 995).
——. *Personal Independence Payment: Early Progress* (HC 2013–14, 1070).
——. *Public Service Markets: Putting Things Right When They Go Wrong* (HC 2014–15, 84).
——. *Managing Business Operations: What Government Needs to Get Right* (2015).
——. *The Impact of State Pension Reforms on People with Guaranteed Minimum Pensions* (HC 2015–16, 907).
——. *Benefit Sanctions* (HC 2016–17, 628).
——. *Investigation into HMRC's Contract with Concentrix* (HC 2016–17, 915).
——. *Investigation into NHS Continuing Healthcare Funding* (HC 2017–19, 239).
——. *Investigation into Errors in Employment and Support Allowance* (HC 2017–19, 837).
——. *Support for Pupils with Special Educational Needs and Disabilities in England* (HC 2017–19, 2636).
——. *Investigation into the Underpayment of the State Pension* (HC 2021–22, 665).
——. *Improving Operational Delivery in Government: A Good Practice Guide for Senior Leaders* (London, NAO, 2021).
——. *Customer Service: HM Revenue & Customs* (HC 2023–24, 726).
——. *Reducing the Backlog in the Crown Court* (HC 2023–24, 728).
——. *Investigation into the Pensions Dashboards Programme* (HC 2023–24, 732).
——. *Report on Accounts: DWP* (2023).
——. *Lessons Learned: Government Compensation Schemes* (HC 2024–25, 121).
——. *DWP Customer Service* (HC 2024–25, 127).
——. *Support for Children and Young People with Special Educational Needs* (HC 2024–25, 299).
——. *Carer's Allowance* (HC 2024–25, 377).
——. *Immigration: Skilled Worker Visas* (HC 2024–25, 745).
Northern Ireland Assembly, *Research and Information Service Briefing Paper: Own-Motion Investigations by Ombudsmen* (Paper 80/15, 2014).
Northern Ireland Public Services Ombudsman, *Human Rights Manual* (Belfast, NIPSO, 2016).
——. *Overview Report: The Use of Restrictive Practices in Northern Ireland Schools* (Belfast, NIPSO, 2021).
——. *PIP and the Value of Further Evidence: An Investigation into Personal Independence Payment* (Belfast, NIPSO, 2021).
——. *Draft Model Complaints Handling Procedure: The Complaints Handling Process* (Belfast, NIPSO, 2022).
——. *'Forgotten': An Investigation into Healthcare Waiting List Communications* (Belfast, NIPSO, 2023).
——. *Strengthening Our Roots: An Overview Report on Tree Protection in the Planning System* (Belfast, NIPSO, 2023).
——. *PIP and the Value of Further Evidence: Own Initiative Follow up* (Belfast, NIPSO, 2023).
——. *Lost in Translation: An Overview Report by the Northern Ireland Public Services Ombudsman on General Practitioner Use of Interpreting Services* (Belfast, NIPSO, 2025).
Northern Ireland President of Appeal Tribunals, *Standards of Decision Making by the Department for Communities* (Belfast, Appeals Service, 2024).
OFSTED, *SEND: Old Issues, New Issues, Next Steps* (2021).
Parliamentary Commissioner for Administration, *Television Licences* (HC 1974–75, 680).
——. *A War Pensions Injustice Remedied* (HC 1977–78, 312).
——. *Rochester Way, Bexley: Refusal to Meet Late Claims for Compensation* (HC 1977–78, 598).

——. *Annual Report for 1979* (HC 1978–79, 402).
——. *Annual Report for 1983* (HC 1983–84, 322).
——. *Second Report Session 1988–89: Annual Report for 1988* (HC 1988–89, 301).
——. *The Barlow Clowes Affair* (HC 1989–90, 76).
——. *Delays in Handling Disability Living Allowance Claims* (HC 1992–93, 652).
——. *Annual Report for 1993* (HC 1993–94, 290).
——. *Investigation of Complaints against the Child Support Agency* (HC 1994–95, 135).
——. *The Channel Tunnel Rail Link and Blight: Investigation of Complaints against the Department for Transport* (HC 1994–95, 193).
——. *Investigation into Delays in Making Payments under the Arable Area Payments Scheme* (HC 1999–2000, 635).
——. *State Earnings-Related Provision (SERPS) Inheritance Provisions* (HC 1999–2000, 305).
——. *State Earnings Related Pension Scheme (SERPS) Inheritance Provisions: Redress for Maladministration* (HC 2000–01, 271).
Parliamentary and Health Service Ombudsman, *'A Debt of Honour': The Ex Gratia Scheme for British Groups Interned by the Japanese during the Second World War* (HC 2005–06, 324).
——. *Tax Credits: Putting Things Right* (HC 2005–06, 124).
——. *Trusting in the Pensions Promise: Government Bodies and the Security of Final Salary Occupational Pensions* (HC 2005–06, 984).
——. *The Parliamentary Ombudsman: Withstanding the Test of Time* (HC 2006–07, 421).
——. *Put Together in Haste: 'Cod Wars' Trawlermen's Compensation Scheme* (HC 2006–07, 313).
——. *Retrospective Continuing Care Funding and Redress* (HC 2006–07, 386).
——. *Tax Credits: Getting it Wrong?* (HC 2006–07, 1010).
——. *Equitable Life: A Decade of Regulatory Failure* (HC 2007–08, 815).
——. *Six Lives: The Provision of Public Services to People with Learning Disabilities* (HC 2008–09, 203).
——. *Injustice Unremedied: The Government's Response on Equitable Life* (HC 2008–09, 435).
——. *Cold Comfort: The Administration of the 2005 Single Payment Scheme by the Rural Payments Agency* (HC 2009–10, 81).
——. *'Fast and Fair?' A Report by the Parliamentary Ombudsman on the UK Border Agency* (HC 2009–10, 329).
——. *A Breach of Confidence: A Report by the Parliamentary Ombudsman on an Investigation of a Complaint about HM Revenue & Customs, the Child Support Agency and the Department for Work and Pensions* (HC 2010–12, 709).
——. *Care and Compassion? Report of the Health Service Ombudsman on Ten Investigations into NHS Care of Older People* (HC 2010–12, 778).
——. *More Cold Comfort: How the Rural Payments Agency Handled Claims to the Single Payment Scheme in 2005–06* (HC 2010–12, 1662).
——. *Report by the Parliamentary and Health Service Ombudsman on Complaints about Disability Issues* (HC 2010–12, 1512).
——. *Responsive and Accountable? The Ombudsman's Review of Complaint Handling by Government Departments and Public Organisations 2011–12* (HC 2010–12, 799).
——. *Report on the Consultation on Direct Access to the Parliamentary Ombudsman* (London, PHSO, 2011).
——. *Ombudsman's Report on the Icelandic Water Trawlermen Compensation Scheme 2009* (London, PHSO, 2012).
——. *Our Strategic Plan 2013–2018* (2013).
——. *Sexual Assault Abroad* (HC 2013–14, 837).
——. *Report on an Investigation into Complaints about High Speed Two Limited* (HC 2014–15, 620).
——. *Breaking Down the Barriers: Older People and Complaints about Health Care* (London, PHSO, 2015).
——. *Report on an Investigation into Complaints about High Speed Two Limited* (HC 2015–16, 620).
——. *Driven to Despair: How Drivers Have Been Let Down by the Driver and Vehicle Licensing Agency* (HC 2016–17, 660).
——. *Complaints about UK Government Departments and Agencies and Other UK Public Organisations 2016–17* (2017).
——. *Maintaining Momentum: Driving Improvements in Mental Health Care* (HC 2018, 906).

——. *Ignoring the Alarms: How NHS Eating Disorder Services are Failing Patients* (HC 2017–19, 634).
——. *Making Complaints Count: Supporting Complaints Handling in the NHS and UK Government Departments* (HC 2019–21, 390).
——. *Women's State Pension Age: Our Findings on the Department for Work and Pensions' Communication of Changes* (HC 2019–21, 444).
——. *Continuing Healthcare: Getting it Right First Time* (HC 2019–21, 872).
——. *The Ombudsman's Casework Report 2019* (HC 2020, 63).
——. *Final Investigation Report of a Complaint about UK Visas and Immigration* (Manchester, PHSO, 2020).
——. *PHSO Stakeholder Survey* (Manchester, PHSO, 2021).
——. *An Investigation into UK Visas and Immigration's Handling of Windrush Man's Status* (Manchester, PHSO, 2021).
——. *An Investigation into HS2's Failure to Communicate with a Family about Acquiring Their Home* (HC 2021–22, 211).
——. *Complaint Standards Framework: Summary of Core Expectations for NHS Organisations and Staff* (Manchester, PHSO, 2022).
——. *Continuing Healthcare: An Investigation into Hounslow Clinical Commissioning Group* (Manchester, PHSO, 2022).
——. *UK Central Government Complaint Standards: Summary of Expectations* (Manchester, PHSO, 2022).
——. *An Investigation into UK Visas and Immigration's handling of Windrush man's status* (Manchester, PHSO, 2021).
——. *An Investigation into UK Visas and Immigration's Handling of Windrush Man's Status* (Manchester, PHSO, 2021).
——. *An Investigation into the Department for Work and Pensions' Handling of the Ms U's Migration to Employment and Support Allowance* (HC 2021–22, 856).
——. *An Investigation into HS2's Failure to Communicate with a Family about Acquiring their Home* (HC 2021–22, 211).
——. *The Earl Report: An Investigation into a Complaint about the Environment Agency* (HC 2021–22, 1233).
——. 'Over 118,000 People Denied Compensation from DWP after Benefits Error Cut Payments' (13 January 2022).
——. *Broken Trust: Making Patient Safety More Than Just a Promise* (HC 2022–23, 1444).
——. 'Woman Assaulted Overseas Told: "Carry on with Your Holiday and Enjoy it" by Foreign Office' (29 April 2022).
——. 'Urgent Action Needed to Prevent Eating Disorder Deaths' (27 February 2023).
——. *Women's State Pension Age: Our Findings on Injustice and Associated Issues* (HC 2023–24, 638).
——. *Complaints about UK Government Departments and Other Public Organisations 2023–24* (Manchester, PHSO, 2024).
——. *Investigation into UK Visas and Immigration* (31 October 2024).
——. *Demand across the Public Service Ombudsman Landscape* (Manchester, PHSO, 2025).
——. *Our Guidance on Financial Remedy* (Manchester, PHSO, nd).
Partington, M and Kirton-Darling, E, *Research Issues Paper: Feedback* (London, AJTC, 2008).
Pensions Commission, *A New Pension Settlement for the Twenty-First Century: The Second Report of the Pensions Commission* (London, The Stationery Office, 2005).
Post Office Horizon IT Inquiry Report Volume 1 (HC 2025, 1119).
Pottakis, A, Englman, M, Keenoy, A and Thomas, R, *Ombudsman Peer Review of the Parliamentary and Health Service Ombudsman, UK* (Manchester, PHSO, 2022).
President of Appeal Tribunals, *Report on the Standards of Decision-Making by the Secretary of State 2004–05* (London, Appeals Service, 2005).
——. *Report by the President of Appeal Tribunals on the Standards of Decision-Making by the Secretary of State 2006–2007* (London, Appeals Service, 2007).
——. *Report by the President of the Social Entitlement Chamber of the First-tier Tribunal on the Standards of Decision-Making by the Secretary of State and Child Maintenance and Enforcement Commissioner 2008–09* (London, Appeals Service, 2009).
——. *Report by the President of the Social Entitlement Chamber of the First-tier Tribunal on the Standards of*

Decision-Making by the Secretary of State and Child Maintenance and Enforcement Commissioner 2008–09 (London, Tribunals Service, 2010).
Prime Minister, *The Parliamentary Commissioner for Administration* (Cmnd 2767, 1965).
——. *The Citizen's Charter: Raising the Standard* (Cm 1599, 1991).
——. *Modernising Government* (Cm 4310, 1999).
Prisons and Probation Ombudsman, *Adjudication Complaints* (London, PPO, 2013).
Public Service Ombudsman for Wales, PSOW, *Ending Groundhog Day: Lessons from Poor Complaint Handling* (Pencoed, PSOW, 2016).
——. *The Ombudsman's Casebook: Issue 31* (Pencoed, PSOW, 2018).
——. *Complaints Standards Authority: Wales Complaint Handling Processes – Statement of Principles* (Pencoed, PSOW, 2019).
——. *Homelessness Reviewed: An Open Door to Positive Change* (Pencoed, PSOW, 2021).
——. *Homelessness Reviewed: Revisited* (Pencoed, PSOW, 2023).
——. *Are We Caring for Our Carers? An Own Initiative Investigation into the Administration of Carers' Needs Assessments in Wales* (Pencoed, PSOW, 2024).
——. *Equality and Human Rights Casebook 2023/24* (Pencoed, PSOW, 2024).
Report of the Public Inquiry Ordered by the Minister of Agriculture into the Disposal of Land at Crichel Down (Cmd 9176, 1954).
Sayce, L, *Independent Review of Carer's Allowance Overpayments* (London, DWP, 2025).
Scottish Parliament Local Government, Housing and Planning Committee, *Oral Evidence of the Scottish Public Services Ombudsman*, 6 December 2022.
Scottish Public Services Ombudsman, *Support and Intervention Policy* (Edinburgh, SPSO, nd).
——. *SPSO Statement of Complaints Handling Principles* (Edinburgh, SPSO, 2011).
——. *SPSO Complaints Improvement Framework* (Edinburgh, SPSO, 2017).
——. *Complaints Indicators Key Performance for the Model Complaints Handling Procedures* (Edinburgh, SPSO, 2022).
——. *Strategic Plan 2024–2028* (2024).
Scottish Tribunals and Administrative Justice Advisory Committee, *Mapping Administrative Justice and Tribunals in Scotland* (2015).
Senior President of Tribunals, *Annual Report 2021* (2021).
——. *Practice Direction Reasons for Decisions* (2024).
Social Fund Commissioner, *Annual Report 2012/2013* (Birmingham, Independent Review Service for the Social Fund, 2013).
Social Security Advisory Committee, *Sanctions in the Benefit System* (London, SSAC Occasional Paper 1, 2006).
——. *Decision Making and Mandatory Reconsideration: A Study by the Social Security Advisory Committee* (London, Occasional Paper No 18, 2016).
Syrett, S, Etherington, D, Ekanem, I and Macaulay, P, *Understanding the Experiences of PDCS Customers Engaged with the Formal Complaints Process* (London, DWP Research Report No 770, 2011).
Treasury Solicitor's Department, *The Judge over Your Shoulder: A Guide to Good Decision Making*, 5th edn (London, Treasury Solicitor's Department, 2018).
Tribunal Service, *Transforming Tribunals: Implementing Part 1 of the Tribunals, Courts and Enforcement Act 2007* (CP 30/07, 2007).
Welsh Government, *Response* (Cardiff, Welsh Government, 2023).
——. *A New Tribunal System for Wales: White Paper* (Cardiff, Welsh Government, 2023).
Welsh Senedd, Local Government and Housing Committee, *Homelessness* (Cardiff, Welsh Senedd, Government, 2023).
Widdicombe, D, *The Conduct of Local Authority Business* (Cmnd 9797, 1986).
Williams, W, *Windrush Lessons Learned Review* (HC 2019–20, 93).

INDEX

www.ingramcontent.com/pod-product-compliance
Ingram Content Group UK Ltd.
Pitfield, Milton Keynes, MK11 3LW, UK
UKHW021454240926
475688UK00009B/164

9 781509 983810